TRIBES AND POLITICS IN YEMEN

MARIEKE BRANDT

Tribes and Politics in Yemen

A History of the Houthi Conflict

HURST & COMPANY, LONDON

First published in hardback in the United Kingdom in 2017 by
C. Hurst & Co. (Publishers) Ltd.,
41 Great Russell Street, London, WC1B 3PL
This paperback edition published in the United Kingdom in 2024 by
C. Hurst & Co. (Publishers) Ltd.,
New Wing, Somerset House, Strand, London WC2R 1LA

Printed in the United Kingdom

A Cataloguing-in-Publication data record for this book is available from the British Library.

ISBN: 9781911723424

This book is printed using paper from registered sustainable and managed sources.

www.hurstpublishers.com

For M

CONTENTS

PREFACE AND ACKNOWLEDGEMENTS

In December 2007, I was standing on a rock ledge of Jabal Mislān in Munabbih which offered a wide view of the surrounding valleys and the Fayfā' massif beyond the Saudi frontier. Suddenly my local companions fell silent and turned their attention to the valley. A volley of gunfire echoed in the mountains. 'The Houthis,' one said. 'No, this is a tribal feud,' objected another. At this point I still didn't know that this issue—of Houthis and tribes—would be with me for many years to come.

Fieldwork, as Jenkins put it, is an apprenticeship of signs, a process of entry into a particular world.[1] My apprenticeship began many years before I started work on this book in fall 2011. During my five-year sojourn in Yemen—from 2003 to 2008 I lived in Sanaʿa, where I studied Arabic and worked in development cooperation—Yemen's extreme north had always caught my special interest. Almost all of my trips led to the areas of ʿAmrān, Saʿdah and al-Jawf. Many times I travelled unaccompanied, and people from the area, in particular families I knew from previous visits, took on the roles of hosts and guides. It was always a great advantage to be a woman, because as a foreign female I could cross the gender divide as no man could do, and got access to all areas of life. The hospitality of these families was so overwhelming that 'travelling' in the strict sense soon became impossible: on many occasions I found myself stuck in the houses of shaykhs whose generosity and splendid sense of hospitality literally forbade letting me go before three days had passed.

I concur with de Regt, who argues that friendship can be a suitable research method, because the insights that ensue from a long-standing personal relationship may provide more depth than conventional research methods.[2] During my early stays in Yemen's extreme north I gathered social and political information indiscriminately while participating in everyday life. I also collected data by more formal methods: I kept diaries and handwritten notes, a folder with press reports on the Houthi conflict (which in 2004 began to complicate my travel plans), and a dossier of influential persons in the Saʿdah area. This dossier originally served to keep track of the numerous names, titles, ranks and grades, tribal and kinship affiliations, phone numbers, children, etc. of my acquaintances in the Saʿdah and al-Jawf regions, whose number grew rapidly. In 2011, these documents and contacts became the very nucleus of my scientific research on the Houthi conflict. By 2015, the dossier had inflated to encompass 351 people, from Shidāʾ in Saʿdah's extreme west to Sharūrah in the Rubʿ al-Khālī.

Nevertheless, the work on this book was challenging. Some areas of the Saʿdah region were relatively well explored by preceding researchers. In other areas I had virtually to start from scratch. What are the tribal structures of Khawlān, Jumāʿah, Wāʾilah, Dahm, Wādiʿah? Who are their important figures and influential shaykhs? Which dynamisms are inherent in their day-to-day politics? Which historical events, kinship relations, alliances, enmities and feuds continue to impact on them? To consider these areas and tribes, extensive preparations were necessary—a slow and step-by-step approach, in order to feel my way into these local societies and navigate their territories. Again and again I had to establish reliable contacts in the remotest areas of Yemen, and the maintenance of existing contacts was time-consuming. I literally processed thousands of pages of Arabic news material. The comprehensible presentation of the ever-expanding Saʿdah wars (2004–10) and their internal and external dynamics, was, too, a tricky task that required a multi-pronged narrative recorded in separate storylines. Finally, I have learned how daunting and emotionally distressing it can be to deal with the reconstruction of a war that has caused enormous destruction and to which some of my friends have fallen victim. Those who survived are now facing each other as bitter enemies. As the work progressed, I found it increasingly difficult to distinguish between the 'good' and the 'bad', between perpetrators and victims, heroes and villains, as all of them got involved in an increasingly brutal fratricidal war.

Since I began work on this book in 2011, the security situation in Yemen has been constantly deteriorating. The immediate outcome of Yemen's 'Arab Spring' or 'Change Revolution', which commenced in 2011, was an epic political muddle, a policy and power vacuum and an economic crisis that invited even more confusion and turmoil throughout the country. My last visit to Yemen was in September 2013. In September 2014 the Houthis seized the capital, and in March 2015 a coalition of Sunni states led by Saudi Arabia began a withering bombing campaign in Yemen dubbed Operation Decisive Storm, among the deadliest and most indiscriminate in the region's recent history. At the time of writing, Operation Decisive Storm was still in full progress.

Despite these dramatic circumstances, I was fortunate to maintain contact with my informants in the field, even if the contact increasingly shifted from face-to-face encounters to online communication, gradually transforming my research into what is called 'digital anthropological fieldwork'.[3] It is no exaggeration to say that without the helpfulness and support of these informants, my work would have been impossible. These people's contribution was so substantial that I consider this book as much theirs as mine. My sources in the field were available for consultation at any time, gathered the rarest and most special information for me, visited and called other people in the remotest parts of the country, to whom no foreigner had ever spoken before. With some of them I worked simultaneously on other issues such as tribal history and genealogy. Their helpfulness was truly unlimited, and they talked to me as if I hailed from their area. I am kind of proud of the nicknames they have given me during my research: *al-ṣundūq al-aswad* ('the black box': stores and processes all sorts of information and data), and *al-akhṭabūṭ* ('the octopus': has her fingers in pies everywhere). Whatever I know, however, I have learned from them.

The Houthi conflict is a sensitive issue. During the Saʿdah wars, the freedom of the press was restricted, journalists were intimidated and arrested. The parties to the conflict have pursued veritable cleansing campaigns among their opponents. One lesson of the Saʿdah wars was that crossing red lines of whatever nature is dangerous. We should therefore expect, as with Herzfeld's Greece, that anything anthropologists might want to know will, by definition, be something they should not—and if they do know, they should at least keep quiet about it.[4] This need for oblique secrecy gave supreme priority to the protection of my Yemeni sources, because here research practice touched on the issue of 'dual use', which arises when research involves or generates knowledge that could be misused for unethical purposes. For this reason I decided, with great regret, to make my Yemeni informants anonymous. This was not an easy decision because my work would never have come so far without them. This book is dedicated to them, in particular to my most erudite source and dear friend, M.

Beyond Yemen, my sincerest thanks go to Andre Gingrich, who invited me to pursue this project at the Institute for Social Anthropology (ISA) of the Austrian Academy of Sciences in Vienna and kindly supervised the anthropological work. In fact there could not have been a better choice for the implementation of this research project, as the ISA has a leading role in the exploration of southwest Arabia. Its research tradition on this region goes back to the nineteenth century and David Heinrich Müller, and is connected with the likes of Eduard Glaser and Walter Dostal. Andre Gingrich's works on southwest Arabia, and on northwest Yemen in particular, were the very starting point of my research. His deep understanding of South Arabia's tribal and non-tribal societies and their histories, based on extensive first-hand experience gained through anthropological fieldwork among the tribes of Khawlān b. ʿĀmir in northwest Yemen and southwest Saudi Arabia, his sensitivity towards his research objects and their environments, and his encyclopaedic knowledge on theoretical matters of Anthropology have enormously influenced and enriched my work. Without him, it would never have come so far. When it came to the Munabbih tribe, I have at times felt that I am not doing much more than writing long footnotes to what he worked out in the first place. My frequent references to his work point to only a small part of what I owe to him.

At the ISA, I was fortunate to have the chance to consult numerous other experts working on modern and medieval Yemen. I owe special thanks to Johann Heiss, Eirik Hovden and Daniel Mahoney, who provided me with valuable information and advice regarding Saʿdah's history, tribal structures and tribal genealogy. Eirik Hovden's extensive and detailed comments on the draft manuscript have been extremely helpful, and have done much to help me clarify my thinking as well as broaden my knowledge and avoid generalizations.

Gabriele vom Bruck, Marie-Christine Heinze, Laurent Bonnefoy, John E. Peterson, Askar al-Enazy, Adam Seitz, Nabeel Khoury, and Hurst's anonymous peer reviewers were all kind enough to read parts or the whole of the manuscript in draft. Their support, suggestions and corrections have been invaluable in improving the book's contents and structure into what they are now. My research has also benefitted from discussions with Shelagh Weir, Gerhard Lichtenthäler, Helen Lackner, Najwa Adra, Daniel Varisco, Nadwa al-Dawsari, Madeleine Wells Goldburt, Lucas Winter, Anne-Linda Amira Augustin, Mareike Transfeld and Fernando Carvajal. I am most grateful for their interest, comments, and suggestions. A great debt is owed to all of them for passing on so much of what they know and think about Yemen.

I owe special thanks to Elke Niewöhner and Huibert Wierda, who have both spent considerable time in Saʿdah. Both have accompanied this book from its very beginnings and have taught me many things on Saʿdah's written and unwritten modern history. Elke Niewöhner provided the cover image for the book from her private archive; it shows Shaykh Fayṣal Manāʿ (left) on Saʿdah's airfield in 1972.

Horst Kopp and Stephan Adler of the Institute for Geography at the University of Erlangen-Nuremburg supported me in the preparation of the maps. I am especially indebted to them as the production of maps on Yemen's remote peripheries is an extraordinary difficult task, because reliable map material for these areas is still lacking. During the production of the maps, I benefited from Horst Kopp's enormous knowledge and experience on Yemen. Beyond this, I would also like to express my deep respect and gratitude to him. Since I first started to work scientifically on Yemen in the early 2000s he became—and still is—a kind of mentor to me. His constant and reliable support and his never-ending helpfulness were always inspiring and have enabled me to persevere through all these years I have been working on Yemen.

Working with Hurst has been an extraordinary fortune. It is a great honour that Michael Dwyer accepted my manuscript proposal without demanding abridgements of its admittedly voluminous text. Jon de Peyer guided me through the work of publishing, and Lara Weisweiller-Wu and Farhaana Arefin have greatly improved the text into what it is now. From 2011 to 2013, the research that led to this book received funding from the People Programme (Marie Curie Actions) of the European Union's Seventh Framework Programme (FP7/2007–2013) under REA grant agreement n° 273978; I greatly value the EU's generous support. I also would like to thank the Austrian Academy of Sciences and the Institute for Social Anthropology in Vienna for having created a suitable working environment for me as a severely disabled person.

I am deeply grateful to all. None, however, has any part in the shortcomings of my work: for those and for the interpretations I offer, I alone bear responsibility.

NOTE ON TRANSLITERATION

For transcribing Arabic, I have used a slightly modified system of the *International Journal of Middle Eastern Studies* (IJMES) for both written and spoken words. The Arabic *tāʾ marbūṭah* is rendered *ah*. Initial *hamzah* is unmarked. I have not distinguished lunar from solar letters when writing the Arabic article. Common words, such as shaykh, imam, Houthi, Quran, al-Qaeda, Yemen, Saʿdah, Sanaʿa, Saudi Arabia, Doha, Qatar, Gaddafi, Shiite, Wahhabi, Hadith, shariah etc. are rendered in an Anglicized version. The Arabic *bin* or *ibn* ('son of'), where it comes between two names, has been given as simply *b.* throughout. The plural of some Arabic words such as shaykh, *hijrah* and *qāḍī* is given in an Anglicized (shaykhs, *hijrahs*, *qāḍīs*) rather than an Arabic (*mashāyikh/shuyūkh, hijar/hujar, quḍāʾ*) version. For better readability some personal names like ʿAbd al-Malik, ʿAbd Allah, etc. have been transcribed as ʿAbdulmalik, ʿAbdullah, etc. May orthodox linguists excuse these liberties.

LIST OF ABBREVIATIONS

AQAP	Al-Qaeda in the Arabian Peninsula
CE	Common Era
CSF	Central Security Forces
CSO	Central Security Organization
CTU	Counter Terrorism Unit
GCC	Gulf Cooperation Council
GIFCA	Gaddafi International Foundation of Charitable Associations
GPC	General People's Congress
IDP	Internally Displaced Person
IED	Improvised Explosive Device
JMP	Joint Meeting Parties
LDA	Local Development Association
LNG	Liquefied Natural Gas
MoI	Ministry of Interior
MP	Member of Parliament
NDC	National Dialogue Conference
PDRY	People's Democratic Republic of Yemen
PSO	Political Security Organization
SCER	Supreme Commission for Elections and Referendum
YAR	Yemen Arab Republic
YR	Yemeni Riyal

LIST OF MAPS AND FIGURES

Maps

Figures

GLOSSARY

āl	people of; descendants of
ʿālim, pl. *ʿulamāʾ*	religious scholar
ʿaṣabiyyah	spirit of tribal solidary
aʿyān	tribal elders
ḍāmin, pl. *ḍumanāʾ*	guarantor
hijrah, pls. *hijar* or *hujar* (*hijrahs*)	person or place under special tribal protection; a settlement or community of sādah under tribal protection
ibn/bin, pls. *abnāʾ* or *banī*	son
jabal, pl. *jibāl*	mountain
khurūj	rising against unjust rulers
madhhab	school of law
muhajjar	under *hijrah* protection
qabīlah, pls. *qabāʾil* or *qubul*	tribe
qabīlī, pl. *qabāʾil*	tribesman
qāḍī, pl. *quḍāʾ* (*qāḍīs*)	hereditary jurist-administrator
sayyid, pl. *sādah*, adj. *sayyid*	male descendant of the Prophet; the pre-republican elite to which the al-Ḥūthī family belongs
shaykh, pls. *mashāyikh* or *shuyūkh* (shaykhs)	tribal leader, representative of a tribal unit
shaykh shaml or *shaykh mashāyikh*	senior tribal leader, 'shaykh of shaykhs'
sūq, pl. *aswāq*	market

ʿurf, pl. *aʿrāf*	tribal customary law
waqf, pl. *awqāf*	religious endowment
zaydi, pl. *zuyūd*, adj. *zaydi*	follower of a branch of Shia Islam whose heartland is in northern Yemen

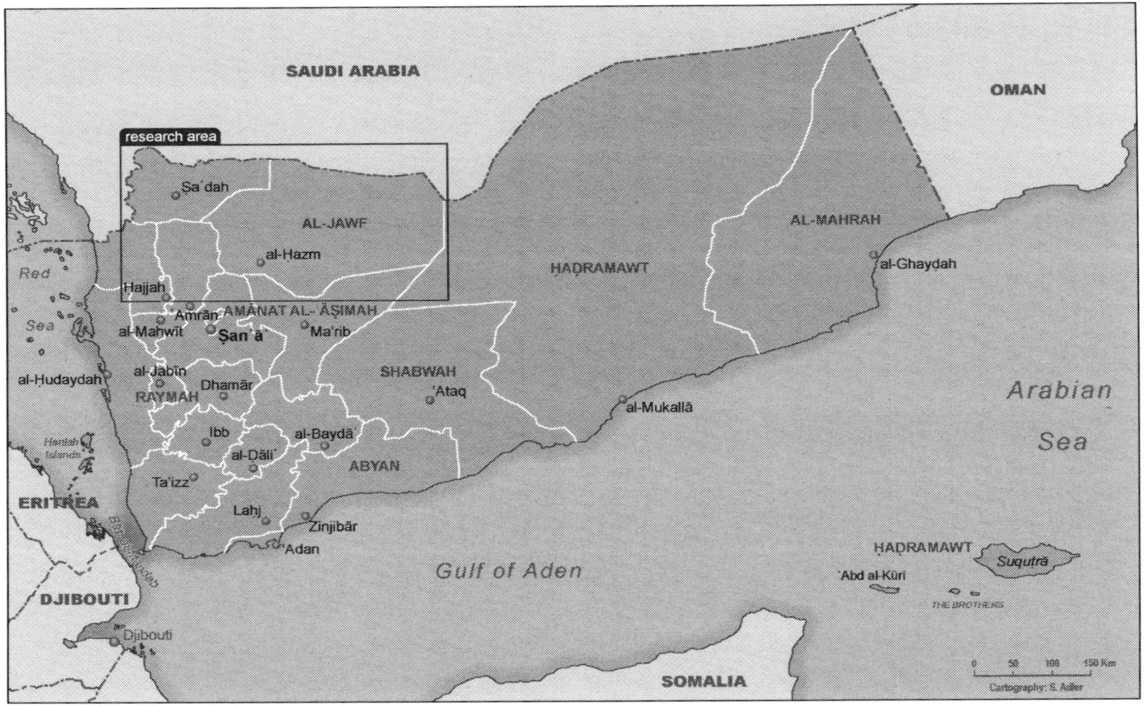

Map 1: Provinces of Yemen

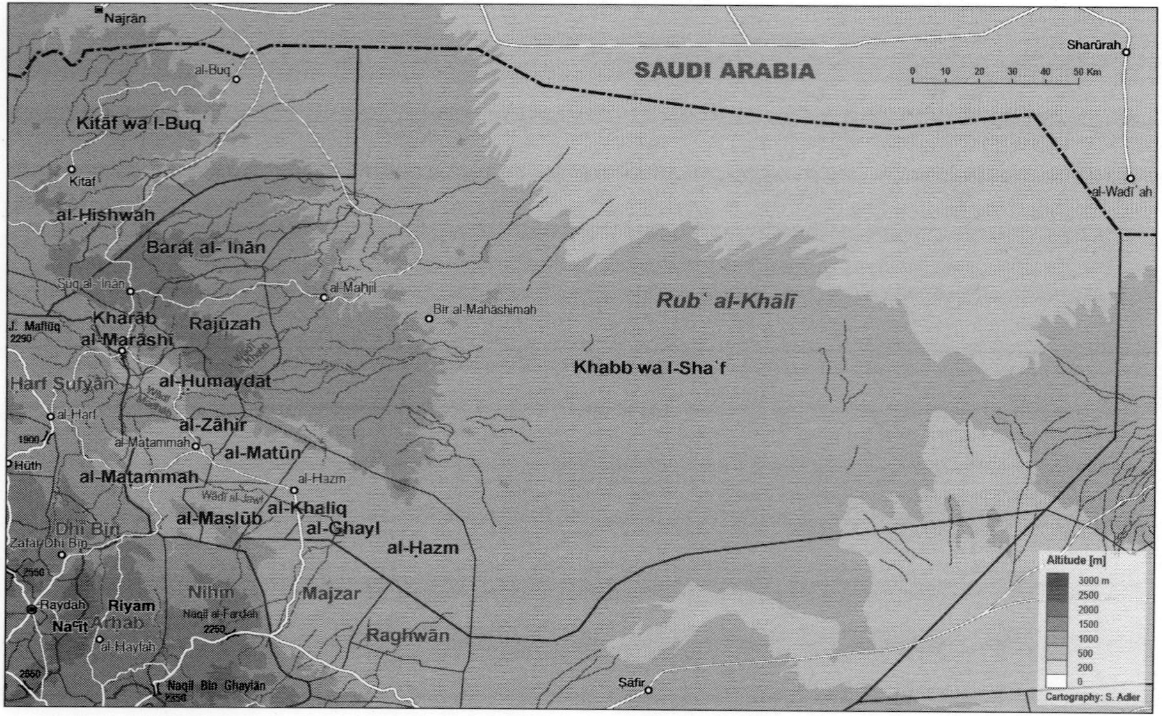

Map 2: Districts of al-Jawf province

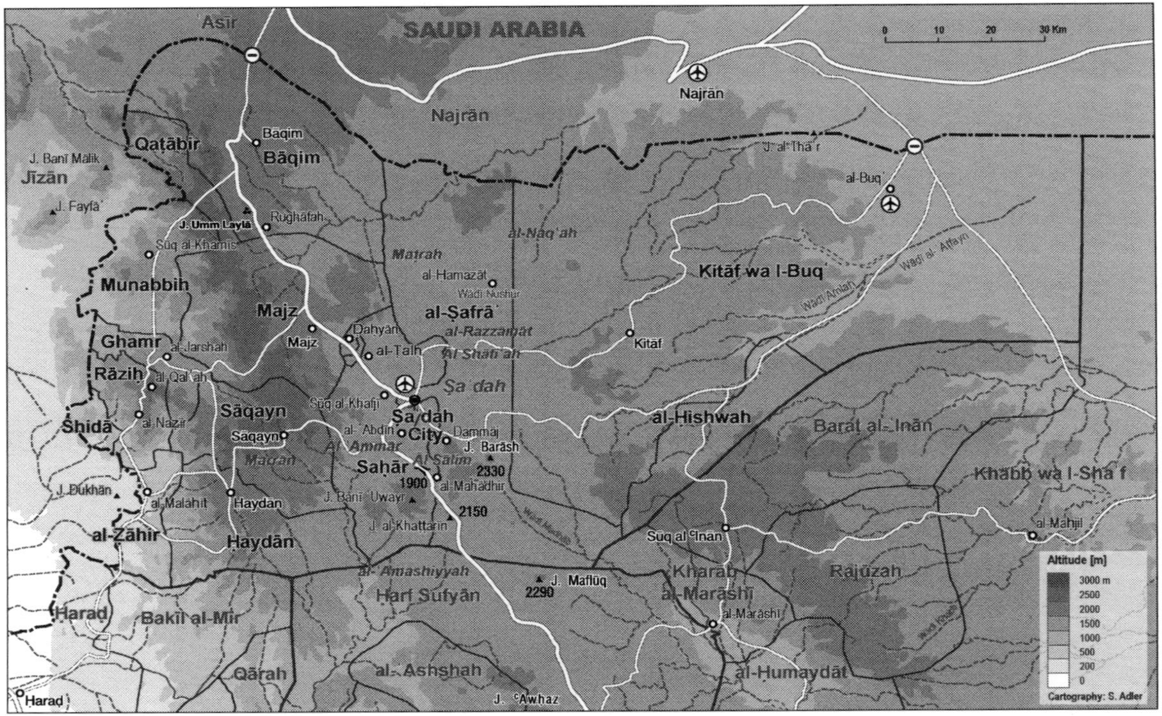

Map 3: Districts of Saʿdah province

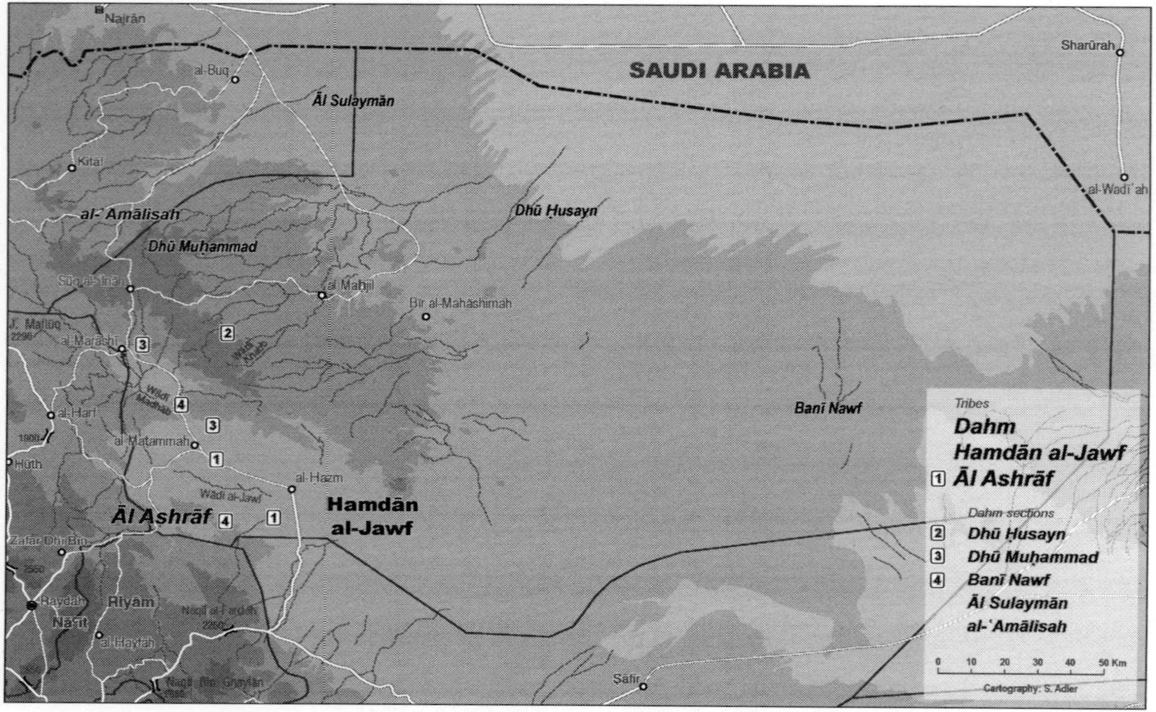

Map 4: Tribes of al-Jawf province

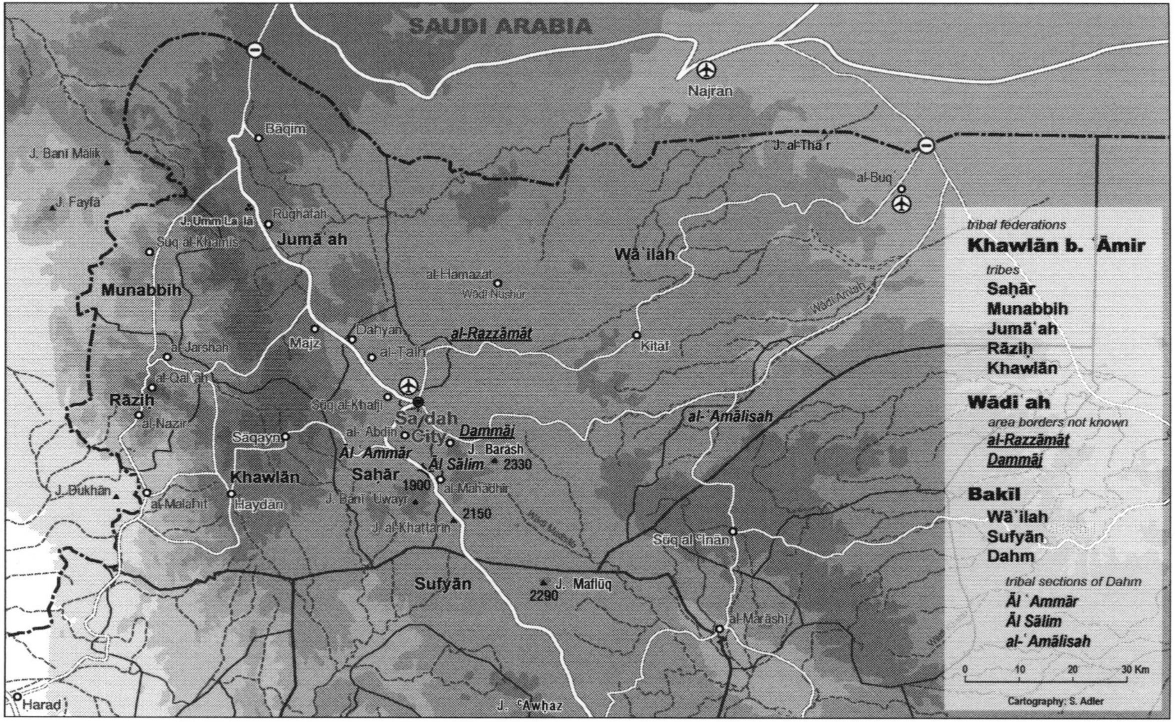

Map 5: Tribes of Sa῾dah province

INTRODUCTION

THE INTERIOR VIEW OF A WAR

If anthropology has any raison d'être [...], it is to allow us to confront the written schema of the intellectuals with the richer and untidy welter of living practice.

Martha Mundy[1]

Al-ḥarb dāʾiman tatruk fī l-nufūs ashyāʾ... wa hādhā mā ẓahara ḥattā al-ān khilāl al-ḥarb bi-mā an al-nās kulluhum fī khandaq wāḥid wa fī makān wāḥid lākin yaẓill fī l-nufūs shayʾ min al-māḍī wa māsīhi wa mukhallafātihi.

[War always leaves something in the souls ... and this is what became evident during the war: all people are in the same place and in the same trench, but in the souls remains something of the past, its tragedies, and its aftermath.]

Former governor of Saʿdah

In March 2015, Operation Decisive Storm put the international community's spotlight on Yemen. Seemingly from one day to the next, a military coalition of predominantly Sunni states led by Saudi Arabia began shelling military installations, arms stockpiles, airports, streets, bridges, and infrastructure throughout the country. Operation Decisive Storm was the coalition's response to the occupation of the capital Sanaʿa and the conquest of further parts of Yemen by the Houthis or, as they call themselves, Anṣār Allah.

A few months earlier, in September 2014, the Houthis had seized the Yemeni capital. They seemed to appear out of nowhere on Yemen's national stage. People had known for some years that an on-and-off war had been waged between the Houthis and the government in Yemen's northernmost provinces, Saʿdah, al-Jawf and northern ʿAmrān, but other domestic challenges—the easily accessible and much more 'vocal' South, the global impact of al-Qaeda in Yemen—had attracted far more attention from researchers, journalists, and the global public. The flow of information from Yemen's extreme north was further impeded by the inaccessibility of its often rugged, mountainous terrain, and of its tribal customs and traditions (often despised and denigrated by urban middle-class Yemeni intellectuals), as well as an information blockade by the government, which had tried to hush up the conflict since its eruption in 2004.

And so it happened that the largest and most brutal conflict in contemporary Yemen, which at the time of writing had been dragging on for twelve years, received at best passing attention from many scientists and journalists. Only in 2014 did public attention turn to the Houthis, when—rather like Gellner's 'wolves'[2]—they left their remote northern strongholds, pushed into central parts of Yemen, seized the capital, and continued their march towards Aden, literally hunting down Yemen's weak transitional government and eventually forcing it into Saudi exile.

The Book

Since the Houthi conflict began to hit international headlines in 2014, it has often been defined against regional contexts, such as the Iranian-Saudi proxy war or the Sunni-Shia divide. This is not to say that these regional conflict drivers were insignificant, but they have primarily served to reduce the Houthi conflict to a catchy denominator, thereby obfuscating its local dynamics and complex nature.

What I wish to do here is to explore these local or 'grassroots' dynamics of the Houthi conflict at its roots: in the Saʿdah region, Sufyān and al-Jawf in Yemen's extreme north. The aim of this book is to reconstruct the conflict's development by giving full play to its local drivers: the micro- and mesopolitical, tribal, and personal dynamics that shaped the manner in which those individuals and communities directly involved in the conflict calculated their interests, concerns and ambitions, vis-à-vis each other, the Houthi movement and the old regime (in itself a complicated set of constantly shifting alliances, often animated by local factors). Rather than focusing on regional and international forces, this book gives attention to the wide spectrum of local causes that explain the conflict's onset, persistence, and expansion: shifting internal power balances, the uneven distribution of resources and political participation, the accumulation of mutual grievances, growing sectarianism and tribalisation. It records, so to speak, the very local narrative of the Houthi conflict.

The research question is related to anthropology's traditional—and, in many ways, enduring—preference for small-scale networks, local communities, and other micro-entities. In pursuing its empirical goals, this book builds on the socio-cultural anthropological theories of Eickelman, Piscatori and al-Rasheed, who emphasize the importance of local people in the implementation of policies, ideologies, and religious hermeneutics. It is often local people (rather than authorities such as religious scholars, states, and so on) who invoke the symbols of those policies to reconfigure the boundaries of civic debate, public life, and conflict.[3] These actors do not lead the debates, but they formulate the local agendas, shape the reality of political practice and enact policy on the ground. On this basis, the present book focuses, in a typically anthropological fashion, on 'peripheral' views and perceptions rather than adopting a more centralized view.

This 'bottom-up' social anthropological approach, as applied here, entails working with individuals and groups not normally taken into account by scientists of those disciplines working with broader theories and using top-down approaches. The bottom-up approach thus invites us to discover issues and interdependencies that are often unseen or marginalized, but which are nonetheless meaningful. Martin has called these individuals and groups, and their specific rituals and actions, 'unidentified political objects' (*objets politiques non-identifiés*).[4] He argues that focusing beyond the repertoire of political and/or sectarian parties, their programmes, representatives, and discourses is a vital and rewarding task, because scientists too often restrict their investigations to a rather limited repertoire of research objects. Research programmes that are 'locked in' on a particular path often reproduce and elaborate already known discourses and fail to identify new questions, as researchers involved in these programmes believe that the main objects of inquiry have already been identified. In such cases, scientists pursue their chosen path, not realizing that they are surrounded by a lively welter of 'unidentified' objects that could be, and often are, politically significant, maybe even more so than 'identified' political objects. On the other hand, and for the same reasons, social anthropologists find it hard to communicate the kind of macro-evidence and abstraction often expected from them by colleagues in other fields.

I am aware of the methodological and epistemological difficulties involved in the task of reconstructing and interweaving the multifaceted narratives of hitherto 'unidentified' objects. My methodology, as outlined below, embraces a combination of literature- and fieldwork-based approaches with the aim of deepening and broadening understanding to give a richer, hopefully 'truer' account. Yet written sources on local details were few, sometimes non-existent, and often I had to rely on competing oral narratives. This work had its rewards, challenges and limitations. People always had a lot to say about their situation, and the categories they used were not always sound and precise. Their narratives were complex, discursive, person-bound, at times even inherently contradictory, and offered subjective viewpoints rather than an 'absolute truth'.

In considering the Houthi conflict, however, it does not suffice to point to the existence of competing narratives and the impossibility of producing 'objective truth'. This book deals with living individuals, most of whom became actively involved in an increasingly brutal and inhumane fratricidal war, a fact that required that I work with the utmost sense of neutrality, carefulness and responsibility. Throughout the research process I have strived to deconstruct my sources' often biased—at times even offending—narratives and representations, and to countercheck and balance their statements. The very fact that this book is about the words and deeds of living people imposed on me an academic and moral obligation to aim for maximum balance and neutrality in my representations and conclusions, despite inevitable doubts about the existence of an 'objective truth'.[5]

The Houthi conflict is multifaceted and complex, and its local narrative as recorded here constitutes only one of manifold ways of approaching and explaining the conflict. The many other narratives of the Houthi conflict sometimes complement each other, sometimes compete: the sectarian narrative, the domestic political narrative, the boundary narrative, the proxy war narrative, and so on. The Yemeni government has its own version. Foreign nations have their different claims. It would be extremely interesting to learn about the internal dynamics and narratives of the subverted armed forces. Certainly none of these narratives—including the 'grassroots' account recorded in this book—can, in isolation, fully explain the conflict. This epic conflict is too large to be read from a single perspective, on a single 'plateau of analysis', whether sectarian, religious, economic, tribal or political.

The Research

The bottom-up approach of social anthropology proved useful for this subject—based on qualitative analysis, fieldwork and micro-studies, it is particularly close to the local details of individual and community life. Consequently, the research methodology applied in this study produced a triangulation of qualitative content analysis, qualitative social science methodology (ethnographic fieldwork) and digital anthropological approaches.[6] This 'mixed method' approach, in addition to the aims stated above of enriching the study, was a response to the deteriorating security situation; the ethnographic and digital anthropological fieldwork could be weighted differently as two components of a 'minimum-maximum' mix.

Qualitative content analysis consisted of literature-based analysis and archival work. The investigation of the state-of-the-art, that is the available, body of 'Western' and Arabic scientific source material focused on the historical roots of the Houthi conflict and the course of the Saʿdah wars. This provided an overview of the main trends and milestones of recent history and of developments in the research area. Archival work served to collect and process local written knowledge at primary and secondary level.[7] Special emphasis was given to the analysis of Yemeni local and national press—of different political affiliations—available in online archives, such as *Mareb Press*, *al-Masdar*, *al-Eshteraky*, *al-Thawrah*, *al-Methaq*, *26th September*, *al-Ayyam*, and *Khawlan.com*. Unfortunately, as of 2012 the online archive of *al-Ayyam* is no longer available; those *al-Ayyam* articles quoted in this book I had downloaded prior to that point. The same goes for the online archives of the Houthi website *al-Menpar*, which was hacked several times and shut down completely between 2012 and 2013. Non-Yemeni press, such as the Saudi *al-Sharq al-Awsat*, *Okaz*, and *al-Riyad*, were also considered. Although many of these newspapers take a clear political stance, the press review helped to complement, scrutinize and balance the often equally biased and incomplete information from local oral sources.

Ethnographic fieldwork was a key tool for achieving the book's objectives and ensuring its empirical approach.[8] As indicated in the Preface, fieldwork had actually begun long before the start of this project. During my five-year sojourn in Yemen from 2003 to 2008, I had the opportunity to establish contacts in the northern regions of Saʿdah, Sufyān and al-Jawf. My visits to these regions were initially brief, but increased in length over time. When I began work on this book in fall 2011, my contacts in this region constituted the original group of 'informal cooperation partners' or 'human sources in the field'. In November 2012 and September 2013, I was able to spend further weeks in Yemen and to meet in the capital, Sanaʿa, with many of my informants from Saʿdah and al-Jawf. I also got invitations to revisit Saʿdah, including by the then governor. However, I was given to understand by people close to the security apparatus who knew about my book that if I followed these invitations to Saʿdah, I would face 'consequences'. After my last stay in Yemen in

2013, the country's rapidly deteriorating security situation and the increasing number of abductions of foreigners made further fieldwork unjustifiable in the eyes of my institute and my family.

This increasingly imposed on me the need to re-adjust my research methods. Insufficient access to the very area at the heart of the research is a problem that does not only affect researchers concerned with Yemen, but rather all researchers who deal with crisis regions, such as Syria, Iraq, Afghanistan, Somalia, Pakistani tribal areas, Libya, and Mali. To overcome this impediment, anthropologists have started to resort to an innovative distance approach called 'digital anthropological fieldwork'.[9] Digital anthropology is not a research area, but rather a methodological approach. Like most other social anthropologists, I am conscious that in situ fieldwork is difficult to replace, but believe that, in times of crisis and difficult access to the field, digital fieldwork can help to continue anthropological work by using the communication opportunities offered by digital media. Indeed, if anthropologists felt they could not measure up to disciplinary standards, or continue to contribute a unique perspective on the world's central crisis zones, without conducting the maximum ethnographic fieldwork that has always been their trademark, then they would be doing a disservice to their field. Anthropological research transcends empiricist realities, and anthropological interpretations at a distance should not be withheld because of methodological standards that cannot be met in times of crisis and in war zones.

Much of the 'distance' empirical data for this project is derived from digital fieldwork—that is, a continuous online exchange with my sources in the field, with whom I had worked to establish solid relationships of trust since 2003. From 2011, the circle of informants has frequently been extended through 'contacts' and 'introductions'. With many of these people I was also working simultaneously on other topics, such as tribal history and genealogy. At times I have spent hours per day chatting with my informants based in Yemen's north, preferably in the late evening and at night, when they were free for conversation. This type of private digital communication was not just a makeshift solution, but also brought great research benefits. Many informants could speak more freely than they would have done face-to-face—in Yemen's highly politicized and conflict-prone environment, the mere physical presence of the researcher can already be compromising. Online, however, no one knew that they were talking to me, and all spoke on condition of absolute anonymity. This completely unobserved conversational situation enabled my informants to communicate freely, to engage in open dialogue without fear of reprisals or other limiting concerns, and to do so without having to censor themselves. In light of these experiences, I believe that, in certain circumstances and for certain research topics, the distance approach can be a suitable means to continue in situ fieldwork when armed conflict temporarily renders field visits too risky.

The Chapters

The Houthi conflict is deeply rooted in the history of Yemen, and its aftershocks will continue to impact on the country for decades to come. This book's research objective—to explore the local dynamics of the Houthi conflict—thus required spanning a broad period, from the 1960s to the present day.

Chapter 1 of this book provides the reader with basic knowledge of the research area and its inhabitants. It starts with a brief overview of its topographical features and its diverse natural landscapes, followed by a discussion of the concept of 'tribe'. This discussion and the development of a viable working definition are necessary because amongst scientists the term 'tribe' is a matter of controversy. The chapter then outlines the basic features of Yemen's tribal system. It introduces the various tribes of the research area, their internal structures and settlement areas, and the peculiarities of the area's other, non-tribal social groups: *sādah* (descendants of the Prophet), *qāḍīs* (hereditary jurist-administrators of tribal descent), non-tribal 'weak' people and urban city dwellers.

Chapter 2 traces the area's profound socio-political and economic transformations since the beginning of the 1962 revolution that led to the overthrow of the imamate, and describes Yemen's transition from the imamic kingdom into the republican order. The chapter first considers the course of the 1960s civil war between royalists and republicans in the Saʿdah area and the loyalties and patterns of alliance among local tribes; this section serves to identify historical continuities in tribal loyalties and allegiances, and to introduce a number of important individuals and families who, having ascended to power during the civil war, then continued to wield tribal, political and economic influence throughout the republican period. This chapter shows that in the decades after the civil war the Yemeni republic did not succeed in building a capable state, and that the process of nation building remained incomplete. The chapter describes the peculiarities of the republican order in the Saʿdah area, which—rather than providing state building, development and investment—was largely based on the political and economic patronage of tribal elites, and led to significant inequality in distribution of income, economic resources, and political participation. Another side effect of incomplete state building was the emergence of a vibrant shadow economy, made possible by the permeability of the Yemeni-Saudi border.

Chapter 3 scrutinizes the various manifestations of Saudi influence in Yemen's extreme north, particularly with regard to the role of Saudi patronage politics in protection of the controversial and vulnerable border between the two countries. By considering the boundary problem through the lens of borderland residents, this chapter focuses on the influence of Saudi patronage politics in the area, the mutual interdependencies between Saudi boundary policy and the emergence of the Houthi conflict, and the vital role that tribes and tribal elites played in this process.

Chapter 4 identifies the sectarian and related political developments that unfolded in this complex and competitive environment. It explores the interplay between Sunni religious radicalization and Shia-Zaydi counter-radicalization, as well as the various sectarian, tribal, and political stages on which this radicalization took place. It explains the local role of the al-Ḥūthī family in its very area of origin, the Marrān Mountains, and reconstructs the emergence of the movement led by Ḥusayn al-Ḥūthī; a movement which, in 2004, entered into open conflict with the Yemeni state.

Chapters 5 and 6 reconstruct the course and the dynamics of the so-called Saʿdah wars: six intermittent phases of armed conflict between the Houthis and the state, from 2004 to 2010. This section shows how the sectarian and social-revolutionary thrust of Houthism fused with existing open and latent conflicts in the area, a process that led gradually to an enormous expansion of the conflict's scope and magnitude. It analyses the course of the Saʿdah wars, the composition of the national military and Houthi armed forces, their respective supporters and opponents among the local tribes, local, domestic and international mediation initiatives, as well as important domestic events such as elections.

The book concludes with an overview of events since the end of the last Saʿdah war in 2010: the Houthi seizure of power in the Saʿdah region and the beginning of Yemen's 'Change Revolution' in 2011; the GCC Initiative and the fall of President Salih; the subsequent rapprochement between Salih and the Houthis; the National Dialogue Conference; and the Houthis' seizure of the capital, Sanaʿa, in 2014. The conquest of Sanaʿa is the landmark event that closes this book. Evidently, the 'fall' of Sanaʿa was far from the end of the story, but rather the beginning of a new chain of events—the Houthi expulsion of the interim government, the beginning of Operation Decisive Storm, the protracted negotiations in Switzerland and Kuwait between the government, Houthis, and the UN—whose consideration will certainly fill other books.

This interior view of Yemen's Houthi conflict has become exhaustive, much more exhaustive than originally intended. Given the sheer mass of material, the accumulation of minute details and names, I considered it important to conclude the book with a comprehensive and meaningful summary. To all those who do not find the time to read the elaborations below, I would instead recommend consulting the summary at the end of this book.

1

TERRITORIES AND SOCIETIES

Saʿdah, Sufyān and al-Jawf in Yemen's extreme north are topographically and socially diverse regions. Their topography is characterized by high mountains, plains, steppes and deserts, and the area's inhabitants belong to different social strata. Much of the population sees itself as tribal, but the area is also home to non-tribal communities.

This chapter provides an introduction to the topographical and social characteristics of this research area. In view of the book's subject, special consideration is given to the social and territorial estates of the tribes. Since the concept of 'tribe' is controversial and disputed, it is essential to discuss and define the term before we can move on to consider the peculiarities of Yemen's tribal system. The area's other social status groups will also be introduced: underprivileged artisan groups, urban city dwellers, and *sādah* (the hereditary Zaydi elite to which the al-Ḥūthī family belongs). The sectarian peculiarities of this region will only briefly be touched upon, as they are the subject of Chapter 4.

Physical Ecologies

Yemen's extreme north is roughly divided into three topographical zones: the western mountain range, the central highlands, and the arid east. Experts make much more precise distinctions of up to seven main zones, but here we confine ourselves to the topographical features that are important for understanding the book's main focus.[1]

The Western Mountain Range

The mountains dominating western Saʿdah governorate are part of the Sarawāt mountain range, which runs parallel to the western coast of the Arabian Peninsula, from the border with Jordan in the north to the Gulf of Aden in the south. In Saʿdah governorate, the Sarawāt peaks reach heights of 2.89 kilometres (Jabal al-Aswad) and 2.819 kilometres (Jabal al-Nawʿah). To the west, toward the Tihāmah coastal plain and the Red Sea, the Sarawāt break off into single massifs, whose peaks still reach heights of 2.79 kilometres (Jabal Ḥurum in Rāziḥ) and 2.39 kilometres (Jabal al-ʿUrr in Munabbih). Jabal Rāziḥ is connected with the Sarawāt's Khawlān massif by a mountain ridge, while Jabal Munabbih is situated below the Sarawāt's edge.

High valleys, *wādīs* (dry valleys) and elevated plains are located between the Sarawāt's peaks and between the mountain range and its foothills to the east and west, including the Bawṣān plateau west of Jabal Munabbih and the fertile Wādī al-Badr in the Jabal Ghamr area between Jabal Rāziḥ and Jabal Munabbih, which drains into Wādī Jīzān. Wādī Ḍamad runs between Jabal Munabbih and Jabal Fayfāʾ, another isolated massif situated across the Saudi border. Several large *wādīs* originate in the area of the Khawlān massif, draining east and southeast into the Tihāmah, including Wādī Ḥaydān, Wādī Khulab (between Khawlān and Rāziḥ), and Wādī Liyyah. As a result of exposure to rain winds, large parts of the Sarawāt range and its foothills are very fertile. In some places, sufficient rainfall and farming on small terraces, supplemented by well and cistern irrigation, enable the cultivation of cereals, vegetables, coffee, bananas, fruit, and *qāt* (*Catha edulis Forsskål*; a stimulant plant).[2]

The western mountain range is crossed by a large number of ancient trade and transportation routes. The rugged terrain, however, renders the construction of modern tarmac roads difficult. In the early 2000s, the government launched the Northern Ring Road construction project (196 kilometres long), called 'President Ali Abdullah Salih Road' (*al-ṭarīq al-dāʾirī al-shamālī ʿAlī ʿAbdullah Ṣāliḥ*) and taking the following route: Saʿdah city-Qaṭābir-Munabbih-Ghamr-Rāziḥ-al-Malāḥīṭ-Ḥaraḍ. This should significantly extend state influence into this remote region and connect it to the central parts of Yemen. The construction works, however, have proved fairly complex, hampered by the challenges of the steep terrain and, since 2004, the deteriorating security situation. The road section between al-Naẓīr in Rāziḥ and Qaṭābir is still unpaved and very tough to pass.

The Central Highlands

The eastern slopes of the mountain range define the western edge of Saʿdah's central highlands. To the east, the mountain range falls steeply down into the Saʿdah basin and, in the Umm Laylā area further to the north, into the Yusnam and Bāqim depression. The Saʿdah basin has approximately the shape of an ellipse pointing to the north; at its southeastern edge lies the city of Saʿdah. The basin extends 30 kilometres from northwest to southeast, at its widest point, and 16 kilometres in the southeast direction and covers a total area of 213 square kilometres. Its elevations range from 2.05 kilometres in the northwest to 1.84 kilometres in the northeast.[3]

The Saʿdah basin is mostly arid. Rainfall is sporadic and often comes in short and intense outbursts whose intensity can vary greatly between local areas.[4] Prior to the introduction of tube wells in the early 1970s, the Saʿdah basin's natural vegetation mainly supported the rearing of livestock.[5] Since the 1970s, artificial irrigation by motor pumps has been widely used and has led to a profitable cultivation of cereals, vegetables, *qāt*, alfalfa, palms, and so on—but at the cost of dramatically falling groundwater levels.[6] The Saʿdah basin is famous for its grapes, citrus fruit and especially its pomegranates, which are exported all over Yemen; Saʿdah city also bears the epithet *Madīnat al-Salām wa l-Rummān*: the town of peace and pomegranates. The Wādī al-ʿAbdīn, a few kilometres southeast of the city, is considered a particularly fertile region.[7]

Important transportation, trade and pilgrim routes have been leading through the Saʿdah basin since ancient times.[8] Today, the only direct highway from Sanaʿa to Saudi Arabia, paved in the late 1970s, passes through the Saʿdah basin and Saʿdah city. At Bāqim, a few kilometres from the Saudi frontier, the Northern Ring Road branches off this highway. Another important tarmac road connects Saʿdah city to the border crossing point al-Buqʿ in the governorate's northeast.

The Arid East and al-Jawf

The decrease in altitude between the Saʿdah basin and the arid eastern regions is not very pronounced, since the erosion level of the South Arabian desert still averages around 1 kilometre in height. East of the Saʿdah basin begins the extended transition zone to the steppe and desert areas of the Rubʿ al-Khālī, the largest contiguous sand desert in the world. Saʿdah's arid east is determined by rocky hillsides and mountainous areas, whose altitudes, however, do not match those of the Sarawāt to the basin's west. Beyond Jabal al-Tha'r and al-Buqʿ, the terrain turns into the sands and dunes of the Rubʿ al-Khālī. The eastern regions are very arid. Climate and topography do not favour agriculture; one finds only small oases with well irrigation.[9] The area is traversed by large *wādīs*: Wādī Nushūr north of Saʿdah city, and to the east the Wādīs al-ʿAqīq, Amlaḥ, Silāḥ, and al-ʿAṭfayn, most of them draining into the Rubʿ al-Khālī.

The Saʿdah basin's southern fringe is bordered by Sufyān's barren rock landscape, called al-ʿAmashiyyah, which belongs to ʿAmrān governorate. The total area of Sufyān's large but sparsely populated territory is one-third of the size of ʿAmrān governorate. Beyond the rocky al-ʿAmashiyyah, Sufyān's terrain is largely flat and sandy, with some cultivation of sorghum and animal husbandry.[10] In the east, across a mountain ridge, Sufyān is bordered by Wādī Madhāb, which originates in the Jabal Barāsh area near Saʿdah city and drains further east into the Wādī Jawf.

In the east and southeast, Saʿdah governorate borders on al-Jawf, a vast governorate of 30.62 square kilometres whose boundaries are roughly defined by the Baraṭ plateau to the west and by the southern tributaries of the Wādī Jawf to the south.[11] To the north and east, the territory of al-Jawf extends into the Rubʿ al-Khālī. Several *wādīs* (Wādī Madhāb, Wādī Khabash, Wādī Khārid, Wādī Hirrān etc.) drain from the north, south and west into the Jawf depression. Depending on rainfalls in the central and northern regions of Yemen, floods regularly inundate large areas of al-Jawf. Thanks to this consistent irrigation the central basin is partly covered with shrubs and bushes, yet is no longer cultivated in the same intensive way as in ancient times.[12] Agriculture in al-Jawf is now mainly subsistence-based, with sorghum being grown over the majority of arable land. Around pumped wells a greater variety of crops can be found, such as wheat, barley, sesame, and some fruit and vegetables.[13] The western part of al-Jawf is dominated by the Baraṭ Plateau, a steep, barren mountain range. The Baraṭ Plateau is bordered in the northwest by Wādī Amlaḥ, in the southwest by Wādī Madhāb; in the east it gradually descends into broken terrain and rock screes and finally changes into the vast sandy areas and longitudinal dunes of the Rubʿ al-Khālī. Parts of al-Jawf are inhabited by semi-nomadic tribes.[14]

Despite al-Jawf's enormous size, few roads connect it to the rest of Yemen: an only partially paved track links Kharāb al-Marāshī and Baraṭ al-ʿInān in western al-Jawf with al-Ḥarf in Sufyān and, to the north, with al-Ḥishwah district in Saʿdah governorate, from where the road divides and runs either west to Saʿdah city or north through Wādī al-ʿAṭfayn to the al-Buqʿ border crossing point. The second asphalt road links al-Jawf governorate's administrative centre al-Ḥazm, either via Dhī Bīn, Raydah and ʿAmrān city or via Arḥab with Sanaʿa. The main access road to al-Jawf, however, is over the Sanaʿa-Maʾrib highway. Near the Naqīl al-Farḍah mountain pass (Nihm area), a tarmac road branches off this highway, reaching al-Ḥazm after 55 kilometres.

Estates of Society

Unlike the central and southern parts of the country, Yemen's extreme north (Saʿdah, al-Jawf, northern ʿAmrān) is dominated by tribal norms and customs. Tribesmen played a pivotal role before and throughout the Houthi conflict, and account for many of its dramatis personae. It cannot be ignored that it was the tribal leaders (shaykhs) who dominated the region's politics, economy, and public discourse; and it was their tribesmen—more than anyone else—who steered the war in the remote, northernmost parts of the country. Tracing the trajectories of tribes and families over decades is a useful tool for understanding the way tribes divided during the Saʿdah wars, and on which sides. Despite this pronounced tribal component, at no time was the Houthi conflict a purely tribal one. Rather, the heterogeneity of the parties and their diverging, often incommensurable objectives and motivations made the conflict a kind of 'hybrid' war, driven by an ever-changing blend of political, ideological, military, economic, tribal, sectarian, and personal causes.

Tribe: A Contested Concept

The term 'tribe' (*qabīlah*) is as common in Yemen as it is disputed among scientists. It is therefore advisable at this point to explain the term in more detail. Entities called tribes are diverse polities which can be found throughout North Africa and the Middle East. Their polymorphism and relative indeterminacy render a universally applicable definition almost impossible. For this reason, the concept 'tribe' is regarded by many as defunct. Besides its conceptual ambiguity, the term 'tribe' is ideologically charged. In colonial times, in sub-Saharan Africa the concept of tribe contributed to portrayal of indigenous populations as 'primitive', which in turn helped to justify missions of development and civilization. During decolonization, therefore, this classical anthropological evolutionism collapsed and, in many parts of the world, the term 'tribe' took on a largely negative and pejorative meaning.[15] Ever since, some researchers have been trying to replace the term 'tribe' with less loaded but more shallow and arbitrary terms with low explanatory value, such as 'ethnic groups', 'indigenous people' or just 'local communities'.[16]

The accusation that the term 'tribe' conveys a negative, ideologically charged image does not apply to the entire world. In parts of central and western Asia and North Africa, particularly in areas influenced by Islam, the term tribe and its local equivalents never had the predominantly pejorative meaning seen in colonial Africa. Here 'tribe' was not an etic, but an emic, indigenous representation; sections of the local population have referred to themselves since time immemorial as 'tribes' (pl. *qabāʾil*) and use the term with pride as a matter of course. Most scholars would therefore agree that the concept is obsolete as a general comparative category, but 'tribe' is still a useful term with particular applications, which should always be empirically determined for different regions and periods. As Gingrich has elaborated, in present discussions the debate is therefore oscillating between complete rejection of the term 'tribe', and its more or less critical, limited use when referring to specific times and regions.[17] Especially in Yemen's rural north, 'tribe' is a historically rooted, emic concept of social representation. While this fact is recognized by almost all scientists, the scientific discussion of researchers concerned with Yemen centres around the definition of the term 'tribe', the theoretical elaboration of the concept, and the varying extent of its applicability in the country's different regions and social spaces.

The segmentary model was an early theory that tried to fit the tribes of Yemen into such a theoretical framework. The model was introduced in the 1940s by Evans-Pritchard with regard to the Cyrenaican Bedouin and further elaborated by Gellner to apply to the Berber of the High Atlas.[18] To an extent, Gellner's functional-segmentary model was founded on Ibn Khaldūn's work (fourteenth-fifteenth century CE). In regard to Yemen, segmentary theory manifested itself particularly in some early works by Dresch.[19] Segmentary theory basically suggests that a tribe comprises a population that claims patrilinear descent from a common eponymous ancestor, and which is sub-divided into a hierarchy of nested lineages or segments named after subsequent ancestors. In the socio-political sphere segmentary theory suggests that no segment has specialized or permanent political functions and no crucial level of social organization; rather, segments work through their 'balanced opposition' to one another—equivalent groups at different levels of the system only mobilize in response to threats, then dissolve when they abate.[20] According to what is known as the Khaldūnian cycle, militarily superior tribes united by *ʿaṣabiyyah* (group solidarity) periodically conquer centres of civilization but eventually become sedentarized and then are themselves conquered; hence, in segmentary theory, tribes only have meaning in contradistinction to the city-state.[21]

Segmentary theory retains its explanatory power because it underscores the tribes' composition of nested groups, the importance of collective action and collective responsibility, and the conceptualization of groups as kin descending from a putative common ancestor. Also, segmentary trees are useful tools for illustrating the tree-like pattern of tribal genealogical-structural representation. However, the socio-political implications of the segmentary model are criticized as too one-sided. Yemen's tribes are not acephalous, anarchic and antagonistic isolated entities working through use of physical compulsion, as the segmentary model suggests. The socio-political implications of segmentary theory have been challenged by many anthropologists, who have demonstrated that, in fact, to varying degrees Yemen's tribes have very important levels of organization; historically evolved, stable, often symbiotic links with state powers; administrative and juridical structures; written laws; durable political alliances; and a culture of mediation and dialogue.[22] However, this criticism of Dresch's notion of tribes in Yemen is short-sighted. Despite his early theoretical inclinations toward segmentary theory, Dresch's groundbreaking and indispensable work actually substantiates the close interrelationship of tribes and state in Yemen, the importance of historically grown and stable alliances, the core role of conflict resolution and mediation and the high degree of development among tribes' jural and judicial systems.

Because of these pitfalls of Gellnerian segmentary theory, today many researchers opt for models in which repetitive cycles are less important than sequences of transformation, and which emphasize aspects of development and interdependence. These models are better placed to consider profound long-term changes in history together with the impact of external flows and long-distance influences. Gingrich calls this theoretical approach the 'cultural historical' model.[23] Besides Dresch's later works, it is reflected in the works of Dostal, Gerholm, Adra, Caton, Gingrich, and Weir, as well as my own preliminary works on tribes in Yemen.[24] Beyond Yemen, the cultural-historical model has also been adopted, among others, by Bonte and Conte, who emphasize the dynamic, variable, and interactive nature of tribes and tribalism.[25]

Against the backdrop of these discussions, I would like to join with Gingrich's working definition, which sees tribes as medium-sized, centralized, or acephalous entities displaying a combination of basic characteristics. First, they are usually associated with a territory, homeland, or tribal area, while using non-territorial criteria (such as *qabyalah*, see below) to distinguish between members and non-members. Second, the genealogical aspect is essential: tribal members usually share some dominant idiom of common origin, such as (putative or real) descent from a single ancestor. This real or imagined common descent emphasizes group cohesion over outside interests and internal differentiation. Third, tribes are not closed, self-contained systems but rather open entities that maintain lively relations with their (tribal and non-tribal) environments.[26]

This open and adjustable definition enables scientific work with the notion of tribe in the consideration of regions where—as in Yemen—'tribe' is an emic concept of social representation. However, 'tribe' is only one of many models of social representation; Yemeni society is composed of different social strata, including but far from limited to tribes. Furthermore, Yemen's growing urban and peri-urban areas, large parts of central and southern Yemen, and even parts of the rural, peasant north do not (any longer) consider themselves tribal societies. An indiscriminate application of the term 'tribe' would direct analytical focus away from the socio-political diversity of the Yemeni context—the members of many rural village communities could today be more usefully identified as farmers than as tribesmen. Mundy, who did her fieldwork in the 1970s in Wādī Ẓahr, a peri-urban area of the capital Sana'a, correctly noted that:

> a model of society of North Yemen cannot stop at Ḥāshid and Bakīl [the two main tribal confederations of northern Yemen], however powerful the leadership of these groups may be, but must take account of the economically central if sometimes politically marginal populations of Tihāma, the Western Mountains and Lower Yemen, that is to say ... of fundamental economic and social diversity.[27]

This is perfectly true, yet the levelling traditions of state dominance within peri-urban areas such as the Wādī Ẓahr have certainly induced researchers to underestimate the persistence and strength of tribal structures in other parts of the country, particularly in the extreme north.

Yemen's Tribal System

In Yemen, the representation of (real or imagined) common ancestry is important to the tribal concept, but it is not the sole representation that defines tribal communities. The 'non-territorial criteria' of our working definition revolve around the concept of 'tribalness' (*qabyalah*). *Qabyalah* is a system of ethical values, a set of ideal characteristics of the tribesman connoting honour, courage, pride, and protection of the weak.[28] The term *qabyalah* is used to refer to a general code of conduct, to which tribesmen claim to adhere.

The maintenance and defence of honour (*sharaf*) plays a special role in the concept of *qabyalah*.[29] A tribesman's honour can be impugned by attacks on any component of his honourable self, but three particular components are metonymically exalted to special iconic status: daggers, women and landholdings (*arḍ*).[30] Thus the protected space on which tribal honour depends is often identified with physical space: that is, with territory. Disgrace (*ʿayb*) is what infringes honour; according to the codes of *qabyalah*, any infringement of honour requires amends. The honour of an individual tribesman is part of the tribe's collective honour and can therefore be defended by the entire tribal solidary group. This is the imperative of *ʿaṣabiyyah*, translated by Dresch as 'tribal solidarity', 'esprit de corps', or a 'cohesive drive against others'.[31]

From the smallest to the largest groups, tribes and tribal sections are usually represented by chieftains (*mashāyikh* or shaykhs).[32] Usually the shaykhs are elected from tribal families in which the office of the shaykh is hereditary. The elective element means that shaykhdom (*mashīkh*) is not necessarily passed from the father to one of his male offspring, but can be transferred to any eligible, prominent and able person of the chiefly lineage. With this interplay of selection and succession, it rarely happens that someone is elected a shaykh without descending from the same genealogical lineage as their predecessor. Once on a track, shaykhly lineages are difficult to derail. This is also due to the fact that shaykhly lineages usually inherit important tribal documents and contracts, knowledge and possession of which is essential for the fullfillment of a shaykh's duties in representation, conflict mediation, and jurisdiction.[33] This explains why many shaykhly lineages in Upper Yemen, despite all historical vicissitudes and rivalries, were able to maintain their positions for centuries.

Shaykhs perform important tasks for the benefit of their tribes. These include administration of their tribal units and promotion of their welfare through representation of tribal interests, both internally and externally—that is, to other tribal groups as well as the state. The shaykhs administer their tribal groups though a second tier of tribal officials, called 'notables' (*aʿyān*) or 'elders' (*kibār*), who both represent and administer their clans and assist and deputize for the shaykh.[34] Shaykhs are therefore part of a 'management team', a practice that helps the institution of shaykhdom survive the inadequacies of individual shaykhs.

Shaykhs do not have supreme or coercive power over their tribal constituencies; they neither 'govern' them nor exercise a restraining influence by force.[35] It is up to every member of the tribe whether or not to agree with the opinion and actions of his shaykh. In very severe cases of disagreement, tribal members may also leave a tribe and entrust themselves to the jurisdiction of another shaykh.[36] The shaykh is therefore obliged to avoid antagonising the members of his group, as any kind of authoritarian behaviour would not be consistent with *qabyalah*.[37] The absence of formal power and command implies that the concept of shaykhly authority should be understood essentially in symbolic terms. Caton has demonstrated that power, such as it exists in this system, must be achieved through persuasion, and a shaykh's ability of verbal suasion is one of the most important prerequisites for a successful tenure of the office.[38] Only through personal influence, not coercion, can shaykhs mobilize large numbers of men in tribal affairs.

Shaykhs' legal obligations comprise the tasks of conflict management, according to tribal customary law (*ʿurf*).[39] Customary law is a set of principles, rules and local precedent cases (*silf*) that regulates the reciprocal obligations of tribesmen, as well as tribal obligations towards people defined as 'weak'. It is oriented towards the peaceful settlement of conflicts. In case of conflict it is applied by way of mediation (*wisāṭah*) and arbitration (*taḥkīm*). The situation in Yemen, however, is characterized by the coexistence of three legal systems: the rules of tribal customary law, Islamic law (sharia), and the state's judiciary.[40] In the rural areas of Upper Yemen, *ʿurf* and sharia law are in many ways complementary and thus coexist. They are, however, represented by different social strata: *ʿurf* is promoted by the shaykhs, whereas a sharia judge belongs to one of two groups: the *sādah* (descendants of the Prophet, sing. *sayyid*), or the *qāḍīs* (hereditary jurist-administrators of tribal descent).

Nevertheless, the relationship between the representatives of sharia and those of *ʿurf* is not free of competition; historically, sharia representatives often condemned *ʿurf* and designated it with pejorative terms such as *ṭāghūt* (wickedness).[41] Tribes' relationship with sharia law varies. For example, in Rāziḥ District, where the homonymous tribe has developed close cooperation with the local *sādah* and the respective state overlords, *ʿurf* is regarded as fully compatible with sharia law.[42] Among the Rāziḥ's immediate tribal neighbours, the more *sayyid*-hostile and isolationist Munabbih, sharia enforcement through the *sādah* is regarded as an unwelcome interference in tribal affairs. In such cases, a situation of rivalry and competition can emerge between *ʿurf* and sharia, between the shaykhs and the *sādah* as arbitrators.[43]

Other Status Groups: *Sādah, Qāḍīs,* 'Weak' People

Beyond the tribal estate, the area's inhabitants are divided into various other social strata: *sāḍah, qāḍīs*, underprivileged artisan groups called *ahl al-thulth*, and non-tribal city dwellers.[44] For our purposes, the *sādah* are particularly relevant because the Houthi movement, albeit largely driven by local tribes, was both initiated and led by members of the *sādah* social stratum.

Sādah

The *sādah* (sing. *sayyid*, also the adjective) are descendants of the Prophet through his two grandsons, Ḥusayn and Ḥasan. They form the religious aristocracy in nearly every Muslim country. In Yemen many *sādah* trace their descent to the first Zaydi imam, Yaḥyā b. al-Ḥusayn (d. 911), a member of the Prophet's family and follower of the Zaydi branch of Islam. He came to Yemen in 897, when the Saʿdah region and large parts of the northern highlands were ravaged by a protracted tribal conflict. The tribes involved had invited him to mediate in their conflict according to sharia law. Yaḥyā succeeded in this mediation, then settled down in Saʿdah city and established the Zaydi state under the Zaydi Hādawī school of law.[45]

Zaydi Hādawī doctrine[46] ascribes to the *sādah* a leadership role in both religious and secular affairs, and *sādah* henceforth occupied the position of imam (the spiritual and secular leader of the Zaydi community) as well as leadership positions in government administration and the military. In the centuries after Yaḥyā's arrival, the rule of the Zaydi imams was often fragile, and often—beyond temporary expansion of their sphere of influence—confined to the tribal north, as their base of power. The tradition of *sādah* leadership elapsed with the overthrow of the imamate in 1962 and the establishment of the Yemeni republic.

Due to their alleged non-Yemeni origin, in genealogical terms the *sādah* are still considered an immigrant community. Whereas almost all South Arabian tribes regard Qaḥṭān (the putative common ancestor of the Southern Arabs) as their progenitor, the *sādah* still trace their descent to the Prophet, an ʿadnānī Arab of the Banī Hāshim clan of the Meccan Quraysh tribe, ʿAdnān being the putative common ancestor of the Northern Arabs.

The *sādah*'s specific marriage patterns enabled them to survive as a coherent descent group among Yemen's southern Qaḥṭānī Arabs.[47] Since their identity and exclusive status derive from their putative descent, they preserve detailed genealogies. They sustain their elevated status within Yemeni society through the principles of patrilinearity and endogamy; endogamy, however, is applied much more stringently to their females (sing. *sharīfah*), even though these practices seem to have changed somewhat in recent years.[48] For *sādah* it is legitimate to marry tribal women, and their offspring will then in turn be of *sayyid* stock.[49] Therefore, many *sādah* have tribal cousins and relatives, and vice versa. Such marriage patterns lead to close kinship ties between *sādah* and tribesmen while simultaneously maintaining their genealogical distinction from one another.

Among the tribes, *sādah* are attributed a superior status while simultaneously being 'weak'; the tribes must protect the *sādah*, because they are vulnerable. Hence *sādah* usually enjoy the protection of the tribe on whose territory they live. In exchange, many *sādah* exercise important religious and legal functions for the benefit of the community. Learned *sādah* act as religious scholars and jurists, sharia judges, writers, and mediators in tribal disputes.

Individual *sādah*, *sayyid* families, and *sayyid* settlements can obtain *hijrah* status—that is, special contractual protection by the tribes.[50] Zaydi tribes, in particular, believe that *sādah* living among them bring with them the additional *barakah* (blessing) and honour of their noble descent, and hold them in special veneration. In return for their performance of mediation and scholarly services, the tribe offers to protect and honour the *sādah* and give them the wherewithal to make a livelihood. The conditions of *hijrah* protection are enshrined in contracts with the leaders of specific tribes, usually those among whom the *sādah* live. Since learned scholars have often historically settled in a *hijrah*, the latter would often take on the character of a *hijrat ʿilm*: a centre of learning renowned as a sort of school for the Zaydi-Islamic sciences, attracting students.[51]

Over the centuries, certain *sayyid* families have come into possession of large landholdings through the Islamic institution of *waqf* (religious endowment).[52] Under the *waqf* system, a tribal member donates to the mosque a piece of land, which becomes the property of the Muslim community. The imam of the mosque then makes a *sayyid* his partner. In this way, *sayyid* families have quasi-permanently acquired large landholdings. Gingrich and Heiss argue that abolishing misuse of this practice was one of the aims of the 1962 revolution.[53]

The fall of the imamate in the late 1960s dealt a blow to the *sādah*'s standing generally. With the 1962 revolution, the *sādah* lost their political claim to power. Under the subsequent republican government, they were overshadowed by tribal shaykhs and *qāḍīs* (hereditary jurist-administrators of tribal descent, see below), and in the countryside *sādah* were considered by many to be reactionary and associated with backwardness.[54] A process of social, political and economic decline ensued among the *sādah*, benefiting the tribal shaykhs in particular. This shift in balance after the 1960s civil war is the subject of Chapter 2 of this study.

Qāḍīs

Another socially and politically important status category is that of the *qāḍīs*, hereditary jurist-administrators, who are considered of tribal stock. Among the tribes, they are given special esteem and status because of their education: the study of sharia law.[55] Indeed the very name *qāḍī* implies the function of judging. In theory, any tribesman can become a *qāḍī* through the study of Islamic law. In practice, however, *qāḍī* status is quasi-hereditary. Some *qāḍīs* are *muhajjar* (under tribal protection) and enjoy special contractual protection by the tribes.[56] Many of them form part of Yemen's administrative class. Certain great *qāḍī* families have played a conspicuous part in Yemen's history for centuries. *Qāḍīs* played a significant role in the imamic state and—unlike the *sādah*—were able to preserve their influence after the 1962 revolution.

'Weak' people

Another social stratum is composed of those professionals of inferior status whom tribesmen consider beneath them. They are the 'lowest' third of the social scale and hence called *ahl al-thulth* (lit. 'people of the third').[57] The occupations of the *ahl al-thulth* are denigrated by tribesmen as filthy, polluting activities: butchery, running cafés, making pottery, polishing daggers and making scabbards, working as a barber, tanning and working with hides, medicinal cupping, circumcising, acting as a herald, drumming and other music-playing.

Despite the immense social value of these products and services, tribesmen tend to deride the *ahl al-thulth* as 'deficient' (*nuqqāṣ*) because of their ancestry and professions. From the tribal point of view, the members of this status group are 'weak' (*ḍuʿafāʾ*, pl. of *ḍaʿīf*), because they do not have the tribesman's ability to intervene in affairs between other tribesmen.[58] The status of the *ahl al-thulth* is considered hereditary; few tribesmen and certainly no *sādah* would intermarry with them.

Nowadays, the stratification of Yemeni society in these principal status groups seems rather obsolete, not to say donnish, as today these categories are nowhere near as obvious or stable as they were, say, twenty or thirty years ago. 'Weak' people may become successful traders or hotel owners—and the wealthy merchant, of course, commands a degree of respect everywhere. After 1962, many *sādah* lost their former source of income—the *waqf*—and became impoverished; *sādah* in general have lost much of their political influence and social prestige. Tribesmen may no longer see anything shameful about buying and selling at market, and entrepreneurs of tribal birth can be found trading alongside those whose fathers were 'weak' traders. All are being increasingly absorbed into the relative egalitarianism of Yemen's enormously growing urban centres.

The Tribes of Saʿdah, Sufyān and al-Jawf

We will end this chapter with a close look at the structures and settlement areas of the tribes within this book's research area, in Yemen's extreme north. The area is home to several tribes, who belong to two distinct confederations (unions based on perceived common descent). Saʿdah governorate is inhabited by five tribes of the Khawlān b. ʿĀmir confederation: Saḥār, Rāziḥ, Jumāʿah, Munabbih, and the homonymous tribe Khawlān. The Saʿdah governorate's east, al-Jawf and the north of ʿAmrān governorate are dominated by the tribes of Wāʾilah, Dahm, and Sufyān, all of them member tribes of the Bakīl confederation. Furthermore, in the east of Saʿdah governorate are some groups of Wādiʿah, an ancient but dispersed tribe of slightly unclear affiliation.

All of these tribes further sub-divide into numerous sub-units, here called sections or segments. In Yemen the nomenclature of tribal units is ambiguous, as there seems to be no obvious privileged level of classification that applies in all circumstances, nor any standard distinction of terminology between one level and the next, and the vocabulary denoting sections and sub-sections varies from place to place.[59] Most tribal sub-divisions are locally referred to as *farʿ* or *ʿashariyyah* (pl. *ʿashāʾir*), both meaning branch or section, rather than as generic terms such as *fakhdh* or *ḥabl*. Applicable to all tribal divisions is the term *qism*, meaning division, part, or segment, which is commonly used by local sources to describe tribal affiliations. In the Saʿdah region people may use the term *qabīlah* (tribe) to describe the Khawlān b. ʿĀmir confederation as a whole, but they may also use it to refer to its constituent tribes, such as the

Saḥār and the Jumāʿah, or sometimes even their sections. For instance, in Rāziḥ not only the Rāziḥ tribe as a whole but also its divisions are called 'tribe', as in 'the tribes of al-Naẓīr'.[60] The same applies to the Bakīl confederation: strictly speaking, Wāʾilah and Dahm are the two divisions of Shākir, which is a Bakīl member. Both Wāʾilah and Dahm, however, are referred to as 'tribes'; the name 'Shākir' is only important to denote their common ancestry. The same applies to sub-divisions of Wāʾilah and Dahm such as Dhū Ḥusayn, or even smaller units such as Shawlān. This ambiguity of nomenclature seems to be highly unusual in all but a few areas of southwest Arabia.

Khawlān b. ʿĀmir

The settlement area of the Khawlān b. ʿĀmir confederation—also called Khawlān b. ʿAmrū, Khawlān b. Quḍāʿah, or Khawlān al-Shām—is located in Western Saʿdah governorate. The confederation is divided into the moieties of Furūd and Yahāniyyah. Yahāniyyah includes Rāziḥ, Khawlān, Jumāʿah, Fayfāʾ and Banī Mālik. Furūd includes Saḥār, Munabbih, and Balghāzī. Each of these eight member tribes again sub-divides into moieties, these being further sub-divided into numerous sub-sections. Since the 1934 Treaty of Ṭāʾif, which defined the boundary between Yemen's former Mutawakkilite Kingdom (1918–62) and the Kingdom of Saudi Arabia, the territory of the confederation has been divided by the Yemeni-Saudi border.[61] Five member tribes (Saḥār, Rāziḥ, Jumāʿah, Munabbih, and the homonymous tribe Khawlān) have since then been located on the Yemeni side, with the other three member tribes (Banī Mālik, Fayfāʾ, Balghāzī) on the Saudi side.

The perceived common ancestry of these tribes and their internal divisions can be displayed using tree diagrams, which suggest descent from a (real or putative) common ancestor. Tree diagrams correspond to the common visual representation of tribes as tree-like structures, which divide and sub-divide in the manner of tree branches—though there is no central and pre-eminent trunk, all branches being equal.

The settlement area of the five Yemeni member tribes of the Khawlān b. ʿĀmir confederation reaches from a few miles east of Saʿdah city, extending northwards over the town's west to the border of the Saudi Jīzān province. To the south, the confederation's territory begins about 10 or 15 miles from Saʿdah city, and extends northwest to the Saudi Arabian border. The member tribes' neighbours are Bakīlī tribes to the east and south, the Tihāmah to the west and tribes of the Saudi ʿAsīr confederation to the north.

Fig. 1.1: The tribal confederation of Khawlān b. ʿĀmir (*Saudi tribes*)

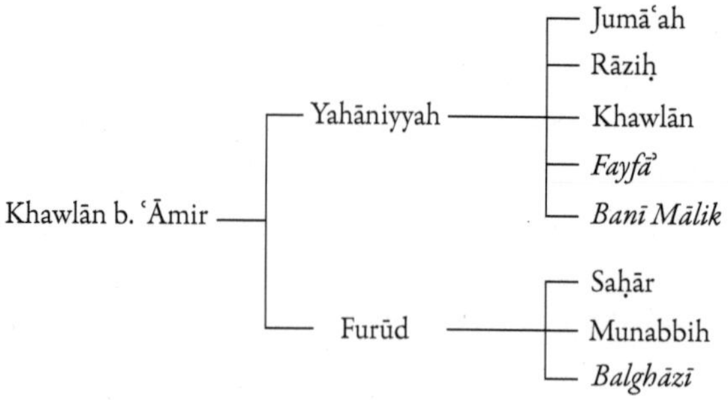

Working on Khawlān b. ʿĀmir is challenging because often neither the chroniclers nor the tribesmen define their terms precisely, and the researcher regularly must rely upon the context to judge whether, by 'Khawlān', an individual is referring to the overall community descended from the eponymous ancestor, or to the confederation's member tribe Khawlān, which retains the ancestral name. Today, Khawlān b. ʿĀmir also must be clearly distinguished from Khawlān al-Ṭiyāl (or Khawlān al-ʿĀliyah), the Bakīl tribe settled east of Sanaʿa. In terms of genealogy, Khawlān al-Ṭiyāl is distantly related to Khawlān b. ʿĀmir.[62]

Khawlān

The Khawlān member tribe dwells on the eponymous massif of the western mountain range. The tribe's territory consists of fertile but steep mountains, famous since ancient times for agriculture and highly developed irrigation techniques.[63] Because of its size and population density, the tribe's settlement area is administratively divided into three districts: Ḥaydān, Sāqayn, and al-Ẓāhir.

The sections of Khawlān are each permanently aligned with one of two conceptually opposed genealogical moieties named Aḥlāf (adj. *ḥilfī*) and Jihwaz (adj. *jihwazī*). The five *ḥilfī* sections are Banī Baḥr, Dhwayb, Zubayd, Walad Nawwār and Shaʿb Ḥayy. The six *jihwazī* sections are Marrān, ʿUraymah, Walad ʿAyyāsh, al-Sharaf, al-Karb and Banī Saʿd.[64] In terms of territory and population, the largest division within present-day Khawlān's tribal structure is the *ḥilfī* section of Banī Baḥr, which occupies the fertile, mountainous territory northwest of Sāqayn city.

Jumāʿah

Jumāʿah is another member tribe of the Khawlān b. ʿĀmir confederation. Its settlement area comprises parts of both the western mountain range and the Saʿdah basin. To the west Jumāʿah extends over the Bawṣān plateau to Munabbih and Wādī Badr of Ghamr located between Jumāʿah and Rāziḥ, and to the south to the Khawlān massif. Almost the entire mountain range north of the Khawlān massif—except the Jabal Rāziḥ and Jabal Munabbih and their foothills—is Jumāʿah territory, including Jabal Aswad and Jabal Umm Laylā in the governorate's far north. To the east, the tribe's territory extends into the depressions of Yusnam and Bāqim north of the Saʿdah basin. Bordered by the Saudi provinces ʿAsīr to the north, Wādī Najrān to the northeast, and Jīzān to the northwest, Jumāʿah shares part of Yemen's border with Saudi Arabia.

Like Khawlān, Jumāʿah sub-divides into two moieties: Aḥlāf (adj. *ḥilfī*) and Naṣr (adj. *naṣrī*). The Aḥlāf further sub-divide into the sections Majz, al-Maʿārīf, Banī ʿUbād, Banī Suwayd, Āl Jābir and Qabāʾil Qaṭābir. The Naṣr moiety comprises Banī ʿUthmān, al-Baytayn, Banī Ḥudhayfah, Banī Shunayf, Ilt al-Rubayʿ and Āl Talīd, the latter being placed on the Saudi side of the international border.[65] The Jumāʿah territory is divided into three administrative districts: Majz, Bāqim and Qaṭābir.

The tribe's settlement area is rich in pre-Islamic historical sites. One of the most famous is Umm Laylā, close to the Saudi border. In Islamic times Jumāʿah played a key role as a pillar of the imamate in Saʿdah. The relationship between Jumāʿah and the imams was close, though not free of competition, and many famous *hijrah* settlements are located on Jumāʿah's territory.[66] One of Yemen's oldest *hijrahs* is located in Qaṭābir: Hijrat Āl Yaḥyā b. Yaḥyā also known as Hijrat Qaṭābir, from which famous imams and other *hijrahs* throughout Northern Yemen have emerged.

Rāziḥ

Rāziḥ is the name of both a Khawlān b. ʿĀmir member tribe and a high massif situated on the western edge of the Sarawāt mountain range, overlooking the coastal plain. Jabal Ḥurum, the highest summit of Jabal Rāziḥ, is crowned by two fortresses and guards the only pass into the Rāziḥ massif from the north or the east. The Wādī Khulab valley creates a formidable border with the Khawlān massif to its southeast. To the west and south the slopes of Jabal Rāziḥ plunge from summits of over 2.5 kilometres to meet the Tihāmah coastal plain, at an altitude of about 500 metres. Fringing the Rāziḥ massif to the west and south is a chain of lower mountains and foothills with altitudes of less than 1.3 kilometres. These constitute a distinct region of Rāziḥ called ʿUqārib. The Yemeni-Saudi border runs along the western edge of the ʿUqārib hills. Jabal Ghamr and Wādī Badr also belong to the tribal territory of Rāziḥ.[67]

Rāziḥ divides into sixteen sections permanently aligned in two moieties named Aḥlāf and Jihwaz (separate from the Khawlān's moieties of the same name). The *jihwazī* tribes comprise Banalqām, Birkān, Ghamr, Munabbih,[68] Banī ʿAbīd, Banī Ṣafwān, and al-Waqir. The *ḥilfī* tribes are Banī Asad, Banī Maʿīn, Banī Rabīʿah, al-Izid, al-Naẓīr, al-Shawāriq, Ālat al-ʿUṭayf, Banī Ṣayāḥ, and al-Wuqaysh.[69] Furthermore, members of the Rāziḥ tribe differentiate between the sections that dwell on the main massif of Jabal Rāziḥ and those on the ʿUqārib foothills. This territorial distinction is ultimately reflected in the tribe's administrative division into Rāziḥ district on the one hand, and Shidāʾ district on the other, where the ʿUqārib section resides. Due to topographical peculiarities, Ghamr section is also allocated a separate administrative district.

Rāziḥ is a remote but fertile and populous region with a productive economy based on agriculture and trade; it bestrides the important trade route across the northern mountains, and in the west it commands the Tihāmah plain.[70] Because of its wealth, and also due to its geostrategical potential, Rāziḥ has always attracted interest from the outside. For fiscal and strategic reasons, therefore, since antiquity Rāziḥ has always been subjected to some kind of supra-tribal or 'state' control and has historically experienced great cultural continuity in state governance.[71] Rāziḥ's governors and garrisons, however, were mostly local representatives of states whose centres of power lay elsewhere. Rāziḥ hosts a large population of *sādah*, who mostly live in and around the more central settlements, some of them *hijrahs* with old mosques.

Munabbih

Munabbih is one of the 'younger' member tribes of the Khawlān b. ʿĀmir confederation. Munabbih and the Saudi Khawlān tribes Fayfāʾ, Banī Mālik and Balghāzī were formed through processes of tribal fission and fusion in medieval times.[72] The tribe dwells on the eponymous massif, Jabal Munabbih, situated beyond the Sarawāt's precipice, and in parts of Jabal Munabbih's foothills. The tribal territory of Munabbih is identical to that of the eponymous district.

The Munabbih, too, are divided into moieties: ʿAliyyin and Shaʿshaʿ. The ʿAliyyin further sub-divide into the sections Ahl al-ʿUrr, Buṭayn and Āl Yazīd, and are settled in the elevated area around Jabal Munabbih's main ridge and its highest peak, Jabal al-ʿUrr. The Shaʿshaʿ consist of the sections Qaharatayn, am-Maqnaʿ (Āl Maqnaʿ), am-Ṭāriq (Āl Ṭāriq), ʿAyyāsh and Banī Khawlī.[73] They live in the mountain's lower areas in two separate zones in the south and northeast, bordering with other Khawlān b. ʿĀmir member tribes in Yemen and Saudi Arabia.[74]

The isolated and remote Jabal Munabbih is connected with central Yemen by a segment of the Northern Ring Road. Historically the territory of Munabbih was a peripheral, almost inaccessible area at the fringes of the region's historical state centres. Hence Munabbih has managed to maintain, over long periods, a position of relative autonomy from state power.[75] Today, Munabbih is the only member tribe of the Khawlān b. ʿĀmir confederation on whose territory neither *sādah* nor *hijrah* settlements are found.[76] In this respect, Munabbih differs significantly from other member tribes of the confederation, which have been exposed to greater external economic and political influence. The extreme dialectal peculiarities and special costume of the Munabbih reflect their historically peripheral status.[77]

Saḥār

The Saʿdah basin is largely the home of Saḥār, the fifth and final member tribe of the Khawlān b. ʿĀmir confederation. Saḥār sub-divides into eleven sections aligned with two moieties: Kulayb and Mālik. The Kulayb sections are Wādī ʿAlāf, al-Uzqūl, al-ʿAbdīn, Ghurāz, al-Abqūr, and al-Dhurriyah. The Mālik moiety consists of Banī Muʿādh, Walad Masʿūd, al-Ṭalḥ, al-Mahādhir, and Banī ʿUwayr.[78]

The Saḥār tribe is of particular importance in the Saʿdah region because it commands vast territories in the central, relatively easily accessible Saʿdah basin, and virtually surrounds Saʿdah city, historically the spiritual and often mundane centre of the Zaydi Imamate and, since 1970, the seat of the municipal government. Prior to the 1962 revolution, the Saḥār tribe had special importance for the imams because it had an important protective function for the city, the *hijrah* and the market.[79] As we will see in the following chapter, during the 1960s civil war some Saḥār shaykhs played a determining role on the republican side. After the civil war, these shaykhs assumed a particularly prominent tribal, political and economic role in the republican Saʿdah governorate.

The tribal territory of Saḥār is essentially identical to that of the homonymous district. Saḥār's settlement area, however, is more heterogeneous than that of the confederation's other member tribes. The unprecedentedly favourable economic and post-civil war conditions—including the agricultural boom of the 1970s following the introduction of artificial irrigation—facilitated migration into the Saʿdah basin by all kinds of tribal and non-tribal people.[80]

Saʿdah city, surrounded by the Saḥār tribe, constitutes its own administrative district. It is the administrative and political centre of the Saʿdah governorate, as well as the centre of political integration: in recent centuries Saʿdah city has always been a marketplace, often a military garrison, sometimes the seat of government, and since 1970 the governor's seat. Saʿdah city is traditionally *hijrah*, a place and a population protected by the surrounding tribes, and has a high proportion of *sayyid* residents.[81] The comparatively urban character of Saʿdah city is further accentuated by the fact that—in contrast with medieval times—its residents' tribal affiliations are now significantly weakened.[82]

Bakīlī Tribes

The other tribal confederation of Yemen's extreme north is the Bakīl confederation, one of two confederations belonging to the grand confederation of Hamdān b. Zayd. There are three Bakīli tribes settled in the research area: Wāʾilah, Dahm and Sufyān.[83]

Fig. 1.2: The tribes of the Bakīl confederation

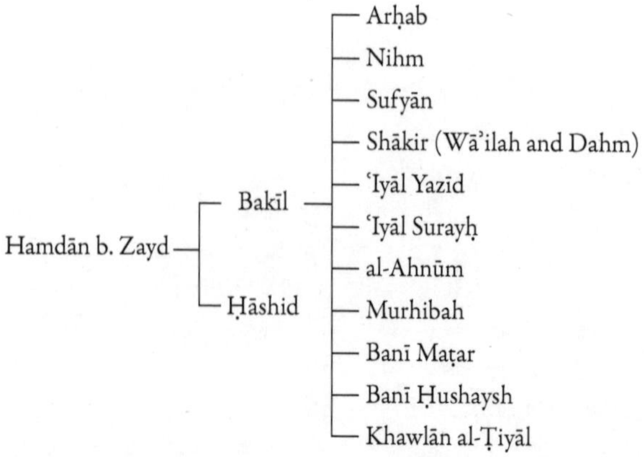

Wā'ilah and Dahm

The eastern borders of Jumāʿah and Saḥār, two of the Khawlān b. Amīr tribes, constitute the western border of Wā'ilah. The eponymous tribe's territory extends all the way east to the Rubʿ al-Khālī desert, where its territory borders that of Dahm (see below) and Yām (another tribe of Hamdān stock, in the Saudi Najrān region) in the east and north, partly overlapping with Yām domains. Wā'ilah territory is defined by the *wādīs* Nushūr, Amlaḥ, Ruḥūb, Kitāf, al-ʿAqīq, al-ʿAṭfayn and al-Faqārah, many of them draining into the Rubʿ al-Khālī.

Wā'ilah, too, consist of moieties: Rijāl ʿUlah and al-Shaʿrāt. Al-Shaʿrāt comprises the sections al-Zubayrāt, Āl ʿAbbās, Āl ʿAbīs, al-Luhūm, Banī Wāhib, Āl Ṣawāb, and Ahl Sanaʿa. The exact sub-division of Rijāl ʿUlah is complex, but broadly speaking it is divided into the segments al-Maqāsh, Āl Bāsān, Āl ʿAmrū, Āl Muqbil, Āl Mahdī, Āl Ḥusayn and Āl Abū Jabārah.[84] The territory of Wā'ilah is home to further tribal groups who are not part of Wā'ilah, but rather belong to the tribe of Dahm, whose central area of settlement is located in al-Jawf (see below). In terms of genealogy, Wā'ilah and Dahm are closely related; both are considered descendants of Shākir b. Bakīl. The Dahm tribes that have settled among Wā'ilah are Āl ʿAmmār and Āl Sālim, who control territories along and east of the highway connecting the Saʿdah basin to the capital Sanaʿa, as well as al-ʿAmālisah, residing between Kitāf city and the Baraṭ plateau.

The primacy of the connection between tribal and political representation is particularly striking in northern Hamdān. The areas with a relatively large proportion of Dahm (Āl ʿAmmār and Āl Sālim) and Wādiʿah (Wādiʿah Dammāj; see below) constitute al-Ṣafrā' district, and the settlement area of al-ʿAmālisah, inhabited by those Dahm east of Kitāf, constitutes al-Ḥishwah district; while the vast Kitāf wa l-Buqʿ district is tribally and politically dominated by Wā'ilah.

A large part of Wā'ilah territory is non-arable; the total percentage of utilized agricultural land is only 10 per cent.[85] Wā'ilah has almost no domestic economic production. The topography of the region results in a natural connection between the two agricultural, commercial and political centres of the region, Najrān and Saʿdah. The majority of trade routes connecting them pass through the territory of the Wā'ilah, who have consequently specialized in trade and smuggling.[86] Tribes and traders alike depend on the tribe for safe passage of their goods; hence it was the religious, commercial and military interest of local states in this route which gave—and still gives—Wā'ilah's shaykhs their bargaining power. The tribe's image of strength and historical autonomy from regional states is supported by the traditional absence of larger *hijrahs* and garrisons on their territory. On the other hand, relative autonomy never stopped the Wā'ilah from taking sides with state forces, if it was considered necessary or advantageous.[87]

Al-Jawf governorate is the settlement area of the Dahm tribe. Its sections are permanently aligned with the Nasr and ʿAmrū moieties. Nasr sub-divides into al-Mahāshimah, Āl Sulaymān, Āl Sālim (located in Saʿdah), and Dhū Ghaylān (further sub-divided into Dhū Muḥammad and Dhū Ḥusayn). ʿAmrū comprises the sub-sections al-ʿAmālisah and Āl ʿAmmār (both located in Saʿdah) and Banī Nawf.[88] Only a few non-Dahm groups reside in al-Jawf. The eight sections of Hamdān al-Jawf, a tribe installed around al-Jawf's administrative and commercial capital al-Ḥazm, are often identified as a Dahm tribe. The members of Hamdān al-Jawf, however, see themselves as an 'independent' tribe of Hamdān b. Zayd pedigree.[89] Through territorial proximity and alliance policy, however, Hamdān al-Jawf is close to Dahm. The Ashrāf, a special tribe of *sayyid* pedigree, reside in lower al-Jawf, with their main settlement area in Ma'rib governorate, further to the south.[90]

In Saʿdah—as in most governorates of Upper Yemen—administrative divisions have usually been drawn along existing tribal territorial borders, so that tribal borders are in most cases congruent with district boundaries. In al-Jawf, the relation between tribal territories and administrative divisions is less clearly pronounced, probably as a result of lesser historical continuity in tribal territories.[91] The Dahm settlement area comprises the largest part of al-Jawf. The Dhū Muḥammad are concentrated in the Baraṭ area (Baraṭ al-ʿInān and Kharāb al-Marāshī districts), but their territory also encompasses the district of al-Zāhir. Dhū Ḥusayn territory comprises the Rajūzah and al-Maṭammah districts and the majority of al-Ḥumaydāt and al-Matūn. It further stretches an indeterminate distance eastward into the enormously large and sparsely populated Khabb wa l-Shaʿf district, towards the Rubʿ al-Khālī desert. The Banī Nawf reside in al-Maṣlūb and part of al-Ḥumaydāt district; their very large main territory, however, begins only a few kilometres east of the provincial capital, al-Ḥazm, and covers the entire southeastern part of Khabb wa l-Shaʿf district. Beyond al-Ḥazm, the Hamdān al-Jawf can be found in al-Khaliq district. The Ashrāf tribe is settled in al-Ghayl district and the southern part of al-Maṭammah. Dahm territory as a whole meets with Āl Murrah (the Yām section) and al-Ṣayʿar (a Saudi desert tribe of Kindah pedigree) near

Sharūrah, just north of today's Saudi-Yemeni Wadīʿah border crossing, at the longitude of central Ḥaḍramawt.

Sufyān

The territory of Sufyān district and that of the homonymous tribe are essentially identical. The Sufyān are a member tribe of the Bakīl confederation and sub-divide into the moieties al-Ṣubārah and Ruhm. Al-Ṣubārah is sub-divided into the sections al-Shumaylāt and Abnāʾ Marzūq. Ruhm moiety is sub-divided into the Baʿlakī and Nuṣfī sections.[92] For much of its length, Sufyān's southern border, along the mountain ridge of Jabal Aswad and Jabal Aḥmar near al-Ḥarf (the district's administrative centre), marks the border between the territories of the al-ʿUṣaymāt and Sufyān tribes, and therefore between the Ḥāshid and Bakīl confederations. The total area of Sufyān's large but sparsely populated territory covers one-third of ʿAmrān governorate in its entirety. Beyond the rocky landscape of al-ʿAmashiyyah, Sufyān's terrain is largely flat and sandy, with some cultivation of sorghum and animal husbandry.[93]

Wādiʿah

The Wādiʿah are a territorially dispersed tribe that also belong to the grand confederation of Hamdān b. Zayd.[94] Their enclaves are located in ʿAmrān (near Khamir) and Saʿdah (Dammāj and al-Razzāmāt areas). Further Wādiʿah enclaves can be found in the Saudi areas of Najrān and Ẓahrān al-Janūb. Opinions on Wādiʿah genealogy and tribal affiliation differ. Local sources argue that Wādiʿah ʿAmrān belongs to the Ḥāshid confederation and Wādiʿah Saʿdah to the Bakīl. This ambiguity may be explained by the tendency of lineage rumps of groups threatened with marginalization to fuse with other lineages (and in so doing to fuse their resources with those of the adopting lineage)—a common process that can be observed throughout Yemen's history.

Hamdān al-Shām

Now it becomes tricky: Wāʾilah and those tribes and sections of Dahm and Wādiʿah settled in the eastern Saʿdah region (Āl ʿAmmār, Āl Sālim, al-ʿAmālisah, Wādiʿah Dammāj, Āl al-Razzāmāt) are referred to as Northern Hamdān, Hamdān al-Shām. Hamdān al-Shām is a genealogical term denoting those tribes settling in the eastern Saʿdah region and whose genealogies meet in the Hamdān b. Zayd confederation. It is primarily used to distinguish the different groups of Hamdānī pedigree from their immediate neighbours in the Saʿdah region—that is, the Khawlān b. ʿĀmir confederation to the west—and thus to draw a distinction between the Khawlānī (descended from Ḥimyar) and Hamdānī (descended from Kahlān) tribes of the Saʿdah region.

PART ONE

LEGACIES OF THE PAST (1962–2004)

The following chapters aim at elucidating the multiple contexts of the Houthi conflict and its complex local history. They explore the conflict's historical roots as well as the tribal, political, sectarian and economic factors that led to its eruption. To this end, they deal with certain topics in great depth, some of which have so far been neglected by researchers. The wide range of issues covered can be pooled into three main subjects: firstly, the elite transformations in Saʿdah province, triggered by the 1960s civil war and then cemented by the republican regime's politics of patronage; secondly, the influence of Saudi patronage politics on local tribal societies; and thirdly, the effects of an influx of radical Sunnism and the emergence of an overtly competitive sectarian environment. All these issues are deeply interconnected and represent the various facets of a complex development, which eventually led to the outbreak of the Houthi conflict in 2004.

The 1960s civil war in the Saʿdah area is a good starting point to measure and interpret the alignment of the region's tribal loyalties and allegiances in times of war. The area has often been portrayed in relation to the civil war in an oversimplifying and perfunctory manner, as a 'royalist bloc' or 'imamic fortress'. On the contrary, Chapter 2 of this volume, exploring tribal allegiances during the civil war, reveals that tribes and tribal sections were never, or almost never, homogeneous blocs or groups following primordial allegiances. Rather, the alignment of allegiances was (and is) driven by a variety of interests and motives: religious convictions, strategic alliances, kinship ties, ancient contractual obligations and protection pacts, economic interests, financial incentives, tribal and personal rivalries and enmities, and resulting struggles for prestige, power and influence. The 1960s civil war set the course for the post-revolutionary elite transformations in the Saʿdah area, which has led to empowerment of tribal shaykhs at the expense of the *sādah*, the former administrative elite. Furthermore, the civil war triggered a reshuffle in power relations among the shaykhs themselves and led to the emergence of certain key actors who—either themselves or through their successors—disproportionately influenced local politics in the decades to come, and eventually became vital players in the Houthi conflict. Thus, considering the dynamics of tribal relations enables us to reconstruct the twisted evolution of the republican order in the Saʿdah area.

The chapter 'Reshuffle of Power Relations' explains how Saʿdah's new tribal elite, which emerged after the civil war, has been cemented by the republican politics of patronage. Many influential shaykhs of the area became easy targets for co-optation, allowing the young Yemeni republic to push its agenda without making substantial efforts at state building. Incomplete state formation, underdevelopment, and the political and economic patronage of certain influential shaykhs resulted in severe imbalances: a vastly unjust distribution of economic resources and a deeply patrimonial political system. These disparities in wealth and power fostered increasing alienation between many ordinary tribespeople and their enriched shaykhs. The politics of patronage also generated new disparities and conflicts between the shaykhs themselves, because not all shaykhs became part of this new stratum of the corporate privileged. In fact, every era in Yemeni history has brought forth privileged and underprivileged groups, and certain shaykhs have wielded considerable power. After the 1960s civil war, however, a largely new development took place in the rural areas of northern Yemen: a systematic economic and political empowerment of shaykhs, at the expense of both the *sādah* and many average tribesmen.

Chapter 3 elucidates the crucial influence of Saudi borderland politics on the tribal, political and economic situation in the Saʿdah area and beyond, as well as the fundamental interdependence of the ongoing Saudi-Yemeni boundary dispute and the emerging Houthi conflict. In addition to Yemeni patronage politics, Saudi patronage also helped to consolidate the post-revolutionary elite in Saʿdah. Saudi patronage, was even more deeply rooted in the area than the new patronage politics of Yemen itself—the beginnings of the Saudi patronage policy can be traced back to the Saudi-Yemeni War of 1934 and the Treaty of Ṭāʾif, which resolved it. After the conclusion of this treaty, the tribal elites in the Yemeni borderlands played a vital role in securing the international boundary between Yemen and the Saudi Kingdom. Since the follow-up Treaty of Jeddah in 2000, however, the loyalty of the borderland tribes has been shaken by the Kingdom's plans to physically enforce and fortify the border. This shift in Saudi policy has triggered the recent re-alignment of allegiances in Saʿdah's tribal environment; the chapter also explains the mutual influence of Saudi borderland policy and the emerging Houthi conflict.

The final chapter of this part, 'Sects and Politics', sketches the dynamics which sectarian and related political developments could produce in this environment, so marked by economic and political inequalities. The recent decades of religious radicalization in Yemen are tantamount to a declaration of failure of Yemen's 'Traditionist Project', as Haykel has called it, which aimed to bridge the differences between domestic Sunni and Zaydi-Shia denominations.[1] The spread of radical Sunnism in the Zaydi heartland, at times promoted by the Yemeni government, triggered the emergence of a Zaydi resistance movement, which not only was directed against the increasing 'Sunnization' of Zaydism, but also addressed the marginalization of the local Zaydi community. The Zaydi revival managed to develop a powerful social revolutionary and political component through its resistance to the post-revolutionary elite described above, and its more or less artificial stabilization by the patronage politics of the Yemeni and Saudi governments. Since the turn of the millennium, the Zaydi revival's sectarian, social revolutionary and political agenda has been significantly influenced and shaped by the Zaydi cleric and former politician Ḥusayn Badr al-Dīn al-Ḥūthī, who has given the Houthi movement its name.

Thus, in the local context of the Saʿdah area, the Zaydi revival movement became a catalyst with the potential to unite all those, in Saʿdah and beyond, who felt economically neglected, politically ostracized and religiously marginalized. This background explains why the Houthi movement gradually developed such powerful dynamics. Furthermore, it then becomes understandable why one of the most striking features of the Houthi conflict was the expulsion of a large number of shaykhs from the Saʿdah area—something that did not happen during the 1960s civil war—and in turn, after the Houthis' seizure of power in the Saʿdah area in 2011, a complete re-definition of tribal leadership.

The Saʿdah wars (2004–10) were thus neither a power struggle of local tribes, nor a social revolution of the economically and politically marginalized, nor a sectarian war. Rather, they were all three at once: social, political, sectarian, economic, tribal and personal interests began to merge. Generalizations of these sometimes overly complex frameworks should be avoided: the dynamics of the Saʿdah wars can only be elucidated through a consideration of individual cases, their historical dimensions and their local causes.

However, what one sees as complex and what one sees as simple is relative, and changes with time. Locals effortlessly navigate this environment, well aware that local constellations, motivations, and allegiances change rather slowly and gradually, and are relatively predictable against underlying historical continuity and the endurance of positions and actions among local elites. Despite their inherent particularism, most tribes have a relatively stable political position over time, with infrequent shifts in position, and the findings of this study substantiate the remarkable degree of historical continuity in tribal positions and loyalties. By referring to the historical dimensions[2] at play in current developments in the Saʿdah area, it is possible to transcend and determine the present—its specific political, sectarian and economic settings—and thus to render contemporary events meaningful and intelligible.

2

ELITE TRANSFORMATIONS

The 1960s civil war was a major event, resulting in a reshuffle of local power structures and the emergence of a new equilibrium. We do not know much about the local developments and events in the Saʿdah area during the period from the end of the civil war to the outbreak of the Saʿdah wars in 2004, as existing information sources on local history and development are limited or incomplete. There was hardly any continuation of the promising, mainly ethnological and anthropological studies conducted in the Saʿdah area between the early 1970s and the mid-1980s.[3] Increasingly the once important Saʿdah province fell into oblivion. Governmental neglect, remoteness and the scarcity of scientific research contributed to the development of the initial Houthi conflict going almost unnoticed by the outside world. The attention of the government, the media and the scientific community shifted back to Saʿdah only in 2004, when the first in a long series of violent confrontations between the Houthis and the central government erupted. These became known as the Saʿdah wars.

Tribal Allegiances during the Civil War (1962–70)

To provide a better understanding of the local dynamics that led to the Houthi conflict's outbreak in 2004, it is useful to revisit the 26 September Revolution of 1962 and the ensuing civil war (1962–70), which led to the abolition of the imamate and the establishment of the Yemen Arab Republic (YAR). A review of the civil war in the Saʿdah area enables us to shed light on patterns of tribal allegiance and the historical relations between tribes and their respective state overlords, thus elucidating the tribal loyalties and allegiances at play during the Houthi wars. Moreover, this chapter serves to introduce a number of key actors of local and national relevance, most of them from shaykhly families who gained importance during the civil war and who still wielded enormous influence over local politics in the Saʿdah area when war broke out in 2004.

Most accounts of the 1962 revolution and the ensuing civil war focus on events in the capital Sanaʿa, and on the role of the surrounding tribal confederations, Ḥāshid and Bakīl. The role of the Saʿdah region's tribes in the civil war remains almost unexplored. As stated above, Saʿdah's role in the conflict has often been reduced to that of a 'royalist bloc' or 'imamic fortress', and its tribes portrayed as 'ammunition' (*dhakhīrah*) of the Zaydi imamate.[4] In point of fact, their role during and after the civil war makes for a complex story. Similar to the tribes of Ḥāshid and Bakīl, the fortunes of many tribal leaders from the Saʿdah area were bound up with those of successive imams, vying with them for power and influence, and supporting or opposing them during conflicts between competing imams.[5] Due to an abundance of political, denominational, strategic and economic constellations and motivations during the civil war, the tribal societies of Saʿdah were traversed by rifts, tensions and conflicting allegiances. The royalist forces in Saʿdah were strong, but there was also considerable resistance to the imamic system. In my interviews with contemporary witnesses from the Saʿdah area, two aspects were given particular emphasis regarding the formation of tribal opposition to imamic rule: the hostage system and the imams' attempts to steer tribal politics through the investiture of particular shaykhs.

Under the 1911 Treaty of Daʿʿān with the Ottomans, the then Zaydi imam of Yemen, Imam Yaḥyā (1918–48), resumed control over the Zaydi heartland in northern Yemen and began to establish an unparalleled degree of order in his dominion.[6] This order partly relied on the age-old Yemeni tradition of taking hostages. State institutions were underdeveloped, and taking hostages became a central element of imamic rule in order to keep the tribes, its ultimate mainstay, under control. Normally hostages were young boys between the ages of five and fifteen—generally the sons of tribal leaders—although in some cases older hostages were also kept. The contemporary conduct of the shaykhs and their tribal groups determined whether the hostage would live in comfort and receive an education, or spend his time in a dungeon, sometimes under appalling conditions.[7]

During the Ḥamīd al-Dīn dynasty, especially during the reigns of Imam Yaḥyā (1904–48) and Imam Aḥmad (1948–62), the imams took tribal hostages in great numbers, and they were particularly careful of their choice when it came to the Saʿdah region. In Rāziḥ, for instance, the imams demanded hostages from every shaykhly family and leading clan.[8] In Munabbih, the number of hostages taken by the imams—when they were able to implement this policy, as Munabbih was outside of state control for long periods—was exactly the number of tribal sections and their shaykhs. Many hostages from the member tribes of the Khawlān b. ʿĀmir confederation were held in the fortresses of al-Sinnārah and al-Ṣamʿ near Saʿdah city.[9] In Rāziḥ, due to the tribe's highly developed local administration and close relationship with the imams, an elaborate system was established in which the hostages were sometimes held only for a few months, then replaced by others.[10] In other cases, such as the Saḥār tribe, the sons of certain shaykhs were separated from their families for longer periods. Some of these 'hostages of obedience' (*rahāʾin al-ṭāʿah*) spent their whole childhood and youth far from their families and tribes, in sometimes very inhospitable fortresses and prisons as distant as al-Ahnūm, Shihārah or Ḥajjah that became notorious and dreaded places of confinement. Some hostages were detained for decades; others were executed and buried in the cemeteries next to the prisons, called the 'hostages tombs' (*maqābir al-rahāʾin*).[11] There are quite diverse and conflicting narratives about the rule of the imams in northern Yemen. The shaykhs' position vis-à-vis the hostage system is reflected in the local historiography of al-Sufyānī, who recorded gruesome deeds by referring to historical cases in which, for instance, an imam ordered amputation of hostages' hands and feet, or a mass execution of Khawlān b. ʿĀmir hostages.[12]

One of Saʿdah's shaykhly lineages less amenable to government control, and hence under the imams' special surveillance, was the Mujallī family of Raḥbān. The shaykhs of Raḥbān are also the senior shaykhs of Saḥār's al-ʿAbdīn section. Al-ʿAbdīn had a special importance for the imams because this section is settled in the immediate vicinity of Saʿdah city and has historically fulfilled an important protective function for the city, the *hijrah* and the market. Hostages from the Mujallī family were held in great numbers. Before the 1962 revolution Ḥusayn, son of the then shaykh Fāyid Mujallī, spent much of his twenties a hostage in different fortresses and jails such as al-Sinnārah, Ḥajjah and Sanaʿa. His age indicates the special importance of the Mujallī family, because usually at the age of fifteen, when a boy was considered to have reached manhood, a hostage would be permitted to return to his family and be replaced by a younger relative. Those over fifteen who remained hostages were often manacled or chained.[13] Ḥusayn Mujallī returned home only shortly before the last imam, Muḥammad al-Badr (September 1962), finally abolished the hostage system. His uncle Ḥamūd Mujallī was also thrown in jail as part of a punitive campaign—he and a Jewish fellow prisoner were chained and shackled to each other by the legs for four months.[14]

Another imamic method of exerting control over disobedient tribes and recalcitrant shaykhs focused on the steering of shaykhly succession, and sometimes the replacement of entire shaykhly lineages. As stated above, among the Khawlān b. ʿĀmir (as among most tribes in Yemen), the shaykhs are usually elected from certain shaykhly families. The election of a successor from among the eligible candidates is subjected to a vote by tribal elders (*aʿyān*).[15] The 1911 Treaty of Daʿʿān had granted Imam Yaḥyā the right to appoint officials and judges in his dominion, and provided a logical basis for the extension of his appointive powers over the shaykhs, who were the judicial heads of their tribes according to customary law (*ʿurf*). Thereafter, Yaḥyā attempted to appoint his own nominees to those positions as they fell vacant, either by promoting a candidate of the shaykhly lineage who proved to be a more reliable partner than his predecessor, or in some cases by marginalizing the entire lineage in favour of another.[16] In case of success, this intervention gave the imam immense power and patronage, as he was able to appoint more 'trustworthy' tribal leaders and to divest authority from less loyal lineages. The tribes violently objected to Yaḥyā's policy, and for nearly twenty years he worked to impose his power of appointment.

In the years before the 1962 revolution, this policy was implemented by the imam's representative in Saʿdah city, Prince ʿAbdullah b. al-Ḥasan, who pursued a policy of replacement and, as some say, 'elimination' (*taṣfiyyah*) of those shaykhs who were disobedient or opposed the imam's rule.[17] Prince ʿAbdullah was a nephew of Imam Aḥmad (1948–62), who ruled after Yaḥyā and was the penultimate imam. Albeit a delicate, small-boned person, ʿAbdullah was called *ṣaqr al-ʿurūbah* (Falcon of Arabness) for his prowess and courage. The policy of replacement aroused fierce opposition among the targeted tribes and shaykhs. During the 1962 revolution and the ensuing civil war, these shaykhs and their families and tribes were among the first to side with the republicans and oppose the royalist system because of—in their words—the tyranny (*ẓulm*) and subjugation (*istiʿbād*) to which it subjected them. Their motivation therefore featured certain characteristics of *khurūj* (lit. departure), a doctrinal Zaydi term for openly challenging an unjust authority.[18]

During the decade preceding the 1962 revolution, Imam Aḥmad's occasionally humiliating and often unpredictable attitude had further weakened the moral basis of the Ḥamīd al-Dīn dynasty's rule among certain tribes from Saʿdah and beyond, not only in the eyes of the notorious 'malcontents', but also among some shaykhs who were once quite close to him. Qāʾid Shuwayṭ from Banī ʿUwayr wrote in his memoirs that he had originally been *ʿarīf* (a 'military shaykh' or 'officer') under Imam Aḥmad, like many other shaykhs from the Saʿdah area who were rallied with their tribesmen for the imam's military campaigns.[19] Because of their closeness to the imam those shaykhs had, according to Qāʾid Shuwayṭ, intimate knowledge of the people's plight and grievances during Aḥmad's reign, and many of them deemed the revolution a 'salvation from an abasing reality' (*al-khalāṣ min wāqʿ muzrin*). The creeping alienation between Imam Aḥmad and certain shaykhs had already culminated in 1959 in open conflict. During his father's medical treatment in Italy, Crown Prince Muḥammad al-Badr had tried to buy the loyalty of some northern tribes. After his return to Yemen, Imam Aḥmad cancelled those large subsidies and attempted to get back some of the money. He summoned the senior shaykh of the Ḥāshid confederation, Ḥusayn b. Nāṣir al-Aḥmar, and his son Ḥamīd under a safe conduct to al-Sukhnah in the Tihāmah lowlands. When they arrived, a heated argument took place, after which Imam Aḥmad ordered the arrest and decapitation of his guests. This was a blatant breach of both confidence and tribal customs, which led to uprisings among many tribes in the country's north and east. These were then violently suppressed by Imam Aḥmad.[20]

Qāʾid Shuwayṭ also recalled in his memoirs that, at the same time as Imam Aḥmad gave the order to execute Ḥusayn b. Nāṣir al-Aḥmar and his son, he also summoned to al-Sukhnah three shaykhs from Saḥār—Musʿad Shuwayṭ, Aḥmad Shuwayṭ and Ḥamūd Mujallī—whose families had also received financial incentives from Muḥammad al-Badr in exchange for their 'good conduct'.[21] When they arrived, Aḥmad imprisoned them for a whole year. To add insult to injury, he paid them a humiliatingly small daily amount of money, equivalent to the price of an animal at the market. After the arrival of a large tribal delegation from Saḥār, Imam Aḥmad released the shaykhs and provided a small plane to bring them back to Saʿdah. However, when the shaykhs boarded the plane, they found some members of the Ḥamīd al-Dīn family already on board, on their way to Sanaʿa. When they were over Manākha in the Ḥarāz Mountains, Ḥamūd Mujallī, fearing that he and the others had been lured to their imprisonment or deaths, entered the cockpit and forced the pilot to turn towards Saʿdah, threatening to gun him down.[22] These incidents indicate that, by 1962, relations between the imamate and many influential shaykhs from the Saʿdah area and beyond were already characterized by the deepest distrust.

After the death of Imam Aḥmad in 1962, he was replaced by Crown Prince Muḥammad al-Badr. The latter adopted a more clement policy than his father, introduced reforms, and abolished the unpopular hostage system.[23] Shortly thereafter, the 26 September Revolution began in Sanaʿa with a coup by army officers, among them several men of *sayyid* and tribal background, and Muḥammad al-Badr—allegedly disguised in women's clothes—fled the capital. It was no coincidence that he headed for the Zaydi heartland of northwest Yemen, where the imamate still enjoyed fairly stable support. During the ensuing civil war, parts of the Saʿdah region became royalist strongholds till 1970. Muḥammad al-Badr set up his two main headquarters in Jabal Qārah in Ḥajjah and Jabal Rāziḥ near the Saudi border (with another headquarters in the Kitāf region in eastern Saʿdah), and the royal princes were prominent in the struggle against republican forces. Muḥammad al-Badr and the princes rallied the local tribes, and distributed arms, ammunition, supplies and money to those who were with them.

The sometimes very great tribal support that Muḥammad al-Badr found in the northern areas of Saʿdah indicates that many Zaydi tribes remained attached to the imamate as the legitimate form of authority beyond the tribe, and that they were willing to defend imamic authority out of conviction. In his memoirs, ʿAbdullah al-Aḥmar (senior shaykh of the Ḥāshid confederation and leading republican) wrote that it was very difficult for the revolution and the Republic to govern and control the Saʿdah region, because of its tribes' deep-rooted loyalties to the institution of the Zaydi imamate.[24] He describes the openly denominational nature of the civil war:

> it was a fight about faith, belief and conviction, and the rest of the princes of the house of Ḥamīd al-Dīn sent us letters which intimidated us to support the 'pharaonic colonists and their slaves', as they said, and which pointed out the royalist role in the resistance against the infidels, and called us to support them and to fight for the sake of Allah.[25]

The expression 'pharaonic colonists' (*al-mustaʿmirūn al-farāʿinah*) indicates that, as long as the Egyptians were involved on the republican side, xenophobia was also a motivator for opposing the revolution; the brutal actions of the Egyptian troops, who had no scruples in using toxic nerve gas against the local population, left continuing bitterness in the Saʿdah region.[26]

ʿAbdullah al-Aḥmar also conceptualized Saʿdah as a sort of imamic bastion, thus distorting the region's nature. When studied more closely, an enormous variety of motivations and positions becomes visible among the area's tribes, indicating that tribal society was deeply fractured. Many factors were at play in the development of diverging loyalties. Some tribes made strategic alliances with the republicans according to practical considerations, as in the past they had allied themselves against Zaydi imams with Yuʿfirids, Rasūlids, Idrīsids and others.[27] Bribes and the opportunity to 'sell' tribal allegiance played a major role in exerting influence on the tribes, particularly since Muḥammad al-Badr had abolished the hostage system.[28] Kinship ties, feuds and enmities significantly steered the alignment of tribal loyalties (when considering the Saʿdah wars of 2004–10, many such cases will be discussed in more detail). Positions could also differ within a tribe; shaykhs and their sections found themselves on opposing sides, or one sub-division of the section sided with the royalists, while the other adhered to the Republic. For reasons of internal power rivalries, even members of the same lineage or clan were at times divided.

This is not the only inaccurate impression given by an over-generalization in ʿAbdullah al-Aḥmar's memoirs. He wrote that in Rāziḥ, one of Muḥammad al-Badr's headquarters, there was 'not a single Republican'.[29] Historically the fertile and strategically favourably situated Rāziḥ mountain area, with its large *sādah* population, had a long-standing symbiotic relationship with the local overlords, including the Ḥamīd al-Dīn imams.[30] During the civil war, however, the tribal society of Rāziḥ was split. Weir explains that most Rāziḥīs were 'royalist' by default as well as conviction and contractual allegiance. Yet a small minority openly and actively supported the republicans, and others undoubtedly did so secretly, variously motivated by resentment of *sayyid* power and privilege, exasperation at Muḥammad al-Badr's inadequacies, and yearning for the development promised by the republicans.[31] During the civil war the senior shaykh of Rāziḥ, ʿAlī Aḥmad al-ʿAzzām, was with the royalists, and so were many other tribal leaders and their tribes in Rāziḥ. On the other hand, some Rāziḥ shaykhs openly supported the revolution, such as the shaykh of al-Izid and Sulaymān al-Faraḥ of Ilt Faraḥ, the shaykhly clan of al-Naẓīr, Rāziḥ's main commercial and administrative centre. That said, Ilt Faraḥ also included active royalists.[32]

Considering this alongside the Jumāʿah and Khawlān tribes, it becomes evident that this pattern was repeated in other tribal areas. While many senior shaykhs sided with the royalists, resistance and revolt was mainly led by rival 'minor' shaykhs. In Khawlān the senior shaykh, Ḥusayn Rawkān, had aligned himself with the royalists. The most active republican tribal leader was Muḥammad Ghatāyah, both shaykh of Khawlān's Walad Yaḥyā section and *shaykh al-shaml* (senior shaykh) of Marrān; during the civil war he established relations with both the republicans and the Nasserite leaders in Sanaʿa. He was assassinated by royalist tribesmen from Khawlān upon his return to his home region.[33]

The Jumāʿah are said to have been particularly characterized by a certain 'lack of cooperation' (*inʿidām al-ʿamal al-jamāʿī*) and political dispersion. The tribe's senior shaykh, Yaḥyā Muḥammad Muqīt, also *shaml shumūl* (senior representative) of the Khawlān b. ʿĀmir confederation, supported the imamate 'with all might' (*bi-quwwah*), although the relationship between the Muqīt dynasty and the imams had never been free of conflict and competition.[34] Other sections of Jumāʿah openly sided with the Republic, notably the Āl al-Ḥamāṭī of Banī Ḥudhayfah. Driven by the historic rivalry between 'tribal' Majz and '*sayyid*' Ḍaḥyān, shaykhs and their followers from Majz also sided with the Republic, among them Muḥammad Muṣliḥ al-Naḥū as well as shaykhs of the al-Lahbī, ʿAbūd and Dihām lineages.[35]

The member tribes of the Khawlān b. ʿĀmir's Furūd moiety, Saḥār and Munabbih, showed the strongest support for the Republic.[36] The Saḥār senior shaykh (also *shaykh al-shaml* of Saḥār's Mālikī moiety), Dirdaḥ b. Jaʿfar, the senior shaykh of Saḥār's Kulayb moiety, Mahdī b. Naṣr Kubās, and Nāṣir b. Qirshah of Wādī Masʿūd were among the strictest pro-monarchy shaykhs, and a majority of the Saḥār sections were with the royalists.[37] Among the Saḥār shaykhs, however, considerable opposition developed, and these anti-royalist Saḥār shaykhs became the central force and main drivers of the revolution in the Saʿdah area. Their resistance was significant because, as stated above, the Saḥār tribe are settled on the outskirts of Saʿdah city, and the Saḥār's al-ʿAbdīn section has historically served an important protective function. The Saḥār shaykhs who supported the revolution from its inception were called the 'Saʿdah Brigade' (*liwāʾ Ṣaʿdah*); many of them participated in the seventy-day siege of Sanaʿa in 1967. Among the most prominent representatives of the Saʿdah Brigade were those shaykhs who had faced humiliating experiences during the reign of Imam Aḥmad—notably Fāyid Mujallī, his brother Ḥamūd and his son Ḥusayn of al-ʿAbdīn, as well as tribal sections and their shaykhs that backed al-ʿAbdīn for alliance or kinship reasons, such as Raḥbān (the home section of the Mujallī family) and Farwah. In addition to these were Musʿad, Aḥmad and Qāʾid Shuwayṭ from Banī ʿUwayr, whom Imam Aḥmad had imprisoned in al-Sukhnah, ʿAbdullah b. ʿAlī Manāʿ from al-Ṭalḥ and his sons Muḥammad and Fayṣal, Fayṣal al-Surabī from Banī Muʿādh, and Bushayt Abū ʿUbayd from al-Mahādhir.[38] These shaykhs were of the utmost importance for anti-royalist resistance in Saʿdah before and during the revolution.

With their historically *sādah*-hostile and isolationist tendencies and determination to keep central authority at a distance, the Munabbih are, to some extent, an exception. During the early phase of the civil war, they declared themselves neutral, and remained so until becoming pro-republican.[39] Munabbih is the only member tribe of the Khawlān b. ʿĀmir confederation whose then senior shaykh, ʿAlī Maḍwāḥ b. ʿAwfān, sided with the Republic. On the other hand, his internal rival Dahbāsh Miṭrī, *shaykh shaml* (highest representative) of Munabbih's Shaʿshaʿ moiety, sided with the royalists. The reasons for this were twofold: firstly, the Miṭrī family had developed ties of marriage and loyalty with the *sādah* of the nearby Hijrat Āl Yaḥyā b. Yaḥyā; secondly, intra-tribal rivalries with the ʿAwfān lineage undoubtedly played a part.[40]

The largest and most powerful group of Hamdān in the Saʿdah area, the Wāʾilah tribe of the province's east, was one of the royalists' strongest allies. Prince Ḥasan had his headquarters in Wāʾilah territory, near Wādī Amlaḥ, and Prince Muḥammad Ḥusayn was in charge of the rear bases near Najrān, from where the imamic ordnance was organized; thus the Wāʾilah became the main guarantors of royalist supplies.[41] Furthermore, the royalists hid in the caves of Qadam in Kitāf—the Egyptians used toxic nerve gas to flush them out, in order to proceed towards Najrān.

Wāʾilah has a history of relative and precarious autonomy, but at the same time significant elements of the tribe are influenced by a strong and powerful correlation to Zaydi belief and doctrine dating back to the early days of Zaydism.[42] There was a close relationship between the Ḥamīd al-Dīn dynasty and one of the then most influential shaykhs of Wāʾilah, Ḥāmis al-ʿAwjarī of Āl Mahdī; when he was a royal prince and imamic field leader in the Saudi-Yemeni war of the 1930s, Aḥmad spent more than two years in Wādī Nushūr, the home area of the al-ʿAwjarī clan.[43] During the civil war Ḥāmis al-ʿAwjarī and his son ʿAbdullah stood firmly on the side of the Ḥamīd al-Dīn.[44] Despite his advanced age, Ḥāmis al-ʿAwjarī led the battles personally (*bi-l-bunduq wa l-khanjar*).[45] Ḥāmis al-ʿAwjarī received support from Maʿbar b. Fayṣal of Āl Abū Jabārah, a Wāʾilah section dwelling in the immediate vicinity of the Saudi border.[46] But even the Hamdān of Saʿdah were no uniform royalist block.[47] Opposition to the royalists came, for instance, from Āl ʿAmmār of Dahm and their shaykhs Yaḥyā al-Ḥusaynī and Hindī Dughsān. Yet both Āl ʿAmmār and the Dughsān clan were divided against themselves. Moreover, the Dughsān and the al-Ḥusaynī clan were embroiled in a blood feud.

The battle for Saʿdah city mirrors these internal struggles among the region's tribal societies. At the beginning of the revolution in 1962, Saʿdah city was immediately occupied by republican forces. During the course of the civil war the city was then twice taken by the royalists, twice re-conquered by the republicans. Locals recall a series of plagues breaking out in Saʿdah city; many of its inhabitants fled to the mountains and caves of the tribal hinterlands.[48] In his memoirs, Qāʾid Shuwayṭ described the hardships of the republican struggle in the city: the pro-republican shaykhs and their supporters fought under dire conditions against strong royalist forces, their families' houses were destroyed several times, and each siege brought starvation, forcing them to drink dirty water from cemetery wells.[49] The republican forces suffered the biggest setback when the Egyptian forces withdrew from Yemen in 1967, leaving behind a vacuum on the republican side. This emboldened the royalists in Saʿdah to advance on Sanaʿa, already besieged by imamic forces.

By February 1968, the siege of Sanaʿa was lifted, and the republicans had essentially won the war. Saʿdah, however, remained a stumbling block for the revolution. In 1969, when Muḥammad al-Badr and the other princes had already gone into exile, Prince ʿAbdullah b. al-Ḥasan, the field leader of the royalists in Saʿdah city and surrounding areas, still refused to leave Saʿdah. His headquarters was al-Sinnārah, a fortress situated on a precipitous mountain slope overlooking both Saʿdah city and Wādī al-ʿAbdīn in Saḥār. In 1969, Saudi Arabia had already cut its material support to the royalists. In the summer of that year, certain Saḥār shaykhs of the Saʿdah Brigade conspired to kill the prince.[50] They set up three ambushes outside the city. When the prince left al-Sinnārah fortress on his way to Saʿdah city's al-Hādī mosque for the Friday prayer, he met the first ambush and was killed. One of these shaykhs has been identified as having 'supervised the last seconds of the prince', as a local source put it. The assassination of Prince ʿAbdullah was seen as the very last knife plunged into the heart of the imamic system, and the memory of his murder is still a vivid part of the collective memory in Saʿdah.

On the royalist side, the assassination of Prince ʿAbdullah elicited feelings of humiliation and anger. The desire for revenge expressed itself in the subsequent looting of Saʿdah city and some areas of Saḥār. The royalist ʿAbdullah Ḥāmis al-ʿAwjarī had demanded that the shaykhs involved ask Prince ʿAbdullah to leave Saʿdah, rather than kill him. After the prince was found dead, ʿAbdullah al-ʿAwjarī took his body and buried him in the al-ʿAwjarī family graveyard in Wādī Nushūr. Then he rallied the Wāʾilah tribes, who responded to his call 'regardless of what is right and what is wrong',[51] and when the last members of the Ḥamīd al-Dīn family had crossed the Saudi border, the Wāʾilah and those tribes who were with them invaded and sacked Saʿdah city, al-ʿAbdīn and Raḥbān.[52] The city's inhabitants, including the shaykhs of the Saʿdah Brigade, fled to Khamir, Sanaʿa and elsewhere.

The republican forces in Saʿdah were weaker than the strong republican tribes of Upper Yemen, with fewer military, material and human resources at their command; their final success was dependent on the support of republican forces from among the Ḥāshid and Bakīl tribal confederations. For some months Saʿdah city remained in the hands of royalist tribesmen until the shaykhs of the Saʿdah Brigade returned from exile, many of them from the republican city of Khamir, accompanied by Amīn Abū Rās, Mujāhid Abū Shawārib, ʿAbdullah al-Aḥmar, and other pro-republican shaykhs. They were able to lift the siege of Saʿdah city and expel the remnants of the imamic forces towards Wādī Nushūr in Kitāf, where one of the last battles of the civil war took place.[53] Wāʾilah and Rāziḥ were the very last regions in Yemen in which the imamic system prevailed, and the revolution could not succeed until those imamic strongholds had fallen.[54] In 1970, the republicans succeeded, and the royalist forces were scattered. The Zaydi imamate was finally, albeit laboriously, replaced by the Yemen Arab Republic.

The preceding overview sketches tribal positions and allegiances in the Saʿdah area during the 1960s civil war. It indicates that it would indeed be difficult to speak of tribal allegiances in the Saʿdah area without taking into account tribal structures, geographical positions, and inter-, intra- and supra-tribal power relations. During the civil war three aspects took on particular importance: the fragmented but relatively stable character of tribal loyalties; the central role of intra-tribal rivalry in the alignment of political positions, and the rise of those tribal 'big men' who became prominent actors in Saʿdah's recent history and whose scions, as we will see, had and still have a crucial impact on the causes, course and outcome of the Houthi wars that erupted in 2004.

The account above has shown that none of the Saʿdah tribes was a uniform bloc, and in some cases loyalties split down to the family level, especially when the leading shaykh's position was contested by internal rivals. Allegiances were governed by a variety of financial, strategic, religious, familial and personal interests and motives.

The frictions during the 1960s civil war were expressions of diverging religious beliefs, political convictions and practical considerations, but also the consequence of intra- and inter-tribal rivalries. When considering the alignment of loyalties, a certain stratification of allegiances becomes evident. As a rule of thumb, the senior shaykhs of Hamdān Ṣaʿdah and Khawlān b. ʿĀmir—except the Munabbih—sided with the imamic system, and thus with the then dominant power, although historically their relationship with the imams was troubled. As stated in Chapter 1, senior shaykhs do not 'govern' their tribes, and their political authority is limited. Nevertheless their position is highly prestigious and gives a strong internal and external signal, because they 'unite' and represent their tribes as a whole, notably in negotiations with other tribes inside and outside the confederation as well as with respective state powers. Historically, cooperation between the senior shaykhs and the Zaydi imams was no reliable constant, but rather a process constantly shattered by conflicts and re-negotiation. During the 1960s civil war, however, this power symbiosis proved to be rather stable. We have seen that some of the Saʿdah area's lower-ranking shaykhs were key figures and 'motors' of the revolution. Some joined the republicans because of competition with other, royalist shaykhs, some out of political conviction—notably those who had faced coercion and humiliating experiences during the imamate. The constellation of allegiances in Saʿdah differed from the situation among, say, the Ḥāshid confederation, whose senior shaykh ʿAbdullah al-Aḥmar took on a proactive leading role on the republican side from the beginning of the revolution.[55]

Finally, by considering the 1960s civil war, we can follow the rise of several families of central importance in the Saʿdah area. Shuwayṭ, al-Surabī, Mujallī, Dughsān, al-ʿAwjarī and Manāʿ are among those shaykhly lineages that influenced and even, to a certain extent, determined post-revolutionary political, social, and denominational developments in Saʿdah. As we will see in the following chapter, some *sādah* influence was able to endure the transition process in Saʿdah, but the local tribes and their shaykhs, especially those who had been with the Republic and were rewarded accordingly, were never more powerful than during the two or three decades after the revolution. In conjunction with the weakness or even absence of state institutions after the system change in 1970, this tribal ascendance generated a patrimonial structure in which political power was bound not to state institutions, but to people. During the post-war period, domestic politics in Saʿdah became a 'big man game', and the heroic exploits and revolutionary glories of those shaykhs who had supported the Republic became central to their tribal and political *haybah* (prestige) and *wazn* (weight). Personalization of politics and political power was not rare in other parts of Yemen and beyond, but it became particularly pronounced in the Saʿdah area, where much policy-making was now in the hands of those influential men of tribal background who had emerged victorious in the civil war.

These tribal leaders and their successors practised politics against the background and under the influence of their personal stories and experiences; political and personal motives overlapped and interpenetrated their actions. In some cases, therefore, decisions and events of the 1960s civil war and even of the more recent Houthi wars reflect the biographies of certain influential tribal leaders and their successors. One obvious example already discussed is the deliberate suppression of certain shaykhly families during the reign of Imam Aḥmad, in Saʿdah notably the Shuwayṭ and Mujallī families, whose utterly humiliating experiences at times resembled what Volkan calls a 'chosen trauma'.[56] A chosen trauma may lie dormant in the family's consciousness for decades, but its influence, according to external factors, can endure.

By considering those same biographies, we may be better able to understand why, for example, Ḥusayn Mujallī, aghast at the appearance of the Believing Youth movement in the 1990s, called them 'the royalists' (*al-malikiyyin*), and deemed it necessary to antagonize this 'resurrected threat' in whatever way he could—an irrational reaction, since the Believing Youth never sought the reinstallation of the imamate. This personal attitude helps in turn to explain why his son ʿUthmān was among the Houthis' bitterest enemies. When, towards the end of the Houthi wars, ʿUthmān Mujallī found himself targeted by the Salih government and in the midst of annihilatory confrontations with the Houthis,[57] he may have witnessed what Volkan calls a 'time collapse': a phenomenon that occurs when perceptions and feelings connected with an ancestor-shared trauma collapse into a current political or military conflict. On this occasion, such a collapse may have meant that during the final battles of the Houthi wars ʿUthmān Mujallī could no longer assert himself in socially or politically adaptive ways, and ended up internalizing a sense of helpless rage that in 2011 led to his expulsion to Saudi Arabia by the Houthis. The Mujallī clan's narrative directly equates the events of 2011 with those of the 1960s civil war, in the course of which ʿUthmān's father and grandfather were temporarily expelled from Saʿdah to (republican) Khamir by royalist forces. After ʿUthmān's own expulsion by the Houthis, a member of the Mujallī family linked this crucial experience to the civil war fifty years earlier:

> History repeats itself. My father and my brother and their tribes have been expelled during the [1962] September Revolution in the same way and because of the same mind-sets and ideas. [...] The issue is a matter of time, the water will return to its normal way, as we will return [to Saʿdah], honoured and dignified as our fathers have returned before us.[58]

These complex intra-tribal fragmentations in times of conflict can occasionally create the impression that tribal allegiances are fluid and fluctuate; indeed, there is a famous proverb from the time of the 1962 revolution: 'Republican by day, royalist by night' (*jumhūrī nahāran wa malikī laylan*). However, at least for the Saʿdah region, this is not necessarily the case. As we have seen in this chapter, most tribes—despite their inherent particularism—hold a relatively stable position over time, with infrequent shifts. The following chapters will further demonstrate this remarkable degree of historical continuity.

Reshuffle of Power Relations

Unlike the failed coup of 1948, the 1962 Revolution did not aim at the replacement of one imam by a more just or capable imam, but at the overthrow of the imamic system as a whole. In consequence not only the imam, but also the *sādah* (adj. *sayyid*) were removed from their ascriptive position of power and influence, which they had obtained over a millennium of imamic rule. The new republican leadership was socially and intellectually heterogeneous, consisting of military officers, members of the *qāḍī* estate (hereditary jurists), modern educated political activists, shaykhs, Arab nationalists of various shades, Muslim brothers, etc. It agreed on vilifying both the *ancien régime* and their former suzerain lords. Despite the fact that numerous *sayyid* scholars had also played a critical role in the movement against the Ḥamīd al-Dīn regime—which they criticized for contradicting Zaydi Hādawī doctrine—and even though the *sādah* contributed many officers to the revolution, they became its main targets, and faced severe harassment in the decades that followed.[59] After the revolution the *sādah* were identified with reactionary backwardness, sometimes despised in a fashion akin to the French Republican aversion to aristocracy and royalty.[60]

In the Saʿdah area, the conclusion of the 1960s civil war was more or less externally enforced through the supporting action of pro-republican Hamdān (Ḥāshid and Bakīl) shaykhs such as Amīn Abū Rās, ʿAbdullah al-Aḥmar, and Mujāhid Abū Shawārib. The majority of the population, however, remained attached to the lost imamic system. Due to this lack of popular support for the Republic, for some years after the end of the civil war the republican government was only able to achieve its targets in Saʿdah in half-coalition with the local *sādah*. Curiously enough, only recognized royalists were able to make their voice heard when enforcing republican policy.[61] In addition, the 1970s marked a period of 'institution building', which required suitably qualified administrative personnel. Thus, in conformity with the government's policy of national reconciliation, the experience of certain *sayyid* administrators continued to be utilized, and senior posts in Saʿdah's municipal and provincial government were filled by both high-status outsiders and educated and highly skilled *sādah*.

The *sādah*'s participation in the political system was based upon connections, education, specialized knowledge, governmental experience, and personal achievements or influence at the local level.[62] Two examples from the early Republic are ʿAbdullah Yaḥyā al-Ṣaʿdī from Ḍaḥyān and ʿAbdulraḥman al-Fayshī, both members of influential *sayyid* families. During the civil war ʿAbdullah al-Ṣaʿdī had been a royalist field commander in Jumāʿah and, in November 1965, a member of the royalist delegation to the Ḥaraḍ peace conference. In 1970 he was appointed governor of Saʿdah, and ʿAbdulraḥman al-Fayshī his deputy. Later on, ʿAbdullah al-Ṣaʿdī attained even higher offices such as minister of public works and minister of endowments and religious guidance.[63]

Many *sādah* had no choice but to work towards an arrangement with the Republic, because much of their property had been sequestered, including large parts of the religious endowments (*waqf*) that had formerly generated their revenues.[64] *Waqf* land had fallen to the state or been seized and divided up among influential shaykhs, many of them belonging to the pro-republican Saʿdah Brigade. The new income of those *sādah* in the Republic's civil service simply did not bear comparison with the lost *waqf* income, leading to a general impoverishment of the *sādah*, who had also suffered great material losses during the civil war. Practically, therefore, many *sādah* in Saʿdah were forced to cooperate with the republican government.

Other *sayyid* religious scholars, such as Majd al-Dīn al-Muʾayyadī and Badr al-Dīn al-Ḥūthī, preferred to live and continue teaching from their respective home regions in rural Saʿdah, according to the Zaydi principle of emigration (*mabdaʾ al-hijrah*)—a principle of precaution applied when the Zaydi community is unable to change an oppressive regime.[65] They continued to live under the protection of the surrounding tribes as they had before the revolution; the 1960s civil war and its aftershocks provoked a rush of renewed protection pacts between *sādah* and the tribes in whose territories they lived.[66]

On the other hand the tribal shaykhs, notably those who had fought on the side of the Republic, reached the height of their power in the 1970s. The warring parties' attempts to buy off tribal loyalties—as well as the enormous financial largesse, weapons and material support provided by the last imam, the republicans, the Saudi Kingdom, and at times the Egyptians and the British to shaykhs on both sides—had greatly strengthened the position of the northern tribal leaders.[67] That position was further boosted by the activation of customary methods of military mobilization, because it was these leaders who had gathered the fighting men for both sides throughout the civil war.

These shaykhs were not just anybody. After 1962, public representations of the *sādah* as 'strangers in the house' and the refusal to recognize them as *awlād al-balad* ('genuine Yemenis') were centered on their "Adnānī origin' (see Chapter 1).[68] The Yemeni tribes, by contrast, reckon themselves descendants of Qaḥṭān, the progenitor of Yemen's indigenous inhabitants, the Southern Arabs. Many shaykhly lineages in northern Yemen are of extremely long standing; family histories of 700 or 800 years are quite common among the shaykhs of Khawlān b. ʿĀmir and Hamdān b. Zayd. Jumāʿah's Muqīt lineage, for instance, can trace its pedigree over a millennium.[69] In reference to this, among Jumāʿah the incumbent shaykh is called 'Prince of Khawlān, known as Ibn Imqīt' (*amīr Khawlān al-maʿrūf bi-Ibn Imqīt*). The Rawkān, al-Surabī, al-ʿAzzām, and ʿAwfān lineages, too, are of extremely long standing.[70] Another famous example is the Abū Rās of Dhū Muḥammad (Bakīl) in the Baraṭ region, who own written genealogies that suggest their lineage goes back to the ancient Prophet Hūd. Thus, rooted in remotest antiquity, the great shaykhs of the Abū Rās lineage are referred to by some as 'kings'.[71]

When a central state creates or recruits local patrons in an attempt to control its peripheries, it can only draw on the existing pools of political talent and experience. Whereas such talent during the imamate and in the first years after the civil war came from among the *sayyid* (and some *qāḍī*) administrators, in the decades that followed the state increasingly drew on the leadership experience of the shaykhs. As Peterson argues, effective political functioning reverted to the near-exclusive domain of the village or tribe, and the shaykhs' newly enhanced political status was partly due to the vacuum of leadership and legitimacy, and the need for the system change to be implemented at grassroots level after the civil war.[72]

The profound transformations that followed the civil war did not only result in empowerment of tribal shaykhs at the expense of the *sādah*; it simultaneously triggered a reshuffle of the deck in tribal power relations. The formative phase of the republic in Saʿdah was closely bound up with the emerging dominance of those shaykhly lineages who were rewarded for their loyalty during the civil war. The republican credentials of those shaykhs and tribes boosted their position and legitimated their future assertions of power on local and national levels. Their names constituted a kind of 'white list', which entailed direct material and status benefits.[73] In Saʿdah this 'white list' included the shaykhs of Saḥār's Saʿdah Brigade and other republican shaykhs, such as Fāyid and Ḥusayn Mujallī, ʿAbdullah and Fayṣal Manāʿ, Qāʾid Shuwayṭ, Fayṣal and Ḥusayn al-Surabī, Bushayt Abū ʿUbayd, Yaḥyā al-Ḥusaynī, Hindī Dughsān, and ʿAlī Maḍwāḥ b. ʿAwfān. After the civil war many of them were able to expand their power and to position themselves more favourably.[74]

The 1970s transition period also facilitated the rise of some entirely new shaykhly lineages that had not existed before 1962, therefore called 'revolution shaykhs' (*shuyūkh al-thawrah*) in contrast to the historically established shaykhly lineages (*al-usar al-ʿarīqah fī l-mashīkh*). Examples include ʿAlī Julaydān of Banī Ṣuraym and, in the Saʿdah area, the al-Munabbihī family from Munabbih. The latter family's pro-republican activism during the civil war promoted the rapid rise of ʿAlī Ḥusayn al-Munabbihī from a simple tribesman to the wealthy and powerful contractor, politician and *shaykh al-sūq* (head of the market) of Munabbih's main commercial venture, Sūq al-Khamīs; later on this ascendance was accelerated by his political assertiveness and economic success.[75] He further strengthened his tribal position by establishing marriage relations (*muṣāhirah*) between his family and Munabbih's senior shaykhly lineage, the ʿAwfān family. The ʿAwfān lineage preferably pursues intra-tribal marriages among the Munabbih—these often reciprocal marriage pacts are a strategy pursued by the ʿAwfān clan to maintain and develop a network of allies.[76]

On the other hand, many anti-republican shaykhs were threatened with marginalization. In the Saḥār area they were literally outmanoeuvred by powerful tribal competitors. For instance, both Dirdaḥ b. Jaʿfar, senior shaykh and *radd* (judicial head) of Saḥār, and Shaykh al-ʿUlābī of the Banī ʿUwayr had supported the royalists during the civil war. In the early phase of the republic these formerly important shaykhly families came under pressure from severe intra-tribal rivalry with the Saḥār 'heroes' of the revolution, notably the Shuwayṭ and Mujallī families, who did not hesitate to use this advantage.[77] They subsequently experienced bitter political intrigue and fell victim to ruthless power games. Although both Dirdaḥ b. Jaʿfar and al-ʿUlābī gradually abandoned their royalist stance after the civil war, they remained permanently marginalized by these competitors.

Finally, there was a large host of 'defector shaykhs' who had vigorously fought the republican forces during the civil war, but in the years or decades after 1970 turned instead towards the now dominant power. These included, for instance, Yaḥyā Muqīt, then senior shaykh of Jumāʿah and head of the

Khawlān b. ʿĀmir confederation; Ḥusayn Rawkān, senior shaykh of Khawlān; Aḥmad al-ʿAzzām, senior shaykh of Rāziḥ; Dahbāsh Miṭrī, senior shaykh of Munabbih's Shaʿshaʿ moiety; and the then most influential Wāʾilah shaykh, ʿAbdullah al-ʿAwjarī. In the course of national reconciliation many of them became members of the Consultative Council (*majlis al-shūrā*), the early legislative assembly of the Yemen Arab Republic formed in 1971, and gradually came to terms with the republic. Yet this shift of loyalties was no uniform process, but rather an ongoing bargain with the republican state in which the conditions of allegiance were constantly renegotiated. These shaykhs were willing, as Weir explains, 'to create a cooperative relationship with the republican government which they had recently violently opposed, on condition they benefited and their system was preserved'.[78] This re-alignment of loyalties was a relatively ponderous process and contributed to the fact that, by the end of the 1980s, the political leadership in Sanaʿa still considered large parts of Saʿdah province 'royalist'.[79]

One well-known defector shaykh was ʿAbdullah Ḥāmis al-ʿAwjarī of Wāʾilah in the east of the province, who remained strongly opposed to the republic for many years.[80] Yet royalist shaykhs had little opportunity to translate their influence into more substantial power, and as the republican system consolidated, being 'royalist' became an increasingly useless and hollow option for the ambitious ʿAbdullah al-ʿAwjarī. The Wāʾilah are an extremely important tribe in terms of licit and illicit trans-border trade with Saudi Arabia, which began to flourish enormously after the end of the isolationist imamate and the country's new economic opening. ʿAbdullah himself was a 'big trader', and the Yemeni government did its best to co-opt him politically and economically, even at a high price.[81] It is hardly surprising that in the context of national reconciliation ʿAbdullah al-ʿAwjarī became a member of the early Consultative Council even though he was still a staunch royalist. With time, however, ʿAbdullah al-ʿAwjarī's loyalty shifted to the republican system which at the end of his life he supported by conviction, even though his political clout on the national level was always constrained by his former royalist stance.[82]

The shift served to place himself, his family and his tribe favourably in the struggle for influence and resources. Aspects of inter-tribal rivalry, too, played a role: at the dawn of the Republic the Wāʾilah, mindful that considerable trans-border trade routes also pass through Saḥār territory, were determined not to cede ground and influence during the transition to the newly strengthened Saḥār shaykhs of the Saʿdah Brigade. It was therefore a matter, as Lichtenthäler argues, of whether Saʿdah would become *Hamdāniyyah* or

Saḥāriyyah—whether Hamdān Bakīl from the east or Saḥār of the Khawlān b. ʿĀmir confederation would take control of Saʿdah's profitable trade flows.[83] This revenue was worth embracing the Republic.

The Politics of Patronage

The shaykhs' ascent to power began to assume additional, supra-tribal forms when President al-Iryānī (1967–74) raised the republicans' collaboration with tribal leaders to the national level and began to recruit shaykhs, who rarely if ever held office under the imams, into the formal and ruling establishment. Following the national reconciliation at the end of the civil war, shaykhs of various persuasions, non-tribal republican and some formerly royalist figures entered the republican government.

This appearance of a body of men with both tribal standing and official rank was in large part new. In the Consultative Council, the early legislative assembly of the YAR formed in 1971, shaykhs held the majority of seats. Moreover, many shaykhs were rewarded with the official rank of colonel (*ʿaqīd*) in recognition of the military services they had provided during the civil war and were placed in command of some key regular army units, particularly the shaykhs of the pro-republican Saʿdah Brigade.[84] The still vulnerable republican government provided an excellent opportunity for several senior shaykhs to extend their influence and power beyond their tribal bases to the national level. For the first time, they began to hold important positions within central government, rather than only influencing government from the outside, as was the case during the imamate.[85]

The integration of members of important shaykhly families into government and the army enabled the state to create a common bond of loyalty and to expand its influence into remote territories with strong tribal traditions. In Saʿdah the government's patronage policy seemed at first glance to have a 'nurturing' effect on the tribal system. Weir argues that historically all state overlords in the region had 'superimposed their administrative structures onto the template of tribal structures [...] Each ruler introduced much the same kinds of judicial, tax, and law-enforcement officials, and these men coordinated in similar ways with tribal officials'.[86] In the wake of the Republic and the decades to come the shaykhs became easily targeted points of co-optation who gave the opportunity to the weak Yemeni state to push its agenda outside Sanaʿa without concentrating on state-building efforts in rural areas.[87]

The disadvantages of tribalism within government soon became evident. Many shaykhs retained their tribal ties and values and imported their rivalries and enmities into the state.[88] During his 'Revolutionary Correctional Initiative', President Ibrāhīm al-Ḥamdī (1974–7) took action to curb the institutionalization of tribal and other parochial influences and hence to curtail certain shaykhs' influence on the state, in particular certain major shaykhs of Upper Yemen, such as ʿAbdullah al-Aḥmar of al-ʿUṣaymāt, Mujāhid Abū Shawārib of Khārif, and ʿAlī, Muḥammad and Dirham Abū Luḥūm of Khawlān al-Ṭiyāl. He began to modernize and reorganize the armed forces and removed powerful tribal leaders from a broad array of key military and political posts.[89] Many shaykhs opposed al-Ḥamdī's Correctional Initiative in an alliance led by ʿAbdullah al-Aḥmar, who moved with 3,000 of his tribal supporters from Khamir to Ṣaʿdah city, which became one of his headquarters in his struggle against al-Ḥamdī.

In 1977 tribesmen of Saḥār and Sufyān blocked roads in protest against al-Ḥamdī's policies.[90] Later that year al-Ḥamdī was assassinated; some believed that ʿAbdullah al-Aḥmar and Saudi figures were behind his assassination.[91] A few months later, the same fate befell al-Ḥamdī's tribal-political ally Amīn Abū Rās of Dhū Muḥammad (Dahm), near-perpetual minister of state and *shaykh mashāyikh* of Bakīl. He was one of the leading pro-republican shaykhs and an outspoken critic of the Saudis and their tribal vassals in Yemen, who had progressive, socialist-inspired visions regarding the social meaning of shaykhdom, as expressed in his famous saying: 'The first and the last word is due to the people' (*al-kalimah al-ūlā wa l-akhīrah li-l-shaʿb*). After his assassination, his legacy was virtually wiped out by his tribal opponents, and his famous lineage was marginalized.[92]

After the brief interlude of Aḥmad al-Ghashmī and ʿAbd al-Karīm al-ʿArashī, in 1978 Lieutenant Colonel Ali Abdullah Salih of the Sanḥān, a small Ḥāshid tribe southwest of Sanaʿa, became president and began to build up his nationwide power base, the General People's Congress (GPC, *al-muʾtamar al-shaʿbī al-ʿāmm*), which later turned into Yemen's dominant political party.[93] He was able to secure his grip on power through astute promotion of his Sanḥān kin and tribesmen into the government and the armed forces, filling the void left by the dismissals and reorganizations of al-Ḥamdī's Correctional Initiative to give the republican government and military a certain Ḥāshidī—and especially Sanḥānī—leaning.[94] The power-sharing agreement called the 'covenant' (*al-ʿahd*) dates from this period, which stipulated that the Sanḥān elite would stand behind Salih, and that the man behind Salih and his successor would be General ʿAlī Muḥsin al-Aḥmar, a relative of Salih who later became commander of the North Western Military Region and the

First Armoured Division, the main governmental force in the Houthi wars.[95] The 'covenant' was broken by Salih in the mid-2000s when he openly began establishing his own son Aḥmad as his successor, and fell apart completely when ʿAlī Muḥsin, then commander of the armed forces in the Houthi wars, joined the anti-Salih protests of Yemen's 'Change Revolution' in 2011.

After Salih took office in 1978, many shaykhs from the Saʿdah area continued to act as vital links between their tribes and the republican government; in the complex interplay of forces between the YAR, Saudi Arabia, and the socialist state in southern Yemen, at times the shaykhs and their tribes have also been militarily in demand. Many shaykhs and tribesmen from the Saʿdah region served in the 1994 civil war.[96] Some shaykhs with no official ties to the military and security apparatus also acted on behalf of the state and conducted smaller 'reserve police' operations in remote border areas, playing an important role in securing the boundary between Yemen and Saudi Arabia.[97] The 'colonel shaykhs'' 'civilian' counterparts were the 'Member of Parliament shaykhs'. Saʿdah's shaykhs developed an almost hereditary entitlement to parliamentary office, as we will see in Chapter 4.

The shaykhs of the Saʿdah region, however, have never gained direct and stable access to the upper echelons of the political executive and military command—these were restricted to the inner power circle of the Salih government. Hence they did not benefit from links to the centre to the same extent as leading figures of the Sanḥān and certain members of the tribal elite from among the Ḥāshid and Bakīl confederations. The issues of tribal segregation in the executive power functions, including vertical segregation (the 'glass ceiling' through which non-Sanḥān and non-Ḥāshid tribal leaders could seldom break), and their relative under-representation in a Sanḥān-dominated government were subjects of continual dissatisfaction. The government compensated these tribal leaders for their exclusion from the inner power circle with generous financial support and by granting them a relatively free hand in their tribal home regions in Saʿdah. The shaykhs acknowledged the state's authority, and in turn their local tribal authority was reciprocally acknowledged and buttressed by the allocation of financial subsidies, which took the form of monthly salaries paid through the Tribal Affairs Authority (*maṣlaḥat shūʾun al-qabāʾil*), a department of the Ministry of Interior.[98] These salaries varied greatly according to different governmental agendas and interests and were based on a shaykh's strategic importance to the government. In addition, many Saʿdah shaykhs received financial subsidies from the Saudi government, because the Saudis also had vital interests in the region.[99] Shaykhs therefore received subsidies from various sources, and their multiple loyalties to different, sometimes conflicting powers made up a complex fabric.

For some shaykhs, the external capital inflow generated through political patronage and their own economic endeavours far exceeded their traditional cash payments received 'from below'—in recognition, for instance, of mediation, arbitration, and dispute settlement according to tribal customary law (*ʿurf*). This new revenue generated further disparities in wealth and power between tribes. Yemen's tribal system is very diverse across time and space, and historically shaykhs have certainly always attracted cashflows from overlords who depended on their cooperation and support. After the founding of the Republic, however, the shaykhs' material and political inclinations were particularly pronounced. Many shaykhs moved from their tribal areas to the capital, Sanaʿa, or stayed there over long periods of time, thus loosening their tribal ties and, consequently, losing their tribal influence. Not only in the Saʿdah region but throughout the countryside in Upper Yemen, tribesmen began to complain of certain influential shaykhs becoming 'absent' or 'distant'; historically, these shaykhs had been based in Lower Yemen,[100] and thus were now criticized for neglecting the principle of representation, a central and pivotal part of their tribal office and authority.[101]

By no means did this affect all shaykhs; many of them remained esteemed leaders closely connected to their tribal home bases, who continued to perform with diligence the key roles of their tribal office, notably representation and conflict resolution. A good example is Salmān ʿAwfān, senior shaykh of the Munabbih.[102] Salmān ʿAwfān neither aspired to public office nor moved to the capital, and his economic situation was simply moderately comfortable. He remained an esteemed mediator and arbitrator. Salmān ʿAwfān was one of few shaykhs whom local *sādah* described as a 'wise man' (*faqīh*), and this despite the fact that parts of the Munabbih tribe and some of their shaykhs, in particular the ʿAwfān clan, had in the past been at odds with the *sādah*.[103]

To sum it up, the Salih regime's policy in Saʿdah province was characterized simultaneously by in situ patronage of selected tribal elites and their exclusion from and segregation within the highest echelons of power. In turn, these tribal elites benefited financially from the patronage network while pursuing a policy of tribal autonomy that aimed to keep governmental interference at bay. Not all shaykhs were equally important to the government, and the uneven allocation of governmental resources resulted in substantial potential for conflict and destabilization, because it produced or enhanced disparities in wealth and influence between the shaykhs, caused or exacerbated resentment and jealousy, and created or widened rifts and enmities between tribes. The creation of conflict among actors on the local and national level was certainly intended by the Salih regime, which based its survival policy on the fomentation of crises. Phillips has called this informal system of creating and exploiting conflict and discord among the government's rivals and foes the 'politics of permanent crisis'.[104] Salih's style of governance also mirrors what Bauman has called 'liquid modernity', whereby those at the top create as much chaos as possible for those lower down, in order to rule more easily.[105] In Yemen's remote north, therefore, the politics of patronage proved to be a double-edged sword: while at the national level it contributed to state building and state formation, at the local level it entailed preservation of tribal autonomy and triggered tribal rivalry and conflict.

Shadow Economy

The state's policy of neglect in terms of development and institution building also shaped the area's economic idiosyncrasies. After 1970, a kind of distorted economy developed which was characterized by a lack of state-run development and investment initiatives on the one hand, and on the other by the development of a flourishing private sector and vibrant shadow economy, made possible by the permeability of the Yemeni-Saudi border. Again, these economic developments favoured the tribal elites and resulted in economic imbalances, including a vastly unjust distribution of economic resources. These imbalances helped prepare the ground for the Houthi movement to later take root and flourish.

Among Saʿdah's citizenry, loyalties to the lost imamic order proved rather resilient to the system change after the 1960s civil war, prompting the republican government in Sanaʿa to consider Saʿdah's population 'royalist' until the late 1980s.[106] The government countered the region's perceived 'unruliness' with punitive measures resulting in decades of economic deprivation, political marginalization, and territorial isolation. State interference remained weak and punctual and mainly focused on financial co-optation of tribal elites rather than on economic development of the province. In consequence, Saʿdah province and large parts of Yemen's extreme north benefited much less than many other parts of the country from government investment and development efforts.[107]

Few national and international development projects were implemented in the period between 1970 and 1990. Instead, the main impetus for rural development in Saʿdah (as in many other regions of Yemen) came from local organizations at grassroots level called LDAs (Local Development Associations; *taʿāwun ahlī li-l-taṭwīr*), which reflected the widespread local desire for development and improvement of living conditions, notably in infrastructure, schools, and health.[108] In 1972, the formerly autonomous LDAs were united in a nationwide umbrella organization called the Confederation of Yemeni Development Associations (CYDA) and subjected to state control, making them instrumental in the extension of state hegemony throughout the country. Shaykhs and religious leaders attempted to position themselves as representatives of the LDAs, although public opinion was often against this new form of elite entitlement.[109] During the 1980s, the LDAs gradually lost influence, perhaps also reflecting the fading out of development models from earlier phases of late modernity. At the same time Yemen faced serious economic problems as a result of world recession and several drought years in the late 1980s.

After Yemeni unification in 1990 and the ensuing political transformation process, Saʿdah province gained more attention and some major state development projects were initiated, especially in the areas of education, electrification, healthcare, water, and road construction. This period saw the start of the Northern Ring Road Project (*mashrūʿ al-ṭarīq al-dāʾirī al-shamālī*) which aims at connecting Saʿdah city with Ḥarad in the Tihāmah lowlands—it continues to drag on and may not ever be completed.[110] The Saʿdah-Kitāf-al-Buqʿ road was also expanded, as was the road connecting the al-Buqʿ border crossing with al-Ḥazm in al-Jawf, in 2002. International development cooperation has also fostered some development projects, especially in the Saʿdah basin's water sector, with German and Dutch support in particular. Saudi Arabia, too, has funded several projects in the governorate, most notably the Saudi Hospital in Saʿdah city.

In comparison with the development projects that have been carried out in other Yemeni provinces, the national and international efforts in Saʿdah have been limited. The government mainly devoted its resources to those more central areas of the country that were under its control and that recognized its authority. The weakness of state structures, the strong emphasis on tribal customary law and the fact that state law enforcement did not really extend to Saʿdah formed a general impediment to development efforts and external investment in the province. Yemeni public and private investment banks refused to give loans to any facilities there, 'as if Saʿdah was no part of Yemen'.[111] Government involvement remained weak and sporadic and mainly focused on political, financial and economical co-optation of the tribal elites, rather than on general and consistent development of the province.

Nevertheless, since the 1970s many parts of the province, especially in the relatively flat, fertile and conveniently situated Saʿdah basin, have experienced considerable growth. This economic development was mainly based on agricultural production and trade in agricultural products. Saʿdah is a climatically and topographically diverse landscape. In particular, the mountainous western parts of the province, inhabited by tribes of the Khawlān b. ʿĀmir confederation, are fertile and populous regions where the raising of livestock and, the farming and trading of small cash crops (notably wheat, citrus, coffee, fruits, grapes, apples, pomegranates, vegetables, and *qāt*) remain most people's primary vocation.[112] The mountainous and steppe regions of Saʿdah province are joined by permanent trade arteries, and are integrated to varying degrees into local trade networks.[113]

During the YAR period, the agricultural sector of the province received boosts from the remittances of Yemeni migrant workers in Saudi Arabia before their expulsion in 1990.[114] These remittances spurred a further proliferation of construction, agricultural expansion and consumer goods in the region and provided the cash for agricultural and drilling equipment, which was brought in cheaply and tax-free from across the border.[115] With the gradual improvement of the region's infrastructure, in particular through the Northern Ring Road Project, but also through incentives such as the fruit import ban of 1984, sales and trade opportunities for agricultural products were further expanded, facilitating long-distance trade with central parts of Yemen and even with Saudi Arabia, where demand for agricultural products is high.

Again, the tribal elites and their business partners benefited most from these developments. Many of them were integrated into the system of Yemeni (and Saudi) patronage. In addition, the 1962 revolution was in part directed against abuse of the *waqf* institution by the *sādah*. As we have seen, after the 1960s civil war much of the *waqf* land, which had been associated with certain *sayyid* families for centuries, was contested by influential shaykhs.[116] Some shaykhs greatly benefited from the redistribution of land and resources—locally referred to as *istīlāʾ ʿalā al-arḍ* ('land-grabbing')—and appropriated large parts of former *waqf* holdings.[117] Among them were shaykhs of the Saʿdah Brigade such as Fāyid and Ḥusayn Mujallī and Ḥusayn al-Surabī, but also, quite tellingly, figures who, at that time, were still strictly royalist, such as ʿAbdullah al-ʿAwjarī.[118] In consequence many influential shaykhs began to invest in agriculture, and with increasing prosperity they started large farm businesses, among which artificially irrigated fruit and citrus orchards possessed the highest prestige. Simultaneously, the '*waqf*-grabbing' of the early days of the Republic entailed the impoverishment of many influential *sayyid* families in Saʿdah. Until the end of the imamate, these families had lived off the revenues from these religious endowments. Although some *sādah* with links to the old regime were accepted into the republican civil service and spent their careers in it, their new salaries were in no way comparable to their previous *waqf* income.[119]

Lichtenthäler argues in his study on water politics in the Saʿdah basin that the financial opportunities available to the shaykhs and the emerging trader class, as well as the remittances of Yemeni guest workers in Saudi Arabia, provided the cash to purchase drilling equipment from across the border. Subsequently all kinds of tribal as well as non-tribal people and local labourers returning from abroad moved into the Saʿdah basin to be close to the emerging centres of tribal, political and economic power. These immigrants did not belong to the long-established tribal communities of the Saʿdah basin, but immigrated from the surrounding tribes of Khawlān b. ʿĀmir, Bakīl and even Ḥāshid. In consequence, the cost of real estate skyrocketed, a development that benefited the incumbent landowners, including many 'big shaykhs'. In the long term, this uncontrolled immigration had a destabilizing influence on local tribal societies because most of these immigrants did not change their tribal affiliations after moving to live among the tribes of the Saʿdah basin. As Lichtenthäler argues, they shared no history of cooperation with their host communities. In fact, a primary reason for moving to the Saʿdah basin may have been to break free from the need to share and cooperate over the scarce and limited water and land resources in their home territories.[120] This influx of farmers from other tribal regions, the competition for land and water and the gradual depletion of the ground water resources (the increase of 'water stress', as Lichtenthäler calls it) entailed an increase in feuds, disputes and drawn-out conflicts, with simultaneous dilution of tribal norms in conflict resolution.

Other shaykhs did not focus on agriculture, but rather on investment. The isolationist imamic regime had been overthrown in northern Yemen, and development and 'modernity' were in the air. In many areas, mainly in the Saʿdah basin and around Saʿdah city (and other emerging commercial ventures throughout the province), a boomtown atmosphere started to prevail in which trade, investment and construction developed rapidly. Development and investment, which the state would not or could not provide sufficiently to the province, were run by private hands. This sector, too, was dominated by local shaykhs and influential traders, some of whom had gained considerable influence at both the regional and national level since the early 1970s, and who had substantial connections and funds at their disposal.

The Mujallī family, for instance, had appropriated large *waqf* holdings in the early 1970s. The combined value of the Mujallī land and property holdings along the main road through the new section of Saʿdah city was enormous.[121] By arguing that Saʿdah needed investment and economic change, Ḥusayn Mujallī became an early espouser of rather modernist views in Saʿdah. By drawing on construction assistance from China, he built the Raḥbān Hotel in 1979, the first in Saʿdah city to host visitors; he would later also build the Casablanca Hotel, built on former *waqf* land. The Mujallī family's real estate included numerous shops and flats, as well as government buildings. After his experiences during eight years of devastating civil war, Ḥusayn Mujallī welcomed a 'change of consciousness' in the conflict-torn local society. He sent his firstborn son, ʿUmar, to study medicine abroad because he wanted him to learn 'something useful' rather than pursuing a military career 'like everyone else'. Yet this shift in attitude did not prevent him from sending his second-born son, ʿUthmān, to the Police Academy in the Yemeni capital.

Tribal hierarchies merged into new business elites, which in part relied on state contracts for their business. Saʿdah's influential shaykhs and their business partners were able to monopolize and capitalize on the Yemeni government's few attempts to expand its presence in the Saʿdah area through steering state contracts to their patch. This tribally dominated business elite has built health and government facilities, schools and water supply systems throughout the province. Thus, republican government influence in the province literally expanded along the patterns of tribal power structures. The tribal and economic sway of local shaykhs and their business partners of the emerging trader class became closely intertwined with the power interests of the state. It is important to appreciate that it was the tribal elites who significantly contributed to state formation and state building in a peripheral, underdeveloped province which has long been dominated by royalist and anti-republican tendencies.

In Munabbih, for instance, the construction of the administrative government compound (locally dubbed *al-mudīriyyah*) on a mountain slope overlooking Sūq al-Khamīs, the million-dollar construction of sections of the Northern Ring Road, and other construction projects within and outside Munabbih's tribal territory were all carried out by the construction company of ʿAlī Ḥusayn al-Munabbihī, the new *shaykh al-sūq* (market head) of Munabbih's emerging commercial venture Sūq al-Khamīs.[122] The resulting inflow of capital enabled him, for instance, to construct a school in Sūq al-Khamīs, the Madrasat ʿUmar bin al-Khaṭṭāb, and to maintain several others on the Munabbih territory—good deeds through which he acquired further local prestige and influence. Such wealth as flowed from external sources augmented the powers of tribal leaders and, as in the case of ʿAlī Ḥusayn al-Munabbihī, elevated them to new positions of authority within the tribal society and contributed to the development of both their area and their tribe.

Besides Saʿdah's shaykhs, after the civil war the basin also became home to a number of rich and influential trading families. These include, for instance, the remarkably successful Jarmān clan of the Banī ʿUwayr, who established the Jarmān Commercial Corporation (*muʾassasat Jarmān al-tijāriyyah*), specialized in arms trade and road construction, and Aḥmad ʿAwaḍ Abū Maksah, owner of the Abū Maksah Corporation for Trade and Construction (*muʾassasat Abū Maksah li-l-tijārat wa l-muqāwalāt*). In most cases the traders have formed partnerships with shaykhs; Jarmān Muḥammad Jarmān, for instance, cooperated closely with both Fāris Manāʿ of al-Ṭalḥ and the late Qāʾid Shuwayṭ of Banī ʿUwayr. As Lichtenthäler put it, many traders have learned to 'convert economic muscle into political power', and, like some of the area's shaykhs, they have gained major social, economic and political influence on regional and national levels.[123]

Besides this, smuggling accounts for a large share of the governorate's trade activities. Saʿdah province shares about a 90 kilometre frontier with Saudi Arabia. Nine out of the province's fifteen districts border Saudi Arabia and its southern provinces of Najrān, ʿAsīr, and Jīzān. The border between Yemen and Saudi Arabia is predominantly a political and not a tribal border, because both member tribes of the Khawlān b. ʿĀmir confederation in the western mountain range and the Saʿdah basin, and the Wāʾilah in the province's east settle on both sides of the border and are connected by descent, tribal affiliation, marriage relations, daily life and trade. Both the Treaty of Ṭāʾif (1934) and the Treaty of Jeddah (2000), which define the boundary between Yemen and Saudi Arabia, entitle the borderland inhabitants within a 20 kilometre corridor to straddle the boundary without visa restrictions. These Saudi concessions to the Yemeni borderland tribes aimed at securing their loyalty and cooperation with the Saudi Kingdom, because the boundary unduly favours Saudi interests and cuts deeply through the territories and pasture lands of the local tribes (we will return to this subject in the following chapter).

Borderlands often provide shadowy landscapes where different social networks cross, legal sovereignty is hazy, and policing is light.[124] Smuggling is indicative of the extent to which states are unable or unwilling to control their peripheries and borders—in the Saʿdah region, rather than benefiting from government investment and development projects, the local population has seen the emergence of a vibrant shadow economy, made possible by the permeability of the Yemeni-Saudi border. Though this shadow economy connected the Yemeni borderland tribes with Saudi Arabia, it simultaneously reinforced the rift between them and the Yemeni state, which was intent on extending its writ to all corners of the country but could not or would not provide similarly profitable alternative sources of income and satisfactory social services.[125]

All districts of Saʿdah province are connected through official and unofficial trade routes with the Saudi Kingdom. Today's trade routes still flow along ancient transportation, trade and pilgrim routes which connect southwest Arabia via Ḥijāz and Nejd to the northern parts of the Arabian Peninsula, such as sections of the Incense Road (*ṭarīq al-bukhūr*), and the so-called Elephant Road (*darb al-fīl*) leading through Jumāʿah territory and the 'Iron Gates' (*abwāb al-ḥadīd*), that is the Bāqim mountains.[126] Today the region's main trade routes towards Saudi Arabia pass through the Saʿdah basin, Wāʾilah in the east, and—in the adjacent Ḥajjah governorate—through Ḥaraḍ in the Tihāmah lowlands.

The difficulties in controlling these trade flows were already evident during the Second Ottoman Occupation in Yemen. Blumi argues that during the Second Ottoman Period in Yemen (1848–1918), Ottoman control was at least partially undermined by regional trading and smuggling transactions of the local parallel economy, which specifically sought to avoid state-building measures and was far greater in size than the formal economy maintained by the imperial power itself.[127] Ultimately the Ottoman Empire's lack of manpower and the sophistication of the local populations endangered the Empire's ability to maintain any meaningful presence in these distant territories.

After the end of the 1960s civil war, the region's shadow economy continued to expand, with improving transportation and access to local and international trade networks. Ever since, the licit and illicit transportation of goods across the international Yemeni-Saudi border has (not for the first time in recent history) taken up a large proportion of the province's trade activities. Smuggling of goods and commodities on the 'grey' spectrum (which are not duty-paid) goes in both directions: wheat, flour, dates, medicines and electronic equipment are smuggled from Saudi Arabia to Yemen; cattle and diesel are smuggled from Yemen to Saudi Arabia.[128] On this 'grey' spectrum, smuggling activities comply with social norms, as smugglers often operate in a zone of socially licit but economically illegal activity.[129] In fact, almost all smugglers in Saʿdah province are also merchants, entwining their activities so that it takes a kind of forensic accounting to untangle their licit and illicit trade activities; many of them are using their illegal profits to help enrich their social or political capital. Where the spectrum is at its lightest, smuggling is considered a socially acceptable crime, and cross-border trade, which interferes with the territorial demands of the bordering nation states but complies with the local tribes' frameworks of plurilocal and transnational kinship networks, is considered legitimate by many locals. Thus, cross-border movements and smuggling activities cannot be reduced to a purely functional meaning, as they are more than just a coping strategy responding to economic constraints. Rather, Saʿdah's borderland inhabitants consider such activity their legitimate right, as governed by the provisions of both the Treaty of Ṭāʾif and the Treaty of Jeddah.

However, besides the smuggling of 'grey' consumer goods, enormous trafficking in 'black' goods such as weapons, ammunitions, *qāt*, liquor, drugs, and humans also emerged as a central part of the province's economic profile, especially in its east. Where the grey and dark grey spectrum fades to black, smugglers operate in a deeply illicit as well as illegal place.[130]

Lichtenthäler notes that from the mid-1970s until the early 1980s at least one third and possibly half of Saʿdah's adult male population was involved in the trans-border trade between Yemen and Saudi Arabia.[131] The large-scale trade flows across the boundary were operated by local tribes and organized by some of Saʿdah's influential shaykhs, many of whom made their fortunes from smuggling. The Wāʾilah and Dahm, in particular, who live on the largely unimplemented boundary in eastern Saʿdah and al-Jawf, became to some extent dark grey and black economy traders involved in licit and illicit cross-border trade activities, including trucking. Their trade networks operate large-scale illegal trade flows from Yemen across the vast and unexplored space of the Rubʿ al-Khālī desert to the Saudi capital Riyadh and the Gulf in the north, using their borderland territories in Saʿdah and al-Jawf as a hub for contraband. As elaborated in Chapter 3, the powerful trader shaykhs of Wāʾilah and Dahm are willing and able, if necessary, to enforce their trade interests by military means against the governments of Yemen and Saudi Arabia.

Since the 1980s, the Yemeni and Saudi governments have increased their efforts to control the trans-border trade flows more effectively. Mobile border patrols were set up and new border crossing points have been opened, which have become four main points: al-Buqʿ in Wāʾilah, ʿIlb near Bāqim, al-Ṭuwāl near Ḥaraḍ, and al-Wadīʿah near Sharūrah in the Rubʿ al-Khālī, as well as some smaller border crossing points. Officials of the two countries maintain that the increase in the border crossing points would restrict smuggling and accommodate both trade and the growing movement of citizens, particularly after Yemen joined the GCC Standard Organization; however, the success of the two governments' efforts to control trans-border trade remains limited.[132]

Saudi authorities complain that smugglers adapt very quickly to every one of their counter-smuggling strategies. Drug smugglers, for instance, are heavily armed and fight to the death when surrounded, because they know that in Saudi Arabia convicted drug traffickers are usually beheaded.[133] In addition, the social, political, and economic links and networks of Saʿdah's trader shaykhs and their partners in Saudi Arabia further obstruct efforts to control the border. Influential people on both sides of the border derive huge financial and political profit from smuggling. The social and political connections and networks of smugglers in Saʿdah's and Saudi Arabia's border regions, and their complicit partners in the Yemeni and Saudi authorities, make it almost impossible to control the lucrative transfer of contraband across the border.

The governments' efforts to better control the trans-border trade simply had the effect that smuggling activities became too risky for many small and average traders, who instead shifted to a future in agriculture.[134] Influential shaykhs were less affected by state control, because many of them had positioned relatives in the administration and military apparatus of the province, who helped to obstruct the government's measures against their clans' obscure trading activities.[135] In addition, many shaykhs are no longer dependent on smuggling; their political links and established networks on both sides of the border help them to import officially for comparable financial gain. The implementation of the planned border fortifications between Yemen and Saudi Arabia will lead to a further advantage of these well connected groups, at the expense of the ordinary population.

The reciprocal relationship between political patronage, tribal clout and transnational economical power can be illustrated by the rise of the Manāʿ clan, although this well-known family is far from being the largest trader clan in the area. The Manāʿ clan is of the shaykhly lineage of al-Ṭalḥ, a section of the Saḥār's Mālik moiety dwelling around 10 kilometres north of Saʿdah city. During the 1960s civil war, members of the Manāʿ family belonged, as we have seen, to the republican Saʿdah Brigade. ʿAbdullah al-Aḥmar mentions

ʿAbdullah b. ʿAlī Manāʿ and his sons Muḥammad and Fayṣal in his 'white list' of the revolution, of those who participated in the seventy-day siege in Sanaʿa and played a key role in the overthrow of the imamic system in Saʿdah.[136]

During the civil war, ʿAbdullah Manāʿ belonged to a delegation of ten Saʿdah shaykhs who went to Egypt to meet with Jamal Abdul Nasser.[137] For this reason the Saudis threw his son Fayṣal into jail in Jīzān, Saudi Arabia, where he suffered permanent injuries. This is one of the reasons that Fayṣal's relations with the Saudis continued to be strained even after the reconciliation between the Saudis and the republicans. In 1982, Fayṣal Manāʿ was among the founders of the GPC, in which he held several political offices. Having been a member of the Consultative Council since the early 1970s, after Yemeni unification in 1990 he was elected as Member of Parliament for the GPC for Saḥār constituency in the 1993 and 1997 parliamentary elections.

The rise of the Manāʿ family is attributable to its political position during the civil war, the associated patronage politics of the republican government, and above all to the economic opening that began in the province in the early 1970s. Historically, the weekly market Sūq al-Ṭalḥ has been a purely intra-tribal market of the Saḥār, which members of other tribes were not allowed to attend.[138] It was the weekly market of Saʿdah city, within the city walls and protected by its *hijrah* status, where the Saḥār had the opportunity to meet with members of other tribes and to sell off contraband from Saudi Arabia.[139] In the 1970s, the rule that Sūq al-Ṭalḥ could not be attended by non-Saḥār tribespeople started to become more flexible, and over the following years Sūq al-Ṭalḥ became one of the largest markets for contraband and arms on the Arabian Peninsula.[140] Hence the modification of the tribal market law (*qānūn al-sūq*) in the 1970s led to the economic rise of the Manāʿ family. Moreover, Sūq al-Ṭalḥ became the home base of several influential traders and entrepreneurs, notably the Abū Maksah and Jarmān clans.

Whereas Fayṣal Manāʿ continued to hold several important political positions after the 1970s, the trading activities of the Manāʿ family were pursued by his relative Fāris Muḥammad Manāʿ.[141] Fāris Manāʿ, a graduate of the Faculty of Economics and Trade in Sanaʿa, was able to establish a veritable trade empire headquartered there and in al-Ṭalḥ; he was recognized as one of the most prominent arms dealers in the Middle East. Under his stewardship, Sūq al-Ṭalḥ became the hub of a global arms trade, with partners from eastern Europe, Iran, China, France and others; this trade mainly supplied the highly profitable local and domestic market, but also became competitive on foreign markets such as the conflict-torn Horn of Africa.

Fāris Manā' has been close with the then President Salih since the beginning of the 1990s, prompting the latter to rely on him for purchases of military equipment and weapons for the Yemeni army. Because of his prominent position in the government's arms purchases, Fāris Manā' is said to have had a private army of tribal warriors at the state's expense, in order to maintain stability and security in al-Ṭalḥ, the location of his main weapons storage.[142] Unlike his kinsman Shaykh Fayṣal Manā', Fāris Manā' never belonged to a political party. Indeed most 'big' traders of the Sa'dah region have tried to maintain more or less neutral positions in times of both peace and war. During the Sa'dah wars (2004–10), they apparently made good bargains with all parties to the conflict—hence they were keen in their aftermath to maintain good relations with everyone. Fāris Manā' and the other trader shaykhs of the area have been criticized for this 'business neutrality'.

On the other hand, his neutral position during the Sa'dah wars enabled Fāris Manā' to act as a highly respected and skilled mediator, with the required tribal *wazn* (weight) and *nufūdh* (influence). In extremely precarious situations, when for the government everything was failing on the ground, he was one of very few people who could provide essential mediation between the government and the Houthis.[143] It is the paradox of Fāris Manā' that he successfully mediated in a war whose weapons he had made available to the population. This contradiction, however, certainly applies far more to Western governments and arms manufacturers who have been selling their weapons to this region for decades. In this regard, Fāris Manā' was just the last link in the chain of the international arms trade with Yemen and the wider region, in which many stakeholders have made their fortunes.

In Sūq al-Ṭalḥ arms were sold which contributed to the destructive power of the Sa'dah wars. These wars belong to those asymmetrical, 'new' wars in which the battlefield is the civilian population—as a target, a strategic object, and an opposing force.[144] Being deeply embedded in local micro-contexts, these wars blur the distinction between combatants and civilians. The arms trade of the grey and dark grey spectrum, which occasionally faded to black, played an essential role in arming the local population for the Sa'dah wars—a population that was already heavily armed before the war erupted in 2004.

As discussed in Chapter 1, tribal self-conceptualization prizes a masculinity of which weapons are considered an integral part; in general terms, tribes consider themselves a sort of 'arms-bearing aristocracy'.[145] Hence, in the tribal context of northern Yemen, arms play an important role that exceeds their sheer function as instruments of violence. The Yemeni 'gun culture', as Heinze calls it, is reinforced through the government's inability to provide security to its citizens.[146] In the absence of the state, the possession and carrying of small arms is essential to uphold security, autonomy, and individual and collective honour. Heinze argues that tribal conflict management is working towards peaceful resolution of conflict, but external circumstances determine whether weapons are locked away or kept in constant readiness for use.[147] During the Saʿdah wars, clearly the latter was the case.

In conclusion, the republican period was characterized by major transformations on the social, political, and economic level. The system change after the 1960s civil war entailed an empowerment of tribal leaders at the expense of the *sādah*, some of whom were politically powerful, while others lived ordinary lives. Moreover, it triggered a reshuffle in tribal power relations themselves, since those pro-republican shaykhs who emerged victorious from the civil war did not hesitate to use their advantageous starting position against their tribal rivals, some of whom were threatened with marginalization.

Yemen's tribal societies are very diverse in time and space. Historically, shaykhs have always been the points of co-optation for respective overlords who depended on their cooperation and support in establishing their own rule and asserting their local agendas. After the founding of the Yemeni Republic in 1962, however, the material and political preference of the shaykhs became particularly pronounced. The new tribally dominated elite was reinforced by the Yemeni government's politics of patronage. Patronage as a governance instrument brought the province both relative autonomy and exclusion from development efforts, as government influence remained inconsistent, selective, and mainly focused on the financial and economic patronage of a narrow range of tribal leaders, rather than on state building through the provision of public infrastructure and services. Few development and investment projects have been implemented in the governorate, most of them after unification in 1990, and during their implementation the shaykhs and their business partners have, again, profited enormously from the opaque system of awarding state contracts and from the graft endemic in procurement processes. This is one of the reasons why tribal leaders have been the ones to contribute significantly to state formation and state building in a politically and geographically peripheral and underdeveloped province, while simultaneously ensuring the limitation of its influence.

In the long run, development, political participation and structural legitimacy are the most durable and important foundations of any state. In this respect the Yemeni government's record in the Saʿdah area has been abysmal. Weak government control led to the emergence of a vibrant shadow economy made possible by a permeable border with Saudi Arabia. Besides the smuggling of 'grey' consumer goods, a huge traffic in 'black' goods has also emerged, contributing to the escalation of militarization in an already heavily armed society. Again, tribal leaders benefited disproportionately from this development. The general population of the province, by contrast, proved to be less economically robust. Ordinary people were more vulnerable to state efforts in trade control and border fortification, because they lacked the domestic and transnational relationships and networks which promoted and protected the licit and illicit trade activities of some influential shaykhs.

These developments have had an ambivalent impact on the tribal system as a whole. Historically, the standing of a shaykh has been measured by his ability to represent his tribe to the outside and to solve tribal problems and disputes.[148] The patronage politics of the republican government led to an alteration of the concept of tribal leadership, since the ability of shaykhs to channel government contracts to their constituencies and to contribute to their economic development has become one of the most important requirements of the office. In the best possible scenario, the parochial business and investment initiatives of the shaykhs and the joint ventures between them and the government have contributed to the creation of transport routes, investment opportunities, education and health facilities, markets and trade flows, which were also to the benefit of their tribal constituencies. In some cases, however, the tribal population has not benefited from the political and economic empowerment of their shaykhs.

I conclude by saying that the patronage policy of the republican government, particularly the Salih government, has not 'nurtured' the local tribal system, but, on the contrary, helped to distort a functioning tribal order by elevating in importance positions of authority and economic favouritism, which have altered the character of tribal leadership. Throughout history certain tribal leaders have managed to draw resources from 'above'. In republican times, however, underdevelopment, growing gaps in income, and intolerable economic and social imbalances have bred considerable resentment and discontent among the people. This creeping alienation between some shaykhs and their tribal home bases was a particularly dangerous development because shaykhs served as the interface or node allowing the Yemeni state to push its agenda in peripheral areas without carrying out state-building efforts. The alienation between shaykh and tribe and the weakening of the tribal system, therefore, left parts of the population virtually detached from state influence. This is one component of the multifaceted local grievances and imbalances which ultimately contributed to the rise of the Houthi movement. The following chapters demonstrate that, wherever shaykhs began to neglect their tribal duties, or wherever a tribal base did not benefit from the empowerment of its shaykh, or wherever government patronage favoured one tribal group or shaykh at the expense of another, the Houthi movement found particularly favourable conditions to take root and flourish.

3

THE SAUDI INFLUENCE

The international boundary between Yemen and Saudi Arabia bisects the territories of the confederation of Khawlān b. ʿĀmir and some sections of the Hamdān al-Shām confederation into Saudi and Yemeni parts. Saudi borderland policy therefore has a crucial influence on what Herzog calls 'transboundary social formation': the extent to which political, economic, and cultural networks overlap in the borderland.[1] The previous chapters have briefly introduced the influence of Saudi patronage politics on the tribal, political and economic situation in Saʿdah province. This chapter will take a broader and deeper view of this issue and explain the historical development of the patronage relations between the Saudi Kingdom and the Yemeni borderland tribes, as well as the fundamental interdependence of the Saudi-Yemeni boundary dispute, the politics of patronage and the emerging Houthi conflict.

As stated in the previous chapter, the 'fluid' character of the Yemeni-Saudi boundary is a consequence of the provisions of the Treaty of Ṭāʾif (1934) and the Treaty of Jeddah (2000) between the two nations, which grant the residents of the Yemeni-Saudi common borderland (within a 20 kilometre corridor) far-reaching concessions on crossing the boundary without visa restrictions. Moreover, after the end of the 1934 Saudi-Yemeni War, many Yemeni borderland tribal shaykhs became well integrated into Saudi patronage networks and thus important aides of the Kingdom in its efforts to secure the contested boundary. Saudi Arabia, however, increasingly perceived the frequent crossings of the borderland residents and their side effects, such as an increase in smuggling and human trafficking, as a threat to its domestic security and stability. After the Treaty of Jeddah in 2000, Saudi Arabia began to conclude a border demarcation, which at that time was still unenforced on the ground; in 2003, its next controversial—and initially hesitant—step was to begin this physical implementation by erecting border fortifications. Thus, as in Jones' general classification, the territorialization of the Yemeni-Saudi boundary slowly proceeded in three stages: establishment, demarcation, and finally control of the border.[2]

In the face of fierce opposition by the affected tribes, no further fortification works were undertaken during the decade between 2003 and 2013—which more or less coincides with the period of the Saʿdah wars (2004–10). In 2013, however, the Saudi government launched a fresh, more determined attempt at securing its border though the construction of a 'fence' (*siyāj*). Securing the boundary at the expense of the free movement of the borderland tribes amounts to a turning point in the history of Saudi borderland politics in Yemen, as Saudi Arabia now—unlike ten years ago—began to see the fortifications along the Ṭāʾif line as non-negotiable. This rupture in Saudi borderland policy was forced by the spread of armed confrontations between the Houthis and the Yemeni army throughout the Saʿdah region and, most importantly, by the Houthis' seizure of power in Saʿdah governorate in 2011. Saudi Arabia, already on alert because of resurgent Shiite movements in its east, feared the expansion of Zaydi-Shiite influence from Yemen to the north—that is, to the Saudi provinces of Jīzān, ʿAsīr and Najrān. By expelling the most influential shaykhs from their areas along the boundary, the Houthis upset this fragile balance and the borderland patronage networks instrumental in asserting Saudi interests. In other words, the Houthi conflict generated a crisis serious enough to destabilize the entire system of bilateral border protection that had evolved since the 1934 Saudi-Yemeni War, which depended heavily on the cooperation and co-optation of the local tribes.

A Contested Boundary

The Saudi-Yemeni boundary dispute concerns a region of more than 1,200 kilometres of strategically and economically important land and maritime territories and spans almost eighty years, a period in which it repeatedly threatened peace and stability in the region. The main point of contention has been the entitlement of both states to the provinces of Najrān, ʿAsīr and Jīzān. After the Saudi-Yemeni War, these fell to Saudi Arabia temporarily through the Treaty of Ṭā'if in 1934, and permanently in 2000 through the Treaty of Jeddah. Yemeni irredentist claims still advocate the annexation of these 'lost' territories on the grounds of common tribal affiliation and prior historical possession, be it actual or alleged.

Indeed, the tribes of the common borderland are interconnected by descent (*insāb*), kinship (*qarābah*), and marriage relations (*muṣāhirah*). Many Yemeni and Saudi borderland tribes are also closely linked in terms of religious practice; Philby observed during his stay in the Saudi borderland that the religious practices of Banī Mālik and Fayfā' were tinged with Zaydism.[3] In the east of the province the Ismaili parts of Wā'ilah maintained close relationships with their co-religionists in Najrān. In Yemen irredentist claims are expressed through the epithet 'Great' (*kabīr*) and expressions such as *al-Yaman al-Kubrā* (Great Yemen) or *al-Yaman al-Ṭabīʿiyyah* (Natural Yemen), conveying the image of a Yemeni national territory at its maximum conceivable extent.[4] The territorial claims are of particularly explosive nature since they also concern the rights for exploration of natural resources, oil, gas and minerals in particular, that are suspected to exist undiscovered in the border area.[5]

The current boundary between Yemen and Saudi Arabia is in part the result of the historic rivalry between the Saudi Arabian Kingdom, the Zaydi imamate of Imam Yaḥyā and the short-lived Idrīsī Emirate, which was mainly based in the geographical region of Jīzān in what is now southwestern Saudi Arabia.[6] The Idrīsī Emirate was established in 1908 by Muḥammad ʿAlī al-Idrīsī in rebellion against the Ottoman Empire. It gained the support of Great Britain during the First World War, and flourished until the death of its founder in 1920. Under the legally controversial Mecca Treaty of 1926, the provinces of the Idrīsī Emirate fell to Saudi Arabia.[7]

In 1934, the Saudi-Yemeni War erupted between the young Saudi Kingdom and the Yemeni Zaydi Imamate. The Saudi Kingdom had started expanding at the cost of areas to which the Yemeni Imamate also laid claim (those named above), while Imam Yaḥyā had begun gathering troops for an expedition against the tribes of the Najrān region, in particular the Yām, who were living in virtual independence and owed allegiance to none. Parts of Wā'ilah and Yām were of Ismaili denomination and thus answered to the authority of the Ismaili leader. In 1934, ʿAbd al-ʿAzīz Āl Saʿūd and Imam Yaḥyā, who had long been rivals, entered into war. During the Saudi-Yemeni War Saudi forces penetrated deep into Yemeni territories.[8] From the Saudi perspective, their 'right column' forces, under the command of Prince Fayṣal b. ʿAbd al-ʿAzīz, advanced into large parts of the Yemeni Tihāmah and occupied parts of Saḥār and Jumāʿah (including Bāqim and Ḍaḥyān).[9] The 'centre column', under the command of Prince Khālid b. ʿAbd al-ʿAzīz, occupied central parts of the Saʿdah area, including the mountainous natural fortresses of Maṭrah and al-Naqʿah (which, sixty years later, would become Houthi strongholds) and Wādī Nushūr in Wāʾilah. The 'main column', under the command of Prince Saʿūd b. ʿAbd al-ʿAzīz, proceeded via al-Naqʿah into Saḥār and to the gates of Saʿdah city. The 'left column' occupied areas of Wāʾilah and Yām close to Najrān. During this offensive the Yemeni forces were practically defeated, and much of the tribal borderland was occupied by Saudi troops.

Despite their dramatic success, the position of the Saudi occupying troops remained precarious; they were clearly occupying enemy territory and neither their supply lines nor state finances were secure enough to permit a continued occupation. Furthermore, the Yemenis were gradually gathering troops in the mountains and awaiting the signal to commence an all-out counter offensive. Whereas ʿAbd al-ʿAzīz had won the battle, his best advantage lay in getting a favourable peace treaty signed as soon as possible and then withdrawing.[10] Rather than pursuing punitive measures, the victorious Saudi Kingdom adopted a strategy of cooperation which, in the long run, proved to be highly beneficial for both Saudi Arabia and the Yemeni border tribes. A British observation report recorded in 1934 that:

> [...] the wise course adopted in accordance with the instructions of HH the King, in not killing those who do not resist and offering safety to the tribes, has had great effect and has encouraged the Saḥār, the Banī Jumāʿah and the Wāʾilah to open negotiations with a view to offering submission.[11]

The peace negotiations between Saudi Arabia and the Yemeni borderland tribes in 1935 marked the beginning of a close relationship between Saudi Arabia and many Yemeni border tribes, and fostered the formation of a Saudi policy of alliance and patronage in the borderlands. The Saudis were well aware that securing the loyalty of the Yemeni border tribes would be vital for implementing the planned boundary between Yemen and Saudi Arabia, since this boundary would unduly favour Saudi interests and cut deeply through the territories of many local tribes. Among the specific and rather unusual provisions of the 1934 Saudi-Yemeni Treaty of Islamic Friendship and Brotherhood (the Treaty of Ṭāʾif), in particular Appendix 3, Article 1 (1936), were the Saudi concessions designed to alleviate the tribes' fears of this new international boundary and secure their cooperation. Furthermore, some Yemeni border shaykhs became heavily involved in the 1934 boundary negotiations between Imam Yaḥyā and ʿAbd al-ʿAzīz Āl Saʿūd, playing a vital role as members of Saudi-appointed committees for border demarcation and border crossing points. Borderland shaykhs also served as signatories and guarantors of supplementary treaties to the Treaty of Ṭāʾif, among them Yaḥyā Muḥammad Muqīt of Jumāʿah, Muḥammad b. Ḍayfallah b. Ghatāyah of Khawlān and ʿAbdullah Manāʿ of Saḥār, as well as Maʿbar b. Fayṣal (Āl Abū Jabārah of Wāʾilah) and members of the Shājiaʿ clan (Āl Ḥusayn of Wāʾilah).[12]

These emerging patronage relations, which had a considerable monetary aspect, ensured the stability of the controversial new border. They also proved militarily beneficial for Saudi Arabia during the 1960s civil war, when loyal borderland tribes formed buffer zones between the Saudi frontier and the early Yemeni republic, perceived as an Egyptian satellite state.[13] During the 1970 'Wadīʿah border incident', the Saudi Kingdom could even mobilize loyal desert tribes of the Yemeni Wāʾilah to fight South Yemeni infiltrators deep in the dunes of the Rubʿ al-Khālī.[14]

The Treaty of Ṭāʾif defined the boundary in both geographical and tribal terms.[15] However, the so-called Ṭāʾif line—the stretch of the international boundary from the Red Sea to Jabal al-Thaʾr near the Saudi city of Najrān—is predominantly a political and not a tribal boundary, because, as we have seen, tribes and tribal sections of the Khawlān b. ʿĀmir confederation and Hamdān Bakīl confederation, who make up the largest proportion of Saʿdah's tribal population, dwelled on both sides of the frontier. The Ṭāʾif line places five out of eight Khawlān b. ʿĀmir member tribes on Yemeni territory (Jumāʿah, Saḥār, Rāziḥ, Munabbih and the homonymous member tribe Khawlān) and three on Saudi territory (Fayfāʾ, Banī Mālik, and Balghāzī). In the east of Saʿdah province, the Ṭāʾif line bisects the Wādiʿah and draws a boundary between the Wāʾilah and Dahm, which both belong to Yemen, and the Yām, who thus became Saudi. In some areas the Ṭāʾif line even cuts through the settlement area of tribes. For instance, it places the Jumāʿah's Āl Talīd section on the Saudi side of the border, with the rest of the Jumāʿah in Yemen.[16] In Wāʾilah, the Treaty of Ṭāʾif made for particularly complicated, criss-cross solutions; the border has been defined in such a manner that some Saudi individuals became situated on the Yemeni side, but remained Saudi subjects, and vice versa. This certainly constituted a major concession to these individuals.[17]

To demarcate the border and to settle controversies over unclear tribal affiliations, a joint committee—with the participation of H. St. J. Philby on the Saudi side—placed more than 200 demarcation markers along the Ṭāʾif line.[18] Yet some stretches in the central, mountainous boundary sections remained undemarcated, because the committee could not reach certain areas due to tribal strife, such as the boundary section that reaches from Munabbih to today's ʿIlb border crossing point near Bāqim.[19] In the east of Saʿdah province, the joint commission halted its demarcation work at Jabal al-Thaʾr, citing a tribal dispute involving the Saudi Yām and the Yemeni Wāʾilah as the principal obstacle to its completing the demarcation there.[20] Beyond Jabal al-Thaʾr, in the vast territories of the Rubʿ al-Khālī, the boundary was not defined at all. In this area, which extends to the Omani border, various, widely differing claims have been made, largely based on old maps dating back to the Ottoman and British Empires: the Violet Line, the Ḥamzah Line, the Riyadh Line, the Philby Line, and so on, representing earlier claims that were rejected by one side or the other.[21]

The Treaty of Ṭāʾif stipulated that in those areas in which territorial demarcation of the exact 1934 Ṭāʾif line had failed, tribal considerations would come into force. Hence the Treaty put the negotiation and demarcation of these sections of the international boundary back in the hands of the borderland tribes. Boundary shifts in tribal territories, primarily resulting from tribal conflict or the material compensation of tribal blood debt, were henceforth tantamount to alterations of the international boundary.

As a special Saudi concession to the Yemeni border tribes, Appendix 3, Article 1 (1936) of the Treaty of Ṭāʾif granted the 20 kilometre corridor residents the right of crossing without restrictions; however, their movements across the border should, where possible, be at designated border crossing points. For this purpose, Saudi authorities issued special *laissez-passer* passes (*fakk*, pl. *fukūk*) for the residents of this corridor. These visa exemptions were granted exclusively to the borderland residents and not to other Yemeni citizens, who now needed regular passports and visas to cross the border. Nor did this agreement apply to inhabitants of the border area wishing to venture beyond the 20 kilometre common border area.

The Treaty of Ṭāʾif was a temporary settlement, to be renewed at intervals of twenty lunar years. In signing the Treaty of Ṭāʾif and renewing it in 1953 and 1973, the Yemeni government seemed to have dropped its claims to the northwestern portions of its historical territory.[22] In 1990 the merger of the northern Yemeni Arab Republic (YAR) and the southern People's Democratic Republic of Yemen (PDRY) triggered a new wave of national sentiment, resulting in calls for the newly constituted Republic of Yemen to resurrect claims to its ceded northwestern territories. In 1990, preliminary talks for the renegotiation of the Treaty of Ṭāʾif were hampered by serious political tensions between Yemen and Saudi Arabia. After the Yemeni vote in favour of Iraq's invasion of Kuwait at the UN Security Council, Saudi Arabia had expelled hundreds of thousands of Yemeni workers, giving rise to a dramatic increase in unemployment and poverty in Yemen. The political crisis also meant that Saudi Arabia withheld economic aid, and other funds, to Yemen. The Saudi government's decision to expel Yemeni migrant workers, however, did not affect the privileges granted exclusively to Yemeni border tribes inhabiting the common border corridor.[23] Tellingly, the Saudi financial support to Saʿdah's border regions, for example to the Saudi Hospital in Saʿdah city, was also unaffected by this decision. This was seen as a clear and positive Saudi signal to Saʿdah's borderland tribes.[24]

In 1992, shortly before renewal of the Treaty of Ṭāʾif was due, Saudi-Yemeni relations reached a new low after the Yemeni government threatened to withdraw from the Treaty, leading to Saudi military mobilizations and several days of Saudi military training exercises near Ḥaraḍ in the Tihāmah lowlands. In addition, as a counter to the unified Yemen's growing power potential, the Saudis actively supported southern secessionists in the May–July 1994 Yemeni civil war, which led to a severe crisis bringing the two countries to the brink of war in December 1994, when Saudi Arabia amassed troops in the provinces of Jīzān and ʿAsīr.[25] Syria and the US, however, were able to broker a renewed Saudi-Yemeni commitment to settle their differences peaceably. The outcome was a Memorandum of Understanding signed in Mecca in February 1995, in which Yemen, internally weakened by the 1994 civil war, accommodated Saudi Arabia with implicit recognition of the 1934 Ṭāʾif line.[26] The Mecca Memorandum of Understanding resulted in clearly improved relations between the two countries and the establishment of regular high-level meetings between Sanaʿa and Riyadh. In 1998, however, Yemen and Saudi Arabia again came to blows over the tiny al-Duwaymah Island in the Red Sea, which lies roughly to the west of Mīdī, a Yemeni port and border town. The possession of this island has little value in itself, but potentially brings its owner extensive mineral rights on the seabed.[27] This new conflict was settled by the Sanaʿa Protocol of 1998.

After 1998, the Salih government began to assist directly in the enforcement of various Saudi border policies, which ultimately led to the signing of the Treaty of Jeddah in 2000, under which Yemen, despite the objections of some opposition parties, gave up its claims to the 'lost provinces' of Jīzān, ʿAsīr and Najrān. This was due to a number of factors: Yemen intended to enter into negotiations for its accession to the Gulf Cooperation Council (GCC), which required the support of the Saudis;[28] Yemen also made significant territorial gains in the Rubʿ al-Khālī region under the Treaty. Financial incentives also seemed to have played a role, because the Saudi concessions to the Salih government included the reduction of Yemen's debt to Saudi Arabia, and a new loan of $350 million to finance development projects.[29] There was also a pragmatic reason for finalizing border demarcation in the late 1990s, as most states in the region had embarked upon accelerated oil and gas exploration drives at the start of that decade. The consolidation of respective authority, right up to the territorial limits of each state, would ensure that exploration and exploitation could proceed smoothly and without incident.[30]

The Treaty of Jeddah incorporated the provisions of the Treaty of Ṭāʾif including all its amendments, but—in contrast with the earlier treaty—described these as final, permanent, and non-renewable.[31] In other words, the Treaty of Jeddah integrates the Treaty of Ṭāʾif in its entirety, including the permanent cession of Jīzān, ʿAsīr and Najrān provinces to Saudi Arabia. It then defines the remaining land and maritime border areas not covered by the Treaty of Ṭāʾif. Furthermore, the Jeddah Treaty delimits the boundary line in terms of exact territorial coordinates, rather than ambiguous tribal affiliations. The setting of boundary markers on the ground was to be conducted, and official maps made, by an international survey company (the German firm Hansa Luftbild AG would later be given this commission). In addition, Article 4 of the Jeddah Treaty lays down the establishment of a 5 kilometre demilitarized corridor along the Ṭāʾif Line, in which only lightly armed police units are allowed to patrol and the erection of any military sites is prohibited. For the boundary sections beyond the Ṭāʾif Line—that is, east of Jabal al-Thaʾr—separate rules are specified stipulating a demilitarized zone of 20 kilometres. In accordance with the Treaty of Ṭāʾif, the Treaty of Jeddah continues to grant the borderland corridor residents the right to move freely through the border checkpoints. This particularly applies to those borderland residents who do not possess Saudi citizenship; from 1934 Saudi Arabia began to implement a policy of 'Saudization' of the borderlands, in order to further secure the loyalty of the local tribes and support Saudi territorial claims in the disputed border area.[32]

Border Guards

Ever since the 1960s civil war, when the risk of violence and instability spilling over from Yemen became evident, Saudi Arabia has remained extremely attentive to shifts in power and opinion in Yemen. Though Saudi Arabia initially considered the war a domestic Yemeni affair, the situation dramatically changed in the aftermath of the November 1962 Egyptian air raids on Saudi border towns, which showed Saudi Arabia's extreme vulnerability to events and developments in Yemen.[33] In addition, the Saudi monarchs have an understandable repugnance for revolutionary movements that aim at the violent overthrow of kings. As a natural outgrowth of this line of reasoning, Saudi Arabia views events in Yemen, and particularly those in northernmost Yemen, as having a major impact on Saudi internal security and stability. Thus securing the loyalty and cooperation of the borderland shaykhs and their tribes was and is a central Saudi objective in the Saʿdah area.

As we have seen, the relationship between Saudi Arabia and many borderland shaykhs and tribes goes back to the Saudi-Yemeni War of 1934, concluded by the Treaty of Ṭāʾif. The relations between Saudi Arabia and many of these shaykhs are much older and more established than the relations between the same shaykhs and the Yemeni republican government in Sanaʿa, whose grip on its northern peripheries developed only slowly in the decades after the 1960s civil war. After the end of the civil war Saudi influence in the Saʿdah area was so strong that the majority of Saʿdah's tribes only recognized the republican system when Saudi Arabia officially did so in 1970.[34] After the civil war, Saudi Arabia continued to pay subsidies to Saʿdah's shaykhs by presenting itself as a patron and protector of Yemeni tribal interests. This arrangement provides the Saudis with a foothold in Yemen, contributes to the securing of the international boundary and gives the tribal leaders of the Saʿdah area additional power and sources of income.[35] Then Yemeni president Salih was well aware that many of Saʿdah's shaykhs were engaged in double-dealings and receiving both Saudi and Yemeni subsidies, reminding the shaykhs of their national duty by saying: 'Eat, but do not neglect the land' (*kulū lākin lā tafriṭū bi-l-arḍ*).[36]

In the Saʿdah region, the long-standing patronage politics and support of the Saudi Kingdom resulted in an almost rock-solid co-optation of most influential tribal leaders, who, we have seen, played a key role in both the ongoing negotiation and securing of the Ṭāʾif Line and the enforcement of Saudi interests in the region. Notably, the then senior shaykh of Jumāʿah and head of the Khawlān b. ʿĀmir confederation, Yaḥyā Muḥammad Muqīt, played a prominent role in the 1934 boundary delimitation and, during the 1960s civil war, in the defence of the initially Saudi-backed imamate. After the civil war, he vowed to King Fayṣal b. ʿAbd al-ʿAzīz, who was assassinated in 1975, that he would defend the boundary established by the Treaty of Ṭāʾif 'to the last man' (his oath, still considered valid today, was passed on to Yaḥyā Muqīt's successor Ḥasan).[37] In return, King Fayṣal acknowledged the religious and cultural diversity of the Saudi borderlands and their interdependences and tribal affiliations with some Yemeni tribes, especially among the Khawlān b. ʿĀmir of ʿAsīr and Jīzān, some of whom adhered to Zaydi doctrine, and Ismaili tribes in Najrān and the eastern parts of Saʿdah governorate.[38]

Another example of the close cooperation between the Saudi government and the shaykhs was that of Ḥāmis al-ʿAwjarī and his son ʿAbdullah of Wāʾilah, who had been staunch supporters of the then Saudi-backed imamic forces during the 1960s civil war. After the assassination of Prince ʿAbdullah b. al-Ḥasan and the last battles between royalists and republicans in the Kitāf area, ʿAbdullah al-ʿAwjarī took refuge in Saudi Arabia. After some months he returned to Yemen, his relationship with the Saudis greatly reinforced. The 'regular salary' that he thereafter received from across the border is said to have been three times that of other shaykhs in the area.[39] Nevertheless the tribes of Wāʾilah are known for their independence, economic and military strength, and for their ability to enforce their trade interests against state powers.[40]

The Yemeni government, too, tried to co-opt the tribes of Saʿdah, and delegated the task of monitoring its land borders to local shaykhs and their tribesmen. As previously mentioned, the then senior shaykh of Munabbih, ʿAlī Maḍwāḥ ʿAwfān, was the only senior shaykh of a Khawlān b. ʿĀmir member tribe to send clear signals during the civil war in favour of the republicans.[41] The republican government elevated his status accordingly, and empowered him to act on its behalf. During the 1970s, ʿAlī Maḍwāḥ ʿAwfān and his tribal escort acted at times as an 'auxiliary police force' both in border disputes in Munabbih and in quite risky actions outside Munabbih territory—in the early 1980s, the Munabbih escort assisted regular state forces in their successful blows against communist rebels operating in some parts of the Wāʾilah territory in eastern Saʿdah of the province, supported by the then communist regime in southern Yemen. This contributed to an improvement of the Munabbih's reputation among many of the region's staunch royalists, who were themselves anti-communist.[42]

After the Treaty of Jeddah in 2000, this informal cooperation with local shaykhs and tribes to secure the international boundary was raised to an institutional level, resulting in 2003 in the formation of the Yemeni and Saudi Border Guard (*ḥaras al-ḥudūd*). The Border Guard was a regular army unit made up of locals deployed along the Yemeni-Saudi land boundary, especially the mountainous frontier of the Ṭāʾif Line.[43] The bilateral security cooperation, supported by a discreet US presence on the King Khālid Air Base in Khamīs Mushayṭ, helped to curb smuggling and human trafficking across the Yemeni-Saudi border. Despite the magnitude of this issue, the efforts of the two countries to prevent the situation from deteriorating and to mitigate its implications came relatively late; such efforts only began to take place in 2003, after the two countries signed a security treaty regulating the border authorities of the two countries and committing the two parties to extradition of wanted persons and exchange of intelligence regarding terrorists' movements, funding sources, whereabouts and so on. Remarkably, the Border Guard has lived up to its commitments, and tens of infiltrators have been extradited, including a number of Yemenis suspected of links to al-Qaeda and nine of the twenty-three prisoners who escaped from the Political Security Jail in Sanaʿa in November 2006.[44]

The substantial importance of the borderland shaykhs and the close intersection of their tribal and national roles are reflected, for instance, in the role of Aḥmad Dahbāsh Miṭrī, who was until his death in 2007 shaykh of the Banī Khawlī (Munabbih) and senior shaykh of the Munabbih's Shaʿshaʿ moiety.[45] During the 1960s civil war, Aḥmad's father Dahbāsh fought with the royalists and later became one of the many 'defector shaykhs' who, from 1970 onwards, accomplished a turn towards the now dominant republican power. Dahbāsh's son and successor Aḥmad had undergone military training in the Yemeni capital, where he was given the rank of colonel. After the Treaty of Jeddah, the Yemeni government appointed him commander of Munabbih's Border Guard. In 2005 and 2006, Aḥmad Dahbāsh served as a mediator in the violent territorial dispute between the Saudi Āl Talīd and Yemeni Āl Thābit (both sections of the Munabbih's neighbour tribe Jumāʿah).

The enmity between Āl Talīd and Āl Thābit stems from a long-standing territorial dispute with components of blood feud and tribal war. In addition, there is '*naṣrī* and *ḥilfī* between them', as locals say, because the two sections belong to different moieties (Naṣr and Aḥlāf respectively) of the Jumāʿah.[46] In 1934, the Treaty of Ṭāʾif placed Āl Talīd on the Saudi side of the boundary but failed to demarcate this section of the border on the ground due to tribal conflict. Āl Talīd and Āl Thābit fought countless battles according to the customs and patterns of tribal feud in order to re-negotiate and adjust their common border. In 2005, Aḥmad Dahbāsh was one of the signatories of a tribal ceasefire document negotiated between the two groups in Jīzān, which provided for the return of land from Āl Talīd to Āl Thābit and therefore from Saudi Arabia to Yemen, a transaction which had been confirmed at the highest level by the involved nations.[47] This is a good illustration that, even since the Treaty of Jeddah, the Ṭā'if Line is still subjected to minor changes and alterations according to treaties and agreements between the borderland tribes.

Since the Treaty of Jeddah, Saudi Arabia's cooperation with many of its Yemeni tribal aides began to take place in a climate of highest recognition and appreciation. These tribal leaders' role in bilateral security cooperation gives them additional powers and revenue and an international political stage. In May 2001, one year after the signature of the Jeddah Treaty, a high-level meeting between representatives of the Yemeni and Saudi governments and influential shaykhs of the Yemeni-Saudi borderlands took place in Riyadh to celebrate the 'remarkable improvement' of political, social and economic Saudi-Yemeni relations. Among the participants were Prince ʿAbdullah b. ʿAbd al-ʿAzīz, then crown prince, deputy prime minister and commander of the National Guard.[48] The Munabbih shaykhs Salmān b. ʿAwfān, ʿAlī Ḥusayn al-Munabbihī and Yaḥyā b. Lazzah, as well as Hamadān Aḥmad al-ʿAzzām, a member of the senior shaykhly lineage of Rāziḥ, appeared alongside the highest representatives of the Saudi borderland tribal elites as speakers, and emphasized in unison the improvement of security and stability in the region since the signature of the Treaty of Jeddah.

Boundary Fortifications

In the last years before the eruption of the Saʿdah wars, however, the situation on the Saudi-Yemeni border was less stable than it appeared. In fact, after the Treaty of Jeddah in 2000, Saudi borderland policy in Yemen became increasingly two-faced, endeavouring to secure, police and fortify the boundary with Yemen. This shift in Saudi policy represented a significant move from what Martínez has called 'interdependent' borderlands, in which the societies on both sides of the border are linked symbiotically through a considerable cross-border flow of economic and human resources, towards 'coexistent' borderlands, in which only limited cross-border contact exists.[49] The project to physically protect the Kingdom's borders was first proposed in the 1990s following the First Gulf War, to secure the Saudi-Iraqi border. The mountainous boundary with Yemen also became a particular concern at this time. As we have seen, in addition to the potential spillover of political developments, the Saudi-Yemeni border has become an emblem of various threats emanating from Yemen: al-Qaeda fighters, smuggled weapons, narcotics and explosives and, well under the world's radar, one of the largest flows of economic refugees on earth. Saudi Arabia claimed that since the early 1990s smugglers from the border area had been providing the weapons and explosives used by radical Islamists operating inside the Kingdom, such as the perpetrators of the 2003 Riyadh 'compound bombings', which killed thirty-five and injured over a hundred. Moreover, al-Qaeda in the Arabian Peninsula (AQAP), which was formed in January 2009 after the merger of al-Qaeda's Yemeni and Saudi branches, had several Saudis in leadership roles and had sworn to bring down the Āl Saʿūd, the Kingdom's ruling family. Some also see the increasing threat from al-Qaeda as a consequence of the policies of Prince Mishʿal b. Saʿūd b. ʿAbd al-ʿAzīz Āl Saʿūd, former governor of Najrān, arguing that during his term (2009–13) Yemenis with extremist links were naturalized and granted plots of land in Najrān, a process which may have helped to turn the province into a recruiting ground for AQAP in Yemen.[50]

Saudi Arabia calls the planned physical border fortification a 'fence'. In reality it more closely resembles a wall consisting of sandbags and concrete-filled pipelines, 3 metres high, and fitted with radar and electronic detection equipment. Given the legally binding provisions of the Jeddah Treaty and the importance of the tribal leaders' loyalty and cooperation, the construction of this fence has been a highly sensitive issue for both Saudi Arabia and the borderland tribes, because it violates their legal right to cross the border without restriction in exchange for their loyalty to and cooperation with the Kingdom. Hence it is no coincidence that the first construction works on the fence, which began in September 2003, focused on an area at the extreme eastern terminus of the Ṭāʾif Line at Jabal al-Thaʾr, where Saudi patronage politics had previously derailed, leaving local elites at least temporarily detached from Saudi state influence. Here the commencement of the fortification works gave rise to a serious conflict between the Yemeni Āl Ḥusayn tribe and the Saudi government, illustrating the potential hazards of disgruntled borderland shaykhs.

The Āl Ḥusayn are a section of the Wāʾilah's Rijāl ʿUlah (adj. *alhānī*) moiety, settling in the area surrounding Jabal al-Thaʾr, where the eastern terminus of the Ṭāʾif Line turns into the undemarcated territory of the Rubʿ al-Khālī.[51] My inquiries on the position of this tribe during the 1960s revolution and civil war went largely unanswered by my sources in Saʿdah. It was commonly believed that the Āl Ḥusayn were at that time fragmented and peripheral and 'appeared on the scene only after the civil war' (*lam yaẓhirū illā baʿd al-ḥarb al-ahliyyah*). Like many tribes of the vast, desert-like area linking Saʿdah, al-Jawf, Maʾrib and the Rubʿ al-Khālī, the Āl Ḥusayn play a central role in the profitable cross-border trade; their territory is known as a hub for large quantities of contraband. Moreover, the Jabal al-Thaʾr and the surrounding desert, which had always been of mere symbolic significance, gained supreme strategic importance in the emerging struggle for oil and gas resources. Local sources indicate that the Āl Ḥusayn possessed a staggering arsenal of heavy weapons, including the finest modern military communications equipment, armoured vehicles and high-calibre machine guns, which, in terms of both quantity and quality, by far exceeded the armaments available in the Yemeni army camps of Saʿdah governorate.

The tribes of this area owe allegiance to none; for centuries their area slumbered in virtual independence from any outside force. Furthermore, the Āl Ḥusayn (not the Wāʾilah as a whole) and parts of the neighbouring Saudi Yām are of Ismaili denomination, thus owing some supreme loyalties to the Ismaili leader.[52] The policy of intolerance towards the Ismaili minority pursued by Prince Mishʿal b. Saʿūd (governor of Najrān 1996–2008) gave rise to a conflict between the Ismaili population of Najrān and the Saudi government which, in April 2000, reached a temporary peak. During the Ismaili uprising many Saudi Ismailis sought refuge with their co-religionists on the Yemeni side, leading to armed clashes between the pursuing Saudi forces and Ismaili Yemeni border tribes.[53] When the Treaty of Jeddah was signed two months later, the Āl Ḥusayn claimed that the boundary coordinates given in the Treaty put the boundary 4 to 7 kilometres beyond the neutral zone inside Yemen and bisected the territory of the Āl Ḥusayn by granting a part of it to the Saudi Yām.

The then senior shaykh of the Āl Ḥusayn, Muḥammad b. Shājiaʿ, claimed that the tribal borders between the Āl Ḥusayn and the Yām, which were tantamount to the international border between Yemen and Saudi Arabia, were set down in 241-year-old tribal documents officially recognized by the first Saudi monarch, ʿAbd al-ʿAzīz Āl Saʿūd, and by Imam Yaḥyā Ḥamīd al-Dīn during the 1934 boundary negotiations.[54] He spearheaded the tribal opposition to the planned boundary demarcation by resorting to martial rhetoric and action; the Āl Ḥusayn violently sabotaged the demarcation works and the installation of the actual boundary markings by the German survey company Hansa Luftbild. In 2003 the Āl Ḥusayn also forcibly obstructed the first Saudi attempts to build the border fence.[55] Much of the region descended into armed conflict, because in order to divert the Wāʾilah's attention from the boundary fortifications and their territorial claims against Saudi Arabia, the Saudi and Yemeni governments readily rekindled the deep embers of perennial conflict between the Wāʾilah and their brother tribe and hereditary enemy, the Dahm.

The sudden deterioration of relations between Saudi Arabia and Muḥammad b. Shājiaʿ did not happen overnight, but had begun after the first news of Saudi plans to police and fortify the border in the early 1990s, in which Muḥammad b. Shājiaʿ and his tribe saw a threat to their trans-border movements and transnational trading activities. As a first step, the Āl Ḥusayn allied themselves with Qatar, an alliance which came naturally in the sense that the Shājiaʿ family also bears Qatari nationality. To build up additional threat and bargaining potential against the Saudi and Yemeni governments, Muḥammad b. Shājiaʿ and some other affected tribal leaders from the desert areas of Wāʾilah and Dahm, among them Amīn al-ʿUkaymī, also received a 1997 delegation from Osama bin Laden, who at that particular time spoke of the possibility of emigrating from Afghanistan to Yemen. Yet the negotiations with bin Laden failed to yield any results.[56]

In 2003, the Yemeni and Saudi governments publicly dismissed Muḥammad b. Shājiaʿ's threats against the implementation of the border fortifications as 'transient bubbles'.[57] Extensive Egyptian and US efforts, however, convinced the Saudi authorities to remove all physical border fortifications and local mobility constrictions, and the Saudi government tried to calm the Āl Ḥusayn by awarding 500 Saudi passports and material compensation.[58] Meanwhile, the Yemeni government distributed additional financial resources related to the 'war on terror', which commenced in 2001, to shaykhs of remote border areas in Saʿdah and al-Jawf—funds which were meant to prevent local tribes from providing refuge to elements of al-Qaeda.[59] Muḥammad b. Shājiaʿ was killed in 2002 in the vicinity of his home base, al-ʿAṭfayn fort, when his car crashed at night into a tank truck; many suspected an assassination plot. Since the Saudis would not let him cross the border into their country to reach Najrān Hospital, he died of blood loss.[60]

Since these incidents in Āl Ḥusayn, the area has been shrouded in rumour and speculation concerning illicit arms deals and terrorism, some of which may be true but much of which are mere hearsay.[61] The fact is that the construction of the fence was halted and stalled for six years, during which five Saʿdah wars took place. It was only in June 2009, shortly before the outbreak of the sixth and last official bout of conflict between the Yemeni government and the Houthis, that the border fortification project witnessed new movement. The European Aeronautic Defense and Space Company (EADS), a systems solution provider for armed forces and civil security entities worldwide, won a major contract to recommence the implementation of the border security system along 9,000 kilometres of Saudi Arabia's land borders with the

UAE, Kuwait, Qatar, Jordan, Oman and Yemen.[62] In spring 2013, the Saudi government announced the continuation of construction works and the mobilization of additional security forces to guard them. The Emir of ʿAsīr, Prince Fayṣal b. Khālid, said there were no more disagreements with the 'Yemeni side'—by which he meant the new Yemeni Transitional Government headed by ʿAbd Rabbuh Manṣūr Ḥādi, at that time mainly preoccupied with its own affairs—over the security fence.[63] Three main factors led to the re-commencement of the controversial project: the enormous increase in both illegal immigration and smuggling of weapons, explosives, narcotics; the merger in early January 2009 of the Yemeni and Saudi al-Qaeda branches into AQAP; and, of course, the emergence of the Houthi conflict and the eruption of the Saʿdah wars in 2004, its initially intermittent violence gradually evolving into a rolling conflict which, by 2009, had dragged most of Saʿdah and its neighbouring governorates into war. When in 2009–10 the Houthis briefly crossed the Saudi border at Jabal Dukhān near al-Malāḥīṭ, Saudi Arabia saw itself obliged to enter the war. After the Houthis seized power in Saʿdah governorate in spring 2011, Saudi Arabia began publicly to interpret the situation along the porous Saudi-Yemeni border as a 'machination' of a Houthi-backed 'foreign country' known for its hostility to the Kingdom: Iran.[64]

Yet, since 2009, the fortification works have not focused on the area at the eastern terminus of the Ṭāʾif Line at Jabal al-Thaʾr, as in 2003. This time, they have included the mountainous boundary sections in the west of the province. This relatively well-defined section of the Ṭāʾif Line had hitherto been broadly stable due to the long-established relations of cooperation and patronage between the Saudi government and the local tribal elites. However, with the beginning of the upheavals brought by Yemen's 'Change Revolution' in the wake of the 2011 Arab Spring, the Yemeni regime lost control of its north-western periphery. The resulting power vacuum led to enormous expansion and empowerment for the Houthis, who expelled the majority of the senior shaykhs, regarded as aides of the Yemeni and Saudi governments. Consequently, the sensitive border regions in western Saʿdah governorate were no longer secured by tribal allies of the Saudi (and Yemeni) government, but rather controlled by Saudi-hostile Houthis. It is no surprise, therefore, that this area became the new focus of Saudi border fortification plans.

Blumi argues that the Saudi attempts to formalize and police the border have provoked the Houthi conflict, because local communities had straddled the border for decades and were now prevented from freely moving and interacting, and the planned border fortifications threatened to cut them off from their livelihoods.[65] According to Blumi, the media have largely distorted the nature of the conflict in the Saʿdah region by making it increasingly synonymous with the Houthi movement; rather, Blumi sees it as the by-product of a process that forcibly imposes previously unknown boundaries upon communities. Indeed, it is indisputable that the boundary fortification plans have produced unrest and concern among the borderland tribes, because the fortifications represent the ultimate violation of their legitimate right to straddle the boundary within the 20 kilometre corridor, as guaranteed by the Treaties of Ṭāʾif and Jeddah.

Yet Blumi's interpretation that the Houthi conflict and the Saʿdah wars were essentially a revolt of local communities against Saudi boundary fortification plans needs to be revised and nuanced, because in most cases the violence of the Houthi conflict and the violence that arose from opposition to the border fortification were two distinct phenomena. This becomes evident through a careful re-assessment of the two empirical examples that Blumi cites in support of his thesis: the temporary closure of the ʿIlb border crossing in Bāqim by a member of the Muqīt[66] clan, and the conflict between the Saudi government and Muḥammad b. Shājiaʿ and his tribe, the Āl Ḥusayn. To further elaborate this issue, we will also take into account a third case, namely the border conflict between the Āl Amshaykh (a Munabbih section) and the Saudi Border Guards, which made the headlines in Yemen throughout the spring of 2013.

In February 2009, a member of the Muqīt clan, the Jumāʿah's senior shaykhly lineage and simultaneously the senior shaykhly lineage of the entire confederation of Khawlān b. ʿĀmir, closed the ʿIlb border crossing north of Bāqim for several hours, in protest against the increasing Saudi boundary restrictions. This is one of the most important border crossings between Yemen and Saudi Arabia. Blumi interprets this incident as an example of local protest against boundary restrictions transforming into the violence of the Houthi conflict.[67] However, localizing the scope of analysis reveals that this matter is much more complex. By considering its local context, it becomes clear that this incident does not necessarily indicate a connection between the post-2000 boundary-related protests and the violence of the Saʿdah wars. The Muqīt clan is, as we have seen, neither opposed to Saudi interests nor loyal to the Houthis. On the contrary, since the 1960s civil war the Muqīt family has played a prominent role in the stabilization of the Ṭāʾif Line. Shortly after the ʿIlb incident, Ḥasan Muqīt, senior shaykh of Jumāʿah and simultaneously *shaml shumūl* (the highest representative) of Khawlān b. ʿĀmir, reaffirmed to the other Khawlānī shaykhs in Saudi Arabia that he and his followers would not permit 'anyone' (by which he meant the Houthis) to cross the border, 'as long as there is a drop of blood in our veins' (*lan natruk aḥadan yaʿbur ṭālamā fī ʿuruqnā qaṭrat damm*).[68] In August 2009, during the sixth Houthi war, Ḥasan Muqīt's son Bandar was captured when he unsuccessfully tried to defend Bāqim (the home area of the Muqīt clan) against Houthi intrusion. The Houthis seized him near ʿIlb as he attempted to flee across the border into Saudi Arabia.[69] Yaḥyā Muqīt, another member of the Muqīt clan, was the founder and chairman of the Tribal Alliance of the Sons of Saʿdah (*al-taḥāluf al-qabalī li-abnāʾ Ṣaʿdah*), a tribal defence community formed to fight the Houthis, and one of the most prominent and active protagonists of Saʿdah's tribal resistance during these wars. After 2011 the Houthis expelled all of them from the Saʿdah area, even the head of the confederation, Shaykh Ḥasan Muqīt, because of their loyalty to the Saudi and Yemeni governments.[70]

Blumi's second example, the border incident in Wāʾilah, must also be carefully re-read in context. Blumi sees the 'revolt in Wāʾilah' (which was a revolt of the Āl Ḥusayn and not of Wāʾilah as a whole) against the planned border fortifications as part of the larger context of the violent Saʿdah wars. A re-assessment of the local complexities suggests a rather different interpretation. During the Saʿdah wars, the majority of the senior Wāʾilah shaykhs—among them Fāyiz al-ʿAwjarī and Muḥammad b. Qamshah—were firmly opposed to the Houthis and positioned themselves on the side of the Yemeni government. On the other hand, Ṣāliḥ b. Shājiaʿ, Muḥammad's son and successor, and his tribe did not join the Houthis, but maintained their historically 'neutral' position throughout the six Saʿdah wars. Because of the remoteness of their territory and their sheer material and military superiority, the Āl Ḥusayn were able to keep the Houthis at a distance and prevent the conflict from spreading into their territory. The neutral position of the Shājiaʿ clan also enabled Shājiaʿ b. Shājiaʿ, another prominent son of the late Muḥammad, to act in 2005 as an intermediary between the Houthis and the government in Sanaʿa.[71] During the Ṣaʿdah wars, the territory of the Āl Ḥusayn became an important buffer zone between the Saudis and the Houthis. And, we must not forget, the Āl Shājiaʿ and the Saudis are connected by close historical relations; despite the border troubles of 2000 and 2003, no one would benefit from a serious long-term deterioration in relations. Accordingly, during the sixth war in 2009–10, when most areas of Ṣaʿdah were plunged into war, parts of the Āl Ḥusayn took action together with Saudi security forces against the Houthis.

The Āl Ḥusayn are primarily adept traders, and their alliances are focused on the assertion of their trade interests. It is therefore not surprising that, with the resumption of Saudi border fortification in 2013, the sons of Muḥammad b. Shājiaʿ entered into mutual negotiations and security cooperation with the Saudi security forces, rather than triggering a violent chain reaction as their father had. Certainly the very nature of such a re-negotiation rests on major mutual concessions regarding the physical border fortifications and local mobility constrictions. ʿAbdullah b. Shājiaʿ, one of Muḥammad's sons, made a robust declaration to the Saudi daily *Okaz* that his tribe would protect the border from all violations by 'bandits, terrorists, illegal immigrants and the smuggling of narcotics, weapons, and other contraband', and that this was both a 'national and a religious duty for the sake of the neighbourly relations with the Saudi Kingdom'.[72] This declaration was a little bizarre, as it was ʿAbdullah b. Shājiaʿ's declared intention to assist Saudi security in tracking infiltrators and smugglers. To this purpose, the Āl Ḥusayn erected tents in the borderland and tribal volunteers began to patrol the boundary—that is, to safeguard the very Saudi security with which the Āl Ḥusayn used to play fast and loose. In this case, the primacy of trade interests clearly helped to dissolve the intricate fabric of multiple dealings, conflicts of interests, and shifting loyalties of local tribes. The primacy of trade interests also explains why the Shājiaʿ clan may open clandestine relations with the Houthis when the Saudis do so, or at least see an economic advantage in so doing.[73] In Wāʾilah political positions and alliances may be 'transient bubbles'; trade interests, however, are not.

In spring 2013, border clashes erupted between the Āl Amshaykh and the Saudi Border Guards along the Ṭāʾif Line in the mountainous western part of Saʿdah governorate. The Āl Amshaykh are a Munabbih section dwelling in lower areas of Munabbih's tribal territory, directly bordering on Saudi Arabia. The media in Sanaʿa quickly interpreted these clashes as epiphenomena of an 'aggressive, Saudi-hostile' Houthi policy, since Munabbih at this time was infiltrated by the Houthis.

Since their power seizure in the province in 2011, the Houthis had more or less forcibly expelled Munabbih's most influential shaykhs, among them Salmān b. ʿAwfān, Munabbih's senior shaykh; Yūsif b. Miṭrī, son of Aḥmad Dahbāsh and senior shaykh of Munabbih's Shaʿshaʿ moiety; and Ḥusayn ʿAlī al-Munabbihī, son of Munabbih's most prominent businessman and 'shaykh of the revolution' ʿAlī Ḥusayn al-Munabbihī.[74] The Saudis responded to this development by deploying police and Border Guards and reinforcing security measures in the region by constructing military centres (*marākiz ʿaskariyyah*) along the border, including one on top of Jabal Fadhdhah, a crest overlooking the lower slopes of Munabbih and thereby situated 'over the heads of Āl Amshaykh', as a local put it.

Jabal Fadhdhah is a Saudi border crest overlooking some lower parts of the Yemeni regions of Munabbih and Ghamr. The crest is located on territory which in 1934 could not be demarcated by Philby's team due to tribal feuding. The feud in Āl Amshaykh, which obstructed the demarcation of this border segment, arose over a dispute regarding tribal grazing rights. In many areas of Sa'dah province (and beyond), the relatively arid, low elevation areas at intra- and inter-tribal borders are used as pasture lands by several tribal groups, all of which hold alternate, reciprocal grazing rights in these area as recognized in tribal contracts. Overgrazing by one side often causes conflict with the other contracting parties, and at the time of writing the Āl Amshaykh are still engaged in such disputes with neighbouring Saudi tribal groups (mostly the Banī Mālik, of Khawlān b. 'Āmir stock).[75]

The newly constructed Saudi military base on Jabal Fadhdhah is not only located on territory on which the Āl Amshaykh claim grazing rights. It is also located within the demilitarized 5 kilometre security corridor designated by the Treaty of Jeddah. Moreover, in the years before the base's establishment, the Saudis began to restrict the freedom of movement of the borderland inhabitants, and even confiscated Yemeni sheep and cattle when crossing the border. Consequently, the Āl Amshaykh accused Saudi Arabia of violating the provisions of the Treaty in multiple ways. The fact that the Yemeni government has signed the Treaty of Jeddah, and has thus drawn a definitive line under the historical territorial claims of the Yemeni border tribes, further embittered the tribespeople. Shaykh Jibrān b. Sawādah of Āl Amshaykh explained:

> We fought over this border for thirty-five years, and many of our men fell in this fight.[76] And when our government signed the Treaty of Jeddah, we said: Enough of this (*khalāṣ*)! We do not continue our fight for this state; we request nothing but the performance of the Treaty. The Saudis shoot us with machine guns, and we have nothing but useless rifles [...]. Munabbih is not dominated by the Houthis, but we may be in need of them if the state does not stand with us to stop the violations of the Saudis [...]. We cannot resist the Saudis alone if they wage war against us. The Houthis called me from Sa'dah [city] and told me: We will come. But I told them: No, I will call you in when I am in need of you, for the time being the men of Munabbih are with me.[77]

On first sight, this situation seems to be perfectly in line with situations in which the weaker side, which felt unsupported or abandoned by the Yemeni government, allied itself with the Houthis, as happened, for example, in the territorial conflict between Sufyān and al-ʿUṣaymāt.[78] Yet in the Āl Amshaykh case, other forces were at work. Little cooperation has so far been established between the Āl Amshaykh and the Houthis, for multiple reasons: First, Munabbih's historical autonomy-oriented and in parts *sādah*-hostile policy has generated a general aversion to 'external interference', in particular regarding the Houthis.[79] Second, locals were well aware that open involvement by the Houthis could turn local border unrest between Saudi Border Guards and the tribesmen of Āl Amshaykh into a large-scale military confrontation between the Saudis and the Houthis—a confrontation that all sides, each for their own reasons, were reluctant to unleash.

These three examples show that Blumi's reasoning falls short when he argues that the Saudi attempts to impose boundaries and to formalize and police the border have provoked the Houthi conflict. Despite their conflict with the Saudis, neither the Āl Ḥusayn of Wāʾilah, nor the Āl Amshaykh of Munabbih and the Muqīt clan of Jumāʿah have allied themselves with the Houthis. In each case, the violence that arose from opposition to Saudi border policy and the violence of the Houthi conflict were separately emerging phenomena.

To sum up, traditionally, consideration of the Yemeni-Saudi boundary dispute has adopted a view from the centre, focusing on its legal provisions and the rhetoric, intentions and negotiations of the Saudi and Yemeni central governments. In contrast, this chapter considers the boundary problem at grassroots level through the lens of the concerned borderland residents and by looking at the social realities it has engendered. It focuses on the influence of Saudi patronage politics in the borderlands of Saʿdah, the mutual interdependencies between Saudi boundary policy and the emergence of the Houthi conflict, and the vital role that tribes and tribal elites have played in this process.

Since the Treaty of Ṭāʾif (1934), the borderland tribes of Saʿdah were responsible for the precise (re-)negotiation of some stretches of the boundary and the protection of the fragile equilibrium along the border. Borderland shaykhs were well integrated into networks of both Yemeni and Saudi state power and became important aides of the states in their efforts to control the borderlands. In return, the shaykhs were granted generous financial support and their tribes enjoyed special cross-border mobility rights, as provided for in the Treaties of Ṭāʾif and Jeddah. As long as their interests were guaranteed, the tribes secured the boundary and minimized the explosive potential of the political sabre-rattling and periodic border skirmishes between the two countries' armies. This mutual cooperation was so beneficial to the local tribes that irredentist claims advocating the recapture of the three 'lost' territories of

ʿAsīr, Jīzān and Najrān seem far more of a goal of urban Yemeni nationalist sentiment than a real objective of the concerned tribes. As long as their legal rights to cross the boundary were secured, it meant little to the tribes whether their territories belonged to Yemen or to Saudi Arabia; instead they derived enormous economic benefit from the presence of the international border that bisected their territories.

Since the 1990s and especially since the conclusion of the Treaty of Jeddah in 2000, Saudi Arabia has endeavoured to impose its jurisdiction and territoriality on the borderland. The Kingdom began to demarcate its boundary with Yemen and to secure a particularly unruly and sensitive area in the east of Saʿdah province through a physical border barrier. The demarcation and fortification works were blocked by fierce tribal resistance, which led to the temporary suspension of the project. The Houthi conflict, which gradually spread through the province from 2004 and in 2009 briefly crossed the international boundary at Jabal Dukhān in Shidāʾ, led to an insistent resumption of Saudi boundary fortification plans. During the Saʿdah wars, the fragile equilibrium in the borderland became increasingly unhinged due to the proliferation of the conflict, and, above all, the expulsion of the tribal elites, whose occasionally rock-solid co-optation by the Yemeni and Saudi states, as we shall see, had long been the main obstacle to the military success of the Houthi movement.

The impact of Saudi border policy on the emergence of the Houthi conflict has been marginal, since the demarcation and especially the fortification works started relatively late and are in most areas still in a state of planning. It has also been shown that the violence against the border fortification and the violence of the Houthi conflict are in most cases distinct phenomena; few of those who protested against the Saudi mobility restrictions later became Houthis. Conversely, the influence of the Houthi conflict on Saudi border fortification plans has been enormous. It is no exaggeration to say that the Houthi conflict generated a crisis serious enough to destabilize the entire system of bilateral border protection which has depended since 1934 on the cooperation and co-optation of the local shaykhs. The expulsion of Riyadh's tribal cooperation partners led to a definitive rupture in Saudi Arabia's long-consistent borderland policy: since 2011, Saudi Arabia has considered the border fortifications non-negotiable.[80]

At the time of writing, the boundary fortification works are still at the planning stage and will not be operational in the near future. Instead of the planned high-tech fortifications, Saudi Arabia has so far erected mainly barbed wire (*islāk*) and simple concrete separation walls (*judrān ʿizālah*). It is still open to question whether the envisaged boundary fence can be realized and to what extent it will prove useful.[81] The construction conditions along the Saudi-Yemeni border are tough: the extreme climate, the rugged topography, and the lack of roads and basic infrastructure all obstruct the implementation of construction works and the use of the proposed sensitive electronic monitoring technology. Moreover, the effectiveness of the Saudi border security system would require the cooperation and skills of the authorities in neighbouring Yemen—but since the Houthis seized power in Saʿdah governorate 2011, the Yemeni state is no longer present in its previous form in the borderlands. The contractors' access to the border areas is made even more difficult by the fact that since 2011 most of the border areas have been controlled by the Houthis. In the end, tribes, traders and smugglers will have an easy time getting past the border and learning its weak points.

4

SECTS AND POLITICS

Throughout history the Saʿdah region, despite its importance as the primordial cell and spiritual centre of Zaydism, has never been Yemen's only 'centre'. The Zaydi imamic state was often weak and fragmented, and Yemen's economic and political centres were often elsewhere—in Sanaʿa and Lower Yemen. The preceding chapters have demonstrated how the system change after the 1960s civil war further peripheralized and disconnected the Saʿdah region from the rest of the country. Peripheralization, conceptualized by Fischer-Tahir and Naumann as 'the outcome of complex processes of change in the economy, demography, political decision-making and socio-cultural norms and values', refers to a spatially organized inequality of power relations and access to material and symbolic goods that constructs and perpetuates the precedence of centres over areas that are marginalized.[1] In that sense, after the 1960s civil war large parts of Yemen's extreme north became peripheralized to the centre Sanaʿa, further to the south—this is similar to what happened to southern Yemen after Yemeni unification in 1990.[2]

This chapter explores the dynamics that could unfold in this environment as a result of sectarian and related political developments. Since the 1980s, the process of socio-political and economic peripheralization was further exacerbated by the increasing marginalization of the Zaydi *madhhab* (doctrine, school of thought). Being promoted by the Saudi and (at times) the Yemeni government, the spread of radical Sunnism in the Zaydi heartland triggered the emergence of a Zaydi resistance movement. In the context of the Saʿdah region, the Zaydi revival had an immensely far-reaching impact, providing the basis for the emergence in the 1990s of the 'Believing Youth'—an organization that transformed the theological discourse of the Zaydi renaissance into religious revival and social activism on grassroots level. A second, less successful mode of Zaydi revivalism also took place on the political stage in the mid-1990s.

Since the turn of the millennium, the Zaydi revival's agenda has been significantly shaped and altered by the Zaydi cleric and former politician Ḥusayn al-Ḥūthī. Under his influence, the revivalism movement has managed to embrace a powerful social revolutionary and political component. Among Yemen's Zaydi scholars, this change of agenda has not always been met with approval. In Yemen's extreme north, however, riven by socio-political and economic imbalances, the revival movement led by Ḥusayn al-Ḥūthī ultimately became a rallying point that could unite the interests of those who felt economically neglected, politically ostracized and religiously marginalized.

The Sunnization of Upper Yemen

Islamic identities in Yemen have historically been divided into two main Islamic orientations: Shiite Zaydism and Sunni Shāfiʿism. There are also numerically smaller groups of Shiite Ismailis (in the Ḥarāz Mountains and among some sections of the Wāʾilah and Yām in northeast Saʿdah and northern al-Jawf), as well as some Jewish communities.[3] Whereas the Zaydis' historical heartland is located in Upper Yemen, especially in Saʿdah, ʿAmrān, al-Jawf, Ḥajjah and Dhamār provinces, Shāfiʿism is the dominant school of jurisprudence in Lower Yemen, the eastern part of the country and the Tihāmah. The settlement areas of the Zaydis and Shāfiʿīs are not always clearly distinguished from each other. The Saʿdah region, for instance, is considered the heartland of Zaydism, but in some areas—notably al-Ḥishwah, al-Ẓāhir, Shidāʾ, and Ghamr—Sunnis make up a considerable part of the population.[4]

The Zaydis belong to a sect of Shia Islam that traces its name back to its eponym Zayd b. ʿAlī, the great-grandson of ʿAlī b. Abī Ṭālib, who revolted against Umayyad rule in 740 CE after Imam al-Ḥusayn's death at Karbala.[5] By recognising Zayd b. ʿAlī as its founder, Zaydism distinguishes itself from Imāmism (Twelver Shia, as prevalent in Iran). The biography *Sīrat al-Hādī ilā al-Ḥaqq Yaḥyā b. al-Ḥusayn* by ʿAlī b. Muḥammad b. ʿUbayd Allah al-ʿAbbāsī al-ʿAlawī, written in the tenth century CE, deals with the arrival and life of the first Zaydi imam in Yemen, Yaḥyā b. al-Ḥusayn (d. 911) and his attempts to establish his rule over the tribes in Yemen's north.[6] Yaḥyā b. al-Ḥusayn managed to establish a Zaydi community in Yemen in 897 CE, when the Saʿdah region and large parts of the highlands had long been ravaged by a protracted tribal conflict. Since the involved tribes found themselves ultimately unable to resolve the dispute, they sent a delegation to Medina, which led to the invitation of Yaḥyā b. al-Ḥusayn, a member of the Prophet's family and a follower of the Zaydi branch of Islam, who managed to solve the conflict through mediation and arbitration according to shariah law.[7] Yaḥyā b. al-Ḥusayn then took up residence in Saʿdah city. He established a kind of Zaydi state (*dawlah*) and adopted the title *amīr al-muʾminīn* (ruler of the faithful), the traditional title of the caliph. His honorary name as imam was *al-Hādī ilā al-Ḥaqq* (guide to the truth). The imam and his followers encountered support, but also hostility and opposition, in the tribal society of the Northern Highlands. In his biography the tribes are sometimes depicted as the imam's allies, and sometimes as adversaries; he regarded his tribal opponents as enemies of Islam.[8] Thus, al-Hādī's fourteen-year reign, though propitiously launched, resembled one of constant warfare to restore discipline over rebellious tribes, to halt renewed intertribal hostilities, and to extend Zaydi influence. Throughout its existence, the Zaydi imamate was a state of varying influence and often intermittent authority, which existed for almost a millennium until the 26 September Revolution of 1962.

The legal teachings and judgements of Yaḥyā b. al-Ḥusayn are the basis for the so-called Zaydi Hādawī school of law. The main emphasis of Zaydi Hādawī teaching is its insistence on righteous rule through the *sādah* ('lords'): the Ahl al-Bayt, or Āl al-Bayt, as the descendants of ʿAlī b. Abī Ṭālib through either Ḥasan or Ḥusayn are called.[9] Hādawī doctrine ascribes to the *sādah* a leadership role in both religious and secular affairs, and the *sādah* henceforth occupied the position of the imam (the spiritual and secular leader of the Zaydi community) as well as leadership positions in government administration and the military apparatus. According to Hādawī doctrine, supreme rulership (*imāmah*) and thus the office of the imam is not hereditary, and therefore not subject to dynastic succession. Any *sayyid* aspiring to the office of imam had merely to assert his claim to leadership through issuing a 'summons' to allegiance (*daʿwah*), and then leading an active 'rising' (*khurūj*) against illegitimate rulers and his own contenders. Unlike Sunnis, Zaydis have always insisted on having a just ruler who must fulfil rigorous qualifications and duties, and the fourteen qualifications of eligibility for the office of imam make up a formidable list of requirements.[10] In sum, the imam should be the best available of the Prophet's kin who successfully claims and asserts leadership in accordance with the Zaydi principle of 'commanding the right and forbidding the wrong' (*al-amr bi-l-maʿrūf wa l-nahī ʿan al-munkar*).[11]

Sunnis of the Shāfiʿī branch are the second major legal school in Yemen. They adhere to the teachings of the Muslim Arab scholar of jurisprudence, Muḥammad b. Idrīs al-Shāfiʿī (d. 820). In matters of jurisprudence the Zaydi and Shāfiʿī schools of law are not far apart, and the main difference can largely be reduced to the question of candidacy for the imamate and the supremacy of the *sādah*. Yet historically this disagreement between Sunnis and Zaydis was not always antagonistic. There were times when Zaydis considered Sunnis to be enemies against whom 'holy war' (*jihād*) was justified; the most recent examples are Imam Yaḥyā's struggle against the Ottomans and, in the 1960s, the royalists' struggle against Egyptian forces. In other, more politically settled times, religious affiliations have made little if any difference. Generally the Zaydis are considered a moderate Shia sect, so moderate indeed that the Zaydi community sometimes described itself as the 'fifth school' (*al-madhhab al-khāmis*), after the four orthodox or Sunni schools of Islam.[12]

Zaydi tolerance of other doctrines facilitated the emergence of a reformist movement within Zaydism, which aimed at a convergence of both Islamic doctrines and in turn challenged some of the foundations of the Hādawī Zaydi school, in particular the issue of righteous rule. This process to bridge the jurisprudential gap between Zaydi and Shāfiʿī sects, called the 'Sunnization of Zaydism' by Cook and the 'Traditionist Project' by Haykel, commenced as early as the fifteenth century CE.[13] From the early nineteenth century, it was predominantly promoted by the scholar-jurist Muḥammad al-Shawkānī (d. 1834).[14] The convergence of Zaydism and Shāfiʿism (and Sunnism in general), and the integration of Sunni elements into the Zaydi school of law, had not only theological motivations, but also a political dimension.[15] The Traditionists rejected some Zaydi theological doctrines, especially the Hādawī doctrine of non-inheritance of supreme rulership (*imāmah*) and rejection of dynastic succession. In contravention of the central Zaydi tenet of the *khurūj* ('rising' against unjust rulers), al-Shawkānī repudiated rebellion even against tyrants: according to him, dynastic rule was acceptable and rebellion against a ruler, no matter how unjust or unscholarly, was forbidden.[16] By the mid-eighteenth century, the rulers of the Qāsimī Imamate (1635–1850s) had become dynastic rulers and no longer fulfilled the rigorous qualifications stipulated by Zaydi Hādawī law.[17] Traditionist doctrine thus facilitated the transformation of Qāsimī structures of rule from their initial Hādawī charismatic style into dynastic and patrimonial modes of domination. Thus some

Zaydi scholars have criticized the two dynasties that successively ruled highland Yemen from the mid-seventeenth century until 1962—that is, the Qāsimī and then the Ḥamīd al-Dīn dynasties—for abandoning the original emphatic style of Zaydi leadership and succession, thereby effectuating an adulteration and decline of Zaydism.[18]

Traditionist doctrine brought about a second fundamental alteration, by facilitating the rise of scholars who abandoned the Zaydi Hādawī school of law, upon which the Yemeni imamate was founded, instead preferring a non-*madhhab* identity. In 1962, the project of non-*madhhab* identity was taken up by republican ideologues whose goal was to create the Republic as an enduring ideological form through the merger of Sunni and Zaydi doctrines, in an effort to create a 'unified' Islam based primarily on the Quran and the Sunna.[19] The republican leadership, which was socially and intellectually heterogeneous (it consisted of Arab nationalists of various shades, army officers, Muslim Brothers, members of the *quḍā'* estate, Free Yemenis, and even *sādah*), was agreed on vilifying the *ancien régime* and the Hādawī-Zaydi school on which its legitimacy was based. This leadership pursued a reorganization of society and a further standardization of religious beliefs and practices, condemning Zaydi doctrines and teachings that had favoured the *sādah*.[20]

Yet this process of doctrinal convergence, which after 1962 was elevated to republican state ideology, has been increasingly undermined by the spread of radical Sunnism. Behind this creeping radicalization also lay political calculations: the important role which the republican state was able to play in the process of sectarian convergence should not mask the fact that power maintains a complex and ambiguous relationship with religious identities. Just as some Zaydi dynasties and later on the republican government took advantage of the Traditionist project, the republican state also developed an interest in playing one identity or *madhhab* off against another in order to divide the different social groups. Thus, state power has not always (or not exclusively) focused on the phenomenon of convergence between the religious groups as discussed above, but at times also supported the spread of radical doctrines. The emergence of radical Sunni groups as well as the emerging Zaydi countermovement in Yemen expressed resistance to the formation of a religious identity to overcome sectarian opposition and generated new tensions and cleavages within society.

The emergence of this competitive sectarian environment began with the spread of radical Sunnism in the historical heartland of Zaydism. In the Yemeni context, the plurality of Sunni Islamism that has emerged in recent decades is today expressed through three main Islamist ideal-types: Muslim Brothers, violent jihadi fringes (some affiliated with al-Qaeda), and Salafis. Each of these groups is structured in a specific way and distinguishes itself from the others through a number of key issues, such as participation in party politics, loyalty to the ruler, attitude towards the state, and overt stigmatization of other religious and political identities.[21] Although these movements are distinct from one another, their adherents cannot always be so clearly distinguished, because these groups can overlap and change quickly due to shifting alliances.

The spread of Sunni Islamism goes far back into the recent history of Yemen. By the turn of the nineteenth century, proselytes of Muḥammad b. ʿAbdulwahhāb's doctrines, seconded by the political acumen and military vigour of the House of Saʿūd, had penetrated much of the Arabian Peninsula and won sympathizers in Yemen.[22] After the 1960s civil war, the use of al-Shawkānī by republicans in establishing their interpretation of Islam had great appeal in Saudi religious and political circles. The Saudis saw the Yemeni Traditionist scholars as sharing the outlook and message of their own Wahhabi scholars.[23]

Since the 1962 revolution, Sunni Islamists in Yemen have concentrated their activities on the education system and the mosques. The most important educational institutions run by Islamists were the so-called *maʿāhid ʿilmiyyah* (Scientific Institutes) founded in the 1970s and financed by Saudi Arabia, which spread rapidly throughout Yemen.[24] The Scientific Institutes were initially created in order to oppose socialist expansion in the regions on the border with South Yemen, and the Saudi government continued to be their main source of funding, despite unification in 1990. Their administration was dominated by Wahhabi proselytizers, members of the Yemeni Muslim Brotherhood and other Sunni Islamists, such as ʿAbdulmajīd al-Zindānī. They represented a parallel and separate system of education to the national school system and were largely independent of government control. Officially they pursued the further convergence of religious doctrines, but in practice they did not have one centralized ideology, as the Institutes' teachers did not necessarily follow one curriculum, sometimes adapting it to local contexts. Many, too, also had an anti-Shia bias. They denounced Zaydis as infidels (*kuffār*) and accused them of heresy.[25] After a harsh debate, the Scientific Institutes, then said to have had around 600,000 pupils, became nationalized and reintegrated into the public education system as recently as 2002.[26]

The Scientific Institutes did not only inculcate a monolithic Sunni version of Islam in Yemen's youth. They were able to prosper because they served political purposes. First, they were a conduit for improving Yemeni-Saudi relations, on which Yemen depended financially.[27] Second, Sunni Islamists were considered a neutralizing force against the Zaydis, whose commitment to the Republic was generally suspected.[28] Third, they formed a bulwark and powerful force against the socialist PDRY (People's Democratic Republic of Yemen, in the south): during the armed conflict between the northern Yemeni Arab Republic (YAR) and the PDRY-sponsored National Front in the early 1980s, and again during the 1994 civil war, the YAR was able to mobilize Sunni Islamists, both ideologically and militarily, against the threat posed by the PDRY and its sympathizers in the north.[29]

From the early 1980s, the Salafi doctrine began to spread in the Saʿdah region and other areas of Yemen.[30] Both Salafis and Muslim Brothers theoretically reject the principle of disorder (*fitnah*) and advocate unity of the faithful. Yet while the Muslim Brotherhood stresses Muslim unity and opposes delving into intra-Muslim differences that might lead to strife among the Muslim community, Salafism is a puritanical theological movement that insists first and foremost on purifying the credal beliefs and practices of errant Muslims. A further specifity of Salafi doctrine is its insistence on respect for power, even if it is corrupt (Salafis legitimate a political ruler only when they themselves benefit from it, naturally). Salafis distrust or entirely reject democratic forms and parliamentary policy and promote instead complete loyalty to a ruler (*wālī al-amr*—president, king, or imam), even when he is deemed corrupt or unjust.[31] In this regard, Salafi doctrine is fundamentally different from the quest for social justice led by many among the Muslim Brothers, jihadis and Zaydis (the latter through the *khurūj* concept—although traditional Zaydi elites in Saʿdah were not themselves very democratically oriented). Salafi teaching has been much more acceptable to political elites and the national leadership in Yemen and beyond, not least because it represents much of what Zaydi Islam is not—above all, the Salafi credo that obedience to the ruler is mandatory. By its rejection of democratic forms, Salafism has commonalities with Saudi Wahhabism; in fact, inside Yemen it is common for Wahhabis to be seen as a subgroup of the Salafis.

In Rāziḥ, for instance, the spread of Salafi-Wahhabi beliefs during the 1970s and 1980s was initiated through Yemeni migrant workers returning from Saudi Arabia, which is why the term 'Wahhabi' is particularly suitable to denote those early labour migrants who brought their new religious beliefs directly from Saudi Arabia to their home areas in Yemen without going through Yemeni Salafi educational institutions as the Dār al-Ḥadīth (see below). During the period of great Yemeni labour migration to Saudi Arabia, many men from the Saʿdah region had converted to Salafism (or its Saudi branch, Wahhabism) and then propagated their beliefs in their home areas.[32] In turn, the Salafi-Wahhabi movement began to flourish in the Zaydi heartland. The abandonment of Zaydi beliefs was a clear rupture with the past, because these men no longer identified themselves with the historical school to which their fathers and forefathers had belonged, and which they now vilified.[33] This conversion offered them new possibilities and roles outside the old, existing Zaydi hierarchy.

The recent development of Salafism in Yemen is less connected to Saudi transnational proselytism than to internal and translocal dynamics of Yemeni society, and is therefore largely adapted to the local Yemeni context. The Yemeni branch of Salafism emerged in the beginning of the 1980s around the figure of Muqbil b. Hādī al-Wādiʿī (d. 2001).[34] Muqbil was born in the late 1920s into the tribal community of Āl Rāshid, a section of the Wādiʿah.[35] The Wādiʿah section of Muqbil al-Wādiʿī is located in the Saʿdah basin, which is dominated by Khawlān b. ʿĀmir tribes. Muqbil's home area, Dammāj, is situated about 7 kilometres southeast of Saʿdah city, near the upper part of the fertile Wādī al-ʿAbdīn, the settlement of the homonymous Saḥār section.

Muqbil al-Wādiʿī's father was a peasant farmer of tribal origin who owned a grape orchard. Historically the people of Wādiʿah were Zaydis, except for a small Jewish community that emigrated in large part to Israel in 1949. As a young man, Muqbil began Zaydi studies at the al-Hādī Mosque in Saʿdah city, the largest and oldest Zaydi educational centre in the region, as a student of the renowned Zaydi scholar Majd al-Dīn al-Muʾayyadī.[36] In his autobiography, Muqbil argued that the local Zaydi religious scholars among the *sādah* did not take him seriously because of his 'inferior' tribal descent.[37]

In 1962, when the civil war between republican and royalist forces broke out, the majority of Āl Rāshid fought with the royalists. Muqbil left Yemen for Saudi Arabia, where he had previously studied. His stay in Saudi Arabia was abruptly ended in 1979, when he was accused of connections to Juhaymān al-ʿUtaybī, a religious activist and militant who, in the same year, led the takeover of the Grand Mosque in Mecca to protest against the Saudi monarchy and their rule.[38] After being expelled from Saudi Arabia, Muqbil returned home to the Saʿdah region to settle permanently in his home area, Dammāj, where he founded the Salafi teaching centre Dār al-Ḥadīth al-Khayriyyah on his family's private landholdings. Since that time, the Dār al-Ḥadīth has propagated the *daʿwah* or 'call' of Salafi Islam from the heartland of Zaydism.

In Saʿdah's religious landscape, the still unbroken dominance of the *sādah* contrasted sharply with the egalitarian Wahhabi doctrine to which Muqbil had been exposed in Saudi Arabia. Against the background of his rejection by Zaydi scholars of the al-Hādī Mosque, Muqbil's shift from Zaydism to Salafism and the foundation of his own teaching centre therefore appears to have been, as Bonnefoy argues, 'a kind of social revenge'.[39]

The Dār al-Ḥadīth became one of the leading centres of Salafi teaching and propagation in the Arab and Muslim worlds. It was funded semi-officially by various institutions and individuals from Saudi Arabia and the Gulf, among them Saudi businessmen of Yemeni origin.[40] With the assistance of these wealthy donors, Muqbil built the Dār al-Ḥadīth, a huge, white painted compound with heavy concrete walls, loudspeakers and satellite dishes, which probably could have doubled as a bunker. The contrast between the Dār al-Ḥadīth and its rural environment resembled, as Padnos noted, 'a seventh-century scene of agriculture and cobblestone towers into which a fortress has been dropped'.[41] Several tens of thousands of students have enrolled there since the early 1980s. The 'foreign' students from other regions of Yemen and beyond accounted for the majority of its residents; when the Houthis displaced Dammāj's 'foreign' students in January 2014, the Dār al-Ḥadīth was virtually empty.[42]

In his teachings, Muqbil al-Wādiʿī followed a domestic rather than an international agenda. He called for support for the mujahidin in Afghanistan, but asserted that fighting abroad was not considered a priority.[43] In fact, he rejected the views and actions of Osama bin Laden, whom he blamed—along with movements like the Muslim Brotherhood—for many of the problems Muslims faced even before 9/11. Instead he focused on fighting the Marxist regime in South Yemen, which led to the participation of Salafis from Dammāj in the 1994 civil war.[44]

Moreover, Muqbil and his successor Yaḥyā al-Ḥajūrī incited their students against their Zaydi co-religionists and neighbours. Salafis, who insist first and foremost on purifying the creedal beliefs and practices of errant (non-Salafi) Muslims, have an obsession with avoiding 'reprehensible innovations' (*bidaʿ*), such as Zaydi traditions of visiting graves, erection of tomb stones and so on, because according to Salafi belief invoking the dead constitutes polytheism. Because of these practices, the Salafis in Saʿdah stigmatize their Zaydi neighbours as *kuffār* (unbelievers) or refer to them by the derogatory label *al-rāfiḍah* (heretics). Their fiery rejection of the Zaydi *madhhab* and its 'reprehensible innovations' took not only rhetorical but also violent forms, which led to the destruction of tombstones and cemeteries in the Saʿdah region and throughout Yemen.[45] The Salafis legitimized these violent actions through the practice of *takfīr*, or allegations of apostasy or heresy; for this reason, Zaydis refer to Salafis as *takfīriyyūn* (takfirists). This sectarian incitement provoked social unrest and violent antagonism with the Zaydis, and also openly challenged the convergence of religious identity in Yemen.

The Salafis' policy of provocation and their aggressive rhetoric and behaviour towards their Zaydi neighbours led to tensions between the students of the Dār al-Ḥadīth and their predominantly Zaydi environment, and made the Dār al-Ḥadīth dependent on tribal protection. In his autobiography Muqbil claimed that his original Wādiʿah tribe defended him against his enemies, the Zaydis. Yet Wādiʿah was never a uniform Salafi block as Muqbil suggested. There are no 'Salafi areas' or even 'Salafi tribes' in the Saʿdah region, and the presence of a Salafi centre in Dammāj does not mean that Salafism dominated the area. The Wādiʿah are a tribe with old Zaydi traditions, and they have a history of resistance against the Dār al-Ḥadīth rather than a history of cooperation. Padnos pointed to a climate of constant threat and to the dangers which emanated from the immediate neighbourhood of the Dār al-Ḥadīth.[46] Even before the outbreak of the Saʿdah wars in 2004, the Salafis in Dammāj at times had to take up arms to defend themselves against a hostile environment; a description that calls into question Muqbil's version of contingent tribal protection by the Wādiʿah. The Ahl Dammāj (as the students and the supporters of the Dār al-Ḥadīth were locally known)[47] were not drawn from certain contingent tribes, but were a motley group from various areas of Saʿdah, Yemen, and even foreign nations. Tribesmen and shaykhs of other Saʿdah tribes, such as Fāyid Mujallī (succeeded by his son Ḥusayn and his grandson ʿUthmān) and Qāʾid Shuwayṭ (followed by his son ʿĀrif), both from Saḥār, played a far greater role in the protection of Dammāj than the shaykhs of Wādiʿah itself; in the August 2013 battles between Houthis and Salafis, at least one Wādiʿah shaykh was killed by residents of the Dār al-Ḥadīth.

Rather than uniting society and leading to tribal bloc formation, as Muqbil implied, his teachings were divisive and split local society from within. Through its egalitarian doctrine aimed at the elimination of social divisions, Salafism held a considerable attraction for some of Saʿdah's ordinary citizens. Salafism challenged the key tenets of Zaydi doctrine, which were still manifest in many regions of Saʿdah, especially Zaydi-Hādawī principles such as the *sādah*'s claim to religious authority and social superiority on the grounds of religious descent, which Salafis felt contravened Islamic ideals by promoting inequality.[48] Thus the *sādah* became a major target of Salafi propaganda. In many areas of Saʿdah the *sādah* were still influential persons who continued to dominate leading positions in the religious sphere, and bad blood persisted among the tribes due to the *sādah*'s refusal to marry their daughters 'down' to tribesmen or their shaykhs, citing the Quranic teaching of *kafāʾah* (equality of marriage partners).[49] The conflict between Zaydis and Salafis split some communities at family level, because in some cases the practice of intermarriage led to family constellations consisting of both Salafis and leading *sādah*.[50] Many of these conflicts could be contained by local mediation, but in the long term their violent and escalatory potential led to a deterioration of the relationship between Zaydis and radical Sunnis.

The shaykhs had special reasons to support the Salafi *daʿwah*. Weir observed that in the late 1970s in Rāziḥ the shaykhs' support for Wahhabism and Salafism had initially been tacit and passive, because the shaykhs' positions, like the *sādah*'s, were underpinned by descent-based clans, hereditary entitlement, and in some cases by strategic marriage alliances with leading *sādah* families.[51] Consequently, Weir argues, the shaykhs could hardly embrace egalitarianism or renounce the descent principle. Yet in the following decades this situation seemed to change fundamentally, because the Salafis, who questioned the *sādah*'s right to spiritual leadership, never questioned the shaykhs' aspirations for political leadership. The shaykhs quickly recognized the political power dimension of the anti-*sayyid* thrust of radical Sunnism, especially that of the Salafi doctrine, and capitalized on it in order to reinforce their own leadership claims against the still influential *sādah*, notably those shaykhs of the Saʿdah Brigade who had asserted their claim to leadership in the 1960s civil war and became influential pillars of the republican system in the Saʿdah area. In addition, since 1934 many shaykhs had been integrated into the Saudis' patronage networks. They demonstrated their allegiance by promoting a Saudi agenda in their tribal constituencies and working 'for the sake of the Saudi interests' (*min ajl al-maṣāliḥ al-saʿūdiyyah*), as one of them put it.[52]

The Salafis' proselytism and anti-*sayyid* thrust, and the political calculations of some shaykhs, made the Dār al-Ḥadīth a symbol of the local struggle for power and hegemony in Saʿdah. As previously stated, the Wādiʿah themselves are a small, fragmented and rather insignificant tribe with Zaydi traditions. They have no prominent senior shaykh who could unite and represent them as a whole or muster them militarily—only a number of minor shaykhs who do not always ensure adequate coordination and sometimes adopt different positions. Due to this particularism, only a minority of the Wādiʿah cooperated with Muqbil, and their protection would never have been sufficient to achieve Muqbil's ambitious projects in the face of local Zaydi resistance. On the other hand, certain influential shaykhs of the pro-republican Saʿdah Brigade, such as the Saḥār shaykhs Fāyid, Ḥusayn and ʿUthmān Mujallī of neighbouring al-ʿAbdīn and Qāʾid Shuwayṭ of Banī ʿUwayr supported Muqbil's objectives. These shaykhs, who had fought for the Republic in the civil war and against the supremacy of the *sādah*, now sought to secure and expand their newly acquired power, and continued to compete fiercely with the *sādah*, still influential locally.

The Dār al-Ḥadīth became the symbol of these shaykhs' 'victory' over the conservative forces in the Saʿdah area. The inflammatory speeches of Salafi preachers provided them with ideological and rhetorical ammunition against the *sādah* (and later against the Houthis). The guardian role which the shaykhs of the Mujallī and Shuwayṭ lineages assumed vis-à-vis the Dār al-Ḥadīth was substantiated by pacts of assistance and protection between them and the Ahl Dammāj. This cooperation not only served the shaykhs' domestic political goals, but was for a long time also in the interests of the government in Sanaʿa and the Dār al-Ḥadīth's powerful donors in Yemen, Saudi Arabia, and the Gulf.

These shaykhs, however, often followed an agenda of 'common goals' rather than sectarian beliefs. They capitalized on Salafi ideology to pursue their own policies, which included strategic objectives and considerations as well as aspects of power politics. In many cases, the shaykhs' support for the Salafis indicated an anti-*sayyid*, rather than an anti-Zaydi, disposition. Many shaykhs of the Saʿdah region come from centuries-old Zaydi dynasties historically known as the 'pillars of the Zaydi community' (*arkān al-mujtamaʿ al-zaydī*). Although these shaykhs started to pursue Sunni or even Salafi agendas in the region, in private they were often more fluid with respect to their Zaydi origins, or adhered to a non-*madhhab* identity. Indeed, it would be wholly inappropriate to describe ʿĀrif Shuwayṭ and the modernist Mujallī family as 'zealous Salafis'.[53] Local merchants denounced the Salafis in private as obscurantist and a threat to Yemen's economic future.[54]

For the Mujallī family of al-ʿAbdīn this policy of common goals also appeared at first sight to pay off militarily after the eruption of the Saʿdah wars in 2004. When ʿUthmān Mujallī entered into military confrontations with the Houthis, fighters of the Ahl Dammāj were among his supporters, and this despite the fact that during the Saʿdah wars the Dār al-Ḥadīth tried to maintain an overall 'neutral' position. Yet when, after the end of the Saʿdah wars in

2010, the Dār al-Ḥadīth was drawn into fierce confrontations with Saʿdah's new Houthi suzerains, it was supported by tribal warriors from al-ʿAbdīn and the followers of some shaykhs of Wāʾilah's Āl Abū Jabārah section.[55] Other shaykhly supporters of the Dār al-Ḥadīth, such as Qāʾid Shuwayṭ and his son ʿĀrif, exercised considerably more caution and restraint in regard to military cooperation with Dammāj, a fact which would benefit them after the Houthis seized power. Through some astute manoeuvring, ʿĀrif Shuwayṭ could not only escape displacement by the Houthis, but also managed to establish himself as a negotiator between the Houthis and the Ahl Dammāj; in a January 2014 open letter to the Ahl Dammāj, ʿAbdulmalik al-Ḥūthī referred to ʿĀrif Shuwayṭ (as well as ʿUmar Hindī Dughsān of Āl ʿAmmār and Fayṣal al-Ḥamāṭī of Jumāʿah) as a neutral guarantor for the safe conduct of the Ahl Dammāj during their exodus to Sanaʿa.

Since the early 1980s, the powerful protection of certain shaykhs using the Dār al-Ḥadīth to assert their own political and hegemonic goals has permitted the Salafi movement to propagate its teachings in relative autonomy, not only from the immediate Zaydi neighbourhood but also from the central government in Sanaʿa. Muqbil mentioned that, without this protection, 'the enemies of our movement, especially the Shi'ites of Saʿdah, would have annihilated us'.[56] When Muqbil al-Wādiʿī died in 2001 in Jeddah, Saudi Arabia, the Dammāj branch of Salafism was losing credit among Yemen's Salafists under the aegis of his even more zealous successor, Yaḥyā al-Ḥajūrī—but it remained popular among foreigners searching for authenticity and drawn to Dār al-Ḥadīth's prestigious past.[57]

The Zaydi Revival Movement

The increasing Sunnization of the Zaydi *madhhab* and the spread of various types of radical Sunnism in the heartland of Zaydism were increasingly perceived as a serious threat to the Zaydi community. Zaydi scholars claimed that the government's policy, euphemistically described as aiming to 'override *madhhab* distinctions', in fact had contributed to deepening doctrinal cleavages. Rather than producing a homogenizing effect, it had served to promote one religious ideology at the expense of another.[58] Across the Saʿdah region, but also in other areas with a large proportion of Zaydi residents, many Zaydis felt increasingly marginalized, under pressure, and alienated, blaming the republican state for supporting a policy which they perceived as undermining their *madhhab*.

Zaydis complained that Salafis were able to pursue their proselyte policy under the nose of the state by publishing their thoughts and establishing their schools and 'Scientific Institutes' across the country. Furthermore, Salafis tried to intervene in the administration of the other schools and universities and to change their curricula according to their own beliefs. They tried to bring Zaydi mosques under their control, a practice that Zaydis referred to as 'mosque grabbing' (*istīlāʾ ʿalā al-masājid*). Zaydis were publicly humiliated and accused of deviation (*inḥirāf*), and the Salafis, themselves supported by wealthy donors in Yemen, Saudi Arabia and the Gulf, taunted them as 'penniless Shia' (*al-fuqarāʾ al-shīʿa*). The most controversial practices, however, were the desecrations of Zaydi graves by Salafi activists. While Salafi preachers publicly threatened to destroy Zaydi graves in order to stop the Zaydis' 'reprehensible innovations', their acolytes were implementing their requests, destroying many of the gravestones in the cemeteries just beyond Saʿdah's city wall.[59]

Ritualized praying gestures became charged with immense symbolic and emotional significance. Whereas previously the differences between Zaydi and Sunni prayer methods were dismissed as unimportant, they now became an expression of religious beliefs and led to confrontations between the worshippers.[60] In these confrontations, the Zaydis perceived the role of the state as hostile and pro-Salafi. Local sources indicate that during confrontations between Zaydis and Salafis, the latter could call in security forces and the police and even, in severe cases, the army, which, since the 1998 appointment of ʿAlī Muḥsin al-Aḥmar as commander of the North-Western Military Region, was considered friendly to the Salafis.[61] The Zaydis, by contrast, could not even appeal to the local authorities, because in many cases the district directors turned a deaf ear to the Zaydis' needs.[62] The perception of the Yemeni state as a hostile power collaborating with their religious opponents contributed to the emerging Zaydi resistance against Sunni proselytism merging early on with opposition to the government—not to the idea of the state and statehood, or the Yemeni Republic as such, but rather to the state as embodied in the policy of the Salih government.

From the early 1980s, a specifically Zaydi response emerged to the influx of Sunnism in the region. The Zaydi revival movement began as a defensive movement to counter the Wahhabi-Salafi onslaught and the continuing government policy of neglect or, at times, active persecution. It involved a great deal of soul-searching and was inspired by a deep sense of peril arising from the spread and increasing popularity of Salafism. The Zaydi revival was not a unified movement, but led to a wide range of activities, including a re-invention of Zaydi ritual and education activities. After Yemeni unification in 1990, it also became active at party-political level. However, factional disputes within the Zaydi revival soon escalated, ultimately leading to an internal split and the emergence of the group which, from 2001, became known as 'Houthis' (*al-Ḥūthiyyūn*) and, from 2011, as Anṣār Allah.

In the mid-1980s, Zaydis began publicly to celebrate Zaydi religious rituals such as *ʿīd al-mawlid al-nabawī* (the Prophet's birthday) and *ʿīd al-ghadīr*—the latter being a profoundly significant feast day for Shiites because it commemorates the Prophet's designation of ʿAlī b. Abī Ṭālib as his successor (*khalīfah*).[63] Since the establishment of the Republic, the Zaydi community in Saʿdah province and adjacent governorates had only been able to celebrate *ʿīd al-ghadīr* in peripheral and remote regions such as Jumāʿah, Marrān in Khawlān, Rāziḥ, and al-Ḥamazāt near Wādī Nushūr, and the large plain between the mountain pass Naqīl al-Ghūlah and Raydah in ʿAmrān. The fact that there were districts in Saʿdah and elsewhere in Upper Yemen that continued to celebrate *ʿīd al-ghadīr* after the abolition of the imamate was seen as an expression of defiance and opposition to the republican rulers in Sanaʿa. The exaltation of these specifically Shia rituals served to create a natural dichotomy between Zaydi revivalists and adherents of Salafism. After Yemeni unification in 1990, the Shia celebrations expanded and evolved to include Saʿdah city, al-Ṭalḥ, Raḥbān, Banī Muʿādh, al-Abqūr, Walad Masʿūd of Saḥār; Ḍaḥyān and Majz city in Jumāʿah, al-Naẓīr in Rāziḥ, Marrān in Khawlān, Sufyān in ʿAmrān and many other areas, even though since 1995 these ended in arrests, because of what the state saw as the feast day's latent anti-republican character.

The Zaydi scholars took different positions on Zaydi revivalism. Numerous scholars—Ṣalāḥ Falītah, Muḥammad al-Manṣūr, al-Murtaḍā al-Maḥaṭwarī, Aḥmad al-Shāmī, Ḥamūd ʿAbbās al-Muʾayyad, and Qāsim Muḥammad al-Kibsī, among others—have contributed to the theological elaboration of the Zaydi revival. Among them, Majd al-Dīn al-Muʾayyadī, Badr al-Dīn al-Ḥūthī and Muḥammad ʿIzzān especially gained prominence among Saʿdah's 'simple' non-specialist Zaydi population.

Majd al-Dīn al-Muʾayyadī (1913–2007) was one of the most influential and respected contemporary Zaydi scholars. Born in al-Raḍmah on the Baraṭ plateau (al-Jawf), he spent most of his life in Ḍaḥyān where he devoted himself to teaching.[64] He held the honorary title *imām al-ʿilm*, one of the highest titles conferred by Zaydism. In the early 1970s, he was appointed grand mufti of Yemen and al-Ḥijāz by King Fayṣal of Saudi Arabia, making him the only

Yemeni scholar authorized to issue legal judgments and learned interpretations pertaining to Islamic law in regard to the Zaydi communities in the Saudi southwest (Jīzān, ʿAsīr, Najrān), whom he visited frequently.[65] After the 1960s civil war, in which al-Muʾayyadī played a prominent role on the royalist side, he became one of those Zaydi scholars who tried to reconcile Zaydi doctrine with republicanism. In 1990, he issued an oath in which he abandoned *sharṭ al-baṭnayn*, the *sādah*'s claim to leadership, as demanded by Zaydi Hādawī doctrine.[66] He and other prominent Zaydi scholars argued that the conditions of Zaydi political doctrine, which restrict legitimate rule to suitable learned descendants of the Prophet (that is, the *sādah*), are only valid under certain historical circumstances no longer present. He and his associates rather saw political leadership as a right vested in the community at large: anyone elected by the people becomes a legitimate ruler, regardless of his noble descent.

Al-Muʾayyadī's public rejection of *sharṭ al-baṭnayn* and the privileged role of the *sādah* earned him the confidence of the republican government, which in its early phase was dominated by non-*sayyid* Zaydis (so-called 'Qaḥṭānī Zaydis'), as well as tremendous sympathy and support from the ordinary non-*sayyid* population, particularly in his home area Jumāʿah and its surroundings—an area characterized more than any other in the Saʿdah region by competition between *sādah* and tribes. Al-Muʾayyadī was among the few Zaydi scholars who advocated marriage between tribesmen and *sharīfah*s (female members of the *sayyid* community), and ruled in the tribesmen's favour in controversial cases—which took on violent, pogrom-like characteristics in at least one instance—by saying: 'What forbids the marriage between a tribesman and a *sharīfah* when the marriage was consummated according to Islam?'[67] In response, conservative Zaydis accused al-Muʾayyadī of leaning towards al-Shawkānī's 'Traditionist' positions and thus facilitating the dilution and adulteration of the Zaydi doctrine, and of remaining silent in the face of the increasing onslaught against Zaydism.[68]

Whereas Majd al-Dīn al-Muʾayyadī's position has been considered 'quietist' by many Zaydi revivalists, the Zaydi scholar Badr al-Dīn al-Ḥūthī (1926–2010) emerged as a strong proponent of Zaydi revivalism. Badr al-Dīn al-Ḥūthī was a student of Majd al-Dīn al-Muʾayyadī, and one of the most influential contemporary Zaydi scholars. He had family roots in the *hijrahs* of Ḍaḥyān and Ḥūth, both renowned for their religious erudition, and lived and taught in the Marrān mountains in the area of the Khawlān tribe (see below). He wrote and edited numerous books and pamphlets, presenting the Zaydi case against its Wahhabi and Salafi opponents on issues of ritual practice, theology and politics.[69] As early as 1979, he began to write rebuttals and refutations of anti-Shia literature produced by Wahhabis and Salafis, such as a rebuttal to Ibn Bāz's fatwa prohibiting prayer behind a Zaydi imam.[70] He also took a keen interest in refuting the intense anti-Zaydi writings of Yemen's foremost and most outspoken Salafi scholar and director of the Dār al-Ḥadīth in Dammāj, Muqbil al-Wādiʿī.[71]

Badr al-Dīn al-Ḥūthī rejected the quietism of al-Muʾayyadī. When it came to *sharṭ al-baṭnayn*, however, his position was less clear. He never renounced publicly the principle of *sādah* supremacy; instead, he differentiated between two types of government: on the one hand, *imāmah* by a representative of the *sādah*, and, on the other, *iḥtisāb* (rule by a kind of 'administrator' who administers Islamic law, but does not have the authority to make law or *ijtihād*, independent reasoning): that is, rule by a democratically elected leader who could also be of non-*sayyid* descent, as long as he was God-fearing, followed the Zaydi principle of 'commanding the good and prohibiting the wrong', and adhered to the constitution. The *muḥtasib* is a substitute for an imam in times where there is no imam, or no one among the ranks of the *sādah* has the appropriate qualifications. Badr al-Dīn al-Ḥūthī's *muḥtasib* model was certainly more artifice than conviction, because it allowed him to keep open the option of tolerating the Salih government; otherwise, Badr al-Dīn would have faced serious reprisals from the state. However, in Badr al-Dīn's eyes, the imamate remained the most preferable type of government.[72] To date, the Houthis' position on the question of governance is still based on this understanding as formulated by Badr al-Dīn: *sayyid* rule is recommended, but not an absolute necessity.

Badr al-Dīn's active role in the Zaydi revival movement and the establishment of the Ḥizb al-Ḥaqq party (see below) landed him and his family in trouble with the Yemeni authorities; after harassment from the government, he spent some years in exile in Islamic Iran.[73] His stay in Iran introduced him to the radical political thought of the Islamic Revolution and its strong emphasis on social justice, liberation and resistance to western hegemony and exploitation—ideas which also found fertile ground in the underdeveloped and neglected Saʿdah region.

Another influential figure of the Zaydi revival movement was Muḥammad Yaḥyā ʿIzzān, one of the younger students of Majd al-Dīn al-Muʾayyadī. ʿIzzān, a scholar of tribal descent from the Rāziḥ area, wrote and edited numerous books and pamphlets on issues of Zaydi ritual practice, theology and politics.[74] In the 1990s, in response to the spread of the Sunni 'Scientific Institutes', 'Izzān participated in the Zaydi revivalists' efforts to establish a Zaydi educational work, and they began to set up Zaydi educational institutions, the so called *madāris 'ilmiyyah* ('Scientific Schools'). In this first attempt in Zaydi history to formalize the educational process into a set curriculum with standard textbooks, new reference texts were edited and issued to reflect a Zaydi education.[75] Muḥammad 'Izzān and Muḥammad al-Ḥūthī, a son of Badr al-Dīn al-Ḥūthī, helped to establish the *Muntadā al-shabāb al-mu'min* (Assembly of the Believing Youth) in the early 1990s, which built on previous Zaydi revivalist efforts.[76] The name Believing Youth was inspired by similar Shia movements in Lebanon and Iran.[77] The Believing Youth managed to transform the theological discourse of Zaydi renaissance into religious revival and social activism at grassroots level. Initially, its administration was rudimentary, consisting of a handful of members and a single rented room. In the words of Muḥammad 'Izzān, the Believing Youth was devoted to 'cultural studies' and publications, being bereft of political experience and orientation. Muḥammad 'Izzān and Muḥammad al-Ḥūthī were also effective in establishing the so-called 'Summer Schools' (*marākiz al-tadrīs al-ṣayfiyyah*), the Believing Youth's educational institutions.[78] In the Summer Schools, which took place during the summer break for public schools (for only two months a year), young men and boys studied Islamic legal and theological sciences in accordance with Zaydi precepts.

The Believing Youth and its Summer Schools were a reaction to the establishment of the Salafi Scientific Institutes in Sa'dah, but this was not their only purpose. Muḥammad 'Izzān explained that Zaydi educational activism aimed to 'fill the void' (*sadd al-farāgh*) experienced by young people, particularly in the Sa'dah area.[79] Muḥammad 'Izzān considered this activism a necessary defence against the palpable threat of Salafism; it had an element of 'rescuing' young Zaydi faith from gradual disappearance. Muḥammad 'Izzān explained that, in the neglected regions of Sa'dah governorate, the Believing Youth and its Summer Schools had not only educational but also social preoccupations. It aimed at gathering young Zaydis during the school holidays, 'so that—and this is an important point— the void does not lead them to drift to deviation (*inḥirāf*) and worse'.[80] The Summer Schools focused on the rural youth, most of them of tribal origin. With their education and employment programme, they intended to avoid Salafism attracting more and more followers out of general discontent and lack of opportunities in the region. According to Muḥammad 'Izzān, the curricula of the Believing Youth were devoted to tolerance, rejecting fanaticism and extremism and instead promoting 'moderation and balance'.

In the official accounts of the Yemeni government, little attention was paid to the Believing Youth and its activities until 2003. Initially the Yemeni government looked favourably on the Believing Youth movement and temporarily supported it financially as a counterweight to both the growing influence of Iṣlāḥ (a party that served as the political rallying point of a number of Sunni Islamist schools of thought—see below) and the Saudi-Wahhabi encroachment in the north of the country.[81] In the 1980s, the Salih government had promoted the spread of radical Sunnism in Yemen's north, in order to limit the power of both the still influential *sādah* and the socialist Yemeni brother state in the south. In the early 1990s, Salih still at times supported the Zaydi revival movement as a means of curbing the growing influence of Salafism and Wahhabism. The financial patronage of various competing sides and the resulting crises were a government strategy to produce conflict among its potential opponents and rivals, engulfing and weakening them in a spiral of violence. This informal ruling system of the Salih regime, based on the sponsorship and exploitation of conflict and discord among rivals, was dubbed the 'politics of permanent crisis' by Phillips.[82] A former government official explained:

> The government has so far supported a large variety of conflicting groups and sectarian movements. The government does not have a particular thought, the issue is political: how to strengthen our party over the other? How do we use a group or groups against other groups? The case was an issue of political interest and not intellectual, because the intellectual culture of the pillars of power is weak [...] The whole deal was a political deal with distinction. The state was not interested in sectarian doctrines; it was only interested in its benefits, which it got even from external sides.[83]

The Believing Youth's influence grew quickly. The Summer Schools started with a handful of students in the early 1990s. By 1994, 15,000 students were participating.[84] Muḥammad ʿIzzān, Badr al-Dīn al-Ḥūthī's sons Muḥammad, Ḥusayn and Yaḥyā, and the tribesmen ʿAbdulkarīm Jadbān and Ṣāliḥ Habrah were among its teachers and guest lecturers. With the exception of Muḥammad ʿIzzān, all of them would play a role in the Houthi opposition to the regime after 2004.

As the Believing Youth grew, Zaydi senior scholars began to take notice of it and attempted to influence the curricula of the Summer Schools. Differences of opinion arose; for example, Majd al-Dīn al-Muʾayyadī accused Muḥammad ʿIzzān of violating the principle that any text, before being taught, must have his approval.[85] Muḥammad ʿIzzān had examined certain Zaydi sources in a critical way, and Majd al-Dīn al-Muʾayyadī accused him of being anti-Zaydi, demanding that Muḥammad ʿIzzān no longer be allowed to teach. As a result, Majd al-Dīn al-Muʾayyadī issued a fatwa against Muḥammad ʿIzzān and other Young Believers.[86] In this particular conflict, Badr al-Dīn al-Ḥūthī intervened in Muḥammad ʿIzzān's favour. But disagreements also arose between Ḥusayn al-Ḥūthī, Badr al-Dīn al-Ḥūthī's eldest son, and Muḥammad ʿIzzān, resulting in 2001 in the Believing Youth's internal split.

From Zaydi Revivalism to Political Competition

The second, less successful mode of Zaydi revivalism took place on a political level. Yemeni unification on 22 May 1990 at first ushered in a considerable degree of liberalization, and the new constitution affirmed Yemen's commitment to free elections and a multiparty political system. Whereas Salih's General People's Congress (GPC) remained the dominant political party in Yemen's north and the Yemeni Socialist Party (YSP) in the south, the atmosphere post-unification also led to the formation of new parties, including the Islamic-tribal coalition of the Iṣlāḥ party, the Zaydi Ḥizb al-Ḥaqq, and several pan-Arab parties such as Baath and Nasserites.

The Yemeni Congregation for Reform (*al-tajammuʿ al-yamanī li-l-iṣlāḥ*), more commonly known as the Iṣlāḥ party, combined a number of Sunni Islamist schools of thought. It comprised an uneasy political alliance that integrated and represented the Yemeni branch of the Muslim Brotherhood, associated with the 'Traditionist' wing, as well as Wahhabi-style religious partisans, tribal leaders and businessmen.[87] Beyond the very broad label of 'Sunni Islamist', it is difficult to attribute any one coherent ideological stance to the Iṣlāḥ party. Until his death in 2007, the chairman of the party's tribal wing was Ḥāshid's senior shaykh, ʿAbdullah al-Aḥmar, while one of its main political figures was ʿAbdulmajīd al-Zindānī, a cleric and president of the Sanaʿa-based al-Imān university.[88] Although the Salafis are the sort of people others would regard as 'quintessentially Iṣlāḥ', many of them reject the Iṣlāḥ party as they do any other form of democratic political activity.[89]

Although the Iṣlāḥ party is supposedly 'fundamentalist', even 'radical', initially it was in fact more a party of the establishment centre. From 1990 to 1994, ʿAbdullah al-Aḥmar stood firmly with President Salih in times of crisis.[90] From 1993 to 1997, Iṣlāḥ was in fact part of the government, in coalition with the GPC.[91] Since that period it has moved in and out of favour with

Salih and the GPC, underlining the ambiguous position of popular Islamist figures within the patronage system of the Salih government. When the Islamists' political fortune and the personal relationships between President Salih and some of the party's elites (particularly the al-Aḥmar family) deteriorated, the party became more divorced from the state-sponsored patronage system of which it once had been a pillar.[92]

The formation and political liberalization of the Sunni-dominated Iṣlāḥ party triggered the establishment of a Zaydi-oriented party, Ḥizb al-Ḥaqq (Party of Truth).[93] Ḥizb al-Ḥaqq was founded in 1990 by Aḥmad al-Shāmī, a court judge of *qāḍī* descent. One reason for its establishment was to avoid accusations of clandestine anti-regime activities and to end 'the history of fear' that had characterized the period between 1962 and 1990.[94] At times, the party was supported by the government, because it was seen as an alternative to the alliance with Iṣlāḥ that ended with the 1997 elections, in which Iṣlāḥ participated for the first time in an opposition coalition. Yet on the whole, the government's relationship with Ḥizb al-Ḥaqq remained confrontational. Ḥizb al-Ḥaqq tolerated a wide range of views and was shaped from the outside as a rallying point of Zaydi and *sayyid* interests, mainly because its list of sixty-seven candidates in the first parliamentary elections of 1993 read like a veritable Who's Who of influential *sayyid* families.[95] In accordance with those Zaydi scholars who tried to reconcile Zaydi thought with republicanism and democratic principles, Ḥizb al-Ḥaqq acted in line with a manifesto issued in November 1990 by the senior Zaydi scholars: Aḥmad b. Muḥammad al-Shāmī, Muḥammad b. Muḥammad al-Manṣūr, Ḥamūd ʿAbbās al-Muʾayyad and Qāsim Muḥammad al-Kibsī. This manifesto abandoned the Hādawī *sharṭ al-baṭnayn* by denying (albeit with some obscure passages) that righteousness in the political realm is linked to the Prophet's descendants' divine right to rule. It was an attempt to pre-empt criticism from the republican state, which sought to root its legitimacy in having ousted the imamate, thus rendering unlawful the principles that underscored it.[96] Badr al-Dīn al-Ḥūthī, however, cultivated some ambiguity—on the one hand refraining from signing the 1990 manifesto, on the other serving as vice president of Ḥizb al-Ḥaqq, which recognized the legitimacy of the republican regime.[97]

Despite the complex and multifaceted fabric of these new parties, political discourse soon came to be dominated by reductionist stereotypes reflecting the overheated competition between the *madhhab*s. Ḥizb al-Ḥaqq labelled the Iṣlāḥ party 'Wahhabi supporters', and Iṣlāḥ countered by accusing Ḥizb al-Ḥaqq of seeking to restore the imamate.[98] Theological doctrines became political concepts. After Yemeni unification, sectarian categories such as 'Salafi' or 'Zaydi' led to the emergence of political solidarities, which in turn were further strengthened and stabilized by rhetoric and political systems. These distinctive categories, although vague in themselves, were reinforced through the political debate, and later through the government-Houthi conflict. Thus Wedeen sees the Houthi conflict as the result of a mobilization process of identification that began with the emergence of a multi-party system after 1990.[99]

Party manifestos and theological discussions were not the whole issue. In the Saʿdah area, the Iṣlāḥ party has been relatively well received by certain influential shaykhs, among them Qāʾid Shuwayṭ and Muḥammad Ḥasan Manāʿ, both from Saḥār, Fāyiz Bishr from Khawlān, and Sulaymān al-Faraḥ from Rāziḥ. The trend for tribalization of politics had become evident even before the first parliamentary elections in 1993, during June 1992 celebrations under the auspices of ʿAbdullah al-Aḥmar marking the opening of Iṣlāḥ's office in Saʿdah city and the surrounding regions. According to Dresch and Haykel, the event resembled a huge tribal gathering, with tribes in full regalia, more than it did a 'civilized political rally'.[100] For some of the Zaydi population, however, the Iṣlāḥ celebration was regarded as a provocation, since Saʿdah was the centre of Zaydi learning and the home of important *sayyid* clans. The tribal feuds of the Sufyān (Bakīl confederation) had a particular impact on the implementation of the Iṣlāḥ celebration. Sufyān is a strategically important tribal territory in northern ʿAmrān governorate that straddles the main road between Sanaʿa and Saʿdah. On his way to Saʿdah city, the convoy of ʿAbdullah al-Aḥmar was stopped by his tribal opponent, Mujāhid Ḥaydar of Sufyān. In revenge, Ḥamūd b. ʿAzīz of Sufyān, a rival of Mujāhid Ḥaydar and ally of ʿAbdullah al-Aḥmar, later held up a contingent of Ḥizb al-Ḥaqq.[101]

During the 1992 Iṣlāḥ celebrations in Saʿdah city, both ʿAbdullah al-Aḥmar, then senior shaykh of the Ḥāshid confederation, and Nājī al-Shāyif, then considered senior shaykh of the Bakīl confederation, attended as part of the Iṣlāḥ leadership. Nājī al-Shāyif left the rostrum at the start of the exchange of speeches, supposedly after a *zāmil* (tribal chant) by Ḥasan Muqīt, senior shaykh of the Khawlān b. ʿĀmir confederation, portraying al-Shāyif as a subordinate of ʿAbdullah al-Aḥmar.[102] Al-Shāyif and Iṣlāḥ were never reconciled. Later on, Nājī al-Shāyif reappeared as part of the GPC. These political manoeuvres had little to do with party politics or differences in theology; rather, they concerned personal animosities and tribal rivalries. Considering the overlap of party interests and tribal rivalries and allegiances makes these volatile changes somewhat more comprehensible.

When the results of the 1993 parliamentary elections were announced, the GPC had won the majority of seats and formed a coalition with Iṣlāḥ. Despite the nationwide nomination of sixty-seven candidates, Ḥizb al-Ḥaqq won only two seats, both in Saʿdah governorate. In the west of the province, in Sāqayn constituency, the seat went to Ḥusayn Badr al-Dīn al-Ḥūthī; in the east, in Kitāf wa l-Buqʿ constituency, to ʿAbdullah al-Razzāmī.

Ḥusayn al-Ḥūthī was the eldest son of Badr al-Dīn al-Ḥūthī. In the 1993 elections he succeeded in asserting himself against his competitor Ḥamūd Mardās (Baath Party), senior shaykh of Banī Baḥr, the numerically greatest section of the local Khawlān tribe. Ḥusayn al-Ḥūthī was influenced by one of his teachers, Muḥammad al-Manṣūr, who maintained that there are two acceptable ways of practising Zaydi *khurūj*: through force or elections—in 1993, Ḥusayn al-Ḥūthī took the position that political change should result from free elections.[103]

In fact, Ḥamūd Mardās' decision to run for the elections had been a wise and consensual decision because he was a respected figure within and beyond the Khawlān tribe. His economic status was considered moderate, which lent him credibility as it suggested that he was not on the Saudi payroll and was therefore not seen as a promoter of Wahhabism or Salafism. In this regard, Ḥamūd Mardās was an exception in Khawlān; local sources from this area indicate that, in the 1990s, the unequal distribution of property and resources between the ordinary population and the influential shaykhs was particularly pronounced in Khawlān. The often extreme underdevelopment of the region stood in sharp contrast to the economic situation of certain powerful shaykhs involved in Yemeni and Saudi government patronage, some of whom supported Wahhabi and Salafi interests in the region. Some of these shaykhs not only became very wealthy, but were also more or less absent from their tribal home areas due to their political and economic ambitions in Sanaʿa. Their absence led to a lack of representation and also had an adverse impact on the system of tribal conflict resolution. Even before the 1993 elections in Khawlān, the void arising from the absence of some senior shaykhs was in part filled by members of the al-Ḥūthī family, *sādah* of famous pedigree, who possessed prestigious reputations, kinship ties with the local population, vast local knowledge and experience in mediation and arbitration of tribal conflict. Tribal sources from the Khawlān area explain that members of the al-Ḥūthī family were able to settle tribal conflicts in Khawlān which neither the shaykhs nor the state judiciary could (or would) resolve.[104]

When Ḥusayn al-Ḥūthī had won the 1993 elections by a wide margin of about 1,500 votes, many shaykhs in Khawlān and beyond considered this victory of a *sayyid* a challenge to their shaykhly authority. It marked the emergence of an open competition between Ḥusayn al-Ḥūthī and Khawlān's senior shaykh, ʿAbdullah Rawkān, which from 2004 onwards would also be pursued by military means. ʿAbdullah Rawkān observed Ḥusayn's activities with suspicion and concern. In the late 1980s, he had been one of the first to take action against Zaydi revivalist activities in Khawlān, and urgently warned the governor of the al-Ḥūthī family's social activities.[105] In return Rawkān himself was 'advised' by Zaydi revivalists to abandon his commitment to the spread of Salafism and Wahhabism in the region, despite the fact that Rawkān himself wasn't a convinced Salafi. Other Khawlān shaykhs, notably Fāyiz Bishr and Ḍayfallah al-Shawīʿ of Ḥaydān, were also openly opposed to Ḥusayn al-Ḥūthī and the activities of the Believing Youth. Al-Shawīʿ even went so far as to prohibit Ḥusayn al-Ḥūthī from entering his territory.

Ḥusayn had similar experiences with the tribal leaders in other areas of Saʿdah, who felt challenged by the political rise of a *sayyid* and the spread of the Believing Youth. The late Ḥusayn Fāyid Mujallī (d. 1997) of al-ʿAbdīn (Saḥār) had been particularly alerted to the Believing Youth's increasing numbers and activities; recalling his bitter struggles against the imamic forces during the 1960s civil war, he dubbed its followers 'the royalists' (*al-malikiyyin*), a term which (for him) carried pejorative connotations. Ḥusayn Mujallī prevented Ḥusayn al-Ḥūthī and later also ʿAbdulkarīm Jadbān on more than one occasion from entering the tribal territory of al-ʿAbdīn. After the 1993 elections, in a meeting with other Saḥār shaykhs, Ḥusayn Mujallī drew their attention to the fact that 'there is a risk of the end of the shaykhs' influence and that the influence of the shaykhs is endangered by the Believing Youth and al-Ḥaqq'.[106]

As stated above, in the 1993 elections Ḥizb al-Ḥaqq won its second parliamentary seat, in the eastern constituency of Kitāf wa l-Buqʿ. On the surface, the parliamentary elections in this constituency appeared to be a political struggle between the GPC and Ḥizb al-Ḥaqq. Yet, examined in greater detail, it becomes obvious that the Kitāf elections were steered by tribal conflict, the rivalry between two competing shaykhs, and the debate about the prerogative of interpretation of Zaydism. The particularity of this situation was that both competing shaykhs, ʿAbdullah Ḥāmis al-ʿAwjarī and ʿAbdullah ʿAyḍah al-Razzāmī, were known for their deep Zaydi convictions.

ʿAbdullah al-ʿAwjarī was, as we have seen, a 'big trader' and one of the most influential shaykhs of Wāʾilah. Having been a staunch supporter of the royalists during the 1960s civil war, in the following decades he changed track, gradually shifting to the republican system of which, by the end of his life, he was a committed supporter. Yet among the al-ʿAwjarī clan, all kinds of everyday politics continued to make reference to the denominational determination of their section of the Wāʾilah, deeply influenced by Zaydi beliefs and aware of its historical role as a pillar of Zaydism.[107] Zaydism was a fundamental issue to ʿAbdullah al-ʿAwjarī; though closely associated with Saudi Arabia, he resisted all Saudi attempts to abandon Zaydism and shift to a Salafi agenda. He was far from opposed to Zaydi beliefs or in support of the Sunni denominations that began to spread in Saʿdah in the 1980s. ʿAbdullah al-ʿAwjarī distinguished himself as a benefactor of Zaydi students of the al-Hādī Mosque in Saʿdah city and the Great Mosque in Sanaʿa, and was bound in friendship to Majd al-Dīn al-Muʾayyadī, who had also fought on the royalist side during the civil war. Majd al-Dīn, who endeavoured after the war to reconcile Zaydi doctrine with republicanism, considered the deeply religious yet power-conscious and politically flexible ʿAbdullah al-ʿAwjarī his mundane alter ego. Thus, he supported al-ʿAwjarī when the latter ran as a GPC candidate in the 1993 elections.[108] Majd al-Dīn al-Muʾayyadī also demanded the support of other Zaydi scholars for ʿAbdullah al-ʿAwjarī's cause, 'for religious and mundane considerations' (*iʿtibārāt dīniyyah wa dunyawiyyah*), and 'because he is with us with his heart and mind, his wealth and breath' (*huwa maʿanā qalban wa qāliban wa mālan wa nafsan*).[109]

The Āl Mahdī—the tribal section of which the al-ʿAwājirah (adj. *al-ʿawjarī*) are part—have a relatively recent history of conflict with a neighbouring tribal group of Wāʾilah, the Āl al-Nimrī. Disagreements in the early 1990s over the construction and management of a school resulted in tribal upset and the death of a member of the Āl Mahdī, which triggered a cycle of violent retaliation and blood feud (*thaʾr*). Since the Āl al-Nimrī were weaker than the Āl Mahdī, they allied themselves with the neighbouring Āl al-Razzāmāt, a section of the Wādiʿah whose shaykh was ʿAbdullah al-Razzāmī. Neighbouring tribes often maintain hostile relations at their borders and ally themselves with their neighbours' neighbours, resulting in larger patterns of spatially interspersed coalitions or blocs.[110]

When ʿAbdullah al-Razzāmī ran as a Ḥizb al-Ḥaqq candidate in 1993, this was not only a provocation to the powerful ʿAbdullah al-ʿAwjarī, who himself ran for the GPC, but also for Majd al-Dīn al-Muʾayyadī and all those Zaydi scholars who were close to al-Muʾayyadī and who supported the candidacy of the more influential al-ʿAwjarī. Being neither an intellectual nor a *sayyid*, al-Razzāmī's loyalty to Ḥusayn al-Ḥūthī was first and foremost based on deep personal friendship; al-Razzāmī was one of Ḥusayn's closest friends and confidants. Local sources often stress the unusual fact that al-Razzāmī's loyalty and allegiance to Ḥusayn al-Ḥūthī were based not on common descent, kinship or intermarriage, but solely on a personal relationship between the two men. Ḥusayn, his father Badr al-Dīn and all who were close to them supported al-Razzāmī's candidacy, which led to tensions among the Zaydi scholars and profoundly angered both al-ʿAwjarī and Majd al-Dīn al-Muʾayyadī.[111] The election turned out to be highly controversial, leaving us with divergent explanations of al-ʿAwjarī's defeat and al-Razzāmī's success. A member of al-ʿAwjarī's own tribe echoed his tribe's version:

> Ali Abdullah Salih played a role [in these elections]. He wanted the success of ʿAbdullah al-Razzāmī and Ḥizb al-Ḥaqq for several reasons. He wanted a radical movement to stand against Muqbil al-Wādiʿī. Moderate Zaydis were not to have armed clashes against Wahhabis in Saʿdah. They disagree with them in their ideas and fundamentals but they do not fight them. Salih needed the Salafis at that time but he was afraid that he would not be able to contain them afterwards. So he wanted a radical Zaydi movement to restore the balance. In 1993 ʿAbdullah al-ʿAwjarī did not want to run for elections, because he knew the game. He even left to Cairo, but Salih insisted that he run. And during the vote count the military got the order to stuff the ballot boxes in favour of ʿAbdullah al-Razzāmī. First, Salih wanted to give Ḥizb al-Ḥaqq places in the parliament, and second, Salih was not happy with ʿAbdullah al-ʿAwjarī's relations with the Saudis. Salih wanted to show that we have a multi-party system and that powerful figures can lose, and ʿAbdullah al-ʿAwjarī turned out to be his pawn.[112]

In other words, al-ʿAwjarī's supporters blamed his defeat on political machinations and electoral fraud. By contrast, for the supporters of al-Razzāmī, the latter's success was due to the strong presence of the Zaydi revival movement in the Kitāf area; they maintained that al-Razzāmī could win the voters' sympathy because he was better able than 'big trader' al-ʿAwjarī to represent the deep religious convictions of the Zaydi parts of Wāʾilah.[113] Even so, al-Razzāmī's narrow victory over al-ʿAwjarī certainly turned matters on their head—a minor shaykh of a small, rather insignificant tribal section of the dispersed Wādiʿah had triumphed politically over a senior shaykh of immense influence, wealth and tribal clout among the pre-eminent Wāʾilah of Kitāf.

In the years after these elections, al-Razzāmī backed Ḥusayn al-Ḥūthī in every political and military move and, under the fighting name Abū Yaḥyā, numbered among the very few shaykhs to support the Houthis militarily from the very beginning; the number of such early pro-Houthi shaykhs can be counted on one hand. After Ḥusayn al-Ḥūthī's death in 2004, al-Razzāmī also supported Ḥusayn's father, Badr al-Dīn, and the al-Razzāmāt area was at the centre of the second Saʿdah war in 2005, when Badr al-Dīn sought refuge there. Al-Razzāmī was also among the early military leaders in the Houthi fortresses of al-Naqʿah and Maṭrah in northeastern al-Ṣafrāʾ district, close to the Saudi border. Nevertheless, after Ḥusayn's death, the alliance between al-Razzāmī and Ḥusayn's successor ʿAbdulmalik deteriorated over time. After the fourth Saʿdah war (February–June 2007), al-Razzāmī withdrew from the conflict.[114]

Again, accounts of this rift are contradictory. Muḥammad ʿIzzān says that al-Razzāmī considered ʿAbdulmalik's policy a deviation (*inḥirāf*) from Ḥusayn's thought; for instance, ʿAbdulmalik cooperated with foreign organizations like the Red Cross, which al-Razzāmī regarded as a 'suspicious Western organization'.[115] Sources from al-Razzāmī's tribal milieu add that he felt passed over when the aged Badr al-Dīn handed leadership of the rebellion on to the rather young ʿAbdulmalik (b. c. 1980); al-Razzāmī felt that he himself was due this role as a faithful friend of Ḥusayn and seasoned military leader of the rebellion. As he witnessed Houthi military leadership positions becoming increasingly occupied by *sādah* rather than tribesmen like him, and the leadership following rigid Hādawism and even beginning to assume dynastic forms, al-Razzāmī became embittered by this suspected 'neutralization of tribal leaders' (*taḥāyyid al-ʿunṣur al-qiyādī al-qabalī*). This was when he finally withdrew from the Houthi conflict.[116]

By that time, tensions between ʿAbdulmalik al-Ḥūthī and ʿAbdullah al-Razzāmī had been further aggravated by the military feud during the Saʿdah wars between the Āl al-Nimrī/al-Razzāmāt and the Āl Mahdī (home section of the al-ʿAwjarī clan). From the second to the fourth Saʿdah wars (March 2005–June 2007), the al-Razzāmāt tribe launched heavy attacks on the Āl Mahdī; several members of the al-ʿAwjarī shaykhly lineage, including a son of ʿAbdullah al-ʿAwjarī, were killed. This was even a decisive element in triggering the third Saʿdah war in November 2005. Al-Razzāmī became increasingly embittered as ʿAbdulmalik issued statements and press releases downgrading these battles and killings to mere 'tribal feuding', declaring that they were due to the feuds of Wādī Nushūr—that is, the revenge issue between al-Razzāmī and the al-ʿAwjarī clan—and had nothing to do with the Houthi cause.[117] ʿAbdulmalik even sent emissaries to the al-ʿAwjarī to assure them that 'the Houthis' had nothing to do with al-Razzāmī's aggression.[118]

However, Houthi sources maintain a different version. For them, after the death of his friend and soulmate Ḥusayn al-Ḥūthī, al-Razzāmī had 'lost his [inner] balance' (*faqada al-tawāzun*). As a firm supporter of 'Hādawī doctrine', he was a firm believer in the *sādah*'s claim to leadership and welcomed the takeover of leadership by Ḥusayn's kin—yet remained convinced that Ḥusayn was still alive. According to this narrative, after the fourth war, he 'withdrew to the hermitage of the inaccessible mountains and waited for the return of Ḥusayn al-Ḥūthī'.[119]

The 1993 electoral results in Kitāf constituency show that political manoeuvres often had little to do with party politics or differences in theology, and more to do with personal animosities and tribal rivalries. The events that unfolded there are exemplary of the complexity of a local setting involving various groups providing contradictory and self-serving versions of one incident. These competing narratives remain ultimately incommensurable. Existing evidence, however, should nevertheless make it possible to deduce at least one factor at play: the coincidence of political struggle and tribal conflict. In these power games, the supposedly weaker side frequently allied itself with the Houthis—a pattern repeated across many regions in Saʿdah and neighbouring governorates.[120]

The rest of the 1993 Ḥizb al-Ḥaqq candidates in Saʿdah governorate ran in vain against strong competition from tribal-political heavyweights. The parliamentarians who emerged from the 1993 elections were largely influential shaykhs of the province: Shaykh Qāʾid Shuwayṭ of Banī ʿUwayr (Saḥār) won Iṣlāḥ's only seat in Saʿdah city constituency. Shaykh Fayṣal ʿAbdullah Manāʿ of al-Ṭalḥ (Saḥār) won for the GPC in Saḥār; Shaykh Ḥasan Muḥammad Muqīt of Jumāʿah (also senior shaykh of the Khawlān b. ʿĀmir confederation) won as an independent in Majz and Bāqim; Shaykh Aḥmad Dahbāsh Miṭrī of Banī Khawlī (also senior shaykh of Munabbih's Shaʿshaʿ moiety) won for the GPC in Munabbih and Qaṭābir; Shaykh Ḥasan Muḥammad Muyassar of Banī Maʿīn (Ghumār) won for the GPC in Rāziḥ (against ʿAbdulwāḥid Sulaymān al-Faraḥ for Iṣlāḥ); Shaykh Ḍayfallah Yaḥyā Rassām of Ilt Rassām (the Walad ʿAyyāsh section of Khawlān) won for the GPC in Ḥaydān, al-Ẓāhir and Shidāʾ; and Shaykh Ṣāliḥ Hindī Dughsān of Āl ʿAmmār (Dahm) won for the GPC in al-Ṣafrāʾ and al-Ḥishwah.

These results point to the localization of power and influence in Saʿdah province. With the exception of Ḥusayn al-Ḥūthī himself, every MP elected was a tribal shaykh. After Yemeni unification in 1990, the shaykhs—as semi-hereditary, elected tribal representatives of their tribes or sections—also lay claim to supra-tribal, political offices. They monopolized the major offices in their tribal constituencies, such as the official function of MP, because only they possessed the necessary experience, national connections and financial means to pursue political candidacies. Many of them had previously been members of the Consultative Council, and their proximity to the regime and other national-level decision makers, as well as the potential political and business connections, made a parliamentary seat an object of desire. This assertion of shaykhly entitlement to national political representation of their respective regions against tribal and non-tribal political rivals would later, in some cases, become dynastic in nature. Burrowes and Kasper argue that, from the 1980s, the trend toward concentrating political power in the hands of tribal shaykhs, military officers, and northern businessmen was briefly 'interrupted and challenged' in 1990–4, but then accelerated after the 1994 civil war.[121] In the Saʿdah region, however, there was no such rupture, as political power remained firmly bound to the social strata of the shaykhs.

Yet, as Phillips noted, within the patronage system, inclusiveness is high but group cohesion is low.[122] Some of Saʿdah's active GPC MPs—known as 'Saʿdah's parliamentary bloc' (*al-kutlah al-barlamāniyyah* or *kutlat Ṣaʿdah*)—were rivals, or even antagonistic towards one another. Some MPs even had a history of blood feud, but were now supposed to chart a new course together in Parliament. Similarly, the relationship between Saʿdah's parliamentary bloc and the central government was not always free of conflict. For instance, the father of Ṣāliḥ Hindī Dughsān, who won for the GPC in 1993 in al-Ṣafrāʾ and al-Ḥishwah, had previously swung around the leftist axis; both father and son have been involved with the socialist movement in the former PDRY. An attempt in 1989 to kill the father inside the perimeter of a government building in Saʿdah city failed, but a number of men from both sides were killed and many were wounded. Following this incident, the government literally besieged the shaykh's house in Āl ʿAmmār with tanks and artillery in order to prevent the outbreak of a major tribal conflict.[123] The Dughsān clan's relationship with the government since can only be described as one of mutual mistrust—yet Hindī Dughsān still became a GPC MP.

Something similar happened with ʿUthmān Mujallī, who entered Parliament in 1997 for the GPC and was re-elected in 2003. Although the scion of a flawless republican shaykhly clan, his criticism of the government's approach during the Saʿdah wars landed him in trouble with the regime; an assassination attempt on his brother Yāsir in December 2007, also inside Saʿdah city's security precinct, injured Yāsir severely and killed some of his companions. The incident prompted a serious parliamentary crisis in Sanaʿa and tribal unrest in Saʿdah, and initiated the decline of the tribal-governmental anti-Houthi coalition.[124]

In the parliamentary elections of 1997, Ḥizb al-Ḥaqq failed to secure a single seat. The party, suffering from internal divisions over religious doctrine, failed to communicate its goals to the electorate.[125] In Sāqayn constituency, the Khawlān's senior shaykh, ʿAbdullah Rawkān (GPC), threw all his weight behind his candidacy, and pushed Ḥusayn al-Ḥūthī out of Parliament. In Kitāf wa l-Buqʿ, ʿAbdullah al-Razzāmī lost his seat to Shaykh Aḥmad Hamadān Abū Mushʿaf (GPC) of al-Maqāsh (Wāʾilah), whose candidacy was supported by ʿAbdullah al-ʿAwjarī. The latter—after his painful defeat in 1993—had decided not to run again. Iṣlāḥ also lost its only parliamentary seat in Saʿdah, as Qāʾid Shuwayṭ was defeated by his rival ʿUthmān Mujallī (GPC); here, too, the exploitation of long-standing rivalries paid political dividends for the Mujallī clan.[126] As in 1993, all other parliamentary seats went to tribal heavyweights such as Shaykh Fayṣal Manāʿ (GPC) in Saḥār; Shaykh Ḥasan Muqīt (independent) in Majz and Bāqim; Shaykh Ḥasan Muḥammad Muyassar (GPC) in Rāziḥ; and Shaykh ʿAlī Ḥasan Jaylān (GPC) in Ḥaydān, al-Ẓāhir and Shidāʾ. In Munabbih and Qaṭābir, shaykh and businessman ʿAlī Ḥusayn al-Munabbihī (GPC) defeated his tribal-political rival, Shaykh Aḥmad Dahbāsh Miṭrī (GPC). In al-Ṣafrāʾ and al-Ḥishwah, Shaykh Ṣāliḥ Ṣāliḥ Hindī Dughsān (GPC), son and tribal-political heir of the late Ṣāliḥ Hindī Dughsān, was elected.[127] In other words, 100 per cent of the parliamentarians elected in 1997 in Saʿdah governorate were 'big' tribal shaykhs.

Furthermore, the GPC managed to strengthen its already preeminent position in Saʿdah in these elections: eight of the nine Saʿdah parliamentarians were GPC, and only one was independent. This failure of Iṣlāḥ and Ḥizb al-Ḥaqq may have been the result of peripheral marginalization in terms of social welfare, and the government's developmental presence was felt even more strongly in this period because of reduced remittances and international aid.[128] In 1997, the electorate accepted the influential GPC shaykhs' promise to enhance relations with the government by their (real, desired, or suppositious) national connections and to provide for more prosperity in their tribal constituencies—apparently hoping that this shaykh-GPC-government triangulation would benefit their regions.

In the years since 1997, the province has seen development of what was virtually a one-party system. Despite the overheating sectarian tensions in the province, the GPC in Saʿdah achieved quasi-Stalinist results in the 2003 parliamentary elections; every MP of the Saʿdah parliamentary bloc was a GPC MP, reflecting the consolidation of the patrimonial system entrenched in Yemen since 1990. Yemeni unification strengthened the power of the Salih regime, which simultaneously tried to co-opt its traditional rivals: an authoritarian rule evolved out of a set of conditions that, at first glance, seemed to guarantee the opposite. The tendency to confine the political landscape led to an increasingly autocratic system, with President Salih, his clan and the ruling GPC party controlling most if not all the levers of power.[129]

In the 2003 elections again seven out of nine GPC deputies came from the ranks of the influential tribal shaykhs: ʿUthmān Mujallī in Saʿdah city, Fayṣal Nāṣir ʿArīj in Saḥār, ʿAbdulsalām Hishūl Zābiyah in Majz and Bāqim, ʿAlī Ḥusayn al-Munabbihī in Munabbih and Qaṭābir, ʿAlī Ḥasan Jaylān in Ḥaydān, al-Ẓāhir and Shidāʾ; Fāyiz ʿAbdullah Ḥāmis al-ʿAwjarī in Kitāf wa l-Buqʿ; and Ṣāliḥ Ṣāliḥ Hindī Dughsān in al-Ṣafrāʾ and al-Ḥishwah. When the latter was killed in 2008 in an armed ambush on the way to the funeral of former MP Qāʾid Shuwayṭ, his brother, ʿUmar Ṣāliḥ Hindī Dughsān, was elected for the GPC in the controversial supplementary elections of 2009, which became a symbol of both arbitrary government and the evolving 'inheritance principle' (*mabdaʾ al-tawrīth*) among Saʿdah's parliamentary bloc.[130]

Saʿdah's only non-shaykh parliamentarians elected in 2003 were Yaḥyā Badr al-Dīn al-Ḥūthī in Sāqayn and ʿAbdulkarīm Jadbān in Rāziḥ. In the electoral lists both are named as GPC members, yet people often say that they actually ran as independent candidates and only joined the GPC after their election. Regardless, both would later play a central role in the Houthi opposition to the regime. When Yaḥyā, a brother of Ḥusayn al-Ḥūthī, stood against Shaykh ʿAbdullah Rawkān in 2003, Ḥusayn was already expanding his influence within the grassroots of the Zaydi revival movement. It is not known whether Ḥusayn supported Yaḥyā's (successful) candidacy as an extension of and complement to his own social activism. We also do not know what ultimately prompted Yaḥyā al-Ḥūthī to join the GPC after the elections rather than remaining an independent candidate or joining the al-Ḥaqq party. Probably, the revolving democratization process and the emergence of what was virtually a one-party system dashed any hopes for meaningful political participation outside the GPC. Yaḥyā al-Ḥūthī and ʿAbdulkarīm Jadbān may also have struck a deal of sorts with the government. Longley Alley explains that the GPC's effective use of local, popular figures was matched by their respect for local traditions and norms: when party organizers found, for example, that any person (a *sayyid*, or a lesser shaykh) was more popular than the senior shaykh of an area, they would sometimes allow the senior shaykh to run on the GPC ticket, while encouraging the other candidate to run as an independent. The other candidate would then promise to switch to the GPC after winning the election.[131]

In any case, through the successful candidacy of Yaḥyā al-Ḥūthī the Zaydi revival movement regained a voice in the political arena. Since Yaḥyā's electoral success, he has been partly responsible for the movement's political and 'diplomatic' activities. Before and during the Saʿdah wars, Yaḥyā al-Ḥūthī was constantly involved in mediation efforts, including the three Doha Agreements in 2007, 2008 and 2010.[132] Yet the wars did not leave Yaḥyā with many opportunities to pursue his domestic political agenda. In 2005, he went to Germany, where he was granted political asylum. After a trip from Germany to Libya in 2007, the government lifted his parliamentarian immunity from prosecution and in June 2008 revoked his membership of the parliament. In exile, Yaḥyā has continued to serve as a spokesperson for the Zaydi revivalists, giving television interviews on pan-Arab news outlets, writing editorials and conducting interviews in foreign newspapers, and participating in mediations. For many years, the Yemeni government sought in vain to have Interpol extradite him to Yemen. Only in 2013 did Yaḥyā return, as a nominated member of the National Dialogue Conference. As soon as his aircraft landed in Sanaʿa, he was shot at. Security concerns and awareness of his highly polarizing personality may explain why he did not ultimately participate in the National Dialogue Conference, instead withdrawing to the Houthis' Saʿdah strongholds.[133]

The other non-shaykhly GPC parliamentarian was ʿAbdulkarīm Jadbān, who won a thin majority of 200 votes in Rāziḥ against Iṣlāḥ's candidate Shaykh Amīn Ḥasan Jābir. Unlike Yaḥyā al-Ḥūthī, however, ʿAbdulkarīm Jadbān was of tribal descent. He was an esteemed scholar and activist of the Zaydi revival movement and was a founding member of the Believing Youth. Jadbān was able to link Zaydi revivalism with loyalty to the regime. Since he reasoned that Zaydi-inspired strife might cause more harm than good to the Zaydi *madhhab*, and that the link between genealogy and political authority reflected bygone social hierarchies that were no longer binding, he represented—from the government's perspective—the 'good Zaydis'.[134] In 2013 he, too, became a member of the National Dialogue Conference, where he acted as a representative of the Houthis (or Anṣār Allah, a name adopted after the end of the Saʿdah wars). In November 2013, he was assassinated in Sanaʿa by unidentified gunmen.[135]

Ḥusayn al-Ḥūthī's proposal that *khurūj* should be undertaken through democratic institutions had added a new, dynamic component to the ongoing debates about Zaydi revivalism and doctrine. Yet, in overall terms, the initial political success of the revival movement has not proven sustainable. Ḥizb al-Ḥaqq achieved promising results in the 1993 elections, and in 1997 it was temporarily represented in government when Salih, attempting to marginalize Iṣlāḥ, appointed a Ḥizb al-Ḥaqq minister of endowments and Islamic guidance. Since 1997, however, the revivalists' political efforts have either been thwarted by the increasingly powerful shaykh-GPC coalition or co-opted by the regime.

The political winners of democratization's stalling were the tribal shaykhs. Saʿdah province is a good example of Mundy's argument that in post-revolutionary Yemen the two hierarchies of power—that is, the major shaykhs and the state—have increasingly merged into one and have ultimately been combined into a ruling coalition, if not a ruling class.[136] That said, the shaykhs' sometimes rancorous struggles against their competitors and machinations for the votes of their constituents show no primordial loyalties among their tribes. We should recall that tribes are far from uniform blocs and rarely adhere to any given political stances. Their shaykhs often possess a considerable degree of tribal authority and personal influence, but they cannot claim their tribesmen's political allegiance; they do not 'govern' their tribes. As Carapico put it, political parties do not represent tribes, nor does party loyalty rest on tribal affiliation.[137] Rather, within each tribe there are many parties, and within each party are people of different tribal (and non-tribal) origins.

The Emergence of the Houthis

After losing the 1997 election, Ḥusayn al-Ḥūthī turned away from party politics. The increasing polarization between Majd al-Dīn al-Muʾayyadī and Badr al-Dīn al-Ḥūthī and his kin and followers prompted the influential Majd al-Dīn to drive Ḥusayn al-Ḥūthī out of Ḥizb al-Ḥaqq.[138] Even before this, during his tenure as an MP, Ḥusayn al-Ḥūthī had not been able to effectuate the changes he had hoped for. In Sāqayn constituency in 1997—as everywhere in Saʿdah governorate—influential GPC shaykhs, some of whom not only defended their 'right' to parliamentary representation, but even began to develop a dynastic entitlement to the position, prevailed. Ḥusayn al-Ḥūthī decided to dissociate himself from Ḥizb al-Ḥaqq and to leave the political arena's well-established dialectic of government and opposition.

In 1999, Ḥusayn al-Ḥūthī temporarily left Yemen to study for a master's degree in Quranic sciences at Khartoum University, Sudan. After his return to the Ṣaʿdah region in 2000, he focused on social activism at the grassroots level on which the Believing Youth was already operating. Ḥusayn had previously participated in the social activism and educational work of the

Believing Youth, but for many years the movement had been far more closely identified with Muḥammad ʿIzzān and Ḥusayn's brother Muḥammad al-Ḥūthī—from 1993 to 1997 Ḥusayn was in Parliament from 1993 to 1997 and in Sudan from 1999 to 2000, and his father, Badr al-Dīn al-Ḥūthī, spent periods in Iran. Ḥusayn's return from Sudan and devotion to the work of the Believing Youth gave a fresh impetus to the Zaydi revival movement at the turn of the century, but also exacerbated an already smouldering factional dispute within the Believing Youth, which in 2001 led to a split within the movement.[139] Much of what might be said about the emergence of this schism is tentative, given the conflicting nature of various sources and their lack of corroboration.

Muḥammad ʿIzzān, for instance, claims in an interview that after his return from Sudan Ḥusayn tried to bring his views and thoughts into the curricula of the Believing Youth. ʿIzzān then critically scrutinized Ḥusayn's views, finding some elements that over-emphasized the role and rights of the *sādah* and undermined the *usūl al-fiqh* (Islamic jurisprudence), and others that were not reflected in Zaydi doctrine at all, but rather reminiscent of Iranian Jaʿfarī doctrine.[140] However, Supreme Court judges who also scrutinized Ḥusayn's lectures did not support this analysis; they failed to find references to Imāmī-Shiism.[141] Some sources argue that Ḥusayn was aiming to politicize the Believing Youth in order to counter the region's various problems—not an approach supported by Muḥammad ʿIzzān, who insisted on the movement's strictly apolitical character. Other sources suggest that Muḥammad ʿIzzān may have been intimidated or coerced during his 2004/5 incarceration in Political Security jail into denouncing Ḥusayn.[142]

In any case, in 2001 the disputes within the Believing Youth led to an internal fraction, those leaning towards Muḥammad ʿIzzān and Majd al-Dīn al-Mu'ayyadī on the one side and those inclined towards Ḥusayn al-Ḥūthī and his father Badr al-Dīn on the other. The group led by Ḥusayn, subsequently dubbed *Aṣḥāb al-shiʿār* (Followers of the Slogan), was the nucleus of the movement that later became known as the 'Houthis' (*al-Ḥūthiyyūn*). 'Houthis' remains the vernacular name of this group, which is used in everyday practice by both the members of this group and their opponents. Only in 2011 did they adopt the official name Anṣār Allah (Partisans of God).

The emergence of the famous slogan (*al-shiʿār*), which was eponymous with respect for the founding group centred on Ḥusayn al-Ḥūthī, marked a turning point in the latter's thinking and became emblematic of the broader Houthi movement. Lux has reconstructed the evolution of this slogan, which was catalyzed by an event that took place in Gaza, Palestine, on 30 September 2000 at the beginning of the second Intifada.[143] On that day, a cameraman captured footage of a gun battle between Israeli forces and Palestinians depicting two civilians—a father and son—pinned against a wall and behind a barrel. The child was killed and died in his father's lap. This iconic clip was broadcast around the world. Among the millions in the Middle East who saw it was Ḥusayn al-Ḥūthī, and he is said at that moment to have uttered the *shiʿār*, which became the emblem of the Houthi movement, for the first time: 'Death to America, Death to Israel, a Curse Upon the Jews, Victory for Islam' (*Al-mawt li-Amrīkā/al-mawt li-Isrāʾīl/al-laʿnah ʿalā al-yahūd/al-naṣr li-l-islām*).

In 2001, when the Believing Youth schism emerged, the rallying potential of Ḥusayn's *shiʿār* was reinforced by the consequences of the September terrorist attacks in New York. After 9/11, US policies toward Yemen and the Middle East in general were driven by the 'Global War on Terror', and President Salih—having been painfully burnt during the First Gulf War (Desert Storm) when he sided with Saddam Husayn—this time came out in support of the United States. The domestic consensus that he imposed on the other parties directly after 9/11 gave the Houthis significant room for manoeuvre: Iṣlāḥ was forced into silence, leaving the Houthis the only Yemeni force to remain vocal against the alliance.[144] From late fall of 2001, Muslims in Saʿdah and beyond were confronted with television images of civilian deaths and war atrocities in Afghanistan and the creation of Guantanamo Bay, to which many Yemeni nationals were sent. The Yemeni government declared combat activities against its enemies to be part of the 'War on Terror', earning then President George W. Bush's praise for its courage in carrying out its promise to stand by him. The government in Sanaʿa, by depicting senior military officials who were to lead the coming campaign against Ḥusayn al-Ḥūthī as contributing to the struggle against terrorism in Yemen, created an opportunity to dispel American suspicion about their links with radical militancy.[145] The US-Yemeni security cooperation was highly unpopular throughout the country, and after the US invasion of Iraq in 2003, such cooperation became even more odious to many Yemenis, who nurtured fraternal feelings for Iraq and its regime.[146]

These developments were an opportunity for Ḥusayn al-Ḥūthī to take the lead in mobilizing the growing movement in Saʿdah and adjacent areas, carried forward by grievances with sectarian, political, anti-imperialist and social revolutionary facets. Over the following two years, widespread dissatisfaction in the region gave Ḥusayn the basic leverage for motivating his audiences through charismatic lectures. His messages cut across tribal and socio-economic lines and also met with an enormous response in areas beyond Saʿdah province. He went spectacularly public during a lecture in January 2002 entitled 'Shouting in the Face of the Arrogant' (*al-ṣarkhah fī wajh al-mustakbirīn*).[147] This was the first of a lecture series whose transcripts were later called the *malāzim* (printed transcriptions of his lectures, literally '[lecture] notes'), which mainly centred on anti-imperialism, Zaydi revivalism, and the marginalization of the Saʿdah region and adjacent areas. Other recurring themes in the lectures were associated with calls to action, in which the Islamic Revolution of Iran and Lebanon's Hezbollah served as models of resistance[148]—according to Wells Goldburt, these references led to a deterioration in the relationship between Ḥusayn and the government.[149] Regardless, the overarching religious referent wielded by Ḥusayn in his mesmerizing lectures, far from being strictly Zaydi, appeared at first sight to be pan-Islamic.[150]

The *shiʿār*'s green-white graffiti began to spread throughout northern Yemen on rock faces and walls. In 2003, the *shiʿār* had already become a visible feature of the streetscapes of Sanaʿa, especially in the Old Town's narrow streets, with their numerous Zaydi mosques. Simultaneously, Ḥusayn al-Ḥūthī organized anti-American demonstrations across Yemen and instructed his followers to shout the *shiʿār* after Friday prayers in mosques throughout the country, a practice that increasingly irked the government.[151] Indeed, the rationale of the slogan-shouting lay in its capacity not to incite violence, but to provoke the authorities.[152] Still, the slogan-shouting at the centre of prayers and protests represented an undisguised critique of power, and symbolized a shift in the nature of the Zaydi-inspired dissent. 'Commanding right and forbidding wrong', the central tenet of Zaydism, now became embodied in modes of mass public expression associated with agitation against US policy in the Middle East. The chants and mass rallies added a new, dynamic component to Zaydism, which in the government's eyes contrasted sharply and dangerously with the affirmative political disposition of many Salafis.

Dorlian sees the initial anti-government stance of Ḥusayn al-Ḥūthī's group as more politically than religiously motivated; a political opposition that found its expression in the 'anti-imperialist' Houthi slogan.[153] Although Ḥusayn also promoted genuine religious positions, in Dorlian's view the sectarian dimension of his confrontation with state power was mainly a product of the government's efforts to 'confessionalize', and so 'de-legitimize', a political conflict. Dorlian argues that the government was unable to counter the Houthis' anti-Americanism, because the position—articulated by no other force—found great approval among the Yemeni population. In response, the government tried to shift the focus of the conflict by accusing the Houthis of seeking to re-establish an imamate, and positioning itself as the defender of the Republic. This not only distracted a receptive public from the anti-US narrative, but allowed Sanaʿa to integrate the fight against the Houthis into the international 'War on Terror', thereby strengthening its strategic partnership with the US and gaining the sympathies of those important Sunni states whose support was crucial for Yemen's efforts to join the Gulf Cooperation Council.

Whereas the Houthis' catchy anti-imperialist and anti-American slogan served to mobilize their followers, the economic and political marginalization of the Saʿdah region, the uneven distribution of economic sources and political participation, and the religious discrimination against its Zaydi population provided fertile soil in which the Houthi movement could take root and blossom. As we have seen, the marginalization of the Zaydis was not only a theological problem. It also had repercussions for Zaydi daily life. In his lectures, Ḥusayn al-Ḥūthī frequently referred to the discrimination suffered by the region's Zaydi population and deplored the government's support, both tacit and open, for Salafi groups.[154] He argued that the lack of social justice, state services and sustainable development in the region ostracized the local Zaydi community. According to him, this discrimination went so far that the government was increasingly seen as a hostile power allied with the Zaydis' sectarian opponents—in case of open confrontations between the denominations, 'the Wahhabis are able to call in [Salafi-friendly military commander and relative of President Salih] ʿAlī Muḥsin directly, whereas the Zaydis are left without a government official to support them'.[155]

Ḥusayn al-Ḥūthī's experiences during the 1997 parliamentary elections, too, left their mark on his lectures. He accused the successful GPC candidates of unfair use of electoral pledges and gifts with the aim of substantially influencing the election, of the buying of votes and of electoral fraud.[156] He also criticized the political leadership in Sanaʿa and the GPC MPs' disinterest in eradicating underdevelopment and poverty in their constituencies. He lamented that during their tenure these parliamentarians channelled government funds to their own patch instead of contributing to the development of the areas they represented: 'The leaders come to agreements—leader after leader—and the members of the Parliament and members of the government—member after member—and yet the land remains uncultivated'.[157] All of these themes were politically explosive issues, because underdevelopment, fraud and the graft endemic within the state budget did not only concern Ḥusayn's home region in Khawlān, but also most other regions of Yemen.

Indeed, local sources from rural areas frequently complain that, after the end of the 1960s civil war, many shaykhs used their shaykhdom to maximize their own wealth and increase their personal influence and power at national level without contributing substantially to the social welfare and development of their tribal constituencies. The al-ʿUṣaymāt of Ḥāshid, for instance, saw their senior shaykh, ʿAbdullah al-Aḥmar, 'transformed [after the 1960s] from a leader and representative of the Ḥāshid to a government insider with his political and financial interests centred in Sanaʿa and less with his tribesmen'.[158] His own tribespeople, the al-ʿUṣaymāt, have not benefited materially from his presence on the national scene. Although the al-ʿUṣaymāt were tremendously proud of their famous senior shaykhly lineage, the contrast between the national importance of their senior shaykh and the underdevelopment of the region was appalling and created social unrest. Accordingly, when the Houthis 'freed' parts of al-ʿUṣaymāt during their expansions in 2013 and early 2014, Houthi sources described the situation they encountered there as 'terrible' (*murʿib*), stating: 'the region needs another fifty years of development to become like Ḍaḥyān. There are no signs of the twentieth century; the conditions prevailing in al-ʿUṣaymāt are reminiscent of the Middle Ages'.[159]

Furthermore, the Republic's patronage of senior shaykhs—and their consequent lack of interest or presence in their home areas—had repercussions for social peace; local sources indicate that some shaykhs (in their customary role as mediators and arbitrators) and the government (that is, the state justice system) could not or would not perform these roles in local conflict resolution. It must be said that many shaykhs did split their time between Sanaʿa and their home areas to stay connected to their tribes. Others, however, were more or less absent, or began to demand enormous financial compensation for their tribal mediation and arbitration services. This void led to an increase in tribal conflict and revenge cases, some of which lasted for over thirty years with neither the shaykhs nor state justice able to resolve them. This phenomenon was not limited to Khawlān, Ḥusayn al-Ḥūthī's home region. In Ḥabūr (ʿAmrān governorate, the constituency of Iṣlāḥ MP Ḥamīd al-Aḥmar, son of Shaykh ʿAbdullah al-Aḥmar and one of Yemen's richest businessmen), this void in tribal conflict resolution and local governance had by the 1990s already generated a situation of dilapidation and chronic feuding, in which the feuding groups had even begun to target each other's cattle and sheep.[160]

In his lectures Ḥusayn al-Ḥūthī did not spare the state's leadership from his criticism. He described then President Salih's promise in the 1980s to provide

Saʿdah province with electricity as 'idle talk', because 'in the end [...] not a single promise has been kept as Ali Abdullah Salih said when he visited [the region]: "God willing, in 1986 Saʿdah will be on a single power grid"; then came 1987, 1988, 1989, 1990 and 1991 and nothing happened—we remained applying for electricity for seven years for a single region'.[161] Accordingly, from 2004 (when the Saʿdah wars began), the Houthis began to tear generators out of military bases, government buildings and certain GPC shaykhs' houses in the territories that fell under their sway, and to install these devices in the villages for public use. A tribal source from the Khawlān area explained that the home village of a Khawlān shaykh whom the Houthis expelled during the conflict 'lived in total darkness, although the shaykh has millions of dollars. But now all [members of the] Khawlān [tribe] get free electricity except the expenses for the fuel, for the first time since the invention of the light bulb. The Houthis seized the generators of the shaykhs, military sites and some government centres, and distributed them to villages and rural areas, and this was a great humanitarian gesture.'[162] In this understanding of events, Ḥusayn's early charitable efforts, including collecting funds for schools, local electrification, clean water supplies, and so forth, were not intended in the first instance to build an insurgent base. Rather, these efforts provided him with a considerable amount of local prestige and social influence, rivalling and outpacing that of many leading shaykhs, the local authorities, and the state itself.[163]

The movement's social revolutionary and political goals thus addressed an agenda of local grievances. They fell within the overarching Zaydi domain of 'commanding what is right and forbidding what is wrong', which can be found throughout Ḥusayn al-Ḥūthī's *malāzim* (lecture notes). In his *malāzim* he frequently invoked Shia principles of justice and of 'commanding what is right and forbidding what is wrong' when discussing what he considered *fasād* (corruption) in contemporary Arab societies, particularly Yemen.

By the beginning of 2003, the Houthi slogan had spread at an alarming rate within Saʿdah governorate, while Ḥusayn's lectures began to circulate among Zaydis in the governorate and beyond. The slogan-shouting particularly needled the president. Salih repeatedly called for Ḥusayn to abandon the slogan. In 2003, he summoned Yaḥyā al-Ḥūthī, ʿAbd al-Karīm Jadbān and Fāris Manāʿ to Sanaʿa and asked them to convince Ḥusayn to give it up, threatening 'relentless persecution' if he would not.[164] In January 2003, Ḥusayn's followers came into direct confrontation with the state for the first time. During a stopover in Saʿdah city on his way to perform the pilgrimage in Mecca, President Salih, accompanied by Iṣlāḥ MPs ʿAbdullah al-Aḥmar and

ʿAbdulmajīd al-Zindānī, joined the prayer in Saʿdah's al-Hādī Mosque. As they left the mosque, Houthi followers angered them by chanting the slogan.[165] The slogan was also heard when the then American ambassador, Edmund Hull, sought to visit al-Hādī Mosque in Saʿdah city.[166] Hull complained to the Yemeni authorities about the incident, persuading the US embassy in Sanaʿa to exert pressure on the Yemeni government, which proceeded to arrest hundreds of Houthi supporters.[167] This incident further strengthened Ḥusayn al-Ḥūthī's anti-Americanism, as sources in the Zaydi community were adamant that the government's ferocious campaign against his supporters was largely instigated by outside pressures, emanating mainly from the US and Saudi Arabia.[168]

Tensions intensified when Ḥusayn's supporters continued chanting the slogan in ever more mosques after Friday prayers, leading to clashes between Houthis and security forces that ended in mass arrests. The government cut salaries of Houthi sympathizers among civil servants and teachers, or forcibly transferred them to other governorates. School students were expelled from schools, and entire schools were even closed down. Still, the Houthis refused to stop chanting considering the act an assertion of their right to freedom of expression in a democratic state.[169]

When Ali Abdullah Salih ordered Ḥusayn al-Ḥūthī to come to Sanaʿa and turn himself in to the government, the two men's relationship approached a crossroads. Rather than coming to the capital, on 27 April 2004 Ḥusayn sent a handwritten letter to President Salih, delivered by an envoy. In this letter, Ḥusayn assured the president, in polite and respectful terms that left everyone's dignity intact, of his loyalty to the Republic—yet circumstances, he continued, left him unable to meet President Salih in the capital. He explained that: 'I do not work against you, I appreciate you and what you do tremendously, but what I do is my solemn national duty against the enemy of Islam: America and Israel. I am by your side, so do not listen to hypocrites and provocateurs, and trust that I am more sincere and honest to you than they are.'[170]

At first glance, this letter resembles a commitment to the government on Ḥusayn's part, and the traditional courtesies and polite phrases of formal Arabic were undoubtedly meant to ease the tension and allow both sides to save face. Yet in his *malāzim* Ḥusayn had already publicly shown utter contempt for the politics of the Salih government. This letter was the expression of a point of no return in the relationship between Ḥusayn and the president: Ḥusayn did not go to Sanaʿa, he would not negotiate with the president, he did not answer to the president's authority. His refusal was thus tantamount to a break with the dialectics of Yemen's political system, based on co-option and patronage, and hence with Yemen's 'accepted and time-tested modes of regime-periphery relations'.[171]

In June 2004, ten of the most eminent Zaydi scholars, such as Muḥammad b. Muḥammad al-Manṣūr, Aḥmad al-Shāmī and Ḥamūd ʿAbbās al-Muʾayyad, published a manifesto, in which they recommended caution toward the ideas of Ḥusayn al-Ḥūthī, describing him as someone who had lost his way, and attributing to him 'words and actions that have no connection to the Āl al-Bayt and to the Zaydi school'.[172] They ended their statement with an outright repudiation of Ḥusayn and a refusal to associate with him. This manifesto, which appeared about two weeks before the eruption of fighting between the Yemeni army and the Houthis, was touted by the government as equivalent to religious approval of the coming military campaign in Saʿdah.[173] By that time, the rift among the Zaydi scholars had already changed in nature and reached a new level of escalation. In the same month, the first Saʿdah war erupted.

The al-Ḥūthī Family

Badr al-Dīn Amīr al-Dīn al-Ḥūthī, the father of Ḥusayn al-Ḥūthī, originated from the Bayt Zayd al-Ḥusniyyah family from Ḥūth, a *hijrah* settlement close to Khamir on the Ḥāshid tribe's territory in ʿAmrān governorate. He was born in 1926 in Ḥūth, but left Ḥūth as a young man to study in the city of Ḍaḥyān, north of Saʿdah city. After his studies, Badr al-Dīn, who suffered from asthma, was forced to leave the arid, dusty Saʿdah basin and move somewhere with a climate more conducive to his health. For his new place of residence, he chose Marrān in the Khawlān Massif, on the territory of the homonymous tribe, about 25 kilometres southwest of Saʿdah city—a fertile, mountainous, well-tempered region favoured by monsoon rainfall, where he pursued a life devoted to righteous living and teaching, on the geographical and political margins of Yemen.

Badr al-Dīn entered into four marriages. Two of his four wives had tribal backgrounds, the other two *sayyid* backgrounds. With his first marriage, he allied himself with a minor shaykhly lineage of Banī Baḥr, the numerically greatest section of Khawlān's Aḥlāf moiety.[174] This union produced four sons: Ḥusayn, Yaḥyā, ʿAbdulqādir and Aḥmad. His second marriage connected him with Āl al-Sittīn, one of Ḍaḥyān's influential *sayyid* families, and produced his sons Muḥammad and Ḥamīd. His third marriage was with a minor shaykhly lineage of Walad Yaḥyā, the numerically greatest section of the Marrān's

Jihwazī moiety, resulting in two sons, Amīr al-Dīn and Ibrāhīm. With his fourth marriage, Badr al-Dīn combined his al-Ḥūthī descent with an Āl al-ʿIjrī pedigree—a *sayyid* clan living in Mashhad near Ḥaydān, on the territory of Khawlān's Zubayd section. This connection produced his sons ʿAbdulmalik, ʿAbdulkhāliq, Najm al-Dīn, ʿAbdulsalām and ʿAlī.

All of Badr al-Dīn's sons, and numerous daughters, were born and raised in Khawlān. His intermarriage (*muṣāhirah*) with local shaykhly lineages was in line with the dominant pattern of local marriage customs in the Khawlān b. ʿĀmir region, which generally coincide in the tribal regions of Saḥār, Jumāʿah, and Khawlān.[175] During his 1980s fieldwork in this area, Gingrich observed that, with regards to the general type of marriage patterns, hypergamous marriage connections between female members of senior shaykhly lineages and locally influential *sādah* were standard practice.[176] In this case, a girl from the senior shaykhly lineage, such as the senior shaykh's daughter, is married to a *sayyid* family of high reputation. The *sayyid* family might be living in the tribal territory, or its vicinity, especially if the *sādah*'s services are needed locally. During most periods of Yemen's Islamic history, up to the end of the 1960s civil war, these marriage alliances with senior shaykhs were vital for the *sādah* for legal, political, and protection purposes. They retained their importance after the end of the war, when the *sādah* felt vulnerable and threatened by the anti-*sayyid* thrust of the Republic and emerging Salafi-Wahhabi groups, all of which made them dependent on tribal protection.

Through his marriage policy, Badr al-Dīn connected his family with both tribal moieties of the Khawlān tribes: Aḥlāf and Jihwaz. However, in something of a deviation from the historically documented trend of marriage customs in this region, he took wives from minor shaykhly lineages. Notably, he did not establish marriage connections with Khawlān's senior shaykhs, such as the senior shaykh of Khawlān, who is also the senior shaykh of Khawlān's Aḥlāf moiety, or other shaykhly lineages that became influential in republican times, and which would, according to custom, have offered the most suitable marriage partner for the al-Ḥūthī family. One reason for this, inter alia, is that it is important to shaykhs whether a *sayyid* family traces its descent to a 'great' imam. In the Saʿdah region, senior shaykhs prefer to marry off their daughters to such lineages. Yet, in spite of his excellent reputation and erudition, the shaykhs of Khawlān considered Badr al-Dīn a 'newly arrived' *sayyid* from Ḥūth or Ḍaḥyān (see below).[177]

There was also another factor in play. Historically, as sources from this family indicate, the Rawkān family—as the most senior shaykhly lineage in Khawlān—

had pursued hypergamous marriages with influential *sayyid* families in the area. But, with the profound socio-political changes and elite transformations that followed the 1960s civil war, which led to an increased importance of the shaykhs at the expense of the *sādah*, the family gradually abandoned this practice. In recent decades, the family of the senior shaykh of Khawlān has instead begun to concentrate on pursuing 'big' intra- and extratribal isogamous marriages (with other senior shaykhly lineages among and beyond the Khawlān tribe). The fall of the imamate in the late 1960s and the gradual assertion of the Republic dealt a blow to the standing of the *sādah*, and in the decades after the civil war the shaykhs emerged as the true source of political power. Elite marriages are a means of forming alliances, and although the *sādah* remained influential actors on the local level, for the influential shaykhs isogamous marriage connections with other shaykhly lineages often became essential to legitimizing and reproducing their shaykhly status and hegemony.

Badr al-Dīn's intermarriage with minor shaykhly lineages in Khawlān served to establish and strengthen close grassroots ties between his growing family and the Khawlān tribe. Having moved relatively recently from Ḍaḥyān in Jumāʿah to Marrān in Khawlān, Badr al-Dīn's marriage patterns quickly produced close kinship ties between al-Ḥūthī family members and their in-laws among the local tribes, on whose territory the family lived and whose special protection they enjoyed. One of Badr al-Dīn's sons explained:

> We grew up in our home and in the homes of our maternal uncles (*akhwāl*), close together, and thereby our connection has strengthened with our community and our companions, with whom we spent our childhood, and who are now the men of the area, and our relationships with many of them have been very close since our childhood. And by these connections we fraternized socially and tribally with the tribe, to the extent that the tribe would worry if we didn't feel a sense of belonging to it. Then the people of Marrān called upon us: 'Say: our land, and say: our companions' (*qūlū bilādnā wa qūlū aṣḥābnā*). We are deeply involved in the life of the tribe, both in Marrān and elsewhere, and serve [the people of] Marrān with all our efforts, with the goal of preserving our culture, religion and history and to protect them from the onslaught of tyranny (*ẓulm*), that has afflicted us and still threatens us.[178]

Interestingly, this source indirectly stressed (whether intentionally or not) that the children of Badr al-Dīn grew up both in the house of their father and in the houses of their tribal maternal uncles—in other words, with their tribal mothers. Furthermore, Badr al-Dīn's tribal in-laws emphasized both the kinship relations that emerged from intermarriage and their own importance in raising Badr al-Dīn's children. In these cases, the matrilateral relationships of

Badr al-Dīn's children facilitated phases of pre-marital residence among their tribal relatives. This obviously served to activate and reinforce the tribes' general obligation of protection vis-à-vis the *sādah*.[179]

In fact, in Sa'dah's tribal society, the relations of kinship still constitute such a tremendous value that it is normally unreasonable for an individual or a group to restrict kinship relations to one lineage only. Thus, the al-Ḥūthī brothers—as both *sādah* and 'members of the Khawlān tribe'—can be genealogically related through both patri- and matriline. Generally, the evidence for the al-Ḥūthī children's occasional residence among their mothers' tribal families does not contradict the dominant patrilocal model, but merely attests to the lineages' close ties with local tribal society. Indeed, we might say that patrilocality is so dominant that Badr al-Dīn's sons continuously refer to their 'maternal uncle's houses' (*buyūt al-akhwāl*), rather than to their 'mother's houses'.

Thus, intermarriage produced close family relations between Badr al-Dīn al-Ḥūthī's family and some sections of the Khawlān tribe. Tribal law gives special protection to particular categories of persons or places defined as 'inviolable' (*muḥarram*). Because of their non-tribal status, the tribes consider the *sādah* dependents of tribal protection, and their defence against outsiders of potential importance. Evolving family connections through marriage provided the al-Ḥūthī family with additional support and protection, because members of related tribal groups protect their kin from intrusion, regardless of whether the kin in question are tribesmen or *sādah*.

This protection is usually sealed by special tribal-*sayyid* treaties, which declare the *sādah hijrah* or *muhajjar* (under protection).[180] This *hijrah* protection is awarded only to specific *sādah* families, referred to as *muhajjarīn*, and its conditions are enshrined in contracts (termed, for instance, *qā'idat al-tahjīr*) with the leaders of specific tribes—usually those with whom the *sādah* live. The protective relationship between the al-Ḥūthī family and the local tribes was sealed in such a document. In the 1990s, local tribes issued a contract of assistance (*waraqat nuṣrah*) that declared the members of the al-Ḥūthī family *ṣuḥbah* (companions) of the tribe; this status, as a member of the al-Ḥūthī family explained, is 'equivalent to *hijrah*'.[181] Thus, whoever commits a wrong against or disgraces the al-Ḥūthī family is considered to have insulted the family's tribal guarantors (*ahl al-tahjīr* or *ḍumanā*) from Khawlān. The imperatives of *tahjīr* and '*aṣabiyyah* ('spirit of tribal solidarity' or 'cohesive drive against others', as Dresch translated it)[182] were also at work during the Sa'dah wars, when tribesmen protected Ḥusayn al-Ḥūthī and his brothers, who were targeted by the government.

Within this given social context, a relationship of mutual benefit evolved. Badr al-Dīn al-Ḥūthī settled in the tribal territory of Khawlān, protected by the tribes. In return, he performed learned and scholarly services for the tribes, such as teaching, scribal work, reading, drafting documents, mediation and arbitration. As a result, he was honoured by the tribesmen and given sufficient land to guarantee himself and his family an income. One of his sons explained:

> My father had great influence and popularity, because he served the people so well throughout his life. At that time he was everything for them: it was he who put everything in order and solved their conflicts, who taught the people, preached to them, guided and advised them. He answered all their questions and corrected them, and people asked him questions about medicine, arithmetic, history, industry, astronomy, geography, and above all about religion and *fiqh*. It was the task of Zaydi scholars like him to broaden the people's education in many aspects, in order to serve the community in the most excellent way possible. After his death his sons did the same in the same way, and, thank God, in the Saʿdah area our family is one of the most important families that serves the community with all its love and advice.[183]

This is a rather common description of the *sādah*'s role and function among the tribal host societies who give them shelter.[184] Due to their image as learned men of Islamic law and due to his neutrality, Badr al-Dīn and other local *sādah*—such as Ibrāhīm al-Shahārī, and also since 1990 Badr al-Dīn's eldest son Ḥusayn—acted as mediators, negotiators, and arbiters according to shariah law in tribal conflicts. Through this service and experience, they gained the same political know-how as the senior shaykhs: how to be impartial, wise and well informed about tribal politics, and how to negotiate face-saving compromises. The Zaydi tribesmen of Khawlān were in serious need of these services—the state's judicial system was weak, corrupt or absent. This absence included the senior shaykh of Khawlān, who, in his function as *radd* (final arbiter) of the Khawlān tribe, should—according to customary tribal law—have played a major role in conflict resolution. Other shaykhs openly supported Iṣlāḥ or Salafi groups in their regions, or demanded high financial compensation for their services beyond the means of ordinary tribesmen. Although the *sādah* did not assume formal leadership roles in republican society, many tribesmen in Khawlān sought out the al-Ḥūthī family's advice and service.[185]

The prominent role of Badr al-Dīn al-Ḥūthī as a 'newly immigrated' scholar aroused envy and resentment among some Khawlān shaykhs. The conflict between them and Badr al-Dīn was primarily one of rivalry over knowledge and power—an almost common feature of the relations between *sādah* and shaykhs. One tribal source described the reaction of a minor shaykh from the Marrān area to Badr al-Dīn's social activities:

> Badr al-Dīn al-Ḥūthī did not hail from this area, but from Ḥūth. He came to this tribe's area as a protected person (*bi-ḥaqq al-hijrah*), and there he acquired the tribal knowledge that actually belonged to the shaykh (*akhadha al-maʿrifah al-qabaliyyah allatī kānat ḥaqq al-shaykh*). Badr al-Dīn al-Ḥūthī attracted a lot of people and was soon able to manage their affairs. During the first Saʿdah war a follower of the shaykh was killed [by the Houthis], and in revenge the men loyal to the shaykh killed two of Badr al-Dīn's followers. There was then a *ṣulḥ* [contractual ceasefire] between the parties, but the conflict over hegemony over the tribe [*al-haymanah ʿalā al-qabīlah*] kept on flaring up during subsequent phases of the war.[186]

This conflict was due to the fact that shaykhly lineages usually monopolize the knowledge essential for performance of the shaykh's duties and responsibilities.[187] Badr al-Dīn's activities certainly had a salutary effect on the tribal community and social peace between ordinary tribesmen in Khawlān, but the long-established shaykhs viewed him as an 'immigrant' interfering in their areas of prerogative and responsibility.

In sum, the local reputation of Badr al-Dīn al-Ḥūthī and his sons was not only based on their famous pedigree and noble descent, but also on their services to the community, their personal merits, and on the fact that they maintained a modest lifestyle that contrasted sharply from that of some senior shaykhs. Their devotion to local communities' affairs both boosted their reputation among many ordinary tribesmen and simultaneously exacerbated existing tensions and rivalries over prestige, prerogatives and power between the *sādah* and not only local shaykhs but even the local state authorities. According to one of Badr al-Dīn's disciples, 'he was the government' (*huwa kāna l-ḥukūma*) in Marrān.[188] When his eldest son Ḥusayn began to address the marginalization of Saʿdah's Zaydis, the developmental imbalances of the region, and the corruption of the government, many local people started to 'gravitate toward him' (*injadhaba ilayhi al-nās*), making the Khawlān tribe the 'first incubator' (*al-ḥāḍana al-ūlā*) of the Houthi movement.[189]

A Divided Society

The social achievements and services of the al-Ḥūthī family were widely respected (and at times contested) among the locals. Yet by no means did a majority of the local people initially support Ḥusayn al-Ḥūthī's cause. The religious-political programme of the emerging movement led by Ḥusayn (which, after his death in 2004, was temporarily continued by his father Badr al-Dīn and in 2005 taken over by his half-brother ʿAbdulmalik) evoked resistance among large divisions of the local people. This resistance mainly came from local Sunnis of various shades, but the Houthi movement also generated profound tensions among Zaydis themselves, who subscribe to diverse political moralities: some adhere to the thought of Ḥusayn, while some consider his followers a renegade group, and some prefer a neutral status. The stronger the Houthi movement grew, the deeper the cleavages became within the Ṣaʿdah region's local communities, and the more passionately the people discussed the al-Ḥūthī family's entitlement to lead and represent the local Zaydis.

The struggle between local Houthi supporters and Houthi opponents only constituted a very distant echo of the great theological discussions that took place at a different level among the scholars.[190] Among tribes and shaykhs, knowledge of basic Zaydi principles and subjects of theological debate tended to be rather rudimentary. The simple, non-specialist population of the province particularly questioned the Houthi movement's justification for its representation of the local Zaydi community and the al-Ḥūthī family's (alleged or real) leadership entitlement within this movement.

In the first instance, the Houthi movement was portrayed as a radicalized deviation of the 'true' Zaydi doctrine, which threatened both the internal unity of Zaydism and its historical ability to coexist with other sects. Whereas the Houthis claimed to represent an authentic Yemeni Zaydism genuinely in need of protection from Salafi encroachment, their local opponents portrayed them as a radical, aggressive renegade group. This criticism was fuelled by prevalent tensions among the Zaydi scholars, such as Majd al-Dīn al-Mu'ayyadī's reportedly negative attitude to the Houthi movement and the words of Muḥammad ʿIzzān, who claimed to have found in Ḥusayn's writings elements with no equivalent in Zaydi doctrine (see above). Pejoratively dubbing the movement *Ḥūthah* (Houthism), a shaykh of the Munabbih tribe complained:

> We in Saʿdah knew nothing of the differences between the sects until the *Ḥūthah* showed up. The Houthis claim that the government is preventing them from practising their Zaydi *madhhab*, but that's not true, it is not a sectarian war (*ḥarb madhhabiyyah*), we are all Zaydis, no one has prevented us from practising our Zaydi *madhhab*. The Houthis themselves are the ones who are a threat to the Zaydi *madhhab*. There were tough discussions between Ḥusayn al-Ḥūthī and the great Zaydi scholars in the governorate, who adhere to the true Zaydi doctrine. The late Majd al-Dīn al-Mu'ayyadī, to whom the [tribal] people went, has warned them that Ḥusayn al-Ḥūthī's writings have no connection with Zaydism and that they undermine the foundations of [Zaydi] jurisprudence (*usūl al-fiqh*). All people know of the dispute between Majd al-Dīn and the Houthis and the quarrels they had. In the Summer Schools they do not study the acknowledged Zaydi sources. They study

> only the writings of Ḥusayn al-Ḥūthī. What they teach in the Summer Schools—the speeches and lectures of Ḥusayn al-Ḥūthī—is not based on the foundations of Zaydism. How can they say, therefore, that they would defend the Zaydi *madhhab*? Also, Muḥammad ʿIzzān, who was among the founders of the Believing Youth, said that the writings of Ḥusayn al-Ḥūthī are not founded on a sustainable basis.[191]

To many Zaydis, the new dynamic, self-assertive Zaydi activism, which had emerged from confrontation with Sunni extremism, was quite unfamiliar; some suspected that the Houthi movement was in fact not a revival of Yemeni Zaydism, but rather an externally operated movement influenced by Iranian Twelver Shiism. This suspicion was an expression of irritation at the gradual transformation of the historically tolerant and moderate Zaydism into ferocious Houthi activism. Criticism increased with the visible re-invention of ritual that accompanied the rise of the Houthis, namely the reinvigoration of the Zaydi versions of great Shiite festivities officially banned since the 1962 revolution, such as *ʿīd al-ghadīr*, *ʿīd al-mawlid al-nabawī*, and, from 2008, *ʿāshūrā* (the commemoration of the 680 CE martyrdom of the Prophet's grandson, Ḥusayn b. ʿAlī b. Abī Ṭālib, in Yemen historically called *yawm al-nushūr*).[192] Since 1962, these festivities had been suppressed by the republican government, so most among the younger Zaydi and *sādah* generations had not experienced them. The reinvigoration of these Zaydi festivities involved a great deal of soul-searching; they were meant as a demonstration of newly acquired Zaydi self-confidence and strength. The exaltation of these specifically Shia rituals served to create a natural dichotomy between Zaydi revivalists and Salafis. Critics, however, have tarred the Houthis with the brush of Iranian proxies because of their newly developed Zaydi activism and public celebration of Shia festivals.

Neither Badr al-Dīn nor Ḥusayn al-Ḥūthī publicly demanded the reinstallation of the imamate or the reactivation of the *sharṭ al-baṭnayn*, although in their eyes the imamate remained the ideal type of government. Still, the rejection of Zaydi hereditary doctrine is another central motif of resistance by many non-Hashemite Zaydis ('Qaḥṭānī Zaydis') against the Houthi movement. From the viewpoint of many non-*sayyid* people, the al-Ḥūthī family's *sayyid* status, in combination with their leadership role in the eponymous movement, is reactionary: anti-democratic, backward-looking, and directed against the social progress of equalization pursued since the 1962 revolution.[193] Indeed, the espousal of such simplistic and overzealous stances by some *sādah* in Yemen can be seen as a direct cause of the antagonism now directed against the Houthi movement. Vom Bruck argues that, before the 1962 revolution, 'rigid Hādawism' had been responsible for much of the frustration felt by many non-Hashemite Zaydis.[194] Since the 1962 revolution, republican discourse had drummed stereotyped anti-*sayyid* argumentation patterns into the people, who despised both the *sādah* and *sayyid* rule; now, at the turn of the century, these were being transformed into anti-Houthi discourse. This rationale focuses on the Houthis collectively, but especially targets the al-Ḥūthī family by asserting that they seek to restore the Zaydi imamate:

> They are convinced of their claim to power far beyond what you can imagine—convinced that only they have this legitimacy, and those who doubt it are doubting religion itself. They say that only the *baṭnayn* are entitled to rule, that is the descendants of al-Ḥasan and al-Ḥusayn, the sons of Imam ʿAlī b. Abī Ṭālib. The al-Ḥūthī family descends from them, and everyone else who claims power is an unbeliever (*kāfir*). The Houthis say that they are the rightful heirs of God on earth, and that ruling is their property and right, but they were robbed of it on 26 September 1962 [....]. They say what happened on 26 September 1962 was a coup d'état (*inqilāb*) and not a revolution.[195]

After the end of the 1960s civil war it had been widely believed that the imamate was consigned to history, but the al-Ḥūthī family's activism and popular appeal stimulated renewed discussion of the imamate's viability. A taboo was broken, and the issue was seized upon by government propaganda, political and sectarian detractors (such as Salafis and Iṣlāḥ) and anti-Zaydi elements in the army.

Houthi opponents delegitimized the al-Ḥūthī family's (alleged and real) claim to leadership and representation of the entire Zaydi community in not only political and religious, but also genealogical terms. As we have seen, the *sādah* in Yemen are seen as an immigrant community of putative ʿAdnānī (northern Arab) descent living among a tribal community of putative Qaḥṭānī (southern Arab) descent, and the *sādah*'s restrictive marriage policy was an appropriate strategy to enable the *sādah* to survive as a coherent group.[196] Since the 1962 revolution, public representations of the *sādah* as 'strangers in the house' and the refusal to recognize them as *awlād al-balad* ('genuine Yemenis') have continued to be based on their supposed outsider origins.[197] By contrast, the tribes, who claim descent from Qaḥṭān, see themselves as rooted in remotest antiquity as the indigenous inhabitants of Yemen. This is a very old line of reasoning against Yemen's *sādah*, already evident in the historical writings of al-Ḥasan al-Hamdānī (tenth century CE) and Nashwān al-Ḥimyarī (twelfth century CE).[198]

After the 1962 revolution and the abolition of the imamate, republican ideologues evoked a tradition that was both Qaḥṭānī and Islamic, as an alternative to the *taqlīd ahl al-bayt* (the verdicts and practices of the scholars who belong to the House of the Prophet) and Zaydi-Hādawī history.[199] A tribesman from Khawlān presented this line of reasoning:

> My head bursts whenever I see Yaḥyā al-Ḥūthī on television and he says from Germany that his community and his people in Khawlān b. ʿĀmir have been robbed and killed! He says: My community in Khawlān and my people and my companions, and so forth. Well, since when is he a Khawlān, and since when are we his people? They do not descend from Khawlān and are not related to Khawlān, neither closely nor remotely, they are only 'neighbours' (*jīrān*)—and you know the meaning of 'neighbour' among the tribes![200]

By addressing the al-Ḥūthī family's genealogical non-membership of Khawlān's local tribal community, this critic echoed the powerful rationale of the local/foreign dichotomy—a representation that also contradicts the al-Ḥūthī brothers' self-perception as 'members of the Khawlān tribe' (see above). By referring to the term *jār* (pl. *jīrān*; lit. neighbour), the source denies any relation between the local Khawlān tribe and the al-Ḥūthī family in terms of descent or genealogy, assigning them to the category of non-tribal people living under the tribe's protection—that is, 'protected clients' of the tribes who inhabit a social space that is properly outside tribal hierarchy.[201] As the term *jīrān* is conventionally used for non-tribal groups such as Jews, who require protection and cannot defend themselves, the use of this label is intended to defame the al-Ḥūthī family.

Many of these lines of reasoning were taken up by the government's anti-Houthi propaganda and were further elaborated in large-scale media campaigns. Since the beginning of the armed conflict in Saʿdah in 2004, the Yemeni government has launched several interrelated propaganda campaigns that sought to distance the Houthis in general and the al-Ḥūthī family in particular from authentic Yemeni society, politics, and even religion. The Houthis were portrayed as a foreign-backed renegade group seeking to sunder hard-won republican unity through brutal actions that oppressed the Yemeni people in hopes of returning the country to the dark ages of the imamate, based on interpretations of Zaydism that were fundamentally incorrect or out of step with the spirit of the times.[202]

Those Zaydis who neither joined the Houthi movement nor agreed with the government's actions faced the most difficult situation. In his exploration of conflicts of identification and loyalty within the Yemeni Zaydi community since the end of the imamate, King sees the Republic of Yemen as a project that originally aimed to neutralize sectarian loyalties and reduce the influence of the *sādah*.[203] As a result, in post-revolutionary Yemen, the Zaydis (in particular members of prominent *sayyid* families) were forced to adopt a regime-affirmative position, because an emphasis on their Zaydi identity and Zaydi activism would be considered subversive and opposed to the dominant republican idea of statehood and societal unity. As a consequence, Zaydis were deprived of the opportunity to criticize the government's military activity in Saʿdah on constitutionality or human rights grounds, because their critics would then have questioned their loyalty to the Republic. A few individuals, such as ʿAlī al-Daylamī and Muḥammad ʿAbdulmalik al-Mutawakkil, managed despite evident repression to hold such a line in Sanaʿa—and many paid dearly for it.[204]

Thus, at the outbreak of the first Saʿdah war (2004), local society was deeply divided. In his documentation of the province's penetration at the grassroots by 'ideas and activities of the Believing Youth', al-Mujāhid provides insight into the area's internal cleavages at the beginning of the armed confrontations between Houthis and government.[205] In no case were tribes or tribal sections uniform blocs; conflicts of allegiance ran through the communities at village level and, in some cases, even within families.

The Houthi movement was rejected particularly strongly in some districts of the governorate's extreme west, such as Shidāʾ and al-Ẓāhir, whose inhabitants were predominantly of Sunni-Shāfiʿī denomination and many of whom held Saudi passports.[206] The Houthis also met with considerable resistance in Munabbih, in the extreme northwest; tribal politics in Munabbih had historically focused on the preservation of relative autonomy, and among some central sections of the Munabbih, hostile attitudes toward the *sādah* prevailed.[207]

In other areas—Khawlān, Rāziḥ, Jumāʿah, Saḥār, Wāʾilah—the Houthi movement was able to count on the support of large parts of the local community, even before the outbreak of war in 2004; throughout the governorate, the Houthis were able to mobilize supporters and controlled numerous mosques and schools. The movement was particularly strong in areas where *sādah* accounted for a large proportion of the population. Ḍaḥyān in Jumāʿah, for example, just a few kilometres from Saʿdah city, is the home of many famous *sayyid* families, such as the al-Ṣaʿdī, al-ʿIjrī, al-Qāsimī, al-Ḍaḥyānī, Āl Ismāʿīl, al-Ḥūthī, Shams al-Dīn, and Ḥumrān families.[208] Ḍaḥyān is also well known for its many religious seminaries and institutes offering advanced studies in Zaydism, making it the country's largest hub for Zaydi scholarship;

Ḍaḥyān is sometimes referred to as the Zaydi 'Qom' in Yemen.[209] Ḍaḥyān's seminarians came from all over Upper Yemen, including some Saudi borderland tribes of Khawlān b. ʿĀmir stock, notably the Banī Mālik, Fayfā', and Balghāzī. In the early 1990s, Ḍaḥyān became the organizational centre of the Zaydi revival movement. The administrative headquarters of the Believing Youth and the management of the summer schools were located in Ḍaḥyān's Ḍakhm compound (*Mabnā Ḍakhm*). However, as a centre of religious learning with a high percentage of *sādah*, the relationship between '*sayyid* Ḍaḥyān' and 'tribal Majz' (Jumāʿah's nearby district capital) was often riven with rivalry and dissension.

Exploiting the millions of small, battery-operated cassette players that had flooded Yemen, in the early 2000s Ḥusayn al-Ḥūthī and his followers broadcast his lectures, exhorting the Zaydi people to resist and to reclaim their endangered Zaydi identity, pride and glory. To many tribesmen, Ḥusayn became a popular hero; but to their leaders, he was a provocative figure, for the shaykhs knew very well that if he managed to rally 'their' tribes to his cause, they would lose much of the supra-tribal power that they had acquired since the 1960s revolution. Consequently, very few shaykhs openly supported Ḥusayn's cause from the outset. A few shaykhs remained neutral, each for his own reasons. The rest were strongly opposed to the Houthi movement, which sooner or later could (and would) challenge their shaykhly status and authority and unhinge the foundations of the republican state.

This was the context of the outbreak of the first Saʿdah war in 2004: a powerful social revolutionary movement had arisen, directed against the political and economic empowerment of a small elite group that was the pillar of the republican order in Yemen's north. This movement featured equally powerful components of Zaydi revivalism and anti-Americanism. It was led by Ḥusayn al-Ḥūthī, a cleric-orator from a respected Zaydi family who was as brilliant as he was stubborn, and who resisted all of then President Salih's attempts to co-opt him. Whereas Ḥusayn's agenda met with approval among many ordinary people in Yemen's north, the Salih regime and its local beneficiaries regarded it as a challenge, a provocation, and a danger.

PART TWO

THE SA'DAH WARS (2004–10)

This part of the book reconstructs the course of the six Sa'dah wars and their aftermath, from the first battles in Marrān in June 2004 to the end of the sixth war in February 2010, the Houthis' seizure of power in Sa'dah governorate in March 2011, and their ascension to power at national level in late 2014. It consists of three chapters: Chapter 5 examines the first three rounds of conflict until the February 2006 mediation, which successfully brought the third war to a halt. Chapter 6 examines the fourth, fifth and sixth bouts, whose principal feature was the conflict's enormous territorial expansion. Chapter 7 summarizes the developments since the end of the sixth Sa'dah war in February 2010 that culminated in the Houthis' seizure of the capital Sana'a in September 2014.

5

INTO THE MAZE OF TRIBALISM

2004–6

In June 2004, the Saʿdah wars began with a police operation against Ḥusayn al-Ḥūthī in Marrān, in Saʿdah's western mountain range—a confrontation which subsequently developed into a conflagration. With hindsight, it can certainly be said that in the first phase of the conflict—during the first three bouts of war from 2004 to 2006—it could well have been possible to resolve or at least contain the conflict through mediation. In fact, several mediation initiatives took place, but their careless implementation by the government rather creates the impression that their failure was intended. However, the successful mediation at the end of the third war, which led to the conflict's first (and only) locally brokered contractual ceasefire, is clear evidence that it was in the hands of the warring parties to channel violence into mediation and contain the conflict. Indeed, at this particular time, the government wanted to end the war, in order to carry out the 2006 presidential and municipal elections. After these were held, the war resumed. After the eruption of the fourth war in February 2007, the internal dynamics of the conflict thwarted all further mediation efforts, including those of foreign governments, notably Qatar.

In light of the obvious lack of domestic political will to find a common solution, many factors contributed to the perpetuation and expansion of the crisis. These included 'external' reasons that drew on separate domestic and international driving forces.[1] The war became increasingly affected by political rivalries, by the emergence of a war economy, and by foreign powers such as Saudi Arabia, Libya and (allegedly) Iran. To a great extent, our image of the Houthi conflict is determined by these 'external' narratives, which highlight the regional and international relevance of the Houthi conflict, but fail to explain the dynamics pushing forward the battles on the ground.

By contrast, Part Two of this volume explores the minutiae of the conflict's local dynamics: it provides the interior view of a war machine which, by 2010, had driven almost the entire north of Yemen into a maelstrom of fratricidal warfare, and which would further expand in the following years. Many causes led to the enormous proliferation of the conflict throughout Yemen's north, though two were particularly noteworthy. First, the government's armed forces waged these wars with such brutality that the Houthi movement continuously grew in size and fighting ability, gaining sympathy from those who were suffering. Specifically, the indiscriminate violence of the armed forces and their deployment of mercenaries from tribes external to the Saʿdah region (notably from Ḥāshid) led to massive military enlistment among the tribes of Saʿdah in favour of the Houthis. Second, prevalent tribal feuds and rivalries began to merge with those of the Houthi conflict, as these tribes allied themselves either with the Houthis or with the government. These dynamics allowed distinctions to become blurred over time, playing into the common social overlap of ideological, political, sectarian, tribal, and personal interests. In particular, the involvement of the tribes, with their strong norms of collective honour and vengeance, unleashed an entirely new dynamic on an already complex and multilayered conflict.

The First War (22 June–10 September 2004)

Opinions vary as to whether the Houthis provoked the outbreak of the first war in Marrān in June 2004, or whether they were surprised by the armed forces' attack. In any case, the excessive force with which the army tried to crush the rebellion in Marrān apparently caught the Houthis largely unprepared. There is no other way of explaining Ḥusayn al-Ḥūthī's futile perserverance in the caves of Jurf Salmān in Marrān until his fatal end. However, in the course of the subsequent bouts of war, Houthi military capabilities developed rapidly, not least due to the increasing collaboration of battle-hardened tribes, and soon posed a serious challenge to the Yemeni army.

A secondary location of this first war was al-Razzāmāt in Wādī Nushūr in Wāʾilah (Kitāf district) east of Saʿdah city, the home region of Ḥusayn's friend and fellow parliamentarian ʿAbdullah al-Razzāmī. In Saʿdah city, too, Ḥusayn's supporters launched a number of operations targeting government forces. For the army, Ḍaḥyān and Āl al-Ṣayfī in the Saʿdah basin became a target as they were considered Believing Youth and Houthi strongholds. Numerous unsuccessful attempts at de-escalation and conflict mediation took place during the first Saʿdah war, clustered around the opening stages of the conflict in February 2004 and the first weeks of combat in June and July. The first war ended on 10 September 2004 with the death of Ḥusayn al-Ḥūthī.

Triggering the War

At the time of the outbreak of military confrontations, Colonel Yaḥyā ʿAlī al-ʿAmrī was governor of Saʿdah province. Born in 1950 in Dhamār, he was a GPC man. Prior to his appointment as governor in 2001, he held a number of sensitive posts in security and administration, including as chairman of the Ministry of the Interior Commissions on Yemen's borders with Oman and Saudi Arabia respectively, commander of Central Security in ʿAmrān, and vice minister of the interior.

Yaḥyā al-ʿAmrī's inauguration as governor of Saʿdah occurred at a time of unrest, coinciding with the rise of Ḥusayn al-Ḥūthī and the Houthi movement's formation out of the ranks of the Believing Youth. He was known as a 'first-class statesman' (*rajul dawlah min al-ṭirāz al-awwal*) who introduced a hitherto unknown efficiency and functional performance to the local authority offices in Saʿdah city and the districts; many of the administrative staff praised his 'strict management' (*idārah ṣārimah*).[2] Outside the local authority, his bold approach was met with distrust. In Saʿdah's highly personalized political system, shaped by tribal norms, al-ʿAmrī's aim to impose the state's sovereignty at all costs collided with the interests of the senior shaykhs, who resisted any attempt to reduce their influence. The local meddling of tribal authority in state administration had already become clear to Governor al-ʿAmrī during his inaugural visits to the districts. He quickly realized that tribesmen of certain influential shaykhs accounted for most of the administrative staff in the province, which led him to make the mocking remark: 'It seems that Saʿdah's entire administrative staff is [from] al-ʿAbdīn' (*yabdū ʿan waẓāʾif Ṣaʿdah kulluhā al-ʿAbdīn*).[3]

Yaḥyā al-ʿAmrī also embarked on a collision course with the province's second influential group, the Zaydi religious establishment. In an effort to curb the official influence of both the shaykhs and the Zaydi revival movement in the governorate, he instructed the administration to reject *sādah* applications to the civil service if the applicant showed an affinity with the Zaydi revival movement.[4] Hamidi reports that al-ʿAmrī, soon after taking up his post, passed a school in Saʿdah city named after Imam Ḥasan b. ʿIzz al-Dīn (d. 1128 in Hijrah Fallalah). Picking up some soil and throwing it at the plaque, he shouted that the age of the imams was over.[5] A local remarked, 'Governor Yaḥyā al-ʿAmrī reminds me of the myth you may have heard from locals about the rat that was the cause of the Ma'rib dam destruction. Colonel al-ʿAmrī is the one who sparked the conflict in Saʿdah with his recklessness and his aggressive behaviours.'[6]

President Salih had obviously installed Yaḥyā al-ʿAmrī in Saʿdah to bring the Houthis to heel, forgetting that his way of keeping adversaries in line had always been to appease, co-opt, listen to their grievances and not to try and force them to toe the Sanaʿa line unless absolutely necessary. Many believe that had Salih been more lenient and understanding of the Houthis' demands, he would not have brought a long war on himself and the country.

After having been appointed governor of Saʿdah, Yaḥyā al-ʿAmrī paid inspection visits to the districts. He returned from Ḥaydān and Sāqayn with 'bad impressions' (*inṭibāʿāt sayyʾiah*), because the state's sovereignty seemed to be weak, checkpoints were not under state security control, and many schools and mosques were under the influence of the Believing Youth. The district director in Ḥaydān informed the governor that Ḥusayn al-Ḥūthī had advised his followers to refrain from paying *zakāt* (a Muslim taxation on income and wealth) to the local authorities, and that much of the *zakāt* was instead being delivered to local *sādah*.[7] Al-ʿAmrī also heard about construction and fortification works by Ḥusayn's followers. Although the Houthis themselves denied any pre-war fortifications, anecdotal evidence of such activities was abundant in the Saʿdah region. A shaykh from Majz recalled:

> In the years leading up to the war, the Houthis had dug trenches in Marrān and Ḍaḥyān, and also in other areas. And when we asked what they were doing there, they said they would search for 'ancient treasures' (*kunūz al-awlayn*). We also asked them this when they were digging in the Ḥikmī Mountains in Marrān, because there were no treasures there. They replied that they were digging cisterns (*birak*) for the people in Marrān, for drinking water. But they were never used as cisterns. This became clear to us from the first to the third war. These 'cisterns' were their main hideouts and weapons storages.[8]

Al-ʿAmrī proceeded to monitor the situation in Marrān, which moved increasingly beyond the state's control. The slogan shouting of the Houthis spread to other districts and mosques, including al-Hādī Mosque in Saʿdah city, and also reached the Grand Mosque in Sanaʿa. On 18 June 2004, Yemeni security forces arrested 640 people for chanting the Houthi slogan outside the Grand Mosque in Sanaʿa after Friday prayers.[9] According to some sources, children and plainclothes officers had been deployed to observe and identify these men prior to their detention.[10]

War Course

On 20 June 2004, President Salih sent Yaḥyā al-ʿAmrī on an expedition (*taḥarruk mīdānī*) to the Khawlān Massif to arrest Ḥusayn al-Ḥūthī, to arm some local shaykhs and—so some say—to identify possible military targets in the region.[11] His passage was blocked by residents as tribesmen fired on a military checkpoint. At the same time, Ḥusayn al-Ḥūthī sent Shaykh Ḥasan Ḥamūd Ghatāyah as his envoy to Interior Minister Rashād al-ʿAlīmī, in order to convince the minister that his intentions were peaceful.[12] On 22 June, Ḥasan Ḥamūd Ghatāyah journeyed again from Marrān to Sanaʿa to meet the minister; he was surprised in al-Malāḥīṭ west of Marrān by the advance of a large military force including heavy weapons and tanks from ʿAbs and the surrounding barracks in the Tihāmah lowlands. He turned for clarification to the military commander of the northwest, ʿAlī Muḥsin al-Aḥmar, only for the latter to arrest him.[13]

Meanwhile, a battalion of regular troops and irregulars or 'volunteers' (pl. *mutaṭawwiʿūn*) from the Ḥāshid confederation were advancing on Marrān from the al-Madarraḥ area in Sufyān, where it had waged a punitive campaign against Shaykh Mujāhid Ḥaydar. Since the 1980s, Mujāhid Ḥaydar of the Sufyān (Bakīl) in northern ʿAmrān governorate was in opposition to both President Salih and the al-Aḥmar clan of al-ʿUṣaymāt (Ḥāshid).[14] Mujāhid Ḥaydar controlled a section of the highway that runs from Sanaʿa through ʿAmrān to Saʿdah city. In 2004, shortly before the outbreak of the first Saʿdah war, Ḥusayn al-Aḥmar wanted to travel on this road, but Mujāhid Ḥaydar blocked his passage. After the exchange of verbal threats and the mobilization of a large number of tribal fighters on both sides, Ḥusayn al-Aḥmar withdrew, but convinced President Salih on his return to Sanaʿa to send a punitive expedition to Sufyān to arrest Mujāhid Ḥaydar for 'highway banditry' and blocking the road. When the armed forces failed to prevail against Mujāhid Ḥaydar, he was asked to negotiate directly with the president in Sanaʿa. Having arrived in the capital, he was kept waiting and eventually returned empty-handed to

Sufyān. While he was in Sanaʿa, the armed forces had been dispatched from Sufyān to Marrān to move against Ḥusayn al-Ḥūthī. Observers suggest that Mujāhid Ḥaydar was held up in Sanaʿa for fear that he would rally his tribesmen to hinder troop movements from Sufyān to Marrān, or would even come to Ḥusayn al-Ḥūthī's aid, although at that time Mujāhid Ḥaydar was not considered a Houthi supporter.

The joint advance on Marrān by the armed forces and the Ḥāshid mercenaries on 22 June 2004 marks the eruption of what became known as the first Saʿdah war. The military campaign's aim was to arrest or kill Ḥusayn al-Ḥūthī in Marrān and to quell the 'rebellion'. This first war concentrated on the Marrān mountains, a partly inaccessible but densely populated and agriculturally intensively utilized region in the Khawlān massif, which was not only the bastion of the Houthi movement but also populated by thousands of civilians. During the first Saʿdah war, the government unleashed the full force of its jets, helicopter gunships, tanks, armour and artillery to pound the lightly armed Houthis in their mountainous hideouts. Houthi supporters claimed that some of the attacks on Marrān by planes and rockets came from the Saudi region, and accused the Saudi air force of bombing villages in support of the Yemeni army, a charge Riyadh denied.[15]

Fighting also escalated in al-Razzāmāt, in Wādī Nushūr in Wāʾilah (Kitāf district) east of Saʿdah city. This was the home region of Ḥusayn al-Ḥūthī's unswervingly loyal friend and fellow MP ʿAbdullah al-Razzāmī.[16] These confrontations were provoked by ʿAbdullah al-Razzāmī and his fellow tribesmen and aimed at distracting a part of the army from Marrān and thus taking the pressure (*takhfīf al-ḍaghṭ*) off Ḥusayn al-Ḥūthī. At the same time, the tribal feud between Āl al-Razzāmāt and Āl al-Nimrī on the one side and Āl Mahdī (led by Shaykh Fāyiz ʿAbdullah al-ʿAwjarī) on the other flared up again, further destabilizing the situation in Wādī Nushūr. At this time, however, the majority of Āl Mahdī were not fighting the Houthis, but rather their own opponents of Āl al-Razzāmāt and Āl al-Nimrī, who thus were subjected to a double attack by the government and their tribal enemies.

Houthi supporters also launched a number of operations in Saʿdah city targeting government forces with the aim of taking the pressure off Ḥusayn in Marrān, who was surrounded by the full military force of the army. In the city, Houthi loyalists strove to show their presence in the governorate's capital, thereby encouraging other supporters. They were able to break through security barriers and to access the central security precinct. A brief government siege of the city, along with clashes with Houthi followers, began a few days after the eruption of the war in Marrān. As a deterrent, the corpses of killed Houthis were tied by their feet to military vehicles and dragged through the streets.[17]

The fourth arena of the first Saʿdah war was Ḍaḥyān and Āl al-Ṣayfī in the Saʿdah basin, a few kilometres north of Saʿdah city. To the west, Āl al-Ṣayfī borders directly on Ḍaḥyān. As we have seen, Āl al-Ṣayfī and Ḍaḥyān were considered Believing Youth strongholds; Badr al-Dīn al-Ḥūthī owned a house in Āl al-Ṣayfī. Locals report that during the attack on Āl al-Ṣayfī and Ḍaḥyān, which was conducted with utmost rigour, dead and injured Houthi loyalists were run over with tanks. This pre-emptive strike, which proved a strong deterrent, and the following military siege of Ḍaḥyān aimed at destroying one of the most important Houthi centres and preventing an influx of fighters from this area into Marrān to support Ḥusayn. For this purpose, roads were blocked throughout the governorate, either by the army or by tribes close to the government.

Composition of the Armed Forces

The majority of troops deployed against the Houthis belonged to the First Armoured Division (*al-firqah al-ūlā madarraʿ*; also called *firqah*) under the command of ʿAlī Muḥsin al-Aḥmar and its subunits, such as the 310th Armoured Brigade stationed in ʿAmrān, led by Brigadier General Ḥamīd al-Qushaybī.[18] The number of soldiers mobilized during the first war is estimated at 20,000.[19] Yet the reliability of such figures, especially those from government sources, is doubtful, as leading commanders of the army were suspected of pervasive use of the practice of 'ghost soldiers'—individuals listed on the military payroll who never or rarely worked, whose pay was pocketed by the military elite and whose equipment was sold on the black market—and stonewalled attempts at audits that would have implicated them.[20]

Hamidi argues that the bulk of the regular forces in action in Saʿdah province were Sunnis, many of them reservists of the former South Yemen army who had been defeated by the northern forces in 1994.[21] In 2004, a decade after their defeat, the Salih government threw them into combat in Saʿdah province, assuming that the occasional domination of the Sunni south by the Zaydis during the imamate had inspired resentment and that southern soldiers would therefore be better motivated to fight armed Zaydi villagers. Salmoni, Loidolt and Wells argue, however, that the Yemeni government employed 'Sunnis from Hashidi areas—and reputed former Afghan Salafi mercenaries that the [Government of Yemen] had previously used in the south'.[22] My understanding of this situation is more akin to the latter interpretation: that the Sunni southerners who did fight against the Houthis in 2004 were a combination of those who had fled the south in the 1980s and returning fighters from the Afghan war of the same decade. Both of these groups fought for the north in 1994, and were patrons of General ʿAlī Muḥsin. Nonetheless, the sources here appear to contradict one another somewhat.

In addition to regular troops, irregular levies participated in the conflict from its inception. During the first Saʿdah war, they did not play as prominent a role as they would in later phases of the conflict; but from the very beginning their impact was crucial. Most of these irregulars came from the Ḥāshid confederation, which, due to its history and the political positioning of many of its shaykhs, has been seen as particularly close to the republican government.[23] Moreover, many Ḥāshid warriors had been directly deployed from a tribal feud in Sufyān to the war scene in Marrān. Many Ḥāshid tribesmen served in the regular forces under ʿAlī Muḥsin (himself a Ḥāshid tribesman from Sanḥān), but most of them participated as volunteers (pl. *mutaṭawwiʿūn*) or mercenaries (pl. *murtaziqah*). During their combat mission in Marrān and other arenas of the first war, some of them were led by their own shaykhs, others fought under the command of the ʿIyāl al-Aḥmar—the sons of ʿAbdullah al-Aḥmar, especially Ḥusayn—and still others fought side by side with radical Sunni 'Religious Committees' (pl. *lijān dīniyyah*), many of whom had already fought for the regime in 1994 against the 'infidel South'.[24] These irregulars, too, enjoyed the backing of General ʿAlī Muḥsin, who had himself embraced Salafism.[25] The systematic recruitment of militant Sunnis increased considerably from the fourth war onwards, when in 2007 the government began to rally them deliberately to its cause.[26]

Despite the fact that tribal leaders of the Ḥāshid confederation and numerous other tribes held senior military positions, the government avoided appointing shaykhs and their tribesmen as regular army officers and soldiers in the Saʿdah wars. The reasons for this exclusion of local tribal leaders were manifold: the army's internal balance of power needed to be preserved, conflicting tribal and parochial interests needed to be kept out of the military, and the army needed to be prevented from becoming involved in local feuds.[27] Therefore, during the six rounds of war, tribal shaykhs were not deployed as regular army officers, but almost exclusively as leaders of irregular militias. These irregulars performed many tasks. They were able to access remote areas that the army, with its heavy gear, could not reach, especially in the rugged mountains of Marrān. They could move easily from one area to another because of their inconspicuous clothing. The military provided the militias with weapons and supplies.

Whereas the Ḥāshid were engaged against the Houthis from the beginning of the war, the shaykhs of the Saʿdah region itself were hesitant to join the battle. When it became clear that the regular army and the Ḥāshid mercenaries were experiencing difficulties in bringing the situation fully under control, on 16 August President Salih gathered tribal shaykhs from the Saʿdah region in the capital and urged them to 'play their role to eradicate this evil seed and to control extremism' in their region. Yet the shaykhs' responses were mixed, ranging from affirmation that the Houthi rebellion was indeed dangerous to the state, to complaints that the tribal leadership of Saʿdah had not been consulted until after the situation had spun out of control.[28] This call to arms was only the first in a long series of government attempts to rally the shaykhs and tribes of Saʿdah to fight as irregulars. Yet this was a controversial matter—although Saʿdah's shaykhs fully agreed on the need to curb and combat Ḥusayn's influence, they could not come to terms with the state's management of the conflict, which disregarded the shaykhs' vital and prestigious role in tribal mediation. Instead, the government was proposing to throw their tribesmen into battle and expose them to the chain reactions of blood revenge and tribal feuding from which it wanted to protect its regular army. The shaykhs knew that the open participation of their tribesmen would lead to further deterioration, not resolution, of the conflict. Moreover, many of them were deeply concerned at the incursions of armed Ḥāshid mercenaries into their tribal territories.[29]

One side effect of the deployment of irregulars was the high level of collateral damage and incidents of friendly fire. On 25 August, 135 were killed in one fell swoop when a group of plainclothes irregulars attempted to infiltrate a suspected Houthi hideout and fell victim to a Yemeni Air Force strike; the number of casualties was downplayed by government media.[30] Coordination between the army, air force, Central Security forces and irregulars was poor throughout the conflict.[31] The armed forces' failure quickly and decisively to end the rebellion sent shockwaves through the military and security apparatus. During the increasingly bloody conflict, sources from the Ministry of Defence reported bitter finger pointing between General ʿAlī Muḥsin and President Salih's son and commander of the Special Forces, Ahmad Salih, as well as arguments between the Ministry of Defence and the Ministry of the Interior over field tactics and deployment techniques.[32]

The violent approach of the Yemeni army was causing considerable collateral damage without achieving substantial military gains.[33] The military leadership, which initially had announced that it would end the rebellion in Marrān within forty-eight hours, began to throw more and more soldiers into the conflict and to expand its attacks to further regions where it suspected Houthi loyalists. The destruction of villages and civilian infrastructure by army shelling, air bombardment and indiscriminate military violence amplified grievances among civilians of the war zone, further ignited the conflict and contributed to its endurance. As a consequence, many who had not originally sympathized with Ḥusayn al-Ḥūthī's cause began to side with the rebels, in some instances taking up arms in solidarity with fellow villagers, relatives or tribesmen harmed in the fighting.

Mediation

As stated above, there were multiple unsuccessful attempts at de-escalation and arbitration during the first Saʿdah war, both in its preliminary phase in February and as combat began in the summer. The appointment of mediators was not surprising, as mediation is a socially accepted and preferred means of conflict management in Yemen's tribal and political environment—setting up mediation teams at times of heightened tensions and eruption of armed conflict is rather common practice. Chapter 1 has outlined the tribes' well-established and often effective mechanisms for channelling crises into negotiation. In the context of the Saʿdah wars, however, nothing conclusive emerged from mediation, as conventional mechanisms of crisis prevention and conflict control found limited application. There were four reasons for this.

First, in 2004, the Houthi conflict was not yet a 'tribal' conflict. Thus the application of what was probably Yemen's most developed method of conflict regulation—mediation according to tribal customary law (*ʿurf*)—was limited. The early Houthi conflict did not correspond to the pattern of a 'traditional' tribal conflict of honour and territoriality, which could be contained and resolved through the procedure of sureties, guarantors, and arbitration according to *ʿurf*. Rather, at this stage it was a political dispute between a *sayyid* and the state. Only at later stages of the Saʿdah wars, with the increasing involvement of tribes, was tribal mediation given a stage.

Second, President Salih obstructed the assignment of mediators with the status and capabilities to mediate at national level. Mediation—particularly successful mediation—is associated with a high gain in prestige and reputation for the mediator himself. Sources close to President Salih have indicated that multiple proposals on notably competent and influential mediators had been submitted to the president, all of which he dismissed.[34] In the years to come, this behavioural pattern solidified. In a cycle repeated throughout the war, any mediator who was too successful was quickly villainized as a disingenuous Houthi supporter, discredited and pushed out of negotiations; in later phases of the conflict, this fate would befall Yaḥyā al-Shāmī, Fāris Manāʿ, and ʿAbdulqādir Hilāl.

Instead, and this is the third reason, Salih appointed far too great a number of mediators, who moreover were all to work together on one team. Most of these people were not neutral for one reason or another. For a mediator to be acceptable, there are certain requirements: he must have personal integrity and prestige, and he cannot be a member of one of the two groups involved; equidistance from the parties to the conflict is essential. Yet almost all mediators appointed by the government had a partisan background: they were Houthis, *sādah*, shaykhs, Zaydi scholars, Iṣlāḥ party members, opposition politicians, or military officers. It was therefore impossible for the team members to reach a common understanding amongst themselves, let alone broker a deal between Ḥusayn al-Ḥūthī and the government. This competition and lack of cooperation led to tensions within the team, rendering a unified stance vis-à-vis Ḥusayn al-Ḥūthī and the state impossible.

The fourth and final obstruction to mediation as a solution was the fact that the armed forces were acting out of sync with the political leadership, and frequently sabotaged mediation endeavours. On several occasions, the armed forces prevented mediation team members from reaching Ḥusayn al-Ḥūthī in Marrān. The government would then communicate to the general public that Ḥusayn al-Ḥūthī had refused to receive the team.

As the International Crisis Group has ably pointed out, it is difficult to determine precisely how many mediation attempts took place from 2004.[35] The overall number ranges from five to eight. Because of conflicting data in the literature and among locals—and even among the mediation team members themselves—it is difficult to reconstruct the complete list of mediators and the total number of their missions.

Mediation endeavours commenced in spring 2004. The government appointed as mediator the Zaydi scholar Muḥammad b. Muḥammad al-Manṣūr (member of Ḥizb al-Ḥaqq's High Committee and deputy mufti of the Republic). A former teacher of Ḥusayn al-Ḥūthī, Muḥammad b. Muḥammad al-Manṣūr was very close to him, despite certain doctrinal differences.[36] He was sent to Marrān three times, but his mediation—often referred to as 'the first mediation'—yielded no results.[37] In an interview with Dorlian, he explained the reason for the failure: 'The problem lies in the Wahhabi presidential advisers. Yaḥyā al-ʿAmrī and ʿAlī Muḥsin al-Aḥmar did not want me to meet with Ḥusayn al-Ḥūthī. I spent several days in Saʿdah and at the end of the eleventh day, I returned empty-handed to Sanaʿa.'[38]

As we know, in the last days before the outbreak of the first war, Ḥusayn al-Ḥūthī sent Shaykh Ḥasan Ḥamūd Ghatāyah as his envoy to Sanaʿa to convince the government that his intentions were peaceful, but Ghatāyah was arrested on the way by General ʿAlī Muḥsin. Immediately after the launch of the military campaign on 22 June, President Salih commissioned Yaḥyā al-Ḥūthī and Ṣāliḥ al-Wajmān to negotiate with Ḥusayn al-Ḥūthī in Marrān; their mission was often referred to as the 'second mediation'. Yaḥyā al-Ḥūthī was Ḥusayn's full brother and an MP.[39] Ṣāliḥ al-Wajmān was a shaykh from the al-Ṣuḥn area near Saʿdah city. Apart from his close connections to both Ḥusayn al-Ḥūthī and President Salih, he was apparently appointed due to his rare status as both *sayyid* and shaykh.[40] Yaḥyā al-Ḥūthī and Ṣāliḥ al-Wajmān travelled to al-Malāḥīṭ in order to proceed to Marrān. Between al-Malāḥīṭ and Marrān, the roads were jammed with military equipment, combat aircraft was operating, and the roads were blocked almost every 100 metres by tribal or military checkpoints. In Wādī Liyah near al-Malāḥīṭ, unable to advance to Marrān, they had to abandon their mission.[41] The government communicated to the general public that Yaḥyā al-Ḥūthī and Ṣāliḥ al-Wajmān had managed to reach Ḥusayn al-Ḥūthī in Marrān, but had failed to convince him to surrender.[42]

A few days later, another mediation committee was formed, which started off a third and a fourth attempt at mediation. This committee was significantly larger; in addition to Yaḥyā al-Ḥūthī and Ṣāliḥ al-Wajmān, it comprised about a dozen members, including ʿUthmān Mujallī (shaykh and MP), ʿAbdulsalām Hishūl Zābiyah (shaykh and MP), ʿAlī Ḥusayn al-Munabbihī (shaykh and MP), Ṣāliḥ b. Shājiaʿ (shaykh), Ibrāhīm Muḥammad al-Wazīr, Ṣalāḥ Falītah, ʿAbdullah al-ʿIzzī, Ismāʿīl ʿAlī al-Ḥūthī, ʿAbdulkarīm Jadbān (MP), ʿAlī Hādī al-Ṣaylamī, Muḥammad Ḥasan Jibālah, and Aḥmad Nāṣir al-Baʿrān.[43] The committee reached Marrān during a brief pause in hostilities, but fighting soon resumed. ʿAbdulkarīm Jadbān called General ʿAlī Muḥsin and urged him to stop the fighting—ceasefire being a prerequisite for any mediation—in order to enable the mediators to reach Ḥusayn al-Ḥūthī in Marrān. Yet ʿAlī Muḥsin replied that this was impossible. As the battles went on, the mediation team was, again forced to withdraw. Government media reported once again that Ḥusayn al-Ḥūthī had refused to receive them.[44]

The mediation team continued to grow. The fifth committee, considerably inflated, included an astounding thirty-four members. The chairman of this committee was again Muḥammad b. Muḥammad al-Manṣūr, and several shaykhs, ministers, representatives of political parties, religious scholars and ex-generals were added into the mix. The government was apparently trying to give all stakeholders a share in the mediation leadership, thereby completely reversing the principle of neutrality and equidistance.

In addition to the members of prior mediations, the committee now comprised the shaykhs Muḥammad Nājī al-Ghādir, ʿAbdullah Nājī Dāris, Muḥammad Nājī al-Shāyif, Ḥusayn al-Aḥmar, Ghālib Nāṣir al-Ajdaʿ, and Muḥammad ʿAbdullah Badr al-Dīn. Also appointed were representatives of political parties: Ḥamūd ʿUbād (minister of endowments and Islamic guidance), ʿAdnān al-Jifrī (former minister of justice), ʿAbdulwahhāb al-Ānisī (assistant secretary-general of Iṣlāḥ), Muḥammad Qaḥṭān (head of Iṣlāḥ's political department), Muḥammad Ḥusayn al-ʿAydarūs (assistant secretary-general of the GPC), Aḥmad Muḥammad al-Shāmī (chairman of Ḥizb al-Ḥaqq), ʿAbdulmalik al-Mihklāfī (secretary-general of the Nasserite Party), Muḥammad ʿAbdulmalik al-Mutawakkil (assistant secretary-general of the Union of Popular Forces Party), and Muḥammad Ghālib Aḥmad (member of the Yemeni Socialist Party's political bureau). There were also religious scholars of the Yemeni Scholars' Association (*jamʿiyyat ʿulamāʾ al-Yaman*): Ḥamūd al-Hitār (chairman of the Religious Dialogue Committee), Ḥusayn al-Hidār, and Ḥamūd ʿAbbās al-Muʾayyad (who was sick). They were joined by ex-generals Muḥammad Ḥātim al-Khāwī and Muḥammad Shāʾif Jārallah, and some others besides.[45]

The ever-increasing size and heterogeneity of the mediation team obstructed its work. Mediators were lacking neutrality: too close to the Houthis, too close to the government, too close to the Salafis. Committee participants were too overtly political, lacked local roots, nurtured preconceived ideas about the parties to the conflict or lacked sufficient knowledge about the Saʿdah region.[46] Rather than finding common ground, the committee members were working at cross-purposes. Many of them were affected in one way or another by the conflict itself. The mediation team might have succeeded had there been consensus among them. Instead, the mediation was sabotaged by disagreement. A committee member recalled:

> Confusion (*labs*) prevailed in the mediation team as the members were divided into three fractions: a group that wanted to solve the conflict, a group that collaborated with the Houthis, and a group that wanted to perpetuate the conflict out of hatred (*nikāyah*) for the other two groups. It was a very complex situation.[47]

This extremely large and diverse committee managed to write a letter and send it on 27 July 2004 to Ḥusayn al-Ḥūthī. They asked for his cooperation with regard to their planned visit to Marrān. Ḥusayn replied three days later, in writing, that the road to Marrān was impassable because of the military campaign.[48] Instead of dispatching the entire committee, smaller sub-committees were set up and sent to Marrān. A five-member sub-committee led by Yaḥyā al-Ḥūthī managed to reach Ḥusayn al-Ḥūthī in Marrān.[49] A second, twelve-member sub-committee headed by Muḥammad b. Muḥammad al-Manṣūr failed in its attempt to reach Marrān, as the helicopter pad provided by Ḥusayn al-Ḥūthī was shelled by combat aircraft.[50] It has been rumoured that the armed forces under ʿAlī Mushin hoped to short-circuit mediation by commencing operations while mediation teams were either with Ḥusayn al-Ḥūthī or travelling to Saʿdah, raising the spectre of internal regime schisms linked to Salafi influence within the military.[51]

The mediation teams and the government gave conflicting versions about the failure of negotiations. On 5 August, Muḥammad b. Muḥammad al-Manṣūr explained the reasons for the failure of mediation in a letter to the president: on arrival in Saʿdah, the delegation was informed by the governor and ʿAlī Mushin that they could not contact Ḥusayn al-Ḥūthī due to combat in the area. Fighter planes had taken off for Marrān just as the delegation was about to do the same. Thus, they could neither mediate nor even meet with Ḥusayn al-Ḥūthī and talk to him.[52] Even so, the government communicated to the public that Ḥusayn al-Ḥūthī was unresponsive and refused to meet with the committee.[53] After this episode, further mediation was terminated, and would only recommence at the end of the second war in April 2005.

Death of Ḥusayn al-Ḥūthī

Mediation attempts had no impact on the first war's military operations, which, apart from a few short-lived ceasefires, grew unabated. On 5 August 2004, the government announced the capture of Ḥusayn al-Ḥūthī's last stronghold in Marrān and said it was conducting door-to-door searches for him.[54] But the affair was far from over. Ḥusayn al-Ḥūthī had taken refuge in the Jabal Salmān region near Marrān, a steep mountain area inaccessible to the army's tanks and other vehicles. Due to its steepness and ruggedness, this mountain was known as Salmān Cliff (Jurf Salmān), its mighty boulders hiding deep caves inside the rock.[55]

On 19 August, military sources claimed that the war had already killed 900 people in total.[56] Among the dead were some Houthi field commanders, but not Ḥusayn al-Ḥūthī himself. On the same day, the government claimed that control had been established over all the regions in which Ḥusayn's followers had previously been positioned and that they had been pushed into the Jurf Salmān area.[57] On 2 September, Brigadier General Ḥamīd al-Qushaybī was seriously wounded. In the last days of the war, the armed forces bombed and shelled the caves of Jurf Salmān in which Ḥusayn had sought refuge with dozens of his followers and family members and more than fifty injured, who had been without food and ammunition for several days. In the battle for Jurf Salmān, the army used excessive force: it was said to have deployed about 3,000 soldiers for this operation alone.[58] Tear gas and petrol were doused into the caves and set alight.[59] Ḥusayn was killed in the early hours of 10 September. His death came at the end of a two-day siege on the Houthi-defended cave by Yemeni Central Security Forces (CSF).[60] The cave's entrance had been bombed and all inmates had temporarily lost consciousness (from either the gas or the smoke). Afterwards, Ḥusayn had emerged from the cave with two followers in order to surrender. Everyone else was evacuated out of the cave, and the women and children led elsewhere. An officer shot Ḥusayn at point-blank range.[61] His body was transported to an undisclosed medical facility in Sanaʿa.[62]

Anxious to put an end to this painful episode, the Republic's leadership was quick to declare military victory and a unilateral end to the fighting. After Ḥusayn's followers challenged government reports about his death, photos of his corpse were released on the website of pro-government newspaper *al-Thawrah*, and large posters were hung up in the streets of Saʿdah city.[63] The government expected that the triumphant plastering of the city with the image of Ḥusayn's body would be regarded by his family and disciples as both sacrilegious and a social insult. The strategy was meant as a deterrent to his followers.[64]

Yet this approach proved to be a grave error—it had the opposite effect. In the specific religious context of Shiism, the 'martyrdom' of Ḥusayn al-Ḥūthī was ultimately hugely conducive to the Houthi movement's development. As Gellner explained in the case of al-Ḥusayn b. ʿAlī (d. 680 in Karbala), a violent death elevated him to almost mythical levels:

> [...] the fact that he [al-Ḥusayn b. ʿAlī] was a victim of an at least putatively Muslim ruler makes it even easier for the religious leaders to de-legitimize political authority and mobilize opposition, in a way which must be the envy of more self-consciously revolutionary ideologies [...] The Shiite Martyrdom was perpetrated by Muslim rulers, and its symbolism can be used to de-legitimize Muslim rulers [...].

The martyrdom was fiercely avenged and revenge is also required when the politico-religious drama is re-enacted.[65]

This testimony to Shiism's capacity for revolutionary mobilization is perfectly logical, given that a cult of the martyred personality is at the very core of Shiism. Thus, the battle for Jurf Salmān and the martyrdom of Ḥusayn al-Ḥūthī became a mise en scène of unfinished Shia history and the beginning of the grand narrative of Ḥusayn al-Ḥūthī's mystification. Remembering the battle for Jurf Salmān, a Houthi commander commented: 'This is a new Karbala, another Karbala. This is Karbala, and this is the Ḥusayn of Karbala. We have given the blood of innocents from the sons of Ḥusayn and the likes of Ḥusayn.'[66] Ever since September 2004, the Houthis have interpreted the events of Marrān and Ḥusayn al-Ḥūthī's death as an invocation of the battle of Karbala and a stand against oppression, using these symbol dynamics to strengthen the resolve of the people against the Salih regime. Far from acting as a deterrent, the martyrdom of Ḥusayn al-Ḥūthī led to 'petrification' (*taḥjīr*) of his followers' convictions. When asked a few months later if he regretted the death of his son Ḥusayn, Badr al-Dīn al-Ḥūthī responded: 'No, I do not regret it'.[67]

First Interim

The first Saʿdah war was not decided by *ṣulḥ* (contractual ceasefire) between the two warring parties, but rather by *ḥasm* (decisive military defeat) of the Houthis. After the *ḥasm* President Salih tried to reach a *ṣulḥ*, too, particuarly to accommodate the Gulf States which felt particularly threatened by the spread of Shiism due to their geostrategic position, but also to strengthen his own position relative to both the Houthis and the domestic opposition, notably General ʿAlī Muḥsin and the Iṣlāḥ party. But the intransigence of Badr al-Dīn al-Ḥūthī and ʿAbdullah al-Razzāmī and Salih's stalling tactics ultimately prevented the negotiation of a *ṣulḥ*.

After the killing of Ḥusayn al-Ḥūthī, the government moved vigorously against Zaydi activists throughout Yemen. About 1,000 alleged Houthi supporters were arrested, many of them teenagers, and measures were taken to restrict or ban Zaydi ceremonies such as *ʿīd al-ghadīr*.[68] Among the detainees were the judges Yaḥyā al-Daylamī and Muḥammad Miftāḥ, as well as ʿAbdulkarīm al-Khaywānī, editor-in-chief of opposition newspaper *al-Shūrā*, who was sentenced to one year in prison for violating the 1990 Press Law.[69] Al-Khaywānī, who was of *sayyid* descent, was found guilty of supporting the Houthi movement, publishing reports damaging to the public interest, and 'public humiliation' of the president.[70] His arrest sparked international media coverage.[71]

In an attempt to ease the tensions in Saʿdah, Salih called on Badr al-Dīn al-Ḥūthī and ʿAbdullah al-Razzāmī to leave the province and to come to Sanaʿa in order to negotiate a *ṣulḥ*. Al-Razzāmī strictly refused to respond to this request.[72] In January 2005, as a signal of goodwill (*ḥusn al-niyyah*) and under a written safe conduct (*wijh amān*) from President Salih, Badr al-Dīn left for the capital. Salih had promised him that, if he attended, the government would compensate the victims of the war in Saʿdah for the damage caused, including amnesty for the political detainees and an end to the persecution of Ḥusayn al-Ḥūthī's followers. But after Badr al-Dīn arrived, along with some family members and guards, he stayed for two months in the house of ʿAlī al-ʿImād, without any of these promises being implemented or an invitation to meet the president. Instead, Salih requested further concessions (*tanāzalāt*) from Badr al-Dīn, for instance that he acknowledge that what Ḥusayn did was wrong, and that his followers were 'misguided elements' (*al-mugharrar bihim*).[73] But here Badr al-Dīn remained unyielding. As a result, he spent two months under virtual house arrest in Sanaʿa, trying to persuade the government to lift the restrictions on Zaydi activists and to obtain amnesty for those arrested. His efforts were in vain. Moreover, the government's refusal to issue firearms licenses for his guards had heightened his sense of peril. Having failed to win an appointment with the president, Badr al-Dīn al-Ḥūthī decided to return empty-handed to Saʿdah and left the capital in greatest secrecy.

Shortly before his clandestine departure on 11 March 2005, however, Jamāl ʿĀmir of *al-Wasaṭ* newspaper conducted an interview with him (the first and only press interview with Badr al-Dīn), which was published on 19 March 2005.[74] For the republican government, this interview was a slap in the face. To start with, in the interview he characterized the movement initiated by his son as a rebellion for the 'defence of Islam'. Badr al-Dīn criticized the Yemeni government's cooperation with the US and its simultaneous promotion of radical Sunnism. In his eyes, both the Yemeni government and violent radical Sunnism were the product of a US policy that aimed to ignite sectarian differences and the conflict between Sunnis and Shiites, 'because the United States hate the Shiites'. According to Badr al-Dīn, the Houthi movement was a defence of Islam itself against the onslaught of US imperialism and its allies and puppets within the Yemeni government, the Iṣlāḥ party and the Salafis. This part of the interview culminated in a provocative declaration that, during the first round of war, 'harm was inflicted on Islam, and most important is the protection of Islam, and what happened [in Marrān] was the defence and the protection of Islam against harm, and this is more important than to protect ourselves'.

Second, Badr al-Dīn stressed the principle of *sayyid* supremacy. As a concession to modern, post-revolutionary times, he differentiated between two types of legitimate government: *imāmah* by a representative of the Āl al-Bayt, and *iḥtisāb* (rule of a 'administrator') by a democratically elected leader who could also be of non-ʿAlīd descent, as long as he was God-fearing, followed the Zaydi principle of 'commanding the good and prohibiting the wrong', and adhered to the constitution.[75] In other words, Badr al-Dīn recognized the Republic, and stressed that a non-*sayyid* president was acceptable as long as he adhered to certain principles. He also made clear that in his eyes *imāmah* was the preferable type of government, while emphasizing that neither he nor his son Ḥusayn had ever demanded the position of imam for themselves. However, once a legitimate imam emerged, he should have priority over a democratically elected president.

The content of this interview was much more radical and uncompromising than the letter that Ḥusayn had sent the president in spring 2004, which had been the ultimate trigger of the first Saʿdah war. After all, father and son had grown up in very different political systems, and did not necessarily share the same ideas. Even worse for the government, Badr al-Dīn was one of Yemen's most respected and prominent Zaydi scholars, whose merits and profound erudition could not be doubted by anyone. His words could not be brushed aside, as with Ḥusayn al-Ḥūthī's *malāzim*, which the government called 'hallucinations'.[76] Instead, the government interpreted Badr al-Dīn's words as a call for a coup (*inqilāb*) against the republican system and in particular against President Salih, and as a call for a return to imamic rule.[77] It further enraged the president that Badr al-Dīn had publicly described him as an accomplice of the US government and an enemy of Islam. In this context, the regime interpreted Badr al-Dīn's secret, unauthorized departure to Saʿdah as part of a formal execution of the Zaydi principle of *khurūj* (rising against a ruler perceived to be unjust).[78]

The Second War (19 March–11 April 2005)

In the second Saʿdah war, the Yemeni government was primarily concerned with dismantling what it perceived to be the Houthis' leadership—in other words, liquidating Badr al-Dīn al-Ḥūthī and ʿAbdullah al-Razzāmī. Indeed, as in the first war, when government forces concentrated on locating and killing Ḥusayn al-Ḥūthī, throughout the second the regime focused on areas where members of the Houthi leadership were alleged to be hiding.

The second war was a rather brief episode, but it exhibited new features. First, it witnessed the rise of ʿAbdulmalik al-Ḥūthī, brother of Ḥusayn, as the new Houthi leader, who henceforth led the rebellion in uneasy tandem with his rival, ʿAbdullah al-Razzāmī. Second, the strategic and tactical approach of both sides evolved, as certain battles relocated from the mountains to the flat and open terrain of eastern Saʿdah governorate. The Houthis' military capacities had begun to develop, posing news challenges for the state military, including well-planned military and sabotage operations in Sanaʿa and Saʿdah city.

Another feature of the second war was the expansion of the fighting due to increased involvement of local tribes. For instance, in Wādī Nushūr and al-ʿAbdīn, the conflict reinforced and re-ignited pre-existing tribal feuds and rivalries; in Banī Muʿādh, too, the armed forces found that they were unable to persecute tribal Houthi individuals without getting into conflict with the entire tribe. These processes of *ʿaṣabiyyah* (tribal solidarity, or a cohesive drive against others) were aggravated by the armed forces' continued partial reliance on Ḥāshid mercenaries, who had a history of tribal conflict with some of the region's tribes.

Attempts at conflict mediation once again failed. In retrospect, the Yemeni government and those involved made no serious efforts to facilitate it, and the Houthi leaders understandably rejected these initiatives. Just as in the first war, the second was decided by *ḥasm* (decisive military defeat of the Houthis). Nevertheless, the very mission of the second war—to eliminate Badr al-Dīn al-Ḥūthī and ʿAbdullah al-Razzāmī—could not be accomplished. Both leaders managed to escape the sweeping and combing operations of the armed forces and to retreat to Maṭrah and al-Naqʿah, a region that would host Houthi headquarters throughout the subsequent wars.

The Houthi Leadership Repositions Itself

Immediately after his interview with *al-Wasaṭ*, Badr al-Dīn al-Ḥūthī headed for al-Razzāmāt in Wādī Nushūr, where he had already spent the first war. There he was welcomed by ʿAbdullah al-Razzāmī, his son ʿAbdulmalik al-Ḥūthī, and other Houthi field commanders and loyalists who had been on the run since the first war the previous summer.

After Ḥusayn's death, ʿAbdulmalik had been able to withdraw from Marrān to al-Razzāmāt in Wādī Nushūr. Many of his family members were dead or in prison; his brother Muḥammad was in detention at the Department of Criminal Investigation in Sanaʿa, and his brother Yaḥyā had been forced into exile.[79] After Ḥusayn's death, therefore, his loyalists were now rallying around ʿAbdulmalik, as Badr al-Dīn's son, Ḥusayn's half-brother and a Khawlān local—although ʿAbdulmalik was very young (b. c. 1980, likely two decades younger than Ḥusayn).

Before the outbreak of the first war in June 2004, ʿAbdulmalik, like most of his brothers, had devoted his attention to religious studies. Yet, unlike most of his brothers, during and after the first war he had established considerable influence over the movement's military 'field' commanders (*fī l-mīdān*), such as Yūsif and Ṭaha al-Madānī, ʿAbdullah al-Ḥākim (also known as Abū ʿAlī) and others. It became clear that ʿAbdulmalik was a gifted strategist and a charismatic orator. Certainly he did not possess the uniquely mesmerizing rhetorical skills of his slain brother Ḥusayn, but he, too, could inspire, rally and lead the people. Only his relationship with al-Razzāmī, who had also developed a claim to the movement's leadership and with whom ʿAbdulmalik disagreed on certain doctrinal issues, remained tense.[80] Now, in the second war, ʿAbdulmalik, al-Razzāmī, ʿAbdullah al-Ḥākim and Yūsif al-Madānī—then just twenty years old—rose to become the movement's field commanders.

Badr al-Dīn's unauthorized departure from Sanaʿa, and especially his interview with *al-Wasaṭ*, had enraged the government, which responded with a series of accusations. The government charged Badr al-Dīn and al-Razzāmī with seeking to re-establish the imamate and resume the 'insurgency'. In an all-out political attack, Salih also accused the opposition—particularly its two Zaydi-based parties, Ḥizb al-Ḥaqq (which al-Razzāmī and the late Ḥusayn had represented in parliament) and the Union of Popular Forces (*ittiḥād al-quwah al-shaʿbiyyah*)—of supporting the Houthi movement.[81]

Course of the war

The second war erupted on 19 March 2005 with a shoot-out between security forces and members of the al-Razzāmāt tribe in the province's largest arms market, Sūq al-Ṭalḥ, a few kilometres north of Saʿdah city. In order to keep a close watch on the area, the collaboration between the government's security forces and some tribes also included cooperation in the intelligence field. Tribal informants had identified a group of al-Razzāmāt members at the market. During the shoot-out, four members were killed and more injured while attempting to flee.

Following the fatal shoot-out, for some days the fighting ceased, but tensions remained high. Demonstrations took place in Saʿdah city with demonstrators shouting the Houthi slogan. Fierce fighting erupted on 27 March when Houthi followers launched attacks on security and army positions in several places in the Saʿdah governorate in retaliation for the victims of the shoot-out in al-Ṭalḥ. They attacked military checkpoints and set up roadblocks on streets that led from Saʿdah city northwards to Ḍaḥyān/Bāqim, southwards to al-ʿAmashiyyah/Sufyān and eastwards to Kitāf/al-Buqʿ. In Saḥār Houthi loyalists attacked a police station.

Strategically and tactically, the Houthis' military approach differed significantly from that of the first war. In Marrān, the terrain had been densely populated, mountainous, steep, and partly inaccessible, leading to a war of attrition (*ḥarb istinzāf*) in which Ḥusayn al-Ḥūthī persevered in the isolated mountain stronghold of Jurf Salmān to his death. But in Wāʾilah and Saḥār, the main arenas of the second war, part of the terrain was spacious, flat and open, allowing the Houthis greater mobility. This partial relocation actually benefited the conventional manoeuvre forces of the Yemeni army, which had air support and armour. Yet the Houthis launched a guerrilla war (*ḥarb ʿiṣābāt*) of surprise attacks (*ghārah*), ambushes (*kamīn*), sniper actions (*qanṣ*) and fast, flexible hit-and-run tactics (*al-karr wa l-farr*), enabling them to inflict damage on the armed forces and then immediately withdraw from the area to hilly and rocky terrain. This tactical approach allowed them to retreat quickly to their strongholds before the armed forces could formulate a counter-attack.

From this second war on, the Houthis started to show remarkable skill with weaponry, inflicting serious casualties on Salih forces. Their guerrilla tactics provoked the army to launch a large-scale operation involving heavy artillery, tanks, and attack helicopters.[82] In order to hunt down the Houthi leadership, the military deployed raids (*dahm*), combing operations (*ḥamlāt tamshīṭ*), and sieges (*ḥiṣār*) of Badr al-Dīn and al-Razzāmī's suspected locations. On 28 March, the government carried out a commando operation to arrest Badr al-Dīn in Wādī Nushūr, but the plan failed. After this, the clashes between the army and Houthi loyalists expanded further.[83]

During the second war, the army cordoned off the Houthi leaders' likely locations in al-Razzāmāt and Āl Shāfiʿah,[84] a few kilometres northeast of Saʿdah city. Al-Razzāmāt belongs to the territorially dispersed Wādiʿah, and the Āl Shāfiʿah are part of the Āl Sālim further to the east, who in turn belong to the Dahm, whose settlement centre is actually located in al-Jawf. The rest of Wādī Nushūr is dominated by sections of the Wāʾilah (Āl al-Nimrī and Āl

Mahdī). Topographically, this region is a contingent area characterized by crests, *wādīs* and caves. To the east and northeast it borders on Āl Sālim and Wādī Āl Abū Jabārah located in Kitāf district.

Faced with these attacks by the forces searching for the two leaders, al-Razzāmāt, Āl al-Nimrī and Āl Shāfiʿah formed an alliance to defend their territories. Simultaneously, the military campaign in Wādī Nushūr rekindled the prevalent tribal feud between the Āl Mahdī, who sided with the government, and the Āl al-Nimrī and the al-Razzāmāt, who both sided with the Houthis.[85] Several thousand soldiers were deployed to the areas of al-Razzāmāt and Āl Shāfiʿah, surrounding them from and shelling them with artillery and tanks.[86] The operations resulted in heavy casualties on both sides.

This emerging tribal involvement was also seen among the al-ʿAbdīn. Al-ʿAbdīn is a section of the Saḥār tribe, which is settled in the immediate vicinity of Saʿdah city. The al-ʿAbdīn's senior shaykh comes from the Mujallī lineage. Fāyid Mujallī and his son Ḥusayn, we recall, had been heroes of the 1960s revolution. Due to their solid revolutionary credentials as well as their merits, after the revolution they rose to become two of the most influential shaykhs in the Saʿdah area.[87] Politically and economically, the Mujallī family had benefited enormously after the civil war, managing to appropriate central, high-quality *waqf* land previously providing income for the local *sādah*, including lands belonging to al-ʿAbdīn's *hijrah*, Raḥbān. On some of these lots, the Mujallī family had constructed buildings that they then rented to the government, such as those of the Oil Company (*sharikat al-nafṭ*) and the Central Bank (*al-bank al-markazī*). After Ḥusayn Mujallī's death in 1997, his second-born son ʿUthmān took over as shaykh.

During the second war, clashes erupted between the Mujallī clan and the Ḥāmid clan, another shaykhly clan in al-ʿAbdīn belonging to al-ʿAbdīn's historical shaykhly lineages (*al-usar al-ʿarīqah fī l-mashīkh*). These two clans form a classic pair of opposites with a long history of conflict. Their rivalry had many causes. First, during the 1960s civil war, the Mujallī had been on the side of the revolution, whereas the Ḥāmid had fought for the royalists. Second, while the Mujallī had become very wealthy and influential after the civil war, the financial resources of the Āl Ḥāmid and their political influence were nil. Third, the Mujallī supported the Salafi Dār al-Ḥadīth in nearby Dammāj (without themselves being Salafis), whereas the Āl Ḥāmid were firm supporters of Zaydi Hādawī doctrine and served an important protective function for the *sādah* in Raḥbān. Last but not least, many citizens of al-ʿAbdīn believed that the Mujallī were 'dominating over the people' (*yuhayminūna ʿalā al-mawāṭin*), and the Āl Ḥāmid were unwilling to accept this 'hegemony' (*haymanah*). The Āl Ḥāmid exercised the role of intra-tribal opposition leaders and gathered in al-ʿAbdīn all those who were dissatisfied with the status quo, particularly in regard to the local distribution of power, political participation, influence and income. A local source summed it up as follows: 'The Āl Ḥāmid and the Āl Mujallī competed for a long time, even before the war and before the emergence of the Believing Youth and the Houthis, and this was a struggle for influence within the tribe, because they were shaykhs.'[88]

In 2005, this feud for tribal leadership (*thaʾr ʿalā zaʿāmat al-qabīlah*) drove them to military confrontation. It remains unclear what exactly triggered these clashes. Regardless, during the second war, the Āl Mujallī (led by Ḥamīd, a brother of ʿUthmān) were able to call in the regular army to assist them, and a military campaign was launched against the Āl Ḥāmid. In these violent clashes between state troops and Mujallī loyalists on one side and the Āl Ḥāmid and their allies on the other, the army surrounded the Āl Ḥāmid neighbourhood and shelled the houses with tanks, on the pretext that the Āl Ḥāmid were Houthis. This clash alone left tens dead and wounded.[89] Local sources say that before the war the Āl Ḥāmid had not, in fact, been Houthis. Rather, they came out of this very confrontation as Houthi loyalists because they and the movement now had a common enemy: the Mujallī clan and their backers, the Yemeni army. As we will see, this classic pattern was to be repeated many times over in the course of the Saʿdah wars.

In many places, the anti-Houthi forces' use of indiscriminate violence aggravated existing tensions. This is reflected by the events in Banī Muʿādh, a few kilometres north of Saʿdah city in the immediate neighbourhood of Sūq al-Ṭalḥ. The Banī Muʿādh, too, are a section of the Saḥār. At the beginning of the second war, many tribesmen of Banī Muʿādh were Houthi loyalists, but not yet whole tribal sections (*bi-shakl jamāʿī*).[90] During the conflict, a shoot-out between Houthi loyalists and security forces erupted in Banī Muʿādh's heavily frequented weekly market, Sūq al-Khafjī.[91] Afterward, security forces encircled Houthi loyalists and other Houthis in turn surrounded the security forces. Each party tried to blockade the other and so the circles continued to expand. In order to break this deadlock, the military leadership deployed army reinforcements to the region including irregular forces (*murtaziqah*) from among the Ḥāshid, who had already participated in the first war in Marrān and al-Razzāmāt and who now resorted to random violence against the local population, thus setting the stage for protracted confrontations and revenge actions for the rest of the Saʿdah war period.[92]

Leading shaykhs were furious with Salih over the amount of indiscriminate killing and destruction perpetrated by the regular army and the Ḥāshid tribal levies in order to suppress the Houthi rebellion in Saḥār, accusing the Ministry of Defence of using 'Darfur-like' scorched-earth tactics against civilians.[93] Faced with the escalating tensions in al-ʿAbdīn and Banī Muʿādh, Governor Yaḥyā al-ʿAmrī tried to intervene on behalf of the government, calling a meeting with leading Saḥār shaykhs in which he demanded that they play a more proactive role in the defence of their territories against the Houthis. In turn, the shaykhs, who felt pressured by the government, convened with their tribesmen in order to negotiate and align their views. In Banī Muʿādh, a poet put his tribe's wrath into dialect verses:

Welcome O people of Saḥār and al-Asās
Each of you is tribesman, free, and in good repute
And offers his support
What has been shattered is beyond repair
Brutality increased and became immeasurable
Its target is no longer al-Ḥūthī or al-Nuwās[94]
It became a gamble
Between those in Sanaʿa who are rich and influential.[95]

The poem points out that the force deployed by the armed forces had been disproportionate and was giving rise to the impression that the military's objective in Saḥār was not to combat the Houthis, but rather to loot the area and its tribes. Between the lines, the poem also refers to the Saḥār tribe's inability to protect its territory from Houthi incursions because the Houthi fighters were themselves elements of the tribe, not invaders from the outside (such as the Ḥāshid mercenaries fighting with the government). In sum, the disproportionate use of force generated an impression among the Saḥār that the government and the Ḥāshid mercenaries were not fighting a military operation against the Houthis, but rather had launched a full offensive against the entire Saḥār tribe.[96]

For the Banī Muʿādh, the deployment of Ḥāshid mercenaries within their territory was a particular provocation. Lichtenthäler has documented the deadly conflict between the Banī Muʿādh (representing Saʿdah tribes) and the Ḥāshid (representing central state power), dating back to the 1980s.[97] This tribal conflict, with components of blood feud, had been decided in favour of the Banī Muʿādh through the bold intervention of their senior shaykh, Ḥusayn al-Surabī, who travelled to Sanaʿa to meet the president and convince him of the Banī Muʿādh's cause. Thus, the presence in this area of Ḥāshid mercenaries from the second war onwards was a particularly sensitive and problematic issue, and led to massive military enlistment among the Banī Muʿādh in favour of the Houthis (*tajayyush li-ṣāliḥ al-Ḥuthī*).[98]

Throughout the conflict, Shaykh Ḥusayn al-Surabī tried to remain neutral. He and his father Fayṣal had fought for the Republic during the 1960s civil war. However, al-Surabī's prestige amongst his tribesmen was not based on his family's loyalty to the government, but—on the contrary—on his proven ability to outwit and resist government control and to keep state power at a distance.[99] At times in the past, he had been vigorously opposed to the government's and General ʿAlī Muḥsin's efforts to establish Salafi mosques and schools in his tribal constituency. Throughout the Saʿdah wars, al-Surabī took a neutral (*muḥāyid*) stance and refused to commit manpower from his tribe to the government's irregular forces. After the second war, he eluded the continued pressure from the government by travelling to France, where he intended to seek medical treatment of old war wounds from his battles against the royalists during the 1960s civil war.

As the noose was tightened around the primary locations of the second war in al-Razzāmāt and Āl Shāfiʿah, the wider arena of operations was expanding further. The beleaguered Houthis changed their tactics again, and switched to actions exhibiting features of sabotage and urban warfare. Amidst reports of escalating fighting in Saʿdah province, six grenade attacks against military personnel were reported in Sanaʿa in the first half of April 2005, most of them in areas bordering on the Old Town such as Bāb al-Yaman and Bāb al-Salām. The targeting of the armed forces in the capital implied that the conflict had started to spread beyond the initial area of military engagement in Saʿdah province. On 29 March, a grenade was thrown from a vehicle into a military transport truck carrying several soldiers in Bāb al-Salām. Another grenade attack against the army took place on 5 April in front of the Ministry of Defence, when a man threw a grenade from his vehicle into a transport truck carrying several soldiers. The grenade, which was thrown back out of the truck, exploded on the sidewalk. On 9 April, in Bāb al-Yaman, a grenade was tossed into a passing air force vehicle. Another grenade attack was rumoured to have occurred on 10 April in the Ḥaddah area. Despite the government's efforts to play down the situation in its public statements, press circles almost unanimously concurred that a Houthi Sanaʿa cell (*khaliyyat Ṣanʿāʾ*) was behind the attacks.[100]

At the height of the fighting in al-Razzāmāt, on 8 April, a platoon-sized group of Houthis (about sixty men) slipped into the city of Saʿdah in the small hours of the morning and stormed a number of government buildings, from which they proceeded to shoot at army and police units. Saʿdah city witnessed twenty-four hours of fierce street fighting in which dozens of people were killed.[101] This change of tactics posed particular challenges for the armed forces. During the urban combat operations in Saʿdah city, the Houthis were able to capitalize on their detailed local knowledge of the area, right down to the layout of buildings, and the tacit support of many residents. Ordinary citizens were difficult to distinguish from Houthi fighters, especially individuals simply trying to protect their homes from attackers, particularly soldiers and looters attempting burglary. While the rebels were able to move from one part of the city to another undetected, the army was more exposed, as they were unfamiliar with the defending Houthis' secret hidden routes and had to use the open streets. The fighting in Saʿdah city dramatically reduced the government's advantages in armour, heavy artillery, and air support. During the clashes, city life was completely disrupted. Shops closed their doors. Security forces combed the city's neighbourhoods.[102] This eruption of urban warfare was a strong show of force by the Houthis that greatly diminished local confidence in the government's combat capabilities. After the fighting had subsided, government troops managed to regain control of the city. Again, the corpses of killed Houthis were tied by their feet to military vehicles and dragged through the streets. A curfew (*ḥaẓr tajawwul*) was declared, lasting for some weeks.

Due to the rapid changes in Houthi tactics in Saʿdah and the acts of sabotage in Sanaʿa, the military advanced relentlessly in al-Razzāmāt and Āl Shāfiʿah, where it still suspected the Houthi leaders of hiding. On 30 March, the government announced that the armed forces had taken over most of al-Razzāmāt and Āl Shāfiʿah, except for the areas of Jabal ʿĪssā and Āl Ṣalāḥ. On 11 April, the army was able to consolidate control and began to conduct combing operations in search of Badr al-Dīn al-Ḥūthī and ʿAbdullah al-Razzāmī. When al-Razzāmī's body was (falsely) found and identified, the government announced the end of major combat operations, arguing that it had now established complete control over all Houthi strongholds. The military leadership did regret, however, that Badr al-Dīn had managed to 'flee from the hole in which he was hiding'.[103]

The rebels in the Houthi strongholds of al-Razzāmāt and Āl Shāfiʿah surrendered. Yet the very mission of the second war—the elimination of the Houthi leadership—had failed. The reports of al-Razzāmī's death turned out to be false. Both leaders had eluded the armed forces and managed to flee northward from the besieged Wādī Nushūr region to the natural fortresses of Maṭrah and al-Naqʿah, close to the Saudi border.

Mediation

There were three mediation attempts during the second war. Like their predecessors, these mediation initiatives were condemned to failure. In practical terms, mediation with the Houthi leaders was by definition virtually impossible during this conflict, because the army was instructed to track down and eliminate them.

Nevertheless, in early April 2005, President Salih commissioned a group of scholars and shaykhs headed by Judge Aḥmad Muḥammad al-Shāmī (leader of Ḥizb al-Ḥaqq and member of the Consultative Council, who had already been a member of mediation committees during the first war) to convince Badr al-Dīn al-Ḥūthī and ʿAbdullah al-Razzāmī to surrender.[104] One member of this committee was Shājiaʿ b. Shājiaʿ, brother of Wāʾilah shaykh Ṣāliḥ b. Shājiaʿ who had been selected due to his Ismaili (supposedly 'neutral') background and his mediation experience—at the end of the first war, he had already accomplished the feat of persuading al-Razzāmī to lay down his weapons after Ḥusayn was killed.[105]

On 7 April, Shājiaʿ b. Shājiaʿ reported through the press that the mediation committee had been able to reach al-Razzāmī on the phone, but that his demands were 'impossible to meet because they are intransigent and unacceptable to intermediaries'.[106] This came as no surprise, as the government had articulated nothing less than non-negotiable maximum demands, aimed at a total Houthi surrender—not genuine mediation. The government openly adopted an inappropriately partisan tone, demanding a 'surrender to justice' (*taslīm anfusihim li-l-ʿadālah*) of the 'misguided elements' (*al-mugharrar bihim*).

The deployment of the Intellectual Dialogue Committee (*lajnat al-ḥiwār al-fikrī*), headed by Judge Ḥamūd ʿAbdulḥamīd al-Hitār, also proved counterproductive.[107] Prior to the conflict, al-Hitār had directed the re-doctrination and de-radicalization programme for Sunni Islamist extremists, including members of al-Qaeda. In the aftermath of 9/11, the committee was viewed in a somewhat positive light both domestically and internationally as an original means of fighting terrorism, including by Western countries like the US, Britain, and France.[108] Al-Hitār seized every opportunity of self-presentation to promote his dialogue concept as an all-purpose weapon against religious extremism. During the second war, he tried to 'persuade [the Houthis] to abandon their wrong ideas based on extremism, intolerance and to return to the right path'.[109] However, the Dialogue Committee's efforts remained ineffective, because al-Hitār (in line with government policy) lumped together Houthi loyalists and al-Qaeda-affiliated jihadis without delving into the specific local context of the rebellion in Saʿdah. Observers opined that al-Hitār had 'no credibility', because he was closely tied to the government and mandated not to negotiate, but merely to repeat Salih's demands.[110]

Their annoyed Houthi counterpart interpreted the government's offensive rhetoric and its non-negotiable demands as evidence of bad faith (*sūʾ al-niyyah*), and responded with deadlock (*jumūd*) and cancellation (*ilghāʾ*) of the talks. Mediation, which had already reached an impasse before it was actually set in motion, failed to produce any compromise through the negotiation of face-saving solutions acceptable to both the Houthis and the government. The government hurriedly declared that it 'is doing everything it can and more than necessary to resolve the problem peacefully', but that the negotiations had failed due to the intransigence (*taʿannut*), fanaticism (*taʿaṣṣub*) and unresponsiveness (*ʿadam al-istijābah*) of the Houthi leadership.[111]

Further mediation initiatives were blocked. In April 2005, ʿAbdullah al-Aḥmar independently launched a mediation initiative and tried to send his envoy Shaykh Aḥmad Nāṣir al-Baʿrān with a message to Badr al-Dīn al-Ḥūthī; yet armed forces under the command of ʿAlī Muḥsin again prevented the envoy's passage. Al-Aḥmar's mediation attempt failed for several reasons. First, General ʿAlī Muḥsin, who had no interest in a peaceful solution to the conflict, had already allowed the mediation attempts during the first war to run into the sand. Second, successful mediators of tribal conflicts gain enormous power and prestige in Yemen, and sources from within the government have indicated that Salih begrudged ʿAbdullah al-Aḥmar this role. This may also have been the reason why Salih frequently declined to involve tribal and non-tribal mediators of particular competence and proficiency. Third, given his leadership role in the Iṣlāḥ party and his closeness to Saudi Arabia, al-Aḥmar did not possess the necessary neutrality and trustworthiness that distinguishes a suitable mediator. When he embarked on his initiative, he publicly referred to the Houthis as an 'aggressive horde of rebels' (*shirdhimah mutamarridah mughālibah*) who possessed no connection with Zaydi doctrine, and called for their elimination.[112]

For the domestic opposition, the government's habit of holding its cards close to the chest was annoying in most cases, but crossed the line into dangerous conceit when the government, and in particular the army under ʿAlī Muḥsin, undermined all external mediation initiatives. The government obviously felt uncomfortable letting externals perform the mediation task, thus allowing them a close look at internal processes, and the authorities frequently accused partisan opposition figures of supporting the 'sedition in Saʿdah'.[113]

Second Interim

The government announced the end of the second Saʿdah war on 11 April 2005, but the conflict kept simmering. After the war, the government carried out an arrest campaign against Houthi supporters in Saʿdah, blocked roads leading to Houthi strongholds in Maṭrah, al-Naqʿah, Ḍaḥyān, Nushūr, and Marrān, and swept these areas for Houthi commanders.[114] The rebel leaders had retreated from Wādī Nushūr and had entrenched themselves in the mountains and caves of the natural fortresses of Maṭrah and al-Naqʿah. On 10 May, Badr al-Dīn al-Ḥūthī and ʿAbdullah al-Razzāmī sent a letter from al-Naqʿah to President Salih in Sanaʿa, delivered by Shājiaʿ b. Shājiaʿ. After the usual greetings, Badr al-Dīn and al-Razzāmī directly addressed the issue:

> It has not escaped your notice that a war has been waged, and we have been surprised that this war has been waged against us. Nothing from our side has occurred that would justify shedding our blood, killing our sons, destroying our homes, and expelling our families. All this was done without justification since neither in the past nor in the present have we rejected the republican system or the president. So don't believe the rumours of hypocrites and the lies of hateful and malicious people. We as citizens call upon you to remove this injustice that has been put upon us. If this is done, we are prepared to attend (*naḥnu mustaʿidūn li-l-ḥuḍūr*), at any time, in person or by a representative. But if this tyranny of murder, destruction, arrest, expulsion, confiscation of our possessions, etc. continues, the problem will not be solved, but will grow and become even more complicated. God is the One whose help we seek.[115]

Pro-government propaganda inaccurately reproduced the content of this letter. The government brushed aside the (more or less veiled) threat to extend the conflict, and in particular distorted the meaning of the term *ḥuḍūr* (coming), that is the willingness of the Houthi leadership to attend negotiations in person or by way of a representative if the government stopped the attacks. Instead, government media replaced the phrase *ḥuḍūr* with *taslīm* (surrender), thereby giving the impression that the leaders had expressed their willingness to turn themselves in. The newspaper *26 September*, the mouthpiece of the armed forces, wrote:

> His Excellency President Ali Abdullah Salih received a letter of Badr al-Dīn al-Ḥūthī and ʿAbdullah ʿAyḍah al-Razzāmī and their rebellious followers, which

> expresses their willingness to lay down their arms, renounce violence and stop the attacks on citizens and members of armed forces, security and public facilities. [...] This gesture came out of the keenness of the political leadership to stop the bloodshed and promote a climate of security and stability in those areas.[116]

Al-Sharq al-Awsaṭ even referred to the letter as *ʿarḍ al-Ḥūthī bi-l-istislām muqābil waqf malāḥaqatihi*: Badr al-Dīn's offer to surrender in exchange for not prosecuting him.[117] This representation intended to support the claims of the Yemeni authorities that they had effectively won a military victory against the Houthis, whose leadership was about to surrender.

On 22 May, Yemen's national unification holiday, President Salih appeared on television to pardon Badr al-Dīn and announced an amnesty for his followers. Badr al-Dīn roundly rejected the president's offer, because security forces were still conducting a sweeping campaign in Saʿdah and a wave of arrests in Sanaʿa.[118] Hundreds of Houthi supporters were arrested, including field commander ʿAbdullah al-Ḥākim (also known as Abū ʿAlī) and Badr al-Dīn's son Amīr al-Dīn. On 30 May, the judge Yaḥyā Ḥusayn al-Daylamī was sentenced to death and his colleague Muḥammad Miftāḥ to eight years in prison on charges of spying, insurrection and backing the Houthi movement.[119]

Thus, neither the Houthi leaders' cautious offer to negotiate nor the government's offer of a pardon had any effect, and the conflict dragged on. Numerous cases of sabotage and attacks on military facilities and senior government personnel were perpetrated throughout this second interim. In the Saʿdah area, local shaykhs were targeted. Thirty-six people of a so-called 'Sanaʿa terrorist cell' (*khaliyyat Ṣanʿāʾ al-irhābiyyah*) of Houthi activists, including a woman, were arrested. The Yemeni authorities accused them of pursuing sabotage against military and security vehicles and of the assassinations of senior military and security personnel, including an attempt to assassinate the head of military intelligence, ʿAlī al-Siyānī, and of plotting to attack the US ambassador's convoy.[120]

In Saʿdah governorate, throughout the second interim phase, violence kept flaring up, often in the form of clashes between Houthi fighters and followers of pro-government shaykhs. Lingering hostilities were exacerbated due to harsh army tactics and the anger and resentment they had caused among the local population. The conflict in Wādī Nushūr between Āl al-Nimrī/Āl al-Razzāmāt and Āl Mahdī, for instance, dragged on. In previous chapters we have explored the history and several transformations of this conflict, the origins of which date back to the 1980s.[121] The initial administrative issue of the construction of a school led to the outbreak of a tribal feud, transformed itself after Yemeni unification in 1990 into a political rivalry, and in 2004 jumped on the bandwagon of the Saʿdah wars. During the first and the second wars, Āl Shāfiʿah joined Āl al-Nimrī and Āl al-Razzāmāt, who fought against Āl Mahdī and the state military. By the second interim period, the conflict had already developed a momentum of its own and would ultimately trigger the eruption of the third Saʿdah war in late November 2005.

Likewise, the conflict that broke out in Banī Muʿādh during the second war had taken on a life of its own. As we know, Shaykh Ḥusayn al-Surabī of the Banī Muʿādh was staying abroad for medical treatment. His rival, Shaykh Yaḥyā Dirdaḥ b. Jaʿfar, sided with the government, yet many of his tribesmen were Houthi loyalists.[122] In Āl ʿAmmār (an enclave of Dahm a few kilometres south of Saʿdah city), Shaykh ʿUmar Ṣāliḥ Hindī Dughsān (brother of GPC MP Ṣāliḥ Ṣāliḥ Hindī Dughsān) moved against the Houthis, but his brother, Aḥmad Ṣāliḥ Hindī Dughsān, later became a Houthi field commander. Thus, the loyalties of both the Dughsān clan and the tribesmen of Āl ʿAmmār were divided, as had already been the case in the 1960s civil war.

Several assassination attempts were perpetrated in Saʿdah during the second interim phase, some of them directed against Ḥasan Manāʿ. As secretary-general of Saʿdah's local council and deputy governor of Saʿdah, Ḥasan Manāʿ was a symbol of the state (*ramz al-dawlah*) and thus a potential Houthi target. Another murder was attempted against Colonel ʿAlī Fanīs al-Ithlah when his SUV convoy left the compound of the al-ʿAwjarī clan in Wādī Nushūr, leaving him wounded and several of his guards dead. Al-Ithlah was a brother of Shaykh Ḥamad Fanīs al-Ithlah of the Āl Abū Jabārah (Wāʾilah), who live in the homonymous *wādī* in the immediate vicinity of the Saudi border. They were related by marriage to the al-ʿAwjarī clan. The al-Ithlah clan played a crucial role both in trans-border trade as well as in the protection of Salafist activities in the Saʿdah area, and had close ties to both Saudi Arabia and the Dār al-Ḥadīth in Kitāf (to which we shall return later). Possibly, he was targeted because of his ties to Salafism; or it might be that the perpetrators were actually targeting Fāyiz al-ʿAwjarī, and confused the two convoys.

On 26 September 2005, the forty-third anniversary of North Yemen's 1962 revolution against the imamate, President Salih made a surprise announcement granting amnesty to all jailed Houthi supporters and ordering financial compensation to the Ḥamīd al-Dīn family, which had ruled Yemen prior to the 1962 revolution. 'We have pardoned them despite the blood that has been spilled', Salih said during a speech in Taʿiz, referring to the war in Saʿdah.[123] Press reports, however, agreed that this decision did not enter into effect, and that those released were in the range of fifty people out of among four or five thousand imprisoned. *Al-Sharq al-Awsaṭ* learned from a Yemeni lawyer that, when the latter asked the responsible authorities in Sana'a why they hadn't released the rest of the detainees, the authorities replied that the amnesty announcement was merely a political speech, and that Salih had not issued a written decree to enforce it.[124] The announced financial compensation for the Ḥamīd al-Dīn family, too, remained unimplemented.

The Third War (30 November 2005–23 February 2006)

External observers often considered the third Saʿdah war less intensive than its predecessors. However, this impression of decreased intensity was most certainly the result of the government's censorship, which led to an almost complete information blackout.[125] The government restricted and criminalized the right of the media to gather and distribute information on the Saʿdah wars, prevented journalists from entering the conflict zone and blocked mobile telephone access in the conflict areas. When the Yemeni newspaper *al-Shūrā* disregarded the censorship and ran stories on the conflict, it was shut down and its editor, ʿAbdulkarīm al-Khaywānī, was arrested.[126]

As a result, the media were largely silent about the battles that took place between 30 November 2005 and 23 February 2006. The coverage from pro-government media focused far more on preparations for the coming presidential elections in September 2006 than on the military confrontations in the north. During the third war *26 September*, the military's mouthpiece, only mentioned 'sporadic skirmishes' between the army and the Houthis. The third war, however, affected far more places than the previous bouts had; during this episode the war expanded in scope and the fighting spread across Saʿdah governorate.

Yet, despite the escalating magnitude of the battles, many peripheral areas still remained unaffected by the conflict, notably Rāziḥ, Munabbih, Shidāʾ, al-Ẓāhir, al-Ḥishwah and the eastern parts of Kitāf. The Munabbih tribe in the far north-west, for instance, was still far more concerned with pursuing its intra- and intertribal feuds and negotiating the Yemeni-Saudi boundary delineation.[127]

The third war raged from 30 November 2005 until 23 February 2006. Since it started as a resurgence of the clashes in Wādī Nushūr, its outbreak was ultimately triggered by a tribal feud. The conflict spread further west, to Saḥār and Jumāʿah, and even touched the neighbouring governorates, ʿAmrān (in al-Ḥarf) and al-Jawf (in al-Matūn). The government faced strong pressure to settle the conflict, even if only temporarily, before the September 2006 presidential and local elections—this allowed, for the first time since the beginning of the Saʿdah wars in 2004, the successful mediation and negotiation of a *ṣulḥ* (contractual peace) between the Houthis and the government. This *ṣulḥ* allowed the province to enjoy a brief period of détente and relative peace, until it was drawn into the maelstrom of the subsequent wars.

The Fortresses of Maṭrah and al-Naqʿah

Badr al-Dīn al-Ḥūthī, ʿAbdulmalik al-Ḥūthī and ʿAbdullah al-Razzāmī had managed to elude the military's combing and sweeping campaigns in Wādī Nushūr and had relocated to the adjacent area of Maṭrah and al-Naqʿah, which was soon considered to be the Houthis' main stronghold and headquarters. Maṭrah and al-Naqʿah are situated in a large area that begins north of Sūq al-Ṭalḥ and extends along Wādī Nushūr to the Saudi border: a barren, rocky landscape characterized by mountains, valleys and an abundance of caves.[128]

Locals and domestic media tended to stylize Ḍaḥyān as a kind of sacred territory or 'Qom' of the Houthis. Around Maṭrah and al-Naqʿah, however, a myth developed of an unconquerable mountain fortress. The Houthi leaders' discretion on this remote place has certainly helped to elevate it to the realms of secrecy and legend. Asked about the nature of the place, one leader responded: 'Maṭrah and al-Naqʿah are regions over which the falcons do not dare to circle' (*Maṭrah wa l-Naqʿah manāṭiq lā tatajarraʿ al-suqūr an tuḥalliq fawq-hā*).[129]

The area of Maṭrah is considered territory of the al-Abqūr and Walad Masʿūd of the Saḥār's Kulayb moiety. The adjacent area of al-Naqʿah—somewhat further to the northeast—belongs to the territory of the al-Razzāmāt (Wādiʿah).[130] The entire Maṭrah and al-Naqʿah area reaches from the Saudi border in the north to Wādī Nushūr in the south. Due to its aridity, inaccessibility and ruggedness, this region is almost devoid of people; only a few pastoralists and their flocks range through the area, which is used as pasture land by several tribal groups of the Saḥār, Jumāʿah, Wāʾilah, and Wādiʿah, all of which hold alternate, reciprocal grazing rights in this area as recognized in tribal contracts.

The few authentic photographic and film recordings of Maṭrah and al-Naqʿah, alongside eyewitness accounts, allow us to suppose that it is a mountainous area with an abundance of caves of enormous depth and space. During the 1960s civil war, the Egyptians used toxic nerve gas in this area to flush royalists out of the caves. A senior military officer described the impossibility of military conquest of the area during the Saʿdah wars:

> The nature of the place determines its importance. Even the air force did not achieve the desired results against the rebels, who entrenched themselves amid the giant mountains where dozens of deep gorges, caverns, overhanging cliffs and caves are cut deeply into the rocks. On the ground you will reach Maṭrah only by limited ways that are controlled by the Houthis.[131]

Other sources indicated that some caves in Maṭrah and al-Naqʿah also served as Houthi prisons. Among the Houthis' opponents in the Saʿdah region, anecdotal evidence of detention in Maṭrah and al-Naqʿah was abundant. A shaykh of Jumāʿah remembered:

> If you had an argument with the Houthis, first those of your tribe who belonged to the Houthis came and called for your loyalty. And if you refused, Houthis came who did not belong to your tribe. Either you solved the problem with them, or they took you with them, blindfolded you and brought you to Maṭrah or al-Naqʿah. The government and the governor should have been warned before the war when the Houthis built Maṭrah and al-Naqʿah and started to detain people there. And when you asked the Houthis how their situation was there, they answered: Thanks be to God, we are content, comfortable and struggling in the cause of God (*al-ḥamd lillāh mabsūṭūn, murtāḥūn wa mujāhidūn fī sabīl allāh*).[132]

During the third war, the dispute between ʿAbdullah al-Razzāmī and ʿAbdulmalik al-Ḥūthī on the movement's leadership and its ideological orientations led to a certain friction within the Houthi forces.[133] While al-Razzāmī and his followers installed his headquarters in al-Naqʿah, ʿAbdulmalik al-Ḥūthī and his followers moved to the area of Maṭrah. This resulted temporarily in two separate command groups, which only resumed full cooperation after the Saʿdah wars, during the battle against the Salafis in Kitāf in 2011.[134]

Throughout the Saʿdah wars, the Houthi fortresses of Maṭrah and al-Naqʿah proved invulnerable from the air and impregnable to ground forces. The Houthis had learned their lesson from the first and second wars. The relative ease with which the army had localized and killed Ḥusayn al-Ḥūthī in the first war didn't seem to bear repetition. From this third war, dozens of military units were deployed to the vicinity of Maṭrah and al-Naqʿah in order to hunt down the rebel leaders entrenched in the mountains and caves, but all attempts to penetrate this area were doomed to failure.[135] The barren mountains and deep valleys formed a natural barrier against intruders. Maṭrah and al-Naqʿah would sustain heavy shelling by the Yemeni air force during subsequent rounds of war, and during the sixth war, the Saudi air force also targeted this area. During Operation Decisive Storm, which commenced in March 2015, Houthis accused the Saudi air force of using cluster bombs in Maṭrah and al-Naqʿah. At the time of writing, no ground troops have ever advanced into the area.

War Course

At the end of November 2005, the assassination attempt on ʿAlī Fanīs al-Ithlah sparked a new series of clashes in the Wādī Nushūr area between the Āl Mahdī, who were allied with the government, and their foes from among the al-Razzāmāt, Āl al-Nimrī and Āl Shāfiʿah, who joined the ranks of the Houthis. The resumption of the conflict in Wādī Nushūr was a decisive element in the outbreak of the third Saʿdah war.

In Wādī Nushūr, we recall, tribal and political fault lines made up a complex set of conflicts, rendering the distinction between tribal feud, political conflict and the violence of the Houthi wars increasingly difficult. One source of concern was that the conflict in Wādī Nushūr had already had a destabilizing impact on the surrounding areas: after an (unsuccessful) Houthi assassination attempt against Shaykh Fāyiz al-ʿAwjarī of Āl Mahdī in January 2006, the army's combing operations in surrounding areas triggered further confrontations between Houthis, security forces, and their respective tribal allies.[136]

The events in Wādī Nushūr and elsewhere suggest that tribal feuds were gradually growing in importance. This development was watched closely by both the government and the Houthi leaders. Controversial discussions were being held among the Houthi leadership on how to deal with the growing number of those among their fighters who were not ideologically motivated but had joined the rebellion for other reasons, namely revenge, tribal enmities and feuds, some of which dated back to the 1960s civil war and had now begun to fuse with the Houthi conflict.[137] The Houthi leaders understood only too well that the ideological drive of these men was not comparable to that of those who had dominated the battles in the first war and parts of the second. The Houthi veterans of the first war had been men who knew Ḥusayn al-Ḥūthī personally and who had studied at his right hand. Now, the increasing impact of tribal feuding led to a massive influx of other fighters, whose priorities threatened to dilute the movement's ideological orientation. Once the war had begun to perpetuate itself along the lines of prevalent tribal feuds, it became increasingly difficult to steer and control. On the other hand, the massive influx of tribesmen into the movement was a welcome development for the Houthis—since it bolstered their military strength and mass support—and was tolerated by the leadership.[138]

Fighting now flared up again in Banī Muʿādh, where much blood had been spilled in the second war. On 30 November, a Houthi ambush on a police patrol near Banī Muʿādh's weekly market al-Khafjī killed three soldiers and wounded fifteen others, and led to massive deployment of armed forces to the area.[139] The unrest and collateral damages in Banī Muʿādh prompted Shaykh Ḥusayn al-Surabī to request the army's withdrawal from the area. The government again convened a meeting with shaykhs of the Saḥār and Wāʾilah tribes and called on them to stand with the state and protect their regions from Houthi attacks.[140]

In January 2006, government forces carried out intense and fierce military operations along the 60-kilometre mountain range west of the Saʿdah-Bāqim road, including the areas Ṣabr, al-Ḥāribah, al-Khazāʾin, *hijrah* Fallalah and Umm Laylā in the extreme north. *Hijrah* Fallalah in particular became the arena of formidable clashes—a 'triangle of horror' (*muthallath al-ruʿb*) in which dozens of people were killed. After a siege that lasted more than a month, government troops re-gained control of Fallalah. *Mareb Press* reported that inside a nearby cave of Jabal al-Khazāʾin, the bodies of twenty Houthi fighters began to decompose as military forces prevented the collection and burial of their corpses for more than two weeks after their death. Locals described the armed confrontations in Saʿdah as a 'humanitarian and social disaster by all standards'.[141]

Many other places saw armed clashes: Marrān, Ḍaḥyān, Āl al-Ṣayfī (which has been virtually eradicated over the six rounds of war), al-Ṭalḥ, Jabal ʿIzzān, and Āl Sālim. Houthis launched offensives and sabotage operations against army and security positions and attacked shaykhs close to the government, such as the security director of Saḥār, whom they managed to wound, and (again) Ḥasan Manāʿ, who escaped unwounded.[142] On 18 January 2006, during the Shia festival *ʿīd al-ghadīr*, Houthi supporters lit bonfires on mountaintops around Saʿdah city and fired joyful shots from hundreds of guns, despite the tight security measures imposed by the authorities, who sought to prevent celebrations altogether.[143]

During the third war, ʿAmrān and al-Jawf were affected by fighting for the first time. In January 2006 the air force bombed the Jabal Ḥām area of al-Jawf's al-Matūn district, where Houthi followers—calling themselves 'Anṣār Allah in al-Jawf'[144]—had been regrouping and using the area to launch their sabotage attacks on military and government sites.[145] In February, armed clashes broke out in al-Ḥarf, Sufyān's district capital, located at the highway between Sanaʿa and Saʿdah city, which led to the wounding of fifteen people. The clashes erupted when people in al-Ḥarf protested against the deployment of a military brigade to al-Ḥarf and attacked a government building with small and medium arms. The situation escalated when the armed forces began to shell the house where the perpetrators were suspected to be hiding. Shaykh Bakīl ʿAbduh Ḥubaysh, son of Sufyān's senior shaykh ʿAbduh Ḥubaysh, told the press that after the army began its shelling, a number of tribal notables (*aʿyān*) intervened to evacuate women and children out of the house before the military proceeded to destroy it. However, the military opened fire on the notables, six of whom were seriously wounded and taken to hospitals in Sanaʿa and Saʿdah city. The situation in al-Ḥarf was teetering on the brink and would have escalated dramatically had one of the injured mediators died, among whom were respected tribal dignitaries of Sufyān's senior Ḥubaysh shaykhly lineage—namely, Aḥmad Ḥusayn Ḥubaysh (former Deputy Security Director of Sufyān), Khamāsh Ḥubaysh, and Ṣāliḥ Yaḥyā Ḥubaysh.[146]

On 24 December 2005, clashes erupted in Saʿdah city's central prison, called Qiḥzah, between prison guards and inmates protesting against their inhumane detention conditions. Many of the inmates were Houthi supporters who had been detained during the two previous rounds of war and the army's sweeping campaigns during the interim periods. Seven prisoners were killed and another fifty injured.[147] The Qiḥzah rebellion broke out after prison guards allegedly mistreated some prisoners, but sources say that the real reason behind it was Houthi dismay at the non-implementation of the 26 September 2005 presidential amnesty. Several months previously, in preparation for the amnesty, many inmates had been transferred from the prisons of al-Ḥudaydah and other governorates to Saʿdah's Qiḥzah prison, but their release had been delayed by the authorities. Governor Yaḥyā al-ʿAmrī set up a mediation committee consisting of Muḥammad ʿAbdullah al-Ṣaʿdī, ʿAbdullah Ḥusayn al-Muʾayyad, Ṣāliḥ al-Wajmān, Muḥammad al-Sharʿaī, and Zakariyā al-Shāmī, who were able to defuse the tensions.[148]

On 27 January 2006, the Criminal Investigation Prison in Sanaʿa witnessed a spectacular prison break in which the Houthi field commanders ʿAbdullah al-Ḥākim (Abū ʿAlī) and Ṭaha al-Ḍalʿaī escaped with the help of hand grenades. In the summer of 2005, during the sweeping campaign that followed the second war, the pair had been arrested in Ḍaḥyān as suspected members of the so-called 'Sanaʿa terrorist cell', which the Yemeni authorities accused of attempting to sabotage military and security vehicles and of assassinating senior military and security personnel. The government accused ʿAbdullah al-Ḥākim of having supported the preparation and processing of explosive materials used by members of the cell. The escapees' breakout was so audacious that it is widely understood to have been impossible without inside assistance. The hand grenades were packed in plastic bags and smuggled into the prison in a large bowl of *ʿaṣīd* (an extra-large wheat dumpling or porridge, eaten with fingers in a communal style). After their escape, they fled in a car waiting for them in the vicinity of the prison, all of which strengthened the belief that the escape was well planned and cleanly executed. In response to this case, the Ministry of the Interior opened an investigation that led to the dismissal of a number of senior officers in Sanaʿa, as well as the replacement of all guard members in the Criminal Investigation Prison.[149]

In those days, however, this was not even the most scandalous of jailbreaks. A few days later, on the morning of 3 February, nearly two dozen men crawled through a tunnel running from the basement of the Political Security Organization's prison in Sanaʿa to a neighbouring mosque.[150] The escapees included Jamāl al-Badwī, leader of the cell responsible for the bombing of the USS Cole in Adan in 2000, and Fawāz al-Rabīʿī, leader of the cell that attacked the French oil tanker *Limburg* in 2002. This escape would prove pivotal in the rise of Yemen's first durable al-Qaeda presence. Just seven months later, al-Qaeda launched synchronized vehicle-borne suicide attacks against Western oil facilities in Ma'rib and Ḥaḍramawt governorates, implemented almost exclusively by men of this breakout.

Mediation

While the third war dragged on, the presidential and local elections of September 2006 moved closer, in which the people of Saʿdah, too, would cast their votes on the continuation of Salih's long-term presidency and the composition of Saʿdah's local councils. The government came under increasing pressure to put at least a temporary end to the Saʿdah wars and to bring the situation under control. This was no easy task, as the governorate was already wartorn.

In order to ease the tensions, to substantiate its goodwill and therewith placate Saʿdah's voters, the government announced the compensation of war damages in the Saʿdah region while the third war was still being waged. It promised the provision of substantial funds for the restoration of public facilities and infrastructure, including the continuation of construction work on the region's most important road project: the Northern Ring Road, which—once completed—would connect Saʿdah city with its mountainous hinterland via Qaṭābir, Munabbih, Ghamr, Rāziḥ, Malāḥīẓ, Ḥaydān and Sāqayn.[151] This was not a completely altruistic project, since this road was essential for the military to control the unruly province and secure the army's supply lines. Furthermore, most of the funds would end up in the pockets of pro-government tribal contractors.[152] The pro-government newspaper *al-Mu'tamar* summed up the announcement's message thus: 'Sa'dah is a privileged region of Yemen, and benefits from development activities more than any other region in Yemen'.[153]

The president also set up a new mediation committee. For the first time since the outbreak of war in 2004, this committee was able to work successfully and managed to reach a contractual ceasefire (*ṣulḥ*) with the Houthis. It was headed by Brigadier General Yaḥyā Muḥammad al-Shāmī, a military man of *sayyid* descent who had been governor of Sa'dah in the 1980s and was now governor of al-Bayḍā'. Yaḥyā al-Shāmī assisted the president in selecting the other committee members. Compared with its predecessors, the composition of this committee was quite unusual. Nine of its eleven members were *sādah*: Muḥammad 'Abdullah al-Shar'ī, Muḥammad 'Abdullah al-Ṣa'dī, Faḍl Muḥammad al-Muṭā', Ibrāhīm Muḥammad al-Manṣūr, Ṣāliḥ al-Wajmān, 'Abdullah Ḥusayn al-Mu'ayyad, Ṣāliḥ 'Awaḍ al-Kibsī, and Aḥmad 'Ayḍah al-Ḥamzī, in addition to al-Shāmī. The tenth and eleventh members were the shaykhs Malfī Ḥumlān al-Ṣayfī (from the devastated Āl al-Ṣayfī) and 'Alī Nāṣir Qirshah (of Walad Mas'ūd, Saḥār), both suspected Houthi sympathizers.

This committee managed to meet with the Houthi leaders. On 23 February 2006, a number of agreements were signed by 'Abdulmalik al-Ḥūthī for the Houthis and Yaḥyā al-Shāmī for the government: the Houthis confirmed their adherence to the constitution, the Houthi slogan 'Death to America, Death to Israel...' was no longer to be chanted in mosques or on marches in the country's largest cities, Houthi hideouts were to be evacuated, the general presidential amnesty decreed in September 2005 was to be fully implemented, victims of the war were to be compensated, everyone would return to work, there would be no more arrests, Zaydi schools would reopen (having been ordered shut following the first war), and permission to teach Zaydi works would be granted, as long as these works agreed with the Quran and the Sunna.[154]

After signing the *ṣulḥ*—and ahead of the upcoming electoral campaigns—the government organized festivities in Ḍaḥyān, Munabbih and Qaṭābir to celebrate the end of violence and turmoil; these were attended by a parliamentary delegation of seventy members led by the GPC's assistant secretary-general, Shaykh Sulṭān al-Barakānī. The government also announced a prisoner amnesty, reconstruction assistance for Sa'dah's districts, and the planned electrification of the entire governorate. In recognition of his services in negotiating the *ṣulḥ* and ending the war, and in response to Houthi demands, President Salih appointed Yaḥyā al-Shāmī governor of Sa'dah. The new governor confidently announced that the *ṣulḥ* had 'ended the rebellion in Sa'dah forever'.[155]

6

THE LANGUAGE OF WAR

2006–11

The February 2006 *ṣulḥ* initiated several months of political détente, during which the government successfully conducted presidential and municipal elections. However, after the polls, the situation deteriorated and the war resumed. The *ṣulḥ* had given rise to great expectations, and its breakdown after a year threw away a unique, and probably the last, opportunity for a peaceful settlement of the Houthi conflict. Although significant mediation initiatives took place in the fourth to sixth wars, three of them brokered by Qatar, none of these initiatives were able to arouse the same local hopes and expectations as the 2006 ceasefire brokered by Yaḥyā al-Shāmī.

After the outbreak of the fourth war in February 2007, the internal and external dynamics of the conflict began to thwart all efforts at mediation and obstructed the implementation of ceasefire agreements. Many factors contributed to the perpetuation and expansion of the crisis. A hybrid, explosive conflict situation was emerging that hardly resembled the initial situation in 2004. Tribal feuding, the emergence of a war economy, domestic political intrigues, foreign meddling, and the increasing sectarian character of the war began to develop inexorably. Strife and discord characterized the relationships among all stakeholders, as the government, opposition parties, the military, shaykhs, tribes, and Houthis lost trust in each other and were often even at odds amongst themselves. As a result, 'the language of war imposed control over every inch of Saʿdah province (*lughat al-ḥarb farraḍat sayṭarah ʿalā kull shibr min anḥāʾ muḥāfaẓat Ṣaʿdah*), as a local put it.[1]

The government's indecision towards the Houthis was growing increasingly obvious. President Salih did not want to close the Saʿdah file forever, because he benefited in many ways from the prolongation of the war.[2] Under no circumstances, however, did he want to lose the war militarily, and from the fourth bout the ever-stronger Houthis began to downright embarrass the government's armed forces. This hesitation, in conjunction with the complex local and national situation, would ultimately lead to the nerve-racking stop-and-start process of the sixth war, deliberately stirred up and then toned down through successive cycles of political manoeuvring. Only Saudi Arabia's entry into the war in November 2009 brought a turning point, providing significant relief for the Yemeni government and military. In February 2010, the sixth and final 'official' Houthi war ended in stalemate: contrary to official statements, there was no written agreement and no document between the parties to the conflict to seal their last ceasefire. Officially, the war was only paused, in standby mode. The following year, in 2011, the Houthis in Saʿdah looked on as the Salih regime collapsed in Sanaʿa, opening a new window for action and alliance.

Third Interim: A Brief Period of Détente

After the *ṣulḥ*, successful negotiator Yaḥyā al-Shāmī and the hated Yaḥyā al-ʿAmrī found their positions swapped: al-Shāmī became governor of Saʿdah, and al-ʿAmrī was transferred from Saʿdah to al-Baydāʾ. Al-Shāmī's inauguration ushered in several months of rapprochement, which—like the stage of retardation in classical Greek tragedy—brought a fatal escalation to a temporary halt in a way that suggested the possibility of a different outcome. However, as we know, this transient phase of détente was only intended to facilitate the presidential and municipal elections scheduled for September 2006, and did not outlast them.

Brigadier General Yaḥyā Muḥammad al-Shāmī, who originated from Ibb, had joined the military corps in 1963 as a student at the Military Academy in Sanaʿa; after completing his studies, he took up numerous leadership positions. In 1985–7, he had been governor of Saʿdah. In 1990, he was appointed governor of Maʾrib. In 1995, after the civil war, he resigned from this post and worked in the GPC administration. In 1997, he was appointed governor of al-Baydāʾ until the beginning of 2006, when he was appointed head of the third war mediation committee in Saʿdah. He served as a governor of crisis management. Despite his early military career, Saʿdah's citizenry regarded him a 'civilian' (*rajul madanī*), in contrast with al-ʿAmrī, whose approach was regarded as that of an 'old-school security man' (*wasāʾil rajul al-amn al-ʿatīq*).[3] The decision to appoint al-Shāmī was a timely signal of hope, because he had the blessing of both the Houthis and the government. Since he had already served as governor in the 1980s, he was familiar with the region and its people.

Saʿdah's senior pro-government shaykhs, however, were not happy with al-Shāmī's appointment. Some had bad memories of his previous governorship, and apportioned to him a share of the blame for the emergence of the Houthi crisis. One shaykh of Jumāʿah recalled:

> In the late 1980s ʿAbdullah Rawkān and some other shaykhs went to Governor Yaḥyā al-Shāmī and warned him of Badr al-Dīn al-Ḥūthī and his activities in Marrān and Ḍaḥyān. ʿAbdullah Rawkān had been one of the first to sense that something dangerous was in progress. But Yaḥyā al-Shāmī replied that the *sayyid* [Badr al-Dīn al-Ḥūthī] only studies the Quran, and that he is a good man (*al-sayyid yadrus al-qurʾān wa huwa min ahl al-khayr*). Because of Yaḥyā al-Shāmī's talk, Yemen descended into mayhem and distress.[4]

The shaykhs suspected Yaḥyā al-Shāmī of being a Houthi sympathizer because during and after the mediation he made concessions to the movement, rather than keeping it on a tight leash. His policy of tolerance and laissez-faire inclinations towards the Houthis irritated the shaykhs. And, lest we forget, Yaḥyā al-Shāmī was a *sayyid*; given the shaykhs' traditional rivalry with the *sādah*, they did not trust him. In essence, whereas al-ʿAmrī had been too much of a statesman for their taste, al-Shāmī was not enough of one.[5]

Indeed, he pursued a difficult line of reconciliation between the warring parties. In the run-up to the September elections, he was just the man the government needed to cool tensions in Saʿdah and to successfully prepare and oversee the presidential elections:

> Yaḥyā al-Shāmī was appointed governor for the purpose of calming the situation until the presidential and municipal elections were peacefully held. He was able to convince the sons of Saʿdah that they need security and stability, that they should stop the war and leave the mountains, return to their homes, and participate in the elections.[6]

On his inaugural tour through the districts, al-Shāmī sought to defuse tensions by encouraging Houthis to come out of their strongholds and hideouts in the mountains, offering them safe return to their home areas. He did not, however, visit the Houthi strongholds of Maṭrah and al-Naqʿah, because 'they were uninhabited'.[7] In order to prove his good faith, he began to implement the promised amnesty, prompting the release of 627 of 1,500 Houthi supporters, including Muḥammad Badr al-Dīn al-Ḥūthī, who had been arrested during the sweeping campaign after the second war. The released Houthis pledged not to shout the Houthi slogan. However, the local authorities delayed the release of further detainees and even imprisoned some of those who returned home from the battlefields and Houthi strongholds.[8] Government troops withdrew from the Saḥār area around Saʿdah city, which generally calmed down—except in Ḍaḥyān, where the conflict kept simmering.

More conciliatory measures in Saʿdah followed. The Houthis insisted on participating in municipal decision-making processes and demanded that a number of them be appointed to important positions, whereupon the government—albeit reluctantly, because it considered this a diminution of its prestige—changed some district directors in the province.[9] As part of President Salih's re-election campaign, the government announced allocation of $150 million for service projects in the province that year.[10] The new district director of Ḥaydān, Shaykh Ṣāliḥ Abū ʿAwjāʾ,[11] announced the long-planned completion of the Northern Ring Road section connecting Saʿdah city with the districts of Sāqayn and Ḥaydān; he also promised construction of schools, and the renewal and expansion of the province's electricity and water network.[12] A parliamentary delegation of seventy MPs, headed by GPC secretary-general Sulṭān al-Barakānī, toured the province and made public appearances in Munabbih, Qaṭābir, and Ḥaydān districts, where they promised generous compensation of war damages. They were welcomed enthusiastically by local GPC MP shaykhs and their loyalists. Yaḥyā al-Shāmī granted the Zaydi population the right to celebrate *ʿīd al-ghadīr*, which had been banned since 1970, and huge public *ghadīr* celebrations took place in January 2007.

On 20 September 2006, the presidential and municipal elections were held. Originally, as tensions increased over an inevitable but hugely unpopular reduction of fuel subsidies in 2005, President Salih had announced that he would not seek re-election in 2006, saying that it was time for 'young blood' to lead the country. His announcement sparked demonstrations by both thousands of Yemenis supporting the decision and thousands urging him to reconsider. Salih retracted his decision in late June 2006, but only after a long dramatic interlude.[13]

In September 2006, Salih was officially awarded 77 per cent of the national vote. His opponent, Fayṣal b. Shamlān (JMP), trailed in second place with 22 per cent, while the combined vote share of three other candidates amounted to less than 1 per cent.[14] In Saʿdah governorate, the elections were a resounding success for the GPC. On average the districts of Saʿdah voted for Salih by 91 per cent. Munabbih was the only district in Yemen where the president received 100 per cent of votes—a clear message, not necessarily in favour of Salih, but against the Houthis. By comparison, Salih's vote share in neighbouring Rāziḥ was only 72 per cent.[15]

The simultaneous municipal elections determined the composition of the local councils at district and governorate level.[16] Again, the GPC, as well as some independent candidates, came out on top.[17] An evaluation of the electoral lists shows that Ḥizb al-Ḥaqq nominated five (unsuccessful) candidates in Saʿdah governorate; Iṣlāḥ did not nominate any. Local sources involved in the electoral process opined that Iṣlāḥ, traversed by internal fractions, had refrained from nominating a candidate because the party did not have sufficient support on the ground, and therefore did not see any chance of electoral success—a phenomenon that also occurred in other governorates, as Iṣlāḥ yielded relatively poor results nationwide.[18]

The GPC's success in the conflict-torn northern governorate, and the low number of municipal opposition candidates, suggest that non-GPC candidates had almost no chance in Yemen's political system, and that Saʿdah governorate, though conflict-ridden, was still largely under state political control at this time. Voting for Salih was a clear signal against the Houthis, who had campaigned for a boycott of the elections, leading to low voter turnout.[19] Moreover, voting behaviour in Saʿdah was certainly influenced by Salih's promise of a veritable bonanza of compensation services and investment in infrastructure in the underdeveloped and war-torn governorate.

We do not know to what extent the official election results were reliable. In fact, they could hardly be monitored, since the Yemeni Supreme Commission for Elections and Referendum (SCER) was unable to undertake a review of local council constituencies ahead of the elections. The European Union Election Observation Mission called the elections 'an open and genuine contest', but with 'important shortcomings' in regard to intimidation at some polling stations, violation of voter secrecy, GPC campaigning, and underage voting.[20]

Immediately after the elections, Yaḥyā al-Ḥūthī raised concerns from exile in Germany about their execution. He publicly condemned the conduct of the electoral process in Saʿdah and complained of forgery, fraud, and voter coercion in favour of the ruling party's candidates. On behalf of the Houthis, he refused to recognize the outcome and demanded a free and fair electoral climate in which the president 'could not control a nation for twenty-eight years'.[21]

Shortly after the elections, in October 2006, President Salih personally visited Sāqayn and Ḥaydān districts. Riding the wave of his electoral success, he even visited the mighty boulder cliffs and caves of Jurf Salmān in Marrān, in which Ḥusayn al-Ḥūthī had stood and perished during the first war. During his visit, the president repeated his promise of extensive assistance for infrastructure, education, electricity, water and health worth about 2 billion Yemeni riyals, including 400 million granted by King Abdullah of Saudi Arabia.[22]

Warmongers

After September, the short period of détente soon ended. True to his policy, Yaḥyā al-Shāmī continued to defuse tensions between the parties to the conflict, but after the elections his policy increasingly lacked government backing. Serious differences emerged between him and General ʿAlī Muḥsin, who fundamentally disagreed on how to solve the Houthi problem. Whereas al-Shāmī unwaveringly sought to implement the terms of the *ṣulḥ*, ʿAlī Muḥsin constantly opted for military solutions. Moreover, ʿAlī Muḥsin was known for his anti-Hashemite views.[23] Al-Shāmī soon felt betrayed by the regime. When tensions came to a head in November 2006 during the Gaddafi 'mediation', al-Shāmī headed for Sanaʿa, where he refused to leave his house, in protest at the government's poor management of the crisis. One observer explained:

> The problem was, he [Yaḥyā al-Shāmī] talked to the president about dialogue and co-opting the Houthi supporters, and then fifteen guys followed him telling the president that we should just shoot them all. [...] The government was divided between two camps: those who called for 'crushing' the Houthis, and those who knew that using only military means will not solve the problems in Saʿdah over the long term. Well, since the elections the 'let's crush them' camp has taken charge again.[24]

Moreover, the conflict had already begun to develop a dynamic of its own, within a wider framework of separate local, domestic and international driving forces. In many places, tribal dynamics had taken over the conflict: wherever blood had been spilled, the conflict threatened to spiral into cycles of retaliatory violence. On the domestic level, the war was fuelled by political rivalries and the emergence of a profitable war economy. External factors, too, led to a continuation of the conflict, as foreign actors such as Saudi Arabia, Libya and (allegedly) Iran began to intervene.

Revenge and Tribal Feuding

From the second war, it became evident that a significant number of those joining the Houthi ranks were no longer religiously or ideologically motivated, but became involved in the conflict for other reasons. The earliest Houthi warriors had been supporters, relatives, friends, and students of Ḥusayn al-Ḥūthī. Most hailed from the Saʿdah region, especially from the Khawlān tribe, yet also among his supporters were people from other regions and governorates with Zaydi populations, such as Ḥajjah, Dhamār, Sanaʿa, ʿAmrān, and al-Jawf. Many had been imprisoned during the first war and the sweeping campaign of the first interim; after their release, they returned in numbers to the Saʿdah region and resumed fighting.

The second, growing group of Houthi supporters had not joined the rebellion primarily for ideological or sectarian reasons. Many of them had been drawn into the conflict because members of their family or tribe had been killed by bombings in the area and the brutal actions of the armed forces. Others had lost their homes or farms. By 2006, thousands of men were fighting for the Houthis, but not all of them shared the Houthi ideology. Rather, they were 'coasting the wave' of the rebellion in order to fight for their tribe, or against their rivals, the government, or a hated shaykh. Thus, many supporters of the Houthi movement had no 'real' loyalty to it; they switched sides based on immediate private interests.

As we have seen, the incursion of armed Ḥāshid warriors as auxiliaries of the Yemeni army was a particularly sensitive and momentous issue. Ever since the outbreak of the first war in 2004, Ḥāshid irregulars had fought alongside regular troops. When the conflict expanded in scope and magnitude, their presence continued to grow and finally culminated in the mass recruitments of the Popular Army during the fourth war (February–June 2007).[25] However, Saʿdah governorate is the settlement area of tribes of the Khawlān b. ʿĀmir confederation (Saḥār, Jumāʿah, Khawlān, Rāziḥ, Munabbih), the Bakīl confederation (Wāʾilah, parts of Dahm), and small enclaves of the Wādiʿah. Saʿdah's west and centre are dominated by the Khawlān b. ʿĀmir, meaning that these areas are subject to the confederation's grand summons (*al-dāʿī al-kabīr li-Khawlān bin ʿĀmir*). Locals would say: *Ṣaʿdah dāʿīhā al-kabīr Khawlān bin ʿĀmir wa mā lahā dakhl min Ḥāshid wa Bakīl*—'Saʿdah is subject to the summons of the Khawlān b. ʿĀmir, and the Ḥāshid and Bakīl should not interfere'. Meanwhile, the eastern parts of the Saʿdah region and al-Jawf are dominated by Bakīl tribes, whose areas are subject to the grand summons of the Bakīl confederation. The armed incursions of Ḥāshid fighters into Bakīl territories constituted a particularly grave issue, because the Bakīl and Ḥāshid have a long history of bitter rivalry for power and influence.

Many tribes of the conflict area were furious at the deployment of Ḥāshid irregulars to their tribal regions. Both the Khawlān b. ʿĀmir and the Bakīl considered these armed incursions an infringement of their sovereignty and territorial integrity, and defended themselves accordingly against the presence of these mercenaries. This was not only an issue of tribal sovereignty, as there was also concern about the plundering that occurred in their regions. The government paid the Ḥāshid mercenaries a small wage via their shaykhs, but they were first and foremost a 'looting force' rewarded with such opportunities in return for their services. However, in the over-heated context of the Saʿdah wars, taking up arms against the Ḥāshid irregulars was tantamount to joining the ranks of the Houthis.

This is not to say that all tribes of the conflict area joined the Houthis. On the contrary, after years of fighting, Saʿdah's tribes became increasingly polarized. Among the Khawlān b. ʿĀmir tribes, this led to a significant increase in intra-tribal conflict as disagreements between tribal groups became wrapped up in the larger Houthi conflict. Before the outbreak of the Saʿdah wars, many sections of the Khawlān b. ʿĀmir were engaged in a variety of petty feuds and ancient antagonisms over land and honour, but seldom (if ever) in large conflicts between the confederation's member tribes—the specific territorial pattern of the confederation and the spatial dispersion of its two moieties usually prevented block formation and so the uncontrolled escalation of large intertribal conflicts.[26]

Many of these petty conflicts among the Khawlān b. ʿĀmir merged with the wider Saʿdah wars as feuding tribal groups involved sought the assistance of either the government or the Houthis. This implies that battles related to the Houthi conflict have been frequent within the territory of the Khawlān b. ʿĀmir confederation—but both the Houthis and their opponents were relatively incoherent groups that could, in some cases, loosely correspond to certain tribal segments, but hardly if ever to whole tribes. One exception is the Munabbih tribe, who formed a relatively homogeneous bloc of anti-Houthi solidarity. During the sixth war (August 2009–February 2010), the Munabbih tried (ultimately unsuccessfully) to ward off the Houthis' endeavours to extend control over their area.

In contrast, among the Bakīl, a confederation historically much more involved in Yemen's national political power struggles than the rather 'peripheral' tribes of the Khawlān b. ʿĀmir, the fusion of tribal feuding with the Houthi conflict at times led to the formation of large blocs and the opening of inter-tribal fronts, as a result of which whole tribes were at times opposed. The situation in northern ʿAmrān (Sufyān against al-ʿUṣaymāt) and al-Jawf (Hamdān al-Jawf and Dhū Ḥusayn, notably its Shawlān section, against Dhū Muḥammad and Āl Ashrāf) are good examples. This is not to say that the Saʿdah wars were bloodier or more brutal among the Bakīl, as the war claimed a high death toll everywhere. Among the confederation's tribes and sections, however, the fronts (the distinction between Houthi and government supporters) tended to be more homogeneous and clear-cut than among the Khawlān b. ʿĀmir.

On this basis, there is no contradiction between the steady expansion of the war zone and the fact that the Houthi leaders, ʿAbdulmalik al-Ḥūthī and ʿAbdullah al-Razzāmī, were entrenched in the inaccessible areas of Maṭrah and al-Naqʿah without sufficient access to communication (the government repeatedly blocked the mobile telephone network in Saʿdah). In many areas, the war began to steer itself by evolving along prevalent tribal fault lines. Violence bred violence, which led to revenge and a slippery slope away from peaceful solutions. Vengeance, normally contained and channelled into litigation by customary tribal mediation, became a casus belli, at times blurring the distinction between tribal revenge and the Houthi conflict. As a result, one area after another descended into war:

> These retaliatory crimes, and especially those that happened during the truce (*hudnah*) following the third war, were a clear sign that the province had already got on the slide into playoffs and reprisals between its sons. Blood has been shed, and the province has been dragged into the mazes of tribalism (*matāhāt al-ʿaṣabiyyah al-qabaliyyah*). That is why we needed tribal mediation in order to address the issues that arose during the wars: cases of murder, robbery, looting, destruction of property, expulsion [...] The imperatives of blood feud gained the upper hand, hearts were angered, and blood was spilled between the tribes and among them, between those who were with al-Ḥūthī and those who were with the government, or with whomever. However, what was important was that blood had been shed.[27]

Despite the important role of tribal feuding, the Houthi conflict never was a purely tribal conflict. By the heterogeneity of its stakeholders (tribesmen, *sādah*, armed forces, mercenaries, etc.) and their numerous, even diverging objectives and motivations, the conflict became a kind of 'hybrid' war—*ḥarb mukhtalaṭah*, as locals say—whose political, ideological, military, tribal, sectarian, and personal motivations kept oscillating. As a result, tribal customs of peaceful conflict settlement were increasingly ignored. The brutalization of the war was not caused by tribal norms, but rather by their erosion. The ferocity of the battles was of a kind and on a scale exceeding all local rules of engagement, and clearly went far beyond the maximum escalation level of tribal conflict as defined by Jamous.[28]

War Economy

By 2006 the conflict had already given rise to a war economy that helped ensure its perpetuation. Many stakeholders—traders, shaykhs, army officers, state officials, and the government itself—benefited from the war and therefore had no interest in its end.

As the International Crisis Group has worked out, this war economy had many faces.[29] Poorly paid soldiers and mercenaries sold their weapons to the Houthis, pretending to their government-backed superiors that they had lost them. At a higher level, the same deals were even more profitable. Leading military officers are said to have facilitated large-scale arms sales from army stocks to the Houthis.[30] In addition, the military campaigns in Saʿdah justified increased military budgets without independent oversight. Throughout the war, army leaders routinely demanded additional weapons; although some were used against the Houthis, a significant proportion was diverted to local and regional (particularly Somali) markets. 'Ghost soldiers' became a problem: individuals listed on the military payroll who never or rarely worked, their pay pocketed by the military elite and their equipment sold on the black market.[31] Lack of oversight in the context of an expanding military budget has encouraged competition and corruption and fostered trafficking within the military. Many weapons have thus found their way to the Houthis they were intended to combat.[32]

The Saʿdah wars were the heyday of the smugglers among military and government officials and some shaykhs. As the military and humanitarian crisis worsened, they appear to have amassed fortunes in the smuggling of arms, food staples, diesel, and consumer products. Due to both the paucity of state investment in the Saʿdah region and its largely unguarded border with Saudi Arabia, smuggling was a major economic activity and source of income, making cross-border trade a critical revenue generator and one of the war's unspoken stakes.[33]

Additional sources of income were generated through enlistment of tribal militias. Although they were conscious of the need to fight the Houthis, many shaykhs were utterly opposed to the recruitment of their tribesmen for the war against them. However, this phenomenon financially benefited others, as the money allocated to fund tribal militias often ended up in the pockets of the shaykhs who led them; this was the case of Ḥusayn al-Aḥmar's Popular Army, which was recruited in the fourth war.[34] Both the Yemeni and Saudi governments were interested in these tribal militias, and Salih's government had asked Riyadh to fund them; they also received support from Islamists such as ʿAbdulmajīd al-Zindānī. A common practice among certain shaykhs was to mobilize a much lower number of troops than required and keep the rest of the money for themselves: more 'ghost soldiers'.

These are only a few aspects of the emerging economy that turned the Saʿdah wars into a lucrative business. Many stakeholders profited from the war, and over time, the conflict became a permanent tool for generating personal wealth. By perpetuating the war and artificially controlling its intensity, they could provide themselves with an almost infinite source of income.

The Iran Narrative

The international war industry's contribution to the perpetuation of the war in Saʿdah was even greater. It is certainly no exaggeration to say that, in relation to the amounts of weapons, budgetary aid, and military support that the Yemeni government received from its strategic partner states—notably Saudi Arabia and the US—the fraud, scam and racketeering activities of the domestic war economy were closer to peanuts.

Since the inception of the Saʿdah wars in 2004, Yemeni officials have accused foreign countries of supporting the Houthis; Iran, in particular, has been highlighted as a foreign state sponsor of the rebellion. Until 2009, however, Iran didn't show much interest in the Houthis, and until 2011 there was virtually no hard evidence for direct Iranian involvement in Saʿdah, as it made far more sense for Tehran to maintain good relations with Sanaʿa than to support a movement that then had little prospect of actually overthrowing the Salih regime, and would probably not be subservient to Tehran even if it did.

Nevertheless, the suspicions about Iranian support for the Houthis, purposely raised by the government from the onset of war, had far-reaching geopolitical consequences. The integration of the Houthi conflict into the larger context of the Sunni-Shia divide, and thus into the rivalry between Saudi Arabia and Iran, had major material and financial benefits for the Yemeni regime. The transformation of Iran into an overtly Shia power after its Islamic revolution (1979) had induced Saudi Arabia to accelerate the propagation of Wahhabism, as both countries revived a centuries-old sectarian dispute over the true interpretation of Islam. Sunni Saudi Arabia and Shia Iran, competing for leadership of global Islam, have used the sectarian divide to further their ambitions. The Yemeni regime's mantra-like warnings since 2004 of the emergence of a Shia crescent—spanning from Lebanon via Iraq and Iran to Yemen—found fertile soil in Saudi Arabia, which faced a growing Shia challenge from increased Iranian influence in Iraq and globally following the fall of Saddam Husayn, Hezbollah's successes in Lebanon, Iran's championing of Hamas in Palestine, and the development of Iran's nuclear programme.[35]

With the onset of war in Saʿdah, President Salih began conjuring the spectre of Iran's growing political influence in Yemen's Zaydi north, purposefully stirring Saudi anxieties over a Shia political revival in Yemen. He was quick to recognize the potential of the Houthi crisis for generating Saudi concern over the conflict, ensuring continued monetary support for Yemeni military operations. Salih viewed Saudi involvement in the war, and the concomitant increase in direct Saudi budget support to Sanaʿa, as an incentive to prolong, rather than seek to mediate, the campaign in Saʿdah.

As a result, from 2004 the regime's rhetoric was front-loaded with anti-Iranian propaganda. It depicted the Houthis as a movement backed and remote-controlled by Iran, at times even as renegades who had abandoned Zaydi Fiver Shiism in favour of Iranian Twelver Shiism, portraying them as a 'foreign' proxy group or Fifth Column of Iranian Imamism in Yemen. By depicting the Houthis as foreign agents supported by Iran, the government raised suspicions that they were importing Iran's Islamic revolution to Yemen.[36] When discussing Houthi motives for a connection with Iran, government spokesmen and media outlets frequently described the al-Ḥūthī family as aligned with Iran's agenda to drive a Shia wedge into the Arab heartland.

Saudi Arabia, too, recognized the benefits of the Iran narrative for the assertion of its strategic objectives in Yemen and for strengthening its influence in Yemen's border areas and beyond. Internally, the Saudis were by no means convinced of Salih's claims regarding Iranian involvement in Saʿdah. Iranian sympathy and diplomatic and political support for the Houthis were undeniable—but until 2011, Iranian military or financial assistance to the movement was impossible to prove. As late as December 2009—when Saudi Arabia had already entered the war—the US Embassy in Yemen reported that members of the Saudi government's Special Office for Yemen Affairs, a committee headed by Crown Prince Sultan, were privately sceptical of Salih's claims of

Iranian involvement and his desire to regionalize the conflict. The Saudi committee members privately shared the view that the Yemeni president was providing a false or exaggerated picture of Iranian aid to the Houthis in order to elicit direct Saudi involvement. One committee member was quoted saying: 'We know Salih is lying about Iran, but there's nothing we can do about it now'. Senior Saudi officials made no secret of their distaste for Salih, but saw him as the 'devil they know'.[37]

When it came to the US, Salih typically followed much the same process, placing emphasis on the Houthis' slogan 'Death to America, Death to Israel....' and portraying the movement as a terrorist organization. Having been painfully burnt during the First Gulf War (Desert Storm) when he sided with Saddam Husayn, the president placed great importance on cooperation with the US in the Saʿdah wars. Numerous Wikileaks cables substantiate Salih's brazen citation of the Houthi slogan and the movement's anti-American strain to extract US budgetary and military support for his regime. Whereas to the Saudis he conjured the Iranian bogeyman, when dealing with Washington he maintained persistently that the Houthis were a terrorist group seeking to target US and Israeli interests, in a bid to incorporate his military campaign in Saʿdah into the Global War on Terror. By depicting the war as a struggle against terrorism in Yemen, the government also had an opportunity to dispel American suspicion about some senior government and military officials' links with radical militancy.[38]

At the time of the second war in 2005, Foreign Minister Abū Bakr al-Qirbī had begun asking for substantial US support for the Yemeni government against the Houthis. On the political level, al-Qirbī said that there was no doubt that they were a 'terrorist organization'—because 'they use terrorist tactics and they have outside financial support',[39] supposedly from Iran and Lebanese Hezbollah. Al-Qirbī maintained that although the rebellion had started as a local Zaydi movement, it had evolved into a militant organization connected with Twelver Shiism and could expand to Saudi Arabia, Bahrain and Kuwait.[40]

A few days after al-Qirbī's diplomatic foray, the US Embassy to Yemen listed Salih's material demands. Under the heading 'President Saleh urgently requests material assistance for his security forces currently engaged with al-Houthi insurgents', the US Embassy conveyed an extensive list of military equipment sought by Sanaʿa. These included armoured high-mobility multi-purpose wheeled vehicles (HMMWVs), night vision devices (NVDs), M-24 sniper systems for target interdiction, grenade launchers and ammunition for use against insurgent forces in caves and on mountain- or hilltops, M-240 machine guns and ammunition, man-portable anti-armour weapons systems with a 1-kilometre stand-off to destroy bunkers and hardened positions, non-lethal riot control gas canisters and launchers, armoured personnel carriers, armoured recovery vehicles, an armoured mobile operations centre capable of transmitting live digital feed via satellite or radio to headquarters or base station, and so on.[41]

As the fighting spread, Salih regularly increased his demands. Just after the end of the second war, the US Embassy cabled to Washington:

> Saleh raised the costs to the ROYG [Republic of Yemen Government] of fighting the second al-Houthi insurrection, claiming (as he has often in the past) that he fought al-Houthi, son and father, on behalf of the U.S. and as part of Global War on Terror. Pitching for USG funds to partially compensate for expenditures of funds and materiel in Saada, Saleh claimed the ROYG has spent a whopping 50 billion YR (approximately 262 Million USD) fighting "your fight." The U.S., insisted the President, has an obligation to pay for some of this damage, "or would you prefer we allow the al-Houthis to chant 'Death to America' on the streets of Sanaa? If you don't care," added the Yemeni President, "then I'll let them say what they want," but warned "it could lead to real chaos." President Saleh also asked Ambassador to weigh in with the UK over reported British objections to the use of Central Security Forces (CSF-CTU) in Saada. Comment: Saleh ended the meeting abruptly, but not uncharacteristically, with a "bye, bye!" before Ambassador could respond to his last request.[42]

The exact figures of US military and budgetary aid to Yemen are unknown, but Salih's constant demands indicate that the support was significant. US diplomats were not blind to his calculations. Washington neither felt threatened by the Houthi slogan—which it took to be 'harmless venting'[43]—nor believed in Iranian backing for the movement, since the 'sloganeering' was the sum total of what Salih could produce in the way of evidence. In 2009, the Obama administration believed that Iranian influence in Yemen had thus far been limited to informal religious ties between Yemeni and Iranian scholars and negligible Iranian investment in the energy and development sectors.[44] It refused to classify the Houthis as a terrorist group, though it still granted the Yemeni government generous military and monetary support, hoping that once the problem in Saʿdah was resolved, Yemen would concentrate its entire strength on its core mission: combating al-Qaeda in the south and east.

Throughout the Saʿdah wars, the notion of Iranian backing for the Houthis was treated as gospel by the Yemeni government. Yet these allegations do not appear to have stunted bilateral relations with Iran. As late as 2008, Yemen's official news agency SABA reported that Foreign Minister Abū Bakr al-Qirbī had negotiated greater economic cooperation while in Tehran. In the same year, Iranian Foreign Minister Manouchehr Mottaki visited Yemen, advancing various Iranian economic projects, especially in the crucial areas of oil and energy. Iranian warships were still allowed to refuel and resupply in Adan during this period.[45]

The situation only changed during the sixth war. After Saudi Arabia intervened militarily in the conflict in November 2009, thus internationalizing it, Iran's full attention indeed turned to the Houthis. From that time, reports on alleged arms shipments from Iran to Yemen grew. Information on these shipments, however, remained vague and unsubstantiated, still solely based on information provided by the Yemeni authorities and impossible to verify by independent observers (such as the UN).[46]

With the beginning of the Arab Spring in 2011, and its impact on Syria, Bahrain and Yemen, the situation changed again. Terrill has argued that the nature of Iranian direct intervention in Yemen seems to have evolved since 2011, when Iran began facing a number of serious geopolitical problems that may have increased its interest in Yemen.[47] Riyadh's relations with Tehran were damaged by the Saudi-led GCC intervention in Bahrain in March 2011, and continued Saudi involvement in Bahrain roiled the Iranians. More significantly, over time, the Iranians have become increasingly concerned over the future of their Syrian ally Bashar al-Assad, who has failed to crush the fierce uprising against him. Adding to the problem, Iran's cold war with Saudi Arabia had intensified strongly as Riyadh has sided with the Syrian rebels, both arming them and helping to lead the successful effort to suspend Syrian membership of the Arab League, thereby further isolating a key Iranian ally.[48]

In early 2011, US government officials and major US media outlets publicly began treating accusations of Iranian weapons being transferred to the Houthis as a serious concern. American officials, having previously dismissed such accusations as baseless, have remarked since 2012 that the Iranians appear to be providing at least limited material support to the Houthis.[49] Suspicion grew in January 2013, when a Yemeni Coast Guard vessel, supported by the destroyer USS *Farragut*, sent a boarding party to search a vessel, the *Jihan I*, which was loaded with a number of weapons and operating within Yemeni waters under the Panamanian flag.[50] However, to date there is still no firm evidence that these weapons came from Iran or were destined for the Houthis; a 2015 UN Security Council Report only 'suggests' that Iran was the origin of these shipments, and that the intended recipients were the Houthis in Yemen or possibly, in some cases, other recipients in neighbouring countries.[51]

Since 2014, Iran has played a much stronger role in Yemen than during the Saʿdah wars of 2004–10. Iran was able to work more effectively with the Houthi movement after it became the de facto authority in Saʿdah province and, at times, even in Sanaʿa. Iran's increased involvement in Yemen also appears to have been spurred by what Tehran perceives as geopolitical pressures resulting from both the fear of encirclement and the potential threats of the Arab Spring, especially the danger that the Assad regime will lose its struggle to remain in power or that Syria will remain destabilized for years.[52]

However, cooperation between the rebels and Iran does not amount to the Houthis becoming Tehran's proxies, since the religious and political differences between the two are considerable. Unfortunately, much of the foreign media and international analysis of the Houthi conflict is still based on the pretence that Yemen has been involved since 2004 in a proxy conflict between Saudi Arabia and Iran. This narrative omits the conflict's much stronger grounding in the Yemeni state's patronage preferences in the country's north. Salisbury has summed this up well: 'At first sight, Yemen appears likely to be another country where Saudi-Iranian tensions further complicate existing home-grown rivalries. At root, however, the latter are local disputes, far more than they are a proxy conflict between Saudi Arabia and Iran'.[53]

The Gaddafi Issue

In November 2006, when the relationship between Governor Yaḥyā al-Shāmī and the government in Sanaʿa had already begun to deteriorate and the Saʿdah region was lurching toward the fourth war, reports on mediation efforts by Libya's revolutionary leader Muʿammar al-Gaddafi were leaked to the press.[54] The Gaddafi issue was so murky that I have decided not to classify it as 'mediation' but rather as 'foreign meddling'. The scarcity of reliable written sources has further challenged the possibility of a balanced presentation of this somewhat bizarre episode. Some said that Gaddafi had offered the Yemeni government his mediation services. Others, however, believed that Salih had asked Gaddafi to mediate, and that this was a ploy to prove that the Houthis had established links with Gaddafi. I myself concur with those who argued that Gaddafi cared about neither the Yemeni government nor the Houthis, and that his 'mediation' initiative seems to have been a scheme to upset his political opponent: Saudi Arabia.

In early December 2006, Gaddafi's son Sayf al-Islām, chairman of the Gaddafi International Foundation of Charitable Associations (GIFCA), travelled to

Sanaʿa to explore possibilities for mediation between the Houthis and the Yemeni government. He also met with Ahmad Salih, reportedly to implement a number of charitable projects in Yemen. That same month, Yaḥyā al-Ḥūthī travelled from Germany to Libya and met with Gaddafi and the chairman of the Libyan Central Bureau of Military Intelligence, ʿAbdullah al-Sanūsī.[55]

Gaddafi's mediation attempt in Yemen quickly turned into a fiasco. Yaḥyā al-Ḥūthī's intermittent presence in Libya was an apparent source of irritation in Sanaʿa. The Yemeni government made an official request to Libya for his extradition, which Tripoli ignored, and also began steps to strip Yaḥyā of his parliamentary immunity.[56] In consequence, relations between Salih and Gaddafi gradually soured as Sanaʿa accused Tripoli of sympathizing with the Houthis. When, in January 2007, Libya's ambassador to Yemen, Khālid al-Shaykh, travelled to Saʿdah to meet with shaykhs and Houthi leaders, he was severely attacked by government-linked media.[57]

In fact, it soon became apparent that Gaddafi's efforts in Saʿdah were not intended to mediate, but instead to exploit the dangerous situation to settle scores with the Saudis. Libyan-Saudi relations have a history of tension, ever since Gaddafi overthrew the Libyan monarchy in 1969 and declared himself a revolutionary leader committed to Arab unification and fighting conservative Arab regimes—Saudi Arabia, which he accused of being subservient to the Americans, was at the top of the list.[58] Libyan agents reportedly planned on several occasions to disrupt the pilgrimage at Mecca, and in 2004 allegedly plotted to assassinate Crown Prince Abdullah (who became king of Saudi Arabia the following year).[59]

In 2006, Gaddafi seems to have applied his leverage in northern Yemen's conflict-ridden tribal environment to destabilize the Saudi Kingdom. About two dozen influential shaykhs of Saʿdah, ʿAmrān, and al-Jawf received very large sums of money from Libya, intended to cause unrest in northern Yemen and create problems for the region's Saudi neighbour. According to *Al-Sharq al-Awsat*, Ḥusayn al-Aḥmar and Fāris Manāʿ were among the recipients.[60] Gaddafi's allocations in Yemen's north were rumoured to have been to the tune of a high double-digit million range in US dollars. Yet his resort to subversion and meddling in Saʿdah proved costly and unsuccessful. An observer from the region recalled the impact of his chequebook diplomacy and 'mediation' endeavours in Yemen:

> Gaddafi has given lots of dollars to the shaykhs in order to create unrest and disturbances and to destabilize the security situation in the areas bordering on Saudi Arabia. When Gaddafi began to dispense his dollar millions in Saʿdah, the shaykhs

> literally freaked out. Some shaykhs commissioned poets to compose odes to Gaddafi, which they conveyed to him through the Libyan ambassador. A very important shaykh of al-Jawf told the Libyan ambassador that he wanted to give a thoroughbred camel as a gift to Gaddafi, and Gaddafi sent a private jet to Yemen to pick it up. Some of the shaykhs were pretty clever. They took pictures of the people in January 2007 at the huge *ʿīd al-ghadīr* celebrations permitted by the new governor, and told Gaddafi that these people were their tribesmen hailing him. You know, Gaddafi was a lunatic and loved to see his followers everywhere. But his money went completely to waste. Gaddafi was not able to wield any influence in Saʿdah. The shaykhs took the money and had no intention of carrying out the mission. Some of the shaykhs built large villas with that money, which you can see in Sanaʿa. Years later, many of these villas were blown up, first by the Houthis during their march on Sanaʿa, then by the Saudis during Operation Decisive Storm.[61]

These shadowy cash transfers from Libya provoked unrest in Saʿdah. The money being poured into the governorate aroused envy and resentment between the Yemeni government and the shaykhs, and among the shaykhs themselves just as many felt betrayed and cheated by other shaykhs who had had their slice of the cake. Several assassination attempts on influential shaykhs—attributed in the war's turmoil to the Houthis—are in fact said to have been conflicts between rival shaykhs in connection with the Gaddafi allocations. In 2010, Fāris Manāʿ's alleged Libya connections were a point of the indictment which brought him to jail.[62] A source commented dryly: 'I remember well the Gaddafi money and the squabbles it caused. Arms deals were also big factors in these squabbles—a lot of shady deals. Someone should make a movie, honestly.'[63]

There is no reliable information as to whether or to what extent the Houthis benefited financially from Gaddafi's 'mediation': Houthi sources deny any Libyan financial support.[64] One diplomatic source, however, has said: 'I'm pretty sure Yaḥyā al-Ḥūthī received a gift also but had no intention of doing Gaddafi any favours, but the Houthis were looking for financing anywhere they could. At the time, Iran was not yet a patron.'[65]

Gaddafi's maladroit diplomacy and provocative tactics did not yield the desired results, but rather provoked the Salih government as well as the Saudis. When, in May 2007 during the fourth war, signs of mediation efforts by (the more prosperous) Qatar arose, the shaykhs of Saʿdah called upon the government to cut ties with Libya and to close Yemen's embassy in Tripoli over 'Libya's support to the Houthis'.[66] During the ensuing diplomatic imbroglio, the Yemeni government recalled its ambassador to Libya. Salih also asked the US embassy if it could press Libya diplomatically to stay out of Saʿdah's affairs.[67]

Domestic Politics and War of Succession

Various persons and groups sought to use the conflict in Saʿdah to their advantage, thus helping to fuel the war. Questions of power and political succession were at play, as internal proxy wars between President Salih and other power brokers in Yemen's fractured political landscape pushed the fighting forward. The existence of such domestic political struggles, notably the internal leadership rivalry at this time between Salih and General ʿAlī Muḥsin, is widely accepted as fact by Yemenis, though it remains very poorly documented. In particular, those who participated in mediation efforts claimed that such competition had obstructed their work, as one faction undermined another, resulting in incoherence on the government's part.[68]

The assumption that domestic political rivalries led to a prolongation of the Saʿdah wars is particularly centred on the role of the opposition parties, especially Iṣlāḥ, Yemen's largest Islamist party. Since 2005, Iṣlāḥ had been part of an oppositional alliance known as the Joint Meeting Parties (JMP; *Aḥzāb al-Liqāʾ al-Mushtarak*), which also consisted of the Socialist Party, the Popular Nasserist Unity Organization, the Union of Popular Forces (a small party consisting largely of liberal Zaydi intellectuals) and Ḥizb al-Ḥaqq. Salih's attempts to control and marginalize opponents by playing them off against each other had ultimately backfired and contributed to the formation of this shaky alliance, although these competing—even hostile—parties shared few programmatic similarities.[69] The purpose of the common political platform was, above all, to set up a single candidate to rival Salih in the 2006 presidential elections. After the poll, consensus and cooperation among the JMP quickly faded.

Ḥizb al-Ḥaqq (perceived as Houthi-friendly) was not the only party to repeatedly demand an end to the war in Saʿdah. Iṣlāḥ was at times very critical of the conflict, which it had never officially supported.[70] The party line was that Iṣlāḥ did not want sectarian struggle in Yemen, and the party repeatedly called for the end to the northern bloodshed. However, tribal sources from the Saʿdah region interpreted Iṣlāḥ's policy differently. They suspected that this anti-war position, given Iṣlāḥ members' particular hostility towards the Houthis and position in opposition to the governing GPC, was aimed at the persistence of the problem rather than its solution. According to these critics, Iṣlāḥ hoped that the war between the Houthis and the Salih regime would continue and lead to the weakening of both warring parties. Shaykhs from Saʿdah, who insisted on a military solution to the problem (yet one led by the state military, not their own tribesmen), found Iṣlāḥ's position 'disingenuous' (*mukhādi*ʿ) and 'pro-Houthi' (*munāṣir li-l-Ḥūthī*); to them, ceasefires and mediation endeavours were looking increasingly like 'artificial prolongations' of the war, not attempts at peace.[71] Criticism of the JMP thus ran through many interviews with shaykhs from the Saʿdah area. Fāyiz al-ʿAwjarī, GPC MP and shaykh of Wāʾilah, reflected in a press interview during the sixth war:

> The parties of the JMP adopted a very negative position. They raised their own partisan interests above those of the nation. They do not know that state interests are not something to gamble with. In many democratic countries the opposition fulfils an essential role in controlling the government, but in Yemen it is exactly the opposite. Whenever the [military] decision is at hand, and whenever we, the sons of Saʿdah, breathe a sigh of relief, the JMP issues a [press] statement against us and launches an initiative which urges the immediate cessation of the combat operations—and then you can draw a line under these combat operations.
>
> *Q: You mean the JMP initiatives aim at the continuation of the war in Saʿdah?*
>
> Exactly. So that the problem continues and both sides [the government and Houthis] wear themselves out in their war against one another. That is why I repeat: the demands of the JMP are void and only aim at maintaining the rebellion. History will tell.[72]

Other groups openly promoted continued hostilities. In Yemen's often opaque and paradoxical political system, the Saʿdah wars served to appease the hawks among those radical Sunnis who saw the war against the Houthis as part of a jihad against the 'godless Shia'. Salmoni et al. argue that internal considerations of regime cohesion may have influenced Salih to approve an aggressive approach.[73] The government and parts of the military apparatus were penetrated by Salafis and Salafi sympathizers, including ʿAlī Muḥsin, who commanded the northwestern military region and the First Armoured Division (*firqah*), and was therefore responsible for all Saʿdah-related operations. Likewise, until about 2005, the leadership of both of Yemen's intelligence agencies, the Political Security Organization (PSO) and the Central Security Organization (CSO), was known for its support of Salafism. In this respect, aggressive prosecution of a war against the Houthis—reportedly strongly advocated by ʿAlī Muḥsin—allowed Salih to deflect Salafi criticism and acted as a hedge against dissent from within his own security services. It is impossible to fully resolve the obvious contradictions between 'pro-war' or 'anti-war' positions among the JMP, Iṣlāḥ, and Salafis. Indeed, these contradictions mirror Yemen's fractured and overcomplex political environment.

Last but not least, issues of power retention and political inheritance had a bearing on the Saʿdah wars. Salih (born in 1942) had been president since 1978—first of the Yemen Arab Republic, and from 1990 of the united Republic of Yemen. During the Saʿdah wars, the succession issue increasingly became a matter of public debate. Salih had tried to delay his departure from power by all means and had even envisaged constitutional amendments for a further extension of his term. However, the idea of such an amendment met with resistance from many parts of the electorate and the ruling elite. Salih worked to groom his son Ahmad, who was head of both the Special Forces and the Republican Guard, to follow his own term in office. His hereditary succession plan similarly lacked unanimous endorsement from the people and the elite.

Moreover, Salih's succession plan appears to have violated his 'covenant' with 'Alī Muḥsin, which stipulated that the latter would be the next president.[74] The two were long-term allies, but also rivals, and their rivalry began to intensify over the succession issue.[75] It is widely believed that Salih was particularly worried about 'Alī Muḥsin succeeding him because the general was a strong leader with Saudi backing, who could mobilize the army behind him. Although 'Alī Muḥsin did not appear to have a direct claim to presidential power—he would likely have faced domestic as well as international opposition if he sought the presidency, as Yemenis generally viewed him as cynical and self-interested—he is said to have been at odds with Ahmad Salih.

In this regard, the Saʿdah wars served to keep 'Alī Muḥsin busy in Yemen's north and, if possible, to diminish his reputation through the brutal fighting and countless instances of collateral damages during the years of clashes and thousands of fatalities, which earned the commander the enmity of many northern tribes and Zaydis. The International Crisis Group argues that the Saʿdah wars were a 'poisoned chalice given to ʿAlī Muḥsin', because they helped cast President Salih and his son as more pragmatic leaders, able to bring the conflict to a peaceful end, while 'Alī Muḥsin was portrayed as both promoting and mismanaging the war in Saʿdah.[76] Furthermore, failed operations, setbacks and internal miscommunications that led the army to strike its own positions prompted rumours of dissent within 'Alī Muḥsin's military command.

Because of this rivalry between 'Alī Muḥsin and the Salihs, the general was given the duty of fighting the Houthis while Ahmad Salih's Republican Guard and US-trained CT units were, with few exceptions, held back—saving them for a rainy day when they would have to defend the president and the palace in Sanaʿa.[77] In 2009, shortly before the end of the sixth and last official war (which would have had dire consequences for the government were it not for Saudi intervention), regime forces were suspected by some of trying to have 'Alī Muḥsin killed by giving the Saudi air force false coordinates.[78] This 'game inside the house', as the International Crisis Group calls it, was an important source of fuel to the Saʿdah wars, driven in part by competition between ruling factions.

These factors, taken together, explain how a complex set of war drivers had emerged by 2006, jeopardizing any hope of a sustainable ceasefire. Boucek has noted that, in its later phases, the reasons for the war in Saʿdah bore little resemblance to the causes of the initial fighting in 2004.[79] By the outbreak of the fourth war in early 2007, the contributing factors in the war's perpetuation had long begun to oscillate between the political and the sectarian, the personal, the tribal and the economic. A source from the Wāʾilah area put it this way:

> There were other conflicts at work: tribal feuds and political haggling, financial aspirations and direction hassles, and one can say: If we want to compare the war in Saʿdah with anything, then [compare it] with a *sūq*, in which everything is available, and everyone deals with what is in his hands and what his interests require. [...] There were conflicts within the parties, within the armed forces, within the tribes, within the villages, everywhere was haggling. The objectives of the war resembled a puzzle, and nothing explained them except struggles for dominance and power.[80]

The Fourth War (16 February–17 June 2007)

After the 2006 elections, the situation quickly worsened. Tensions were on the increase, violations of the ceasefire ran rampant, and skirmishes erupted. A series of assassinations and revenge killings led to chain reactions of retaliatory violence. Both parties to the conflict positioned themselves for a new round of conflict. However, in the short term, the outbreak of the fourth war in February 2007 was triggered by a rather unusual event: the expulsion of the Jews of Āl Sālim by Houthi supporters.

During the fourth war, the action came dangerously close to the Saudi border, as many battles centred on control over the Northern Ring Road straddling the border districts of Rāziḥ, Ghamr, Munabbih, Qaṭābir, and Bāqim. With the exception of Munabbih, these districts came wholly or largely under Houthi control. Fierce clashes erupted in Saḥār, Kitāf, Ḥaydān, Sāqayn, Shidāʾ, al-Ṣafrāʾ and Majz. The army faced the stiffest resistance in Ḍaḥyān, even though it threw thousands of soldiers and Ḥāshid mercenaries into battle.

In the first half of 2007, the armed forces were in utter distress. Since the military proved unable to get the conflict under control by itself, the government encouraged further enlistment of tribal irregulars, notably of Ḥāshid, which led to the creation of the 'Popular Army' led by Ḥusayn al-Aḥmar. For the first time, the government also began systematic recruitment of radical Sunni militants. In Saʿdah, however, mass enlistment of local shaykhs and their tribes proved somewhat trickier than among Ḥāshid in ʿAmrān. The region's shaykhs were anatagonized by the regime's disastrous crisis management, which, rather than solving the problem, had led to a constant expansion of the conflict. Moreover, they interpreted the government's endeavours to muster their tribesmen as a means of forcing them into a quagmire of tribal retaliation, thereby weakening shaykhly power against the state. These disagreements eventually led some of the region's most influential shaykhs, formerly Salih's strongest allies and pillars of the Republic in Saʿdah, to break with the regime. The fourth war ended with a ceasefire agreement brokered by Qatar. The war itself, however, kept the upper hand: neither the first Doha Agreement of June 2007 nor the second Doha Agreement of February 2008 saw serious implementation.

The Blame Game

After the presidential elections, tensions increased again. Areas that had seen fighting and bloodshed remained unsettled. The conflict dragged on at low intensity. In response, the mediation team chaired by Yaḥyā al-Shāmī—now governor of Saʿdah—remained active as a task force despite the conclusion of the *ṣulḥ* earlier in the year, hoping to defuse tensions throughout the conflict area.

Saʿdah's society was deeply divided. Enduring conflicts of loyalty within tribes, villages and families fostered a continued climate of suspicion and mistrust. The governorate was infiltrated by plainclothes officers and mercenaries who—like the local tribes—monitored movement on the ground. During the interim between the third and fourth wars, sudden shootouts and assassination attempts were daily occurrences. The two sides continually passed the buck back and forth, each accusing the other of deliberately fuelling the conflict's progression into a fourth war. Due to the large number of anonymous attacks and assassination attempts, local observers characterize this interim as the period of the 'ghost battles' (*ḥarb al-ashbāḥ*).

Sufyān in northern ʿAmrān, which had been shattered during the third war in February 2006 by a confrontation between the army and local tribes, did not come to rest. In April 2006, two months after the conclusion of the *ṣulḥ*, battle resumed when tribesmen of Shaykh Mujāhid Ḥaydar, Sufyān's lingering malcontent and uncompromising troublemaker, attempted to prevent with force the imposition of an Egyptian Salafi imam on a mosque in al-Ḥarf. He denied any cooperation with the Houthis—he was simply het up about the Yemeni authorities' plans to 'implement the Saudi agenda in Sufyān and spread Salafi extremism at the expense of the Zaydi doctrine', as he said to the press.[81] A few days later, soldiers shot at civilians in al-Ḥarf, allegedly because they had shouted the Houthi slogan. After the incident Mujāhid Ḥaydar convened a meeting of 400 shaykhs and dignitaries of Sufyān to discuss the situation and take a unified stand. He demanded to speak to Fayṣal Rajab, commander of the 119th Infantry Brigade stationed at Jabal Aswad, threatening to apply his well-tested and effective leverage—to block the Sanaʿa-Saʿdah highway, which was of vital importance for the army.

At local level, the chain reactions of retaliation became ever more complex. In early June 2006, Houthi loyalist ʿAlī Saʿīd al-Nimrī of Wādī Nushūr was assassinated by gunmen dressed in civilian clothes in Rughāfah (between Ḍaḥyān and Bāqim). Clashes then erupted between Houthis and soldiers in nearby Qaṭābir, and the Houthis managed to capture the army's weapons.[82] Al-Nimrī's murder triggered a further assassination attempt on members of the al-ʿAwjarī clan—a few days later, on 5 June, a civilian SUV belonging to Shaykh Fāyiz al-ʿAwjarī got into an ambush in Āl Shāfiʿah. Four of its passengers were killed in a hail of bullets, including Yaḥyā Mahdī al-ʿAwjarī, his brother Sulṭān (both army officers) and Yaḥyā's sons Mujāhid (aged fourteen) and Mahdī (eight). A member of the Āl Mahdī, the home section of the al-ʿAwjarī clan, recalled the principles of retaliation and joint liability—the imperatives of blood feud—that now prevailed throughout the region:

> In those days we were expecting the targeting of anyone of Āl al-ʿAwjarī at anytime. And of course Fāyiz was on the top of the list. Fāyiz was well protected. Sulṭān and Yaḥyā, however, were easy to target because their movement was on an almost daily basis and with the same car and on the same road and without escorts. This turned out to be fatal.[83]

ʿAbdulmalik al-Ḥūthī refuted any involvement of his followers in the assassination, which he put down to problems and feuds among the tribes of Wādī Nushūr.[84] The shaykhs of Wāʾilah convened in an emergency meeting with Governor al-Shāmī to discuss the incident. Many of the tribal leaders also doubted that the matter was genuinely related to the Houthi conflict, although at that time the feuds in Wādī Nushūr could no longer be separated from the wars in any meaningful way.

On 10 June 2006, three people were killed in Umm Laylā in the far north of the province: Shaykh ʿAlī Saʿīd ʿArafaj, Ḥusayn Ṣāliḥ al-Kibsī and a security officer. Shaykh ʿAlī Saʿīd ʿArafaj from Wāʾilah and al-Kibsī's father were members of al-Shāmī's mediation team. Al-Kibsī may have been confused with his father and killed in error. Though the assailants could not be identified, the objective of their attack was clear: to sabotage the mediation team's work. This incident led to finger-pointing in the direction of those stakeholders considered uninterested in a peaceful solution to the conflict, particularly the army and ʿAlī Muḥsin. Battles were joined in several areas near the crime scene: Umm Laylā, Qaṭābir, al-Quṭaynāt, Rughāfah, and Yusnam.

After the September elections, the already worrying security situation rapidly deteriorated further. Areas that had been affected by the conflict—Ḍaḥyān, Āl al-Ṣayfī, Qaṭābir, al-Ṭalḥ, Banī Muʿādh, al-ʿAbdīn, Āl Sālim, Āl Shāfiʿah, Nushūr, Ḥaydān, Kitāf, and others—remained unsettled. Houthi slogan shouting increased and led to further arrests. Non-implementation of the promised amnesty and, worse still, the waves of new arrests provoked widespread irritation (*iḥtiqān*, lit. 'congestion') among the Houthis, who complained about incoherent government policy in Saʿdah:

> There prevailed a contradiction between the executive leadership in Saʿdah and the military in terms of coping mechanisms with regard to the Houthis. The government has issued an amnesty and Governor Yaḥyā al-Shāmī tried to release the prisoners, but at the same time the military arrested people en masse under the pretext that they were shouting the Houthi slogan or just supporting the Houthis.[85]

To defuse mounting tensions, in November 2006 the government released 180 prisoners. On 30 November, a further 140 Houthis were released from Saʿdah's Qiḥzah prison and immediately began to shout the Houthi slogan as they roamed through Saʿdah city.[86] In December 2006, riots erupted again in Qiḥzah prison when hundreds of prisoners rebelled against the prison guards and chanted the slogan. The prison guards cut off power and the prisoners' food and water. Unable to suppress the rebellion, they called in security forces of the Rescue Police and the Anti-Riot Battalion. Tear gas was lobbed into the cells.[87] The Qiḥzah riots were repeated during the fourth war in March 2007. After two prisoners were deliberately starved, the prisoners revolted against the inhumane conditions and abuses by the guards, who opened fire on them.

In early January 2007, during the festival of *ʿīd al-aḍḥā*, ʿAdnān Mahdī al-Nimrī and ʿĀdil Ḥubaysh al-Razzāmī were killed in a shootout in the al-Ṭalḥ area of Saʿdah city. The perpetrators reportedly fled towards the security precinct, which gave rise to speculation about their identity. In a subsequent shootout between Houthis and government forces, several soldiers were killed. Shortly after, Houthis were observed in the Sūq al-Ṭalḥ arms market, buying over forty light trucks and so many weapons that arms prices in Sūq al-Ṭalḥ started to rise noticeably.[88] At the same time, the Saudis intensified their efforts to secure the border segments along the Ṭā'if Line between Ẓahrān al-Janūb and Najrān; by force of arms, ʿAbdullah al-Razzāmī prevented Saudi Arabian workers from constructing a tarmac road in the area of Jabal Fard, a Yemeni border mountain, on the grounds that this road would overlook his tribe's villages and homes in al-Naqʿah. In the dispute over these construction works, al-Razzāmī set fire to two Saudi military vehicles (sing. *ṭaqm*), prompting Saudi Border Guards and soldiers to march up into Jabal Fard. Armed battles broke out between al-Razzāmī's followers and Saudi Border Guards.[89]

On 17 January 2007, there was another shootout between Houthi loyalists and supporters of Fāyiz al-ʿAwjarī in the al-Ṭawīlah area (between Saʿdah city and Wādī Nushūr); Fāyiz was unhurt. In the ensuing blame game, both sides claimed that they had been fired upon first. The vicious cycles of retaliatory violence that had taken hold of the province rendered any distinction between cause and effect increasingly difficult. However, the question of who had fired the first shot was of some importance, because the situation in Saʿdah was teetering on the brink—any provocation could lead to the outbreak of a new war.

The Jews of Āl Sālim

In midst of this volatile security situation, one event became the catalyst for the fourth Saʿdah war: the expulsion of forty-five members of the Jewish community of Āl Sālim. Āl Sālim is a small enclave of Dahm a few miles south of Saʿdah city, in the Saʿdah basin.

After Operation Magic Carpet (June 1949–September 1950), which brought 49,000 Yemeni Jews to the new state of Israel, only small scattered Jewish communities remained in Upper Yemen.[90] In the country's tribal society, Jews belong to the non-tribal people, traditionally considered 'weak' *jīrān* (tribal protégés).[91] Living under tribal protection, Jews are usually forbidden to carry arms at all. The protégé is under the honour of his protector, or in his charge, and must be defended by him. To harm one's own protégé would be *ʿayb*, a disgrace for which heavy amends would be due.[92]

On 18 January 2007, the Jewish community of Āl Sālim received a threatening letter from a man called Yaḥyā al-Khuḍayr (alias Abū al-Thāyir), in which he accused the Jews of 'work[ing] for Zionism and corrupt[ing] the morals of the people'. He urged the Jews of Āl Sālim to leave within ten days and threatened consequences for the whole Jewish community if he found a single Jew in the region thereafter.[93] In the signature, Yaḥyā al-Khuḍayr referred to himself as 'Houthi field commander of Āl Sālim'; the letter closed with the Houthi slogan ('Death to America, Death to Israel, Curse Upon the Jews, Victory for Islam').

The deeply frightened Jewish community rushed to exit Āl Sālim, leaving all possessions behind.[94] They headed for Saʿdah city, where they stayed for fifteen days in the Paris Tower Hotel (*Burj Bāris*). During their flight, the Jews of Āl Sālim received support from certain senior shaykhs of Saḥār, namely ʿĀrif Shuwayṭ, Ḥasan Manāʿ and ʿUthmān Mujallī. Mujallī in particular, whose father had concluded a protection treaty with the Jewish community of Āl Sālim after the 1960s civil war, took care of the refugees' needs, providing their food and spending money on them.[95]

Shortly after their arrival in Saʿdah city, the governorate's security director asked Shaykh Nājī Ṣāliḥ Bukhtān and Shaykh Ṣāliḥ al-Wajmān to solve the problem with Yaḥyā al-Khuḍayr, but the Jews refused to return to Āl Sālim. This was not surprising, as al-Wajmān was considered to be close to the Houthis. The relationship between Bukhtān and the Jewish community also seems to have been problematic.[96] The Yemeni government decided to evacuate the Jews to Sanaʿa and accommodate them in apartments in the Tourist City complex, across the street from the US Embassy.[97]

In an interview with US Embassy staff, the refugees characterized relations with their Muslim neighbours as good until the emergence of the Houthi movement. The group's representative, Yaḥyā Yūsif Mūsā, explained that Muslim friends and neighbours had attempted to protect them, but regretted that they were too weak against the threat of the Houthis. However, the same neighbours continued to be loyal to their Jewish brethren by taking care of their livestock and property. The refugees also explained that they had not experienced problems before the emergence of the Houthis, having been protected by the tribes for generations.[98]

The government was well aware of the significance of this incident's international dimensions. When the US government learned of the incident, the State Department summoned Yemen's ambassador to Washington. The chairman of the US House of Representatives Subcommittee of the Middle East Council, Gary Ackerman, demanded that the Yemeni government protect the Jewish community on its territory and sent an envoy of the Office to Monitor and Combat Anti-Semitism to Sanaʿa to follow up the case.[99] The Israeli government also expressed concern. Against the backdrop of the expulsion of the Āl Sālim Jews, the EU threatened to add the Houthis to its terrorist organizations blacklist.[100] The government in Sanaʿa saw this chance to make its mark abroad as a patron of the Jewish community, and provided generous shelter, food and funds. In other words, after the expulsion everything went perfectly for the Salih regime. The Jews of Āl Sālim expressed their gratitude to the president, saying, 'All we have is God and Salih'.[101]

When the Houthis grasped the foreign policy dynamics of this incident, ʿAbdulmalik al-Ḥūthī backpedalled and warned the Yemeni authorities against posturing as protectors of the Jewish minority in a bid for international credit, saying that Yaḥyā al-Khuḍayr, who had expelled the Jews, 'does not represent the Houthis, but was acting for himself'.[102] He accused the government of seeking to 'gloss over and falsify facts'. Although the Houthi slogan was meant to facilitate the promotion of a revolutionary self-image more than to incite violence against any particular group (in 2013 the Houthis were the only party to demand that Jews be represented at the National Dialogue Conference), it proved virtually impossible to wash the movement's hands of the matter, given that 'Death to Israel, Curse Upon the Jews' had been incorporated in its slogan. Dorlian refers to 'visceral anti-Jewish sectarianism' running through Ḥusayn al-Ḥūthī's writings: Ḥusayn used the expression 'brothers of monkeys and pigs' in reference to Jews, and, according to Dorlian, went as far as denying democracy in principle, if such democracy would guarantee citizenship to both Muslims and Jews on an equal basis.[103]

Since the Houthi leaders were entrenched in Maṭrah and effective communication proved difficult (the government having disconnected the province's mobile phone network), Yaḥyā al-Ḥūthī backed his brother from his German exile, accusing the Yemeni government in the international media of deluding international parties for its own benefit.[104] Yet these Houthi protestations were to no avail. The incident and its international reception were an enormous boost for the Yemeni government. On the pretext of the Āl Sālim episode, the army was mobilized to launch the fourth war.

The Fourth Saʿdah War

On 27 January 2007, government troops moved into upper Wādī Madhāb. Wādī Madhāb begins a few kilometres southeast of Saʿdah city and traces a wide arc to the southeast towards the Wādī Jawf. The army's strategic foray into upper Wādī Madhāb had several purposes. First, the army presumed the existence of Houthi training camps and bases in the mountains along upper Wādī Madhāb at the height of Jabal al-Ṣafrā', west of Baraṭ.[105] Second, the army intended to block alternative Houthi supply routes and bypaths that ran from al-Ḥarf in Sufyān and al-Maṭammah northward through the vast, sparsely populated area between Sa'dah and al-Jawf.[106] In addition, the army wanted to surround Houthis in Wā'ilah led by 'Abdullah al-Razzāmī and Shaykh Al-A'ṣar al-Ka'bī (in Kitāf) with a pincer movement and divert their attention from the Saudi border. Last but not least, it made sense to search for alternatives to the vulnerable Sana'a-Sa'dah highway, to circumvent, inter alia, the tribal territory of Mujāhid Ḥaydar, who was perfectly aware of the power he wielded with his well-proven ability to block the highway where it straddled his territories in Sufyān. In addition to this strategic foray, the government erected several new military camps in the conflict region: in Sufyān, Āl 'Ammār, and al-Mahādhir, all of them supposedly to 'protect the Jews'.[107]

The army's advance was the prelude to the fourth Sa'dah war. First, however, a two-week war of nerves took place. The government repeatedly demanded that the Houthis turn in their heavy and medium weapons and—this was new—form a political party to resolve the conflict non-militarily. To emphasize its demands, government communiqués repeatedly used the phrase 'forewarned is forearmed' (*u'dhira man andhara*).

Clearly, laying down their arms was no option for the Houthis, but they discussed the establishment of a political party. The Houthi leaders initially agreed with the suggestion, if—Yaḥyā al-Ḥūthī emphasized—the government 'provided the appropriate atmosphere'.[108] However, they changed their mind when other government demands emerged that were impossible for them to accept, including disarmament, evacuation of their strongholds in Maṭrah and al-Naq'ah, and extradition of 'Abdulmalik al-Ḥūthī to the state.[109] Moreover, the proposal to form a Houthi political platform was opposed by certain senior groups and individuals of the establishment, especially among the armed forces; officers close to the president, notably General 'Alī Muḥsin and his loyalists, refused categorically to accept the formation of a Houthi party and insisted on continuation of the military campaign to eradicate this 'cancerous tumour' (*waram sarṭān*).[110] The disagreements within the regime did not go unnoticed by the Houthis, in whose eyes the government's conditions were in any case unacceptable. On behalf of the movement, Yaḥyā al-Ḥūthī withdrew his consent to form a Houthi party, saying that the government was not serious and that its 'extremism and hostility will not tolerate the existence of a Houthi opposition party'.[111]

It was now the Houthis' turn to issue an ultimatum. On 1 February, ʿAbdulmalik sent a warning letter to Governor Yaḥyā al-Shāmī and Fayṣal Rajab, commander of the Jabal Aswad military camp in Sufyān, and called on the armed forces to depart from the three areas where security forces had recently been stationed.[112]

On 10 February, during a closed session, the parliament in Sanaʿa gave Salih backing for a new military campaign in Saʿdah. Members of the ruling party authorized the president to use military force against the Houthis, outvoting opposition JMP MPs, who were overwhelmingly against the measure.[113] Against the backdrop of the Saudi-Houthi border unrest in al-Naqʿah, Salih sent King Abdullah two letters concerning the security situation, delivered by ʿAbdullah al-Aḥmar and Deputy Prime Minister and Minister of Interior Rashād al-ʿAlīmī.[114]

On 16 February, the government again extended a deadline for the Houthis to hand over their weapons. Altogether, the government issued three ultimatums—all of which were ignored. Each side threatened the other and was unwilling to work towards finding common ground. An observer recalled:

> The government and the Houthis shared the blame for the eruption of the fourth war. The Houthis, who had benefited from several months of *ṣulḥ*, felt strengthened for a new confrontation with the state. The government, too, was not serious in its efforts to find a political solution to the conflict. Rather, it was determined to take military action. Particularly, the government did not show consistency in how to deal with Saʿdah versus other governorates in the disposition of security forces. The government treated Saʿdah differently from other governorates. If areas under tribal control were respected in al-Jawf and Maʾrib, for example, then they should also have been respected in Saʿdah. The government cannot insist on controlling every weapon and every mountain-top in Saʿdah when it does not insist on the same conditions elsewhere. Likewise, the government did not respect tribal traditions when dealing with the Houthis—whose supporters were above all else tribesmen—and dealt with them solely on a military basis. However, this confrontation became a very emotional and personal issue for President Salih and ʿAbdulmalik al-Ḥūthī, a fact that indicated to us that another major military confrontation would probably take place before both sides would be willing to sit down for serious negotiations again.[115]

On 16 February, the fourth war started with a bang: on the same day that the government issued its last ultimatum, Houthi warriors hidden in a tree shot down a helicopter escorting a military convoy on the Sanaʿa-Saʿdah road in Sufyān, and blew up a bridge on the same street, killing dozens of soldiers of the 103rd Brigade, which had been summoned from Maʾrib to Saʿdah as reinforcements.

The army responded with a major offensive targeting all locations suspected of hiding Houthi supporters—in other words, everywhere. In the following four and a half months, large parts of the governorate descended into war. In February, the army had nearly doubled its troop presence in Saʿdah to between 12,000 and 15,000 regular troops, most of them from the First Armoured Division commanded by ʿAlī Muḥsin. By April, the number of soldiers was estimated at 30,000.[116] The armed forces used all weapons at their disposal, including Apache helicopter gunships, aircraft type MiG and Sukhoi, heavy artillery, rockets and tanks. Surveillance measures and checkpoints were reinforced, in particular at the entrances to Saʿdah city and along the roads connecting the city to other regions. These measures aimed at preventing Houthi warriors from infiltrating Saʿdah city. Nevertheless, on 19 February, clashes erupted between Houthis and government troops in front of the Presidential Palace, within Saʿdah city's security precinct.

The Houthis were noticeably stronger than in past fighting. Though still modest in comparison with the armed forces, during the first three wars the movement's military had undergone strategical and tactical evolutions. The horrors and atrocities of the previous wars and the deployment of tribal mercenaries from outside the Saʿdah region had driven many new followers into the Houthis' arms, and the long period of relative ceasefire between the third and fourth wars had helped them to regroup.

Violent battles erupted again in the previous wars' hotspots: Wāʾilah (Nushūr, al-Ḥamazāt, Kitāf), Saḥār (al-ʿAbdīn, Banī Muʿādh, al-Ṭalḥ, Jabal ʿIzzān, al-Mahādhir), Jumāʿah (Ḍaḥyān, Āl al-Ṣayfī, Majz, Bāqim, Qaṭābir), Khawlān (Marrān, Banī Fāḍl), Sāqayn, Āl ʿAmmār, and Sufyān. The army called on the inhabitants of Banī Muʿādh and Ḍaḥyān to leave the area in preparation for major airstrikes and military operations. Gruelling strikes were carried out from al-Naqʿah near the Saudi border to Sufyān in northern ʿAmrān.

The Houthis, for their part, continued to engage in guerrilla-style warfare, using ambushes and attacks on senior military and government personnel and state-owned facilities. They conducted psychological operations targeting the government's security and military services, reportedly using the scare tactic of dumping the corpses of army and police officers killed in Saʿdah in the capital.[117]

The time was certainly past in which the war could have been decided by *ḥasm* (military defeat) of the Houthis. Rebels and government forces fought grim battles for strategically important crests and mountains: Jabal Ghumān and Jabal Āl Ghubayr in Saḥār, Jabal 'Izzān north of al-Ṭalḥ, and Jabal Dukhfash in Āl 'Ammār. After heavy fighting, in March 2007 the latter fell to the military. From Germany, Yaḥyā al-Ḥūthī scoffed in the media: 'The mountain is of no strategic importance... the goal was not the mountain itself but rather the attempt to restore the army's morale, which collapsed on all fronts'.[118] The army could not hold Jabal Dukhfash; in early May the Houthis would recapture it. Also in March, the Houthis shelled the Salafi teaching centre Dār al-Ḥadīth in Dammāj, with casualties among its students.

In Kitāf, the army tried to hunt down 'Abdullah al-Razzāmī, whom they considered the Houthi military mastermind, responsible for the border skirmishes in the area of Jabal Fard. A government official explained:

> The goal of the [fourth] war was to kill 'Abdullah al-Razzāmī and to eradicate the rebellion. 'Abdullah al-Razzāmī was the de facto military leader of the rebellion, and many tribes followed him in the war. 'Abdullah al-Razzāmī was number one, because he had been number two under Ḥusayn al-Ḥūthī, and after Ḥusayn's death he became the man who led the military confrontations in Wādī Nushūr. The tribes followed him. The problem with this man was that he did not accept dialogue. He refused to receive any state officials, including the governor, and did not agree to meet shaykhs or any other person. Even the members of the mediation committees never met him or even reached him on the phone.[119] We have negotiated with his son Yaḥyā and sent his son to him, but to no avail. He even refused to answer the phone. His behaviour became unbearable and could not be tolerated any more. If he would not accept communication, how could we establish dialogue with him?[120]

The air force shelled areas in which 'Abdullah al-Razzāmī was suspected to be hiding. Brutal confrontations took place, again, in Wādī Nushūr, where the same pattern repeated itself as in previous rounds of war. In Kitāf, east of Wādī Nushūr, the military fought against Shaykh Al-A'ṣar al-Ka'bī (Āl Muqbil of Wā'ilah), who had gathered a large number of Houthi warriors around him. Al-A'ṣar al-Ka'bī's followers were stationed near the town of Kitāf, within walking distance of a military camp.[121]

Again in Bāqim district in the extreme north, confrontations came dangerously close to the Saudi border. Armed tribesmen of Ḥasan Muqīt (senior shaykh of the Khawlān b. 'Āmir confederation and an MP) had gathered near a military camp in order to assist the army and prevent the Houthi advance, but the rebels had managed to seize the camp. The surrounding border areas had then witnessed a massive exodus of persons fearing major confrontations and retaliatory air strikes by the armed forces; hundreds of internally displaced persons (IDPs) had fled to the 'Iron Gates'—the Bāqim mountains—without food or shelter, and were now surviving in precarious conditions in the mountains. The Houthis gained control of Bāqim and the Yusnam depression and besieged Majz city, near Ḍaḥyān.[122] In Qaṭābir, they were able to seize the district's security headquarters after bloody clashes with the armed forces and their tribal allies.[123]

The great battles of the fourth war, however, were fought in Ḍaḥyān, Rāziḥ and Ghamr. Much blood had already been spilled in Ḍaḥyān during the first to third wars. Rāziḥ and neighbouring Ghamr, in contrast, had not yet been affected by the war. It was no coincidence that Rāziḥ and Ḍaḥyān became the largest focal points of the fourth war: both had supreme strategic importance because they straddle the Northern Ring Road, the only feasible route linking the remote borderlands along the Saudi-Yemeni border, whose security became a decisive factor in the fourth war. Reaching the peripheral borderlands in the Western mountain range and establishing control over it required boots on the ground. When Ghamr, Qaṭābir, and parts of Bāqim and Majz had fallen into Houthi hands, the army feared losing control of this vital transport connection.

Ḍaḥyān has a large number of sacred Zaydi buildings, a high proportion of its residents are *sādah*; from the outset, both the Zaydi revival and the Houthi movement could count on the support of Ḍaḥyān's citizens. The city had already been the scene of heavy fighting in the earlier wars, so further clashes were very much expected. Yet, during the fourth war, the military met with far stiffer resistance there than it had expected. The determination and acrimony with which the Houthis defended Ḍaḥyān proved an insurmountable obstacle for the army.

In early February, government troops started to besiege the city and set a deadline of eighty-four hours for the residents to evacuate the city before it was stormed and searched house-by-house for Houthi loyalists and weapons. The citizens of Ḍaḥyān considered this ultimatum a prelude to seizure of the city and looting of their property by thousands of armed Ḥāshid mercenaries who had been rallied from outside the province, among them three battalions of over 3,000, notably from al-ʿUṣaymāt and Banī Ṣuraym.[124] Many residents left the city and sought shelter in nearby Āl al-Ṣayfī and Banī Muʿādh, but a considerable number of inhabitants and fighters remained in Ḍaḥyān and put up fierce resistance to the city's would-be captors.

For the fourth war's duration, dreadful battles took place in Ḍaḥyān, which remained under siege throughout, resulting in hundreds of dead and wounded on both sides. Government forces shelled the city with all weapons at their disposal—heavy artillery, tanks, fighter jets and helicopters—and destroyed much of it, including its civil infrastructure (schools, water tanks, health facilities) and sacred buildings (notably al-Thiqlayn Mosque). During the fighting, dozens of dead bodies were dumped on the streets and could not be recovered, leading to the outbreak of infectious diseases. The military launched numerous offensives to seize the city. In its search for Houthi supply routes, the air force raided the corridor between Ḍaḥyān and Maṭrah. The Houthis entrenched themselves in houses, ruins and self-dug caves and repeatedly recaptured neighbourhoods that had been cleared by the army. Firearms, daggers and knives were used in the fight for every street and every house. At the end of the fourth war in June 2007, Ḍaḥyān was still largely under Houthi control.

Unlike Ḍaḥyān, Rāziḥ and Ghamr had not previously been affected by major battles. Rāziḥ, in the governorate's extreme northwest, is the settlement of the eponymous Khawlān b. ʿĀmir member tribe. In the west, it borders on the 1934 Ṭāʾif Line, which defines the boundary between Yemen and Saudi Arabia. Jabal Rāziḥ and Jabal Munabbih to its north are connected by the elevated basin of Ghamr and the Wādī Badr.[125] Ghamr itself borders on four tribal areas: Rāziḥ to the south and southwest, Munabbih to the north, Jumāʿah to the northeast, Khawlān to the southeast—and Saudi Arabia to the west. The Northern Ring Road passes through the district capitals: al-Naẓīr in Rāziḥ, al-Jarshah in Ghamr and Sūq al-Khamīs in Munabbih. In 2007, parts of the Ring Road were still under construction—the section between al-Naẓīr in Rāziḥ and Qaṭābir via Sūq al-Khamīs in Munabbih was not yet asphalted, closer resembling a nerve-rackingly bumpy dirt track through the magnificent mountain scenery of Rāziḥ and Munabbih. Nevertheless, it was the only viable link road between Saʿdah city and the remote western mountain range.

Rāziḥ has always been a stronghold for Zaydi interests.[126] In the 2006 presidential elections, Rāziḥ was the district in Saʿdah with the lowest levels of support for President Salih. The Houthi movement had gained a strong foothold among Rāziḥ's youth and *sādah*. During the fourth war, about 350 Houthi warriors gathered in the nearby regions of Shidāʾ and ʿUqārib.[127] Most of them hailed from Rāziḥ itself and had previously participated in the war in other areas, such as neighbouring Khawlān.

As was the case in other regions, most shaykhs of Rāziḥ were loyal to the government. The government had encouraged them to take charge of their own defence and to prevent the Houthis from entering Rāziḥ or concentrating in the surrounding mountains.[128] Consequently, the district's pro-government shaykhs distributed large quantities of weapons to their followers. During the fourth war, a large contingent of Ḥāshid mercenaries under the command of Ḥusayn Abū Ḥalfah, a Ḥāshid shaykh, was sent to Rāziḥ to proceed from there via the Northern Ring Road to embattled Ḍaḥyān, a strategic move that would enable the armed forces to surround Ḍaḥyān in a pincer movement. After Ḥusayn Abū Ḥalfah and his irregulars arrived in Rāziḥ, they were drawn into clashes with Houthi loyalists, which quickly turned into conflagration and would ultimately prevent Abū Ḥalfah and his men from proceeding further north.

By the end of March 2007, the Houthis had managed to surround the security forces and Ḥāshid irregulars in al-Qalʿah; Abū Ḥalfah eluded them by crossing the nearby Saudi border. By mid-April, the Houthis had brought the greater part of Rāziḥ under their control. The air force launched devastating air strikes. Both the army and the Houthis tried to blockade the Northern Ring Road in Rāziḥ in order to prevent enemy troop movements. In an attempt to prevent pro-government tribal warriors from Munabbih led by Shaykhs ʿAlī Ḥusayn al-Munabbihī and Aḥmad Dahbāsh Miṭrī from joining battle, the Houthis blocked the Ring Road in Ghamr and occupied al-Jarshah, the district's administrative centre, where they blew up the government compound. Like Abū Ḥalfah, the senior shaykh of Ghamr, ʿAlī Ẓāfir, fled with a number of army officers across the Saudi border.[129] Munabbih—wedged between fierce confrontations in Ghamr, Rāziḥ and Qaṭābir—responded by closing the borders and roads of its tribal territory (*taghlīq al-ṭuruq wa l-ḥudūd*). At the end of April, the government deployed the 29th Mechanized Brigade, called the Giants Forces (*quwwāt al-ʿamāliqah*) to Rāziḥ, under the command of ʿAlī al-Jāyfī.[130] On 13 June, shortly before the conclusion of the First Doha Agreement, the Giants Forces managed to gain control over central regions of the district. The Houthis withdrew to the surrounding mountains.

The fighting also flared up again in al-Jawf during this war. In late May, a Houthi group tried to break into a military camp in al-Ghayl district. One week later, Houthi fighters attacked the 9th Brigade stationed in al-Ḥazm with medium and heavy weapons, reportedly in an attempt to relieve pressure on their comrades in Saʿdah. A few days later, a third incident took place in al-Jawf when Houthis attacked a Central Security checkpoint in al-Salāmāt. According to press reports, remote areas in upper al-Jawf began to witness large movements of Houthi troops.[131]

The Popular Army

March and April 2007 were dramatic months for the Yemeni army. Four districts of Saʿdah governorate came entirely or largely under Houthi control: Rāziḥ, Ghamr, Qaṭābir and Bāqim. Saḥār, Kitāf, Ḥaydān, Sāqayn, Shidāʾ, al-Ṣafrāʾ and Majz saw heavy fighting. The greatest military challenge was in Ḍaḥyān, although the armed forces used every weapon at their disposal and threw thousands of soldiers and Ḥāshid mercenaries into battle. ʿAbdullah al-Razzāmī was still very much alive, and the Houthis' forays into Saʿdah city humiliated the army. As if that were not enough, Yaḥyā al-Ḥūthī's provocative statements from Germany—broadcast from a rentable television studio in front of the 'official' backdrop of the German Reichstag in Berlin—ceaselessly castigated the brutal approach of the armed forces, increasing the government's anger. The Houthis were putting the army in a serious hurt locker, and any predictions of the war's outcome were grim. In short, things were going wrong for the government. New measures were needed to ensure that the fourth war did not degenerate into disaster.

As a first measure, in mid-March the Yemeni Authorities announced the dissolution of the Ḥizb al-Ḥaqq party in order to deprive the Houthis of their—supposed—political platform.[132] Ironically, this came just a few weeks after the government had ultimately prompted the Houthis to set up their own political party (see above). The process of the party's dissolution was murky. On 14 March, Secretary-General Aḥmad al-Shāmī reportedly sent a letter signed by several other founding party members, including the scholars Muḥammad al-Manṣūr and Ḥamūd ʿAbbās al-Muʾayyad, to the Parties Affairs Committee, informing it of the decision to dissolve in light of the party's failure to agree on its general goals. After this surprise move, which had not been discussed with other party members, the party leadership announced that Aḥmad al-Shāmī had no right to dissolve it, noting that its internal bylaws didn't empower him to make such a decision.[133] According to a Ḥizb al-Ḥaqq politician, al-Shāmī's action was invalid because the only party authority able to do so was the General Conference. He further asserted that al-Shāmī's announcement had been made under pressure, saying that the secretary-general had been subjected to a harsh campaign by political opponents, including harassment aimed at blackmailing party leaders in an attempt to subvert the democratic process in Yemen. This source cited that campaign as the principal reason for al-Shāmī's resignation.[134] He also attributed his behaviour to pressure related to the ongoing war in Saʿdah and Ḥizb al-Ḥaqq's ideological closeness to the Houthis. The party's executive committee nominated Ḥasan Zayd, head of its political department, to act in al-Shāmī's place, interpreting the secretary-general's actions as a personal resignation. The party itself has never been informed officially to cease work and has kept on working.

As a further measure to cope with the province's deteriorating crisis, Governor Yaḥyā al-Shāmī was sacked. He had firmly maintained his position of rapprochement and mediation, even after the governorate sank back into war in February. The central government regarded the outbreak of the fourth war as evidence that al-Shāmī's conciliatory approach had failed. Furthermore, the relationship between al-Shāmī and the military leadership, particularly General ʿAlī Muḥsin, had worn very thin. Informed sources said that differences of opinion between the two men on the conduct of the war had led to scuffles between their escorts in the war room in Saʿdah city.[135]

On 17 April, al-Shāmī was sacked and Vice Minister of the Interior Major General Muṭahhar al-Miṣrī was appointed governor of Saʿdah. Al-Miṣrī was a graduate of the Police Academy and held a Bachelor's degree in Law from Sanaʿa University and a Master's from the Command and Staff College. He had had a long career in the security sector. Known for a bold approach, he was widely regarded a hardliner, a proven 'hawk' among the many raptors of the Salih regime. He was expected to take a robust line and to assist the armed forces in crushing the Houthis.

The rebels instantly accepted the challenge. On the very day of al-Miṣrī's appointment, they stormed the Presidential Palace in Saʿdah city,[136] and only heavy shelling could drive them out again. Once again, the war had broken into the city's security precinct. And worse was yet to come: shortly thereafter, on 29 April, the Houthis attacked a First Armoured Brigade camp in Saʿdah city.[137] Al-Sinnārah fortress and parts of al-ʿAbdīn near Saʿdah city fell to the Houthis. From Germany, Yaḥyā al-Ḥūthī threatened: 'There will be no military solution even if the battle lasted 400 or 500 years. There will either be freedom and dignity and pride, or death with dignity and pride'.[138]

Despite the large-scale deployment of armed forces from other regions to the crisis area, the government's scope for military mobilization was exhausted, and the brutal actions and indiscriminate violence of the armed forces were pushing more and more people into the arms of the Houthis. When it became clear that the crisis was continuing to escalate and that the regular army would ultimately be unable to defeat the Houthis, the government began systematically enlisting further 'popular' support among those who were loyal, particularly Ḥāshid tribesmen in ʿAmrān and radical Sunnis. As we know, Ḥāshid irregulars had participated in the Saʿdah wars from 2004. During the fourth war, however, given the looming disaster, the enlistment of tribal irregulars became central to the regime's strategy. In April, the National Defence Council officially approved opening the military's doors to popular recruitment and set a target of 10,000 new tribal volunteers. Moreover, the Council also stated its goal to involve the largest possible number of Salafis; newspapers spoke of the planned recruitment of 20,000 'mujahids'.[139]

These irregular forces were called *jabhah shaʿbiyyah* (People's Front) or *jaysh shaʿbī* (People's Army).[140] Joining conditions for the People's Army were simple: the will to fight the Houthis and the ability to use a weapon. None were committed to a fixed term of service or registered on the army's payroll. This initiative led to the recruitment of the Popular Army, which was gathered by the al-Aḥmar clan of al-ʿUṣaymāt in Qaflah ʿUdhar.[141] The Popular Army rallied more than 3,000 tribal irregulars, most of them from the ranks of the Ḥāshid tribes, notably al-ʿUṣaymāt and Banī Ṣuraym.[142] Its commander-in-chief was Ḥusayn al-Aḥmar. Equipped with government weapons and led by less prominent al-ʿUṣaymāt and Banī Ṣuraym shaykhs, these auxiliaries were sent into battle.

For the army, the assistance of tribal irregulars had many advantages.[143] They served to strengthen the army's fighting capacity and to re-establish military balance (*muʿādalah ʿaskariyyah*) with the Houthis. The government's inability to win the war through the regular forces, and its desire to spread the blame for an increasingly unpopular war, were behind its drive to pursue this risky strategy. The tribal irregulars could access remote areas that the army, with its heavy gear, was unable to reach, especially in the rugged mountains. They were able to move easily from one area to another because of their inconspicuous dress. Their casualties were not included on official lists.

The government also sought to mobilize Yemen's state-funded and state-monitored hierarchy of Islamic functionaries for its military campaign in Saʿdah, to rally sectarian support for the army. Indicating the seriousness of the Houthi threat, the regime mobilized government-affiliated Shāfiʿī and Salafi scholars to publish a flurry of fatwas (legal rulings) condemning the Houthis in terms aligned with the government's rhetoric.[144] Islamic scholars disagreed about whether or not the state had the right to crush the rebellion by force. In March 2007, the press reported that Muḥammad Ismāʿīl al-ʿAmrānī, a Zaydi scholar, had issued a fatwa saying that all citizens were obliged to participate in the government's 'jihad' against Zaydi activists in the north of the country. He allegedly argued that the killing of those he described as 'idolaters who drifted away from the community of Muslims' was religiously justified.[145] In this fatwa, which was distributed by official media, he purportedly said that the Houthis did not represent the Zaydi sect, that the state must fight the Houthis, and that Muslims must support the state in that fight.[146]

Yet this fatwa turned out to be a fake. Muḥammad al-ʿAmrānī issued a handwritten statement that made it clear that he had never issued any fatwa on the subject of fighting Houthis.[147] He complained that the government had used his name and reputation to stimulate public opinion and try to form a negative impression of its political rivals. But it was too late—al-ʿAmrānī's alleged fatwa was discussed controversially among Yemen's religious scholars. Ḥamūd al-Hitār, chairman of the Religious Dialogue Committee, defended fatwas of this kind.[148] Al-Murtaḍā al-Maḥaṭwarī, a professor at Sanaʿa University and a Zaydi scholar, criticized the fatwa and accused scholars who issued such fatwas of being government, not religious, loyalists. He argued that the issuance of such fatwas for political ends diminished scholars' status. The sectarian wound was still bleeding in Yemen, he said, citing examples from history of Sunni and Shia scholars, inspired by rulers, issuing fatwas against each other.[149]

Beyond fatwas, the Ministry of Endowments and Islamic Guidance issued directives for Salafi preachers in mosques throughout the country to step up their rhetoric against the Houthis. Such efforts to criminalize and excommunicate the Houthis have been particularly strong in the army. Salmoni et al. reported that forty military chaplains had echoed the government's pronouncements to both Zaydi and Sunni troops, offering an Islamic justification for a war against their fellow Yemenis.[150]

As a result of this policy, the Saʿdah wars took on an openly sectarian hue. Under the influence of inflammatory speeches against 'Safavid Shiites', Sunni jihadis began to participate in the conflict through the Popular Army, including a militant group close to al-Qaeda known as Haṭāṭ, led by Khālid ʿAbdulnabī, which had waged the most fierce armed confrontations against the government in earlier years in Abyan.[151] The sectarian nature of parts of the Popular Army became obvious when radical Sunni Islamist mercenaries in its ranks threatened to punish the Zaydi Houthis with 'divine retribution'.[152] The jihadis of the Popular Army (like the state military) enjoyed the backing of General ʿAlī Muḥsin, who had ties to radical Salafis; he not only tried to convince shaykhs to send tribes into battle, but also to involve jihadis in the war. As such, the Popular Army cannot be characterized as an outright tribal force. Its specific confluence of military-governmental, tribal, and sectarian elements led to a 'hybridization' of the armed forces and of the conflict itself.[153]

Essentially, the build-up of the Popular Army and the mobilization of various tribes and jihadi groups was a desperate act by the government, and one which did not, ultimately, produce any practical advantages. Instead of coming to grips with the Houthi problem, the regime lost even more control over the war. It was impossible to predict the outcome of a conflict between such heterogeneous and numerous factions, with diverse regional, tribal, political and doctrinal allegiances. A commentary in *Mareb Press* summarized the government's tribal-sectarian strategy during the fourth war:

> [...] pushing the Ḥāshid tribes into the Saʿdah war and involving religious fatwas reflects not only the army's inability to resolve the Saʿdah issue militarily after more than a month of fierce fighting [which has led to] the expansion of the war zone and an ever higher number of victims, but also the desire of the government to draw the sons of our country into a fratricidal war without any national responsibility, a conflict that transforms itself into an all-devouring civil and sectarian war which shatters the country's security and stability and tears apart the fabric of national unity.[154]

The government, however, did not only focus on ʿAmrān's Ḥāshid tribes, but also on the tribes of Saʿdah itself. Here, too, the government saw untapped potential and a need for action. Although large parts of the governorate had already plummeted into war and mayhem, in the eyes of the regime the engagement of Saʿdah's shaykhs and tribes left a great deal to be desired. However, enforcing mass mobilization of Saʿdah's tribes as auxiliary forces proved somewhat trickier than with the Ḥāshid in ʿAmrān. This was not due to any lack of loyalty on the shaykhs' part (the vast majority being Houthi-hostile), but due to erratic, incoherent and ultimately disastrous government policy in the region, which had enraged many shaykhs and their tribes.

On 15 March 2007, President Salih gave a telephone speech to mark the inauguration of a new radio station in Saʿdah city, Radio Saʿdah. Many of the invited guests were influential shaykhs of the region. With this patriotic speech Salih wanted to rally the shaykhs to the government's cause and convince them to fight alongside the army. Yet many important shaykhs, although invited, did not attend the opening ceremony. Conspicuous by their absence were, among others, Qāʾid Shuwayṭ, Ḥusayn al-Surabī, Ḥasan Muqīt, Salmān ʿAwfān, and Muḥammad al-Ṭuḥāmī. No shaykh of the Wāʾilah showed up; only Ṣāliḥ b. Shājiaʿ had sent his youngest son. Irritated, Salih lashed out, wondering publicly why they 'did not agree with their participation [in the war]'.[155] This was a rather unfortunate and insulting formulation, which gave the impression that the shaykhs of Saʿdah had been deliberately steering clear of armed confrontations. With this wording, Salih dealt a tremendous slap in the face to the shaykhs, who felt publicly vilified as cowards and tacit Houthi supporters—although many were already in the war up to their necks, were exposed to assassination attempts, and had made immense sacrifices in fighting the Houthis.

The shaykhs were discontent with the government's crisis management for numerous reasons. First, they found that the government's call for mass tribal mobilization unduly interfered in their internal affairs and degraded them to mere auxiliaries of the regular army. Their free rein in their tribal constituencies had always been part of republican order in Saʿdah.[156] They did not like to accept explicit commands, no matter their source. Second, the army's indiscriminate and disproportionate violence against the tribes had angered the shaykhs and had already driven many of their tribesmen to support the Houthis. Hence, for many shaykhs, 'total war' against the movement would have meant antagonizing their own tribesmen and pushing their tribes ever deeper into the swamp of intra-tribal feuding and fratricidal war—and it was obvious that it was the shaykhs and their tribes who would later be left to pick up the pieces. Third, they were furious at the presence of Ḥāshid mercenaries on their territories, and the vast majority were also strictly opposed to the presence in their regions of militant Salafis, who had spilled over from ʿAmrān with the Popular Army. The shaykhs were concerned about the plundering that was likely to occur, given the Popular Army's reputation as a 'looting force'.

Fourth, they found that the government had ignored tribal efforts to mediate in the conflict and, by failing to try and resolve this issue in 'the traditional way', had neglected the shaykhs' traditional and prestigious role as mediators. Fifth, and despite the martial rhetoric of the president and the governor and the army's brutality, they had doubts as to whether the government really wanted to end the war, or to prolong it in order to acquire further arms and money from the US and Saudi Arabia. Why should they throw their tribal brethren into battle if the state did not want to solve the problem? Last but not least, lack of financial incentives probably also played a role: the shaykhs had not received a cut of the government's 2006 supplemental budget request.[157] Their lack of engagement may also have been out of anger at not receiving the kind of outlays they had been privy to in previous years.

In May, the fourth war entered its fourth month without any sign of a quick solution to the conflict. The government was in dire need of the Saʿdah tribes' local knowledge and manpower to get the conflict under control. Salih launched a new initiative to enlist them, seeking the help of the Ḥāshid's senior shaykh and Yemen's self-proclaimed 'shaykh of shaykhs' (*shaykh mashāyikh al-Yaman*), ʿAbdullah al-Aḥmar, whose son Ḥusayn could already point to considerable success in recruiting to the Popular Army in ʿAmrān. He asked ʿAbdullah al-Aḥmar to issue a tribal summons (*dāʿī qabalī*) to the Khawlān b. ʿĀmir tribes in Saʿdah, in order to rally them to the government's cause and terminate their perceived 'lack of cooperation'.

Al-Aḥmar sent a handwritten letter with a tribal summons to the Khawlān b. ʿĀmir shaykhs, in which he urged them to fight as a bloc with the Ḥāshid alongside the government. He threw all his tribal and political weight behind this letter. He pointed to the central role of the shaykhs in the Republic and warned that 'these young mindless adolescents', as he called the Houthis, 'tarnish your reputation and undermine your status'. He urged the shaykhs to join the government in its battle and to 'purify your country from these vandals who want to turn back the wheel of history'.[158]

The armed incursions of Ḥāshid mercenaries were already bad enough—for the tribes of Saʿdah, al-Aḥmar's attempt to summon them added insult to injury. Rather than enhancing cooperation, the letter further aggravated animosities. It was sharply rebuffed by the shaykhs of the Khawlān b. ʿĀmir confederation, who—by virtue of their distinct descent and tribal affiliation—saw no reason to respond to the tribal call of the Ḥāshid.[159] They perceived al-Aḥmar's call for action against the Houthis as a gross insult, as many of them had long been stuck in bloody confrontations with the Houthis, whereas the members of the al-Aḥmar clan had not yet lifted a finger to defend the Republic: none of ʿAbdullah al-Aḥmar's sons had personally participated in battle. Their response was 'harsh and accusatory' (*qāsiyan wa ittihāmiyan*). Shaykh and MP Fayṣal b. ʿArīj of the Saḥār replied on their behalf that, although they did not reject the crux of the matter (the importance of the fight against the Houthis), they were agreed that ʿAbdullah al-Aḥmar 'has no tribal summons over us' (*laysa lahu dāʿī qabalī ʿalaynā*):

> Tell him [ʿAbdullah al-Aḥmar]: Where has he been over the past four years? And what right does he have to summon us by a tribal summons when we are Khawlān b. ʿĀmir b. Quḍāʿah and he is Ḥāshid? And are we that hesitant that ʿAbdullah al-Aḥmar comes and calls us to action with his summons? And is his summons more important than the summons of the president? Has Shaykh ʿAbdullah al-Aḥmar taken into account our martyrs and our sacrifices?[160]

Fayṣal b. ʿArīj further pointed to the fact that al-Aḥmar was representative of the Iṣlāḥ party, which many suspected of viewing the conflict as an opportunity to weaken both Salih and the Houthis, and consequently sharing no interest in a swift resolution to the conflict.[161] He also lashed out against the al-Aḥmar clan itself, especially against Ḥusayn al-Aḥmar, nominal leader of the Popular Army, expressing his suspicions that Ḥusayn al-Aḥmar had recently been in Tripoli, where Muʿammar al-Gaddafi had allocated him a very large sum of money in order to cause trouble and chaos in the region: 'The shaykh [ʿAbdullah al-Aḥmar] knows those who are bringing money from abroad, and his sons know even better [...] Our martyrs will call Shaykh ʿAbdullah and his tribe to account and this is why [the summons of al-Aḥmar] is unacceptable.'[162] Finally, he gave vent to his annoyance about the Ḥāshid mercenaries in Saʿdah. He pointed out that a considerable number of Houthi warriors in Saʿdah came from the ʿAmrān region, notably Sufyān, so that the historical feud between Sufyān and al-ʿUṣaymāt was already being fought in Saʿdah in the guise of the Houthi conflict. He bluntly warned al-Aḥmar that he would do better to withdraw his Ḥāshid mercenaries from the region and 'fight his battle in his own territory'.[163]

In short, this was a resounding failure. Though the government had received it with no small amount of malicious glee (Salih had always been jealous of al-Aḥmar's tribal power and tried to undermine it whenever he could), the president still would not and could not do without the local expertise of Saʿdah's shaykhs, their capacity to organize and mobilize their people, and the combat power of their men. He tightened the screws for the third time and commissioned Governor Muṭahhar al-Miṣrī to force the shaykhs into line. On 17 May, al-Miṣrī convened a meeting with the shaykhs, *aʿyān* and notables of the province. In a speech, he referred to the Houthis as 'enemies of the revolution, the Republic, and unity', who wanted to 'induce the people to kiss the [*sādah*'s] feet as it was the case in imamic times in Yemen'. He demanded that the shaykhs help 'eradicate this malicious virus before it spreads and infects others'. He called on the shaykhs assembled to unite and actively support the armed forces' efforts to 'write their immortal epic in eliminating the elements of extremism and diabolic terrorism'. Shaykh Fayṣal Manāʿ, a GPC veteran from al-Ṭalḥ, rushed to the governor's side and stressed the importance of enhancing coordination and cooperation among the province's shaykhs in order to address the 'elements of diabolical sedition' side-by-side with their 'brothers' in the military.[164]

But then the incredible happened: the government was loudly criticized. Some shaykhs complained about intimidation by senior army personnel urging them to send tribal levies into the war. Other shaykhs protested against the abuse of their tribesmen as mere auxiliaries of the army and refused to throw them into battle without any consideration of the customs of tribal conflict resolution. One asked the governor what his reaction would be if the army and its tribal supporters had fought the Ḥāshid for more than three years without 'plain reasons known to you or others'. 'Uthmān Mujallī complained about the mismanagement of the war. ʿAbdullah Aḥmad Muʿawwad Shabīb of Wādiʿah Dammāj reportedly ranted: 'Are the citizens required to protect the army or is the army required to protect the citizens?!'[165]

The government considered criticism of its policy in Saʿdah a red line, and some shaykhs had now crossed it. A series of 'accidents' and 'murder mysteries' (*qatl ghāmiḍ*) followed. ʿAbdullah Aḥmad Muʿawwad Shabīb was assassinated shortly after the meeting; sources in Saʿdah suggested that the authorities were behind his assassination.[166] In May, a helicopter gunship 'erroneously' bombed the house of Salmān ʿAwfān in Munabbih, killing one of his relatives.[167] Obviously the helicopter attack was a warning to ʿAwfān, who strived to maintain a neutral role and not to interfere personally in the war—and therefore, in the government's eyes, was insufficiently engaged in the battle against the Houthis.[168] Several shaykhs had been warned not to permit Houthi loyalists to enter their regions, so as not to be exposed to bombardment.[169] Even after the fourth war had ended, an assassination attempt took place in December against ʿUthmān Mujallī's brother Yāsir within the security precinct of Saʿdah city. This incident would lead to a crisis between Saʿdah's tribal leaders and the government, which had hardly seen anything like this since the end of the 1960s civil war.

The Houthis, too, closely watched the words and deeds of the shaykhs. ʿAbdulmalik al-Ḥūthī gradually increased pressure on them to stay out of the conflict. In June 2007, under the shadow of the Bāqim battles in which tribal warriors loyal to the Muqīt clan fought alongside the army, he sent a threatening letter to the shaykhs of Bāqim:

> We are following your meetings and we know the efforts of the tyrannical government and Ḥasan Muqīt to get you enmeshed in bloodshed and war. No cause deserves this bloodshed. You would behave in a better way if you chose to be neutral and to protect your blood and the blood of your followers and to stay out of the unlawful crimes of assault and murder. They [the government] want now to purchase your loyalty, and your followers, and your conscience. Don't go astray! Fear God! Fear God, because God watches you, He rewards and punishes, and He punishes the wrongdoers. His punishment in this world is shame, and His punishment in the hereafter is great suffering. And one day you will see the punishment of the criminal traitor Ḥasan Muqīt. We have decided to take revenge on him and his

> fellow traitors and to beat them, even after a long period of time. The day will come that he and his followers will regret their crimes [...] I advise you to save your blood, the blood of your followers, and the blood of your country, and stay away from the ravages of war, because it is better for you.[170]

In sum, during the fourth war, the rift between the government and Saʿdah's tribal establishment became evident. The shaykhs' lack of cooperation was not born of disloyalty to the state or to the Salih regime—indeed, the shaykhs were creatures of that regime, to which they owed their elevated status and prominent role in republican society. They were simply embittered by the government's approach to the conflict, particularly its newly adopted strategy of *ḍarab abnāʾ Ṣaʿdah bi-baʿḍihim* ('fighting the sons of Saʿdah through themselves'). The shaykhs were keenly aware of the political machinations, erratic positions and counterproductive approaches of the government, which had led to the steady perpetuation and brutalization of the war—a war now to be fought at their expense.

At the same time, the shaykhs also managed to withstand the increasing pressure from the Houthi leadership. Both Houthis and shaykhs were aware of their insurmountable differences regarding shaykhly status, roles and responsibilities, which—for the time being—virtually precluded any cooperation between them. Beset on all sides and threatened by military attacks and assassinations, the shaykhs were caught right in the middle of the war.

The First Doha Agreement

By the end of May 2007, the armed forces had slowly and at great cost gained the upper hand; their main success was the recapture of Rāziḥ through the Giants Forces. After months of intense fighting, the war had claimed a high human, financial, and material toll. Both sides were exhausted. At the end of the fourth war in June, foreign observers estimated the number of IDPs at 35,000.[171] The number of Houthi prisoners had reached a record level of nearly 4,000, many of them teenagers.[172] The long battles and the many setbacks and failures had also left their mark on the armed forces, which appeared dangerously divided and vulnerable to growing internal attrition—a reflection of the government's multiple and overlapping power centres. One indicator of the mounting internal tensions was the clashes that took place on 25 May between Central Security Forces and Rescue Police in Saʿdah city, which erupted after disagreements in relation to conflicting leadership directives and were fought with machine guns and mortars. Government sources described the state of the military as 'dilapidated' (*mutahālik*) and 'based on chaos and improvisation' (*qāʾim ʿalā al-fawdā wa l-irtijāliyyah*).[173] One government official expressed his deep concern to the US ambassador, giving the military and the Ministry of the Interior 'a D-minus or worse' for their performance in Saʿdah.[174]

The Libyan 'mediation' had turned into a fiasco, and broader domestic mediation initiatives held no promise of success after the sacking of Yaḥyā al-Shāmī as governor. In May, the first signs of Qatari mediation efforts began to emerge. Following a visit to Sanaʿa on 12 May by Qatari emir Shaykh Ḥamad b. Khalīfah Āl Thānī, heading a high-level Qatari delegation, media sources speculated that the visit was linked to an attempt at mediation between the Yemeni government and the Houthis. This visit came a few days after Salih's return from Washington, where he had discussed the Saʿdah issue with a number of US officials. Yemeni press confirmed that he had met with US Secretary of State Condoleezza Rice, who had asked him to end the war.[175] The US government believed that the longer the conflict in Saʿdah persisted, the more difficult it would become for the Yemeni regime to put down unrest in other parts of the country and to combat al-Qaeda, given all of the human and financial resources it had committed in the province.[176]

The choice of Qatar was a result of the strong relations between that country and the US. In recent years the microstate of Qatar had strengthened ties with Washington in order to improve its position regionally. Qatar had raised global awareness by hosting major international conferences, enhancing its involvement with international organizations, and engaging in mediation and peacekeeping missions in the Near and Middle East. Qatar appealed to a number of actors within Yemen's political arena because of its deep pockets and (unlike Saudi Arabia) relative lack of historical baggage in Yemen, all of which positioned it well to mediate in Yemen's most virulent conflict.[177] Past experience demonstrated that lasting peace in Saʿdah could only come with a comprehensive political settlement followed by significant economic development—areas where Qatari assistance would be very helpful indeed. Thus the US administration regarded Qatar as the right mediator for Yemen: no partisan agenda, good experience in mediating regional conflicts, and the largesse to offer financial incentives to those at war.

Qatar has always mediated in regional conflicts, to the envy of Saudi Arabia, which has often thwarted Qatar's efforts. Now, Qatar was preparing to rummage in Saudi Arabia's hypersensitive files in Yemen—hence Qatar's wish to avoid publicity until a deal was done. The government tried to keep the Qatari mediation secret until a few days before its conclusion. However, though government officials frequently issued denials, the Yemeni press sensed and reiterated that something was afoot, and the Houthis, too, indicated their willingness to participate in Qatar-brokered negotiations.

Immediately after the emir's visit in May 2007, Qatar started its crisis diplomacy in Yemen. The Qatari government sent a delegation to Saʿdah to meet with the Houthi leaders. Yaḥyā al-Ḥūthī travelled from Germany to Qatar to convey the movement's demands. Yemeni presidential advisor ʿAbdulkarīm al-Iryānī also travelled to Qatar. On 16 June, after two months of negotiations, the signing of a Qatar-brokered ceasefire agreement between the Houthis and the government was announced. This became known as the 'First Doha Agreement' (*ṣulḥ Dawḥah al-awwal*).

The agreement had nine provisions.[178] These included, inter alia, the Houthis' agreement to relinquish their positions and to turn in medium-weight arms, while the government was committed to declaring an amnesty and launching Qatari-supported reconstruction projects in Saʿdah. Safe haven in Qatar was guaranteed for ʿAbdulmalik al-Ḥūthī, Yaḥyā al-Ḥūthī, ʿAbdulkarīm al-Ḥūthī, and ʿAbdullah al-Razzāmī, in exchange for their staying quiet and for their backers accepting the republican regime. To help sweeten the deal for both sides, Qatar pledged a huge amount of development aid for Saʿdah, wisely only to be disbursed after implementation of the ceasefire. This pledge was at the core of the agreement, possibly amounting to US$300–500 million, although figures were never released.[179]

After the Doha Agreement had been signed, the government set up a nine-member high-level committee, composed of the heads of parliamentary blocs of political parties and members of the Consultative Council, to oversee its implementation. The committee was chaired by Muḥsin al-ʿUlufī, vice president of the Consultative Council. Its spokesperson was Yāsir al-ʿAwāḍī, a senior GPC official. Other members of the committee included Sulṭān al-ʿAtwānī, Ṣādiq al-Aḥmar, Aḥmad Muḥammad al-Shāmī and Muḥammad Shāyif Jārallah.[180] In addition, Saʿdah governor Muṭahhar al-Miṣrī issued a decree to form nine sub-committees in nine districts to draw up a tight timetable for the implementation of the ceasefire agreement, in particular the Houthis' withdrawal from their strongholds and the handover of heavy and medium weapons.

After the demanding peace negotiations, the implementation of the Doha Agreement proved just as complex. A member of the Houthi delegation described it as a 'difficult agreement whose implementation was even more difficult' (*ittifāq ṣaʿb wa taṭbīqhu aṣʿab*).[181] This was not only due to the negotiation of the ceasefire conditions, which, after all, were not particularly innovative and largely resembled those of previous ceasefire agreements, with the exception of the safe haven for Houthi leaders. This was mainly due to the fact that radical groups had emerged on both sides of the mediation that rejected any kind of ceasefire or compromise and instead insisted on the military solution and total defeat of the enemy. Hardliners in the armed forces continued to opt for military solutions rather than political deals, while certain Houthi field commanders sought to derail the peace process, making the Doha Agreement a crucial test for the movement. Salih's and ʿAbdulmalik's public commitment to the ceasefire had little impact on these dissenting voices, much less on the countless feuds and revenge issues which had arisen throughout the conflict zone. In short, the dynamics of war and the hatred between the warring parties jeopardized the implementation of the Doha Agreement.

While negotiating its implementation, the security situation remained extremely volatile and tense. On 22 June, Shaykh Aḥmad Dahbāsh Miṭrī, senior shaykh of the Munabbih's Shaʿshaʿ moiety, was killed in Qaṭābir when his vehicle drove over a landmine. During the fourth war Miṭrī and his tribal warriors had played a crucial role in fighting the Houthis in Qaṭābir, Ghamr and Rāziḥ. In his view, the Doha Agreement would only enable the Houthis to regroup and start another war.[182] On the day he died, he had angrily walked out on a meeting concerning the agreement's implementation in the Qaṭābir region. The mine killed him as he was heading towards the frontline in Qaṭābir in order to resume the fight against the Houthis.

Upon ʿAbdulmalik al-Ḥūthī's orders, in early July the Houthis handed over large parts of three districts: Majz, Qaṭābir, and Bāqim. In Bāqim, they withdrew from their stronghold on Umm Laylā Mountain, which overlooks the road from Saʿdah city to Saudi Arabia. In Ḍaḥyān, they evacuated the police department from which they had expelled government forces months earlier. They also vacated large parts of Saḥār (Banī Muʿādh, al-Ṭalḥ, Walad Masʿūd and al-Jaʿmalah), Sāqayn and al-Ṣafrāʾ. They opened streets that had been under their control and turned in heavy state military equipment that they had captured in battle.

Despite these gestures of accommodation and compliance, the Houthis could not dispel the military's distrust. Whenever they made a step to implement the Doha Agreement, the government suspected them of covert repositioning and regrouping in preparation for renewed battle. For example, the Doha Agreement stipulated that the Houthis should return to their home areas. Many Houthis, however, were ultimately unable to return to their villages because a number of them found their homes destroyed and uninhabitable, or occupied by the army and/or Ḥāshid mercenaries who had not been withdrawn. In addition, the army suspected that those Houthis who had left their strongholds and returned home were now militarily occupying their home villages—a rather odd logic that wholly distorted the provisions of the Doha Agreement.[183] The handover of weapons to the government proved problematic, too: the Houthis were no regular army, and many medium- and heavy-calibre weapons were tribesmen's private property. The hand-ins were therefore limited to heavy equipment that the armed forces had 'lost' in battle; privately and tribally owned weapons, regardless of their calibre, were not delivered.

The seventh provision of the Doha Agreement, which determined the relocation of ʿAbdulmalik al-Ḥūthī, Yaḥyā al-Ḥūthī, ʿAbdulkarīm al-Ḥūthī, and ʿAbdullah al-Razzāmī to Doha, proved impossible to implement. To spare the Houthi leaders the dangerous trip to Sanaʿa, the government suggested relocating them via Ẓahrān al-Janūb from Maṭrah to Doha, and the Giants Forces providing safe passage from Maṭrah to Ẓahrān.[184] Yet the Houthi leaders remained in Maṭrah and al-Naqʿah, with no indication that they intended to relocate to Qatar.

Due to these procrastinations, the government's dissatisfaction increased. In early July, the parliamentary committee released a statement giving the Houthis another deadline of three days to implement the terms of the agreement, notably to hand over their weapons and vacate their strongholds. ʿAbdulmalik expressed his deep dissatisfaction with the work and attitude of the implementation committees, accusing them of 'ignor[ing] all the positive steps that have been made [to implement the ceasefire]'[185] and complaining that 'after its arrival in Saʿdah city the Committee has stayed behind closed doors and did not communicate with us'. His brother Yaḥyā added that the Houthis had taken significant steps in implementing the Doha Agreement, but the problem lay in the partiality of the committee members, who misinterpreted or simply ignored such progress: 'They do not recognize the facts and they say, for example, we did not hand over Qaṭābir, Majz, Rāziḥ and Ghamr. They stay in a hotel in closed rooms and tell [the president]: "do not believe that they handed it over"'.[186] Only on 28 July, six weeks after the conclusion of the Doha Agreement, the members of the committee met with ʿAbdulmalik al-Ḥūthī for the first time.

On 9 July, the Houthis passed the committee a detailed list that meticulously documented the steps they had taken to implement the Doha Agreement. They listed fifty-three strategically important hills and mountains in six districts (Qaṭābir, Bāqim, Majz, al-Ṣafrā', Kitāf, Ghamr) that had been under their control during the fourth war and which they had vacated after the conclusion of the ceasefire.[187] As a further gesture of goodwill, on 10 July the Houthis released war prisoners (but continued to hold dozens of others).

On 15 July, a convoy including representatives of Qatar was ambushed in al-Ghubayr, Saḥār; two bodyguards were wounded. The blame game resumed once again: government media outlets suspected that Houthi supporters were behind the attack. ʿAbdulmalik, on the other hand, issued a statement in which he condemned the attack and categorically denied any involvement on the Houthi side, suspecting that 'the other party was behind the incident in order to exacerbate the situation'.[188] After the incident, Qatar's envoys decided to withdraw from the Saʿdah region out of frustration with the lack of progress and the deteriorating security situation. On 23 July, the Qatari Embassy confirmed that it was recalling its delegation from Saʿdah for 'further consultation and evaluation of the situation'.[189] The controversy over implementation of the ceasefire conditions dragged on, new deadlines were issued and elapsed without progress. The security situation deteriorated, and in Saʿdah and neighbouring Ḥajjah—where the Houthis had set up 'beachheads'—localized fighting resumed.

On 17 August, after the implementation process had virtually come to a standstill, the Qatari delegation departed for Doha under the pretext of the approaching holy month of Ramadan. The government considered that the Houthis had broken the agreement, while the Houthis accused the government of not implementing anything. Qatar in turn suspended the financial reconstruction and development assistance in Saʿdah governorate, whose disbursement had been conditional upon implementation of the Doha Agreement.

Fourth Interim

During Ramadan in September 2007, the tensions between the warring parties and their respective tribal allies increased. Qatar's mediators had withdrawn from Yemen. In November, the Committee for the Implementation of the Doha Agreement declared that the peace process had failed.[190]

The outbreak of renewed fighting was beyond the control of both the government and the Houthi leaders: driven by processes of feuding and retaliatory violence, as in the third interim period, the war had already begun to perpetuate itself. The armed forces, again, began to relocate military reinforcements to the Saʿdah region. In December, the battles came so close to Saʿdah city, the military's main stronghold, that the army imposed a state of emergency on the city. In anticipation of a looming Houthi attack, the armed forces set up checkpoints on roads entering the city; security cars with speakers tore through the city's streets and called on the residents to stay in their homes. The harbingers of the fifth war had already appeared: a 'harsh winter' (*shitāʾ qāris*) lay ahead.

Once again, the government tried to counteract the looming war, this time—for lack of alternatives—with some shaykhs of Saʿdah. In December, some of the region's influential shaykhs formed a tribal mediation committee and endeavoured to mediate between the government and the Houthi leaders. Yet this initiative was ill-fated. Fāris Manāʿ, who served as head of the committee, apparently was not well received by the Houthis, who still reckoned him a government supporter. At the same time, he had already lost the regime's confidence because of his alleged involvement in the Gaddafi issue; the arms purchases of the regime were now being processed 'directly' or via Salih's relatives.[191] ʿAbdulmalik al-Ḥūthī agreed to receive the mediation committee in Maṭrah, but on condition that ʿUthmān Mujallī be excluded from it. Yet before the mediation team was able to begin its work, the situation in Saʿdah derailed dangerously.

The Government Loses its Last Cards

On 16 December, an attempt was made on the life of Yāsir Mujallī in the security precinct of Saʿdah city. Yāsir was GPC chairman of Saḥār district and a brother of ʿUthmān Mujallī. Six people died and as many were injured; Yāsir and his brother Ṭaha suffered extremely painful injuries but survived. Eyewitnesses reported that gunmen had fired simultaneously at Yāsir and his escort from the rooftops of nearby government buildings, and identified the gunmen as belonging to the bodyguards of the governor and the director of Public Works, Jamīl al-Aṣbaḥī.

Yāsir Mujallī and his escort had been on the way to see al-Aṣbaḥī, to follow up the case of a ground wall close to Raḥbān Hotel in Saʿdah city, which belongs to the Mujallī family. Prior to the incident, there had been heated debates and verbal altercations between Yāsir and al-Aṣbaḥī, which further aggravated existing tensions between the Mujallī clan and the government—ʿUthmān had repeatedly criticized the government's crisis management in Saʿdah, drawing upon himself the wrath of Governor Muṭahhar al-Miṣrī and the state leadership.

This assassination attempt on the brothers of one of Saʿdah's most influential shaykhs and Houthi opponents marked a turning point in the relationship between Saʿdah's tribal elites and the Salih government. In a time of fear over eruption of a fifth war, the incident opened up a new front between the government and its local tribal allies. An observer recalled:

> The assassination attempt [on Yāsir Mujallī] was a political issue. The attack was a message of some persons of the regime represented by the then governor of Saʿdah, Muṭahhar al-Miṣrī, to anyone who criticized or disagreed with some of the regime's actions regarding the war with the Houthis. It was a clear message to ʿUthmān and the other shaykhs of Saʿdah.[192]

Thousands of tribesmen attended the victims' funeral. In anticipation of revenge actions, the funeral took place under the state's intense security alert. After the funeral, ʿUthmān Mujallī struck back. The extreme vehemence of his reaction can only be explained as the result of years of frustration; the assassination attempt on his brother Yāsir was the straw that broke the camel's back. ʿUthmān issued a summons to all tribes of Saʿdah governorate (both the Khawlān b. ʿĀmir and Hamdān al-Shām confederations). On 18 December, two days after the attack, he convened a huge tribal gathering in al-Salām Park in Saʿdah city. Spearheaded by ʿUthmān Mujallī, after extensive discussion of the incident the tribes issued a statement:

> The assault of the government's gunmen belonging to [the security staff of] one of the [government] officials, backed by the leadership of the province, served to implement a plan which aims at marginalizing and undermining everything that is from Saʿdah and to settle political scores with [Saʿdah's] influential persons through the use of violence and force in order to humiliate, insult and bring to their knees those who demand to save Saʿdah from the quagmires of bloody wars and spirals of violence, which have been haemorrhaging the governorate for four years.[193]

During the tribal gathering, ʿUthmān Mujallī called for the investigation of this 'heinous crime in the courtyard of the government complex', as he called it. He made clear that he expected the authorities to investigate the incident and to bring the perpetrators to justice, in order to ease the anger of the Mujallī clan and the tribes loyal to them. Otherwise, he threatened to follow up the matter in accordance with tribal customary law. This was the first time in the history of the Yemeni parliament that an MP (ʿUthmān Mujallī was GPC member for Saʿdah city) had threatened the government in drastic language with taking revenge on the state's representatives for the victims, by—in the words of ʿUthmān—'liquidating senior state officials and targeting the depths of the system', stressing that 'the hand of vengeance is not unable to reach out to the depths of the system and the state's organs by focusing on hitting its vulnerable points'.[194]

In the following days, a continuous flow of tribal gunmen flocked to the region of al-ʿAbdīn, expressing their solidarity and loyalty with the Mujallī clan. In the presence of the victims' parents, a second huge tribal gathering was held in the home compound of the Mujallī clan in al-ʿAbdīn. The gathering ended with another sharp statement from ʿUthmān Mujallī, warning senior state officials in Saʿdah of retaliation if there was procrastination and cover-up of the perpetrators and their backers. The statement, which was distributed to the press, created additional pressure with the declaration of an 'oath of loyalty and blood unity between the families of the victims and the Mujallī clan' (*ʿahd al-wafāʾ wa wāḥidiyyat al-damm maʿ ahālī al-ḍaḥāyā wa Āl Mujallī*). By equating the blood of the victims with the blood of the clan, the latter took responsibility for the crime's atonement under tribal customary law, and ʿUthmān had made it clear that in case of failure or procrastination of prosecution, he would not hesitate to target senior representatives of the state. The other shaykhs present gave ʿUthmān—since he had become the representative of the victims' families and the wounded—sureties such as 'rifles of good faith' (*banādiq al-wafāʾ*), and took an oath of support and assistance (*ʿahd al-ghawth wa l-nuṣrah*) according to tribal customs.[195]

The government had been walking straight into a confrontation with one of its most influential allies in the war on the Houthis—and was now surprised by the consequences. In an attempt to defuse the tensions, ʿUthmān was given a surprise visit from Minister of Interior and Deputy Prime Minister Rashād al-ʿAlīmī and General ʿAlī Muḥsin, who offered condolences and tried to calm him down. According to informed sources, they tried to dissuade ʿUthmān from his proposal of arbitration to settle the issue according to tribal customary law, because the blood pact between the victims' families and the Mujallī clan would potentially trigger a spiral of violence between the state and its former allies among the tribes.[196]

The state's judiciary did not really seriously pursue the case, because of the involvement of Governor Muṭahhar al-Miṣrī and probably the state leadership itself. To appease the anger of the Mujallī clan, their tribe and tribal allies, Jamīl al-Aṣbaḥī and six soldiers from his and al-Miṣrī's entourages were thrown in prison. Ironically, after the Houthis seized Saʿdah city in 2011 and many of the prisoners had escaped, these detainees would refuse to leave the prison because, according to tribal customary law, the matter was still unatoned for and the case could still lead to revenge actions.[197] In Yemen this form of voluntary detention is a phenomenon directly related to the existence of blood feud: Prisons can also serve to protect the perpetrators from tribal retaliation. If the police arrest and jail a tribesman who has committed a crime, those from the offended tribe may raid the prison to release the accused, in order to have him put on trial under the tribal justice system.[198]

In January 2008, a situation of undeclared war began to prevail in Saʿdah. A further worrisome issue for the government was the siege of the 17th Brigade by Houthi forces in Marrān. The government sent military reinforcements from Sanaʿa to Saʿdah in order to break the blockade in Marrān, which was witnessing fierce battles and the displacement of large numbers of citizens.[199] In spite of the official Qatar-brokered ceasefire, Marrān and Maṭrah were bombed by warplanes. Throughout the province, the government was losing support due to its erratic proceeding, arbitrary actions and violent tactics. In January 2008, the US embassy commented: 'All is not well in Saʿdah'.[200]

Wāʾilah and al-Jawf were also in turmoil. Since 2006, those sections of the Wāʾilah tribe living close to the Saudi border had resumed their protests against the demarcation and fortification works on the border, with which the Saudis were pressing ahead due to the expanding Houthi conflict. The Wāʾilah equated the physical implementation of the border, especially in the area of Jabal al-Thaʾr,[201] with the 'looting of the territory of Wāʾilah' (*salb arāḍī qabāʾil Wāʾilah*) and threatened the use of force to restore the integrity of their territory. They warned the Yemeni government against 'collusion' (*tawāṭuʾ*) with Saudi authorities in demarcating the border and reiterated their rejection of the regime's perceived 'disregard and negligence' (*tahāwun wa tafrīṭ*) towards them.[202] Yaḥyā al-Ḥūthī put the boot in by airing his suspicions that the government had sold Yemen's lost territories in Najrān, ʿAsīr and Jīzān for US$200 million to Saudi Arabia, and announced that the case was still far from closed.[203]

Further east, in al-Jawf, parts of Dahm began protesting in autumn 2007 against failed government policies and government neglect. Since the 1960s civil war, the development of al-Jawf governorate followed a similar path to that in Saʿdah as the republican state actively countered the region's perceived unruliness with covert but drastic punitive measures, resulting in decades of economic deprivation, political marginalization, and territorial isolation. State intervention in this province remained weak and sporadic and mainly focused on financial co-optation of the tribal elites, rather than on consistent development of the province. In September 2005, Fayṣal Abū Rās, scion of al-Jawf's most prominent shaykhly linage, had resigned as an MP. He publicly justified his resignation by pointing out the corrupt practices of the government (denouncing it on TV as a 'government of mass destruction').[204]

Also in autumn 2007, members of the Dahm tribe threatened the Yemeni government with mass emigration to Saudi Arabia. For the Dahm, especially in the central region of Khabb wa l-Shaʿf in the Jawf basin, lack of revenue opportunities, the aggravation of famine, poverty, and the spread of diseases were obviously the last straw. This was not just an empty threat: a larger group of people (about 100 individuals) from the Khabb wa l-Shaʿf area moved to the Saudi border and requested humanitarian asylum, which was granted.[205]

The far south of Yemen, too, was in turmoil. In May 2007, government employees and pensioners who had not been paid for years began to organize small demonstrations calling for equal rights and an end to the economic and political marginalization of the south. As the popularity of such protests grew and more people began to attend, the demands of the protests also developed. Instead of solving the problem politically, here too the government resorted to violence, with the result that from 2008 calls were being made for the full secession of the south and the re-establishment of South Yemen as an independent state.[206]

The Second Doha Agreement

In November 2007, these mounting nationwide problems led to a reinvigoration of the stalled Qatari mediation efforts in Saʿdah. Although the mediators were reluctant to resume negotiations, Yemen's negotiator in Qatar, ʿAbdulkarīm al-Iryānī (former prime minister and political advisor to President Salih), managed to persuade Doha to re-engage, arguing that their efforts thus far had succeeded in saving lives and that, conversely, their definitive withdrawal would remove any inhibitions of either party about unleashing further violence.[207] Since ʿAbdulmalik al-Ḥūthī and ʿAbdullah al-Razzāmī had repeatedly refused to leave Saʿdah for Doha, Yaḥyā al-Ḥūthī travelled from Germany to Qatar to convey the Houthis' demands. On 1 February, ʿAbdulkarīm al-Iryānī, Ṣāliḥ Habrah (a tribal Houthi representative of Banī Muʿādh/Saḥār who regularly carried messages between the Yemeni government and the Houthis) and Qatari Prime Minister Ḥamad b. Jāsim Āl Thānī signed the Second Doha Agreement (*sulḥ Dawḥah al-thānī*). The provisions of Doha II were kept confidential, but the agreement's text soon leaked to the press.

Despite Qatar's good intentions, the Second Doha Agreement was a sham. It was not a new peace agreement, but rather amounted to a reactivation of

Doha I, as there were only minor modifications in comparison with the ceasefire agreement brokered in June 2007. Provision 7 of the agreement was slightly modified: ʿAbdulmalik al-Ḥūthī, ʿAbdulkarīm al-Ḥūthī and ʿAbdullah al-Razzāmī were only obliged to spend a period of six months in Qatar after the 'stabilizing of the situation and implementation of the agreement and return of the situation to the status quo ante'.[208] Experience showed that such vague, obscure phrases in treaty texts usually resulted in non-implementation. And so it was here: because the situation did not stabilize, let alone return to whatever the 'status quo ante' was meant to be, this conditionality of the Houthi leadership's relocation to Qatar was unfeasible from the outset, and unfeasible provisions inevitably lead to failed agreements. Doha II also provided that, in order to ensure its neutrality, four additional members would be added to the 'Presidential Committee' (*lajnah riʾāsiyyah*), whose task was to supervise, follow up and document the implementation of the agreement on the ground. These four were Ḥasan Thawrah, Muḥammad Muḥammad al-Muʾayyad, ʿAlī Nāṣir Qirshah and Ṣāliḥ Shirmah—all reckoned to be tacit Houthi sympathizers.[209]

Doha II did not have much positive impact on the ground. After its conclusion in February 2008, both the Houthis and the government made occasional steps to demonstrate their goodwill. Yet soon the negotiations again reached a deadlock. The differences centred mainly on Provision 7 of the agreement, which required the Houthis to leave all sites they occupied, while the government was to gradually release Houthi prisoners. The Houthis were refusing to hand over certain strategic positions, which led to the government's refusal to release more detainees, provoking renewed fatal riots in Qiḥzah prison in Saʿdah city.[210]

Shortly after the signing of Doha II, the blame game and the armed conflict resumed. In Marrān, the Houthis continued to besiege the 17th Brigade. On 3 February, two days after the conclusion of the agreement, the Houthis shot down a combat helicopter in Ḥaydān, resulting in the injury of General ʿAbd al-ʿAzīz al-Shahārī and a number of military officers, who had to make an emergency landing in enemy territory.[211] A few days later, tribal mediators from among the local Khawlān shaykhs managed to rescue them from their predicament. Meanwhile, the Houthis obstinately refused to leave certain mountain strongholds, including their headquarters of Maṭrah and al-Naqʿah. The government in turn refused to pull troops from areas where battles had taken place.

In the same month, Shaykh Shāyaʿ Bukhtān of Āl Sālim died in a mysterious accident. Since he was viewed as a government loyalist, the Houthis were suspected.[212] Clashes between Houthis and supporters of Shāyaʿ Bukhtān ensued, and as a result parts of Āl Sālim fell into the hands of the Houthis. In al-Ṭalḥ, the rebels fought a grim battle against ʿAbdulkarīm Manāʿ and his supporters. In Marrān, they tightened the siege of the 17th Infantry Brigade.

In early March, gunmen (apparently from among the Jalḥā tribe) assassinated Walīd Thawrah, son of the recently appointed Presidential Committee member Ḥasan Thawrah, and two of his companions in Yusnam (Bāqim).[213] Since Ḥasan Thawrah was considered a Houthi loyalist and the Jalḥā as government loyalists, suspicion this time fell upon the supporters and henchmen of General ʿAlī Muḥsin. As with the assassination of Yaḥyā al-Shāmī's mediation committee members in June 2006 and the attempted assassination of the Qatari mediators in July 2007, the objective of this attack was obvious: it aimed at sabotaging the Presidential Committee's work and at dealing a mortal blow to the already moribund peace process. Indeed, after Thawrah's assassination, the Presidential Committee withdrew from Saʿdah to Sanaʿa.

Given the continued failure of ceasefire implementation, Qatar's US$300–500 million pledges in reconstruction aid for Saʿdah province were still held back by the Qatari government. Another point of contention was that President Salih apparently had insisted on these funds being controlled by the government, while the Qataris felt that there were too many Yemeni officials with authority to access funds without sufficient accountability. The episode caused a great deal of friction between the two governments. In consequence, Qatar withdrew its pledges of assistance.[214]

A Memorable Funeral

When the coming of the fifth war became evident, the chains of retaliatory violence and blood feud had already assumed such complex and ramified patterns that they could hardly be understood by an external observer. For the outsider, they resembled the processes inside a pinball machine. A good example of the impact of tribal feuding, wrapped up in the larger Houthi-government conflict, was the events on the margins of Qāʾid Shuwayṭ's funeral in April 2008.

Shaykh Qāʾid Shuwayṭ of Banī ʿUwayr, whom we encountered in previous chapters of this book, died in April 2008 of natural causes. Qāʾid Shuwayṭ was one of those seasoned veterans of the so-called Saʿdah Brigade or *Aḥrār* who had backed the Republic from the onset of the 1962 Revolution. During the 1960 civil war, he had fought under the most adverse circumstances against the royalists and, after eight years, triumphed over them in 1970.[215] After the civil war he had become one of the most influential shaykhs of the Saʿdah region. When he died in April 2008, shaykhs and notables travelled from near and far to Banī ʿUwayr to pay their last respects to this tribal personality.

The rush of numerous tribal leaders into Saʿdah, which was riven by war, turned out to pose a major security problem. In Sufyān, Mujāhid Ḥaydar reverted to his old habit and blocked the Sanaʿa-Saʿdah highway when Ṣādiq al-Aḥmar tried to cross Mujāhid's territory on his way to Banī ʿUwayr. This came as no surprise, as the Ḥaydar and al-Aḥmar clans were at odds. Because Mujāhid accused the late ʿAbdullah al-Aḥmar and the Salih government of involvement in the assassination of his father Aḥmad and three of his brothers in 1987, he bore on his shoulders the enmity of both the regime and the al-Aḥmar clan. In consequence, the feud between the Ḥaydar and the al-Aḥmar led to frequent roadblocks, carried out by followers of Mujāhid Ḥaydar whenever a member of the al-Aḥmar clan travelled to Saʿdah. In 1992, ʿAbdullah al-Aḥmar passed through Sufyān on his way to a tribal meeting in Saʿdah; fearing Mujāhid's revenge actions, he was accompanied by a very large convoy of more than 300 cars. In 2004, en route to the funeral of Shaykh Muḥammad Ḥāmis al-ʿAwjarī (Wāʾilah), his son Ḥusayn was forced to travel to Saʿdah via the long alternative Ḥaraḍ/al-Malāḥīṭ road through the Khawlān massif, because Mujāhid Ḥaydar's followers had blocked the Sufyān route. After his return to the capital, the al-Aḥmar clan organized a Ḥāshid military campaign against Mujāhid Ḥaydar, which began in the same week in June 2004 that the first Houthi war erupted in Marrān.[216] Now, on the way to Qāʾid Shuwayṭ's funeral in Banī ʿUwayr, Ṣādiq al-Aḥmar again found himself trapped in Sufyān, as Mujāhid Ḥaydar's tribe blocked the road in front of him and would not allow him to cross. After several hours of mediation, Qāʾid's son and successor ʿĀrif Shuwayṭ and Ṣāliḥ b. Shājiaʿ (Wāʾilah), who also came to attend the funeral, persuaded Mujāhid Ḥaydar to allow him to pass.

Meanwhile, north of Sufyān, unidentified persons set up an ambush in al-Mahādhir and took down with machine guns Shaykh and MP Ṣāliḥ Ṣāliḥ Hindī Dughsān of Āl ʿAmmār, who, too, was on the way to mourn the death of his father-in-law, Qāʾid Shuwayṭ. Likewise, his son Amīn and a bodyguard were killed and some others wounded.[217] Immediately after the attack, finger pointing began between the Houthis and the government. Eyewitnesses said that the gunmen were wearing military uniforms, but this didn't mean much in Saʿdah's over-complex conflict environment. Governor Muṭahhar al-Miṣrī declared in a statement to al-Jazeera that the Houthis were behind the assassination. ʿAbdulmalik al-Ḥūthī issued a press release blaming the government, suggesting that the assassination may have been due to the fact that a brother of the deceased, Aḥmad Ṣāliḥ Hindī Dughsān, was active on the Houthi side.[218] Ṣāliḥ Ṣāliḥ Hindī Dughsān himself, though a GPC MP for al-Ṣafrā' and al-Ḥishwah, had taken a neutral stance. He had not been sufficiently vocal against the Houthis for the government's liking (*iltazama al-ṣumt*, he was 'committed to silence'), and after all the Dughsān clan's relationship with the government was marked by deep mistrust.[219] On the other hand, as a GPC MP and thus a symbol of the state, he could equally have been on the Houthi blacklist. Hence his assassination could have been related to the wave of 'mystery murders' by both sides to which the shaykhs of Saʿdah were exposed at that time.

In reality, however, the matter was even more complicated, and its mere reduction to an episode of the Houthi conflict distorted the facts. It is believed that in December 1978 followers of Ṣāliḥ Ṣāliḥ Hindī's father had killed Shaykh Yaḥyā al-Ḥusaynī, who was linked by marriage ties to the Mujallī clan, with a landmine in Āl ʿAmmār. After al-Ḥusaynī's death, the Mujallī clan took care of his son Muʿammar, and ever since there had been a blood feud between the Dughsān clan on the one side and the Mujallī and al-Ḥusaynī clans on the other.[220] Apart from this, the Dughsān clan was involved in other feuds, both old and new, which likewise posed an ongoing threat to the life of Ṣāliḥ Ṣāliḥ Hindī Dughsān. Lichtenthäler mentions the Dughsān clan's involvement in numerous conflicts for land and water runoff claims.[221] Local sources thus ruled out either the government's or the Houthis' responsibility, stressing that Ṣāliḥ b. Ṣāliḥ Hindī Dughsān had been involved in numerous tribal revenge issues. A local explained:

> Shaykh Ṣāliḥ b. Ṣāliḥ Hindī inherited many problems from his father. It was always risky for him to travel. If they [the members of the Dughsān clan] came into [Saʿdah] town there were sometimes shootouts. There had been shootouts before in Saʿdah related to this feud [with the al-Ḥusaynī and Mujallī clan], near the governor's palace. And there were even further tribal feuds which Ṣāliḥ had inherited from his father and which were a permanent threat to his life.[222]

While Shaykh Qā'id Shuwayṭ's funeral took place with great pomp (the procession was led by his son ʿĀrif and Governor al-Miṣrī), military units began to track down the putative suspects (that is, Houthis), even though the identity of the perpetrators was and still is unclear. Meanwhile, thousands of armed Dahm tribesmen from among Āl ʿAmmār, Āl Sālim and al-ʿAmālisah gathered and made for the house of Ṣāliḥ Ṣāliḥ Hindī Dughsān in Āl ʿAmmār, announcing that they all stood behind the Dughsān clan and that they would not rest until they took revenge on those who had ambushed and gunned down their shaykh and MP.[223]

After the assassination of Ṣāliḥ Ṣāliḥ Hindī Dughsān, the members of the Qatar delegation travelled—'for the last time', they emphasized—from Sanaʿa to Saʿdah in order to end the impasse, to reach a breakthrough with the parties to the conflict and to prevent the outbreak of a fifth war.[224] Yet on the following day the Qatari mediators left again, having reached a 'dead end' (*ṭarīq masdūd*), with both parties to the conflict, rather than working together, continuing to accuse one another of failing to implement the terms of Doha II. A few days later, on 1 May, General ʿAlī Muḥsin and the minister of defence arrived in Saʿdah city in a helicopter. On the same day, large military supplies arrived in the province, while others were still on the road. 'Alī Muḥsin's arrival in Saʿdah was considered a bad omen (*nadhīr shuʾm*), as the situation was teetering on the brink and resembled the period immediately before the outbreak of the fourth war.

The parties to the conflict had already got themselves into position. It only took a small provocation to unleash the fifth war, and this took place the following day: the bomb attack on Bin Salmān Mosque in Saʿdah city on 2 May.

The Fifth War (2 May–17 July 2008)

The fifth war was a rather brief episode of two months, but in two respects it was fateful. It determined the future direction of the Houthi conflict, as the war expanded from Saʿdah into ʿAmrān, al-Jawf and—temporarily—into Banī Ḥushaysh on the outskirts of Sanaʿa. Moreover, in his attempt to secure his grip on power and to steer the course of the war, President Salih was treading on very thin ice. As conventional loyalties and alliances in Saʿdah had begun to disintegrate below the surface, the pillars of Salih's autocratic rule in the Saʿdah region began to falter. He had already lost the comforting stability of the patronage networks with Saʿdah's shaykhs that, in times past, had channelled or stifled tensions arising between the government and its local partners. Army brutality and government incoherence had engendered disappointment, protest and resistance in such dimensions that they threatened to destroy the political consensus. Also, in the south of Yemen, smouldering fires thought to be under the state's control were being kindled anew. More than ever, governance resembled a nervous balancing act. It is no coincidence that President Salih, in an interview from that time, likened governing Yemen to 'dancing on the heads of snakes', echoing Imam Aḥmad's famous expression: 'you don't understand that I am sitting on a nest of snakes and scorpions, and you will see what happens once I am gone'.[225]

The enormous enlargement of the war was related to a directive from ʿAbdulmalik al-Ḥūthī, who, at the beginning of the fifth bout in May 2008, had threatened to 'expand the scope of war' (*tawsīʿ al-ḥarb*) and to target 'sensitive government areas' (*manāṭiq ḥassāsah li-l-sulṭah*). It was evident that the Houthis felt more confident than ever. He had declared:

> We are now much stronger than in the past, in regard to both our numbers and our possibilities. [...] We have established good internal alliances, whose fruits will be reaped at the appropriate time. We have the experience of the past wars, and we have access to sensitive information, which serves us well. We have the ability to fight a protracted war, and the ability to continue the conflict across generations. [...] We have become far more ready and present on the ground and will open fronts of confrontation in more than one place in order to defend ourselves.[226]

These were no hollow phrases. At the outbreak of the fifth war, the Houthis began pushing from Saʿdah into Sufyān in ʿAmrān governorate, into al-Jawf governorate and into Banī Ḥushaysh, a district near the International Airport just 20 kilometres northeast of Sanaʿa. All of these new areas of conflict were on territories of the Bakīl confederation. To garner support among the Bakīl tribes, the Houthis applied one of their greatest skills: grafting local tribal grievances throughout the north onto a core narrative of resistance to the government. After dramatic battles in Marrān and a successful tribal mediation led by Fāris Manāʿ, the fifth war ended abruptly and somewhat unexpectedly with the declaration of a unilateral ceasefire by President Salih. The ceasefire, however, had little impact on the ground. The volatile interim period after the fifth war led almost seamlessly into the sixth war.

Saʿdah

On 2 May, a blast during Friday prayers at Bin Salmān Mosque in Saʿdah city left at least eleven people dead, most of them soldiers, and injured dozens of others. The improvised explosive device (IED) was rigged to a parked motorcycle at the mosque's gate. The target seemed to have been a number of army officers and/or the Salafi imam ʿAskar Zuʿayl, an aide to General ʿAlī Muḥsin.[227] The government claimed that the Houthis had repeatedly threatened the mosque's imam (who escaped unharmed) because he had attacked Houthis from his podium. ʿAbdulmalik denied any involvement of his followers in the attack and blamed 'hateful [persons] who are blinded by hatred'.[228]

However, the parties to the conflict were already geared for the fifth war, and the mosque blast was the signal to start it. In the days to follow, Saʿdah city saw heavy fighting. The day after the attack on the mosque, the Houthis began to besiege the provincial capital. On the outskirts of the city, they tried to seize the airport. To restore control, for the first time the government deployed two units of the well-trained and -equipped Republican Guard.[229]

Also for the first time, Wādī Āl Abū Jabārah in Kitāf region witnessed Houthi troop movements. Munabbih, too, saw combat: a few days after the attack on Bin Salmān Mosque, a two-day skirmish broke out between Houthis and Central Security Forces (CSF) after the rebels attacked a CSF checkpoint near Sūq al-Khamīs.[230] Thus far, the crisis in Munabbih had been contained through tribal mediation—only later, during the sixth war, would Munabbih become a major theatre of war.

The fifth war saw Ḍaḥyān, Ḥaydān, Marrān, Rāziḥ, Shidāʾ, Saḥār, Āl Sālim, Āl ʿAmmār, Āl Shāfiʿah, Qaṭābir, Bāqim, Nushūr and others raided by air strikes and shelled by tanks and armoured vehicles. Ferocious clashes centred on Jabal ʿIzzān in Saḥār, a mountain of great strategic importance since it overlooked the road to Houthi headquarters in Maṭrah. In Marrān, the Houthis further intensified the siege of the 17th Infantry Brigade (see below). The whole Saʿdah region experienced a large exodus of citizens.

Fighting resumed in almost all areas that had previously seen battle and bloodshed. These confrontations largely followed the same patterns as in the earlier wars. However, the new fronts that opened up during this war in fact became its main battlegrounds: Banī Ḥushaysh, al-Jawf and Sufyān.

Banī Ḥushaysh

On 14 May, the security director of Sanaʿa governorate, Brigadier General Muḥammad Ṣāliḥ Ṭurayq, was ambushed by Houthi loyalists in the Bayt al-Sayyid area of Banī Ḥushaysh district, northeast of the capital. Two of his bodyguards were killed. Ṭurayq himself escaped unharmed, but was forced to seek shelter in a village until military reinforcements arrived from Sanaʿa to rescue him.[231] He took refuge in the house of a Banī Ḥushaysh shaykh who had been accompanying him when the ambush took place. The government sent troops to free him from his predicament, but they, too, were caught in a Houthi ambush. As Ṭurayq and the murdered bodyguards hailed from the Murād tribe in Maʾrib, Murād tribesmen rallied in Maʾrib and Sanaʿa and discussed the option of going to Banī Ḥushaysh to lift the siege themselves.[232]

Ṭurayq, however, managed a secret escape to the capital along small mountain paths. Yet the affair was far from over. About 100 local Houthi loyalists had gathered in Banī Ḥushaysh, supported by some Houthi fighters from the Saʿdah region. The attack on Ṭurayq opened a new front in the immediate vicinity of the capital: an indication that ʿAbdulmalik's threats to expand the war had been serious.

Banī Ḥushaysh is a Bakīl tribe that gives its name to a densely populated district of Sanaʿa governorate, east of Sanaʿa city.[233] To the north, Banī Ḥushaysh borders on the tribal territory of the Nihm, to the east on Khawlān al-Ṭiyāl, and to the south on Sanḥān. Sanaʿa International Airport is situated in the triangle between Sanaʿa city and the tribal territories of the Arḥab, Nihm and Banī Ḥushaysh. The airport shares structures with al-Daylamī Airbase, where part of the Yemeni air force was stationed. Banī Ḥushaysh's Jabal Jumaymah mountain is overlooking the airport's tarmac. Banī Ḥushaysh also hosted a military base of the Republican Guard—the highly trained elite troops commanded by President Salih's son Ahmad, tasked with defending the regime.

The battles in Banī Ḥushaysh continued until the end of the fifth war. The Houthis continued to block the road from Banī Ḥushaysh to Sanaʿa, and the government dispatched units of the Republican Guard, the Military Police and the Central Security Forces to Banī Ḥushaysh.[234] There was an enormous cacophony from artillery fire, tanks and fighter jets that crossed the city to the northeast, dropped their bomb load and then returned. For the first time, the sound of war became audible in the capital.

In the battle for Banī Ḥushaysh, President Salih assigned the fighting to his son and commander of the Republican Guard, Brigadier General Ahmad Salih, rather than relying on the First Armoured Division under the command of General ʿAlī Muḥsin. Many believe that Salih Senior was seeking, in deploying his son near to the capital, to burnish Ahmad's military credentials, which would serve him well should he 'inherit' the presidency. Given its duty to protect the regime and the close proximity of its military base, the Republican Guard's deployment was reasonable. Yet it had been kept as far as possible from the conflict in Saʿdah—Ahmad Salih sent only two units to Saʿdah city and Sufyān upon eruption of the fifth and sixth wars. A military source explained that if the Republican Guard were deployed to Saʿdah on a large scale, and if Ahmad were to go with it, the Guard would fall under ʿAlī Muḥsin's command.[235] For President Salih, this clearly was no option, since ʿAlī Muḥsin and his son were considered rivals for the succession, and a strong showing by either one in this war could pave their way to the Presidential

Palace. President Salih was hoping for an easy and prestigious victory in Banī Ḥushaysh, while 'Alī Muḥsin's First Armoured Division, bogged down in the north, would continue to fritter away its reputation and clout in the tenacious morasses of Saʿdah.[236]

Victory, however, proved difficult, and the Republican Guard found fighting the Houthis in Banī Ḥushaysh a hard slog. Each time the government proclaimed its success, other news sources reported renewed Houthi resistance, suggesting that these victories were not quite as decisive as they were announced to be. Long after Banī Ḥushaysh was declared won, the Republican Guard units continued to bomb and 'root out' Houthis there. The government's pronouncements of victory in Banī Ḥushaysh in the second half of May were considerably premature, as three days of air strikes and shelling at the end of the month were required to stem a Houthi advance to within 12 miles of Sanaʿa.[237] Defensive precautions were taken in the capital and new checkpoints were set up, with soldiers searching all incoming and outgoing vehicles for weapons. After the Houthis temporarily occupied Jabal Jumaymah, which overlooked the airport, five staff members of al-Daylamī Airbase were arrested on suspicion of spying for the Houthis.[238] Obviously ʿAbdulmalik's ominous remark on his 'access to sensitive information which serves us well' kept ringing in the government's ears. In June, the Houthis dominated large parts of Banī Ḥushaysh. Fighting in the district only ended with Salih's unilateral ceasefire on 17 July.

Al-Jawf

Houthi fighters from al-Jawf governorate had already taken part in previous rounds of the Saʿdah wars; during the third and fourth wars, skirmishes and sporadic fighting had taken place there. Yet with the beginning of the fifth war, the Houthis started to push deliberately and forcefully into al-Jawf. On its eruption in early May, they focused on fighting the regular army, but, a few days before the end of the war in July, the dreaded fratricidal war between Houthi- and government-allied local tribes broke out and confrontations developed into conflagration. More than anywhere else, these confrontations were driven by an inexorable impetus; in 2015, al-Jawf was still unsettled by battles and smaller fights.

The governorate's topographical features and infrastructure were discussed in the first chapter of this study. Its main tribal groups belong to the Dahm tribe and its sections Banī Nawf, al-Mahāshimah, Āl Sulaymān, and Dhū

Ghaylān, the latter being sub-divided into the Dhū Muḥammad and Dhū Ḥusayn. Other sections of Dahm—the Āl Salim, al-ʿAmālisah and Āl ʿAmmār—are located in Saʿdah governorate. The Dhū Muḥammad are concentrated in the Baraṭ area, but their territory also continues south and encompasses the adjacent districts of Kharāb al-Marāshī and most of al-Zāhir. The territory of the Dhū Ḥusayn comprises the Rajūzah, al-Ḥumaydāt, al-Maṭammah and al-Matūn districts south of the Baraṭ plateau and stretches an indeterminate distance further east of Baraṭ, into the Khabb wa l-Shaʿf area towards the Rubʿ al-Khālī. The Banī Nawf reside in enclaves in al-Ḥumaydāt and al-Maṣlūb districts, but their main territory begins only a few kilometres east of al-Ḥazm, al-Jawf's provincial capital and main commercial centre, and covers al-Jawf's entire southeast (lower Khabb wa l-Shaʿf) and east. There are only a few groups outside the Dahm genealogy in al-Jawf, such as the Hamdān al-Jawf and their eight segments, a tribe installed around al-Jawf's main administrative centre, al-Ḥazm. The Āl Ashrāf, a special tribe of *sayyid* pedigree, are settled in lower al-Jawf, their main settlement area being located in the Ma'rib area further to the south.[239]

Al-Jawf is perhaps the most isolated and impoverished of Yemen's twenty-one governorates. The prevailing underdevelopment is appalling: in 2009, only 4 per cent of al-Jawf's residents had access to government-provided electricity, and just four registered physicians were responsible for a population of more than 400,000. Because of a lack of schools, 59 per cent of the population remained illiterate.[240] Yemeni security forces have traditionally enjoyed a weaker presence in al-Jawf than in other governorates, the reasons for which are not surprising. Beyond the relatively affluent Baraṭ area, the rocks and *wādīs* of central al-Jawf and the lunar landscapes of northern and eastern al-Jawf, which extend into the vast space of the Rubʿ al-Khālī, are so remote that instability in the governorate represents far less of a threat to the capital than in, say, Saʿdah or Ma'rib. In consequence, al-Jawf remained isolated from almost all signs of state building, development, and investment.[241] Given the government's reluctance to invest in development of infrastructure and government institutions in al-Jawf, and the almost total absence of foreign companies (notably in the oil and gas sector), there are also fewer national, international and economic interests than in any other governorate.

The coexistence of al-Jawf's tribes is considered particularly precarious and uneasy. Since ancient times, the region's tribes have served as a symbol of courage and bravery, embodying timeless qualities that still pertain to Yemeni tribal society's ideals: honour, strength, and noble protection of the weak.[242] Yet the downside of their heroism is that the Dahm (even more so than their sister tribe, the Wāʾilah) are known for their recalcitrance and truculence. They are seen as indomitable avengers whose exaggerated code of honour easily turns into rancorous feuds.[243] Given their mobility and recurring raids (indeed, the Arabic phrase *dahm* means 'raid'), the tribes of al-Jawf have always been dreaded, particularly in Lower Yemen.[244] To the north, the Dahm's raids have reached as far as Dirʿiyyah, the historical capital of the Āl Saʿūd.[245]

Despite strong tribal customs and traditions and the prominent role of skilled and highly respected local shaykhs almost constantly involved in mediations, it was evidently impossible to establish a functioning system of tribal conflict prevention in this period. The main reason for this was that the conflicts and rivalries prevalent in al-Jawf were deliberately fuelled by outsiders, notably the Yemeni and Saudi governments, with the aim of fragmenting and weakening al-Jawf's dreaded tribes. A shaykh of Dhū Ḥusayn explained:

> For more than forty years the state has meddled in al-Jawf in order to weaken the tribes by sowing discord among them. The state played off one tribe against the other and sought to expand the differences between them. It endeavoured to exacerbate issues of feud and revenge among them in order to widen the gap between the tribes and prevent any convergence between them. The government is the main sponsor of revenge issues in al-Jawf and nurtures its feuds. The government deliberately worked towards the proliferation of rivalries and enmities among [the tribes] and even distributed weapons and ammunition among them. [...] The Houthis then gained these weapons and used them directly against the state. [At the time of the fifth war] al-Jawf was an area flammable at any moment, because it borders on Saʿdah and Sufyān and the presence of the Houthis [in al-Jawf] was visible to everyone.[246]

As it was the case in the Saʿdah area, in al-Jawf, too, the government mainly exerted its influence through financial patronage of certain influential shaykhs and the allocation of posts for them and their tribesmen in the municipal government. The Saudi government, concerned for its vulnerable frontier, the transnational mobility of the Dahm and their historical raids deep into Saudi territory, also tried to purchase the loyalty of numerous Dahm and other shaykhs of the region. Thus, despite their malevolent policies in al-Jawf, the constant largesse of Riyadh and Sanaʿa facilitated some very durable alliances with local shaykhs and tribes.

For instance, the Hamdān al-Jawf, a tribe dwelling around the provincial capital al-Ḥazm and al-Khaliq district in Lower al-Jawf, have traditionally played significant roles in the Yemeni government, as municipal administrative staff, security officers and so on. As al-Ḥazm is the governorate's administrative centre and al-Khaliq boasts one of its only paved roads, it is unsurprising that the Hamdān al-Jawf would enjoy deeper relations with Sanaʿa than their neighbours. Most Hamdān al-Jawf shaykhs were firmly co-opted by the Salih regime. As long as Salih fought the Houthis, the shaykhs did so, too. When the ousted Salih allied himself with the Houthis in 2013 against the new interim president ʿAbdrabbuh Hādī, the shaykhs again followed suit.

The Dhū Ḥusayn, on the other hand, have had rather cool relations with Sanaʿa, instead maintaining strong connections with transnational smuggling networks. Populating vast stretches of desert well suited for shadowy trading activities, it is not surprising that the Dhū Ḥusayn have forged strong relations with their wealthier neighbour to the north: Saudi Arabia. During a huge tribal gathering in 1981 in Bīr al-Mahāshimah (in northern al-Jawf), Nājī al-Shāyif of the Dhū Ḥusayn was named the 'paramount' shaykh of the Bakīl confederation (*shaykh mashāyikh Bakīl*).[247] This position had previously been held by Amīn Abū Rās of the Dhū Ḥusayn's sister tribe and fiercest rival, the Dhū Muḥammad, until his assassination in 1978. Al-Shāyif never gained the tribal clout wielded by Amīn Abū Rās. Another influential shaykh of the Dhū Ḥusayn was Amīn al-ʿUkaymī of the Shawlān. Based in al-Matūn district, he was a prominent Iṣlāḥ MP, and a unique ally of the Saudi royal family. Because al-ʿUkaymī had been among those shaykhs who received Osama bin Laden's Afghan envoys in 1997, he was labelled an al-Qaeda supporter.[248] He fell out of favour with Sanaʿa in 2001 under disputed circumstances, when he attempted either to negotiate a resolution to the government's search for Yemeni citizen and al-Qaeda operative Abū ʿAlī al-Ḥārithī, or to facilitate his escape.[249] Al-ʿUkaymī remained a deeply polarizing figure, winning praise from some for helping to mediate tribal disputes as far afield as central Maʾrib, and criticism from others for allegedly harbouring al-Qaeda fighters and brokering 'a deal with the devil if it served him'.[250]

The Dhū Ḥusayn's nemesis is their sister tribe, the Dhū Muḥammad. The senior shaykhs of the Dhū Muḥammad hail from the Abū Rās lineage, one of Yemen's most famous and ancient shaykhly lineages. Many believe that Amīn Abū Rās was poisoned in 1978 by his rivals in the al-Aḥmar clan. Ever since his death, the Abū Rās family has cultivated an intimate enmity towards both the clan and its allies, the Saudis, whom they accuse of complicity in Amīn's death. Relations between Amīn's sons and al-Shāyif, the Bakīl's new 'paramount shaykh', have also been plagued by petty jealousies and mutual antipathy. As a kind of atonement for their father's death, but also because of the family's immense symbolic importance for the Bakīl tribes, Amīn's oldest son Ṣādiq held various high offices in the Salih government, including the post of deputy prime minister.[251] His brother Fayṣal was GPC MP for Baraṭ al-ʿInān and al-Marāshī, but resigned in 2005, complaining about government neglect and corruption.[252] During the Houthi conflict, both took a neutral position, Ṣādiq of course leaning more toward the government, in whose power structures he was deeply entrenched. Yet it should come as no surprise that the most prominent Houthi leader of al-Jawf would emerge from this famous Zaydi shaykhly lineage: ʿAbdulwāḥid Nājī Abū Rās.[253]

Underdevelopment, unemployment, deterioration of security and protracted tribal feuding, all artificially generated through malevolent external meddling, rendered large parts of al-Jawf susceptible to Houthi influence, in particular the Zaydi areas adjacent to Saʿdah governorate. A shaykh from Upper al-Jawf explained:

> There is an incubator environment (*biʾah ḥāḍinah*) in al-Jawf. There are many tribal links between al-Jawf and Saʿdah. Dahm [in al-Jawf] and Wāʾilah [in Saʿdah] are the sons of Shākir. Many segments of the Dahm tribe, such as al-ʿAmālisah, Āl Sālim, Āl Shāfiʿah and Āl ʿAmmār, are located in Saʿdah. Since 2004, the fighting in Saʿdah has sent shockwaves through al-Jawf. Many residents of al-Jawf live in Saʿdah city and its environs, where they have shops and farms. Hence al-Jawf is closely associated with the interests of Saʿdah. In Baraṭ and its environs, for example, many tribes are sympathetic to the Houthis. But there are also loyalists of President Salih and Ahmad Salih and ʿAlī Muḥsin, for example among those who work in the Border Guard, the Republican Guard and the *firqah* [First Armoured Division]. In Lower al-Jawf many shaykhs are allied with ʿAlī Muḥsin and Saudi Arabia, such as Amīn al-ʿUkaymī and Ḥasan Abkar, they are men of Iṣlāḥ. For many years President Salih, ʿAlī Muḥsin, the Āl al-Aḥmar, and Saudi Arabia have invested in some shaykhs of al-Jawf, and these are unpopular among their tribesmen, because they took care only of their own interests and lost their popularity and their support. For this reason they have a lot of enemies, and the Houthis then invested in their enemies. The Ashrāf tribe in al-Jawf also has followers and relations, after all they are *sādah*! Others remained neutral—like me. Alas that these evil days should be mine.[254]

The Houthis appear to have tentatively expanded their reach east through a deft use of soft power. Local sources suggest that they used the promise of support in resolving al-Jawf's intricate tribal conflicts to win initial acceptance among the tribesmen. As early as the 1990s, particularly capable *sayyid* mediators, among them Badr al-Dīn al-Ḥūthī himself, temporarily relocated from Saʿdah to al-Jawf to help certain tribes resolve their disputes.[255] They served as mediators and arbiters in village disagreements and tribal conflicts and hence worked to solidify their positions in these areas. In Marrān, too, Badr al-Dīn and his family earned credibility among the average population by offering the same service.[256] As a result, both the Zaydi revival movement and later the Houthi movement met with strong support among the population in parts of al-Jawf, especially the western and northern areas dominated by Zaydis. Nevertheless, the number of active Houthi fighters in al-Jawf had been negligible in the first three or four wars. A Houthi veteran from al-Jawf recalled:

> In the early phases of the Houthi conflict the number of Houthis in al-Jawf did not exceed seven individuals. They went to Saʿdah in order to participate in the war. During their participation in the last events of the second war in al-Jawf, their leader was Abū Ḥaydarah, who also led the Jawf team during the third war. Before the front finally erupted in al-Jawf in the fifth war, everyone was afraid of the government, and therefore the Houthis initially didn't get much of a response. When events in Saʿdah heated up, the government launched a campaign of pressure and threats in al-Jawf and mobilized its security forces and intelligence agents. [...] The events lasted until a mediation attempt was made to convince Abū Ḥaydarah to reverse his movement. The government offered him a state post, but he refused categorically. Then he came to me, and I sat down with a number of shaykhs of our tribe. The shaykhs said to me: 'Oh my son, we will get involved in a war for which we are not prepared. Go to Abū Ḥaydarah and try to convince him to change his mind.' But I answered: 'How could I convince him to change his mind! I was a prisoner before the first war in the Central Security Prison, and it was me who initially brought these [Houthi] ideas to Abū Ḥaydarah.' [...] After the shaykhs failed to achieve anything in conversation with me, they started to tell me that their situation was difficult and would obviously become even more difficult because the government would mobilize members of the tribes of al-Jawf against them, and that they were not strong enough for such a confrontation.[257]

In its endeavours to suppress the Houthi movement in al-Jawf, the government initially focused on al-Zāhir district, inhabited by the Dhū Muḥammad and almost entirely by Zaydis. The residents of al-Zāhir were considered particularly attached to Badr al-Dīn, as he had stayed in the district in the 1990s and had also spent some time there during the third war. Al-Zāhir was the nucleus of the Houthi front in al-Jawf. The same Houthi veteran recalled:

> In the fourth war we thought of building a [Houthi] military base in al-Jawf, although we were not very numerous. ʿAbdulmalik al-Ḥūthī had the idea for the base. Initially its headquarters was in al-Mabnā village in al-Zāhir, but then we decided to move the base to Jabal Ḥām [in al-Matūn] in order to take government pressure off the sons of al-Zāhir. Jabal Ḥām was far from people and tribal gatherings. We used the base to receive and train the volunteers from Sanaʿa, and we sent them from this base to the fronts in Saʿdah.[258]

From the fifth war, there was a considerable influx of fugitives and Houthi fighters from Saʿdah, Ḥarf Sufyān and Banī Ḥushaysh, heading for the rugged mountains and open areas of al-Jawf.[259] The streets of al-Jawf were of strategic importance for the Houthis, because it was possible to circumvent ʿAmrān governorate via al-Jawf when ʿAmrān's streets were embattled, blocked or controlled by ʿAlī Muḥsin or the al-Aḥmar clan. Thus the Houthis pushed into al-Jawf, where they encountered both support and opposition from the local tribes. Baraṭ and al-Zāhir were particularly Houthi-friendly, but there were also hostile tribes and shaykhs, such as the Shawlān in al-Matūn and their shaykh Amīn al-ʿUkaymī, and the Hamdān al-Jawf in al-Ḥazm and al-Khaliq, whose shaykhs were mostly loyal to President Salih and/or Saudi Arabia.

Looking at the Houthi strategy in al-Jawf during the fifth war, it becomes obvious that it served to implement ʿAbdulmalik's directive to extend the war:

> In the fifth war, the aim of the Houthi operations in al-Jawf was to ease the pressure on Saʿdah and to confuse the government (*irbāk al-ḥukūmah*). The warriors moved to al-Jawf in order to attack the military bases [of the government] and then returned to Sufyān in ʿAmrān and Āl ʿAmmār in Saʿdah.[260]

Initially, the Houthis' tactical approach in al-Jawf aimed at provoking the government's armed forces and to distract them from the front in Saʿdah. The most appropriate means to achieve this goal was to attack government military bases and to target senior military and government personnel (the Houthis used the same approach in Banī Ḥushaysh).

On 17 May, Houthi forces attacked a military camp in al-Maṣlūb, a district of al-Jawf predominantly inhabited by the Banī Nawf. On 2 June, it came to clashes between Houthis and the district director of al-Ghayl, Shāyif Dirham, after which the Houthis established control over the al-Sāqiyah area between al-Maṣlūb and al-Ghayl. In the early hours of 6 June, a platoon-sized group of Houthis attacked the government compound in al-Maṭammah district and engaged security forces and a number of the Dhū Ḥusayn in battles. On 26 June, clashes erupted between Houthis and members of the Āl Kathīr, a section of the Hamdān al-Jawf, when the Houthis attacked a military base near al-Ḥazm.[261]

In the middle of July, however, a terrible turn of events began to unfold and led to the eruption of armed clashes between the tribes of al-Jawf: the fratricidal war of which the shaykhs had been warning. A few days before the government's proclamation of a unilateral ceasefire, the armed forces in al-Zāhir targeted the car of Houthi field commander ʿAbdulwāḥid Abū Rās on its way from Baraṭ at night. One of his companions was killed, another wounded.

Abū Rās himself was declared dead (it later turned out that he was unharmed). A Houthi field commander recalled the events that followed:

> The next morning, tribal allies of the government drove to al-Ḥazm to ask the governor for help. When they returned, they got into a Houthi ambush, in which five people were killed: the secretary-general of the Local Council of al-Jawf, ʿAbdulwahhāb al-Ḍumayn, ʿAbdullah Ḥasan al-Ḍumayn, Shaykh ʿAbdullah al-Jayshī [of Shawlān] and his brother ʿAlī, and Shaykh Ṣāliḥ al-Qannāṣ. This was the first Houthi operation in al-Jawf that targeted the government's tribal allies, and then things moved on between the sons of the province and the Houthis, who were themselves sons of the province. In this way, through the expansion of the revenge circle (*tawsīʿ dāʾirat al-intiqām*), al-Jawf descended into war.[262]

With this incident, confrontations had begun between the Houthis and tribal allies of the government—tribes whose warlike traditions and stamina in pursuing revenge issues were the stuff of proverbs. The assassination attempt on ʿAbdulwāḥid Abū Rās and the ensuing Houthi ambush of prominent tribal supporters of the regime pushed the tribes of the targeted shaykhs and officers to violence, marking the beginning of a fatal downward spiral, as the ensuing battles generated ever more revenge issues.

The conflict in al-Jawf, therefore, had only just gathered momentum immediately before the declaration of the unilateral ceasefire on 17 July. It should, then, come as no surprise that the ceasefire did not have much impact in the region. In the months to come, the Houthis managed to press deep into al-Jawf and east into the Banī Nawf's vast territory in southern Khabb wa l-Shaʿf. This area marked the eastern limit of the Houthis' sphere of influence. Beyond this point, from 2009/10 onwards the Houthis were increasingly confronted by tribes allied with al-Qaeda in the Arabian Peninsula (AQAP), who countered with considerable resistance as Houthi expansion southeast appeared to hurt AQAP's operations.

Sufyān[263]

After ʿAbdulmalik al-Ḥūthī issued the directive for extension of the conflict's scope, Sufyān became the third area deliberately pushed into war. As we have seen in earlier chapters, Sufyān is an area of supreme strategic importance, since it straddles the Sanaʿa-Saʿdah highway. Blockades of this strategic artery and main transport route leading to the fronts in Saʿdah have always had a direct impact on the course of the Saʿdah wars. Sufyān had already been affected by unrest and skirmishes in previous rounds. Since the eruption of the fifth war, however, the unstable situation in Sufyān has been further inflamed and exacerbated by deliberate fuelling of Sufyān's latent conflicts: the historic feud between the Ṣubārah of Sufyān and the al-ʿUṣaymāt of Ḥāshid, and the feud between the al-Ṣumaym and Āl al-Qaʿūd in al-ʿAmashiyyah.

Ḥarf Sufyān, commonly known as Sufyān, is the largest and northernmost district of ʿAmrān governorate. The territory of the district and its homonymous tribe are essentially identical. Sufyān's crescent-shaped territory stretches from the border of Ḥajjah governorate in the west to Sanaʿa governorate in the southeast. In the north, Sufyān's territory runs along to the border of Saʿdah governorate, this area being called al-ʿAmashiyyah. To the east, across a mountain ridge, it is bordered by Wādī Madhāb, which drains further to the east into the Wādī Jawf. The administrative centre of Sufyān district is al-Ḥarf. Sufyān's terrain is sparsely populated and largely flat and sandy. For much of its length, the mountain ridge of Jabal Aswad and Jabal Aḥmar near al-Ḥarf marks the border between the tribal territories of the al-ʿUṣaymāt and the Sufyān, and therefore between the Ḥāshid and the Bakīl.

The strategic importance of Sufyān became particularly evident during the 1962 revolution and the resulting civil war, with both royalist and republican forces focusing all their offensives on this area. At the end of the civil war, Prince ʿAbdullah b. al-Ḥasan Ḥamīd al-Dīn advanced from Saʿdah towards Sanaʿa—at that time besieged by his cousin Muḥammad b. al-Ḥusayn—through al-Ḥarf, which was held by Brigadier Aḥmad ʿAlī Fāḍl of the Dhū Muḥammad, along with other pro-republican shaykhs and their followers from within and beyond the region.[264] Prince ʿAbdullah b. al-Ḥasan is reported to have said: 'To be sure, if we can pass al-Ḥarf city and Jabal al-Aswad, then victory is ours'. After the end of the 1960s civil war, however, Sufyān lost its formerly immense strategic importance and became—from the capital's perspective—the unsettled backyard of ʿAmrān governorate, bordering on a region that was even more neglected: Saʿdah.

The Sufyān are a member tribe of the Bakīl confederation, divided into the moieties of Ṣubārah and Ruhm; these are further sub-divided into a number of sections and clans.[265] The senior shaykh of Sufyān always comes from the Ṣubārah moiety and its senior shaykhly lineage, the ancient and famous Ḥubaysh clan.[266] The senior shaykh of the Ruhm moiety comes from the Ḥaydar shaykhly lineage, which originates in the Ruhm's Dhū Aḥmad section; during the Saʿdah wars the incumbent shaykh was Mujāhid Ḥaydar, who, we recall, gained notoriety for his well-proven ability to block the vital Sanaʿa-Saʿdah highway.

With a majority of Sufyān's tribal groups remaining loyal to their deep-rooted Zaydi faith and traditions, the Zaydi revival movement had managed to establish a solid presence in Sufyān long before the eruption of the first Saʿdah war. In reaction to Iṣlāḥ activities, the Believing Youth began their activities in Sufyān in the mid-1990s by establishing the Imam Zayn al-ʿĀbidīn school in al-Ḥarf city. In 1997, *ʿīd al-ghadīr* was publicly celebrated in Sufyān's al-Mazḥāṭ area. In this district the Believing Youth managed to achieve what the governing and opposition parties—notably the GPC and Iṣlāḥ—had not, namely to build a solid support base. However, when the Saʿdah wars erupted in 2004 and began to spread from Marrān throughout the governorate of Saʿdah, Sufyān was removed from the conflict, although clearly one of the places where the Houthi movement enjoyed greatest support in material, strategic, and ideological terms. However, despite the success of the Zaydi revival movement in addressing much local discontent and dissatisfaction, initially many shaykhs of Sufyān did not support the Houthis, but were co-opted by the Salih regime. ʿAbduh Ḥubaysh, the senior shaykh, and his sons were initially enemies to the Houthis. His oldest son, Bakīl Ḥubaysh, was the leader of the Popular Army in Sufyān.

When military confrontations started in al-Ḥarf city in the fifth war, the Houthi followers did not consist of certain tribal sections led by a specific shaykh. Although there was considerable support from the Āl al-Qaʿūd during the fifth war (see below), at first the rest of the Houthi supporters in Sufyān were a motley crew of diverse Houthi sympathizers, in addition to a number of Houthi warriors who had come from the Saʿdah region to assist them.

With many influential shaykhs of Sufyān ostensibly co-opted by the regime, the government initially seemed to be in an advantageous position in the district, which perhaps gave it a false sense of security. It is a mark of the Houthis' astute strategy, based on detailed knowledge of the territory and its tribes, that they could gain control over and among both of the Sufyān's moieties during the fifth and sixth wars. Their stratagem to gain control over the Ṣubārah moiety was through interference in the ancient feud between the Ṣubārah and the neighbouring Ḥāshid section, al-ʿUṣaymāt. Meanwhile, within the Ruhm moiety, the Houthis successfully profited from the prevalent blood feud between two rival shaykhs and their supporters. Moreover, in each of these sub-conflicts, the maladroit policies of the al-Aḥmar sons—notably Ḥusayn and Ḥamīd—played a particularly reprehensible role.

For the army and its large troop movements—entire brigades with their heavy gear were dispatched from other parts of the country to the Saʿdah region—the highway between Sanaʿa and Saʿdah city was in fact irreplaceable. The transport of arms and troops to the conflict areas in Saʿdah was carried out through the Sufyān's territory, and any blocking of the supply lines would have dire consequences for the course and outcome of the war. There was no alternative to this route: beyond Ḥaraḍ, the Tihāmah route was poorly constructed, and some sections were extremely steep and winding, passing through mountainous regions, which made it susceptible to ambush. For the same reason, the tracks through the Baraṭ region in al-Jawf were not a viable alternative to the Sanaʿa-Saʿdah highway.

The Sanaʿa-Saʿdah highway had already been a weak point of the armed forces' logistics in previous rounds of war. In the fifth, with the rapid expansion of combat into Sufyān, the problem increased. Throughout this bout, Houthis attacked the armed forces in the Sufyān section of the highway and interrupted or blocked its convoys with ambushes, roadblocks and sabotage. A few days after the outbreak of war in May 2008, the Houthis blocked a bridge north of al-Ḥarf. Since that time, the Houthis have controlled, with some interruptions, this portion of the highway to Saʿdah. They also managed during the fifth war to besiege the 119th Brigade commanded by Fayṣal Rajab, which was stationed in Jabal Aswad camp near al-Ḥarf. At the end of June, the newly elected governor of ʿAmrān, Kahlān Abū Shawārib,[267] travelled to al-Ḥarf to gain a clearer picture, but found himself trapped in the camp. Tribal mediation endeavours by local shaykhs—including ʿAbduh Ḥubaysh and Muḥsin Maʿqil (a locally important shaykh from the Ṣubārah's al-Shumaylāt section)—failed.[268]

The battles and air attacks seen by areas along the highway inflicted heavy loss of life. The result was an extremely costly war that ruined much of Sufyān's infrastructure and human settlements. Army carpet bombing destroyed villages. Bulldozers and tanks razed houses to the ground. Sufyān's district capital al-Ḥarf, home to 20,000 before the war, was virtually razed to the ground. Its inhabitants fled the city.[269] Families were torn apart on the run. Refugees from Sufyān fled all the way to al-Jawf, where they lived under dire conditions. The army constantly lost troops to friendly fire. The Popular Army, in particular, was perpetually countering friendly fire, which had a very negative effect on morale.

The Houthis were hardly squeamish. They focused on blocking the highway and destroying bridges in order to cut off reinforcements and supplies for the troops stationed in Saʿdah, some of which (in Marrān, notably) were caught in extreme distress. An observer recalled:

> In Sufyān the Houthis waged a gang and street war (*ḥarb ʿiṣābāt wa shawāriʿ*) based on sniping (*qanṣ*), attacks (*mubāghatāt*), ambushes (*kamāʾin*), and feints (*khudaʿ ḥarbiyyah*). They used methods of attrition (*istinsāf*) by installing phantom goals (*ahdāf wahmiyyah*) for the army, mines, and digging trenches (*khanādiq qitāliyyah*) in streets and neighbourhoods.[270]

In Sufyān, the brutality and indiscriminate violence of the armed forces had the same effect as in Saʿdah: it angered the people and turned them against the government. In the fifth war, growing popular dissatisfaction with the army's approach became obvious and alienated many of the government's local allies. For instance, Shaykh Muḥsin Maʿqil of the Ṣubārah was a firm ally of the regime, for which his tribe, the Dhū Maʿqil, made many sacrifices in the fifth war. However, they became increasingly discontented with the government, which paid neither salaries to the tribal volunteer fighters nor compensation to the families of victims killed in the war, and did not look after the wounded: this would push the Dhū Maʿqil to switch allegiances and stand with the Houthis in the sixth war.[271]

An additional factor was the old Bakīl resentment towards the Ḥāshid confederation. As tribal levies of the armed forces in ʿAmrān, the many influential shaykhs of Sufyān siding with the regime were automatically subject to the command of Ḥusayn al-Aḥmar, the nominal leader of the Popular Army. Yet Bakīl tribes of Sufyān being placed under the supreme command of a Ḥāshid shaykh was a basically untenable, if not absurd, situation—the resentment of the Sufyān towards the al-ʿUṣaymāt, the home section of the al-Aḥmar clan, was simply too great. In Sufyān, therefore, the Popular Army had no sound basis and would eventually collapse after the fifth war. As a Ṣubārah shaykh commented, 'Bakīl is always aware what Ḥāshid is doing, and conflict intervention by Ḥāshid makes Sufyān side with the other side.'[272]

In the fifth war, the irreconcilable differences between the Ḥāshid and Bakīl materialized in the resurgence of the long-standing territorial conflict between the al-ʿUṣaymāt and the Ṣubārah, which had begun more than a hundred years earlier. When, a few months later, this territorial conflict escalated out of control, the Houthis were able to expand their hegemony over the whole Ṣubārah moiety (see below). The other moiety, Ruhm, ultimately fell under Houthi control due to the erratic policies of the al-Aḥmar sons, notably Ḥamīd and Ḥusayn. After their father's death in December 2007, his sons—who had already achieved considerable economic and political success—also tried to gain visibility in Yemen's tribal environment. Yet none was able to assume the same level of importance as had been attributed to their father: *'Iyāl al-Aḥmar mesh ziyy abāhim*, 'the sons of 'Abdullah al-Aḥmar don't match their father', as one local source put it.[273] Ḥusayn al-Aḥmar, in particular, claimed parts of his father's tribal legacy, hereby competing with his brother Ṣādiq, who had nominally inherited the office of the shaykh—but, in his endeavours to distinguish himself, Ḥusayn's inconsistent and contradictory policies and machinations mostly backfired on himself. This was the case in Ruhm.

Ruhm is located in northern Sufyān, close to the border of Sa'dah governorate. During the 1960s civil war, Ruhm was almost entirely royalist, with few—albeit famous—exceptions, such as the shaykhs Aḥmad Dhaybān and Ḥamūd b. 'Azīz who, at the end of the civil war, took part in the military campaign led by Amīn Abū Rās, 'Abdullah al-Aḥmar, Mujāhid Abū Shawārib, and other pro-republican shaykhs to free Sa'dah from the royalists. In contrast, Aḥmad Ḥaydar, the then senior shaykh of Ruhm, was opposed to both the Republic and President Salih's rule after he seized power in 1978, and resisted all Salih's attempts to co-opt him. In 1987, he was assassinated with three of his sons; his son and successor Mujāhid has accused 'Abdullah al-Aḥmar and the Salih government of involvement.[274]

The Ḥaydar and al-Aḥmar clans remained obdurately at odds. 'Abdullah al-Aḥmar, however, also had an ally in Ruhm, as he cultivated a close relationship with his former comrade-in-arms Ḥamūd b. 'Azīz of the al-Ṣumaym. The al-Ṣumaym tribe controls a territory in al-'Amashiyyah, the large but sparsely populated barren, rocky landscape close to the border of Sa'dah governorate. Ḥamūd's son and successor Ṣaghīr is said to have been the 'spiritual son' of 'Abdullah al-Aḥmar, whose influence and patronage allowed Ṣaghīr b. 'Azīz to rise to a leading position within the Republican Guard in Sana'a, where he was given the rank of brigadier general in 2007. Nicknamed *ḥaras jumhūrī bi-libās shaykh* ('a Republican Guard in the guise of a shaykh'), Ṣaghīr also gained political power in 1997, when he became the GPC MP for Ḥarf Sufyān/Dhī Bīn/Arḥab; he was re-elected in 2003. After his election, his father, Ḥamūd, also presented him prematurely with the office of shaykh, apparently to concentrate and maximize tribal, military and political power in Ṣaghīr's hands.

The close relationship between Ṣaghīr b. 'Azīz and 'Abdullah al-Aḥmar was of mutual benefit. It provided al-Aḥmar with an ally in Sufyān, since Ṣaghīr helped him to counteract the roadblocks and other harassments thrown at his clan by Mujāhid Ḥaydar. Al-Aḥmar's patronage efforts in turn strengthened Ṣaghīr's position in Sufyān and beyond, to the extent that he started referring to himself publicly as senior shaykh (*shaykh mashāyikh*) of Sufyān—a brazen affront against both Mujāhid Ḥaydar, who was senior shaykh of Sufyān's Ruhm moiety, and ʿAbduh Ḥubaysh, who was senior shaykh of the whole Sufyān tribe as well as its *naqīb* and *marāghah* of the Ḥāshid and Bakīl confederations.[275] During his remarkable career within the Republican Guard, Ṣaghīr also became a close friend of President Salih and his son Ahmad. Salih also worked to strengthen and co-opt Ṣaghīr for his own purposes, as a card he could hold against the powerful al-Aḥmar clan in ʿAmrān.

However, since 2006, Ṣaghīr b. ʿAzīz and ʿAbdullah al-Aḥmar's sons, especially Ḥusayn, have become estranged from one another. We recall that Ḥusayn al-Aḥmar was both trying to distinguish himself as leader of the Popular Army, and taking a great deal of money from Gaddafi in order to 'create problems' for the Yemeni and Saudi governments.[276] This had repercussions for the relationship between Ḥusayn al-Aḥmar and Ṣaghīr: whereas Ḥusayn al-Aḥmar had fallen into disfavour, Ṣaghīr remained Salih's staunch ally. Locals agree that for this reason—to weaken Ṣaghīr—Ḥusayn al-Aḥmar covertly supported his enemy, Shaykh ʿAbduh Yaḥyā al-Qaʿūd (also from Ruhm). When ʿAbduh al-Qaʿūd ran as an independent in the 2006 municipal elections in ʿAmrān, Ḥusayn al-Aḥmar supported him as a provocation aimed at Ṣaghīr, who was himself a GPC MP in the governorate.[277]

It is important to note that ʿAbduh al-Qaʿūd, parts of his family and many members of his tribe, the Āl al-Qaʿūd, were Houthi veterans. Two of his brothers were involved with the Believing Youth and the Houthis from their first days of operation and had participated in the Saʿdah wars since the first bout of conflict in Marrān in 2004. When ʿAbdulmalik al-Ḥūthī left Marrān after the first war, according to hearsay he spent several months incognito in Ruhm with the Āl al-Qaʿūd.[278]

We do not know exactly what happened at the polling station in al-Ḥarf in September 2006. Eyewitnesses recall that ʿAbduh al-Qaʿūd appeared, questioned the good conduct of the ballot and called for a halt to vote counting.[279] After this was refused, he stormed the polling station with a canister of gasoline and threatened to burn the ballots because of suspected electoral fraud. The result was a clash between his escorts and security forces at the polling station, which ended in the killing of ʿAbduh al-Qaʿūd on polling day—he burned to death when security forces shot the petrol canister. Because the security forces had belonged to Ṣaghīr b. ʿAzīz's escort, this death marked the beginning of a blood feud between the al-Qaʿūd and ʿAzīz clans. Needless to say, the relationship between Ṣaghīr and Ḥusayn al-Aḥmar is beyond repair.

The ensuing feud between the Āl al-Qaʿūd and Ṣaghīr b. ʿAzīz provided the Houthis with a fresh opportunity to bring Ruhm under their control. They organized support and assistance for the Āl al-Qaʿūd in enforcing the blood feud. Ṣaghīr (himself of Zaydi denomination) said in an interview in 2010 that when he became involved in the war there was actually no dispute or conflict between him and the Houthis: he simply fought for the regime in order to ensure security and stability in Sufyān and to quell the 'insurgency'.[280] Yet, as I understand it, the reality was somewhat different. In spring 2007, followers of Ṣaghīr abducted the thirteen-year-old Amīn ʿAbdulqādir Badr al-Dīn al-Ḥūthī in Sanaʿa in order to force the freeing of one of Ṣaghīr's brothers, whom the Houthis had arrested in al-Mahādhir.[281] After two months in custody, both were exchanged in a hostage swap. This is just one example of the frequent tit-for-tat retaliations that continued throughout Ṣaghīr's life.

The killing of ʿAbduh al-Qaʿūd greatly reinforced the existing alliance between the Houthis and the Āl al-Qaʿūd, who sought revenge on Ṣaghīr, and furthermore roused those of Sufyān's tribesmen who sympathized with the Āl al-Qaʿūd. During the fifth war, there were numerous clashes between the two side's respective followers. Since Ṣaghīr claimed to be fighting a war with the Houthis, rather than a tribal feud, he could call in the army—units of the First Armoured Division stationed at Jabal al-Aswad—to assist him. ʿAbduh al-Qaʿūd's brother, ʿAbdullah Yaḥyā al-Qaʿūd, became a field commander during the fifth war and fell in battle; regime tanks and bulldozers razed his house to the ground.[282] Following ʿAbdullah Yaḥyā's death—and a brief interlude under ʿAzīz Ṭālib (called al-Saḥārī, as he was of Saʿdah governorate's Saḥār tribe)—the Houthis astutely installed exclusively *sayyid* field commanders in Sufyān (namely Yūsif al-Madānī, then a member of the Abū Ṭālib family), to prevent a recurrence of the internal squabbles that had arisen during the 1960s civil war over 'external interference' and 'balance of power'.[283] The feud between the Āl al-Qaʿūd and the ʿAzīz clan, each supported by their respective allies, continued after the end of the sixth war. When Ṣaghīr b. ʿAzīz was wounded in battle and evacuated from Ruhm in summer 2010, the Houthis were finally able to bring the whole of Sufyān under their control.[284]

Gubernatorial Elections

On 17 May 2008, for the first time in the history of Yemen, nationwide gubernatorial elections were held. As early as February 2000, the parliament had passed Law 4/2000, the so-called Local Authority Law, after protracted parliamentary debates and under the pressure of foreign donor organizations and domestic opposition (especially in Yemen's south). The Local Authority Law decentralized the state's authority by establishing locally elected district and governorate councils. However, after its enactment, the government continued to appoint the governors, as the state's highest political authorities at provincial level.

In a sudden paradigm shift that came as a surprise to the administration (but which was not untypical of President Salih's style of governance), in 2008 the legal framework of the Local Authority Law was amended by Law No. 18/2008, which introduced the indirect election of governors by the members of the Local Councils.[285] As Day observes, the gubernatorial elections had been a persistent demand of political opponents in southern provinces, in order to attenuate northern dominance; the decision to allow indirectly elected governors of the twenty-one provinces was above all a 'carrot' dangled in front of the southern opposition (indeed, the fixing of the polling date, 17 May, came after intense fighting in Laḥj and al-Ḍāliʿ provinces).[286] During the gubernatorial elections, the GPC was able to consolidate its dominance, mostly because the opposition coalition of the Joint Meeting Parties (JMP) lacked control of the councils in many provinces.[287] Only three governorates (al-Jawf, al-Bayḍāʾ, Maʾrib) were won by independent nominees.

In Saʿdah, two prominent candidates ran against each other: Ḥasan Manāʿ and ʿUmar Mujallī. Ḥasan Manāʿ belonged to the extended family of the senior shaykh of al-Ṭalḥ, Fayṣal Manāʿ. At that time, Ḥasan Manāʿ was deputy governor and secretary-general of Saʿdah's Local Council; he had excellent relations and a solid support base among the members of the Local Councils who were to elect the governor. Moreover, he benefited from his clan's prominence in Yemen: Shaykh Fayṣal Manāʿ was a hero of the 1962 revolution and one of the founders of the GPC, in which he held various political offices. Ḥasan's brother Fāris was, as we have seen, one of the biggest arms traders of the wider region and one of the wealthiest men in the governorate. At the time of the elections, Fāris' fame as a mediator between the Houthis and the government had reached its zenith in June 2008, when he successfully negotiated the safe passage of the besieged 17th Infantry Brigade during its withdrawal from Marrān.[288] Even though Fāris' once strong relationship with Salih had already suffered from his alleged involvement in the Gaddafi issue, Ḥasan was still in line with government policy and took every opportunity to verbally attack the Houthis. He had already been the target of several assassinations attempts.

His rival, ʿUmar Mujallī, was the eldest brother of Shaykh ʿUthmān Mujallī of al-ʿAbdīn. ʿUmar had studied abroad and was an expert on public health. The Mujallī family, too, had solid republican credentials from the 1960s. However, a few months before the elections, the Mujallī family had a serious run-in with the government when Shaykh ʿUthmān criticized its management of the Saʿdah wars; soon after, gunmen from both the governor's bodyguard and the bodyguard of the director of Public Works tried to assassinate his brother Yāsir.[289] Probably for this reason, ʿUmar ran as an independent, even though ʿUthmān was the GPC MP for Saʿdah city.

Ḥasan Manāʿ won the elections with 171 of the 285 votes cast.[290] In Saʿdah, the elections were celebrated as the dawn of a new age, because the most important political and administrative post in the governorate had been filled by a 'son of Saʿdah'. People hoped that the new governor, by virtue of his local origin and knowledge, would be able to direct the governorate more competently than his predecessors, who always had been outsiders.

Yet the election of a governor from among the locals had its drawbacks, as the elections further aggravated the already intense competition among the shaykhs of Saʿdah. One shaykh from the region recalled:

> At that time Saʿdah went through an unprecedented situation. As I have said, there were many disagreements and conflicts between the constituencies and even between the tribes of the same district. They competed with each other, and every tribe wanted the governor to come from its ranks. But this was not a matter of personal desires and tribal preferences. The governor was elected by members of the Local Authority, which is the electoral body (*al-hayʾah al-nākibah*), and both the Local Council and the governor should stand beyond regionalism and tribal particularism. The appointment of a governor from the outside, therefore, had been better for Saʿdah governorate.[291]

In fact, the gubernatorial elections added new fault lines to already existing ones: a new rift opened within the neither uniform nor harmonious bloc of Saʿdah's shaykhly MPs, who increasingly became polarized between the Manāʿ clan and its allies (Shuwayṭ, Dughsān) and the Mujallī clan and its allies (al-ʿAwjarī, Rawkān, Miṭrī, al-Munabbihī). In particular, the influential Fāyiz al-ʿAwjarī of Wāʾilah, MP and brother-in-law of ʿUthmān Mujallī, ruthlessly gave vent to his dissatisfaction with Governor Ḥasan's administration. His public criticism was vitriolic and weighed heavily, especially when a few months later Ḥasan's brother Fāris got into trouble—Ḥasan was sacked.[292]

After the election, former governor Muṭahhar al-Miṣrī returned to Sanaʿa, where he was appointed minister of the interior by republican decree. As one source put it, *Ghādara al-wizārah nā'iban wa ʿāda ilayhā wazīran*: he had left the Ministry of the Interior as vice minister and returned as minister.

Mediation and Unilateral Ceasefire

The fifth war saw several mediation initiatives. Shortly after the attack on Bin Salmān Mosque and the subsequent battles, the Qatari mediation team returned to Saʿdah and engendered a sense of urgency to prevent the fragile truce from breaking down completely. The Qatari mediators met with Houthi representative Ṣāliḥ Habrah but failed to reach a satisfactory solution. As a result, the Qatari mediation collapsed once again, although frantic negotiations were said to be going on in the Presidential Palace in Sanaʿa.[293]

In mid-June, a few days after the Qataris' departure, the government charged the National Solidarity Council (*majlis al-taḍāmun al-waṭanī*) with mediation in Saʿdah.[294] The Council had been created and chaired by Ḥusayn al-Aḥmar in 2007 as a tribal association dominated by shaykhs from all over the country, which aimed to act as a conservative forum and pressure group representing tribal interests. The appointment of al-Aḥmar to lead the domestic mediation team might seem surprising, because the Gaddafi issue had poisoned his relations with Salih. Yet after this estrangement, the president watched with horror as Ḥusayn gravitated towards the ʿAlī Muḥsin/Iṣlāḥ axis. Salih tried to change course again, giving al-Aḥmar this prestigious role. The mission, however, was doomed to failure from the outset: he was expected to go to Saʿdah and persuade ʿAbdulmalik al-Ḥūthī to evacuate Jabal ʿIzzān, Maṭrah, al-Naqʿah and Ḍaḥyān within a period of thirty to sixty days—an impossibility. In addition, al-Aḥmar and his National Solidarity Council lacked credibility among both government and Houthis.[295] His mediation failed to yield any results.

The war continued to heat up. A particularly worrisome development was the continued siege of large military units in the Saʿdah area. The Houthis were besieging a battalion in al-Ghubayr, Saḥār, while in Marrān, the Houthi epicentre and home region, disaster continued to unfold. Since the winter of 2007 the Houthis had been besieging hundreds of soldiers and officers of the 17th Infantry Brigade under the command of ʿAbd al-ʿAzīz al-Shahārī in Marrān; from early June 2008, the Brigade was totally sealed off from the outside world. Since the outbreak of the first war in 2004, the Brigade had been spearheading the fight against the Houthis in Marrān, where the Brigade had erected a number of military sites.[296] In the fifth war, the battles there became so ferocious that the Houthis managed to cut off all roads to the region, hermetically sealing off the Brigade. They prevented the arrival of supplies and military reinforcements and even brought down combat helicopters with large-calibre fire. By early July, the 17th Brigade had run out of food and drinking water. The soldiers began to drink rainwater from Marrān's desolate cisterns, which—as alleged Houthi arms caches—had been the targets of repeated air strikes in the earlier wars. Government media conveyed an image of heroic resistance: despite the Brigade's predicament, its commander al-Shahārī reportedly threatened to 'teach the remnants of the rebels a lesson they will never forget'.[297] But at the same time dramatic reports of the Brigade's situation leaked to the press. Rumours stubbornly persisted that al-Shahārī had in fact threatened to surrender if no one took action to lift the siege.

The situation in Marrān contradicted all news of 'military progress' and 'imminent victory' with which government media daily inundated its citizens. Shaykhs from Shihārah, al-Ahnūm, Ḥajjah and ʿAmrān—linked by kinship ties to soldiers and officers of the 17th Brigade—arrived in the region to put pressure on the authorities and to accelerate the rescue of hundreds of trapped soldiers. The situation took such a dramatic turn that Salih finally agreed to a group of Saʿdah shaykhs' offer to mediate. The team, chaired by Fāris Manāʿ, included Shaykhs Ḍayfallah Rusām, ʿAlī Nāṣir Qirshah, Dughsān Aḥmad Dughsān, ʿĀrif Shuwayṭ and ʿAbdulsalām Hishūl Zābiyah. In an attempt to save his own mediation efforts, Ḥusayn al-Aḥmar also offered to collaborate, but the team turned him down.[298]

The special feature of this particular tribal mediation team was that one could no longer ascertain what its members really stood for. Fāris Manāʿ's once close relationship with President Salih was already troubled. ʿĀrif Shuwayṭ's recently deceased father Qāʾid had been an Iṣlāḥ loyalist, but ʿĀrif was not his father and had his own agenda. ʿAlī Nāṣir Qirshah was an open Houthi supporter. The other members had previously been GPC MPs or government supporters. But this was the fifth war, not the first, and the regime's botched crisis management had already broken a fair quantity of china. The team's Houthi counterpart in Marrān was Muḥammad ʿAbdullah Muṣliḥ, field commander in the region.[299] The mediation was successful and the Houthis lifted the siege. In return, the 17th Infantry Brigade withdrew from Marrān, where it had been stationed since 2004.

Despite its success—or because of it—this mediation team faced a great deal of criticism. The government reproached the mediators for obliging the armed forces to withdraw without requiring the Houthis to do the same, ultimately enabling the Houthis to seize areas in the region to which they previously had not had access. A government official commented: 'One can say that the mediators have worked more than anyone else for the escalation of the conflict'.[300]

On 17 July 2008, the thirtieth anniversary of his rule, President Salih abruptly ended the war by declaring a unilateral ceasefire. The announcement came in a brief speech during his inauguration of summer camps for GPC-affiliated youths. Apparently, he had coordinated the ceasefire by telephone with ʿAbdulmalik al-Ḥūthī, but he had consulted neither government officials nor the military leadership. The ceasefire came as a shock to the army, as the war was still raging in Saʿdah, Sufyān, al-Jawf and Banī Ḥushaysh.[301]

We can only try to fathom the reasons for this sudden development. Observers from various political and tribal camps identified six possible causes. First, US and EU criticism of the humanitarian situation in Saʿdah had increased, and the indictment of Sudan's president ʿUmar al-Bashīr at the International Criminal Court shortly before the ceasefire announcement may have contributed to Salih's decision.[302] Second, the ceasefire may have been due to Salih's fear that the situation in Saʿdah could spin further out of control. After debilitating blows, not only the 17th Infantry Brigade but also other military units (notably in Rughāfah and Ḍaḥyān) had been removed from the region altogether. The abrupt cessation of hostilities may have served to secure the safe withdrawal of these units.

Third, after the events in Banī Ḥushaysh, the president may have feared an imminent opening of new fronts in areas close to the capital, especially in Sanḥān, Khawlān al-Ṭiyāl, Dhamār, and the capital itself. At this time, numerous Houthi loyalists were arrested on suspicion of forming armed cells in Sanaʿa.[303] Fourth, some observers suggest that Salih was forced to slam on the brakes after Saudi Arabia had begun—seven days earlier—to distribute funds to Ḥusayn al-Aḥmar and Iṣlāḥ representatives such as ʿAbdulmajīd al-Zindānī, in order to support the recruitment (*tajnīd*) of tribes and radical Sunnis to the battle against the Houthis. For this purpose, Ṣādiq and Ḥusayn al-Aḥmar and ʿAbdulmajīd al-Zindānī had recently joined forces.[304] As we have seen, Salih himself had cooperated with the al-Aḥmar clan and Iṣlāḥ on recruitment of these groups, but he wanted to prevent the Saudis from channeling funds to anyone but himself.

Fifth, important elections were again on the horizon: the country's fourth parliamentary elections were scheduled for April 2009 (but would end up being postposed in February 2009 due to ongoing nationwide instability).

Sixth, many suspected that Salih wanted to give the parties to the conflict time to recuperate. It was not in his interest to fight the war to a decisive end. On the contrary, he needed the war to keep General ʿAlī Muḥsin away from Sanaʿa, to maintain international military and financial support from Saudi Arabia and the US, and to bring his son into position to inherit the presidency. Thus, some see the unilateral ceasefire as his attempt to direct and prolong the war, rather than resolve it, to ensure that the war was managed to his liking and to keep credit for any victory out of both the Houthis' and Muḥsin's hands.

There were many reasons to interrupt the war. Certainly no one can know what was really in Salih's mind when he announced the unilateral ceasefire, but in his endeavour to secure his grip on power he continued with his proven practice of playing one side off against the other—as Clarke has put it, 'dancing on the head of snakes rather than setting out to destroy the reptiles has always been more his style'.[305] The fact is that the ceasefire had hardly any impact on the ground, and the ensuing interim period escalated almost effortlessly into the sixth war. To quote Macbeth: 'We have scorch'd the snake, not kill'd it: She'll be close, and be herself; whilst our poor malice remains in danger of her former tooth'.[306]

Fifth Interim

The thirteen months of the fifth interim period resembled a state of undeclared war more than a period of ceasefire. Indeed, it would have been highly unlikely for the president's sudden unilateral ceasefire declaration to produce a significant pacification of the situation. Observers describe the immediate aftermath of the ceasefire as a time of 'calm' (*hudūʾ*) rather than of 'peace' (*salām*).

Exhausted by the brief but intense fifth bout of war, both sides welcomed the truce but remained on full alert. The government tried to show that it was serious and carried out a series of measures to stabilize the ceasefire. Meanwhile, it also began to prepare for the parliamentary elections scheduled for April 2009. Its goodwill efforts included the establishment of the Presidential Committee for Reconstruction and Mediation, whose work, however, soon became undermined by personnel changes and political manoeuvring in Sanaʿa. Moreover, the regime seemed to be pursuing a dual strategy, as its peace initiatives were out of sync with military kinetic operations.

At the beginning of 2009, after the parliamentary elections had been postponed and the Committee for Reconstruction and Mediation had ceased its activities, tensions intensified and armed battles developed into conflagration. Vast and continuous conflict zones emerged in central Saʿdah, the western mountains along the Ṭāʾif Line, Sufyān and al-Jawf. Clashes in these areas further exacerbated existing tensions and catalyzed both rhetorical and kinetic conflict escalation. The kidnapping and murder of a group of foreigners in Saʿdah in June 2009 ultimately paved the way for the sixth and last 'official' round of war.

Peace and Reconstruction Efforts

In the first weeks after the fifth war ended in July 2008, both sides initially made efforts to show their commitment and maintain the ceasefire. On several occasions, prisoners were released or exchanged—yet a considerable number remained in detention.[307] As a further gesture of goodwill, the government established two new committees: the Presidential Reconstruction Committee (*lajnat al-iʿmār al-riʾāsiyyah*) and the Presidential Mediation Committee (*lajnat al-wiṣāṭah al-riʾāsiyyah*).

The Presidential Reconstruction Committee, chaired by Minister of Local Administration ʿAbdulqādir Hilāl, was tasked with the survey and compensation of the damages caused by four years of excessive fighting, which had already wrought havoc in the war zone. The Reconstruction Committee was given access to a $55 million special fund under the prime minister's authority—a sum far less than anticipated or needed, but a start nonetheless.[308] In September, the government appealed for another $190 million from international donors to rehabilitate infrastructure and to support the internally displaced (IDPs).[309] Donors, however, were cautious, as there was a consensus in the international community that they should wait for guarantees of a lasting peace before launching reconstruction or development projects in Saʿdah. Western donors were reluctant to back a government-controlled fund intended to repair what government forces themselves had destroyed and were likely to destroy again if another war erupted—which was itself likely, unless conditions on the ground stabilized.[310] Local and international relief organizations, however, launched a humanitarian assistance drive in Saʿdah immediately after the end of the fifth war: the Qatari Red Crescent Society as well as the presidentially-established Salih Foundation distributed goods to refugees, while Oxfam, Médecins Sans Frontières, Médecins du Monde, the International Committee of the Red Cross and Islamic Relief pursued their own relief programmes, including in zones that remained under rebel control.[311]

The Presidential Reconstruction Committee established four sub-committees tasked with the assessment of war damages in Saʿdah, ʿAmrān, al-Jawf and Banī Ḥushaysh and encouraging the IDPs to return home. The sub-committees received a mixed response. Many IDPs balked at the notion of return, either because their original areas of residence had been destroyed, mined or occupied, or because they feared reprisals from both the Houthis and the army.[312] The Houthis accused the sub-committees assessing damages on the ground of lying about their objectives and spying on the Houthis and their supporters. They claimed that some areas and tribes that had supported the Yemeni army—such as al-Ẓāhir in Saʿdah governorate's extreme west—would receive priority for reconstruction and would benefit from the provision of electricity, water and paved roads.[313] Equally, in the Wādī Nushūr area, pro-government tribesmen prevented the local sub-committee from surveying the damages in al-Razzāmāt, home of ʿAbdullah al-Razzāmī, and accused the Reconstruction Committee of focusing on Houthi areas. As a result of such obstruction, the Presidential Reconstruction Committee was unable to assess the damages fully and failed to make progress on the ground.

The Reconstruction Committee's work was further thwarted by regime and military hardliners who opposed reconciliation and took steps to undermine it. They might well have been behind the forced resignation of ʿAbdulqādir Hilāl as head of the Committee in September 2008. Through his impartial attitude and professional work, Hilāl had contributed to calming the situation. He had, inter alia, demanded that the government lift the state of emergency, restore the power supply, unblock the mobile telephone network, and release prisoners, as these were the Houthis' key demands. President Salih rejected these appeals and security officials accused Hilāl of excessive leniency toward the rebels, expressing suspicions that he lacked the 'resoluteness' (*ḥazm*) required to deal with the Houthis. In September, after two months, Hilāl was sacked and replaced by Minister of Public Works ʿUmar al-Kharashī. The government justified this castling by claiming that al-Kharashī and the Ministry of Public Works possessed more practical experience for the now imminent technical reconstruction phase than Hilāl's Ministry of Local Administration.[314] For independent observers, however, Hilāl's dismissal was another sign of internal regime divisions, a hesitation to end the war, and a setback to peace efforts in Saʿdah. As a result, the Reconstruction Committee lost dynamism and much of the credit it had gained.[315]

Parallel to the Presidential Reconstruction Committee, the Presidential Mediation Committee comprised members of the team that had negotiated the 17th Infantry Brigade's safe passage out of Marrān: Fāris Manāʿ, ʿAlī Nāṣir Qirshah, and Dughsān Aḥmad Dughsān. The Committee was mandated to solve disputes between the various parties throughout the conflict zone, and in the following months was active as a task force for defusing tensions throughout the zone, including in Sufyān, Ghamr and Jumāʿah.

Again, despite or perhaps because the Presidential Mediation Committee worked successfully—Fāris Manāʿ, in particular, was an able and seasoned mediator—it suffered the same fate as the Presidential Reconstruction Committee. After verbal altercations with certain shaykhs of Saʿdah, who accused Fāris Manāʿ in Salih's presence of lying, misleading public opinion and favouring the Houthis, on 24 November 2008 he was dismissed and replaced as head of the Committee by Brigadier General Yaḥyā al-Marrānī, then director of the Political Security forces in Saʿdah.[316]

The Western Mountains

The Houthis regarded these reshuffles in the Presidential Committees as evidence of the government's insincerity in implementing the ceasefire. The dismissal of Fāris Manāʿ and ʿAbdulqādir Hilāl, and their replacement by anti-Houthi hardliners resulted in a further hardening of attitudes. Particularly troublingly, hostilities were rekindled and further flash points created throughout the conflict zone. The government started to dispatch troops and military reinforcements. After the dismissal of Hilāl in September, Houthi spokesperson Ṣāliḥ Habrah warned: 'The monster is about to wake up: the monster of war'.[317]

The Houthis began pushing into the tribal territories of the Khawlān b. ʿĀmir confederation. Locals reported that the rebels were asserting the expansion of their influence with very heavy-handed military action.[318] In December, Houthi forces under the command of ʿAbdullah al-Ḥākim entered into violent confrontations with the Āl al-Ḥamāṭī, a section of the Banī Ḥudhayfah of Jumāʿah who were led by their young shaykh, Fayṣal al-Ḥamāṭī Shinwāḥ. During the 1960s civil war, the Āl al-Ḥamāṭī had largely supported the Republic, and during the Saʿdah wars most of them sided with the Yemeni government. The Houthis got support in their conflict with the Āl al-Ḥamāṭī from the Āl al-Dhīb, another section of the Banī Ḥudhayfah that had been engaged in blood feud with the Āl al-Ḥamāṭī for many years.[319]

The Houthis imposed a twelve-day siege on Āl al-Ḥamāṭī. An attempt at mediation by Fayṣal Nāṣir ʿArīj and ʿAlī Nāṣir Qirshah failed to stop the confrontations. Thereupon other shaykhs of Jumāʿah entered the mediation process and set up a tent in the line of fire between the Āl al-Ḥamāṭī and the Houthis. It is common practice in Yemen for mediators to rush with some armed men to the place of the shooting and station themselves in the middle to prevent further shooting. As soon as they arrive in that area they flag a white cloth, or, as in this case, place a tent. This signals a request for the conflicting tribes to stop shooting and accept mediation. According to tribal custom, conflict parties should then stop shooting until they have spoken to the mediator. However, Houthi field commander al-Ḥākim ignored the mediation attempts and continued to shell Āl al-Ḥamāṭī. Eventually, Fāris Manāʿ arrived on the battlefield and managed to stop the bloodshed. His mediation endeavours led to the signing of a ceasefire agreement between the Houthis and the Āl al-Ḥamāṭī.

In spring 2009, the border areas along the Ṭāʾif Line began to develop into a vast conflict zone, when existing flash points and centres of conflict began to expand and merge. The nucleus of this conflagration was Ghamr district in Saʿdah. The resumption of fighting in al-Jarshah, Ghamr's administrative and commercial centre, was a perfect sequel to the deadly clashes between supporters of Shaykh ʿAlī Thāfir and the Houthis that had gripped Ghamr in the fourth and fifth wars. In Ẓāfir March 2009, a shaykh from Ghamr, Ḥusayn Ḥasān, warned the government that the Houthis were about to seize the district. Indeed, a few days later, the rebels managed to occupy Jabal ʿArʿar, which overlooks the district's centre. By early April, they controlled large parts of Ghamr, including government buildings and Ghamr's administrative centre, Sūq al-Jarshah.[320]

In order to bring a halt to these clashes, the government commissioned Salmān ʿAwfān, senior shaykh of neighbouring Munabbih, to mediate in Ghamr. ʿAwfān was a respected and experienced mediator who had had success in numerous conflicts both within and outside the Khawlān b. ʿĀmir confederation in Yemen, as well as the Saudi borderlands along the Ṭāʾif Line.[321] From the beginning of the Saʿdah wars he had signalled his loyalty to the government, and throughout the conflict the Munabbih tribe has shown remarkable unity in its rejection of the Houthi movement. However, ʿAwfān did not take a proactive role in combating the Houthis. This was due to the fact that the senior shaykh of the Munabbih is defined as a 'shaykh of peace': in order to maintain his role as the neutral and impartial head of the tribe, he never participates in armed conflict. Instead, he delegates the conduct of war to minor shaykhs of his tribe.[322] During the Saʿdah wars, these 'shaykhs of war' were Aḥmad Dahbāsh Miṭrī (who was killed in Qaṭābir in June 2007) and ʿAlī Ḥusayn al-Munabbihī. ʿAwfān's restraint, however, had caused irritation among both the government and the Houthis, and created doubt as to his political orientation. As a barely concealed warning, in May 2007 an army combat helicopter had 'accidentally' shelled his house in Munabbih.[323]

The mediation in Ghamr was therefore a particularly delicate diplomatic mission for Salmān ʿAwfān, because he was under close monitoring by the government. Unfortunately, his attempts at mediation failed because, as Munabbih sources argue, the Houthis lacked the will to enter into a ceasefire and negotiate a political settlement.[324] On the contrary, a member of the mediation committee was shot at by the Houthis—attacking a mediator is a major disgrace (*ʿayb*) under tribal customary law. Despite this Houthi hostility, because the Houthis continued their conquest of Ghamr unimpeded, Yemeni press again suspected ʿAwfān of clandestine complicity with the movement.[325] ʿAbdulmalik al-Ḥūthī, however, blamed the escalation on Shaykh ʿAlī Ẓāfir and the state military, considering these events in Ghamr the prelude to a sixth war.[326] After ʿAwfān's failed mediation, Salih commissioned Fāris Manāʿ. Yet his mediation team encountered difficulties in advancing from Saʿdah city through the conflict areas of Ḍaḥyān, Jumāʿah and Qaṭābir to Ghamr district; upon arrival, they were confronted with a fait accompli.[327] Soon after, the Houthis expelled ʿAlī Ẓāfir from Ghamr.

In June, the battles spread from Ghamr to Rāziḥ and expanded along the Ṭāʾif Line. By early August, the Houthis were in virtual control of almost the entire border area from Bāqim in the north to Shidāʾ in the southwest. After they managed to block all roads between the war zone and the capital, the military found itself unable to bring supplies and reinforcements into the combat zone and to transport their casualties out. Saudi Arabia offered first aid and allowed the initial treatment of wounded soldiers in medical facilities in the Saudi borderlands, and the transport of the wounded on Saudi streets along the frontier to the border crossing at al-Ṭuwāl near Ḥaraḍ.[328] In August, when the Houthis managed to establish control over Sāqayn and al-Ḥārubah in Shidāʾ, the military was forced to withdraw even further. In al-Ḥaṣāmah in Saḥār district, the Houthis seized a military base.

In the far north, too, the battles continued expanding along the Ṭāʾif Line. In Bāqim, Houthis clashed with a group led by Bandar Muqīt and Ḥusayn Ḥaydar. Bandar Muqīt was a son of Ḥasan Muqīt, the senior shaykh of the Khawlān b. ʿĀmir confederation, who had sided early on with the Yemeni government and in particular with the Saudi Kingdom.[329] The Houthis set up a checkpoint near the ʿIlb border crossing in order to cut off escape routes and prevent Muqīt and Ḥaydar and their followers from withdrawing to Saudi territory. Both were captured.[330]

Only Jabal Munabbih remained an island controlled by tribes loyal to the government—for the time being. Embattled on three sides, the Munabbih tribe had closed the borders of its tribal territory. Side by side with Central Security forces, the Munabbih's 'shaykh of war' ʿAlī Ḥusayn al-Munabbihī fought on the fronts in Ghamr and Qaṭābir. After the fall of Ghamr, ʿAbdulmalik al-Ḥūthī and ʿAlī Ḥusayn al-Munabbihī started to exchange belligerent statements and mutual threats. ʿAbdulmalik called al-Munabbihī a war profiteer and puppet of the Salih regime. Al-Munabbihī and his loyalists responded with serious insults of the Houthis and their leader.[331] It was obvious that a direct confrontation between the Munabbih and the Houthis was imminent, and that Munabbih would become one of the main arenas of the sixth war.

Sufyān[332]

In October 2008, the conflict between the Houthis and the followers of Ṣaghīr b. ʿAzīz resumed in a fatal concatenation of events that were as arbitrary as they were brutal. The problem started when members of the al-Ṣumaym, Ṣaghīr b. ʿAzīz's home section, went from al-ʿAmashiyyah in Sufyān to Āl ʿAmmār in Saʿdah. In the market of Āl ʿAmmār, they came across the director of al-Ṣafrāʾ district and his bodyguards, who mistook the Ṣumaymī tribesmen for Houthis. One, Muḥsin al-Ḥaqawnah, was killed, tied by his feet to a military vehicle and dragged through the market. Only later did it transpire that the victim belonged to the same tribe as Ṣaghīr b. ʿAzīz, who had fought in the fifth war against the Houthis. Ṣaghīr, outraged by the killing of his kinsman and the public display of his body, condemned this action as a 'heinous murder and extreme disgrace (*ʿayb aswad*) according to tribal customary law'.[333]

In retaliation, some members of the al-Ṣumaym resorted to blood revenge. Without Ṣaghīr's knowledge, they waylaid a military convoy in al-ʿAmashiyyah and killed five members of the 72nd Infantry Brigade, a unit of the Republican Guard.[334] Since Ṣaghīr himself was a leading officer of the Republican Guard, this was another grotesquely ironic incident. Local sources suggest that the aim of this action was not only to avenge the death of al-Ḥaqawnah but also to drive a wedge between Ṣaghīr and Ahmad Salih, the commander of the Republican Guard. Ṣaghīr, however, who was with good reason nicknamed *ḥaras jumhūrī bi-libās shaykh* (a Republican Guard in the guise of a shaykh), remained unwavering in his loyalty to Salih Junior.

Nevertheless, confrontations resumed between Houthi loyalists and government supporters in Sufyān's Ruhm area. ʿAlī Nāṣir Qirshah, member of the Presidential Mediation Committee, attempted to mediate. Since the conflict concerned a sensitive, strategically important area that straddled the Sanaʿa-Saʿdah highway, the minister of defence and General ʿAlī Muḥsin also intervened, demanding from Ṣaghīr the extradition of two suspects. When the suspects refused to appear, ʿAlī Muḥsin instead demanded nine hostages from Ṣaghīr's tribe.[335] For the state to demand hostages from a tribe is a most unusual practice in post-revolutionary Yemen and indicates both the immense importance of this area for the government and the regime's deep distrust of the tribes of Sufyān, whom Ḥāshid tribes denounce as 'people with black hearts'.[336]

Things turned worse in October 2008, when the long-standing territorial conflict between the Sufyān's Ṣubārah moiety (Bakīl) and the al-ʿUṣaymāt (Ḥāshid) flared up again and started to fuse with the Houthi conflict. The Ṣubārah share a disputed border with the al-ʿUṣaymāt, who, as we know, are not just any Ḥāshid tribe. Their senior shaykh comes from the al-Aḥmar shaykhly lineage, and is the senior shaykh (*shaykh mashāyikh*) of the whole Ḥāshid confederation. The former incumbent, ʿAbdullah al-Aḥmar, was also head of the tribal wing of the Iṣlāḥ party and speaker of the Parliament; he was certainly the most influential and powerful tribal personality in Yemen. Following his death in December 2007, he had been succeeded by his oldest son, Ṣādiq.

The enmity between the two tribes began more than a hundred years ago. The arena of this incessant conflict is al-Suwād, a fertile tributary of Wādī Mawr with an abundance of thermal springs. In Yemen's tribal society, the concept of territory (*arḍ*) is closely related to the concept of honour (*sharaf*). The honour of an individual tribesman is simultaneously part of the tribe's honour, and the protected space on which this honour depends is often identified with physical space: that is, with territory. This honour can be impugned by attacks on any component of the tribesmen's honourable selves, and landholdings have a special status and significance for a tribesman's honour. The borders of tribes are therefore portrayed as sacrosanct, and any insult to territory seriously threatens a man's honour and the honour of his tribe. Hence any insult to tribal territory (and therefore to tribal honour) may lead to blood feud.[337]

According to local sources, the Ṣubārah and al-ʿUṣaymāt reached an agreement to end this feud about a century ago, with the Ṣubārah granted the right to use the land of al-Suwād. In spite of this, implementation of the agreement floundered, because of widely differing interpretations of some of its clauses (the al-ʿUṣaymāt rejected the presence of Ṣubārah in al-Suwād, saying that the land was still under dispute). This has led to protracted battles, causing the death and injury of hundreds to date. Tribal conflicts can usually be settled, or at least contained, through mediation. This conflict, like the Houthi conflict, is an example of the rare repeated failure of such mediation efforts.

In October 2008, the conflict was rekindled, and by the beginning of December had already killed forty-one and wounded over 100.[338] The government was well aware of the risks to the outcome of the Saʿdah wars posed by fanning the flames of this feud, as both Sufyān and al-ʿUṣaymāt were of central strategic importance. The two tribes were expected to cooperate in recruiting the Popular Army led by Ḥusayn al-Aḥmar; Bakīl ʿAbduh Ḥubaysh of the Ṣubārah was the Popular Army's leader in Sufyān. It was therefore particularly alarming that the al-ʿUṣaymāt was using weapons earmarked for the Houthi wars in its territorial dispute with the Ṣubārah. As a result, the Popular Army, which had been on feet of clay in the first place, was about to collapse.

In March 2009, under the watchful eye of President Salih, a high-ranking mediation committee headed by General ʿAlī Muḥsin and several senior Sufyān and al-ʿUṣaymāt shaykhs was duly established, and was able to bring a temporary halt to the feud. The president supervised a ceasefire agreement that provided—just as in Ruhm—for the delivery of twelve hostages (*rahāʾin*), five of them from Sufyān, to ensure implementation of the agreement.[339] Both sides signed the agreement. However, ten days later, violent confrontations broke out again. After two weeks of clashes and dozens of dead and wounded, a new mediation initiative was launched by a large number of Ḥāshid and Bakīl shaykhs. After trying for three days to stop the armed clashes and contain the feud, the negotiators withdrew, without achieving any results and without announcing the reasons for their failure.[340]

During the renewed clashes in al-Suwād, the al-ʿUṣaymāt had fought with heavy weapons, whereas the Ṣubārah had only light- and medium-calibre weapons. This military superiority raised questions about the actual source of the armaments. The Ṣubārah accused the government of arming the al-ʿUṣaymāt via the Popular Army. Mujāhid Ḥaydar of the Ruhm (Sufyān's other moiety) put the Sufyān's grievances in a nutshell:

> The war [between the Ṣubārah and al-ʿUṣaymāt] entered its fourth month, and all the government says are flimsy excuses, pretences, and manoeuvring in its attempt to justify its financial and military support for Ḥāshid against Bakīl. This is nothing

> new; this has been going on since 1978 when Ḥāshid [i.e. Ḥāshid tribesman Ali Abdullah Salih] came to power.[341]

ʿAbduh Ḥubaysh of Ṣubārah, the senior shaykh of Sufyān, took a similar line: 'This state is a Ḥāshid state, and the weapons came from the army's magazines, and it is their state'.[342] He threatened to call in the other Bakīl tribes to support the Sufyān on the grounds that the Ḥāshid was backing the al-ʿUṣaymāt. Standing together with other tribes against outsiders who attack their shared borders is not an unusual practice, but in the larger context of the Saʿdah wars, the other Bakīl tribes joining the Sufyān and the other Ḥāshid tribes joining the al-ʿUṣaymāt would represent a very serious form of 'ganging-up' warfare (*ḥarb ʿiṣābāt*), an offence under tribal law.[343]

This was not only a territorial conflict over possession of the al-Suwād area, but also a tribal rivalry and a proxy war over perceived discrimination against the Bakīl tribes in a Ḥāshid-dominated state. By the outbreak of the sixth war in August, the Ṣubārah's tribal and political grievances had already fused with the Houthis' expansionist thrust, enabling them to extend their control over the whole of Sufyān.

Al-Jawf

In July 2008, a few days before the unilateral ceasefire announcement that ended the fifth war, the secretary-general of al-Jawf's Local Council, ʿAbdulwahhāb al-Ḍumayn, and Shaykh ʿAbdullah al-Jayshī of Shawlān were assassinated, sending shockwaves through the province. This incident had ultimately pushed al-Jawf governorate into fratricidal war among its tribes, known for their truculence and bellicosity.

For this reason, the government was reluctant to deploy regular troops in al-Jawf and instead pressed ahead with the recruitment of local tribes, to be thrown into battle against their brethren. The enlisting of tribal irregulars was supervised by Khālid al-Sharīf, the chairman of the Supreme Commission of Election and Referendum. Al-Sharīf hailed from the province's al-Ẓāhir district. He was a confidant of President Salih and one of the few really influential people from impoverished and politically marginalized al-Jawf. Personal reasons also played a role in his activism against the Houthis: ʿAbdulwahhāb al-Ḍumayn, one of the victims of the assassination, had been his cousin. Furthermore, another branch of the al-Sharīf clan (members of the al-Ashrāf tribe) was active on the Houthi side, and Khālid seemed to need to prove his loyalty to the government. A Houthi field commander in al-Jawf recalled:

> The front in al-Jawf has been opened only after the fifth war. The attack [on ʿAbdulwahhāb al-Ḍumayn] set in motion the conflict between the sons of al-Jawf and the Houthis, who themselves were sons of al-Jawf. The government worked out a new plan for the establishment of military bases and the recruitment of the sons of al-Jawf and Khālid al-Sharīf implemented the government's plan. Khālid al-Sharīf was the godfather (*ʿarrāb*) of the front in al-Jawf. He spent lots of money to recruit the tribes and to set up security checkpoints (*niqāt amniyyah*), one of them in the centre of [Houthi-dominated] al-Zāhir district, and provided them with money and weapons for the purpose of fighting against the Houthis and preventing the presence of anyone from outside al-Jawf. I remember when I was sitting together with ʿAbdulmalik al-Ḥūthī and I was explaining the situation in al-Jawf, ʿAbdulmalik told me: 'My brother, issue a statement (*bayān*) and make public that Khālid al-Sharīf is responsible for the bloodshed in al-Jawf.'[344]

In November 2008, the war between the Shawlān and the Houthis erupted in al-Matūn and al-Zāhir. After the July double assassination, the Shawlān had plotted their revenge. Their retaliation campaign against the Houthis was led by the murdered shaykh's brothers. Members of the Dhū Muḥammad and al-Ashrāf tribes joined in on the Houthi side, and the conflict quickly grew.

After years of frosty relations worthy of the Ice Age, President Salih and Amīn al-ʿUkaymī were growing closer in their fight against the Houthis, as the president announced their close collaboration in the field of 'security and stability'.[345] This was, however, born of a limited unity of purpose. Only a short time later, al-ʿUkaymī could not restrain himself in an interview from mocking the deplorable lack of security and stability in al-Jawf, which he asserted was due not to the local tribes, but to the government's divide-and-rule tactics, which ensured that everything remained 'off track' (*khārij al-miḍmār*).[346] For the time being, there was not yet any military cooperation between the two sides; throughout the Saʿdah wars, al-ʿUkaymī remained strictly opposed to the recruitment of Shawlān tribesmen as irregulars against the Houthis (see below).

The Yemeni government expected the tribes of al-Jawf to play a central role in the fight against the Houthis, hence the president worked hard on bringing the shaykhs into line. Consultative meetings with shaykhs from al-Jawf and neighbouring Ma'rib became regular practice. In these consultations Salih frequently reminded the shaykhs of the ruination of Saʿdah province, in which the war had wrought havoc, as a deterrent. Mutual distrust remained deeply rooted on both sides. During a surprise presidential visit to Ma'rib in February 2009, the shaykhs were taken to him by bus after security forces denied their personal vehicles access to the government compound and its surroundings.[347]

In al-Jawf, meanwhile, the revenge killings went on, claiming a high toll of lives. Also in February 2009, five Houthi field commanders were killed in al-Zāhir district in an ambush set by Shawlān tribesmen: Zayd ʿAlī al-Ḍumayn,[348] Aḥmad ʿAbdullah ʿAbadān al-ʿIzzī, ʿAbdullah Aḥmad Jibrān, Nājī Muḥammad Abū ʿUshāl, and Ḥamūd Aḥmad al-Ḥaydarī.[349] Khālid al-Sharīf denied any government involvement in this incident, which he blamed on tribal vendettas.[350] Shortly after, the Houthis killed Shaykh Aḥmad al-Turkī of Shawlān, who was considered a government supporter, and the violent cycle of retaliation dragged on.[351]

Both sides tried to make their presence felt in al-Jawf. In a kind of race, they began to set up checkpoints, called 'hegemony points' (*niqāt al-haymanah*), which served to show 'boots on the ground' and to monitor the enemy's movements. A Houthi field commander recalled:

> Through the establishment of checkpoints, Khālid al-Sharīf tried to hermetically seal al-Jawf off from the outside world and to prevent the penetration of invaders (*ghazzāh*) from Saʿdah. One of these government checkpoints was planned to be set up between al-Jawf and Sufyān, another in Khabb wa l-Shaʿf district, and the third one in al-Multaqā in al-Maṭammah. When I heard that, I called the [Houthi] military supervisor in al-Jawf and told him to set his people in motion and to anticipate the government's plans by erecting checkpoints in these areas. And within two hours the Houthis erected two checkpoints, the first one in al-ʿAsharah [between Sufyān and al-Jawf] and the second one in al-Multaqā. In al-Shaʿf we threatened the shaykh in charge and he retreated from setting up a checkpoint against us. That way we have thwarted the [government's] plan to cut off al-Jawf from ʿAmrān and Saʿdah in order to prevent the movements of the Houthis. This greatly angered the government, which resorted to fomenting conflict among the tribes of al-Jawf in order to mobilize them against the Houthis. In the front in al-Jawf hardly any regular troops took part.[352]

On 17 February, Salih convened another huge consultation meeting with shaykhs of Dahm and Hamdān al-Jawf. The meeting turned out to be strikingly reminiscent of his failed meeting with the Saʿdah shaykhs on the occasion of the radio station inauguration in March 2007.[353] More than 100 shaykhs from al-Jawf attended, yet most were minor. Many senior shaykhs sent one of their younger sons, or simply their apologies. When the president expressed his surprise at the absence of the senior shaykhs, he angered those present, who replied: 'Do we mean nothing to you, Excellence?' (*wa naḥnu hal mā malaynā ʿaynak yā siyādat al-raʾīs?*) The Banī Nawf seized the opportunity to launch a tirade about the preference given to the Hamdān and the Dhū Ḥusayn in government appointments. Others undermined the very purpose of the meeting by flatly denying the presence of any Houthis in al-Jawf; Shaykh Ṣāliḥ al-ʿIjjī of Hamdān al-Jawf purported that his tribal area was safer than the Presidential Palace in Sanaʿa. Observers took note that the shaykhs of Dahm, instead of answering 'yes' or 'no', frequently resorted to the vague phrase: 'We will bring [your] arguments before God' (*wa naḥmil al-ḥajjah amām Allāh*). One result of the meeting was the establishment of a committee chaired by Nājī al-Shāyif (at that time considered senior shaykh of the Bakīl), and comprising, inter alia, Amīn al-ʿUkaymī (Shawlān), Manṣūr Haḍabān (Dhū Ḥusayn) and ʿAbdulsalām Shayḥāṭ (Hamdān al-Jawf). This committee was charged with mediation in the virulent conflict between the Shawlān and the Houthis. Yet this initiative came to nothing, because the committee members could not agree on the way forward, or how to contain the growing Houthi tide in al-Jawf.[354]

Meanwhile, beyond their tribal dynamics, confrontations in the province also assumed an overtly sectarian character. In May, Houthis sabotaged a meeting of the Iṣlāḥ party in a mosque in al-Matūn by mixing themselves with the Iṣlāḥ audience members. After a speech by Shaykh ʿAbdullah Ṣaʿtar, they shouted the Houthi slogan. After a short moment of confusion—the Houthi slogan by no means contradicted the party's political positions—the Houthis were beaten up by the crowd. Only an intervention via loudspeaker by Ḥasan Abkar, a *sayyid* from Yarīm resident in al-Ghayl district and head of Iṣlāḥ's al-Jawf branch, prevented things from getting worse.[355]

By contrast, in July a similar confrontation in Zayn al-ʿĀbidīn Mosque in al-Khazīʿ (al-Zāhir) had dire consequences. After the evening prayer, Houthis shouted their slogan. Shortly thereafter, a number of gunmen stormed the gates of the mosque and fired indiscriminately on worshippers. Clashes erupted in which the Houthis managed to occupy and destroy Khālid al-Sharīf's house in al-Zāhir. After the 'bloody night of al-Khazīʿ', the Houthis seized large parts of al-Zāhir, al-Maṭammah, al-Ghayl, al-Matūn and Baraṭ districts. Local mediation initiatives—notably by Mujāhid Ḥaydar of Sufyān and ʿAlawī al-Bāshā b. Zabaʿ (secretary-general of the Alliance of the Tribes of Maʾrib and Jawf)—were unable to bring the clashes to a halt.[356] Al-Jawf threatened to descend into disaster. Journalist Muḥammad al-Ṣāliḥī commented in *Mareb Press*: 'The province has become a hotbed of playoffs, murder, and bloodshed. It is awaiting the zero hour to announce the upcoming confrontations, which will be the gate to the sixth war'.[357]

The European Hostage Saga

On 12 June 2009, nine foreigners working at al-Jumhūrī Hospital in Saʿdah city (seven Germans, a Brit and a South Korean) disappeared in Saʿdah province while returning from a picnic. According to eyewitnesses, three armed men ambushed the group near Jabal al-Tulummuṣ in Ghurāz south of Saʿdah city by blocking their way with a black Suzuki Vitara SUV. On 14 June, shepherds found three of them—two German nurses and the South Korean, a teacher—dead in al-Razzāmāt in the Wādī Nushūr area. After almost three days' exposure in Saʿdah's summer heat to both decomposition and dogs and carrion birds, the bodies of the three women were difficult to identify. All of them had been killed by gunshot wounds to the head and each had been shot multiple times. With the exception of some tearing caused by animals, the women's clothing was intact and there were no signs of torture.[358] The rest of the foreigners had been abducted: the Brit and a German couple with three children (two female toddlers, Anna and Lydia, and a baby boy not even a year old). In the overheating governorate, lurching towards the sixth war, an abundance of rumours and theories began to circulate about the perpetrators of the crime. As everyone tried to point the finger at an adversary, no responsibility could definitively be placed.

The first suspicions about potential suspects were drawn from the location of the three bodies in al-Razzāmāt. One story went that ʿAbdullah al-Razzāmī had kidnapped and killed the foreigners. Another rumour said that al-Razzāmī, at that time already alienated from ʿAbdulmalik al-Ḥūthī, no longer obeyed any of ʿAbdulmalik's orders and acted at his own discretion; one of his objectives was to weaken the state and to work against Westerners and their organizations. However, apart from the corpses' discovery in his territory, there was no other indication that al-Razzāmī had anything to do with the crime. And, of course, it was possible that the foreigners were not killed there, but had only been dumped in the area, which was considered a Houthi stronghold, to compromise al-Razzāmī and the Houthi movement.

Shortly after the incident, tribal heavyweight Ṣāliḥ b. Shājiaʿ of Wāʾilah, who maintained informal links to various radical groups in the Saʿdah region, intervened in the search for perpetrators and handed over two men to the authorities. Both men were previously convicted members of the Āl Mahdī section of the Wāʾilah; apparently they were arrested on the grounds that they possessed a black Suzuki Vitara. Yet forensic crime scene investigators found no traces of those killed or abducted in their car. Moreover, Ṣāliḥ b. Shājiaʿ ruled out the possibility that the six abductees were in al-Razzāmāt, as some media had suggested. Indeed, their fate was growing more and more mysterious.[359]

As ever, the government and pro-government shaykhs continued to point to the Houthis, arguing that al-Razzāmāt was under Houthi control (omitting that the site of the abduction, Ghurāz in Saḥār district, was under state control). Minister of the Interior Muṭahhar al-Miṣrī, former governor of Saʿdah and anti-Houthi hardliner, called the incident an 'act of terrorism' and suspected that with this crime the Houthis had sought to blacken the good name of the Yemeni government and increase international pressure on the regime.[360] Sources added that the government was working seriously to have the Houthis designated as a terrorist group in order to get more US support, and to create problems for Yaḥyā al-Ḥūthī, who continued to enjoy asylum in Germany.[361]

The Houthis, as ever, denied any involvement in the incident. ʿAbdulmalik issued a press statement in which he strongly condemned the assault. The rebels organized mass marches and demonstrations to protest against the kidnapping and killing of the nurses, condemning the crime as a 'serious conspiracy against the people of Yemen in general and the sons of Saʿdah in particular'.[362] The Houthis saw the incident as a conspiracy to harm them politically and to legitimize the looming sixth war.

Foreign embassies, too, doubted the Yemeni government's intimations that the crime was perpetrated by the Houthis. Michael Reuss, German deputy ambassador to Yemen, dismissed the regime's attempts to blame Houthis for the kidnapping, telling the US Embassy that, in his opinion, the action neither fitted their mode of operation nor would make any sense in terms of achieving their goals.[363] In particular, given that Yaḥyā al-Ḥūthī was still being sheltered by the German governemnt (his parliamentary immunity having been lifted in 2007 when Sanaʿa sought Interpol's assistance in extraditing him), the Houthis would certainly be cautious about ruining relations with Berlin with violence against German civilians. Yaḥyā's statements from Berlin—as virtually the only Houthi leader who was able to speak unhindered and uncensored to international media—have long disturbed the Yemeni government.

ʿAbdulḥakīm al-Iryānī, director of the Foreign Minister's Office, told the US Embassy that he thought it much more likely that some Salafi group had committed the crime, because the kidnapped foreigners were believed to be involved in proselytizing.[364] Indeed, the abducted foreigners had been affiliated with a Dutch-based charity called World Wide Services. Michael Reuss confirmed that diaries and other items found among the possessions of the deceased strongly indicated that they were involved in evangelist outreach that went beyond doing good works—according to Reuss, the crisis unit of the German Foreign Office had reason to suspect that furious Muslims had threatened the father of the kidnapped German family and asked him to stop his missionary efforts.[365]

Reuss believed that the kidnapping/murder had achieved three visible results: stirring up anti-Houthi sentiment, discomfiting President Salih, and acting as an implicit threat to Christian evangelists. He asserts that each of these results may have benefited ʿAlī Muḥsin, in the following ways: he was generally believed to have profited financially from the fighting in Saʿdah and stood to profit again should conflict with the Houthis recommence in earnest; he had been increasingly marginalized in recent years as Salih handed more and more military power to members of his immediate family; discrediting Salih in front of Germany, Yemen's largest donor, would serve the dual purpose of weakening the president's power base and exacting a certain revenge; and, finally, striking a blow against evangelical Christians would likely appeal to ʿAlī Muḥsin's Salafist tendencies.[366]

Indeed the German nurses had said in their last phone call, just before their murder, that they were being harassed by 'bearded men'.[367] Furthermore, a Salafi military training centre with links to al-Qaeda—the Dār al-Ḥadīth in Kitāf district—was located near al-Razzāmāt in the Wādī Āl Abū Jabārah area northeast of Wādī Nushūr. Officially, the camp was a Salafi teaching institute. However, it had had a different trajectory from the other, well-known Salafi teaching centre in the Saʿdah region, located in Dammāj near Saʿdah city. The camp in Kitāf had distinct military features.[368] The issue was that it had multiple allegiances and that its identity kept oscillating. The armed men of Kitāf have at various times been labelled jihadis, mercenaries, and al-Qaeda operatives, and the distinctions between them and their alliances appear to have been rather blurred. Since 2007, Salafis and al-Qaeda operatives from Wādī Āl Abū Jabārah had been deployed by ʿAlī Muḥsin and the Popular Army against the Houthis. AQAP had partially ceased its previous attacks on security forces, and several high-ranking al-Qaeda figures were involved in combat with the Houthis.[369]

A few weeks before the incident, the then leader of AQAP, Nāṣir al-Wuḥayshī, had demanded the killing of non-Muslim foreigners and the purging of 'infidels' from the Arabian Peninsula; he believed that foreigners in Yemen were either 'spies' or 'Christian proselytizers'. Shortly before the attack on the foreigners in Saʿdah, AQAP had called for vengeance for the participation of Western governments in wars against Muslims to be carried out against tourists.[370] In addition, the level of violence distinguished this abduction from previous incidents. It was more like al-Qaeda-style abductions, such as those seen in Iraq and Pakistan, and may have been conducted by al-Qaeda fighters from Iraq or Afghanistan, who had returned to Yemen. Some observers thus suggested that Islamist militants had staged the kidnapping to provoke the regime into restarting the war in Saʿdah—and/or to divert focus from the parallel fight against AQAP itself.[371]

Yet al-Qaeda usually harnesses such actions for propaganda purposes and produces videos of hostages to give more emphasis to its demands. None of this happened here; for a long time, there was no claim of responsibility, no video, no explanation, and no sign of life of the German family. It is possible that the kidnappers were close in ideology to al-Qaeda, but not part of al-Qaeda's command structure, or that they kept the family as a kind of insurance policy, to guarantee future demands. According to the Berlin crisis team, the case was one of the most complex and enigmatic the Federal Government had ever had to deal with.[372]

In autumn 2009—by which time the sixth Saʿdah war had already begun—two videos of the three children, Lydia, Anna and Simon, were passed to the German Embassy in Sanaʿa, once again through the Shājiaʿ clan. There was still no trace of the parents. In January 2010, the kidnappers got in touch again and demanded, inter alia, the release of several prisoners affiliated with al-Qaeda.[373] In early May 2010, there was evidence of secret negotiations between the Yemeni government and the abductors, without German involvement. Some Yemeni men demanded a ransom of several million US dollars for all the hostages. Their interlocutor was a man who apparently operated from within Saudi territory. In May 2010, the two girls, Anna and Lydia, were finally handed over to a Saudi special commando in Shidāʾ district, in the west of Saʿdah governorate. The parents and the boy were never found; in September 2014 the German government declared them dead.

To this day, the incident remains mysterious. Involvement of Salafis or al-Qaeda seems likely. The Yemeni government itself seemed to be caught off guard. In contrast to the Bin Salmān Mosque bomb attack in 2008, which instantly triggered the eruption of the fifth war, there was no immediate fallout from the European hostage crisis. Nevertheless, it left its traces on the sixth war, for instance in the Six Points, the government's conditions for a ceasefire.[374] Asked about the incident, an influential shaykh from the eastern Saʿdah region suggested an ex-post solution of the case and commented dryly: 'Anyone who wants to know who kidnapped the Germans should ask the Saudis. After all, the Saudis have redeemed the girls from the kidnappers.'[375] However, until some individual or group takes responsibility for the incident, or until the remaining victims are found, theories will continue to proliferate. Whatever the truth may be, the European hostage saga remained a contentious issue for the warring parties and an embarrassing setback for the Yemeni government.

An Undeclared War

Given the war-like situation in Saʿdah, northern ʿAmrān and al-Jawf, the secessionist uprising in the south, and the threat of an electoral boycott by the JMP opposition, on 24 February President Salih postponed the country's fourth parliamentary elections, which had been scheduled for 24 April 2009.

In July 2009, four GPC MPs of Saʿdah's parliamentary bloc—ʿUthmān Mujallī, Fāyiz al-ʿAwjarī, ʿAbdulsalām Hishūl Zābiyah, and Fayṣal b. ʿArīj—resigned from the party, thereby further weakening the government's political and tribal support base in the region. They presented a list of displeasures and grievances.[376] First, neglect of the needs of the 'sons of Saʿdah'. Second, the persistent underdevelopment of the province, despite the government's bombastic electoral campaign promises. Third, the lack of compensation for those killed or wounded in the war against the Houthis. Fourth, the lack of respect displayed by the government for its supporters in the Saʿdah region (who felt rather treated 'as if they were [Houthi] rebels'). Fifth, incidents of robbery and looting and disregard of civil rights committed by the armed forces and its mercenaries. Finally, the MPs cited the exclusion of the 'nobles' (*shurfāʾ*, here meaning Saʿdah's tribal elite) from the processes of mediation, reconstruction, and reconciliation. The resignation of these shaykhs, especially in the case of ʿUthmān Mujallī, had been long overdue after the events of recent years, but marked another milestone in the alienation and estrangement between Saʿdah's tribal elites and the Salih government.

At the national level, too, the president faced increasing open resistance. In an al-Jazeera interview of 5 August 2009, Ḥamīd al-Aḥmar called on him to step down, criticizing his growing autocratic tendencies and his attempts to establish his son Ahmad as his successor. He castigated Salih's unsuccessful crisis management in Saʿdah and accused him of having 'lost Saʿdah, reversed the [1962] revolution, distorted [Yemeni] unity and become engaged to separate [Yemen] through killing citizens demanding their rights'.[377] Moreover al-Aḥmar accused the government of having caused the peace settlement of the Doha Agreements to fail, out of belief that the promised Qatari financial aid would not end up in its pockets.

Rather than receiving approval from the Houthis, al-Aḥmar got a sharp response. In a press release, ʿAbdulmalik al-Ḥūthī accused Ḥamīd al-Aḥmar of exploiting the crisis in Saʿdah for his personal benefit. He argued that Saʿdah was not outside the control of the state, as Ḥamīd had said, but rather resembled a barrack of the state's army. He also argued that the Ḥāshid mercenaries of the al-Aḥmar brothers had ravaged the province, and that the checkpoints and road blocks set up by Ḥamīd's brother Ḥusayn in southern ʿAmrān had imposed an embargo on Saʿdah that barred supplies from reaching the province and prevented the free movement of its people. ʿAbdulmalik further called al-Aḥmar a 'key partner and pillar of the corrupt government who got the lion's share in the looting of the national wealth'.[378] He failed, however, to mention that the Houthi blockades of the Sanaʿa-Saʿdah highway were also keeping essential goods from reaching the war-torn governorate.

By the beginning of August 2009, international relief organizations estimated the number of IDPs in Saʿdah at more than 100,000.[379] Saḥār and the western mountains along the Ṭāʾif Line had already become a huge contiguous war zone. The roads leading to Saʿdah city were under Houthi control. Bāqim district witnessed bloody battles between Houthis and some sections of the Jumāʿah supported by Salafis. In Marrān, the Houthis had trapped the 105th Brigade. After heavy battles, the rebels gained full control over Sāqayn district. In Shidāʾ district, Brigadier Thābit Muthannā Jawās faced stiff Houthi resistance in his attempt to restore government control. During the Shidāʾ battles, the Houthis blocked the Northern Ring Road between Ḥaraḍ and al-Malāḥīṭ; in turn, Central Security Forces (in coordination with the Saudi army) retreated to al-Khawbah (Jīzān) in Saudi territory in order to attack from the rear.[380] Thereupon, the Houthis threatened to expand the battleground proper into Saudi territory, because it was obvious that Riyadh was already participating in the war. Al-Jawf had also descended into conflict; in Sufyān, the Houthis continued to block the Sanaʿa-Saʿdah road and prevented the arrival of military reinforcements from the capital. When, on 11 August 2009, the Yemeni government announced Operation Scorched Earth, its last 'official' war against the Houthis, the northwest had been well and truly at war for months.

The Sixth War (11 August 2009–11 February 2010)

During the interim period the Houthis had worked constantly to extend and consolidate their control over Saʿdah, Sufyān district in ʿAmrān, and al-Jawf.

They set checkpoints on the roads, including the Sanaʿa-Saʿdah highway, and controlled access and security across almost all of Saʿdah. By August 2009, the rebels were stronger than ever. Given this situation, the government was not particularly eager to begin the sixth war, but found itself forced by hardliners such as ʿAlī Muḥsin, Interior Minister al-Miṣrī and Rashād al-ʿAlīmī to resume the war.[381] The constant drumbeat of violent clashes in these three provinces forced the reluctant government to resume the military campaign.

The sixth war began on 11 August 2009. Operation Scorched Earth (*ʿamaliyyat al-arḍ al-maḥrūqah*), as the government called its sixth campaign, became the longest and bloodiest round of fighting since the inception of the war in 2004. A 'scorched earth policy' is a military strategy used while advancing through or withdrawing from an area; it involves destroying anything (including civilian infrastructure) that might be useful to the enemy. This practice has been banned by the Geneva Conventions. Yet despite the regime's seeming default setting of 'overkill', in the first months of the sixth war the armed forces found it particularly hard to prevail against the Houthis. Although the government announced that it would end the war within two weeks and government-related media claimed 'important victories', the war dragged on and many of these 'victories' could not be confirmed. On the contrary, the military suffered humiliating defeats and was forced to evacuate areas of strategic importance and even military bases. With the pullback of the armed forces to Saʿdah city and fighting on its outskirts, the army seemed in the short term to concentrate on defending its most critical bases in Saʿdah city and Sufyān, along the Saʿdah-Sanaʿa highway. Rather than a swift and decisive Operation Scorched Earth, the sixth war resembled a ponderous, erratic process, constantly slowed down by ceasefire and foreign mediation initiatives, all of which embittered the government's tribal allies, whose fate ultimately depended on the military outcome of this war.

After five years of fighting, citizenry and tribes in the war zone had become increasingly polarized along government-Houthi lines. The random and arbitrary air strikes of Operation Scorched Earth were perceived as a strategy of 'retaliatory punishment against everyone' (*ʿiqāb intiqāmī ḍidd al-jamīʿ*). By inflicting collective punishment on civilians, while trying to pin the blame on the Houthis, the government was creating more grievances and further exacerbating its lack of credibility among Yemeni citizens and the international community. Moreover, many disagreements, feuds and antagonisms between tribal sections had long since become wrapped up in the larger conflict and had become proxy wars between government and Houthi forces. During the sixth war, the rebels managed to consolidate their control in Sufyān and parts of al-Jawf. After they had gained ground in al-Jawf, they began to look toward the Ma'rib region, where they set up 'bridgeheads' and colluded with certain tribal leaders. In this respect, the Houthis' strategic moves and secret dealings in the sixth war were already setting the stage for the seizure of Sanaʿa in 2014.

After its unfortunate and disruptive start, the army was forced to change strategy. One shift was the wider use of Special Forces and the Republican Guard. The government hoped that these forces would make a difference, because they were better trained and more professional than 'Alī Muḥsin's First Armoured Brigade (the *firqah*), which led the charge in Saʿdah. Some observers concluded that the *firqah* had withdrawn from the fighting; there was even wide speculation of collusion between the Houthis and 'Alī Muḥsin.[382] In fact, the deployment of these 'elite' forces was not very significant. In the sixth war, the Republican Guard was only dispatched to Saʿdah city and Sufyān (in the fifth war it had been active in Banī Ḥushaysh), and the *firqah* was really worn down. The truth of the situation was that the government's military campaign was on the brink of failure. Though it served many of Salih's interests for the war in Saʿdah to continue, by no means did he wish to end up its loser. Meanwhile, the rivalry between Salih and 'Alī Muḥsin kept smouldering: as spelled out in a diplomatic cable released by Wikileaks, a few days before the end of the sixth war the powers that be tried (unsuccessfully) to rid themselves of 'Alī Muḥsin by giving the Saudi Air Force coordinates of the base where the general was staying during the last round of fighting.[383]

Saudi Arabia's entry into the war in November 2009 marked the turning point in the government's muddled and hapless sixth campaign in Saʿdah. For the Yemeni government and the army, which had already lost control of vast areas, the Saudi air campaign against the Houthis was a huge relief. Indeed, for the Houthis, the two-front war turned out to be a heavy burden. After Saudi military intervention began, the first serious negotiations to find a political solution to the conflict opened between the government and the rebels. Yet the decision to stop the war was no longer in Salih's or the Houthis' hands: it was now in Riyadh. Hence, the big breakthrough only came when Saudi Arabia ceased its aerial bombing campaign in early 2010. The sixth and last 'official' Saʿdah war ended in February 2010 with a stalemate: contrary to official announcements, there was no written agreement and no document between the parties to the conflict to set a seal on the cessation of hostilities.

Central Saʿdah

After the government had announced Operation Scorched Earth in August 2009, the armed forces and their allies launched a major offensive. In the coming months, air, artillery, and missile attacks would target areas across the entire war zone: Al-Mahādhir, al-Khafjī, al-Ṭalḥ, Sūq al-ʿAnad, Banī Muʿādh, Ṣaʿdah city, Āl Sālim, Āl ʿAmmār, al-Maqāsh, Ḍaḥyān, Yusnam, Maṭrah and al-Naqʿah, Bāqim, Qaṭābir, Rāziḥ, Marrān, Ḥaydān, Sāqayn, al-Malāḥīṭ, Shidā', al-Ḥaṣāmah, Sufyān, al-Jawf, and Banī Ḥushaysh, to name a few.

During Ramadan, which began on 21 August, combat aircraft launched devastating airstrikes in the Saʿdah basin, especially in the densely populated areas of al-Ṭalḥ and al-Mahādhir, where at times up to thirty attacks were flown a day.[384] In a fit of indignation at these attacks on civilian targets during the holy month, ʿAlī Nāṣir Qirshah, member of the Presidential Mediation Committee, telephoned Salih and allegedly called him a war criminal. He was arrested and thrown in prison. Fāris Manāʿ and some other Saḥār shaykhs tried to calm things down and killed twenty calves according to tribal custom in order to obtain a presidential pardon for Qirshah.[385] Their efforts were in vain, and Qirshah remained in custody.

In Bāqim district, Houthi loyalists continued fighting against followers of Bandar Muqīt and Ḥusayn Ḥaydar. Both families paid a high price in deaths. By the end of August, Muqīt was on the defensive and was forced to flee northward to Saudi Arabia, as all escape routes to the south had been cut off by the Houthis' control of both the Saʿdah-Bāqim highway and the Northern Ring Road. The Houthis also displaced Bandar's father, Ḥasan Muqīt, the senior shaykh of the Khawlān b. ʿĀmir confederation, and his cousin Yaḥyā, both of whom played a particularly proactive role in rallying Yemeni and Saudi Khawlān b. ʿĀmir tribes against the movement.

In September, heavy fighting continued to shake Bāqim. Government loyalists among the tribe of Jumāʿah complained about the lack of military equipment and the resulting Houthi military superiority.[386] Despite the air strikes, the Houthis and their field commanders, ʿAbdullah Yaḥyā al-Ḥākim and ʿAbdulbāsiṭ al-Hādī, managed to consolidate control over the district. Saudi Arabia began to secure the border with barbed wire in order to prevent an influx of Houthi infiltrators (*mutasallilūn*) and displaced civilians fleeing the fighting.[387]

The Houthis continued to expand and to hold onto conquered territories. The army was suffering setbacks and losing ground, pulling back towards Saʿdah city. The city itself, albeit fiercely embattled, was one of few places that the armed forces managed to hold throughout the sixth war. The city was under a state of emergency as it was crowded with IDPs from the surrounding areas, who had fled from the shelling and clashes in their home areas. Schools became refugee collection centres, and prices hiked due to the closures of shops and businesses. Bombardment, missile strikes, gunmen, snipers, and a government-imposed curfew complicated civil life and hindered the work of the city's al-Jumhūrī Hospital. Throughout the sixth war, Saʿdah city remained under siege, with severe shortages of food, diesel, and other supplies; residents were trapped, unable to flee because of blocked roads and fighting in neighbouring regions. The UN called for the opening of safe corridors to deliver aid and to allow civilians trapped in the combat zones to escape the violence.[388]

By the end of August, the Houthis controlled much of the region surrounding Saʿdah city, while the army tried to hold the city itself and the Kahlān barracks, to its northeast. The Old Town (notably Ḥārat al-Tūt, Ḥārat al-Jirbah, Ḥārat al-Sifāl, Ḥārat al-Sūq near al-Hādī Mosque, and Bāb Najrān) was believed to be a major rebel stronghold and suffered frequent shelling from tanks and artillery. The Houthis tried several times to storm the Presidential Palace in Saʿdah city, especially after *ʿīd al-fiṭr* in September and *ʿīd al-aḍḥā* in November. The Palace had special symbolic meaning for both sides, since control of the building was tantamount to control of the whole city.

In November, the armed forces continued to launch direct attacks on the Old Town, where a group of Houthis had entrenched themselves in barricaded strongholds. In December, again, Central Security forces, in cooperation with Republican Guard and Counter Terrorism Unit (CTU) forces, launched a large-scale military operation in the Old Town called Operation Blow to the Head (*ʿamaliyyat ḍarbat al-raʾs*). The military closed the gates of the Old Town and combed through the city looking for Houthi 'sleeper cells' (*khalāyā nāʾimah*). After this operation, one CTU platoon remained in Saʿdah city, trying to help Central Security Forces to rid the governorate's capital of rebel fighters.[389] Intermittent clashes in Saʿdah city continued until the end of the sixth war in February 2010. Unlike nearby Ḍaḥyān, which firmly remained in the hands of the Houthis, the government forces succeeded in holding the provincial capital.

Dammāj district, too, saw battle. These battles, however, were not yet military confrontations between the Houthis and the students of the Salafi teaching centre Dār al-Ḥadīth, most of whom hailed from regions outside Saʿdah or from abroad: these confrontations only began after the end of the sixth war. During the Saʿdah wars, Yaḥyā al-Ḥajūrī had worked hard to keep the

Dār al-Ḥadīth out of the conflict—certainly no easy task, given the hostility between the Houthis and the Salafis. In typical Salafi fashion, he argued that there was a state in Yemen, and that fighting the Houthis was the responsibility of that state, not of the Ahl Dammāj, as the centre's students were called.[390] In the first five wars, skirmishes in Dammāj had been intermittent, but had never posed a serious challenge to the teaching activities at Dār al-Ḥadīth.[391] In the sixth war, however, battles in the district had a different cause: the Houthis' several attempts to seize Saʿdah city and the Kahlān barracks were conducted from the direction of Wādī Dammāj. During such strategic forays, the Wādiʿah Dammāj got in their way—the tribal section settled in the Dammāj area, part of which performed a protective function for the Dār al-Ḥadīth.

Sufyān[392]

The sixth war in ʿAmrān's Sufyān district was a sequel of the battles that had shaken the area during the fifth war and the ensuing interim period. The interference of the Popular Army and the Houthis in the long-standing tribal conflict between the Ṣubārah of Sufyān and the al-ʿUṣaymāt of Ḥāshid greatly aggravated the feud and transformed it into a main battleground of the sixth Saʿdah war. Simultaneously, in Ruhm, tribal irregulars under the command of Ṣaghīr b. ʿAzīz fought alongside the army for control of the Sanaʿa-Saʿdah highway. Both al-ʿUṣaymāt and Ṣaghīr ultimately lost their fights against the Houthis, whose numbers were on the rise as devastating collateral damage of state operations horrified many locals and drove them into the Houthis' arms. As a result, at the time of the ceasefire in February 2010, the Houthis were stronger than ever.

At the beginning of the sixth war in late August, Ḥusayn al-Aḥmar rallied the Popular Army in Qaflah ʿUdhar (Ḥāshid territory, close to the border of Sufyān) and directed it against the Ṣubārah. As we have seen, the Popular Army was an irregular mercenary force funded and armed by the Yemeni and Saudi governments, which mainly consisted of Ḥāshid tribesmen and radical Sunnis.[393] Now al-Aḥmar used this force to pursue the tribal territorial conflict over Wādī al-Suwād while claiming that it was fighting Houthi rebels. After the Popular Army's attack on the Ṣubārah, Zāyid al-Ṣubārī (a Ṣubārah shaykh from the contested area) issued a tribal summons (*dāʿī al-qabīlah*) for the whole of the Sufyān to support Ṣubārah in its struggle. Confronted with the overpowering strength of the Popular Army and its superior weapons (which came from the army's magazines), he also called in the Houthis, who had no hesitation over joining the Ṣubārah's ranks. Dozens were killed in these clashes.[394]

After the clashes in Ṣubārah, the shaykhs of Sufyān again complained of the government's preference for the Ḥāshid over the Sufyān and the Bakīl confederation more generally. Specifically, Mujāhid Ḥaydar accused al-Aḥmar and his allies of trying to pocket Saudi and Yemeni funds on the grounds that they were fighting Houthis in Sufyān, when in fact they were pursuing the al-ʿUṣaymāt's feud with the help of the Popular Army.[395] Another feature of this round of the conflict was an emerging sectarian dimension, which became obvious when radical Sunni Islamist mercenaries among the Popular Army threatened to punish the Zaydi Houthis with 'divine retribution'.[396] This extremely bloody conflict set off a series of deadly and destabilizing clashes that continued throughout the sixth war. In the end, the Ṣubārah, supported by the Houthis, succeeded with much bloodshed in forcing the withdrawal of al-ʿUṣaymāt warriors and the Popular Army to Qaflah ʿUdhar.

Interestingly, when Ḥusayn al-Aḥmar assembled the Popular Army and led it to war in Ṣubārah, his brother, the Iṣlāḥ MP Ḥamīd al-Aḥmar, tried to complicate matters by encouraging the Houthis and the Southern Movement to work together with the aim of further stretching the government's already strained military resources and throwing President Salih off balance. The US Embassy, informed by Ḥamīd al-Aḥmar personally of these plans, internally described his initiative as 'embarrassing' and saw in Ḥamīd an 'almost schizophrenic change in attitudes towards his would-be political allies from one meeting to the next'.[397] This political foray is another example of the maladroit policies and high-wire acts of the al-Aḥmar brothers, which ultimately would backfire and force them in 2014 into exile.

The Sanaʿa-Saʿdah highway, where it straddles Sufyān, remained an important battleground. In earlier wars the Houthis and the armed forces had already fought bitterly for control of this strategically important road. In the sixth war, too, securing the road was their key concern in the district. Al-Ḥarf and al-Ḥayrah in Dhū Ṣumaym saw heavy fighting, which became so fierce that the 119th Infantry Brigade, stationed at Jabal Aswad and commanded by Fayṣal Rajab, had to call in the Giants Forces and units of the Republican Guard for help.[398] On the ground, the army's regular troops were supported by tribal irregulars who had rallied around Ṣaghīr b. ʿAzīz. These were a ragtag force consisting of government loyalists from different Sufyān tribes and members of Ṣaghīr's own tribal section, the Dhū Ṣumaym.

Al-Ḥarf had already witnessed extreme battles during previous phases of the war, which left hardly any stone unturned. Now, in the battle for the highway, al-Ḥarf was literally flattened by aerial bombardment. Shortly after the outbreak of the sixth war, al-Ḥarf fell to the Houthis, who managed to seize military equipment left behind by the retreating army. A few days later, al-Ḥarf was recaptured by government forces. The army's cleansing operations killed hundreds. Locals found more than 100 bodies rotting on the sides of the roads including two of the then most important Houthi commanders in Sufyān, Muḥsin Hādī al-Qaʿūd and Ṣāliḥ Jarmān.[399]

A particularly tragic incident took place on 16 September, when eighty-seven IDPs were killed in an air raid near al-Ḥarf. At that time, as many as 52,500 people were displaced in Sufyān district alone. Relief organizations estimated that an additional 17,150 were still in al-Ḥarf, unable to flee due to the ongoing military campaign.[400] The air raid took place after displaced families, mostly women and children, had gathered beneath trees at a school in order to seek shelter from the glare of the midday sun. The eighty-seven victims of the airstrike were buried in mass graves dug by bulldozers. Local witnesses said the situation was 'horrendous'. To appease outrage about the attack, President Salih announced that a fact-finding committee led by Shaykh ʿAbduh Ḥubaysh, Sufyān's senior shaykh, would investigate the airstrike. Such measures, however, were insufficient to overcome the local population's progressive renunciation of the regime in Sanaʿa and the increasing drain of fighting forces towards the Houthis.

At the time of the February 2010 ceasefire, the Houthis still held the strategic high ground and controlled makeshift checkpoints in Sufyān along the embattled Sanaʿa-Saʿdah road. For several weeks, they were reluctant to open the Sufyān section of the highway. The ceasefire, however, could only temporarily contain the battles. A few months after the end of the sixth war, in July 2010, the Houthis managed to expel Ṣaghīr b. ʿAzīz, who had entrenched himself with supporters in his home compound in al-ʿAmashiyyah.[401] When Ṣaghīr and the last representatives of the local authorities were expelled from Sufyān, the Houthis were able to bring the entire district under their control, eradicating all signs of the state.

Al-Jawf

Since the fifth war, the Houthis had begun to push forcefully into al-Jawf province in order to relieve the pressure on their fellow combatants in neighbouring Saʿdah, and to expand their own room for manoeuvre. Because of the truculence and warlike traditions of the local tribes, the government considered al-Jawf a particularly risky and dangerous environment. For this reason, it was reluctant to deploy regular troops there, instead pressing ahead with the recruitment of local tribes as in the fifth war.

As everywhere else, however, to recruit the tribes of al-Jawf against the Houthis would require the consent and cooperation of al-Jawf's shaykhs. Rallying Ḥāshid tribesmen had been an easy task. However, as we have seen, it had proven difficult—if not impossible—to bring the Saʿdah shaykhs into line, though there were hardly any differences between them in substance (that is, their need to check the Houthis). In al-Jawf, Salih's search for tribal allies mutated into a confrontation with the Bakīl's infallible collective memory and implacable rancour towards a government that the confederation viewed as 'Ḥāshid-dominated'. When he tried to rally the shaykhs of al-Jawf, the most polite voices among the senior shaykhs were neutral, and called on both the government and the Houthis to lay down their arms.[402] The less softly-spoken voices judged the government very harshly. ʿArafaj b. Haḍabān of Dhū Ḥusayn, a powerful Bedouin shaykh from the margins of the Rubʿ al-Khālī and later president of the Bakīl Council for Peace and Reform (*majlis Bakīl li-l-silm wa l-iṣlāḥ*), was utterly opposed to the recruitment of Bakīl tribesmen as auxiliary forces in the ongoing war. He wryly argued that this was a matter for Ḥusayn al-Aḥmar, in other words for the Ḥāshid tribes, because 'he who enters into a military contract with the state has to implement it [by himself]. Bakīl will not work as sub-contractor'.[403] Amīn al-ʿUkaymī, who had recently positioned himself as a new partner of the government, also dismissed Salih's request: the ongoing battles between the Shawlān and the Houthis, that had erupted at the end of the fifth war were not yet led by him, but by minor Shawlān shaykhs.[404]

During the sixth war, the battles in al-Jawf focused on the governorate's western parts: the Baraṭ Plateau and the relatively affluent and densely populated districts of al-Zāhir, al-Maṭammah, al-Matūn, al-Ghayl, al-Khaliq and al-Ḥazm, which are inhabited by spatially interspersed enclaves of tribes and tribal sections whose centres of settlement are located in other parts of al-Jawf: the Dhū Muḥammad, Dhū Ḥusayn, Banī Nawf, Āl Ashrāf, and Hamdān al-Jawf. These regions saw the perpetuation of conflicts that had broken out during the previous rounds of war. The Houthi conflict aggravated prevalent rivalries and catapulted them into larger political (and later on sectarian) contexts, which meant increased magnitude, more manpower, more weapons, and more victims.

Al-Ghayl and al-Zāhir became the scene of fierce confrontations. The biggest conflict, however, had been raging ever since the fifth war in al-Maṭammah and al-Matūn. Here, the situation was quite complex. Many members of the Āl Abū Ḥusayn, a section of the Shawlān (Dhū Ḥusayn), were allies of the government. The Houthis were largely supported by another section of the Shawlān, the Āl Abū ʻUshāl, as well as many members of the Dhū Muḥammad and Āl Ashrāf. Those among the Shawlān who fought on the government's side were more or less close to Salafism; they were led by minor shaykhs who were themselves supervised by Khālid al-Sharīf.[405] Hence, in addition to elements of tribal infighting, this conflict also had a sectarian hue. The government, however, sent no ground forces to support its tribal allies in al-Jawf, but only granted aerial assistance.

In December 2009, the Shawlān suddenly found themselves stuck in a war on two fronts when a twenty-five-year-old border dispute re-emerged between the Āl Mahdī (another Shawlān section) and the Hamdān al-Jawf. The latter maintained good relations with Sanaʿa and had managed to manoeuvre many of their members into important security and military positions; thus artillery and heavy weapons were used in this sub-conflict. The Hamdān-Shawlān conflict alone displaced 600 families.[406] A shaykh of Hamdān al-Jawf explained: 'This is an old on-and-off war between the Āl Mahdī of Shawlān and the Hamdān al-Jawf which is rekindled from time to time for political reasons.'[407] The situation further grew in complexity when the Āl Ṣaqrah,[408] yet another section of the Shawlān, joined the Āl Abū Ḥusayn in their struggle against the Houthis.

One month earlier, in November, the Houthis had imposed a tight siege on al-Maṭammah and shelled Shawlān with captured tanks. The air force bombed Houthi positions in al-Zāhir and al-Maṭammah, inflicting heavy losses. Despite their critical situation, the Shawlān still did not receive any regime support on the ground.[409] A few days before the end of the sixth war, the Shawlān conflict was successfully contained by tribal mediation through Ṣāliḥ Darmān, a 'neutral' Shawlān shaykh, and Mujāhid Ḥaydar of the Sufyān. Numerous guarantors (*ḍumanāʾ*) from among the tribes of al-Jawf and surrounding areas were involved in this mediation, following which the Houthis lifted the siege and cleared checkpoints in Baraṭ, al-Maṭammah and al-Ḥazm. However, this ceasefire would not last.

Beyond al-Jawf's densely populated western fringes and some large *wādīs*—such as the Wādī Jawf and the Wādī Khabb—towards the Rubʿ al-Khālī the province's landscape takes on full desert character. Since the fifth war, the Houthis had been pressing deeper into the desert and pushing east into the Banī Nawf's vast territory in southern Khabb wa l-Shaʿf. How might one demonstrate one's presence, let alone dominance, in a sparsely inhabited lunar landscape of shifting sand dunes and dust-dry saline lakes? For example, by setting up checkpoints—here called 'hegemony points' (*niqāt al-haymanah*)—on roads and smuggling paths running through the area. Hence, everywhere in al-Jawf makeshift checkpoints began to pop up, manned and maintained by tribesmen allied with the regime or the rebels. A Dhū Muḥammad shaykh explained that in 2009 no fewer than twelve checkpoints surfaced along the road linking al-Jawf with Sufyān. According to him, the rivalry deteriorated to the point that he was not sure whether to address the men manning the points with the salutation *ahlan wa sahlan* for government loyalists or *Allahu akbar* for Houthis.[410] Numerous battles for the erection or removal of such checkpoints took place. The so-called 'intersection points' (*niqāṭ al-taqaṭṭuʿ*), which aimed at blocking roads including the trade and smuggling routes to Saudi Arabia, became quite a bothersome issue for the local tribes: one Houthi intersection point on the road to the al-Buqʿ border crossing was forcibly removed by Dhū Ḥusayn tribesmen.[411]

Al-Jawf's strategic importance, however, is due to the fact that this large governorate—precisely because of its vast desert spaces—is, more than any other area in Yemen, predestined as a transit corridor for swift movement to and from Saʿdah, ʿAmrān, Sanaʿa, Maʾrib, Ḥaḍramawt, and Saudi Arabia's Najrān and Eastern Province. In the sixth war, the Houthis managed to expand their influence via al-Jawf into Maʾrib governorate, and set up clandestine bridgeheads in Majzar, Raghwān, and Ṣirwāḥ districts. One of their strategic targets was Naqīl al-Farḍah, a mountain pass on the Sanaʿa-Maʾrib highway near the road junction to al-Ḥazm in al-Jawf. Blocking the highway would have been tantamount to cutting off oil and gas supplies to Sanaʿa. This would allow the rebels to gain a grip on the capital after the 'checkpoint strategy' in al-Jawf essentially failed to have any effect on the capital or the central parts of Yemen.

Maʾrib, however, continued to remain difficult terrain for the Houthis. The majority of the men and shaykhs of its pre-eminent Sunni Madhḥij tribe had no affinity with the rebels. Nevertheless, ʿAbdulmalik al-Ḥūthī received a number of shaykhs and dignitaries from Maʾrib, who travelled through al-Jawf to Saʿdah, and who were either Zaydis or otherwise aggrieved by the Salih regime. These meetings revealed that some of the tribes surrounding Sanaʿa were so fed up with the regime that they would not think twice about supporting the Houthis if invited to do so.[412]

In al-Jawf, the Houthis continued to expand further east and managed to push deep into the vast territory of the Banī Nawf in southern Khabb wa l-Shaʿf area. This area became the easternmost point of the Houthis' sphere of influence. Here, the rebels were increasingly confronted by tribes allied with AQAP, as al-Qaeda operatives from al-Baydāʾ, Shabwah, Abyan, and other governorates were drawn to Maʾrib and eastern al-Jawf by the prospect of fighting Houthis whom they considered 'infidel Shia'.[413] Moreover, Houthi operational expansion southeast appears to have hurt AQAP operations: the nascent Houthi presence in eastern al-Jawf and northwest Maʾrib may have posed serious logistical problems for AQAP, which depended on reliable passage into Saudi Arabia across Yemen's northern border. The front between the Houthis and AQAP, however, was only opened after the end of the sixth war, when in December 2010 dual suicide bombings targeted Houthi religious processions in al-Jawf and Saʿdah. Both attacks were claimed by AQAP under the banner 'Operations in Defence of Ahl al-Sunnah'.[414]

Munabbih[415]

In Saʿdah's Munabbih district, at the northwestern fringe of the conflict zone, the events of the sixth war took a particularly tragic turn. Since the fourth war, Munabbih had been wedged between battles in Ghamr to its south and Qaṭābir to its northeast. The Munabbih tribe responded by closing its borders and roads, which connected its territory with the outside world. In accordance with the Munabbih's custom of delegated war leadership, throughout the Saʿdah wars the senior shaykh, Salmān ʿAwfān, sought to maintain a neutral position elevated from the bloody events taking place around him.[416] From the fourth war onwards, the tribe's war leaders, Shaykhs ʿAlī Ḥusayn al-Munabbihī and Aḥmad Dahbāsh Miṭrī, fought alongside the government in Ghamr and Qaṭābir, districts that had already turned into veritable flashpoints of the Saʿdah wars. Miṭrī had been fiercely opposed to the conclusion of the First Doha Agreement; like many other shaykhs, he suspected that ceasefires would only give the Houthis breathing room, allowing them to regroup. In June 2007, shortly after the First Doha Agreement, he had been killed in Qaṭābir by a mine.[417]

Despite the large-scale Operation Scorched Earth, in September 2009 the Houthis were able to seize the central parts of Munabbih. Under the leadership of their ruthless military mastermind ʿAbdullah al-Ḥākim, they besieged the large administrative building in Sūq al-Khamīs, the district's capital and administrative centre, located on the mountain of Jabal Mislān. The Munabbih defended themselves together with units of the Central Security

Forces. Observers report that, during the siege of Sūq al-Khamīs, the Houthis were shouting their slogan from their positions, while the Munabbih responded with the Yemeni Republic's national anthem 'Echo, O world, my anthem' (*raddadī ayyatuhā al-dunyā nashīdī*) and other patriotic songs such as 'O skies of my country' (*yā samāwāt bilādī*) and 'I am the people, a strong earthquake' (*ana al-shaʿb zalzalah ʿātiyah*), amplified by loudspeakers.[418]

During the siege of Sūq al-Khamīs, war leader ʿAlī Ḥusayn al-Munabbihī passed away in a hospital in Sanaʿa. The Houthis' seizure of Sūq al-Khamīs and the occupation of the government's administration building coincided with the spreading news of the shaykh's death. His eldest son and successor, Ḥusayn ʿAlī al-Munabbihī, recalled in an interview:

> The Houthis did not seize Munabbih by strength but rather by stealth. As long as my father was alive, the Houthis could not advance into the centre of Munabbih, whatever their military equipment. But they took advantage of it when they saw that we were busy with the death of my father, the shaykh. When the Banī Munabbih learnt of his death, they left the barricades in Sūq al-Khamīs and the surrounding mountains and went to their villages to mourn the shaykh. And then the Houthis, when they saw that the barricades and the mountains lay deserted, said to themselves: This is an opportunity to seize Munabbih that isn't going to happen again.
>
> *Question: But how is it possible that your fighters left the barricades, though you had to know the consequences? You knew that the Houthis were making every effort to conquer Munabbih.*
>
> [...] We believed, however great the wickedness of the Houthis, that tribalness and humaneness would set a limit on the war. But when the Houthis saw the Munabbih descending from the mountains and everyone being busy with the condolences, they seized the opportunity to attack Munabbih's centre.[419]

On 7 October, the Houthis announced total control (*sayṭarah tāmmah*) over Munabbih. Disastrous scenes occurred during their conquest of Sūq al-Khamīs. Residents of the area reported confrontations of hitherto unknown violence that left dozens dead and hundreds displaced. In the presence of his family, the Houthis killed the ninety-five-year-old father of the recently deceased ʿAlī Ḥusayn al-Munabbihī at his home near Sūq al-Khamīs. They sacked the large administrative building, looted it and blew up this symbol of state prestige (*ramz wahībat al-dawlah*) in a huge explosion.

The Munabbih tribe's reaction to the news of their shaykh's death—leaving the war scene in order to mourn him—suggests that this type of war was new to them. Normally, Munabbih's conflicts concerned matters such as the defence of the territory (*arḍ*) and honour (*sharaf*) of tribal subgroups or the whole tribe. The parties to the conflict were linked by tribal affiliation and the canon of common tribal values: *qabyalah*.[420] They strived to channel conflicts into litigation, or, if that failed, to limit their violence and destructiveness through the system of delegated war leadership. Often, truces were negotiated for high religious holidays and other important occasions, such as the death of an honoured person. In the sixth Saʿdah war, however, the Munabbih were drawn into a kind of confrontation in which the enemy was no equal and familiar opponent with whom they could resolve their affairs of honour in accordance with fixed tribal rules and customs. Wrapped up in and exacerbated by the larger conflict between the Houthis and the government, this conflict was no affair of honour at all, but of a scale well beyond what Jamous defined as a maximum escalation form of tribal conflicts.[421]

To be able to attend the shaykh's funeral in Sanaʿa, his sons had to withdraw to Saudi territory because of the Houthis' control of large parts of the Northern Ring Road, the only road connection to the more central parts of Yemen. When they crossed the border, they were received by the Border Guards of the Fayfāʾ, another member tribe of the Khawlān b. ʿĀmir confederation, who escorted them to the al-Ṭuwāl border crossing in the Tihāmah, whence they managed to travel via Ḥaraḍ and Ḥajjah to the Yemeni capital. After an act of state in the Jāmiʿ al-Ṣāliḥ (the giant, newly constructed President Salih Mosque), which was attended by the president himself, ʿAlī Ḥusayn al-Munabbihī was carried to his grave in the Martyrs' Cemetery.

Since the Houthi seizure of Sūq al-Khamīs, the al-Munabbihī shaykhly lineage has remained displaced from Munabbih. The conquest precipitated clashes in other areas of Munabbih. In November 2010, nine months after the end of the sixth war, the Houthis also expelled Yūsif Miṭrī, successor of the late Aḥmad Dahbāsh Miṭrī, from Banī Khawlī, in the lower-lying areas of Munabbih.

Saudi Arabia Enters the War

In the fifth war, the Marrān region had seen the hermetic siege of the 17th Infantry Brigade, which was ultimately resolved through mediation by Fāris Manāʿ. In the sixth war, the Houthis again besieged a military brigade in Marrān—the 105th Infantry Brigade—and again Manāʿ was the only one able to broker a deal to bail out the armed forces. After his mediation, the rebels allowed the 105th Brigade to withdraw from Marrān, but the soldiers were only permitted to take their lightweight 'personal' arms with them: the heavy equipment had to remain in the base. Thus, the huge arms cache of the 105th

Brigade—tanks, anti-aircraft guns, heavy artillery and machine guns plus ammunition, equipment and supplies—fell to the Houthis.[422] Although the military leadership denied the loss of the Marrān camp, a few days later Brigadier Muḥammad Ṣāliḥ ʿĀmir was arrested in ʿAbs barracks near Ḥaraḍ on grounds of having let the camp fall into the Houthis hands.[423]

In neighbouring al-Ẓāhir district, the fighting moved steadily towards the Saudi frontier, which is in the immediate vicinity of the district capital, al-Malāḥīṭ. Al-Khawbah in the Saudi province of Jīzān is only a few kilometres away; both al-Malāḥīṭ and al-Khawbah are connected through the Wādī Khulab. A few kilometres south begins the area in which Jabal al-Dawd, Jabal al-Rumayḥ and Jabal Dukhān are found. Jabal al-Dawd and Jabal al-Rumayḥ are situated on Saudi territory. Jabal Dukhān is dissected by the international border. South of Jabal Dukhān runs Wādī Liyah, which drains into the Saudi Tihāmah.

In the area of al-Malāḥīṭ and al-Khawbah, the international frontier is particularly permeable and vulnerable. Al-Malāḥīṭ's daily market is a major transit point for contraband between Yemen and Saudi Arabia. Qāt, cattle, and agricultural products were smuggled from al-Malāḥīṭ into the Jīzān region. In the opposite direction, consumer goods, medicines, wheat, flour, dates, electronic equipment and so on were smuggled from Saudi Arabia into Yemen. Since 2008, the illegal import of gasoline and flour from Jīzān to Yemen had been a particularly profitable business; these goods reached record prices because of Houthi roadblocks and the embargo imposed by the Yemeni and Saudi governments, all of which isolated the Saʿdah region from the outside world.

In autumn 2009, a confluence of factors exposed the vulnerable border in this area to an extreme stress test. Countless refugees were fleeing from al-Malāḥīṭ's battle zones to Saudi Arabia, where they were arrested by Saudi Border Guards who then sent them back into Yemen via the al-Ṭuwāl border crossing near Ḥaraḍ. Because of Ramadan, thousands of (legal and illegal) Yemeni workers were also trying to return from Saudi Arabia to their home areas in order to spend the holy month and the upcoming Islamic feast with their families. Trans-border smuggling increased due to the high demand of *qāt*, cattle, consumer goods and so on for the upcoming feast. Moreover, border crossings of Houthi 'infiltrators' (*mutasallilūn*) into Saudi territory seem to have occurred more frequently. This uncontrolled cross-border movement of not simply goods but large numbers of people—smugglers, refugees, returning legal and illegal workers, Houthi fighters—confronted the Saudi security forces with a serious challenge.

One week after the start of Operation Scorched Earth in August, the Houthis had seized al-Malāḥīṭ and all military sites in the area. After Bāqim, Rāziḥ, Ghamr and Munabbih districts, in al-Malāḥīṭ, too, the war had entered into the 5-kilometre demilitarized corridor along the border in which, according to Article 4 of the Treaty of Jeddah, only lightly armed police patrols were permitted and the erection of military sites was prohibited.[424] Thus, almost the entire border region along the Ṭā'if Line, from Shidā' in the south to Jabal al-Tha'r in the east, was affected by war.

Saudi Arabia's extreme vulnerability to events and developments in Yemen and the risk of a spillover of violence and instability had already become obvious in the 1960s. Then, Saudi Arabia had initially considered the Yemeni civil war a 'domestic affair'. The situation changed dramatically in the aftermath of the November 1962 Egyptian air raids on Saudi border towns in Najrān, ʿAsīr and Jīzān, which prompted the Kingdom to enter the war in Yemen.[425] Likewise, in late autumn 2009, the continual provocations at the border eventually drew Saudi Arabia into Yemen's Houthi conflict.

The Yemeni army, which had lost control of the important military base at al-Malāḥīṭ, launched numerous attempts to recapture it. As previously in Bāqim, Rāziḥ and Ghamr, Saudi Arabia allowed the Yemeni military to transit through Saudi territory in order to flank Houthi positions and attack from the rear. In late August, there had been increasing indications that some of the warplanes bombing al-Malāḥīṭ had taken off from an air base in the Saudi part of Jabal Dukhān area, and had returned to Saudi Arabia after the assaults.[426] The existence of a 'joint operations room' of the Yemeni and Saudi armies, however, was denied by the respective governments.[427]

After the security situation along the border continued to deteriorate, on 1 November the Saudis officially opened their territory to the Yemeni army.[428] The Houthis responded by slipping systematically into Saudi territory in Jabal Dukhān and forcing Saudi Border Guards to combat. At this point, Saudi Arabia entered the war and began bombing targets inside Yemeni territory. The Saudi air campaign was not just a matter of targeted airstrikes to take pressure off the common border and to establish a buffer zone along it. Rather, the Saudi air war led to two months of heavy shelling of Houthi positions throughout the conflict zone. Massive air raids were flown well beyond Jabal Dukhān and al-Malāḥīṭ and targeted Sāqayn, Marrān, Ḥaydān, Shidā', Munabbih, Bāqim, Majz, Saḥār, Saʿdah city, Maṭrah and al-Naqʿah. Rāziḥ was repeatedly bombed during the sixth war: on 13 December a single Saudi airstrike took as many as seventy lives and wounded up to 100 others.[429] At the same time, Saudi Arabia focused on imposing a naval blockade on northern Yemen. The Royal Saudi Naval Forces bolstered their presence in the Red Sea in order to prevent arms shipments to the Houthis via the port of Mīdī.[430]

The Saudi aerial campaign seemed to be pre-planned, not reactionary. Its unusual swiftness suggests that Saudi forces had been prepared to respond, needing only a pretext—such as the attack on a Saudi border post—for action. On the ground, however, the advance of Houthi infiltrators into Saudi territory turned out to become a real dilemma for Saudi ground forces. The Border Guard was lacking manpower; officers had to be called back from retirement. The Saudi border areas along the Ṭā'if Line are tinged with Zaydism, and some Shia-dominated units of the Border Guard seem to have refused to fight the Houthis.[431] In the largest deployment of Saudi land forces since the First Gulf War, ground forces were transferred to al-Khawbah from other parts of the country (notably the Tabūk military base in northern Saudi Arabia, the Najrān base, and the al-Sharūrah base in the Rubʿ al-Khālī).[432]

The Houthi infiltrators proved more difficult to dislodge from Saudi territories than expected. Residents of al-Khawbah and 400 other Saudi settlements along the border (15,000 persons in total) were forcibly evacuated by Saudi security forces. Houses and entire villages along the border were flattened by bulldozers in order to prevent the Houthis from entrenching themselves.[433] Despite the massive air raids, and due to the weakness of the Saudi ground forces and the mountainous terrain, which was unsuitable for the use of heavy weapons, on 12 November the Houthis seized al-Khawbah city, Jabal Dawd and parts of Jabal Dukhān and Banī Mālik further to the north, which they managed to hold for about a month.[434]

Riyadh sought assistance from its Arab allies. In late November, Jordan sent several hundred troops from its special operations forces to help the Saudi military contain the Houthis. Sources said the Jordanian king was acting on an urgent request from his Saudi counterpart for elite soldiers who were able to hunt down the rebels in both Saudi Arabia and northern Yemen. The *World Tribune* commented: 'The Saudis are in a panic mode and don't have the troops or capabilities to stop the Yemeni Shi'ites'.[435]

In a diplomatic cable, the US Embassy in Sanaʿa disclosed that President Salih was thrilled that the Saudis had become militarily involved in the conflict. For the beleaguered Yemeni army, which had already lost vast areas in Saʿdah to the ever stronger Houthis, Saudi involvement was a positive development, as it believed that this would bring the war to a swifter conclusion. Salih's enthusiasm was evident in his 7 November speech at a ceremony launching the first shipment of Yemen's Liquefied Natural Gas (LNG) project.

He said the 'real war' against the Houthis had only begun with the Saudis' entry into the war, describing the previous rounds of the conflict as 'a rehearsal to test our capabilities'.[436]

At the same time, the participation of Saudi Arabia spurred on the Iranians, and sparked a vociferous exchange of accusations and counter-accusations of foreign interference in the conflict in Yemeni, Saudi, and Iranian media. The Saudi military intervention in Shia-dominated northern Yemen prompted Iran to give the conflict unprecedented media coverage. Yemeni government-linked media accused Iran of directly supporting the Houthis. Saudi outlets largely echoed the Yemeni regime's talking points on Saʿdah, implying Iranian involvement. Though there remained no hard evidence of direct Iranian involvement in Saʿdah, the war of words in the press shows how the Houthi conflict had become a rhetorical proxy war between the two antagonistic regional powers, Saudi Arabia and Iran.

Jabal Dukhān and al-Khawbah remained the focal point of many clashes between Saudi and Houthi forces throughout much of November. Both sides repeatedly claimed to have either captured or recaptured the mountains. The Houthis continued to slip into Saudi territory, where they dug a series of camouflaged bunkers and caves that Saudi forces in turn methodically searched and destroyed. By the end of November, the Saudi army, backed by Jordanian Special Forces, had slowly managed to re-establish control over its borderlands.

December By-Elections

While the war raged on, on 3 December 2009, supplementary elections (*intikhābāt takmīliyyah*) were held in Yemen in order to fill twelve vacant parliamentary seats, three of them in Saʿdah. The government's decision to hold elections in only twelve constituencies, rather than holding the full parliamentary elections postponed in February, came as a surprise for the opposition JMP, which called for a boycott. This was reflected in a low turnout of just 10 per cent.[437]

The by-elections were of the utmost importance for the government. Due to the dual crisis in Saʿdah and in southern Yemen, the government feared for its majority in Parliament. However, a majority was indispensable for the unpopular constitutional amendments envisaged by Salih, including a further extension of his term. According to Article 158 of the Yemeni Constitution, constitutional articles can only be amended if the call for an amendment is supported by at least three quarters of MPs. Yet due to the blockade politics between the GPC and the JMP, domestic politics had come to a stalemate.

The government was bent on pushing the controversial constitutional reform through Parliament, if necessary single-handedly, by filling the vacant parliamentary seats with GPC loyalists.

The December by-elections became a symbol of both arbitrary government and the evolving 'inheritance principle' (*mabdaʾ al-tawrīth*) in Yemeni politics, especially in the Saʿdah region, where since the beginning of the multiparty system in 1990 the influential shaykhs had tended to distribute political posts amongst themselves and to pass them down to their sons. This inheritance principle was never as evident as in the 2009 supplementary elections. One observer recalled:

> During the supplementary elections we could observe an extension of the inheritance principle, which became the norm among the political forces and the parliamentarians of the GPC. It was clear that most candidates would inherit membership of Parliament from their fathers, whereas others received support from influential figures within the ruling party. Inheritance, kinship and patronage were the GPC's admission tickets to Parliament. We faced a system of quasi-feudal dominance (*niẓām iqṭāʿī sulṭawī*) based on control of the state apparatus.[438]

In these elections, the inheritance principle manifested itself in Taʿiz, Aden, Ḥaḍramawt, Raymah and al-Ḥudaydah.[439] In ʿAmrān's Banī Ṣuraym/Khamir constituency, for example, Hāshim al-Aḥmar 'inherited' the seat of his deceased father ʿAbdullah. Henceforth, the sons of ʿAbdullah al-Aḥmar held sway in a total of five constituencies in ʿAmrān: Hāshim in Banī Ṣuraym, Ḥamīd in Ḥabūr, Ḥusayn in Ḥūth, Ḥimyar in Qaflah ʿUdhar, and Madhḥij in al-Madān.

In Saʿdah governorate, three parliamentary seats were vacant: Yaḥyā al-Ḥūthī, MP for Sāqayn, had been in exile in Germany since 2004; the death of Shaykh ʿAlī Ḥusayn al-Munabbihī in the summer of 2009 had left the parliamentary seat for Munabbih/Qaṭābir vacant; and the murder of Shaykh Ṣāliḥ b. Ṣāliḥ Hindī Dughsān in April 2008 had likewise left the seat for al-Ṣafrāʾ/al-Ḥishwah empty.

Nationwide, the by-elections were accompanied by irregularities: phantom voters, voter buying, missing ballots, even armed clashes in al-Ḍāliʿ. Yet nowhere did the elections take such arbitrary forms as in Saʿdah. In Sāqayn, Yaḥyā al-Ḥūthī's constituency, the elections were cancelled by the Supreme Commission of Election and Referendum, officially for security reasons. Yet in truth victory for a GPC candidate in Sāqayn—the nucleus of the Houthi movement—would have been more than unlikely.

In Munabbih, the Supreme Commission of Election and Referendum postponed the elections, also for 'security reasons', despite the fact that at that time the situation in Munabbih was similar to that in al-Ṣafrāʾ/al-Ḥishwah, where the election went ahead.[440] There was likely another reason for the postponement: in this district, the parliamentary seat of the deceased Shaykh ʿAlī Ḥusayn al-Munabbihī was to be 'inherited' by his eldest son and tribal successor Ḥusayn ʿAlī al-Munabbihī. The latter, however, had agitated during the gubernatorial elections for 'Umar Mujallī and against Ḥasan Manāʿ, who won. Governor Manāʿ now exacted his revenge by thwarting the parliamentary election of Ḥusayn ʿAlī al-Munabbihī.[441] To the great displeasure of President Salih, this manoeuvre also obstructed the election of an ultra-loyal GPC MP.

In al-Ṣafrāʾ/al-Ḥishwah constituency, the election took place amidst a tense security situation: during the gubernatorial elections the Dughsān clan, in historic blood feud with the Mujallī clan, had stood firmly by the side of the Manāʿ clan.[442] Oddly enough, after the assassination of Ṣāliḥ b. Ṣāliḥ Hindī Dughsān MP, two of his sons competed for the parliamentary seat: ʿUmar Ṣāliḥ Hindī Dughsān (GPC) and Shihāb Ṣāliḥ Hindī Dughsān (independent). Apart from this blatant case of inheritance, there was a veritable scandal when Governor Manāʿ quietly advanced the elections to 2 December, instead of holding them on 3 December as officially scheduled. He also moved the polling station from al-Ṣafrāʾ district to a hotel in Saʿdah city. When voters appeared on the morning of 3 December at al-Ṣafrāʾ, the election had already taken place. This was in contravention of electoral law and clearly confused voters, an attempt to legitimize the elections and make it look as if they had taken place fairly, although ʿUmar Dughsān had no rival except his own brother, Shihāb. It is unknown how many votes were cast on 2 December. ʿUmar Ṣāliḥ Hindī Dughsān emerged victorious.[443]

The supplementary elections in Saʿdah revealed a grotesque set-up that lacked legal legitimacy. The members of the local sub-committee of the Supreme Commission of Election and Referendum condemned the governor's practices, calling them 'a scandalous trickery violating the electoral law'.[444]

The Manāʿ Case

Turbulent times were ahead for the Manāʿ clan. At the time of the December by-elections, the Manāʿ brothers Ḥasan and Fāris were already in the vortex of another, much greater political affair. Governor Ḥasan Manāʿ's brother Fāris, we recall, was a relative of the shaykh of al-Ṭalḥ, Fayṣal Manāʿ.[445] He was one of the region's biggest arms dealers and by far the most popular member of his family. After the 1994 civil war he rose to become an important partner of the government. He became director general of procurement for the Presidency of the Republic of Yemen and played intermediary roles in government weapons deals.[446]

His relationship with Salih had already been soured in 2007, not solely but at least partly because of his alleged involvement in the Gaddafi issue—there is no hard evidence of Fāris' connection to this episode, which he flatly denies. Nevertheless, his association with Libya—whether perceived or real—was a thorn in the sides of the government, the Saudis and some rival shaykhs.[447] As a result, the regime in Sanaʿa ended its business cooperation with Fāris and began to purchase its weapons either directly or through alternative intermediaries.

After he fell out of favour with the president, Fāris remained a skilled, successful and immensely influential tribal mediator, with the necessary *haybah* (prestige) and *wazn* (weight) among Saʿdah's tribesmen. He was an insider mediator, a type of mediator generally known as the 'insider-partial' as opposed to the 'outsider-neutral'. The insider mediators' greatest strength is that they are more flexible than official mediators. They have more room for manoeuvre, being free from the long command chain and mandate-driven mindsets of states and inter-governmental organizations. Fāris Manāʿ's importance for conflict management in the Saʿdah region grew even greater after the sacking of Governor Yaḥyā al-Shāmī in 2007 and the failure of the Doha Agreements in 2007–8. During the fifth war, Fāris had successfully brokered a ceasefire enabling the 17th Brigade's safe withdrawal from Marrān, after which he had been criticized by the government because this deal eventually enabled the Houthis to extend their control over the whole of Marrān.[448] Nevertheless, after this success and because of his outstanding mediation skills, Fāris Manāʿ was appointed chair of the Presidential Mediation Committee. Yet the government still suspected him of colluding with the Houthis.

In November 2008, after verbal altercations with military leaders and certain Saʿdah shaykhs—notably from the Mujallī/al-ʿAwjarī axis—Fāris lost the chairmanship of the Committee to Saʿdah's director of Political Security, Brigadier General Yaḥyā al-Marrānī. The trope was a familiar one: in a cycle repeated throughout the conflict, any mediator who was too successful or perceived as 'too close' to the Houthis was quickly discredited and pushed out of negotiations (the same had happened to al-Shāmī and former minister of local administration ʿAbdulqādir Hilāl). The government, however, could not do without Fāris; he continued—now unofficially—to mediate in the crisis zone, where he tirelessly intervened to bail out the armed forces and their local allies.

Fāris Manāʿ's second mediation in Marrān, in the sixth war, was a case of déjà vu. Thanks to him, the 105th Brigade was able to escape the Houthi siege and to withdraw unharmed from Marrān. According to the terms of the deal he brokered, all regime soldiers were released along with their personal weapons, but the rebels kept the brigade's tanks, artillery, anti-aircraft guns, and other heavy weaponry. The consequences of this deal soon became clear. A Yemeni Air Force MiG fighter jet crashed on 30 September and a Sukhoi fighter jet crashed on 5 October.[449] It is unclear whether the planes were downed with the 105th Brigade's guns, other battlefield captures or black market purchases. Nevertheless, President Salih was reportedly very angry at the negotiation of a deal that allowed the Houthis to obtain heavy weaponry.[450]

The government started to put Fāris under close surveillance. On 4 October, the Yemeni government seized a large shipment of Chinese-origin weapons and ammunition in al-Ḥudaydah port, allegedly destined for Fāris, who would hand it over to the Houthis. Yemeni media reported that traffickers had attempted to use forged official documents to smuggle the shipment into the country.[451] Two days later on 6 October, the government announced that seven Yemeni arms dealers had been 'blacklisted', including Fāris Manāʿ and his partners, Jarmān Muḥammad Jarmān and Aḥmad ʿAwaḍ Abū Maksah from al-Ṭalḥ.[452] The timing—immediately after the 5 October Sukhoi crash and just days after the seizure of the arms shipment in Ḥudaydah—suggests that either incident, or both, could have prompted Salih to issue the blacklist. He may also have been responding to recent pressure from the US government to take action against arms traffickers.[453] Regardless, the blacklist appeared to be a warning to important arms dealers who had fallen out of favour with the government for apparently supplying both sides in the war.

Tensions intensified on 25 October, when the Yemeni Navy and Coast Guard seized an Iranian vessel named *Mahan 1* in Yemeni waters west of Mīdī seaport.[454] According to Yemeni authorities, five Iranians were among the crew. Yemeni prosecutors issued a writ confiscating the ship and weapons found on board. The First Instance Court in Sanaʿa convicted the crew of smuggling arms from Iran into Yemen. According to the authorities, the ship was heading to a location near Ḥaraḍ in order to offload the weapons for delivery to the Houthis. The reality of the situation remained unclear, but if this account were true, it would have marked the second arms shipment blocked by the Yemeni government in October. It also remained unclear if this incident was in any way related to the blacklist of Saʿdah arms traffickers, or, for that matter, to the Houthis at all.[455] In its internal correspondence, the US embassy dismissed allegations that the Houthis were receiving weapons and other aid from Iran, considering this incident the Yemeni regime's 'latest disingenuous attempt to garner Western and Sunni Arab support by casting the Houthis as terrorists, religious extremists, and allied with a hostile power'.[456]

In December, the Houthis robbed and plundered Fāris Manāʿ's main arms stockpile in Sūq al-Ṭalḥ. Local sources reported that the rebels then transported the weapons in twenty trucks, and that Fāris only reported the incident two days later.[457] In an interview with the pro-GPC *al-Mīthāq*, his rival Fāyiz al-ʿAwjarī accused him of complicity with the Houthis, on the grounds that 'the robbery of arms magazines cannot have happened unless there was an agreement between the merchant and the Houthis, and the merchant was informed one week before that the Houthis planned or intended to seize his weapons stores, but the merchant did not do anything and this shows that the merchant who imported the arms may have agreed with the Houthis on the theft of the arms'.[458] The government reacted by shelling Fāris' properties in Sūq al-Ṭalḥ.[459]

On 28 January 2010, shortly before the unilateral ceasefire that ended the sixth war, National Security (*amn qawmī*) arrested Fāris in Sanaʿa and threw him in jail. In an attempt to defend his brother, Ḥasan Manāʿ, then governor of Saʿdah, risked his neck with his reckless discourse. In an interview with Arabic international newspaper *al-Sharq al-Awsat*, he denied his brother's involvement in illegal practices, unlawful commercial transactions or forgery of documents used in the 4 October Chinese weapons shipment. He added:

> Arms trading isn't potato trading, and the talk of forgery of official documents cannot be true because embassies and officials of both countries were involved in the deal. These deals are not that informal. When you carry a document case, you're carrying more than a carton of biscuits.[460]

This interview angered the government to such an extent that on 6 February Ḥasan was replaced as governor by Ṭaha Hājir.[461] Hājir was a management expert and GPC veteran and had previously been governor of both Ḥaḍramawt and ʿAmrān. This change, made by presidential decree (*qarār jumhūrī*), came as the government and the Houthis were heading for the ceasefire to end the sixth war. The appointment of Hājir, however, was a violation of the Local Authority Law, which, as we know, had been amended in 2008 and now provided for indirect election of governors through the Local Councils.[462] In spite of his personal and professional qualifications, therefore, Ṭaha Hājir was not considered a legitimate governor.

On the morning of 20 February, acting according to tribal custom, shaykhs and *aʿyān* (tribal notables) from Saʿdah brought a number of camels and bulls to the Presidential Palace in Sanaʿa, to solicit a presidential pardon for Fāris

Manāʿ and his release from prison. Their gifts were accepted by the Palace guards.[463] However, when Ḥasan Manāʿ, eight other Saʿdah shaykhs—including Nāṣir al-Tays, ʿAbdullah b. Shājiaʿ, Ḥaydar Shawqah, and Muḥammad Muḥsin ʿUbādah[464]—and a large number of supporters organized a sit-in (*iʿtiṣām*) that afternoon in front of the Presidential Palace to protest against Fāris' imprisonment, the Republican Guard dispersed them with truncheons and water cannons.[465]

The sacking of Ḥasan and the imprisonment of Fāris opened a bout of veritable mud-slinging between the hostile factions of GPC shaykhs in Saʿdah—those close to the Manāʿ clan and those on the Mujallī/al-ʿAwjarī side. Fāyiz al-ʿAwjarī, in particular, inundated Ḥasan Manāʿ with criticism. In early 2010, when Ḥasan's career had already begun to falter, al-ʿAwjarī prompted the parliament to form a 'Fact-Finding Committee' in Saʿdah (*lajnah li-taqaṣṣī al-ḥaqāʾiq fī Ṣaʿdah*), with himself as its head. He accused Ḥasan's administration of arbitrariness, electoral fraud and corruption, and embezzlement of the humanitarian aid pledged by humanitarian and relief organizations for the displaced in the market. He announced his investigation of this matter through the Fact Finding Committee.[466]

Ḥasan Manāʿ, seething with anger, in turn accused the military leadership and the security organs in Saʿdah—notably Major General Muḥammad ʿAbdullah al-Qūsī, first undersecretary of the Ministry of the Interior—of having themselves delivered weapons to the Houthis, and threatened to reveal publicly 'the truth about the Saʿdah wars'. Al-Qūsī—vocally supported by Ḥusayn ʿAlī al-Munabbihī and ʿAbdullah Rawkān, who were part of the Mujallī/al-ʿAwjarī bloc—called these accusations 'ridiculous', adding that 'everyone knows who we are, and everyone knows who the Manāʿ are'.[467]

To make matters even worse for the Manāʿ brothers, in April 2010 the US Treasury Department froze Fāris' assets under Security Council Resolution 9904, on the grounds of him selling weapons to armed factions of al-Shabab, the Somalia-based branch of al-Qaeda, despite a UN arms embargo.[468] The Security Council statement said that he had 'directly or indirectly supplied, sold or transferred to Somalia arms or related material in violation of the arms embargo'.[469] This international action against Fāris Manāʿ was, however, connected with his activities in Somalia, rather than in Yemen.

February 2010 marked the downfall of Fāris Manāʿ and precipitated that of his brother, then governor of Saʿdah. Fāris' defeat, however, was provisional. In March 2011, after the Houthis seized power in Saʿdah, he rose from the ashes and became governor himself.[470]

The Struggle for Peace

Given the Houthis' ever increasing strength and numbers, in late summer 2009 the regime had been reluctant to begin the war anew and start a sixth military campaign in Saʿdah. Yet hardliners and the continuation of violent clashes across the conflict zone forced the government's hand. Given the war's scope and magnitude and its grandiose announcement as 'Operation Scorched Earth', one might easily lose sight of the fact that the sixth war rather resembled a hapless, ponderous stop-and-go process continuously slowed down by ceasefire and foreign mediation initiatives.

Despite these interruptions, both the Houthis and President Salih continued to send signals that they were committed to a military conclusion to the conflict, rather than to a political deal. Most of their attempts at reaching a political solution have, to date, been less than serious. Both sides seemed to pursue a dual strategy, as their peace initiatives were not synchronized with kinetic military action. The government's approach to solving the conflict was full military force, precisely because the Houthis were bringing its forces to utter distress. And after Saudi Arabia entered into the war in November, Salih had little reason to end the military campaign in Saʿdah, as long as he continued to receive funding and military support from the Saudi government. Only after Saudi Arabia ceased its aerial campaign in January 2010 did he feel the necessary impetus to give peace a chance.

On 13 August, two days after the beginning of the sixth war, the Supreme Security Committee demanded that the Houthis meet six conditions, called the Six Points, in order to negotiate a ceasefire: 1) withdrawal from all mountains, fortifications, and districts of Saʿdah; 2) removal of all checkpoints; 3) cessation of all acts of banditry and destruction; 4) return of all seized military and civilian equipment; 5) clarification of the situation of the six kidnapped foreigners, 'as information indicates the Houthis are responsible', and release of all kidnapping victims; and 6) refraining from intervening in the affairs of the local authorities.[471]

The Houthis instantly rejected the Six Points. They argued that, by declaring the sixth war, the government itself had violated the Second Doha Agreement, which required a halt to all military operations. In addition, from the Houthi perspective, the Six Points 'did not propose a comprehensive solution to the Saʿdah crisis in a way that ensures it will not re-emerge'.[472] Moreover, they regarded the fifth point ('release of all kidnapping victims') as a pitfall (*ʿathrah*), because they had always denied any involvement in this incident, and accepting this condition would be tantamount to an admission of guilt. Houthi spokesperson Muḥammad ʿAbdulsalām explained that the movement 'categorically refutes any link between the case of the abductees and the Saʿdah crisis'.[473] In any case, the Houthis, who felt stronger than ever, seemed to be eager to gauge their strength in combat with the enemy.

Two days later, on 15 August, after a horrific bombing campaign in Saʿdah, Fāris Manāʿ managed to convince the Houthis to temporarily revise their position. The rebel leaders signalled their willingness to accept the government's Six Points, except for the fifth point concerning the foreign abductees. But the parties to the conflict failed to reach a final agreement, and the war resumed. On 19 August, in a speech at the Military Academy, President Salih reiterated his intention to 'wipe out' the Houthis.[474] On 26 August, a temporary, verbal ceasefire was enacted to allow humanitarian aid to reach regions affected by the conflict. Yet this only lasted for a few hours. The following night, the Supreme Security Committee announced that it would continue military operations.

September 2009 saw no fewer than five attempts to end the war. After the arrival of Gulf Cooperation Council (GCC) Secretary-General ʿAbdulraḥman al-ʿAṭiyyah in Sanaʿa and a phone call from King Abdullah of Saudi Arabia, the Yemeni government again temporarily suspended its military campaign in Saʿdah.[475] A day later, the war resumed. On 13 September, offers of mediation from the Iranian government and Iraq's Shiite leader Muqtadā al-Ṣadr were interpreted in Riyadh and Sanaʿa as proof that Iraq's Sadrists were providing guidance and support to the Houthis.[476] While these accusations of Iranian support for the rebels were not new, the suggestion that Iraq's Sadrist movement was also supporting the rebels came as a surprise to many. This mediation initiative was strictly secret and only became known after it had failed.[477]

Given the fierce fighting and the dire humanitarian situation in the crisis area, foreign governments and humanitarian organizations increased pressure on the regime to end the war. However, a sustainable ceasefire and/or a political solution to the conflict had become virtually impossible: after six years of war, the parties to the conflict had lost all confidence in each other. This did not only concern the Houthis' relationship with government and opposition, and vice versa. The tribal leaders of the crisis area, too, felt deceived by all sides: by the Houthis, who had pulled the rug out from under the shaykhs' feet by 'playing' and forging alliances with their tribesmen, by the military leadership, by the presidency, and by the opposition parties of the JMP. Maintaining the prestigious supra-tribal role that many of them had achieved after 1962 required the elimination of the Houthis, their total military defeat, and so the shaykhs were both alienated and angered by the plethora of foreign and domestic ceasefire initiatives. As a shaykh of Wāʾilah put it:

> That's all fraud and falsehood. This is the sixth war and not the first. The Houthis have always shown willingness to talk when they saw that they were trapped or that they had run out of weapons and ammunition, and they used the ceasefires as a respite to begin the war anew. A Hadith says: *lā yuldagh al-muʾmin min juḥr wāḥid marratayn* ['A believer is not bitten from the same hole twice': someone won't redo the same mistake]. For our part, we have already been bitten five times, and if we allow ourselves to be bitten a sixth, then we'll really get what we deserve.[478]

Many shaykhs of the Saʿdah region, who in previous rounds of the war had vocally complained about the disregard of tribal mediation, had already reached the point where they no longer even desired any negotiation with the Houthis. They instead demanded a military final solution to the conflict. In mid-September 2009, their anger at the stuttering progress of the sixth war, the numerous interruptions of the fighting, and the mediation attempts by foreign third parties resulted in a declaration signed by ninety-nine Saʿdah shaykhs and dignitaries, in which they called for the termination of any mediation initiatives and the 'eradication of this cancerous tumour', as they described the Houthis. The declaration reads as follows:

> [...] We, the sons of Saʿdah, categorically reject mediation unless al-Ḥūthī and his followers surrender and are brought to justice. The state must fulfil its duty to root out this malignant cancer which has wrought havoc and hampered construction and reconstruction efforts and hurts the interests of the nation and citizens, in particular those of the sons of Saʿdah.[479]

The document, which was signed by tribal shaykhs, politicians, and social figures from all areas of the province, reads like a Who's Who of influential persons of the governorate (many of them in personal union): Fāyiz al-ʿAwjarī, ʿUthmān Mujallī, ʿAbdulsalām Hishūl Zābiyah, Fayṣal b. ʿArīj, Ḥusayn ʿAlī al-Munabbihī, Salmān ʿAwfān, ʿĀrif Shuwayṭ, Ḥusayn al-Surabī, Jaʿfar Ḥusayn Kubās, ʿĀmir Bushayt Abū ʿUbayd, ʿUmar Ṣāliḥ Ṣāliḥ Hindī Dughsān, Yaḥyā Muḥammad al-Ithlah, Muḥammad al-Ṭuḥāmī, Nāṣir al-Tays, ʿAlī Qāʾid Qamshah, Ḥasan Muḥammad Muqīt, Yūsif Aḥmad Dahbāsh Miṭrī, ʿAbdullah Rawkān, Fāyiz Bishr, Ḥamūd Mardās, Aḥmad Shāyaʿ Bukhtān, Sulaymān al-Faraḥ, ʿAbdulnāṣir al-Faraḥ, ʿAlī Ḥasan Jaylān, Ḍayfallah Rusām, Aḥmad Shabīb, Muʿammar al-Ḥusaynī, ʿAlī Ḥamūd Ẓāfir, and seventy-one more.

This uncompromising stance won support from hardline senior military leaders such as the commander of the Giants Brigade, ʿAlī al-Jāyfi, and the 15th Infantry Brigade's commander Thābit Muthannā Jawās, who threatened to reject any political solution and not to implement any orders to stop the war. They promised not to return from the battlefield without 'the head of ʿAbdulmalik al-Ḥūthī' as their 'gift to the children of the Yemeni nation on the occasion of *ʿīd al-fiṭr* and the [commemoration of the 26 September] revolution'.[480]

Regardless, the military campaign continued to stumble. On 17 September, a few days before the Islamic holiday *ʿīd al-fiṭr*, ʿAbdulmalik al-Ḥūthī sent a letter to then UN Secretary-General Ban Ki-moon, in which he expressed his readiness to agree to an immediate cessation of the war for humanitarian reasons.[481] Again, Fāris Manāʿ assumed the role of envoy. The following day, Hezbollah Secretary-General Ḥasan Naṣrallah called on President Salih to stop the fighting and also offered to mediate, an offer that was met with contemptuous silence.[482] On 19 September, the government again enacted a ceasefire in commemoration of the Islamic holiday *ʿīd al-fiṭr*. President Salih announced on television that the ceasefire would be in effect for three days, with the possibility of becoming a permanent ceasefire if the Houthis accepted the Six Points. The offer coincided with a Houthi attack on Saʿdah city; both sides claimed that neither ever laid down arms.

The Saudi entry into the war in November 2009 polarized the regional powers. Whereas Iranian Foreign Minister Manouchehr Mottaki warned Saudi Arabia against interfering in Yemen's internal affairs, the GCC announced that it would stand by the Kingdom.[483] Manouchehr Mottaki confirmed Iran's readiness to mediate in Yemen, but the Yemeni government, now thrilled by the Saudis' direct military support, rejected any 'Iranian tutelage' in Yemen.[484]

Several mediation initiatives overlapped in November 2009, but reaching a ceasefire had been complicated by direct Saudi military involvement. President Salih did not have the power to announce a ceasefire alone as long as the Saudis were fighting the Houthis, nor did he have any incentive to do so while Riyadh continued supplying cash and weapons to the war.

The opening of this second front and the hostility of two state armies was a heavy burden for the Houthis. In November they again declared their readiness to accept the Six Points, except for the fifth. The subsequent negotiations were the first serious effort to bring the sixth war to an end politically. The Houthis chose Ḥizb al-Ḥaqq party secretary and JMP chairman Ḥasan Zayd to act as their intermediary. On 19 November, Zayd met with Salih to discuss conditions for a ceasefire. A mediation committee was formed (consisting of General ʿAlī Muḥsin, head of the Giants Brigade ʿAlī al-Jāyfī, and 119th Infantry Brigade commander Fayṣal Rajab for the government, and ʿAbdulkarīm Amīr al-Dīn al-Ḥūthī, Ṣāliḥ Habrah, and Ṣāliḥ al-Ṣumād for the Houthis), in the event that hostilities ceased. But there was no progress or tangible outcome. Zayd told the US embassy that Salih would not end the war as long as the Saudis continued funding and supporting it.[485]

Separate lines of communication between the Houthis and the Saudi government were also established at this time. A mediation attempt by Ḥusayn al-Aḥmar on behalf of the Saudis again failed, because al-Aḥmar lacked the Houthis' trust and the Saudis did not want to make any concessions to the rebels.[486] There were also indications that the Houthis had chosen Amīn al-ʿUkaymī (Iṣlāḥ MP and shaykh of Shawlān with close ties to Saudi Arabia) to open up secret channels and serve as a mediator with Riyadh. In contrast to his own Shawlān tribe, which had long been stuck in fierce confrontation with the Houthis, until that point al-ʿUkaymī had personally managed to steer clear of fighting the movement. However, any ceasefire agreement between the Yemeni government and the Houthis would have to be agreed to by the Saudis and coordinated with their forces so that all hostilities could cease at the same time. In other words, the power to stop the war now lay in Riyadh.

In December, fighting of the fiercest nature took place between Houthis and the Republican Guard in Saʿdah city. Although the Houthis were battered and war-weary after four months of non-stop fighting, they continued to register victories against Saudi and Yemeni forces. ʿAbdulmalik al-Ḥūthī again announced his readiness to accept the Six Points other than the fifth. The government, however, suspected this as a Houthi tactic to ease the pressure they were facing in Saʿdah city, Sufyān, and al-Malāḥīṭ and on the border with Saudi Arabia. It pushed ahead with the military campaign.[487]

Security events and general developments in Yemen were high on the agenda of the GCC summit held in Kuwait on 14–15 December. Saudi Arabia and Yemen used the summit to drum up support.[488] The Council discussed the need to use the 'GCC Peninsula Shield Force' in Saʿdah, which was intended to deter, and respond to, military aggression against any of the member countries: Bahrain, Kuwait, Oman, Qatar, Saudi Arabia, and the UAE. Observers reported that during the summit the Yemeni government was 'playing the Houthi card and the Iranian card' with the US and the Gulf states, all of whom were concerned about Iranian expansionism.[489] The summit revealed that, despite earlier indications of Salih's willingness to consider a political solution to the conflict, recent events suggested that the president, sensing a new wave of regional support, had redoubled his commitment to a military solution in Saʿdah. Salih chose not to call an end to hostilities, either out of mistrust of the Houthis, or the belief that they were starting to weaken. Instead, he and his regime upped the anti-Iran rhetoric, sent more troops into battle, sought to buy significant caches of new weaponry and embraced Saudi Arabia's ongoing involvement.[490]

The US has appeared increasingly dissatisfied and concerned about the ongoing military commitment in Saʿdah. Since the war exhausted Yemen's conventional military, the Yemeni government has looked to its US- and UK-funded and trained Counterterrorism Units (CTUs) to provide some relief to the battered regular forces of the army. Washington complained that the Salih regime was increasingly resorting to deployment of the American-trained CTU to the war zone. As the US did not regard the Houthis as a terrorist group, it considered it an abuse to pit CTU forces against them. The units had first been sent to Saʿdah in July 2009 to investigate the kidnapping and murder of the Western aid workers. After the outbreak of the sixth war the following month, the CTU was drawn into the Saʿdah wars. It was trained to detect small terrorist cells and to investigate and prevent terror attacks on civilian targets, which made it a poor tactical choice for use against a long-term domestic insurgency. Yet the Yemeni government, desperate not to lose the war against the Houthis, has largely ignored US concerns regarding deployment of the CTU to Saʿdah. In consequence, the CTU, tied down in Saʿdah, has been derailed from its principal mission: to combat genuine terrorist targets like AQAP.[491]

In a New Year's speech on 1 January 2010, President Salih again called on the Houthis to cease hostilities and abide by the proffered Six Points. Interestingly, for the first time, the fifth point concerning the foreign abductees had been replaced with a condition concerning non-aggression on Saudi territory and withdrawal from all positions within a 10-kilometre buffer zone along the border.[492] The Houthis accepted these modified Six Points, including the cessation of attacks on Saudi Arabia. Although the ball was then in the government's court as to when and under what conditions to begin negotiations, the regime remained concerned about the rebels' intentions. On the military front, the government's 'Blow to the Head' operation was still in full swing and continued to focus on clearing Saʿdah city of Houthi warriors.

However, a ceasefire seemed to be within grasp. The prospect of a new permanent ceasefire horrified local tribal leaders, whose fate depended crucially on the military outcome of the conflict. ʿUthmān Mujallī, ʿAbdullah Rawkān, Fayṣal b. ʿArīj and ʿAbdullah al-Maḥdūn reiterated their reservations regarding any domestic or foreign-brokered deal with the Houthis and again demanded the rebels' full military defeat (*ḥasm ʿaskarī*). The shaykhs made it clear that after all their sacrifices to beat the Houthis, they would consider the cessation of hostilities as their 'perdition' (*bawār*), 'doom and displacement' (*ḍayāʿ wa izāḥah*).[493]

On 25 January, just two weeks after Saudi Arabia announced victory against the Houthis and reduced military operations against them (Saudi air attacks only fully ceased in early February), ʿAbdulmalik al-Ḥūthī announced that the rebels were initiating a unilateral ceasefire and were willing to withdraw from Saudi territory.[494] A deal between the government and the Houthis looked promising, especially in light of the government's hopes for capitalizing on the upcoming London Conference to secure potential funding for Yemen. After the Saudis had downscaled their air attacks, President Salih was left alone again to fight the Houthis, encouraging him to consider a more concerted effort at peace. The Houthis, too, were feeling the toll of six months of fighting.

Ahead of the International Conference of the Friends of Yemen in London on 27 January, the Yemeni government sent conciliatory signals on a number of fronts, expressing enthusiasm for tackling AQAP, resuming dialogue with opposition parties and, potentially, striking a deal with the Houthis. The Friends of Yemen, comprising over forty countries as well as international organizations, emerged out of a conference organized by then UK Prime Minister Gordon Brown in response to the threat posed by AQAP, which had attempted to bring down a US airline on Christmas Day 2009. The Friends of Yemen were inspired by a counter-terrorist agenda, but with the aim of dealing with AQAP by helping to build a better Yemen that would address the economic and social causes of discontent.[495] The Salih regime recognized the London Conference's potential for securing additional donor funding to deal with Yemen's many challenges, including the Houthis.[496] However, in London, the US government reiterated its concerns that Yemen paid the Houthis too much attention, instead of taking resolute action against al-Qaeda. Moreover, prosecuting the Saʿdah wars had hampered the Yemeni military's effectiveness, preoccupied the central government to the exclusion of nearly every other issue, led to widespread humanitarian suffering, and rapidly accelerated the country's economic crisis. Foreign Minister Abū Bakr al-Qirbī again tried to convince the US that the Houthis were a terrorist group, but the Obama administration continued to refuse to designate them as a foreign terrorist organization.

Ending hostilities between Saudi Arabia and the Houthis was the most important precondition to a ceasefire between the Yemeni government and the Houthis. The government was once more alone in fending off the rebels, and heightened international attention on Yemen's multiple crises, as well as the potential of hundreds of millions of Qatari and other donor dollars flooding into Yemen for Saʿdah's reconstruction, provided a substantial incentive to end the war and begin the peace process.

After the London Conference, the decisive negotiations between the Yemeni government and the Houthis were set in motion. The ceasefire announcement was precipitated by secret negotiations and weeks of shuttle diplomacy involving two influential mediators—the Qatari government and (according to some) Amīn al-ʿUkaymī.[497] Ultimately, however, the sixth war was not ended by a contractual peace (*ṣulḥ*) between the warring parties based on the modified Six Points, but rather by verbal 'communication' (*tawāṣul*) of the parties to the conflict, and then a sudden decision (*qarār*) by Salih to suspend hostilities at midnight on 12 February. This abrupt unilateral decision overrode the final negotiations with the Houthis. Neither the government nor the rebels have signed any document to seal the ceasefire and their agreement on the modified Six Points.

Ceasefire Sequencing and Third Doha Agreement

Salih's unilateral ceasefire overrode the final stages of negotiations and obstructed the conclusion of a written ceasefire document, which would have converted the Houthis' verbal acceptance of the modified Six Points into a written contract. The modified Points required the following concessions: 1) withdrawal from government buildings, 2) removal of checkpoints and road blocks, 3) return of all seized military and civilian equipment, 4) release of all prisoners, 5) abandonment of mountain positions, 6) cessation of attacks on Saudi Arabia and withdrawal from Saudi territory.

Nevertheless, the reconciliation and reconstruction process continued to inch forward. Although both sides initially appeared in sync in their desire to end the sixth war, a ceasefire agreement's long-term success would have required a concerted, patient effort from both sides to move forward together. One consequence of the abrupt termination of negotiations was that the sequencing of the ceasefire implementation was completely unclear. However, a timetable was agreed for implementation of the Six Points within one month. Five supervisory committees were established to oversee this: the Sufyān Committee, the Saʿdah Committee, the al-Malāḥīṭ Committee, the Committee on the Border with Saudi-Arabia, and the Committee on Arms Delivery.

The humanitarian situation in Saʿdah was appalling: the entire region was a scene of destruction, ruin and havoc. The deterioration of conditions there had resulted in an estimated 250,000 IDPs.[498] The Houthis were intentionally delaying implementation of the Six Points. When the one-month period elapsed, they had not met even a quarter of the conditions. Although they had opened portions of the Northern Ring Road in al-Malāḥīṭ and Bāqim, their presence persisted along the roadsides. In Sufyān, the Sanaʿa-Saʿdah highway was opened only temporarily and reluctantly, although the opening of roads was a central provision of the Six Points. Mines were cleared only in sensitive areas and on main roads. Observers warned that the Houthis wanted to use the opening of the streets in al-Malāḥīṭ and Bāqim to provide themselves with weapons and food. On the other hand, the rebels were reluctant to open the main Sanaʿa-Saʿdah highway, because this would benefit the armed forces in Saʿdah city.[499] Disagreements on questions of detail led to a deliberate slow-down of the ceasefire implementation, such as the question of how many soldiers should form the escort of security chiefs or district directors. After the implementation schedule had lapsed, several members of the Supervisory Committees resigned, annoyed by the Houthis' deliberate procrastination.

The crisis zone was still shaken by fighting. Hours after the ceasefire announcement, there was an assassination attempt against Major General Muḥammad al-Qūsī, under-secretary of the Ministry of the Interior.[500] In al-Maṭammah (al-Jawf), the Houthis tried to assassinate the district director and imposed a suffocating siege on the Āl Ṣaqrah tribe of Shawlān.[501] Despite the ceasefire, the rebels devastated homes and farms of the Muqīt clan and its tribal allies in Bāqim. In Rāziḥ, too, they destroyed houses of pro-government shaykhs. A local recalled:

> These were revenge acts (*aʿmāl intiqāmiyyah*). [During the sixth war] the Houthis were busy on all fronts of the war, but with the end of the war the Houthis turned towards those whom they considered to have supported the government. They wanted to take swift revenge on these people before the ceasefire took effect.[502]

In Sufyān, too, tribes loyal to the Houthis were reluctant to implement the ceasefire and deliberately sabotaged the implementation of the Six Points. In this area the tribal dynamics of the conflict were particularly pronounced:

> Even if the Houthis had implemented the Six Points of the ceasefire, the war [in Sufyān] had returned, as a tribal war (*ḥarb qabaliyyah*) between the tribe of Sufyān and the tribe of al-ʿUṣaymāt, between Ḥāshid and Bakīl. The truce was only a respite for the fighters, the war has started each time anew, and every time it has been more violent than before.[503]

Another factor that rendered the situation in Sufyān so complicated was that the Bakīl tribes felt outmanoeuvred by the presidential decision to stop the war. As we know, the sub-conflict in Sufyān was above all a war between the Ṣubārah (Bakīl) and the al-ʿUṣaymāt (Ḥāshid), the continuation of a conflict over territory and ultimately over the question of whom the republican state patronized in the north. The Bakīl had apparently expected to be involved in some form in the ceasefire negotiations to bring their conflict to a halt, but they were neither involved nor even mentioned in the ceasefire agreement. Now, the ever-suspicious Bakīl felt excluded from the crucial talks between the Houthis and the government:

> The Houthis entered into an agreement with Saudi Arabia and the Yemeni government without having consulted or involved the Bakīl, hence some say the Houthis made fools of the Bakīl. Since when do the Houthis seek the advice of the Bakīl, and since when do the Houthis meet with the Bakīl to discuss their decisions? The Houthis have turned the Bakīl into their henchmen. They deal with the Bakīl as if they were the commander and the Bakīl were the soldiers, they give the orders and the Bakīl carry them out. And I suppose that the non-implementation of the ceasefire in Sufyān was in part due to this fact.[504]

Three months after the ceasefire, the dynamics of the Sufyān sub-conflict in Ruhm led to a new provocation between Ṣaghīr b. ʿAzīz and the Houthis. A traffic accident involving one of Ṣaghīr's family members in al-Mahādhir, Saḥār district, led to renewed battles with the rebels, and the conflict quickly spread into Ruhm, where the Houthis besieged Ṣaghīr and his followers for two months in his home compound. Ṣaghīr's former allies—ʿAlī Muḥsin's *firqah*, the Republican Guard, and Ḥusayn al-Aḥmar's Popular Army—who were endeavouring to abide by the ceasefire terms, stood idly by.

While Ṣaghīr and his followers were desperately defending against the Houthis, the Yemeni government tried to reinvigorate the stalled Qatari mediation efforts in Saʿdah. The prospect of a third round of Qatar-sponsored peace talks inspired horror and dismay among Yemen's shaykhs. Dozens of shaykhs and MPs from Saʿdah and ʿAmrān—including ʿUthmān Mujallī, Fāyiz al-ʿAwjarī, and ʿAbdulsalām Hishūl Zābiyah—started a sit-in at the parliament to draw the government's attention to the deteriorating northern security situation and the Houthis' increasing attacks on tribal leaders. They demanded government action to end the siege against their colleague Ṣaghīr, enforcement of the Six Points implementation, and strongly cautioned against any re-activation of Qatar's role in mediating the conflict.[505] Sixty-two MPs signed a petition demanding that the administration 'assume responsibility in ending the violations committed by the Houthis', and threatened to suspend their parliamentary membership if the authorities failed to help Ṣaghīr.[506] In a speech in Parliament, ʿUthmān Mujallī stressed on behalf of the shaykhly MPs of Saʿdah and ʿAmrān:

> The return to the Doha Agreements has put the people of Saʿdah at the mercy of the Houthis while the state has not done its job in protecting the lives of the people in Saʿdah from their attacks [...] The Houthis seem to fight an organized battle, launching attacks against the tribes and besieging others with the objective of suppressing the tribes and the shaykhs who stood by the government during the last confrontations.[507]

Nonetheless, Qatar again sponsored a meeting in Doha, at which the Yemeni government and the Houthis agreed to an 'explanatory appendix', associated with the Second Doha Agreement of February 2008. This so-called Third Doha Agreement hammered out a twenty-two-point agenda that would guide both sides to meeting obligations under the February 2010 truce, which had been thwarted by violence from both sides.[508] The Houthis' main goal was to obtain the release of around 1,000 prisoners. The government agreed to this, in return for the rebels agreeing to surrender captured government weapons to Qatari mediators.[509] The signing of the Third Doha Agreement on 27 July 2010 by representatives of both the Yemeni government and the Houthi leadership was dutifully witnessed by Qatari Prime Minister Ḥamad b. Jāsim. Some observers have pointed to the significance of b. Jāsim and President Salih remaining in the background during this mediation; this may have been related to Saudi Arabia's now weighty presence in the conflict, as Saudi interference had frequently undermined the efficacy of past Qatari mediation efforts in Yemen.[510]

On the same day as the Third Doha Agreement was signed in Qatar, Ṣaghīr b. ʿAzīz was wounded by shrapnel and evacuated by military helicopter to Sanaʿa. The Houthis looted and burned his properties, and in the overall chaos they managed to capture more than 200 soldiers, seventy of them at the al-Zaʿlāʾ fort in al-ʿAmashiyyah, of which they took full control.[511] When Ṣaghīr and the last representatives of the state had been expelled from Ruhm, the Houthis were in control of the whole of Sufyān. One day after Ṣaghīr's expulsion from Sufyān, the Houthis ambushed and killed Maʿīn ʿAbdullah al-ʿAwjarī, brother of Fāyiz al-ʿAwjarī, in Wāʾilah.[512] Fāyiz vowed to take revenge on the Houthis for his brother's death. Despite all ceasefire endeavours and agreements, such protracted revenge killings and 'playoffs' (*taṣfiyāt*) between the parties to the conflict still made peace more than unlikely.

The Tribal Alliance

In Saʿdah governorate, after the 2010 ceasefire, Saʿdah city alone remained under the army's control. The armed forces were passive and disinclined to confront the Houthis. The rebels, by contrast, worked towards the expansion of their sphere of control and forced their last opponents among the local tribes into deadly battles while the military stood idly by. Discontent and resentment prevailed in almost all alliances between the government and shaykhs. After the ceasefire, the government watched its tribal allies being beaten down by the Houthis, who, according to a local source, 'snap their flesh and break their bones' (*yanhishūna laḥmahum wa yukassirūna ʿiẓāmahum*). Many of them were displaced and fled to Sanaʿa.

The remaining government loyalists among Saʿdah's shaykhs and tribesmen were fighting with their backs to the wall. Now, coping alone with the Houthi threat, for the first time since the beginning of the Saʿdah wars they realized the importance of working with, rather than against, each other. The important thing was to put aside old rivalries and feuds and to hold together. A shaykh from Wāʾilah argued:

> I assure you that there are major problems between the shaykhs in Saʿdah, and this is one of the reasons why the Houthis have been able to prevail. The shaykhs have evaded their responsibilities. They went to Sanaʿa and have left their tribal people alone. Many of these shaykhs found themselves abandoned by everyone after the Houthis had played with their tribesmen, and of their shaykhdom nothing was left (*lam yuʿidd lahum min al-mashīkh ayy shay*ʾ). There are hundreds of conflicts between the shaykhs. Since the beginning of the war in 2004 they have worked hard to convince the political leadership that their rival, Shaykh So-and-So, was with the Houthis. Each shaykh tried to stab the other in the back, so each shaykh challenged the Houthis alone. Their scheming against each other brought Saʿdah to this tragic situation. But now it was necessary to close ranks against the threat, because from Sanaʿa there was nothing but the deafening silence of the state (*al-ṣumt al-muṭabbaq min qibal al-dawlah*).[513]

Given this 'deafening silence', tribal particularism turned out to be the major obstacle to a common defence against the Houthis. The shaykhs were too divided and competitive to form a common front. Under normal conditions, there was no need for unified leadership or joint action. There was a Council of Shaykhs (*majlis al-shuyūkh*) of the member tribes of the Khawlān b. ʿĀmir confederation, but this was convened on very rare occasions that mainly concerned internal inter-tribal issues.[514] Now, however, the situation required concerted and swift military action by an entire region, transcending the boundaries of tribes and confederations, because the state—nominally the region's overall ruler—had declined in authority and assertiveness. A distinctly different kind of leadership was required.

The period between the February 2010 ceasefire and the seizure of Saʿdah city in March 2011 witnessed a series of efforts by shaykhs and tribes to enhance joint action. In June 2010, the Tribal Alliance of the Sons of Saʿdah (*al-taḥāluf al-qabalī li-abnāʾ Ṣaʿdah*) was launched, a supra-tribal defence alliance against the Houthis.[515] The chairman and founder of the Tribal Alliance was Yaḥyā Muḥammad Muqīt, a relative of the senior shaykh of Khawlān b. ʿĀmir, Ḥasan Muqīt. The Tribal Alliance was an attempt to overcome the particularism that had prevented the shaykhs from working in unison to assert their common interests against the Houthis. Among the signatories of the Alliance's written charter were numerous shaykhs of both the Khawlān b. ʿĀmir and the Hamdān al-Shām (Wāʾilah, Wādiʿah, Dahm).

Signatories of the Jumāʿah were ʿAbdulraḥman Muḥammad Thābit, Ṣāliḥ Yaḥyā Qirwash, ʿAzīz Kharazān al-Ḥudhayfī, Misfir Fāḍl al-Ḥudhayfī, ʿĀdil Yaḥyā Farwān; for the Munabbih, Yūsif Aḥmad Dahbāsh Miṭrī and Ḥusayn ʿAlī al-Munabbihī; for the Khawlān, ʿAbdullah Rawkān, ʿAbdulkhāliq Bishr, Ḥasan al-Shawīʿ and Muḥammad ʿAbdullah ʿUqbah. For the Rāziḥ, ʿAbdulkhāliq Suwādī, ʿAbdullah Nāṣir al-Faraḥ and Jamāl al-ʿAzzām signed; for the Ghamr, ʿAlī Ẓāfir. For Saḥār: ʿĀrif Shuwayṭ, Yaḥyā Jaʿfar, Masʿūd Qirḥish; for the Āl Sālim, Aḥmad Shāyaʿ Bukhtān; and for the Wāʾilah, Muḥammad Nāṣir Qamshah, Shāyiq ʿAbdullah Abū Mushʿaf, Hādī Ṭirshān, Muḥammad ʿAyḍah Shabībah, ʿUmar ʿAlī al-ʿIrāqī, and ʿAbdulrabb al-Tays. Also among the signatories were academics, writers, religious scholars (*mashāyikh ʿilm*), and military officers from the Saʿdah region. The Tribal Alliance had a statute and a four-part structure consisting of media, finance, military and intelligence departments. Its military department was composed of ten members and was to take an advisory role among the armed forces.[516]

Yet not all Houthi-hostile shaykhs of Saʿdah joined the Tribal Alliance. The shaykhly clans of Manāʿ, Mujallī, al-Surabī, Dughsān, al-ʿAwjarī, Shājiaʿ, Zābiyah, ʿArīj, and ʿAwfān were conspicuous by their absence, each for their own reasons.

The difference between the Tribal Alliance of the Sons of Saʿdah and the Popular Army was that the latter had been composed of tribal and non-tribal mercenaries from areas outside the war zone, under the nominal command of Ḥusayn al-Aḥmar, who fought as irregulars with the army. The Tribal Alliance, in contrast, consisted of shaykhs and tribesmen of the conflict area acting independently from the state. Critics of the Alliance suspected that the mastermind pulling its strings was ʿAlī Muḥsin, who used the Alliance to continue his war against the Houthis after the 2010 ceasefire had condemned the armed forces and the Popular Army to ceasefire.[517] Members of the Alliance, however, categorically denied any involvement of the general.[518]

The Houthis reacted with outrage. They regarded the formation of the Tribal Alliance as a 'declaration of war' that would lead to a further deterioration of relations between shaykhs and Houthis. Houthi spokesperson Muḥammad ʿAbdulsalām stressed that the signatory shaykhs did not represent their tribes—on the contrary, they were in conflict with their own tribes. He warned that this 'ganging up' (*harb ʿiṣābāt*) and 'tribal bloc formation' (*takattul qabalī*) in an area dominated by a 'culture of revenge' (*thaqāfat al-thaʾr*) would have disastrous consequences for everyone.[519] ʿAbdullah Rawkān, piqued, responded by saying that the tribes of Saʿdah were no 'gangs' (*lasnā ʿiṣābāt*).[520]

Yet, after the formation of the Tribal Alliance, the conflict between the shaykhs and the Houthis did heat up, leading to countless confrontations. In November 2010, under the leadership of ʿAbdullah al-Ḥākim, the Houthis rallied their followers from different districts of Saʿdah, al-Jawf and Sufyān and led them to war in Munabbih. The Houthis had already managed to seize the district's administrative centre, Sūq al-Khamīs in the sixth war. Now they put large parts of Munabbih's Shaʿshaʿ area under siege in order to impose control over the district's lower areas along the Yemeni-Saudi border. Houthi field commander ʿAbdullah al-Ḥākim ignored all mediation endeavours, even those by the Houthi leadership itself, and worked instead towards a decisive battle similar to the confrontations which had displaced Ṣaghīr b. ʿAzīz from Sufyān. The clashes led to the expulsion of Yūsif Aḥmad Dahbāsh Miṭrī, senior shaykh of Munabbih's Shaʿshaʿ moiety and successor of Munabbih's 'shaykh of war' Aḥmad Dahbāsh Miṭrī, who had been killed in 2008.[521]

In December 2010, extremely violent battles erupted between Houthis and followers of Shaykh Muḥammad Nāṣir Qamshah in al-Maqāsh, Wāʾilah, which claimed a high toll (at least fifty dead and hundreds injured). Qamshah's house was seized, looted and burned to the ground.[522] Also in December, there was a bomb attack on Yaḥyā Muqīt, the chairman of the Tribal Alliance, in Saʿdah city centre. He, ʿAbdullah Ḥusayn Muqīt, Fayṣal Aḥmad Qirwash, and two others were injured; Ṣaddām Rawkān—brother of the senior Khawlān shaykh, ʿAbdullah Rawkān—was killed.[523]

The Tribal Alliance failed to achieve its objectives. A tribal source attributed this failure to the Alliance's attempt to beat the Houthis at their own, military game, deviating from the tribal practices and customs of conflict prevention and mitigation that should have been the Alliance's greatest strength:

> The tribes did not apply their tribal rules in their war with the Houthis. Instead, they resorted to army methods in these confrontations, and this is one of the main reasons why the Houthis were able to dominate them. [...] In tribal customs there is the principle of 'give and take' and the principle of dialogue in resolving differences, but the Tribal Alliance did not adhere to it, so the tribal side could not withstand. They reached a stage where they did not have any principles; they just did their work without giving priority to the tribal aspect and its generally accepted customs.[524]

In the months following the formation of the Tribal Alliance, many of its signatories and members were either killed or displaced by the Houthis. By March 2011, when the Houthis seized Saʿdah city, the Tribal Alliance had virtually collapsed.

Seizure of Saʿdah City

In January 2011, shortly after the popular ouster of the Tunisian government, major street protests materialized in Sanaʿa to demand changes to government—the 'Arab Spring' had found its way into Yemen.[525] The protests quickly grew and took on an increasingly pointed tone of criticism toward President Salih, with many demonstrators beginning to call openly for system change and new leadership in Yemen. The Houthis were among the first to join the uprisings. In a way, it was a battle they had been involved in for years.

On 18 March—remembered as the 'Friday of Dignity'—close to fifty protesters were shot dead in Sanaʿa and hundreds were wounded. As tens of thousands finished praying near the capital's Change Square, close to the protest movement's epicentre, Sanaʿa University, men stationed atop roofs and inside buildings, dressed as civilians, opened fire indiscriminately. This incident prompted the declaration of a state of emergency and international condemnation, and ultimately culminated in mass defections and resignations of formerly loyalist politicians and military officers.

Among those who defected to side with Yemen's 'revolution' were the al-Aḥmar brothers and General ʿAlī Muḥsin.[526] In consequence, the Houthis in Sanaʿa suddenly found themselves on the same side as their historical adversaries. The *firqah*—the First Armoured Division under ʿAlī Muḥsin's command, responsible for the war in Saʿdah—also joined the revolution and change axis. Whereas the *firqah* units in Sanaʿa would become for some time a kind of protective force for ʿAlī Muḥsin and protesters, ʿAlī Muḥsin placed the units in Saʿdah in the hands of General al-Ẓāhirī al-Shaddādī, at that time chief of staff (*raʾīs arkān*) of the North Western Military Region.

In Sanaʿa, the Houthis demonstrated more or less peacefully with their former adversaries for a system change. Alongside many members of Iṣlāḥ and other stakeholders, they sat in Change Square, participating in a broad-based movement that called itself the 'Change Revolution'. Though Houthis and Iṣlāḥ loyalists were still fighting each other vigorously in al-Jawf and other fronts outside the capital, over the eleven months of Yemen's popular uprising, Houthi and Iṣlāḥ supporters managed to cooperate on a number of issues, particularly outside of top leadership circles.[527]

In Saʿdah, the Houthis took advantage of the power vacuum and used it for a further expansion of their control. Now their strategic plans were focused on Saʿdah city, the last bastion outside their dominion. In March, two days after the 'Friday of Dignity', the Houthis expelled ʿUthmān Mujallī from al-ʿAbdīn, a few kilometres southeast of Saʿdah city. In the battle for al-ʿAbdīn, the rebels acted with extreme brutality. Medium and heavy weapons were used; dozens of people on both sides were killed. Mediation initiatives by Fāyiz al-ʿAwjarī and Ṣāliḥ al-Wajmān failed. Mujallī—in extreme conflict and left high and dry by both Salih and ʿAlī Muḥsin—defended himself fiercely and desperately. When the Houthis gained the upper hand, he fled via al-Buqʿ to Saudi Arabia. After seizing al-ʿAbdīn, the Houthis blew up the house of the Mujallī clan. Casablanca Hotel, built on former *waqf* land that Mujallī's father and grandfather had appropriated after the 1960s civil war, was also blown up, and Raḥbān Hotel was looted. All family properties were confiscated.[528]

After Mujallī's expulsion, the Houthis focused on Saʿdah city. Anticipating his own expulsion, Governor Ṭaha Hājir left Saʿdah city aboard a helicopter. After his departure, a council for administration of the governorate (*majlis idārat shuʾūn al-muḥāfaẓah*) was formed, chaired by Fāris Manāʿ. On 23 March, the Local Council elected Fāris without competition as governor. Whereas Hājir had been appointed by presidential decree—in violation of the Local Authority Law—Fāris was now hailed as a governor chosen by the people.

On the following day, 24 March, the Houthis took the city without a fight. Under the gaze of the *firqah*, hundreds of Houthi warriors moved in, established control, set checkpoints on arterial roads, and organized a huge demonstration of tens of thousands of supporters against the Salih regime. In fact, their victory in Saʿdah city was so complete and so effortless that it resulted in constant rumours of a deal (*ṣafqah*) or non-aggression pact between the Houthis and ʿAlī Muḥsin, to prevent clashes with the *firqah* units in the city—enabling Alī Muḥsin to focus on the political crisis in Sanaʿa and the Houthis on expanding their grip on Saʿdah city.[529] This alleged agreement would have allowed Alī Muḥsin a degree of comfort as he withdrew some of his troops from Saʿdah to fortify his position in the capital. Not only had he promised to 'protect' protesters at Change Square, but he also had to guard his Sanaʿa headquarters against possible retaliation by Central Security or Republican Guard forces. However, the existence of such a deal could never be proved—according to the Houthis, it never existed.[530]

As the new governor, Fāris Manāʿ held a series of consultation meetings with various stakeholders to determine the province's future: the Houthi leadership, represented by ʿAbdullah al-Ḥākim, members of the Local Authority, shaykhs who had given in to the pressure and shifted to the Houthi side, and security and military leaders. General al-Ẓāhirī al-Shaddādī, Alī Muḥsin's deputy in Saʿdah, assured Fāris that 'the armed forces and security of Saʿdah are with the revolution and change axis'.[531]

In the ensuing months, the Houthis consolidated their rule in Saʿdah. Without infringing the existing administration structures, they managed to impose control over the governorate with a skilful infiltration of state authorities:

> The security services, military and general managers of the executive offices and the leaders of the local authority had only a formal existence, no more. In every executive office and every district was a Houthi delegate (*mandūb*). It was they who were commanding, not the general and district directors. The Houthis fulfilled all functions of the security agencies; they even organized the traffic on the streets of Saʿdah city. The ruler of Ḍaḥyān was the true engine (*al-muḥarrik al-fiʿlī*) of the province of Saʿdah; he was the one who ran the governorate.[532]

The 'ruler of Ḍaḥyān' (*ḥākim Ḍaḥyān*) is a pun referring to the Houthis' supreme field commander, ʿAbdullah al-Ḥākim (Abū ʿAlī) from Ḍaḥyān: a *sayyid* who had formerly worked as a primary school teacher. In the course of the Saʿdah wars, he rose to field commander in Ḍaḥyān and then, after the marginalization of ʿAbdullah al-Razzāmī, to second-in-command of the Houthi movement. Al-Ḥākim was known for his intelligence, his brilliant strategic skills, and his relentless heavy-handed approach to his opponents.

During the six Saʿdah wars, ʿAbdullah al-Ḥākim had led most major Houthi military campaigns, including the conquest of Sūq al-Khamīs in Munabbih in 2009 and now the seizure of Saʿdah city.[533] From 2011 onwards, he would lead the siege of Dammāj, the violent takeover of ʿAmrān governorate, and, in 2014, the seizure of Sanaʿa. Because of his powerful position and swift strategic moves, some likened him to the queen piece in chess. Al-Ḥākim's prominent role in battle earned him numerous blood feuds, and he was (wrongly) declared dead countless times. His verbal attacks on critics and journalists were legendary and have contributed significantly to the Houthis' bad relationship with the media.[534]

Whereas the rest of the country was slowly but steadily sinking into chaos and violence, with the Houthi takeover security in Saʿdah governorate increased dramatically and unprecedentedly. By 2011, the province was safer and more stable than any other Yemeni province—and the Houthi shadow state came into being.

7

FAUSTIAN BARGAINS

2011–14

Law maʿī liwāʾ min al-Ḥūthiyyin la-ḥarrartu bihim al-Quds
('If I had a Houthi division, I would liberate Jerusalem with them')
Quote ascribed to General ʿAlī Muḥsin

With the end of the sixth Saʿdah war and the Houthis' seizure of Saʿdah city one year later, an era came to a close, and a turbulent new phase began whose consideration could certainly fill an entire book. The period from March 2011 until the seizure of Sanaʿa in September 2014 was marked by an enormous territorial expansion of the Houthi dominion, made possible by military coercion, astute political activism at national level, shadowy deals, and adjustment and renegotiation of alliances.

During this period, fighting in al-Jawf and parts of Maʾrib took on an openly sectarian character as the Houthis were increasingly confronted by radical Sunnis and their allies, drawn into the conflict by the Houthi expansion to the east and southeast. In Ḥajjah governorate, which the Houthis gradually brought under their control from 2010 onwards, they entered into confrontations with tribes allied with both Salafis and the Iṣlāḥ party. In winter 2010, they overran the northern part of the Tihāmah plain so effortlessly that observers compared their military advance with a 'miraculous favour from heaven'.[1] From 2011 onwards, the Salafi teaching centre at Dammāj, Dār al-Ḥadīth, which had managed to stay more or less out of the fighting during the six Saʿdah wars, became another focal point for the Houthis; in January 2014, intermittent battles and sieges resulted in the evacuation of its students.[2] Around the same time, the rebels seized another Salafi camp in the remote Wādī Āl Abū Jabārah in Kitāf. Unlike Dammāj, the Kitāf camp had a pronounced military background—it was therefore razed to the ground.[3]

Under the leadership of their ruthless military genius ʿAbdullah al-Ḥākim, the Houthis also brought large swathes of ʿAmrān governorate under their control. As we have seen, by 2010, Sufyān was already completely in their hands. From 2011 onwards, driven by local political calculations and tribal feuds, many areas of ʿAmrān fell into the Houthis' laps without a fight.[4] During that time, their main adversaries in the province, the al-Aḥmar brothers and Sunni Islamists, were weakened by the absence of Saudi aid, as Riyadh remained passive and kept its distance from all parties to the ʿAmrān battles.[5] In January 2014, the Houthis seized the ancestral home compound of the al-Aḥmar clan near Khamir and demolished it. This was certainly another 'game changer': a highly visible and humiliating event for the clan that perfectly symbolized the shift in the balance of power in Yemen's north, likened by Yemeni press to the 'fall of the Pharaohs' (*suqūt al-farāʿinah*).

In July 2014, ʿAmrān's provincial capital fell to the Houthis. By this time, Sanaʿa was already encircled on all sides by Houthis in ʿAmrān, Arḥab, Banī Maṭar, Khawlān al-Ṭiyāl and Sanḥān. Within the city itself, they had a vast base of support. That said, not all sympathizers were staunch defenders of Houthism; many were simply frustrated with the prevailing political stalemate.[6]

While the Houthis had been forcefully expanding their dominion, Yemeni national politics had undergone profound transformations. In November 2011, the power transfer deal mediated by the GCC forced President Salih to resign and regulated the temporary transfer of the presidency to former vice president ʿAbdrabbuh Manṣūr Hādī, in return for domestic immunity for Salih. A UN-sponsored implementation document outlined a transition roadmap that included three principal tasks: holding a national dialogue with the goal of producing a new constitution before elections to be held in February 2014; addressing issues of transitional justice; and unifying as well as reforming the armed forces.[7]

Salih long resisted his disempowerment. Many noted his malicious smile when he finally signed the GCC agreement organizing his departure from power. And in fact, after his ouster, this master of both mischief and political manoeuvring sought to collude with ʿAbdulmalik al-Ḥūthī in order to weaken his rivals: Interim President Hādī and the Iṣlāḥ party. In his absolute desire for power, al-Ḥūthī entered into a pact with his former arch-enemy, a pact that resembled the medieval legend of Faust who made a contract with the devil, exchanging his soul for worldly gains. The alliance between Salih and the Houthis, as outrageous as it was artful, was initially kept secret. It was the result of the profound changes in Yemen's power structures since the beginning of the 'revolution' in 2011. There had been indications of secret cooperation between Salih and the rebels even before the conclusion of the GCC deal: collusion had begun to surface as early as late autumn 2011 in Ḥajjah and in al-Jawf, where Houthis fought against Salafis and Iṣlāḥ supporters with Republican Guard weapons.[8] How had it come about?

Salih, ailing and pressurized by the emerging Change Revolution's calls for his resignation, secretly began to arm the Houthis and facilitated their expansion. He hoped, by causing chaos and disorder, to distinguish himself as the only anchor of stability and Yemen's saviour, especially in the eyes of foreign countries. This alliance also explains why, in December 2012, the Houthis opposed the restructuring of the Republican Guard and the *firqah*: restructuring the army would weaken the influence of Salih and his family, and prevent the smuggling of weapons and heavy equipment from the Republican Guard to the Houthis.[9] In October 2014, a leaked phone conversation between Salih and Houthi field commander ʿAbdulwāḥid Abū Rās proved that the rebels had long been coordinating militarily and politically with the country's autocratic ex-leader to undermine the transitional government and to facilitate Houthi military expansion.[10]

On 18 March 2013, the National Dialogue Conference (NDC) commenced, a landmark event in Yemen's political transition. It was to include representatives of all political parties, civil society, the Southern Movement, Houthis, women and youth groups. A total of 565 delegates representing different sections of society were involved in the NDC, to discuss the roots of the country's problems and to facilitate reconciliation and peaceful transition in the aftermath of the revolution. The NDC's work was divided according to nine thematic sub-committees or working groups that ran the portfolio of political, institutional, and social issues facing the country.[11] The complexity of the conflict in Saʿdah and its sheer territorial dimension justified the establishment of its own sub-committee.

The Houthis had rejected the GCC initiative, but despite their immense reservations they did participate in the NDC. While the Houthi military 'hawks' slowly but surely established a stranglehold on the capital, the movement's delegation to the NDC was dominated by moderate and consensus-oriented 'doves', notably ʿAlī al-Bukhaytī, Aḥmad Sharaf al-Dīn, and ʿAbdulkarīm Jadbān. Around the negotiating table, they met Sunni Islamists with whom Houthi hardliners were at that very moment engaged in deadly battle.

In the NDC, the moderate Houthi delegates dusted off Ḥusayn al-Ḥūthī's social revolutionary agenda, which had moved somewhat into the background during the ordeals of the six Saʿdah wars. Ḥusayn's calls for equality of all groups and sects and for the end of patronage and corruption greatly influenced the political programme of the Houthi NDC delegates. They demanded the establishment of a 'participatory state' (*dawlat al-shirākah al-waṭaniyyah*) or—in the words of ʿAlī al-Bukhaytī—a 'Second Republic' (*al-jumhūriyyah al-thāniyyah*): a state which was neither the imamate of the *sādah*, nor the shaykhs' republic that had governed Saʿdah in recent decades, but one that ensured participation and representation of all people and groups.[12] In political terms, the Houthi delegates were largely in line with youth groups and the Southern Movement, who also called for a 'civil state' and opted for fundamental change and disempowerment of the old elites. The Houthi delegates managed to see their vision of statehood included in full in the NDC's final report.[13]

This agenda came as a surprise to many who were not familiar with the Houthis' roots: for the past ten years, the dominant narrative advocated by the state and government-linked media had hammered into its citizens that the Houthis were a movement remote-controlled by Iran, a 'foreign' proxy group or Fifth Column of Iranian imamism, aiming at re-installation of the pre-1962 imamate.

As expected, the dialogue between the Houthis and their Sunni Islamist nemeses was fraught with difficulties.[14] Three assassination attempts against Houthi delegates took place (two successful), which temporarily brought the Saʿdah working group to the brink of failure. Nevertheless, the Houthis worked towards the successful conclusion of the NDC. Yet upon that conclusion, the moderate Houthi wing had de facto disbanded, after the assassination of ʿAbdulkarīm Jadbān and Aḥmad Sharaf al-Dīn.

After the NDC, tensions intensified over the drafting of the federal system, which was seen as a possible solution to the country's various regional challenges. In February 2014, a fairly unrepresentative committee, handpicked and chaired by Interim President Hādī, delineated six federal regions: Āzāl, Sabaʾ, al-Janad, Tihāmah, Adan and Ḥaḍramawt. Most major political movements, including the Houthis, publicly rejected or expressed reservations about the six-region division. The Houthis argued that the plan distributed natural wealth unevenly. It deprived the Āzāl region, in which the Houthis' historical homeland of Saʿdah was situated, of significant resources and access to the coast. Here the Houthis were referring, respectively, to the hydrocarbon-rich governorate of al-Jawf and the Red Sea province of Ḥajjah, both of which the movement has traditionally considered within its sphere of influence.[15]

The Houthis' outrage at this plan and the growing strength of the movement's hardliners at the expense of the moderates brought the Hādī government under increasing pressure. The rebels reinforced their military presence and further tightened their grip on the capital. When they had encircled the city from all directions, they stepped up both their rhetoric and their actions. In his long speeches, broadcast at increasingly frequent intervals by the Shia TV station al-Masīrah, ʿAbdulmalik al-Ḥūthī impressed upon the transitional government in Sanaʿa that the Houthis were now a powerful, well-organized force to be reckoned with. Even if the discourse of self-defence still determined their political rhetoric, the Houthis had long begun to focus on the military seizure of the capital.

After a fuel subsidies reduction in July 2014, ʿAbdulmalik was able to seize the moment of national outrage and raise a list of demands including the sacking of the cabinet and its replacement by a competency-based technocratic government that would include all factions and thus also the Houthis, as well as implementation of the NDC outcomes—demands to which the government initially refused to respond.

As a result, the country witnessed a live political thriller, whose events were controlled by a master plan, carefully elaborated and orchestrated by ʿAbdulmalik, which engendered a series of concerted measures or escalation levels (*marāḥil al-taṣʿīd*) to gradually increase the pressure on the government in Sanaʿa and so force it to meet his political demands. The government reacted erratically. After months of stalemate, frantic political negotiations took place. Houthi representatives refused all offers the government made in order to defuse the crisis, and continued to pursue their provocation strategy in the capital.

By autumn 2014, the Houthis could credibly claim the strongest fighting skills of any sub-state group on the Arabian Peninsula. Their mastery of terrain, weaponry and small unit tactics was the product of ten years of insurgency. Those in Saʿdah who had endured the withering bombing campaigns of the Yemeni army—and, in the sixth war, of the Saudi air force—represented some of the most battle-tested fighters in the region. At that time, no other group was capable of matching the Houthis in ground combat.

On Sunday 21 September 2014, the inevitable happened: after violent confrontations between security forces and Houthi protesters, provoked by the Houthis' escalation strategy, the rebels overran Sanaʿa. In a swift coup de main, they seized the Yemeni capital. Those military and security units still loyal to Salih—the Central Security Forces and the Republican Guard—stood aside and watched the rebels take the town. The Houthis seized the campus of the ultra-conservative Sunni al-Imān University, a number of government institutions, including the Central Bank and several ministries, and homes belonging to members of the Iṣlāḥ party and the al-Aḥmar clan. They gained strategic advantage over a number of army units, and overpowered parts of the First Armoured Division headed by General ʿAlī Muḥsin. After ten years of war, the Houthis held the reins of power in their hands.

CONCLUSION

Anthropologists conduct intensive analyses of political, economic, sectarian and historical processes on a small scale. How can the micro-sociological study of an anthropologist contribute to the understanding of larger conflicts with regional impact, such as the Houthi conflict? As Geertz once asked, with characteristic irony, 'Are the petty squabbles of barnyard notables really what we mean by politics? Are mud huts and goat-skin tents really where the action is?'[1] The answer is yes. This book underlines the anthropologists' claims to study specific places, not for themselves or for the love of scrupulous description of daily life and local politics in remote places, but to learn something beyond them.

The petty squabbles of barnyard notables, pastoralists in Munabbih or shaykhs in Wādī Nushūr and Sufyān may not in themselves offer a more advantageous means of determining the components of a political system than the more formal deliberations of parliaments and cabinet meetings, or the viewpoints of urban middle-class intellectuals. As Eickelman and Piscatori have admirably shown, the link between the unit of the anthropologist's study and the larger whole is not necessarily that of microcosm and macrocosm, but merely of an arena of study that permits the elaboration of hypotheses about certain social and cultural processes.[2] Anthropologists seek an understanding of what is distinctive about general processes operating in specific historical and cultural settings. To this end, anthropological studies of recent years and decades reflect more directly than their predecessors how the 'background' themes of religious understandings, kinship and family, loyalty and alliance, gender relations, political authority, and the linkages between villages, regions, and states are linked to the hard surfaces of national politics and economics.

It was my aim here to widen the scope of interpretation of the Houthi conflict by giving fuller play to the complexities of local politics. It was obvious that the study of the conflict's local dynamics would require a sufficient contextual backdrop of the society and recent history of Saʿdah province and adjacent areas as a whole. The core of the discussion of these themes, therefore, was set against an account of these areas and their residents and a review of their recent past. Rather than adopting a more centralized view and concentrating on authorities such as states, political parties, religious scholars, and so on, this analysis focused on the role of the region's people in the implementation of policies, ideologies, and religious hermeneutics. These people did not lead the overarching debates, but it was they who formulated the local agendas, shaped the reality of tribal, political and sectarian practice and implemented these policies on the ground.

The notion of locality represented here—the study of the Houthi conflict in its very local context—implies what, from the anthropologist's perspective, is obvious: that religion, ideology, and national politics are elaborated, understood and subsequently reproduced in particular places and at particular moments. Yet, like any complex phenomenon, the Houthi conflict has had many ramifications and has developed in manifold, sometimes even incongruous ways. Mundy once wrote that 'if anthropology has any raison d'être [...] it is to allow us to confront the written schema of the intellectuals with the richer and untidy welter of living practice'.[3] After five years of research into the complexities of the Houthi conflict, I might add, with all humility, that this epic, ever expanding conflict sometimes appeared too abundant to be read.

The starting point for my consideration of the conflict's historical roots was the eight-year civil war between republican and royalist forces that commenced with the September Revolution of 1962. The civil war in Saʿdah is a good lesson in the practice of shaping tribal loyalties and alliances on the ground. Considering tribal alliances during the 1960s civil war reveals that in no case were the tribes of Saʿdah homogeneous blocs following any primordial political loyalties. Rather, during the 1960s civil war, tribes were riven by conflicts of opinion and other cleavages. This is not unusual, since tribes are not political entities and shaykhs are seldom backed by any political consensus among their tribal constituencies: they do not 'govern' their tribes. Ideally, a shaykh is meant to represent and unite his tribe in its entirety, rather than to assert it as a unitary political (or even military) entity on the national stage. Some shaykhs may develop enormous personal influence, and some shaykhs may even abuse their tribal influence to mobilize their tribesmen as military units (as the al-Aḥmar clan frequently did), yet except in cases of customary mediation and arbitration of tribal conflict under tribal law, shaykhs generally do not have a great deal of coercive power over the members of 'their' tribe or tribal section. This became particularly apparent in the Houthi conflict.

The 1962 September Revolution had pledged to the Yemeni people the abolition of social inequality and birthright privilege, and a more equitable distribution of political participation, economic resources and development. In the years and decades to come, the Republic was not able to keep many of these promises. After the civil war, in Yemen's extreme north *sayyid* hegemony was more or less substituted by shaykhly hegemony. The shaykhs had shaken off their former *sayyid* overlords, the administrative elite of the imamate claiming descent from the Prophet, and when the Yemeni Republic began to recruit shaykhs into the formal ruling establishment, for the first time in Yemen's modern history they became part of the government. The shaykhs benefited disproportionately from the republican system: at local level, in many respects they *were* the Republic.

Throughout history, tribal elites have been important for any government in northern Yemen. The tribes of the northern highlands have always lived together with states and tribal elites have always benefited from acting as 'nodes' or interfaces between the state and the northern tribes. Historically, states have frequently superimposed their administrative structures onto the template of tribal structures, with each ruler introducing much the same kinds of judicial, tax, and law-enforcement officials, and these men coordinated in similar ways with tribal officials. Nevertheless, the shaykhs, particularly those who had backed the nascent Republic during the civil war and were rewarded accordingly, had never been more powerful than in the post-revolutionary period. In conjunction with the weakness or even absence of state institutions in Yemen's north, a patrimonial structure emerged in which political power was bound to persons, rather than to institutions.

After Yemeni unification in 1990 and the emergence of a multiparty system, the political arena remained characterized by the continuing weakness of the state and subordination of its fragile institutions to excessive dependence on these dominant tribal personalities. In particular, in the municipal and parliamentary elections held after 1990, local politics became a 'big man' game in which the lion's share of policy-making power fell consistently to Saʿdah's influential shaykhs.

By no means did this entitlement to power and political representation touch all tribal leaders in the Saʿdah region, as many shaykhs remained closely connected to their tribal home bases, continued to perform diligently the central tasks of their office—representation and conflict resolution—and neither aspired to public office nor possessed economic enterprises or a second home in Sanaʿa. Yet, in the decades after the civil war, many of the more influential shaykhs began to consider the traditional concept of shaykhdom—as a social service beyond the struggle for national political participation and economic empowerment—unsuited to 'modern' post-revolutionary times. After the assassination of President Ibrāhīm al-Ḥamdī and the subsequent suspension of al-Ḥamdī's Correctional Initiative in the late 1970s, visions of a separation between tribal and political office and of economic prosperity for all citizens were increasingly doomed to oblivion. Instead, the trend was towards political and economic empowerment of influential tribal leaders: a vision which, in ʿAmrān, the Ḥāshid's senior shaykh ʿAbdullah al-Aḥmar and his sons expertly put in practice.

The politics of patronage was a double-edged sword: rather than 'nurturing' the tribal system, governmental patronage has driven a wedge between some influential shaykhs and their tribal home constituencies and has generated discontent and alienation among many ordinary tribal members, whose economic situation and living conditions have not always improved substantially after the 1960s civil war. This creeping alienation, as well as the underdevelopment of vast areas in Saʿdah province, was a particularly dangerous development, because shaykhs were the point of co-optation and the major interface allowing the Yemeni state to push its agenda in peripheral tribal areas without carrying out substantial state-building efforts. The estrangement of shaykhs and their tribes, therefore, left parts of the population virtually detached from state influence. As a rule of thumb, it can be observed that wherever shaykhs began to neglect their tribal duties, or a tribal base did not benefit from the empowerment of its shaykh, or government patronage favoured one tribal group or shaykh at the expense of another, the Houthi movement and its predecessors found particularly favourable conditions to grow.

The patronage exerted by the Saudi government had a similar preservative effect on the elite constellation in Saʿdah. Saudi patronage can even be traced back further, to the end of the Saudi-Yemeni War in 1934 and the subsequent conclusion of the Treaty of Ṭāʾif. Since 1934, shaykhs and their tribes in the Yemeni borderlands had played a central role in securing the international border between the two countries, and decades of Saudi financial largesse left their mark in the Yemeni borderlands. Since the turn of the millennium, the loyalty of the borderland tribes and shaykhs to the Saudi Kingdom has been shaken to some extent by the final demarcation of the boundary in 2000, and particularly by Saudi plans to police and fortify the border. Yet the present analysis has revealed that the post-2000 Saudi border fortification policy had less influence on the emergence of the Houthi conflict than the social and economic imbalances generated by the Yemeni and Saudi governments' patronage policies. The violence against Saudi border fortification and the violence of the Houthi conflict have often been separate phenomena. Conversely, the spread of the Houthi conflict throughout the province and the post-2011 Houthi suzerainty in Saʿdah and beyond have had an enormous impact on Saudi border fortifications, which recommenced in 2013 after being stalled for ten years by tribal resistance. It is no exaggeration to say that the Houthi conflict generated a crisis serious enough to destabilize the entire system of bilateral border protection that had depended since 1934 on the cooperation and co-optation of the borderland shaykhs.

In this volatile situation, characterized by social discontent and the struggle over resources and political participation, a sectarian element eventually triggered the emergence of a multifaceted resistance movement that later developed into the Houthi rebellion. The prevailing social and economic grievances among large parts of Saʿdah's citizenry were further aggravated by the marginalization of the locally prevalent Shia Zaydi doctrine and the spread of radical Sunnism, sponsored by Saudi Arabia and, at times, Sanaʿa. From the early 1980s, a specifically Zaydi response to the influx of radical Sunnism emerged in the region. This Zaydi revivalism began as a defensive movement to counter the radical Sunni and Salafi onslaught and the government policy of neglect. It involved a great deal of soul-searching and was inspired by a deep sense of peril arising from the spread and increasing popularity of Salafism.

A number of shaykhs supported Salafism on political grounds. During the 1960s civil war, most of them had fought for the Republic and against *sayyid* rule, and after the end of the civil war became influential people who struggled to maintain and consolidate their newly won power and influence. In the decades following the civil war, they continued to compete with the *sādah*, and the inflammatory speeches of Salafi preachers provided them with the ideological and rhetorical anti-*sayyid* ammunition needed to assert their own supremacy. Naturally, shaykhs quickly recognized the power dimension of the anti-*sayyid* thrust of radical Sunnism, especially Salafi doctrine, and some of them capitalized on it to reinforce their own empowerment and leadership claims.

Although the main Salafi teaching centre in the Saʿdah area, Dār al-Ḥadīth in Dammāj, was mainly attended by Yemenis from other regions and by foreigners, Salafism also found supporters among the local people, who were attracted by its ostensibly egalitarian doctrine. Yet, in the Saʿdah context, the fundamental problem of Salafism was that it questioned the *sādah*'s entitlement to spiritual leadership, but never questioned the shaykhs' entitlement to political leadership and economic enrichment: Salafism served to reinforce the existing status quo and the post-civil war class distinctions, which were perceived by many as undemocratic and unjust.

Across the Saʿdah region, but also in other areas with a large proportion of Zaydi residents, many Zaydis felt increasingly marginalized and alienated, blaming the republican state and its shaykhly vassals supporting a policy that they perceived as undermining their doctrine. In consequence, since the mid-1980s, a Zaydi resistance movement emerged and grew rapidly. From the turn of the millennium, this movement was significantly influenced by Ḥusayn al-Ḥūthī, a Zaydi cleric of famous *sayyid* pedigree based in Khawlān's Marrān mountains. In his charismatic lectures, Ḥusayn not only addressed the marginalization of the Zaydi community, but also articulated the economic neglect and underdevelopment of the area, the Republic's class-ridden system, and thus the local population's utter dissatisfaction with the existing state as embodied by the Salih government. Ḥusayn could credibly address the region's political and developmental imbalances, because part of the respect and influence he commanded among the local people derived from the al-Ḥūthī family's modest rural lifestyle, provision of various social services to the people, and status as protected clients with kinship relations to the local tribal population. In the local context, the Zaydi revival was far more than a sectarian movement: under Ḥusayn's direction, it also embraced powerful social-revolutionary and political components. The movement ultimately became a rallying point uniting the interests of those in the Saʿdah area (and beyond) who felt economically neglected, politically sidelined and religiously marginalized. The Zaydi revival movement managed to mobilize the people to demand their rights—in Saʿdah, something that neither political parties, nor civil society organizations nor the shaykhs could or would do.

Yet by no means did a majority of the Saʿdah population initially support Ḥusayn's cause. The religious-political programme of his emerging movement (continued after his death in 2004 by his half-brother ʿAbdulmalik) has not always met with approval. This tough resistance did not only come from the ranks of the shaykhs, Sunni Islamists and Salafis who also had a basis of support among the local population. The Zaydi revival movement, and especially the group around Ḥusayn, also generated profound tensions among Zaydis themselves, who subscribed to various political moralities. The stronger the Houthi movement grew, the deeper the divides in Saʿdah's society became.

This was the situation at the beginning of the first Saʿdah war in 2004: a powerful social revolutionary movement had arisen, directed against the political and economic empowerment of a small elite that served as the northern mainstay of the republican order. This movement featured equally powerful components of Zaydi revivalism and anti-Americanism. It was shaped and led by Ḥusayn al-Ḥūthī, a cleric-orator from a respected Zaydi family who was both brilliant and stubborn and resisted all attempts by President Ali Abdullah Salih to channel his resistance into the well-established and proven dialectics of government and (contained) opposition. Whereas many ordinary people in Yemen's north approved of Ḥusayn's agenda, the Salih regime and its local beneficiaries regarded it as a challenge, a provocation, and a danger. When, in summer 2004, Ḥusayn's unresponsiveness to Salih's summons reached new heights, the president turned to sheer force, and the first Saʿdah war erupted.

The third part of this book traces the course of the six Saʿdah wars (2004–10), with special consideration of the dynamics that led to its enormous territorial expansion: the conflict started in 2004 as a police operation in a village in the remote Marrān mountains. By 2011, the Houthis held sway in the entire Saʿdah province, as well as northern ʿAmrān and western al-Jawf. By 2014, the rebellion had overrun almost all of Yemen's north, including the capital Sanaʿa, and was about to provoke the multi-national foreign intervention which became known as the Saudi-led Operation Decisive Storm.

The first Saʿdah war in 2004 mainly focused on the Marrān mountains in the Khawlān massif in western Saʿdah governorate. This first round of war led to the death of Ḥusayn al-Ḥūthī and thus produced a martyr, a fact that greatly reinforced the Houthi movement's capacity for revolutionary mobilization. Given that a cult of the martyred personality is at the very core of Shiism, Ḥusayn's death became the mise en scène of unfinished Shia history and the beginning of a grand narrative of mystification of the movement's leader.

Instead of putting down the rebellion, the government's military campaigns triggered destructive cycles of violence and counter-violence in Saʿdah's tribal environment which, step by step, engulfed Yemen's north. During these battles, Saʿdah's citizenry became increasingly polarized along government-Houthi lines. From the second war, it became evident that a significant number of people joining the Houthis' ranks were no longer religiously or ideologically motivated, but were drawn into the conflict for other reasons.

The first-hour Houthi warriors had consisted of supporters, relatives, friends, and students of Ḥusayn al-Ḥūthī; most hailed from the Saʿdah region, especially from the Khawlān tribe, though his supporters also numbered people from other regions and governorates with Zaydi populations, including Ḥajjah, Dhamār, Sanaʿa, ʿAmrān and al-Jawf. The second, growing group of Houthi supporters consisted of people who did not join the movement for primarily ideological or sectarian reasons. Many had been drawn into the conflict after members of their family or tribe had been killed by bombings and other aggression by the armed forces. Others had lost their homes or farms. By 2006, thousands of men were fighting for the Houthis, not all of them sharing the Houthi ideology. They simply 'rode the wave' to fight for their tribe, or against their enemies and rivals, the government, or a hated shaykh. Thus, many Houthi fighters had no 'real' loyalty to the movement or its leaders; they switched sides based on interests that were direct, immediate and private.

Ever since the outbreak of the first war in 2004, the government had deployed mercenaries of the Ḥāshid confederation to the Saʿdah region to fight alongside regular troops. In Saʿdah's tribal environment, dominated by member tribes of the Khawlān b. ʿĀmir confederation and the Bakīl confederation, the incursion of armed Ḥāshid warriors as regime auxiliaries was a particularly sensitive and momentous issue. Many tribes of the conflict area were furious at the deployment of Ḥāshid irregulars into their tribal regions. Both the Khawlān b. ʿĀmir and the Bakīl considered these armed incursions an infringement of their sovereignty and their territorial integrity, and defended themselves against the presence of these mercenaries. In the overheated context of the Saʿdah wars, however, taking up arms against the Ḥāshid irregulars was tantamount to joining the Houthis.

This is not to say that all tribes of the conflict area joined the Houthis. On the contrary, after years of fighting, Saʿdah's tribes have become increasingly internally polarized. Among the tribes of the Khawlān b. ʿĀmir, this polarization has led to a significant increase of intra-tribal conflict, as disagreements between tribal groups became wrapped up in the larger Houthi conflict. Before the outbreak of the Saʿdah wars, many sections of the confederation had been engaged in a variety of petty feuds and ancient antagonisms over land and honour, but seldom (if ever) in large inter-tribal conflicts between member tribes—the specific territorial pattern of the confederation and the spatial dispersion of its moieties had usually prevented bloc formation and hence the uncontrolled escalation of large inter-tribal conflicts.

During the Saʿdah wars, many of these petty tribal feuds merged with the Houthi conflict, as those involved sought the assistance of either the government or the Houthis. This implies that during the Saʿdah wars battles related to the Houthi conflict have been frequent within Khawlān b. ʿĀmir territory, but both the Houthis and their opponents were relatively incoherent groups that could in some cases loosely correspond to certain tribal segments, but hardly, if ever, to whole tribes. One exception is the Munabbih tribe in Saʿdah governorate's extreme northwest, who formed a relatively homogeneous solidarity group against the Houthis. In the sixth war, the Munabbih fought hard (though ultimately unsuccessfully) to ward off the Houthis' endeavours to extend control over their territory.

In contrast, among the Bakīl, a confederation historically much more involved in Yemen's national power struggles than the rather 'peripheral' tribes of the Khawlān b. ʿĀmir, the fusion of tribal feuding with the Houthi conflict at times led to the formation of large blocs and the opening of inter-tribal fronts, as a result of which whole tribes were at times opposed to one another. The situation in northern ʿAmrān (the Sufyān against the al-ʿUṣaymāt) and al-Jawf (the Hamdān al-Jawf and Dhū Ḥusayn, notably the Shawlān section, against the Dhū Muḥammad and Āl Ashrāf) are good examples. This is not to say that the Saʿdah wars were bloodier or more brutal among the Bakīl, as the war claimed a high toll of lives everywhere. Among the confederation's tribes and sections, however, the fronts (the lines between Houthi and government supporters) tended to be more homogeneous and clear-cut than among the Khawlān b. ʿĀmir.

Yet, despite the important role of tribal feuding, the Houthi conflict was never a purely tribal conflict. By the heterogeneity of its stakeholders (tribesmen, *sādah*, armed forces, mercenaries, etc.) and their numerous, even diverging objectives and motivations, the conflict rather became a kind of 'hybrid' war—*ḥarb mukhtalaṭah*, as locals say—whose political, ideological, military, tribal, sectarian, and personal motivations kept oscillating. As a result, tribal customs of peaceful conflict settlement increasingly came to be ignored. The brutalization of the war was not caused by tribal norms, but precisely by their erosion. The ferocity of the battles was of a kind and on a scale exceeding all local rules of engagement, and clearly went far beyond the maximum escalation level of tribal conflict as defined by Jamous.[4]

During the Saʿdah wars, both sides deliberately worked at recruiting local tribes to capitalize on their combat experience, local knowledge and sheer manpower. In the fourth war, as it became increasingly clear that the situation was continually deteriorating and the regular army alone couldn't get the situation under control, President Salih deliberately pushed forward the formation of large tribal militias to supplement the regular army. His endeavours led to the creation of the Popular Army in al-ʿUṣaymāt, which was recruited by the al-Aḥmar clan. The Popular Army comprised Ḥāshid mercenaries, but also Sunni radicals and mercenaries from other areas; it never was a purely tribal force.

In the Saʿdah region itself, the shaykhs proved less amenable than the al-Aḥmar clan, whom the Saʿdah shaykhs blamed for abusing shaykhly power to force Yemen's tribes into fratricidal warfare. In this province, therefore, mass enlistment of shaykhs and their tribes as auxiliaries to the regular army proved a greater challenge than among the Ḥāshid in ʿAmrān. Though the shaykhs of Saʿdah by no means refuted the necessity of defeating the Houthis, they were alienated by President Salih's disastrous crisis management, which had led to a steady expansion of the war zone. Moreover, they interpreted the government's endeavours to recruit their tribesmen as a means to deliberately trigger blood feud and fratricidal warfare among the tribes, thus causing chaos and weakening them by exploiting the chain reactions of retaliation and revenge. Though many of the shaykhs and tribes were already heavily involved in the war against the Houthis, military mass recruitment of whole tribes for the government's political purposes was seen as going too far. In the shaykhs' opinion, the defence of the country against the Houthi threat was the duty of the state military, not the local tribes. Between the fourth and fifth wars, these disagreements and misunderstandings between the government and the shaykhs eventually led to a break between the regime and some of Saʿdah's and al-Jawf's most influential shaykhs, who had previously been Salih's ultimate mainstay in this remote region.

External factors, too, contributed to the prolongation and proliferation of the war. The conflict developed a momentum of its own within a wider framework that drew on separate local, domestic and international driving forces. Domestically, the war was fuelled by political rivalries—notably between President Salih and General ʿAlī Muḥsin—and the emergence of profitable domestic and international war economies. Foreign actors, too, led to a continuation of the conflict as Saudi Arabia, Libya and (allegedly) Iran began to interfere in the conflict.

Since the onset of the Saʿdah wars in 2004, multiple attempts at de-escalation and conflict mediation have taken place to defuse the crisis and to restore peace and stability in Yemen's north. The appointment of mediators and mediation teams is not surprising, as mediation is the socially and politically preferred means of conflict management in Yemen. Setting up mediation teams in times of crisis is common practice. The Yemeni tribes, in particular, have effective mechanisms for channelling crises into litigation. Thus, the Houthi conflict has continuously been accompanied by mediation endeavours by religious scholars, tribal shaykhs, politicians, and foreign actors, notably Qatar. Despite intensive efforts, however, the conflict could only be temporarily halted, and no sustainable results have emerged from mediation to date. Conventional mechanisms of crisis prevention and control seemed to have limited application: among other obstacles, the regime's poor conflict management, the lack of political will to definitively end the war, political intrigues, rivalries, unauthorized military action, lack of local knowledge, obscure phrasing, impossible conditions and pitfalls inherent in ceasefire agreements together generated such a fiasco that, in 2009, local stakeholders to the conflict ultimately demanded the cessation of any mediation with the Houthis. Analysis of the composition, approaches and success of the mediation teams and of the reasons for their (short-term) success or failure revealed that de-escalation of the Houthi crisis has been sabotaged not only by the warring parties' lack of commitment, but also by non-compliance with fundamental prerequisites of mediation, thus impeding restoration of stability in Yemen.

The government's inability or unwillingness to end the bloodshed has severely damaged the prestige and the reputation of the state among its citizens and its remaining allies. As Gingrich argues, historically mediation has always been a key asset and sign of the quality of good governance in state activities in northernmost Yemen, as the state was historically largely operating within a wider tribal environment where addressing and mediating smaller and larger conflicts was a routine part of ruling, wherever the state had at least some influence.[5] I would add that the same still pertains to modern Yemen, and the Salih regime (motivated by envy, political gambles, and material greed) failed miserably to maintain this model integrated into the normative pantheon of good governance in Yemen over several centuries.

The Saʿdah wars called into question many putative certainties in Yemen's north. Among the crisis zone's local population, the government's mismanagement of the war caused an increasing drain towards the Houthi forces. The government's clumsy and insidious response to the crisis also pushed forward the disintegration of the once strong alliance between the Salih regime and many northern shaykhs. This is particularly tragic as both the state and most shaykhs had the same ultimate goal—to combat the Houthis. After the disintegration of their alliance, each continued to fight the Houthis alone. The rebellion benefited enormously from this fragmentation and the ensuing lack of unity or concerted action among its opponents.

By the outbreak of the sixth and last 'official' Saʿdah war (Operation Scorched Earth) in August 2009, the Houthis had already become so strong that the Yemeni army averted its final defeat only thanks to Saudi intervention. The rebels used the phase between the end of the sixth war and the beginning of Yemen's 'Change Revolution' in spring 2011 to consolidate their power and to suppress or eliminate their last adversaries among the local population of areas where they held sway. Since the beginning of the Change Revolution, they have embarked on a dual strategy of both political participation in Yemen's transition process and further military expansion: in spring 2011, they seized Saʿdah city and three years later, in September 2014, Yemen's capital.

The conquest of Sanaʿa is the landmark event with which this book concludes. Its fall, however, is far from the end of the story, but rather the beginning of a new, even more prominent chain of events: the Houthis' expulsion of the new interim government, Operation Decisive Storm, and the protracted negotiations between the Yemeni government, Houthis, and the UN in Switzerland and Kuwait. Consideration of these developments will no doubt fill other books to come. It is understandable that the dramatic turn in Yemen since 2014 has received far more international attention and coverage than the petty squabbles of shaykhs and tribes in Yemen's remote north—Geertz's 'barnyard notables', who started it all, and with whom this book deals.

NOTES

PREFACE AND ACKNOWLEDGEMENTS

1. Jenkins 1994: 445.
2. De Regt 2015.
3. On the approaches of digital anthropological fieldwork (also called the 'distance approach'), see Introduction: The Research.
4. Herzfeld 1987.

INTRODUCTION: THE INTERIOR VIEW OF A WAR

1. Mundy 1995: 5.
2. Influenced by segmentary theory, Gellner pictured tribes as an outer circle of 'wolves' absorbed by antagonisms and local feuds. According to what is known as the Khaldūnian cycle, militarily superior tribes united by *ʿaṣabiyyah* (group spirit) periodically conquer centres of civilization. Once united under the leadership of a group possessing both *ʿaṣabiyyah* and a religious message (*daʿwah*), they turn into 'sheepdogs' and attack the central government, causing the fall of the state and the rise of a new dynasty. These tribes are then conquered in turn; see Gellner 1981: 29–30. Because of its inherent inconsistencies, segmentary theory is today regarded as defunct; see the discussion of segmentary theory in Chapter 1 of this book.
3. Eickelman 2002; Eickelman and Piscatori 2004; al-Rasheed and Vitalis 2004; al-Rasheed 2007.
4. Martin 2002.
5. The issue of epistemology has vexed anthropologists for a long time, and no conclusive answers have yet been found. On different opinions in regard to anthropology and epistemology, see Toren and Pina-Cabral 2011.
6. On triangulation of research methods, see Flick 2008.
7. On archival work, see Platt 2012.
8. DeWalt et al. 1998; Emerson et al. 2001.
9. See Boellstorff 2012; Sanjek and Tratner 2015; Robben 2009.

1. TERRITORIES AND SOCIETIES

1. For an elaborate account of Yemen's topography, see Kopp 1981: 29–56 and 2005: 31–44. For topographical features of special areas of the Saʿdah region, see Gingrich and Heiss 1986 (Saʿdah basin, Munabbih, Rāziḥ, Saḥār, Wāʾilah); Gingrich 1989a, 1994a (Munabbih); Lichtenthäler 2003 (Saḥār); Weir 2007 (Rāziḥ).
2. Gingrich and Heiss 1986: 71; Gingrich 1989a: 43–71, 1994a: 45–67; Weir 2007: 14–16. On *qāt* in Yemen, see Weir 1985; Gatter 2012.
3. On topographical features of the Saʿdah basin, see Lichtenthäler 2003: 33–37.
4. Lichtenthäler 2003: 37.
5. Gingrich and Heiss 1986: 15, 27.
6. Gingrich and Heiss 1986: 27. On water depletion in the Saʿdah basin, see Lichtenthäler 2003.
7. Gingrich and Heiss 1986: 87–88.
8. Philby 1952: 408; Forrer 1942: 321.
9. Gingrich and Heiss 1986: 28.
10. Dresch 1989: 27.
11. The southern border of al-Jawf has no distinctive topographical features. It is defined by the border between the tribal territories of Bakīl and Madhḥij.
12. Brandt 2016: 127.
13. Steffen 1978: II/169.
14. Steffen 1978: II/121–4, 198.
15. For a summary of this scientific discussion, see Gingrich 2015.
16. In regard to Yemen, Wedeen (2008) and Blumi (2011) have called for replacement of the term 'tribe' by 'community'.
17. Gingrich 2015.
18. Evans-Pritchard 1940; Gellner 1969: 41–4.
19. See, for example, Dresch 1986.
20. Gellner 1981: 117.
21. Al-Wardī 1962: 143–144.
22. See, for example, Adra 1982; Caton 1987, 1990; Gingrich 1989a, 1994a; Weir 2007.
23. Gingrich 2014b.
24. See Dresch's main works, e.g. 1989. See also Dostal 1974; Gerholm 1977; Adra 1982; Caton 1987, 1990; Gingrich 1989a, 1994a; Weir 2007; Brandt 2012, 2013, 2014a, 2014c.
25. Bonte and Conte 1991.
26. Gingrich 2015.
27. Mundy 1995:9.
28. Adra 1982: 139–58.
29. On the concept of tribal honour, see, for example, Serjeant 1977: 227–8; Adra 1982: 142–4, 185–6; Caton 1987, 1990: 161–5; Dresch 1989: 38–70; Gingrich 2002: 148–52; Weir 2007: 49–51.

30. For a comprehensive account of the social significance of the Yemeni dagger, see Heinze 2015.
31. Dresch 1986: 312.
32. The role of shaykhs in the tribal societies of Yemen is well documented; see, for example, Serjeant 1977: 228–30; Adra 1982; Dresch 1984a; Dresch 1989: 97–106; Gingrich 1989a: 105–36, 1989b; Weir 2007: 95–120. The term shaykh can denote either a tribal or a religious leadership position, as expressed in the terms *shaykh al-qabīlah* (tribal leader) and *shaykh al-dīn* (religious scholar). In this book, the term is exclusively used to denote tribal leaders.
33. Gingrich 1989a: 131–2; Weir 2007: 101.
34. Dresch 1984a: 36; Dupret 2000b; Weir 2007: 68, 102.
35. Dresch 1984a: 41; Weir 2007: 79.
36. Weir 2007: 112–20.
37. Adra 1982: 144.
38. Caton 1987, 1990.
39. Gingrich 1989a: 117–23; Messick 1993: 140, 182–4; Dupret 2000a; Dresch 2006; al-Zwaini 2006: 9–10; Weir 2007: 144–7.
40. Al-Zwaini 2012.
41. Glaser 1913; Rathjens 1951: 4; Serjeant 1969: 11; Dresch 1989: 184–8; 2006: 3.
42. Weir 2007: 145–6.
43. Gingrich 1989a: 124–6.
44. Information on social strata in Yemen can be found in all ethnographic works on Yemen. See, for example, Dostal 1974; Serjeant 1977; Gerholm 1977; Adra 1982; Niewöhner-Eberhard 1985; Mermier 1985, 1993; Meissner 1987; Dresch 1989; Gingrich 1989a, 1994a; Weir 2007.
45. Van Arendonk 1960; Heiss 1989: 63–74.
46. The legal teachings and judgments of Yaḥyā b. al-Ḥusayn are the basis for the so-called Zaydi Hādawī school. The main emphasis of Zaydi Hādawī teaching is its insistence on righteous rule through the *sādah*; for details, see Chapter 4, 'The Sunnization of Upper Yemen'.
47. Puin 1984: 484.
48. Vom Bruck 2005: 160–2.
49. On *sayyid* and tribal marriage patterns, see Serjeant 1977: 227, 238–9; Mundy 1995: 48, 173–5; vom Bruck 2005: 131–62. For special tribal marriage patterns in the Saʿdah region, see Gingrich 1989d.
50. Serjeant 1962: 41–57; Gochenour 1984: 165–74; Puin 1984: 483–94; Dresch 1989: 140–5, 159–60, 165–6; Madelung 1991; Albergoni and Bédoucha 1991; vom Bruck 2005: 38–9, 76; Weir 2007: 52–8, 156–7.
51. Al-Akwa' 1996.
52. Hovden 2018.
53. Gingrich and Heiss 1986: 21.

54. Vom Bruck 2005: 199–215.
55. Serjeant 1977: 237; Dresch 1989: 136–40; Weir 2007: 52.
56. Dresch 1989: 131, 137, 139.
57. Serjeant 1977: 230–5; Dresch 1989: 118–23; Gingrich 1989a: 137–44; Mundy 1995: 45–6; Weir 2007: 58–9.
58. Dresch 1989: 118. Note that for a tribesman to offend against a weak person is a disgrace.
59. Dresch 1989: 78.
60. Weir 2007: 66.
61. On the Treaty of Ṭā'if of 1934 and its renewal by the Treaty of Jeddah in 2000, see Chapter 3.
62. Brandt 2014b: 70–1.
63. Ibid.: 63.
64. Ibid.: 64.
65. Ibid.: 67.
65. Al-Ḥajrī 1984: 475–7; Gingrich 1989b: 75–85.
66. Weir 2007: 11–12.
68. Rāziḥ's Munabbih section is distinct from the Munabbih member tribe of the Khawlān b. ʿĀmir confederation.
69. Weir 2007: 131.
70. Gingrich and Heiss 1986: 71; Weir 2007: 5–6.
71. Gingrich 1993: 267–72; Weir 2007: 5–6.
72. Gingrich 1994a: 14–16.
73. Ibid.: 25.
74. Ibid.: 25–6.
75. Gingrich 1989a: 85; Gingrich 1994a: 18–20.
76. Gingrich 1994a: 12.
77. On Munabbih's dialect, see Behnstedt 1987a: 93–107; Behnstedt 1987b: 1–128, 173–223, 227–316. On Munabbih costume, see Gingrich 1989e.
78. Lichtenthäler 2003: 41.
79. Niewöhner-Eberhard 1985: 8.
80. Lichtenthäler 2003: 73–101.
81. Niewöhner-Eberhard 1985: 58–64.
82. On the medieval inhabitants of Saʿdah city, see Heiss 1998, 2014. On the inhabitants of modern Saʿdah, see Niewöhner-Eberhard 1985.
83. The large Hamdān confederation (consisting of the tribes of Ḥāshid and Bakīl) must be distinguished from the homonymous member tribe Hamdān of the Ḥāshid confederation (usually called Hamdān Sanaʿa to distinguish it).
84. Brandt 2016: 133.
85. Gingrich and Heiss 1986: 112.
86. Gingrich and Heiss 1986: 130; Dresch 1989: 309; Gingrich 1993: 263–7; Lichtenthäler 2003: 62, 80–1.

87. Gingrich 1993: 263–7.
88. Brandt 2016: 129.
89. Brandt 2016: 132.
90. The Ashrāf tribe claims direct descent from the Prophet Muhammad. Despite maintaining a degree of independence from the tribal environment within which they live, the Āl Ashrāf nonetheless maintain many of the structural characteristics of a conventional tribe; see vom Bruck 2005: 141–2.
91. Brandt 2016: 136–8.
92. Dresch 1989: 340.
93. Dresch 1989: 27.
94. The Wādiʿah are not included in Figure 1.2 because their precise genealogical affiliation is unclear.

2. ELITE TRANSFORMATIONS

1. Haykel 2003.
2. That is, elements of the *longue durée*, as introduced by Braudel and elaborated by Gingrich. Braudel 1958; Gingrich (forthcoming).
3. The situation encountered by Elke Niewöhner-Eberhard (1985) in Saʿdah city during her fieldwork (1971–4) in many respects represented the 'zero hour' after the civil war. She observed that state influence was limited to the city, and that both the city and the surrounding area were only marginally touched by the profound economic, social and political transformations that were then taking place in the more central parts of Yemen. A car drive from Sanaʿa to Saʿdah city often took days, and from the perspective of Saʿdah city's inhabitants the political entity called 'Yemen' began only south of Khamir. Likewise, in Rāziḥ, where Weir (1986, 1997, 2007) conducted fieldwork in 1977–80, tribal norms and values were still largely unaffected by the influence of the central government. This applies even more to the tribal society of Munabbih, which is historically characterized by strong isolationist tendencies; during his fieldwork in Munabbih in the mid-1980s, Gingrich (1987, 1989 a-e, 1993, 1994a, 1996, 2001, 2002, 2011, 2014a) encountered a society practically decoupled from direct government influence. By contrast, in more central areas such as Saʿdah city, Saḥār, and Wāʾilah, Gingrich and Heiss (1986) were able to witness clear signs of social and economic change in the early 1980s. However, about a decade later, Gerhard Lichtenthäler (2003), whose field research in the Saʿdah basin concentrated on the period between 1996 and 1999, depicted a society that was already characterized by severe struggles for land, economic resources, and political participation.
4. Expressions used by a local interviewee. Interview, November 2012.
5. On the mutual alliances and interdependences between imams, tribes and shaykhs, see Dresch 1989: 198–230; Dresch 1990.

6. Serjeant 1983: 96–7. For a more detailed analysis of the Daʿʿān treaty, see al-Saqqaf 1999: 141.
7. The description of the hostage system is based in part on the accounts given by Pawelke 1959: 74–5; Wenner 1967: 78–80; O'Ballance 1971: 27–8; Dresch 1989: 229; Dresch 1990: 273–4; and Weir 2007: 273–5.
8. Weir 2007: 273.
9. Information given by a shaykh from Munabbih whose father was among the hostages held by Imam Aḥmad.
10. Weir 2007: 274.
11. According to several sources from Saḥār, including one whose brother was held as a hostage before 1962.
12. Al-Sufyānī 2004 (1): 172. He refers to 600 executed hostages from Khawlān b. ʿĀmir.
13. Wenner 1967: 79.
14. A local source from the Saʿdah area explained that the method of shackling one prison inmate to another was frequently applied in imamic prisons in order to 'settle disputes between them'. Interview, March 2013.
15. For a comparative elaboration of the fundamentals of tribal leadership among the Khawlān b. ʿĀmir and Hamdān b. Zayd (Ḥāshid and Bakīl), see Brandt 2014c.
16. Wenner 1967: 65; O'Ballance 1971: 27–8.
17. According to several interviews with shaykhs from the Saʿdah area.
18. Ibid.
19. Parts of his memoirs were published in *14th October* newspaper; see Shuwayṭ 2006. Qāʾid Shuwayṭ refers to these 'military shaykhs' as *ʿarāʾif* (sing. *ʿarīf*). *ʿArīf* is a term to denote the leaders of the imamic *jaysh al-barrānī*, a kind of paramilitary force made up of tribal levies that complemented the regular imamic forces. These tribal forces were divided into groups, each under the leadership of a shaykh. Fattah notes that *ʿarīf* is a Turkish military title; see Fattah 2010: 27–8. Among the tribes of Khawlān b. ʿĀmir federation, however, the term *ʿarīf* or *ʿarīfah* is traditionally used to denote 'minor' or 'young' shaykhs. In the Saudi ʿAsīr region beyond the border, the term denotes mayors and 'small' representatives of the central government (I thank Andre Gingrich for this information).
20. Stookey 1978: 205–6; Wenner 1967: 125.
21. As recorded in al-Sufyānī 2004: 110–13.
22. This is seen as the second plane hijacking incident in Yemen, the first having been carried out by ʿAlī b. Nāṣir al-Qardaʿī of Murād in the 1930s. See Dresch 1995.
23. O'Ballance 1971: 66, 82.
24. Al-Aḥmar 2007 (3): 85.
25. Al-Aḥmar 2007 (3): 85.
26. Gingrich 1994b: 106. See also O'Ballance 1971: 91, 126–8 on punitive campaigns during the civil war in Saʿdah's western mountains.
27. Stookey 1978: 243–4; Dresch 1989: 223.

28. O'Ballance 1971: 66, 81.
29. Al-Aḥmar 2007 (3): 85.
30. Weir 2007: 256–83.
31. Ibid.: 281.
32. Al-Sufyānī 2004: 119; Weir 2007: 281, 291.
33. According to local sources from Khawlān and ʿAbdullah al-Aḥmar—see al-Aḥmar 2007 (3): 85. Also, al-Sufyānī mentions 'Qāsim Ghatāyah' being a pro-republican shaykh; see al-Sufyānī 2004: 119.
34. The late Yaḥyā Muḥammad Muqīt still earns tremendous admiration from certain tribes and *sādah* in the Saʿdah area for his active royalism during the civil war, yet a famous *zāmil* (tribal chant) dating back to the reign of Imam Yaḥyā indicates that the latter temporarily threw either him or his predecessor in prison.
35. Local sources from Saḥār and Jumāʿah stressed the pro-republican role of Āl al-Ḥamāṭī as well as some tribal divisions and their shaykhs from Ahl Majz. Al-Sufyānī mentions Muḥammad Muṣliḥ al-Naḥū's republicanism during the 1960s civil war; see al-Sufyānī 2004: 119.
36. In his habilitation thesis, Gingrich considers the strategic coalitions of the tribes of Khawlān b. ʿĀmir in the context of the relative imbalance between the confederation's two moieties, the Furūd and the Yahāniyyah. The dominance of Yahāniyyah tribes within the confederation and the relative weakness of Furūd tribes tend to lead more frequently to alliances between Furūd tribes and others outside the confederation; see Gingrich 1989a: 164–5. Indeed, during the 1960s civil war, Munabbih and Saḥār (both belonging to the Furūd moiety) were the first Khawlān b. ʿĀmir tribes to renounce the imamate; see Gingrich 1989a: 103, 576 n. 121.
37. Local sources from Saḥār and Khawlān. Also, Lichtenthäler mentions Dirdaḥ's royalist stance during the civil war; see Lichtenthäler 2003: 57.
38. In addition to several interviews with local sources from Saḥār, Jumāʿah, Khawlān, Sufyān, and Najrān, this information is taken from al-Sufyānī 2004: 19; al-Aḥmar 2007 (3): 94–5; and Lichtenthäler 2003: 57–66. The Saʿdah Brigade cooperated with the well-known pro-republican shaykhs of Ḥāshid and Bakīl, such as Amīn Abū Rās, ʿAbdullah Nājī Dāris, ʿAbdullah al-Aḥmar, Mujāhid Abū Shawārib, Ḥamūd b. ʿAzīz, ʿAbdullah b. Ḥusayn Dhaybān, etc., whose support played a central role in the 'liberation' of Saʿdah.
39. Gingrich 1993: 273; 2011: 40.
40. On the intra-tribal competition between Ibn ʿAwfān and Ibn Miṭrī, see Gingrich 1989a: 199; Gingrich 1994a: 26, Brandt 2012: 56–8.
41. O'Ballance 1971:110.
42. The Wāʾilah and the Dahm reckon themselves descendants of Shākir b. Bakīl, see Brandt 2016. Wāʾilah sources told me about the local belief regarding the 740 CE Battle of Kūfah between Imam Zayd b. ʿAlī (eponym of the Zaydis) and the

Umayyads: supposedly Shākir tribesmen were among Imam Zayd's allies, who protected and sheltered him in their tents when he was injured and dying, and this generated a strong affiliation between the Wā'ilah sections and Zaydism. Some northern sections of the Wā'ilah, however, are—like large parts of Yām—of Ismaili denomination.

43. Niewöhner-Eberhard 1985: 71; al-Sufyānī 2004: 113.
44. Lichtenthäler 2003: 61–3, 83.
45. According to several members of the Wā'ilah tribe.
46. Since 1934, the Dāyil b. Fayṣal shaykhly lineage of the Wā'ilah has established a particularly close relationship with the Saudi government. According to members of the Dāyil b. Fayṣal clan, Maʿbar believed that the Egyptian armed forces, in their attempt to advance on Najrān through Wā'ilah, did not intend to support the revolution in Yemen, but rather to wage war against Saudi Arabia. During the battle between Wā'ilah and the republican forces in Wādī Nushūr, Maʿbar is said to have shouted at the enemies that the latter 'would not withdraw even if only girls of Wā'ilah were left' (*lā insiḥāb ḥattā law lam yabqā siwā al-banāt min Wā'ilah yuḥāribūna!*). To this day, his descendants relate with pride and bravado this poignant anecdote, suggesting that Maʿbar and his followers had inflicted on the enemy 'losses so disastrous that the Egyptians finally retreated to Egypt'. Interview, September 2014.
47. The Wā'ilah and the Dahm have a history of tribal conflict; see Dresch 1989: 347; Brandt 2016.
48. Niewöhner-Eberhard 1985:12, 21, 62; al-Sufyānī 2004: 115–19.
49. Shuwayṭ 2006.
50. This account is based on information available in al-Sufyānī 2004: 116–19; Shuwayṭ 2006; al-Dawlah 2009; and local sources from Saḥār. Lichtenthäler mentions Ibn Ḥaydar of Sufyān being one of the conspirators, see Lichtenthäler 2003: 71 n.13. According to my sources he was not involved but rather active on the royalist side.
51. According to a Wā'ilah source, with typically hyperbolic rhetoric. Interview, April 2013.
52. Niewöhner-Eberhard reported that Saʿdah city's eastern gate (Bāb Juʿrān) was bricked up in the 1970s and an alternative aperture in the eastern city wall closed again because of Hamdān (Wā'ilah) tribal members causing 'uncontrolled disorder' in the city; see Niewöhner-Eberhard 1985: 255 n. 32. According to Huibert Wierda, who worked in Saʿdah hospital from 1973 to 2007, Bāb Juʿrān was closed from the time of the civil war, presumably for fear of Wā'ilah tribes from the eastern province, and only reopened around 2004.
53. Local sources from that area indicate that when Mujāhid Abū Shawārib reached Kitāf, there was word among the Wā'ilah tribes that 'Ḥāshid has occupied the land of Hamdān'. For this reason, he did not proceed further, in order to avoid provoking the imperatives of ʿ*aṣabiyyah* (tribal solidarity).

54. Al-Sufyānī 2004: 117–18; Weir 2007: 280–3.
55. Burrowes 1987: 49–51; Dresch 1989: 102–4.
56. Volkan 2004.
57. See Chapter 6, 'The Government Loses its Last Cards' and 'Seizure of Saʿdah City'.
58. Interview, July 2012.
59. Stookey 1978: 233; Dresch 1989: 140; vom Bruck 1998: 153; 2005: 199–236.
60. Vom Bruck 2005: 199–202.
61. Stookey 1974: 249; Niewöhner-Eberhard 1985: 6, 12, 57; Weir 2007: 286; Weir 2011.
62. Stookey 1974: 249; Stookey 1978: 233, 254–5; Niewöhner-Eberhard 1985: 64; vom Bruck 1998: 167–9; vom Bruck 2005: 207; Weir 2007: 286; Peterson 2008b: 5.
63. Niewöhner-Eberhard 1985: 64; al-Sufyānī 2004 (1): 133; Sharaf al-Dīn 1995: 58. In recognition of his contribution to the liberation of the Saʿdah area and the overthrow of the imamate, in 1969 Mujāhid Abū Shawārib became the first republican governor of the province. Niewöhner-Eberhard mentions that his successor, ʿAbdullah al-Ṣaʿdī, was subjected to hostility from some of Saʿdah's tribal republican camp; see Niewöhner-Eberhard 1985: 201–2.
64. Stookey 1974: 249; Niewöhner-Eberhard 1985: 60–4; Lichtenthäler 2003: 46.
65. Haykel 1995; Haykel 1999: 199–200.
66. Dresch 1989: 142; Weir 2007: 157, 284–5.
67. Dresch 1984b: 169; Dresch 1990: 275–6; Burrowes 1987: 31; Mundy 1995: 15; Weir 2007: 283; Hart-Davis 2012.
68. Vom Bruck 2005: 53, 56.
69. The incumbent Shaykh Ḥasan Muqīt can trace a pedigree of sixty-four ancestors (sing. *jadd*), which certainly goes back to the tenth century, if not earlier.
70. As indicated by sources from among these families, the Rawkān (Khawlān), al-Surabī (Saḥār), and al-ʿAzzām (Rāziḥ) lineages have family pedigrees of approximately 800 years. The emergence of Munabbih's ʿAwfān shaykhly lineage goes back to the sixteenth century; see Gingrich 1989a: 133.
71. The Abū Rās and certain other shaykhly lineages of Bakīlī stock carry the epithet *naqīb* (lit. 'captain'); see Serjeant 1982: 14; Dresch 1989: 405; Dresch 2006: 13 n. 43, 115 n. 38; Brandt 2014c: 104–5.
72. Peterson 1982: 91.
73. The frequent listing of the names of those shaykhs who sided with the republic is a typical feature of memoirs dealing with the revolution and the civil war; see for example the memoirs of ʿAbdullah al-Aḥmar published in 2007.
74. The strong conviction of Zaydi supremacy and the special privileges enjoyed by members of the Ahl al-Bayt by birth has also been shaken to some extent by the expensive and often excellent secular education of the offspring of shaykhs, businessmen and politicians (mostly in personal union). As certain shaykhs began to

enjoy greater wealth and government patronage, they started to send their sons to expensive private schools in Sanaʿa, notably the Sanaʿa International School (SIS), or to foreign boarding schools. One prominent shaykh of Saḥār sent a son to the British military academy, Sandhurst, where he received an elite military training similar to that of Khālid, son of former President Salih; see Brandt 2014a: 111. The son of another influential Wāʾilah shaykh received outstanding training in the UK as a fighter pilot.

75. Brandt 2010: 58–62.
76. Gingrich 1989a: 113; 1989d.
77. Lichtenthäler 2003: 45, 57, 64.
78. Weir 2007: 285.
79. Al-Sufyānī 2004 (1): 134, 137. The Republic's distrust of many shaykhs from the Saʿdah area proved to be rather resilient. Weir mentions that in 1992 twenty gun-mounted trucks and two armoured cars came to Rāziḥ on behalf of the state, after a rumour reached the government that Imam Muḥammad al-Badr had 'returned to Rāziḥ' and was being sheltered by a local shaykh; see Weir 2007: 301.
80. Niewöhner-Eberhard 1985: 158, 218.
81. Lichtenthäler 2003: 81.
82. Ibid.: 63.
83. Ibid.: 56. On the historical rivalry between the Saḥār and the Wāʾilah, see also Bédoucha 1987: 143.
84. Burrowes 1987: 31–2.
85. Peterson 1982: 105.
86. Weir 2007: 310.
87. Phillips 2008: 92–3. Selznick defines co-optation as 'absorbing new elements into the leadership or policy-determining structure of an organization as a means of averting threats to its stability or existence'; see Selznick 1949: 13–15.
88. An incident reported by Niewöhner-Eberhard illustrates the Saḥār shaykhs' power over the governmental military in Saʿdah in the early 1970s. During a tribal dispute between Saḥār and Sufyān, the Saḥār forced the state troops stationed in Saʿdah city to advance into Sufyān where it coerced the Sufyān, under threats of violence, to hand over a defendant, see Niewöhner-Eberhard 1985: 8.
89. Peterson 1982: 114–21; Burrowes 1987: 59–61; Dresch 1989: 263–5, 2000: 126–47; Glosemeyer 2001: 53–4; al-Sufyānī 2004: 119–20.
90. Weir 2007: 293.
91. Rondot 1978.
92. Later on the Salih government provided Amīn's firstborn son Ṣādiq with a remarkable career within the General People's Congress (GPC); sources indicate that this was to prevent him from 'opening the file of his father's assassination'.
93. Phillips 2008: 50–5.
94. Phillips 2011a: 87–104.

95. General ʿAlī Muḥsin al-Aḥmar, a tribesman from Sanḥān and relative of Ali Abdullah Salih, is not related to the homonymous al-Aḥmar shaykhly lineage of al-ʿUṣaymāt (Ḥāshid confederation).
96. Al-Sufyānī 2004: 127–30.
97. Gingrich 2011: 43.
98. Weir 2007: 288; Lichtenthäler 2003: 56–7; Brandt 2012: 60–2; al-Zwaini 2006: 14; Fattah 2010: 41.
99. See 'Border Guards', Chapter 3.
100. Dresch 2000: 160.
101. Brandt 2014c: 110–11.
102. Gingrich 1989a: 105–36; Gingrich 1994a: 23–4; Gingrich 2011; Gingrich 2014a; Brandt 2012.
103. Interview with *sayyid* sources from Qaṭābir, September 2012. See also Gingrich 1989a: 124–6.
104. Phillips 2011a. For a similar approach, see Wedeen 2008: 148–85.
105. Bauman 2000.
106. Al-Sufyānī 2004 (1): 134, 137.
107. Gingrich and Heiss 1986: 8; Kopp and Schweizer 1984; Tutwiler and Carapico 1981.
108. On Local Development Associations in Yemen, see Stookey 1974: 255; Swanson and Hebert 1982; Tutwiler 1984; Stevenson 1985; Burrowes 1987: 67–76, 108, 124, 132; Swagman 1988; Carapico 1998: 110–14; Weir 2007: 289–96.
109. Weir 2007: 291.
110. Al-Sufyānī 2004 (1): 135–6. In 2008, the expansion of the route section Bāqim-Munabbih-Ghamr-Rāziḥ had not been completed; see Brandt 2012: 52. On the difficulties of road construction in Rāziḥ and its tribal implications, see Weir 2007: 292–3.
111. Interview with a trader from the Saʿdah region, August 2012.
112. Salmoni et al. 2010: 31–3.
113. Schweizer 1984; Knupp 2000; Lichtenthäler 2003; al-Sufyānī 2004 (1): 188–9; Weir 2007: 21–4.
114. Halliday 1977; Peterson 1982: 16–20, 147–50; Stevenson 1993; Van Hear 1994.
115. Lichtenthäler 2003: 74.
116. Lichtenthäler 2003: 60, 91.
117. After 1962, other kinds of endowment belonging to the *sādah* in Saʿdah and beyond were given to tribal leaders and others loyal to the regime. In Sanaʿa, for instance, the government allowed a leading member of the Sunni Islamist Iṣlāḥ party to build al-Imān University on *waqf* land belonging to the al-Ḥūthī family. Al-Imān University, established in 1993 and dominated by Salafi thinking, was the first of its kind in the Arab world. See Hamidi 2009: 168, 183 n. 12.
118. Lichtenthäler 2003: 60.
119. Niewöhner-Eberhard 1985: 60, 64.

120. Lichtenthäler 2003: 29.
121. Lichtenthäler 2003: 60.
122. Brandt 2012: 58–62.
123. Lichtenthäler 2003: 66–8.
124. Baud and van Schendel 1997: 214; Ceccato and Haining 2004: 808; Bolt 2012: 112.
125. Detalle 2000: 69–73.
126. On the Elephant Road in pre-Islamic times the San'a-based Christian king Abrahah led a military expedition through Saḥār and Jumāʿah territory against the Quraysh in Mecca in 570 AD, taking with him a number of war elephants, see Philby 1952: 408; Forrer 1942: 321ff.
127. Blumi 2003, 2009b, 2010.
128. Al-Rammah and Awass 2009: 12.
129. Wiegand 1993; Jarvis 2010; Rupert 2012.
130. Campbell 2009.
131. Lichtenthäler 2003: 87–88.
132. Al-Rammah and Awass 2009: 12.
133. Worth 2010.
134. An additional incentive to shift from smuggling to agriculture was the government's ban on the import of fruit and vegetables in 1984 which provided new economic incentives and raised hopes for a livelihood in agriculture, see Lichtenthäler 2003: 89.
135. Lichtenthäler 2003: 88–89.
136. ʿAbdullah al-Aḥmar 2007 (3): 95.
137. Interview, November 2012.
138. On similar regulations in Baraṭ, see Dresch 2006.
139. Niewöhner-Eberhard 1985: 8, 180. On the market within Saʿdah's city walls, see Niewöhner-Eberhard 1976; Niewöhner-Eberhard 1988.
140. On Sūq al-Ṭalḥ's market segments, see al-Sufyānī 2004 (1): 189–90.
141. Fāris Muḥammad Manāʿ is a relative of Fayṣal ʿAbdullah Manāʿ, the incumbent shaykh of al-Ṭalḥ, but not his son or nephew.
142. Interviews with a Saʿdah-based military official and Saḥār tribesmen, November 2012.
143. For further details on Fāris Manāʿ's mediation endeavours during the Saʿdah wars, see the following sections of Chapter 6: 'Mediation and Unilateral Ceasefire', 'Saudi Arabia Enters the War', and 'The Manāʿ Case'.
144. On the concept of 'new' wars, see for example Smith 2005, Robben 2011.
145. Serjeant 1977: 227.
146. On 'gun culture' in Yemen, see Heinze 2014a.
147. Heinze 2014a: 82.
148. For a discussion of the major roles of shaykhs in Yemen's tribal societies, see Brandt 2014c.

3. THE SAUDI INFLUENCE

1. Herzog 1990: 135.
2. Jones 1945.
3. Philby 1952: 501.
4. Koszinowski 1999: 64. On ancient Yemen and its territorial extension, see al-Enazy 2005: 76–7; Schofield 2000: 18–20.
5. Whitaker 1997, 1998a, 1998b; Koszinowski 1999: 69; Schofield 2000: 16–17; Kopp 2000: 80–95.
6. On the Idrīsī Emirate, see Baldry 1977; Reissner 1981; Ghanem 1990; Bang 1996; Dostal 2006: 90–1.
7. Al-Enazy 2005: 8–9.
8. See 'Extract from the 'Umm-Al-Qura' No. 488 of April 20th 1934: Victories of the troops commanded by H.R.H. the Amir Saʿud the Heir Apparent' as reproduced in Schofield 1992: 613–15.
9. Since one of the Saudi commanders in the field was a person called 'Ibn ʿĀyyiḍ', the Saudi-Yemeni War of 1934 is locally referred to as *ḥarb Bin ʿĀyyiḍ wa Banī Jumāʿah*.
10. Peterson 1982: 59.
11. 'Extract from the 'Umm-Al-Qura' No. 488 of April 20th 1934: Victories of the troops commanded by H.R.H. the Amir Saʿūd the Heir Apparent' as reproduced in Schofield 1992: 613–15, here p. 614.
12. 'Annex to the Ṭāʾif Agreement for the Demarcation of Borders between the Kingdom of Yemen and the Kingdom of Saudi Arabia, 1937' as reproduced in Schofield 1992: 643–72, here p. 653, and local evidence.
13. De Gaury 1967: 114.
14. Interview with a Wāʾilah shaykh, September 2013.
15. See Article 4 of the Treaty of Ṭāʾif. For the Arabic text with an English translation, see Ingrams and Ingrams 1993: 191–228. For an English translation, see al-Enazy 2005: 157–70.
16. Brandt 2014b: 67–8.
17. 'Annex to the Ṭāʾif Agreement for the Demarcation of Borders between the Kingdom of Yemen and the Kingdom of Saudi Arabia, 1937' as reproduced in Schofield 1992: 643–72, here p. 671.
18. Philby 1952.
19. This is the section that Philby's expedition then tried to examine in 1936–7; see Philby 1952.
20. See also al-Enazy 2005: 14.
21. On the various demarcation claims in the Rubʿ al-Khālī, see Schofield 2000: 22–5; Heinze 2010: 148–51.
22. Schofield 1999; 2000: 21.

23. Al-Enazy 2005: 69–70.
24. Fustier 2000: 102.
25. Schofield 1999; Whitaker 1995.
26. Schofield 2000: 33; al-Enazy 2005: 32.
27. Whitaker 1998a, 1998b; Schofield 1999.
28. Fustier 2000: 100.
29. Blumi 2011: 111.
30. Schofield 1999.
31. For an unofficial English translation of the Treaty of Jeddah, see al-Enazy 2005: 183–7.
32. Al-Enazy 2005: 125.
33. Badeeb 1986: 51–2.
34. Al-Sufyānī 2004: 48.
35. Burrowes 1987: 32; Koszinowski 1999: 64; al-Sufyānī 2004: 48, 131.
36. Al-Sufyānī 2004: 130–3. Interestingly, in 2013 Yemeni opposition groups unearthed various documents showing Salih himself heading, for a long time, the extensive Saudi list of 'double-dealing eaters'. Thousands of Yemenis received stipends, including politicians, tribal shaykhs, religious leaders and military officers. At its height the annual Saudi budget for financial patronage in Yemen was estimated at $3.5 billion, until it was drastically cut following the Treaty of Jeddah in 2000. Saudi Arabia at that time had financial problems and the government pushed through the border agreement in order to be able to cut the budget; see Stenslie 2013.
37. Interview with a member of the Muqīt lineage, September 2013.
38. Yamani 2008: 144.
39. Lichtenthäler 2003: 62.
40. Gingrich and Heiss 1986: 130; Gingrich 1993.
41. Gingrich 1993: 273; Gingrich 2011: 40.
42. Gingrich 2011: 43.
43. Al-Rammah and Awass 2009: 9.
44. Al-Rammah and Awass 2009: 6–7. On this jail break, see Chapter 5, 'The Third War: War Course'. On al-Qaeda in the Yemen-Saudi borderlands, see Brandt forthcoming (a).
45. On the Miṭrī shaykhly lineage, see Gingrich 1989a: 199, 208; Gingrich 1993: 26; Brandt 2012: 56–8; Brandt 2013b.
46. Brandt 2014b: 67–70.
47. 'Amīr Jāzān yukrim wafd qabīlatay Āl Thābit wa Āl Munabbih', *Okaz*, http://www.okaz.com.sa/okaz/osf/20060714/Con2006071432091.htm, 14 July 2006, last accessed 21 July 2016; 'Inhā al-khilāf bayn qabīlatay Āl Talīd wa Āl Thābit', *al-Riyadh*, http://www.alriyadh.com/2005/12/09/article114024.html, 9 December 2009, last accessed 21 July 2016.

48. 'Maḍā 'āmm 'alā taūqī' mu'āhadat al-ḥudūd', *Al-Riyadh*, http://www.alriyadh.com/Contents/2001/06/02-06-2001/page13.html, 2 June 2001, last accessed 14 March 2013.
49. Martínez 1994: 5–10.
50. Human Rights Watch 2008a; Burke 2012: 12.
51. Not to be confused with Dhū Ḥusayn, the Dahm section. On the contemporary tribal structure of the Wā'ilah, see Brandt 2016.
52. On the Ismailis of the Wā'ilah, Najrān and 'Asīr regions, also called *makārimah* (sing. *makramī*), see Dostal 1983: 53–5; Tuchscherer 1992; on Ismailis in Yemen in general, see Wachowski 2012.
53. Al-Enazy 2005: 124 n. 7; Human Rights Watch 2008a. The confrontation at the Holiday Inn in Najrān city on 23 April 2000 marked a watershed in Ismaili relations with the Saudi government. Over the following weeks, security forces detained several hundred Ismailis, who claim that local intelligence officers tortured them. Najrān has a history of atrocities against religious minorities. In 524 CE the Christians of Najrān were massacred by a Ḥimyarite king, see Moberg 1924.
54. Feldner 2004; al-Enazy 2005: 124 n. 7.
55. Feldner 2004; al-Enazy 2005: 124.
56. Osama bin Laden considered taking sanctuary somewhere in these shaykhs' domains. The negotiations failed because Muḥammad b. Shājia' asked Osama bin Laden's envoys to refrain from any political or military activities directed 'against other countries' (by which he meant Saudi Arabia) in case of residence in his territory; see Brandt forthcoming (a).
57. Al-Enazy 2005: 124.
58. Feldner 2004.
59. Interview with a Ḥazm al-Jawf shaykh, July 2008.
60. According to local sources from the Wā'ilah and involved foreign medical staff. Saudi media gave a different version of the incident, according to which Muḥammad b. Shājia' died in Najrān Hospital.
61. The events of 9/11 and the quest for Osama bin Laden triggered a close to hysterical media hype surrounding Muḥammad b. Shājia', who was, among other things, falsely accused of having assisted al-Qaeda in the purchase of 'nuclear weapons'.
62. Gale 2009; al-Hilaly 2009.
63. 'Asir Emir accuses hostile country for staging southern border infiltrations', *Saudi Gazette*, http://www.saudigazette.com.sa/index.cfm?method=home.regcon&contentid=20130317157178, 18 March 2013, last accessed 24 April 2014.
64. 'Asir Emir accuses hostile country for staging southern border infiltrations', Saudi Gazette, http://www.saudigazette.com.sa/index.cfm?method=home.regcon&contentid=20130317157178, 18 March 2013, last accessed 24 April 2014.
65. Blumi 2011: 91–115.

66. Blumi spells the name 'Muqa'it'.
67. Blumi 2011: 115.
68. Interview, September 2013.
69. 'Mawājahāt 'anīfah fī Bāqim', al-Eshteraki, http://www.aleshteraki.net/news_details.php?lng=arabic&sid=6533, 5 August 2009, last accessed 21 September 2012.
70. On these events, see Chapter 6 of this volume.
71. Muḥammad b. Shājia' is said to have had twenty-three sons. On the mediation role of Shājia' b. Shājia', see Chapter 5, 'First Interim'.
72. 'Qabā'il Wā'ilah al-ḥudūd tata'qqab al-muharribīn', Okaz, http://www.okaz.com.sa/new/Issues/20130102/Con20130102560931.htm, 2 January 2013, last accessed 21 July 2016.
73. During the Saudi-led Operation Decisive Storm, which commenced in spring 2015, Ṣāliḥ b. Shājia' refused to mobilize his tribesmen for the Saudis. His brother 'Abdullah b. Shājia' was killed in summer 2015 in a Saudi airstrike in al-'Aṭfayn.
74. The fathers of both Yūsif Miṭrī and Ḥusayn al-Munabbihī were members of parliament for the GPC and died during the Sa'dah wars; see the following chapters of this study.
75. I thank Andre Gingrich for pointing this out.
76. He refers to the period between the establishment of the Republic and the conclusion of the Treaty of Jeddah: c. 1965–2000.
77. 'Al-shaykh Jibrān b. Sawādah... ākhir al-muḥāribīn ḍidd al-Sa'ūdiyyah', Saadahpress, http://www.saadahpress.net/news/news-12318.htm, 4 April 2013, last accessed 13 January 2014. Other Munabbih shaykhs have confirmed to the author the statement made by Jibrān b. Sawādah.
78. Brandt 2013. On the conflict between Sufyān and al-'Uṣaymāt, see also Chapter 6 of this volume.
79. On Munabbih's isolationist tendencies, see Gingrich 1989a: 85, 124–5, 136, 1994a: 12, 17–20; Brandt 2012: 51–2.
80. Some sources from al-Jawf suggested a different interpretation. From their perspective, Saudi Arabia used the Houthi wars as a pretext to rid the Saudi borderlands of tribal populations of both Bakīl and Khawlān b. 'Āmir stock living on both sides of the border, and to see them deported to regions further to the north, for 'security reasons'. The result were empty, isolated regions—military no-go areas, where oil and water resources were exploited uncontrolled, far from the attention of the world and without local witnesses.
81. On the advantages and disadvantages of border fences, see Jellissen and Gottheil 2013.

4. SECTS AND POLITICS

1. Fischer-Tahir and Naumann 2013.

2. Augustin 2015.
3. Most Jews (around 49,000 individuals) left Yemen for Israel during 'Operation Magic Carpet' (1949–50). There remain some small Jewish groups in Saʿdah governorate (mainly in Saʿdah city and its vicinity), ʿAmrān governorate (ʿAmrān city and Raydah), and Lower Yemen; see Serjeant 1977: 235. On Operation Magic Carpet, see Parfitt 1996; Ahroni 2001; Meir-Glitzenstein 2011, 2012.
4. Al-Mujāhid 2007a: 118–19, 200–4. No accurate and trustworthy statistics exist, but Shāfiʿīs are usually considered to represent a clear majority of the 25 million Yemenis, while Zaydis form around 35 per cent of the population.
5. For further details on the history of Zaydism and the evolution of Zaydi thought, law, and doctrine, see van Arendonk 1960; Madelung 1965; Serjeant 1969; Kohlberg 1976; vom Bruck 1998, 1999, 2005, 2010.
6. Al-ʿAlawī 1981. For a partial translation of the *Sīrah*, see Arendonk 1919 (Dutch) and 1960 (French). On the relationship between al-Hādī and the tribes of Saʿdah, and on tribal societies and tribal self-governance under al-Hādī, see Gochenour 1984; Heiss 1989, 1998.
7. Van Arendonk 1960; Heiss 1989, 1998.
8. Gochenour 1984; Heiss 1998: 7, 10.
9. The descendants of al-Ḥasan and al-Ḥusayn are referred to as *al-baṭnayn*; their eligibility to rule is called *sharṭ al-baṭnayn*.
10. Serjeant summarizes the qualifications of eligibility for the office of Imam as follows: 'In facing the task of government an Imam must combine the qualities of a courageous and resolute warrior with those of a scholar, diplomat and administrator. He must be an arbiter of upright character, and he must have an almost encyclopaedic knowledge of people, especially of the tribes and families with intricacies of their relationships'; see Serjeant 1983: 78.
11. On the principle of 'commanding the right and forbidding the wrong', see Cook 2000.
12. Serjeant 1969: 285.
13. Cook 2000: 247; Haykel 2003.
14. For an extensive elaboration of al-Shawkānī's intellectual biography, which is interwoven with the political history of the Qāsimī Imamate (1635–1850s CE), see Haykel 2003.
15. Whereas the Zaydis found authority in the sayings of an imam, the Traditionists' concerns lay in the Hadith sciences and the elaboration of normative legal rulings based principally on the Prophetic Traditions, see Haykel 2003: 109, 231.
16. Cook 2000: 250; Haykel 2003: 219.
17. Haykel 1999: 194.
18. Haykel 1999: 194; vom Bruck 2010: 192.
19. Haykel 2003: 226; vom Bruck 2010: 187.
20. Haykel 1999: 195; vom Bruck 2005: 52–63.

21. For a comparative overview of Islamists in Yemen and their different political goals, see Bonnefoy 2009b.
22. Stookey 1978: 156.
23. Haykel 1999: 196.
24. On these Scientific Institutes, see Gause 1990: 112; Detalle 1997: 278–9; Mermier 1997: 6–19; Haykel 1999: 196; vom Bruck 1998: 154–6, vom Bruck 1999: 178; Bonnefoy 2011a: 155–7.
25. Weir 1997; vom Bruck 1999: 178.
26. Bonnefoy 2011a: 156.
27. Haykel 1999: 196.
28. Vom Bruck 1998: 158.
29. Vom Bruck 1999: 177. On the National Liberation Front see, for example, Peterson 1982: 103, 186.
30. On the Salafi movement in Yemen, see Dresch and Haykel 1995: 413; Haykel 2002; Burgat and Sbitli 2002; Bonnefoy 2008, 2009a, 2009b, 2009c, 2011a; Yadav 2013.
31. Bonnefoy 2011a: 88–97.
32. Weir 1997; Weir 2007: 296–7.
33. Haykel 1999: 197.
34. Various authors provide information on Muqbil al-Wādiʿī; see, for example, Burgat and Sbitli 2002; Haykel 2002; Bonnefoy 2011a: 54–61; vom Bruck 2010: 188–9. Muqbil himself wrote an autobiography: see al-Wādiʿī 1999.
35. As outlined in Chapter 1's section,'Social Spaces', the Saʿdah basin's pre-eminent tribes belong to the Khawlān b. ʿĀmir confederation; only its eastern and south-eastern peripheries are inhabited by sections belonging to the Wāʾilah and the Wādiʿah. The territories of Wādiʿah Saʿdah are situated in the southeast of the Saʿdah basin, in the Dammāj area in upper Wādī al-ʿAbdīn. Another section of the Wādiʿah, Āl al-Razzāmāt, dwells in Wādī Nushūr area.
36. Hamidi 2009: 183 n. 10.
37. Al-Wādiʿī 1999; see also Haykel 2002; Bonnefoy 2011a: 55.
38. Lacroix and Hegghammer 2007; Bonnefoy 2011a: 57.
39. Bonnefoy 2008: 250.
40. Bonnefoy 2011a: 58.
41. Padnos, a journalist, spent several weeks in Dammāj in mid-2000 on the pretext of pursuing religious studies; see Padnos 2011: 217.
42. See Chapter 7', 'Faustian Bargains (2011–14)'.
43. Bonnefoy 2008: 254.
44. Bonnefoy 2011a: 60.
45. Haykel 1999: 197; Haykel 1995; Haykel 2003: 127–38.
46. Padnos 2011.
47. The designation *ahl* reveals the specific nature of this group, namely a 'gathering'

of various elements with attenuated or unclear tribal descent. For the same reason, the term *ahl* is also applied (often in combination with a toponym) to specific tribal sections whose genuine tribal affiliation is mitigated or diluted, so that they appear under a toponym within the tribal structure. See Heiss 1998: 75–83; Gingrich 1989a: 192–4; Brandt 2014b: 68. In contrast, among the tribes the term *āl* (or *ilt*) designates a claim of representing a descent group. The descendants of the Prophet, the *sādah*, are a special case, referred to both as *Ahl al-Bayt* and *Āl al-Bayt*; see vom Bruck 2005: 65.

48. Weir 1997; Weir 2007: 296–303.
49. Weir 2007: 297; vom Bruck 2005: 131–5, 145–62.
50. Weir 2007: 303.
51. Weir 2007: 297.
52. Interview, July 2013.
53. Qā'id Shuwayṭ, for instance, only began personally to embrace Salafi doctrine at an advanced age.
54. Interview, April 2014.
55. Brandt forthcoming (a).
56. Al-Wādiʿī 1999: 18; see also Haykel 2002: 29.
57. Bonnefoy 2011a: 70–1.
58. Vom Bruck 2010: 187.
59. Haykel 1995.
60. Weir 1997, 2007: 298–9.
61. ʿAlī Muḥsin al-Aḥmar was a relative of President Ali Abdullah Salih. According to some, one of his sisters was married to Ṭāriq al-Faḍlī, a prominent Islamist and 'Afghan Arab' of southern elite background. A career army officer and long-time commander of the First Armoured Brigade, he played a prominent role in defeating southern forces during the 1994 civil war. As the commander of military forces in northern Yemen, he has been in charge of the campaign against the Houthis since eruption of the Saʿdah wars in 2004. He has also been accused of supporting al-Qaeda and held responsible for the spread of Salafism in the Saʿdah area and beyond.
62. Prior to the 2008 modification of the Local Authority Law, members of government-friendly shaykhly clans from other governorates (ʿAmrān, Ma'rib, etc.) were often appointed district directors in Saʿdah; many of these brought with them their own private tribal escorts from their home areas.
63. *ʿĪd al-ghadīr* (*Ghadīr Khumm*) is a Shia festival which commemorates the designation of ʿAlī b. Abī Ṭālib by the Prophet Muhammad as his immediate successor (*khalīfah*). *ʿĪd al-ghadīr* is celebrated through huge open air gatherings, speeches that affirm the succession rights of the Āl ʿAlī (descendants of ʿAlī), and shooting in the air. Sunni Muslims, by contrast, deny the Shia belief that ʿAlī was appointed successor by the Prophet. On *ʿīd al-ghadīr* in general, see Vaglieri 1983. On *ʿīd*

al-ghadīr in Yemen, see Gochenour 1984: 131–2; Gingrich and Heiss 1986: 165 n. 43; Mermier 1991:177–80; vom Bruck 1999: 184–7; Haykel 2003: 39–40; Weir 2007: 298–9.

64. A brief overview of the life and work of Majd al-Dīn al-Mu'ayyadī can be found in al-Sufyānī 2004: 641–4.
65. There was no grand mufti under the imamate, excepting periods of Ottoman rule; see vom Bruck 1998: 168.
66. Dorlian 2013: 37–8.
67. Interview with a tribal source from Majz, May 2014.
68. Houthis, who strive for a semblance of internal unity, normally explain Majd al-Dīn al-Mu'ayyadī's quietist position as a consequence of his advanced age.
69. A brief overview of Badr al-Dīn al-Ḥūthī's life and work can be found in al-Sufyānī 2004: 638–40.
70. ʿAbd al-ʿAzīz ʿAbdullah b. Bāz (d. 1999) was a Saudi Islamic scholar and a leading proponent of Salafism.
71. Haykel 1995; Dorlian 2013: 161–6.
72. For a transcript of the interview with Badr al-Dīn al-Ḥūthī, see ʿĀmir 2005. See also vom Bruck 2010: 186 n.1 and Chapter 5 of this volume, section 'First Interim'.
73. Al-Ṣanʿānī 2005: 10, 18; Hamidi 2009: 170, 184 n. 5.
74. Haykel 1995; Dorlian 2013: 200–3.
75. Haykel 1995.
76. Lux 2009: 375–8.
77. On the influence of the Iranian Revolution and Lebanese Hezbollah on Ḥusayn al-Ḥūthī's political-religious ideology, see Lux 2009.
78. Lux 2009: 376; Salmoni et al. 2010: 99
79. 'Mu'assis al-shabāb al-mu'min Muḥammad ʿIzzān li-l-Jumhūr, Al-Jumhor, http://www.aljumhor.net/portal/news-572.htm, 23 August 2009, last accessed 21 July 2016.
80. Ibid.
81. Al-Ṣanʿānī 2005: 34–5; Peterson 2008a: 2; Hamidi 2009: 167; Lux 2009: 376; International Crisis Group 2009: 6 n. 30; Salmoni et al. 2010: 99; Wells Goldburt 2013; Wedeen 2008: 153.
82. Phillips 2005; Phillips 2008; Phillips 2010.
83. Interview, September 2012.
84. 'Mu'assis al-shabāb al-mu'min Muḥammad ʿIzzān li-l-Jumhūr, Al-Jumhor, http://www.aljumhor.net/portal/news-572.htm, 23 August 2009, last accessed 21 July 2016.
85. Al-Ṣanʿānī 2005: 26.
86. Dorlian 2013: 46 n. 104.
87. For further details on the Iṣlāḥ party, see, for example, Carapico 1993a; Dresch and Haykel 1995: 405–31; Schwedler 1998; Schwedler 2008; Bonnefoy and Ibn

Cheikh 2001; Bonnefoy and Poirier 2010; Phillips 2008: 137–66; Yadav 2013; Yadav 2014b.

88. On ʿAbdullah al-Aḥmar's career and his political involvement since 1959, see Koszinowski 1993. On ʿAbdulmajīd al-Zindānī see, for example, Dresch and Haykel 1995: 410–12.
89. Dresch and Haykel 1995: 413.
90. Dresch and Haykel 1995: 405.
91. On the 1993 parliamentary elections, see Carapico 1993a, 1993b; Detalle 1993a, 1993b; Glosemeyer 1993; 1995: 55–70.
92. Bonnefoy and Poirier 2010; Phillips 2011b: 42.
93. On Ḥizb al-Ḥaqq, see Dresch and Haykel 1995; Haykel 1999: 198–201, 2003: 226–8; vom Bruck 1998: 171–2.
94. Hamidi 2009: 166–7.
95. Detalle 1993a: 8; vom Bruck 1998: 171; vom Bruck 2010: 201.
96. Haykel 1999: 198–9; vom Bruck 1998; vom Bruck 1999; vom Bruck 2010: 203; Dorlian 2013: 29–43.
97. Dorlian 2013: 38.
98. Dresch and Haykel 1995: 412.
99. Wedeen 2008: 152–7.
100. Dresch and Haykel 1995: 416–19.
101. Dresch and Haykel 1995: 417. The feuds of Sufyān continued to have national impact (see Brandt 2013). For further details on these feuds, their historical background and their importance for the Saʿdah wars, see the discussion of Sufyān in Chapter 6.
102. Dresch and Haykel 1995: 417. Ḥasan Muqīt participated as representative of the local tribes who hosted the high-level tribal delegation of Iṣlāḥ. Ḥasan Muqīt himself never was a member of the party; in 1993 he became an independent MP.
103. Hamidi 2009: 169.
104. Interview, January 2015.
105. See also Chapter 6's section 'A Brief Period of Détente'.
106. 'Ṣaʿdah… al-ḥikāyah al-kāmilah', Yemen Press, http://yemen-press.com/news915.html, 13 July 2007, last accessed 27 July 2016.
107. As elaborated above, the collective memory of some parts of Wāʾilah goes back to the birth of Islam and the formation of the Zaydiyyah. Not all parts of Wāʾilah adhere to Zaydism; some northeastern sections are of Ismaili denomination (see Chapter 3's section on 'Boundary Fortifications').
108. Al-Mujāhid 2007 (1): 194–6.
109. Al-Mujāhid 2007 (1): 194–6.
110. This block formation applies to many tribes in Yemen; see Gingrich 1989a: 163–4; Gingrich 1994a: 22; Brandt 2012: 53. These patterns of alliances are also

known among other tribal societies of the Near and Middle East (see Tapper 1991: 64).

111. Al-Mujāhid 2007 (1): 194–6.
112. Interview, March 2016.
113. Interview, November 2012.
114. After an interval of four years, ʿAbdullah al-Razzāmī only returned to combat during the 2011 Kitāf battles between Houthis and Salafis. On these battles, see Chapter 7, on 'Faustian Bargains (2011–14)'.
115. 'Mu'assis al-shabāb al-mu'min Muḥammad ʿIzzān li-l-Jumhūr, Al-Jumhor, http://www.aljumhor.net/portal/news-572.htm, 23 August 2009, last accessed 21 July 2016.
116. Interview with two sources close to al-Razzāmī, February 2013.
117. See Chapter 6's section 'The Fourth War: The Blame Game'.
118. Interview, March 2016.
119. Interview, July 2013.
120. A good example of this pattern of alliance is the historical border dispute between Ṣubārah (Sufyān, Bakīl) and al-ʿUṣaymāt (Ḥāshid); see Chapter 6's discussion of Sufyān.
121. Burrowes and Kasper 2007: 264.
122. Phillips 2011b: 50.
123. Lichtenthäler 2003: 63.
124. See Chapter 6, 'Fourth Interim: The Government Loses its Last Cards'.
125. Haykel 1999: 199; Salmoni et al. 2010: 94–6.
126. Lichtenthäler 2003: 65.
127. His name was actually Ṣaghīr Ṣāliḥ Hindī Dughsān, but he was called Ṣāliḥ.
128. Salmoni et al. 2010: 113.
129. Phillips 2011b; Blumi 2009a.
130. See Chapter 6's section 'The Sixth War: Supplementary Elections'.
131. Longley Alley 2007.
132. On the numerous mediation initiatives during the Saʿdah wars, see Chapters 5 and 6.
133. Brandt forthcoming (b).
134. King 2008; see also vom Bruck 2010: 19.
135. Brandt forthcoming (b).
136. Mundy 1995: 203.
137. Carapico 1998: 166.
138. Al-Ṣanʿānī 2005: 22–4.
139. Lux 2009: 376.
140. 'Mu'assis al-shabāb al-mu'min Muḥammad ʿIzzān li-l-Jumhūr, *Al-Jumhor*, http://www.aljumhor.net/portal/news-572.htm, 23 August 2009, last accessed 21 July 2016. See also Lux 2009: 377. Most Shia Muslims adhere to the Jaʿfarī school of thought, which derives its name from Jaʿfar as-Ṣādiq, the sixth Shia imam.

141. Hamidi 2009: 170.
142. In July 2004, ʿIzzān participated in a human rights training course in Lebanon. Upon his return to Yemen, he was thrown in prison. After his discharge in May 2005, he gave a series of statements criticizing the Houthis. Thus, ʿIzzān distanced himself from Ḥusayn al-Ḥūthī soon after the Saʿdah wars had started. In 2007 he was made director of Saʿdah's radio station and given an office in Sanaʿa; see Lux 2009: 377; Hamidi 2009: 181, 187 n. 86.
143. Lux 2009: 390.
144. Burgat 2006.
145. Du Bouchet 2007: 149.
146. Salmoni et al. 2010: 114–15.
147. Al-Ḥūthī 2002a.
148. Salmoni et al. 2010: 117–21; Lux 2009.
149. Wells Goldburt 2013.
150. Dorlian 2013: 146.
151. Wedeen 2008: 153.
152. Hamidi 2009: 175.
153. Dorlian 2011: 190–3.
154. Al-Ḥūthī 2002c.
155. Al-Ḥūthī 2002c.
156. Al-Ḥūthī 2002d.
157. Al-Ḥūthī 2002d.
158. Peterson 2008b: 17.
159. Interview, February 2014.
160. Interview, February 2014.
161. Al-Ḥūthī 2002b.
162. Interview, July 2012.
163. Salmoni et al. 2010: 123.
164. Al-Dirwānī 2013: 67.
165. Al-Ṣanʿānī 2005: 32; Lux 2009: 375; Dorlian 2011: 185; Dorlian 2013: 134.
166. Al-Dirwānī 2013: 44–5. During his tenure, Hull visited the Saʿdah region several times. His agenda there included the buy-back of MANPADS (Man-Portable Air Defense Systems). MANPADS owned by non-state actors in Yemen could have been used to bring down drones deployed in Yemen against al-Qaeda from 2002 in the War on Terror. In cooperation with Saʿdah's main arms dealers in al-Ṭalḥ, the US government pursued a programme in Yemen to buy back and destroy illicit MANPADS; see al-Dirwānī 2013: 59–61; 'Scenesetter For Visit Of A/s Bloomfield To Yemen', Wikileaks, http://wikileaks.org/cable/2004/08/04SANAA2055.html, 24 August 2004, last accessed 27 July 2016.
167. Hamidi 2009: 169.
168. Al-Dirwānī 2013: 76–8.

169. Al-Dirwānī 2013: 37–43.
170. The letter is dated 8 Rabīʿ Awwul 1425H. For a facsimile and transcription of the handwritten note, see al-Dirwānī 2013: 66–7. After the outbreak of military confrontations, Ḥusayn al-Ḥūthī's letter was translated into English and published by the *Yemen Times* on 28 June 2004.
171. Salmoni et al. 2010: 111.
172. Dorlian 2011: 195–6.
173. Dorlian 2011: 195–6.
174. The names of these tribal sections are often equivalent to family and clan names. Since the disclosure of close Houthi kinship ties with individual members of tribal clans can endanger the safety of these persons and groups, this study refrains from the publication of further details.
175. The marginal type of this marriage pattern is that of the Munabbih: the Munabbih's senior shaykhly lineage, the ʿAwfān clan, does not maintain any direct relations with the *sādah* at all. see Gingrich 1989d; Gingrich 1994a: 12.
176. Gingrich 1989d: 80–1.
177. I thank Andre Gingrich for sharing this information.
178. Interview, July 2012.
179. The special importance of the maternal family in housing and raising Badr al-Dīn's children was further enhanced by some secondary aspects of post-marital ambilocality among certain isolated tribal groups of Khawlān b. ʿĀmir.
180. On the *hijrah* institution in Yemen, see Chapter 1's section on 'Estates of Society'.
181. There are no data on which sections of the Khawlān tribe have signed this contract.
182. Dresch 1986: 312.
183. Interview, July 2012.
184. See Chapter 1, 'Estates of Society'.
185. Al-Dirwānī 2013: 29.
186. Interview, November 2015.
187. Gingrich 1989a: 131–2; Weir 2007: 101.
188. Hamidi 2009: 167.
189. Expressions derived from an interview, July 2012.
190. For an elaboration of the scholarly discussions, see Dorlian 2013.
191. Interview, November 2011.
192. For *yawm al-nushūr* in Yemen, see Mermier 1991. In contrast with the occasional celebrations of *ʿīd al-ghadīr* in post-revolutionary Yemen, rituals to commemorate *yawm al-nushūr* or *ʿāshūrā* have not been performed since 1962. In any case, they were never as elaborate (or bloody) as in countries with Shia Imāmī majorities, nor did gathering places built for these occasions (*ḥusayniyyāt*) exist; see vom Bruck 1999: 186 n. 55.
193. Hamidi 2009: 174.

194. Vom Bruck 2005: 199–215; vom Bruck 2010: 208.
195. Interview with a Khawlān tribesman, October 2009.
196. Puin 1984: 484.
197. Weir 1997: 23; Weir 2007: 297; vom Bruck 2005: 53, 56; Bonnefoy 2011a: 227.
198. See, for example, al-Akwaʿ 1987; vom Bruck 2005: 53–4.
199. Vom Bruck 2005: 200.
200. Interview, October 2009.
201. On the term *jār*, see Gochenour 1984: 10.
202. Salmoni et al. 2010: 169. Examples of this interpretation are al-Aḥmadī 2006 and Sarī al-Dīn 2010, who consider the Houthi movement solely in the context of an alleged revival of the imamate.
203. King 2012.
204. International Crisis Group 2009: 11; King 2012.
205. Al-Mujāhid 2007 (1): 77–204. Al-Mujāhid's report on the Believing Youth's presence in the districts of Saʿdah probably reflects the situation shortly after the first Saʿdah war in 2004. Though at times informative, the report is strongly biased and must be treated with a great deal of caution.
206. Al-Mujāhid 2007 (1): 200, 203, 209.
207. On Munabbih's isolationist tendencies, see Gingrich 1989a: 124–6; Gingrich 1989b; Gingrich 1993: 12.
208. Al-Sufyānī 2004 (2): 347–9.
209. Al-Mujāhid 2007 (1): 104–6.

5. INTO THE MAZE OF TRIBALISM: 2004–6

1. For an elaboration of these 'external' driving forces of the Saʿdah wars, see Chapter 6's section, 'War mongers'.
2. Interview, December 2007.
3. Interview, December 2007.
4. After the 1960s civil war, the civil service had been the only income-generating opportunity for many educated *sādah* after their *waqf* incomes declined; see Chapter 2.
5. Hamidi 2009: 183 n.15.
6. Interview, February 2015.
7. Hamidi 2009: 169–70. In Yemen's north, after the 1960s civil war *zakāt* was collected by Local Development Associations (LDAs), later by the local authorities; see Dresch 1989: 22. According to du Bouchet, Ḥusayn al-Ḥūthī had permission from the government to collect *zakāt*; see du Bouchet 2007: 149. However, people in the area, often mistrusting the government, would customarily give the *zakāt* to *sayyid* families, before and after the revolution; see Hamidi 2009: 183 n.17.
8. Interview, February 2012.
9. Glosemeyer and Reneau 2004: 44; Boucek 2010: 5.

10. Al-Dirwānī 2013: 45.
11. Glosemeyer and Reneau 2004: 44–5; al-Dirwānī 2013: 68.
12. Al-Dirwānī 2013: 69. Shaykh Ḥasan Ḥamūd Ghatāyah was shaykh of the Walad Yaḥyā of Marrān in Khawlān and is said to have been particularly close to Ḥusayn al-Ḥūthī. He was killed by government forces during the sixth war in December 2009.
13. Al-Dirwānī 2013: 69–70.
14. Mujāhid Ḥaydar accuses the late ʿAbdullah al-Aḥmar and the Salih government of being involved in the assassination of his father Aḥmad and three of his brothers in 1987; for further details see Chapter 7's section 'A Memorable Funeral'.
15. McGregor 2004; Hamidi 2009: 185 n 36.
16. On ʿAbdullah al-Razzāmī and the historical background of his feud with the al-ʿAwjarī clan, see Chapter 4's section 'From Zaydi Revivalism to Political Competition'.
17. Interviews, June and July 2013.
18. Brigadier General Ḥamīd al-Qushaybī was widely seen as an Iṣlāḥ party ally. The 310th Armoured Brigade, under the command of the First Armoured Division, was located in the town of ʿAmrān. Ḥamīd al-Qushaybī was killed in July 2014 by the Houthis during their military expansion in ʿAmrān.
19. 'Yemen: Al-Houthi Insurgency Continues Unabated', Wikileaks, http://wikileaks.org/cable/2004/08/04SANAA2006.html, 18 August 2004, last accessed 27 July 2016.
20. For a discussion of the 'ghost soldier' phenomenon, see USAID 2006: 4; International Crisis Group 2013 passim; Seitz 2016: 164–5, 168.
21. Hamidi 2009: 173.
22. Salmoni et al. 2010: 253–4.
23. See Chapter 2's section on 'The Politics of Patronage'.
24. Hamidi 2009: 173–4; al-Dirwānī 2013: 92.
25. Hamidi 2009: 173–4.
26. See Chapter 6's section 'The Fourth War: The Popular Army'.
27. Brandt 2014a.
28. 'Yemen: Al-Houthi Insurgency Continues Unabated', Wikileaks, http://wikileaks.org/cable/2004/08/04SANAA2006.html, 18 August 2004, last accessed 27 July 2016.
29. This controversy between the government and the local shaykhs is discussed in Chapter 6; see the section 'The Fourth War: The Popular Army'.
30. 'Update On Sa'da Fighting', Wikileaks, http://wikileaks.org/cable/2004/08/04SANAA2225.html, 25 August 2004, last accessed 27 July 2016.
31. Ibid.
32. 'ROYG Forces Kill Rebel Cleric Al-Houthi In September 10 Raid', Wikileaks, http://wikileaks.org/cable/2004/09/04SANAA2421.html, 12 September 2004, last accessed 27 July 2016.

33. 'Yemen: Al-Houthi Insurgency Continues Unabated', Wikileaks, http://wikileaks.org/cable/2004/08/04SANAA2006.html, 18 August 2004, last accessed 27 July 2016.
34. This account is based on several interviews with government officials and shaykhs from the Saʿdah and ʿAmrān regions in 2014 and 2015.
35. International Crisis Group 2009: 19.
36. See Chapter 4. Muḥammad b. Muḥammad al-Manṣūr was among the signatories of the 1990 manifesto that Badr al-Dīn al-Ḥūthī refused to sign.
37. Al-Aḥmadī 2006: 158; Sarī al-Dīn 2010: 67.
38. Dorlian 2013: 135.
39. See Chapter 4.
40. In 2008, before the outbreak of the fifth war in May, Ṣāliḥ al-Wajmān was detained by the government; after his release he openly sided with the Houthis.
41. Al-Dirwānī 2013: 99–100.
42. According to a report by the National Security to Parliament and Consultative Council. See: 'Sibtambar net tanshur naṣṣ qarār al-amn al-qawmī', *26 September Net*, http://www.26sep.net/news_details.php?lng=arabic&sid=23234, 15 February 2007, last accessed 27 July 2016.
43. Ibid.
44. Al-Dirwānī 2013: 100–3.
45. For a list of the mediation team members, see, with due caution: 'Sibtambar net tanshur naṣṣ qarār al-amn al-qawmī', *26 September Net*, http://www.26sep.net/news_details.php?lng=arabic&sid=23234, 15 February 2007, last accessed 27 July 2016. These lists tend to be inaccurate. For example, *26 September* erroneously mentions Badr al-Dīn al-Ḥūthī as member of the mediation committee.
46. International Crisis Group 2009: 20.
47. Interview, September 2015.
48. Al-Dirwānī 2013: 104.
49. Ibid.
50. Al-Dirwānī 2013: 104–5; International Crisis Group 2009: 20–1.
51. Salmoni et al. 2010: 182.
52. Hamidi 2009: 184 n. 19.
53. Al-Dirwānī 2013: 106.
54. Peterson 2008a: 5.
55. The mortal remains of Ḥusayn al-Ḥūthī were buried in 2013 near Jurf Salmān in Marrān, in a dedicated mausoleum, which was heavily damaged in May 2015 by the Saudi Air Force during Operation Decisive Storm.
56. Peterson 2008a: 5–7.
57. Peterson 2008a: 6.
58. Hamidi 2009: 171.
59. Al-Dirwānī 2013: 97–8. Local sources claim that during the battle for Jurf Salmān,

toxic nerve gas was used, causing the victims' skin to peel off. Dorlian writes that Ḥusayn al-Ḥūthī was killed by gas; see Dorlian 2013: 135. A foreign doctor who worked during the first war at the Salām Hospital in Saʿdah city, however, said that he never heard about the use of nerve gas, and he would certainly have seen some proof.

60. Wikileaks has reported that a US-trained Counter Terrorism Unit (CTU) team led the final operation; see 'ROYG Forces Kill Rebel Cleric Al-Houthi In September 10 Raid', Wikileaks, http://wikileaks.org/cable/2004/09/04SANAA2421.html, 12 September 2004, last accessed 21 July 2016.
61. Account of an eyewitness who accompanied Ḥusayn al-Ḥūthī in Jurf Salmān. Another source said that the CTU was quite brutal when they got to Ḥusayn in his cave—one reason why the body was not returned. The officer who shot Ḥusayn was later identified as Thābit Muthannā Jawās, who was originally from Laḥj governorate and became commander of the Bā Suhayb Brigade following Yemeni unification in 1991. In March 2015, the transitional president ʿAbd Rabbuh Hādī (elected for two years in February 2012) fled to Adan and appointed Jawās to head the Special Security Forces there. Jawās denied any sort of personal responsibility for the killing of Ḥusayn al-Ḥūthī and said that he was only following orders from the regime, opining that this charge was a fabrication by ex-president Salih to reinforce tensions between Houthis and the transitional government. For an interview with Thābit Muthannā Jawās on the events of Jurf Salmān, see: 'Al-ʿamīd Jawās: Ana man qatala Ḥusayn al-Ḥūthī', *al-Masdar*, http://almasdaronline.com/article/71676, 17 May 2015, last accessed 21 July 2016.
62. Ḥusayn al-Ḥūthī's mortal remains were not released for burial until January 2014.
63. Al-Mujāhid has reported local beliefs that Ḥusayn al-Ḥūthī ascended to heaven and appeared to his followers on the occasion of Shia feasts, particularly at *ʿīd al-ghadīr*, see al-Mujāhid 2007 (2): 131–2.
64. Hamidi 2009: 176–7.
65. Gellner 1981: 42–3.
66. Interview, December 2014.
67. ʿĀmir 2005.
68. 'Fighting Escalates In Saada: Al-Houthi Lives On', Wikileaks, http://wikileaks.org/cable/2005/03/05SANAA726.html, 28 March 2005, last accessed 21 July 2016.
69. Article 103 of the 1990 Press Law prohibits members of the media from printing, publishing or broadcasting anything that: prejudices the Islamic faith; spreads a spirit of strife among the people; harms national unity; undermines public morals; or criticizes the personality of the head of state. By international standards, the law is vague and overly broad, allowing too much room for discretion in its implementation.
70. International Crisis Group 2009: 21.

71. In 2008, after his release, ʿAbdulkarīm al-Khaywānī was again sentenced to six years in prison. After being tortured during his incarceration, al-Khaywānī received a presidential pardon and was released in 2009. On 18 March 2015 he was assassinated by unknown assailants in Sanaʿa while participating in the National Dialogue Conference as a Houthi delegate.
72. Despite some media reports to the contrary, ʿAbdullah al-Razzāmī never turned himself in, neither in 2004 nor in 2005.
73. Dorlian 2011: 186; Dorlian 2013: 135.
74. ʿĀmir 2005.
75. On Badr al-Dīn's concept of *iḥtisāb*, see Chapter 4's section on 'The Zaydi Revival Movement'.
76. Brandt 2006.
77. ʿĀmir 2005.
78. Dorlian 2011: 186; Dorlian 2013: 135.
79. On Yaḥyā al-Ḥūthī, see Chapter 4's section, 'From Zaydi Revivalism to Political Competition'.
80. On the relationship between ʿAbdullah al-Razzāmī and Ḥusayn and ʿAbdulmalik al-Ḥūthī, see Chapter 4's section 'From Zaydi Revivalism to Political Competition'.
81. International Crisis Group 2009: 3.
82. Peterson 2008a: 7–8; Salmoni et al. 2010: 136.
83. 'Al-Yaman: mi'at qatīl fī 24 sāʿah', *al-Hayat*, daharchives.alhayat.com/issue_archive/Hayat KSA/2005/4/8/, 8 April 2005, last accessed 23 February 2014.
84. In Salmoni et al. 2010: 137, 139, Āl Shāfiʿah is drawn incorrectly on the map; it is placed near al-Ḥishwah district in the governorate's far southeast.
85. On the history of this tribal conflict, see Chapter 4's section 'From Zaydi Revivalism to Political Competition'.
86. 'Al-Yaman: mi'at qatīl fī 24 sāʿah', *al-Hayat*, daharchives.alhayat.com/issue_archive/Hayat KSA/2005/4/8/, 8 April 2005, last accessed 23 February 2014.
87. See Chapter 2's section 'Reshuffle of Power Relations'.
88. Interview, December 2014.
89. Salmoni et al. 2010: 136.
90. Interview, October 2014.
91. The Banī Muʿādh's main commercial venture is Sūq al-ʿAnad; see Lichtenthäler 2003: 126. Sūq al-Khafjī has been established relatively recently, named after the Saudi city of Khafjī, which Iraq's former leader Saddam Husayn occupied during his short-lived 1991 war of expansion against Kuwait and Saudi Arabia.
92. Interview with a tribal source from Saḥār, October 2014.
93. 'ROYG Insiders Increasingly Frustrated With Saleh Clan', Wikileaks, http://wikileaks.org/cable/2005/05/05SANAA1352.html, 23 May 2005, last accessd 21 July 2016.
94. Al-Nuwās is the name of an area between Ḥaydān and Sāqayn in Khawlān, whose residents were considered particularly pro-Houthi.

95. *Yā marḥaban bi-l-qawm barr Saḥār wa l-Asās/yatajammʿūkum man qabīlī ḥurr wa ibn nās/waqt al-muzāḥamah/mā ḥaylnā najmil idhā qad fī l-wīʾāʾ shurūkh/ qad kathurat al-quwwah wa qad hiyā shayʾ bilā qiyās/māʿ ādahā tarjīʿ ṣalā al-Ḥūthī wa lā Nuwās/qad hiya muzāqamah/bayn ahl Ṣanʿāʾ mālikayn al-ʿush wa l-furūkh.* This poem was sent to the author by a Saḥār tribesman.

96. 'Al-Houthi Leaders Flee Yemen, Rebellion Near End But Violence Continues', Wikileaks, http://wikileaks.org/cable/2005/04/05SANAA1037.html, 25 April 2005, last accessed 21 July 2016.

97. Lichtenthäler 2003: 57–60.

98. Interview with a tribal source from Saḥār, October 2014.

99. Lichtenthäler 2003: 127.

100. Al-Aḥmadī 2006: 145–6; Peterson 2008a: 7–8; see also 'Grenade Attacks In Sanaa Persist Amid Saada Fighting', Wikileaks, http://wikileaks.org/ cable/2005/04/05SANAA906.html, 12 April 2005, last accessed 21 July 2016.

101. Salmoni et al. 2010: 136, 211.

102. Salmoni et al. 2010: 211; see also 'Al-Yaman: Ittibāʿ al-Ḥūthī yakhūḍūna ḥarb shawāriʿ', *Al-Sharq al-Awsat*, http://archive.aawsat.com/details.asp?section=1 &issueno=9629&article=292653&search=%C7%E1%CD%E6%CB%ED&s tate=true#.VQa7IOFCg80, 9 April 2005, last accessed 21 July 2016.

103. 'Maʿlūmāt ʿan maṣraʿ al-Razzāmī', *26 September Net*, http://www.26sep.net/ news_details.php?lng=arabic&sid=6056, 12 April 2005, last accessed 21 July 2016.

104. Markaz 2008: 198–203.

105. On the Shājiaʿ clan, see Chapter 3's section on 'Boundary Fortifications'. Shājiaʿ b. Shājiaʿ is the oldest of twenty-three sons of the slain Muḥammad Ḥamad b. Shājiaʿ; the brothers all look similar and are often confused. After the violent death of Muḥammad b. Shājiaʿ in 2002, he was succeeded as shaykh of Āl Ḥusayn by his son Ṣāliḥ b. Shājiaʿ. Besides this, Ṣāliḥ b. Shājiaʿ held serious ambitions to become senior shaykh of the Bakīl confederation, competing with Nājī al-Shāyif and Amīn al-ʿUkaymī, both of the Dahm. Due to his Ismaili identity, the historically 'neutral' stance of the Shājiaʿ clan and their outstanding importance and tribal clout in Saʿdah and al-Jawf, and not least because of their close relationship to the Yemeni, Saudi and Qatari governments, the Shājiaʿ clan has played a pivotal role in many sensitive mediations, in the Houthi conflict from 2004 and during the abduction of foreign hostages in Saʿdah in 2009 (see Chapter 6's section 'The European Hostage Saga').

106. 'Juhūd al-wisaṭah', *26 September Net*, http://26sep.net/news_details.php? lng=arabic&sid=5940, 7 April 2005, last accessed 21 July 2016.

107. Ḥamūd al-Hitār had personally been affected by the conflict as his brother, Lt. Col. ʿAbdulʿalīm al-Hitār, was killed by Houthi rebels in August 2004; see al-Ṣanʿānī 2005: 71.

108. Dostal 2008: 189–92; Brandt 2006.
109. 'Al-intihā min ikhmād fitnat al-takhrīb', *26 September Net*, http://26sep.net/news_details.php?lng=arabic&sid=6064, 13 April 2005, last accessed 21 July 2016.
110. Interview, November 2012.
111. Markaz 2008: 198–203; see also 'Juhūd al-wisaṭah', *26 September Net*, http://26sep.net/news_details.php?lng=arabic&sid=5940, 7 April 2005, last accessed 21 July 2016.
112. 'Al-Shaykh al-Aḥmar: Al-Ḥūthī aḥdath fitnah', *Al-Sharq al-Awsat*, http://archive.aawsat.com/details.asp?section=4&issueno=9637&article=294119&search=%C7%E1%CD%E6%CB%ED&state=true#.VSzkoJP568h, 17 April 2005, last accessed 21 July 2016.
113. 'Al-ra'īs al-yamanī yuqallil al-Ḥūthī', *Al-Sharq al-Awsat*, http://archive.aawsat.com/details.asp?section=4&issueno=9665&article=299389&search=%C7%E1%CD%E6%CB%ED&state=true#.VRPLmeFCi8g, 15 May 2005, last accessed 21 July 2016.
114. Salmoni 2010: 137–8.
115. For a transcript of the complete letter, see al-Ṣanʿānī 2005: 116.
116. 'Fī risālah ḥamalahā al-shaykh Bin Shājiaʿ', *26 September Net*, http://www.26sep.net/news_details.php?lng=arabic&sid=6712, 12 May 2005, last accessed 21 July 2016.
117. 'Al-ra'īs al-yamanī yūfiq ʿalā ʿarḍ al-Ḥūthī', *Al-Sharq al-Awsat*, http://archive.aawsat.com/details.asp?section=1&issueno=9664&article=299288&search=%C7%E1%CD%E6%CB%ED&state=true#.VRPK—FCi8g, 14 May 2005, last accessed 21 July 2016.
118. Peterson 2008a: 8.
119. 'Al-Yaman: al-iʿdām wa l-sijn li-l-Ḥūthiyyīn', *Al-Sharq al-Awsat*, http://archive.aawsat.com/details.asp?section=1&issueno=9680&article=302553&search=%C7%E1%CD%E6%CB%ED&state=true#.VRPLqeFCi8g, 30 May 2005, last accessed 21 July 2016.
120. 'Al-Yaman: al-sijn min 2 ilā 4 aʿwām li-aʿḍā' khaliyyah', *Al-Sharq al-Awsat*, http://archive.aawsat.com/details.asp?article=316739&issueno=9751#.V5FEyzX57K0, 9 August 2005, last accessed 21 July 2016.
121. See Chapter 4's section 'From Zaydi Revivalism to Political Competition'.
122. Interview with a tribal source from Saḥār, October 2014.
123. 'Ḥaththa al-mushārikīn ʿalā tadwīn tārīkh al-thawrah', *26 September Net*, http://www.26sep.net/news_details.php?lng=arabic&sid=9518, 25 September 2005, last accessed 21 July 2016.
124. 'Risālah maskūnah bi-l-qalaq', *Al-Sharq al-Awsat*, http://archive.aawsat.com/leader.asp?section=3&issueno=9871&article=337018&search=%C7%E1%CD%E6%CB%ED&state=true#.VRPL1-FCi8g, 7 December 2005, last accessed 21 July 2016.

125. On information policy during the Saʿdah wars, see Shuja al-Deen 2009.
126. See the section 'Second Interim' in this chapter. Because of the information blackout, which was particularly pronounced during the second interim and the third war, information on this period is fragmentary. In some cases even Saudi newspapers such as *Al-Sharq al-Awsat* were more informative than Yemeni newspapers.
127. Brandt 2012: 56–8.
128. Salmoni et al. placed Maṭrah incorrectly in the Munabbih area, in the governorate's extreme northwest; see Salmoni et al. 2010: 142.
129. Interview, January 2014.
130. In administrative terms, Maṭrah belongs to Saḥār district, and al-Naqʿah to al-Ṣafrāʾ district.
131. Interview, March 2014.
132. Interview, October 2009.
133. See Chapter 4's section 'From Zaydi Revivalism to Political Competition'.
134. On these battles, see Chapter 7.
135. 'Ṣanʿāʾ: Maqtal thamāniyah fī ishtibāk maʿ anṣār al-Ḥūthī', *Al-Sharq al-Awsat*, http://archive.aawsat.com/details.asp?article=335933&issueno=9864#.VWg8Skb568g, 30 November 2005, last accessed 21 July 2016.
136. 'Maqtal 6 min al-Ḥūthiyyūn wa ʿadad min al-junūd fī ishtibākāt jadīdah', *Mareb Press*, http://marebpress.net/news_details.php?lng=arabic&sid=376, 21 January 2006, last accessed 22 July 2016.
137. Interview with a Houthi source from Ḍaḥyān, February 2014.
138. Ibid.
139. 'Maṣdar bi-l-dākhiliyyah: istishhād 3 min afrād al-amn', *26 September Net*, 30 November 2005, http://www.26sep.net/news_details.php?lng=arabic&sid=10988, last accessed 22 July 2016.
140. 'Tajaddud al-ishtibākāt fī Ṣaʿdah', *Mareb Press*, 29 December 2005, http://marebpress.net/news_details.php?lng=arabic&sid=209, last accessed 22 July 2016.
141. 'Fullah…arḍ al-maʿrakah fī Ṣaʿdah', *Aleshteraki Net*, 5 March 2006, http://www.aleshteraki.net/nprint.php?lng=arabic&sid=87, last accessed 3 March 2014.
142. Salmoni et al. 2010: 141.
143. 'Yaḥtafil bihi fī rūuʾs al-jibāl bi-ishʿāl al-nīrān ʿalā qimam al-jibāl', *Mareb Press*, 19 January 2006, http://marebpress.net/news_details.php?lng=arabic&sid=362, last accessed 22 July 2016.
144. This may have been the first mention of the term *Anṣār Allah* in connection with the Houthi movement. At the end of the Saʿdah wars in 2010, Anṣār Allah became its official name.
145. 'Al-ṭāʾirāt taqaṣṣuf tajammʿāt al-Ḥūthiyyīn fī l-Jawf', *Mareb Press*, 31 January 2006, http://marebpress.net/news_details.php?lng=arabic&sid=482, last accessed 22 July 2016.

146. 'Fī mawājihāt 'askariyyāt fī Ḥarf Sufyān juriḥa 15 shakhsān', *Mareb Press*, 5 February 2006, http://marebpress.net/news_details.php?lng=arabic&sid=544, last accessed 22 July 2016.
147. 'Media Reaction—Violence In Saada, Assassination Suspects On Trial, Etc', Wikileaks, http://wikileaks.org/cable/2005/12/05SANAA3600.html, 28 December 2005, last accessed 22 July 2016.
148. Interview with a Houthi source from Ḍaḥyān, July 2014.
149. 'Harabat ithnayn min akhṭar ittibā' al-Ḥūthī', *Mareb Press*, 28 January 2006,http://marebpress.net/news_details.php?lng=arabic&sid=449, last accessed 22 July 2016.
150. Phillips 2011a: 43; Johnsen 2013: 191–6.
151. On the Northern Ring Road project, see Chapter 1's section on 'Physical Ecologies'.
152. See Chapter 2.
153. 'Wakīl al-muḥāfaẓāh yataḥaddath 'an ṣarf al-ta'wīḍāt li-l-mutaḍarrirīn', *al-Mutamar Net*, 3 February 2006, http://almotamar.net/news/27752.htm, last accessed 22 July 2016.
154. Dorlian 2011: 186–7; see also 'Lajnat al-wisāṭah tawaṣṣalat ilā waqf al-munāwashāt bi-Ṣa'dah', *26 September Net*, 23 February 2006, http://www.26sep.net/news_details.php?lng=arabic&sid=13003, last accessed 22 July 2016
155. Al-Aḥmadī 2006: 146.

6. THE LANGUAGE OF WAR: 2006–11

1. Interview, March 2013.
2. See the below section 'Warmongers'.
3. Interview with a civil servant from Sa'dah city, November 2006.
4. Interview, September 2012.
5. Based on several interviews with sources from the Sa'dah area.
6. Interview with a civil servant from Sa'dah city, November 2006.
7. Ibid.
8. Markaz 2008: 208; Dorlian 2013: 137.
9. 'Iṣrār 'alā taghyīr thamāniyah min mudarā' al-'umūm fī Ṣa'dah', *Mareb Press*, 1 March 2006, https://marebpress.net/news_details.php?lng=arabic&sid=818, last accessed 22 July 2016.
10. Ibid.
11. Ṣāliḥ Abū 'Awjā' was a shaykh of al-'Uṣaymāt (Ḥāshid). He participated and was wounded in the first war as leader of the Ḥāshid auxiliaries. After his recovery, he was appointed district director of Ḥaydān at General 'Alī Muḥsin's behest.
12. 'Akkada al-mawāṭinūn iltizāmihim bi-l-thawābit al-waṭaniyyah', *26 September Net*, 1 March 2006, http://www.26sep.net/news_details.php?lng=arabic&sid=13140, last accessed 22 July 2016.

13. Phillips 2008: 16.
14. Poirier 2008.
15. Government of Yemen 2006.
16. Local councils are elected at both governorate and district levels for a three-year term. Councillors at both levels are directly elected from their constituencies in a single round, on a 'first-past-the-post', or 'winner-takes-all', basis; see European Union EOM 2006: 10–11. By its nature, this majoritarian electoral system can produce results that are highly unrepresentative of the popular vote, whereby political parties or candidates that win a sizeable proportion of votes can fail to win any seats in an elected assembly.
17. In Saʿdah governorate, 735 candidates stood for district-level election to the local councils (*al-hayʾāt al-maḥalliyyah bi-l-mudīriyyāt*). 685 of them—in roughly equal proportions—ran as GPC and independent candidates. Only fifty ran for other parties: 17 Baath, 15 Socialists, 5 Nasserite, 5 al-Ḥaqq, 4 Khaḍar, 3 Union of Popular Forces, 1 Septemberist. The ninety-five successful candidates consisted almost exclusively—and again, in roughly equal measure—of GPC and independent candidates.
18. Longley Alley 2007. In the municipal elections, Iṣlāḥ suffered a resounding nationwide defeat at the hands of the GPC. Yemeni Islamists seem to have lost their edge in an area formerly considered their strength: grassroots politics.
19. Interview with a member of the Houthi leadership in Saʿdah, January 2015.
20. European Union EOM 2006.
21. 'Al-Huthi yunaddid bi-sayr ʿamaliyyāt al-intikhābāt fī Ṣaʿdah', *Mareb Press*, 22 September 2006,http://marebpress.net/news_details.php?lng=arabic&sid=3015, last accessed 22 July 2016.
22. 'Raʾīs al-jumhūriyyah yuwajjih bi-surʿah muʿālijat āthār fitnat al-Ḥūthī fī Marrān', *26 September Net*, 9 October 2006,http://www.26sep.net/news_details.php?lng=arabic&sid=19206, last accessed 22 July 2016.
23. Dorlian 2011: 187; Dorlian 2013: 137.
24. Interview, November 2014.
25. See the below section 'The Fourth War: The Popular Army'.
26. Gingrich 1994a: 22; Weir 2007: 131. Among the member tribes of the Khawlān b. ʿĀmir confederation, the extent of interspersion of tribal moieties can vary; see Gingrich 1994a: 25; Weir 2007: 131.
27. Interview with a Houthi source from Saʿdah city, October 2015.
28. Jamous 1991.
29. International Crisis Group 2009: 15–17.
30. 'Ḥarb Ṣaʿdah taftaḥ malaf tijārat al-silāḥ fī l-Yaman', *Mareb Press*, 21 April 2007, http://marebpress.net/news_details.php?lng=arabic&sid=5569, last accessed 22 July 2016.
31. For a discussion of the 'ghost soldier' phenomenon, see USAID 2006: 4; International Crisis Group 2013 passim; Seitz 2016: 164–5, 168.

32. International Crisis Group 2009: 15; Salmoni 2010: 197–8.
33. International Crisis Group 2009: 16; Salmoni et al. 2010: 44.
34. International Crisis Group 2009: 15–17.
35. Gause 2011.
36. Al-Aḥmadī 2006: 175–8; Markaz 2008: 103–14 and passim; Salmoni et al. 2010: 169–71.
37. 'Yemeni tribal leader: For Saleh, Saudi Involvement in Sa'ada comes not a moment too soon', Wikileaks, 28 December 2009, https://wikileaks.org/cable/2009/12/09SANAA2279.html, last accessed 22 July 2016.
38. Du Bouchet 2007: 149.
39. 'Ambassador discusses terrorist threat, Saada with FM Qirbi', Wikileaks, 12 April 2005, https://wikileaks.org/plusd/cables/05SANAA917_a.html, last accessed 22 July 2016.
40. Ibid.
41. 'Saada-related military assistance to Central Security Forces CT Unit', Wikileaks, 13 April 2005, https://wikileaks.org/plusd/cables/05SANAA935_a.html, last accessed 22 July 2016.
42. 'Saleh and Ambassador discuss Koran desecration allegations, FMF, and al-Houthi rebellion', Wikileaks, 15 May 2005, https://wikileaks.org/plusd/cables/05SANAA1301_a.html, last accessed 22 July 2016.
43. Interview with a US diplomat, June 2015.
44. 'Iran in Yemen: Tehran's shadow looms large', Wikileaks, 12 September 2009, https://wikileaks.org/plusd/cables/09SANAA1662_a.html, last accessed 22 July 2016.
45. 'Al-Houthi rebellion: No end in sight', Wikileaks, 14 July 2008, https://wikileaks.org/plusd/cables/08SANAA1165_a.html, last accessed 22 July 2016.
46. See United Nations Security Council Report S/2015/401, Annex 1.
47. Terrill 2014.
48. Terrill 2014.
49. Schmitt and Worth 2012.
50. Terrill 2014: 436.
51. United Nations Security Council Report S/2015/401: 14.
52. Terrill 2014: 439.
53. Salisbury 2015: 12. For a similar thesis see Boucek 2010: 10.
54. 'Yaḥyā al-Ḥūthī li-Mareb Press: al-ra'īs yarfuḍ wisāṭah Mu'ammar al-Qadhāfī', *Mareb Press*, 21 April 2007,http://marebpress.net/news_details.php?lng=arabic&sid=3655, last accessed 22 July 2016.
55. 'Anbā' 'an da'm lībī li-Yaḥyā al-Ḥūthī li-bad' ḥarb jadīdah', *Mareb Press*, 16 December 2006, http://marebpress.net/news_details.php?lng=arabic&sid=3869, last accessed 22 July 2016. Yaḥyā al-Ḥūthī had been living abroad since 2005, mainly in Germany, where he successfully applied for asylum. He returned to Yemen in

July 2013 when he was nominated as delegate for the National Dialogue Conference.

56. Peterson 2008a: 9–10.
57. 'Al-safir al-lībī yanfī ittihāmāt', *Mareb Press*, 16 January 2007, https://marebpress.net/news_details.php?lng=arabic&sid=4207, last accessed 22 July 2016.
58. See, for example, Chapin Metz 1987.
59. 'Libya indignant over Saudi rebuke', *BBC News*, 22 September 2004, http://news.bbc.co.uk/2/hi/middle_east/4119719.stm, last accessed 22 July 2016. Allegations of Gaddafi's involvement in subversive activities were numerous. Over the years, Gaddafi has been accused of subversion by several Arab countries, including Egypt, Sudan, Tunisia, Morocco, and Jordan; see Chapin Metz 1987.
60. 'Maṣādir yamaniyyah: muḥākamat ra'īs lajnat al-wisāṭah maʿ al-Ḥūthiyyīn', *Al-Sharq al-Awsat*, 15 April 2010, http://archive.aawsat.com/details.asp?section=1&article=565387&issueno=11461#.V44MEzX57K1, last accessed 22 July 2016. See also the entry on Fāris Manāʿ on Arabic Wikipedia.
61. Interview with a US diplomat, May 2015.
62. 'Maṣādir yamaniyyah: muḥākamat ra'īs lajnat al-wisāṭah maʿ al-Ḥūthiyyīn', *Al-Sharq al-Awsat*, 15 April 2010, http://archive.aawsat.com/details.asp?section=1&article=565387&issueno=11461#.V44MEzX57K1, last accessed 22 July 2016.
63. Interview, May 2015.
64. Interviews, May and June 2015.
65. Interview, May 2015.
66. 'Tamhīdan li-qaṭaʿ al-ʿalāqāt', *Mareb Press*, 10 May 2007, http://marebpress.net/news_details.php?lng=arabic&sid=5848, last accessed 22 July 2016.
67. 'DAS Carpenter and Saleh focus in forum for future and Saada', Wikileaks, 12 June 2007,http://wikileaks.org/cable/2007/06/07SANAA1099.html, last accessed 22 July 2016.
68. See Chapter 5's section on 'The First War: Mediation'.
69. Durac 2011.
70. Markaz 2008: 247–64; International Crisis Group 2014: 8.
71. Interviews, December 2015.
72. 'Al-nā'ib al-ʿAwjarī li-l-Jumhūr: Fāris Manāʿ "Ḥūthī"', *Al-Jumhor*, 30 January 2010, http://www.aljumhor.net/portal/news-1864.htm, last accessed 22 July 2016.
73. Salmoni et al. 2010: 126.
74. See Chapter 2's section on 'The Politics of Patronage'.
75. International Crisis Group 2009: 15; Phillips 2011a: 93–5.
76. International Crisis Group 2009: 15.
77. Phillips 2011a: 93–5; Day 2012: 218; Seitz 2014: 62–4.
78. See Chapter 6's section 'The Sixth War: Introduction'.
79. Boucek 2010: 4.

80. Interview, November 2012.
81. 'Shaykh yattahim al-sulṭāt al-yamaniyyah bi-tanfīdh raghbah saʿūdiyyah bi-nashr al-salafiyyah', *Mareb Press*, 22 April 2006, http://mail.marebpress.com/news_details.php?lng=arabic&sid=1436, last accessed 22 July 2016.
82. 'Tajaddud al-ishtibākāt maʿ ittibāʿ al-Ḥūthī', *Elaph*, 7 June 2006, http://elaph.com/ElaphWeb/Politics/2006/6/154112.htm#sthash.Vj9tjGJO.dpuf, last accessed 22 July 2016.
83. Interview, September 2013.
84. 'Tajaddud al-ishtibākāt maʿ ittibāʿ al-Ḥūthī', *Elaph*, 7 June 2006, http://elaph.com/ElaphWeb/Politics/2006/6/154112.htm#sthash.Vj9tjGJO.dpuf, last accessed 22 July 2016.
85. Interview, September 2013.
86. 'Al-Ḥūthiyyūn yakhrujūna fī muẓāharāt tajūb shawārʿ Ṣaʿdah', *Mareb Press*, 30 November 2006,http://marebpress.net/news_details.php?lng=arabic&sid=3713, last accessed 22 July 2016.
87. 'Iṭlāq al-nār wa qanābil musaylah li-dumūʿ li-mawājihat iṣyān fī sijn Ṣaʿdah', *Mareb Press*, 19 December 2006, http://marebpress.net/news_details.php?lng=arabic&sid=3916, last accessed 22 July 2016.
88. 'Al-Ḥūthiyyūn yashtarūna akhthar min 40 sayyārah shāṣṣ', *Mareb Press*, 7 January 2007, http://marebpress.net/news_details.php?lng=arabic&sid=4114, last accessed 22 July 2016.
89. 'Lajnat al-ḥiwār waṣalat Ṣaʿdah li-l-tawassuṭ bayn al-ṭarfayn', *Mareb Press*, 11 January 2007, https://marebpress.net/news_details.php?lng=arabic&sid=4150, last accessed 22 July 2016.
90. On Operation Magic Carpet, see Parfitt 1996; Ahroni 2001; Meir-Glitzenstein 2011, 2012.
91. On 'weak' people, see Chapter 1's section on 'Estates of Society'.
92. Dresch 1981: 75–8; Dresch 1989: 59–60, 118; Kuczynski 1985: 277–302.
93. "ʿAbd al-Malik al-Ḥūthī yanfī ʿalāqatahu bi-tahdīd yahūd Āl Sālim', *Mareb Press*, 22 January 2007, https://marebpress.net/news_details.php?lng=arabic&sid=4306, last accessed 22 July 2016.
94. The account given here is based on several interviews with shaykhs involved and a Houthi field commander. It also includes the description of Yaḥyā Yūsif Mūsā, the community leader of the Jews of Āl Sālim, given in Wikileaks; see 'Jewish Community's Security Perceptions Increasingly Pessimistic', Wikileaks, http://wikileaks.org/cable/2007/05/07SANAA852.html, 8 May 2007, last accessed 22 July 2016.
95. 'Saada Jews safe in Sanaa', Wikileaks, http://wikileaks.org/cable/2007/03/07SANAA395.html, 14 March 2007, last accessed 22 July 2016.
96. On the role of Nājī Bukhtān, see 'Jewish community's security perceptions increasingly pessimistic', Wikileaks, https://wikileaks.org/cable/2007/05/07SANAA

852.html, 8 May 2007, last accessed 22 July 2016. The Bukhtān clan is politically divided; whereas Nājī Ṣāliḥ Bukhtān was considered a Houthi supporter, his cousin Shāya' Bukhtān was loyal to the government. Shāya' Bukhtān died in 2008 in a mysterious accident. After the Sa'dah wars, his family was displaced to Sana'a.

97. 'Saada Jews safe in Sanaa', Wikileaks, https://wikileaks.org/plusd/cables/07SANAA395_a.html, 14 March 2007, last accessed 22 July 2016. The Tourist City complex is a gated community with small parks, swimming pools, shops—and soldiers guarding the entrances. Despite its name, Tourist City is not a major tourist destination, but a mixed-use residential and commercial complex housing a variety of Yemenis and foreigners. The complex is owned by a relative of Salih.
98. 'Saada Jews safe in Sanaa', Wikileaks, 14 March 2007, https://wikileaks.org/plusd/cables/07SANAA395_a.html, last accessed 22 July 2016.
99. 'Jewish Community's Security Perceptions Increasingly Pessimistic', Wikileaks, 8 May 2007, http://wikileaks.org/cable/2007/05/07SANAA852.html, last accessed 22 July 2016.
100. 'Muṭālabāt ūrūbiyyah bi-idrāj tanẓīm al-Ḥūthī ḍimna al-munaẓẓamāt al-irhābiyyah', *Mareb Press*, 7 February 2007, http://marebpress.net/news_details.php?lng=arabic&sid=4521, last accessed 22 July 2016.
101. 'Saada Jews safe in Sanaa', Wikileaks, 14 March 2007, https://wikileaks.org/plusd/cables/07SANAA395_a.html, last accessed 22 July 2016.
102. 'Al-Ḥūthiyyūn yaḥdharūna al-sulṭāt al-yamaniyyah', *Mareb Press*, 22 January 2007, https://marebpress.net/news_details.php?lng=arabic&sid=4306, last accessed 22 July 2016.
103. Dorlian 2011: 197–8; Dorlian 2013: 150–1.
104. 'Yaḥyā al-Ḥūthī: al-mawājihāt yumkin an tatawass'', *Al-Eshteraky*, 25 February 2007, http://aleshteraky.com/archive/news_details.php?lng=arabic&sid=1838, last accessed 22 July 2016.
105. Interview with the commander of a group of tribal irregulars involved in the advance, July 2015.
106. Markaz 2008: 213. For roads in al-Jawf, see Steffen 1978: II/171.
107. 'Wajjaha tahdīdān khaṭiyyān li-l-muḥāfiẓ', *Mareb Press*, 1 February 2007, http://marebpress.net/news_details.php?lng=arabic&sid=4457, last accessed 22 July 2016.
108. 'Yaḥyā al-Ḥūthī yu'ayyid fikrat inshā' ḥizb siyāsī', *Mareb Press*, 30 January 2007, http://marebpress.net/news_details.php?lng=arabic&sid=4426, last accessed 22 July 2016.
109. Markaz 2008: 232–4.
110. 'Al-Huthi yuwāfiq 'alā maṭālib al-ra'īs', *Al-Eshteraky*, 9 February 2007, http://aleshteraky.com/archive/news_details.php?lng=arabic&sid=1771, last accessed 22 July 2016.

111. 'Wajjaha tahdīdān khaṭiyyān li-l-muḥāfiẓ', *Mareb Press*, 1 February 2007, http://marebpress.net/news_details.php?lng=arabic&sid=4457, last accessed 22 July 2016.
112. Ibid.
113. 'Saada: Parliament votes for war, but over what?', Wikileaks, 12 February 2007, https://wikileaks.org/plusd/cables/07SANAA243_a.html, last accessed 22 July 2016.
114. 'Fī aqall min usbūʿ risalāh khaṭṭiyah min Ṣāliḥ li-ʿAbdullah', *Mareb Press*, 15 February 2007, http://marebpress.net/news_details.php?lng=arabic&sid=4614, last accessed 22 July 2016.
115. Interview with a government official from Sanaʿa, September 2013.
116. 'Maṣādir tu'akkid mushārakat 30 alf jundī min al-jaysh al-yamanī', *Mareb Press*, 12 April 2007, http://marebpress.net/news_details.php?lng=arabic&sid=5438, last accessed 22 July 2016.
117. 'Saada: Fighting intensifies with troop surge', Wikileaks, 21 February 2007, https://wikileaks.org/plusd/cables/07SANAA285_a.html, last accessed 22 July 2016.
118. 'Al-Ḥūthiyyūn yuqallilūna min ahammiyyah Dukhfash', *Al-Eshteraky*, 18 March 2007, http://aleshteraky.com/archive/news_details.php?lng=arabic&sid=1924, last accessed 22 July 2016.
119. This part is not accurate: in fact, Shājiaʿ b. Shājiaʿ had negotiated with al-Razzāmī after the first war.
120. Interview, September 2013.
121. 'Quwwāt al-jaysh taʿthur ʿalā makhzan silāḥ', *al-Ayyam*, 22 March 2007, http://www.al-ayyam.info/default.aspx?NewsID=fb7dd6f0–923c-406b-bb03–188c6be4ebdb, last accessed September 2012.
122. 'Al-maʿārik tamtadd ilā al-ḥudūd al-saʿūdiyyah', *Al-Eshteraky*, 7 May 2007, http://aleshteraky.com/archive/news_details.php?lng=arabic&sid=2147, last accessed 22 July 2016.
123. 'Fīmā qīl ʿan taḥqīq taqaddum li-l-Ḥūthiyyūn fī baʿḍ al-mawāqʿ', *Mareb Press*, 19 April 2007, http://marebpress.net/news_details.php?lng=arabic&sid=5548, last accessed 22 July 2016.
124. 'Taṭawwurāt al-ḥarb', *Al-Eshteraky*, 5 March 2007, http://aleshteraky.com/archive/news_details.php?lng=arabic&sid=1874, last accessed 22 July 2016.
125. The Ghamr are a tribal section of the Rāziḥ. In administrative terms, Ghamr is a separate district.
126. Weir 2007.
127. 'Maṣraʿ 3 ʿaskariyyīn fī ishtibākāt wasaṭ Ṣanʿā'', *al-Ayyam*, 16 April 2007, http://www.al-ayyam.info/Default.aspx?NewsID=4c787a52–4aa1–4226-be3c-8de6aec64a21, last accessed February 2012.
128. 'Quwwāt al-jaysh taʿthur ʿalā makhzan silāḥ', *al-Ayyam*, 22 March 2007, http://

www.al-ayyam.info/default.aspx?NewsID=fb7dd6f0–923c-406b-bb03–188c6be4ebdb, last accessed September 2012.

129. 'Al-ṭayarān yaqṣif al-Jarshah ba'd istilā' al-Ḥūthiyyīn 'alayhā', *Al-Eshteraky*, 10 April 2007, http://aleshteraky.com/archive/news_details.php?lng=arabic&sid=2028, last accessed 22 July 2016.

130. 'Rāziḥ... suyūl al-tadmīr wa sarāb al-ta'wīḍāt', *Al-Ahale*, 12 November 2007, https://alahale.net/mobile/article/2358, last accessed February 2012.

131. 'Huwa al-hujūm al-thālith lahum khilāl aqall shahr', *Mareb Press*, 5 June 2007, http://marebpress.net/news_details.php?lng=arabic&sid=6219, last accessed 22 July 2016.

132. 'Amīn 'āmm ḥizb al-ḥaqq yuṭālib bi-ḥall ḥizbihi, *Mareb Press*, 18 March 2007, http://marebpress.net/news_details.php?lng=arabic&sid=5106, last accessed 22 July 2016.

133. According to a Western researcher, a party official commented on the notion of dissolution: 'A political party is not a grocery shop which you can simply close down'.

134. Interview, September 2015.

135. Interview, August 2015.

136. 'Al-Ḥūthiyyūn yusayṭirūna 'alā al-qaṣr al-jumhūrī li-sā'atayn', *Al-Eshteraky*, 19 April 2007, http://aleshteraky.com/archive/news_details.php?lng=arabic&sid=2071, last accessed 22 July 2016.

137. 'Al-jaysh yu'zil Ghamr 'an Rāziḥ', *Al-Eshteraky*, 30 April 2007, http://aleshteraky.com/archive/news_details.php?lng=arabic&sid=2113, last accessed 22 July 2016.

138. Ibid.

139. 'Ikhtiṭāf al-ṭifl Amīn 'Abd al-Qādir Badr al-Dīn al-Ḥūthī (13 sanah) fī Ṣan'ā'', *Al-Eshteraky*, 13 April 2007, http://aleshteraky.com/archive/news_details.php?lng=arabic&sid=2044, last accessed 22 July 2016.

140. Tribal auxiliaries in Yemen often bear this or a similar name.

141. Qaflah 'Udhar is situated in Ḥāshid territory close to the Sufyān border. On the Popular Army of Qaflah 'Udhar, see also Hamidi 2009: 173–4,185 n. 45.

142. Number given by *Mareb Press*, see 'Murāqibūn: zajj al-qabā'il fī l-ḥarb', *Mareb Press*, 6 March 2007, http://marebpress.net/news_details.php?lng=arabic&sid=4928, last accessed 22 July 2016.

143. For further details on the use of tribal levies during the Sa'dah wars, see Brandt 2014a.

144. Salmoni et al. 2010: 169; Bonnefoy 2011a: 274.

145. Hamidi 2009: 165.

146. 'Al-Maḥaṭwarī yantaqid al-fatāwā al-latī tad'w l-jihād al-Ḥūthiyyīn', *Mareb Press*, 14 March 2007, http://marebpress.net/news_details.php?lng=arabic&sid=5059, last accessed 22 July 2016.

147. Interview with a source from the al-ʿAmrānī family, August 2015.
148. Hamidi 2009: 186 n. 60.
149. 'Al-Maḥaṭwarī yantaqid al-fatāwā al-latī tadʿw l-jihād al-Ḥūthiyyīn', *Mareb Press*, 14 March 2007, http://marebpress.net/news_details.php?lng=arabic&sid=5059, last accessed 22 July 2016.
150. Salmoni et al. 2010: 169.
151. 'Dukhūl jamāʿāh jīhādiyyah ʿalā khaṭṭ al-nār', *Mareb Press*, 20 February 2007, http://marebpress.net/news_details.php?lng=arabic&sid=4707, last accessed 22 July 2016. Khālid ʿAbdulnabī, an 'Arab Afghan', was a Yemeni jihadi who was once part of the Islamic Army of Adan-Abyan and is considered the original founder of Anṣār al-Sharīʿah.
152. Salmoni 2010: 162.
153. Brandt 2013 and 2014a.
154. 'Al-jaysh yastaʿayn bi-qabāʾil min Ḥāshid', *Mareb Press*, 6 March 2007, http://marebpress.net/news_details.php?lng=arabic&sid=4928, last accessed 22 July 2016.
155. 'Al-raʾīs tasāʾal ʿan dawr mashāyikh Ṣaʿdah', YE1, 15 February 2007, http://www.ye1.org/forum/threads/173630/page-34, last accessed 22 July 2016.
156. See Chapter 2's section on 'The Politics of Patronage'.
157. 'Saada: Casualties mount, Saleh prepares for offensive', Wikileaks, 6 February 2007, https://wikileaks.org/plusd/cables/07SANAA221_a.html, last accessed 22 July 2016.
158. 'Al-Ḥūthiyyūn ḥafnah min al-murāhiqīn', *Mareb Press*, 9 May 2007, http://marebpress.net/news_details.php?lng=arabic&sid=5836, last accessed 22 July 2016.
159. See the present chapter's section on 'War Mongers: Revenge and Tribal Feuding'.
160. "Alā ʿaks al-tawaqquʿāt al-mutafāʾilah bi-inhā al-maʿārik', *Mareb Press*, 14 May 2007, http://marebpress.net/news_details.php?lng=arabic&sid=5905, last accessed 22 July 2016.
161. See the present chapter's section on 'War Mongers: Domestic Politics and War of Succession'.
162. "Alā ʿaks al-tawaqquʿāt al-mutafāʾilah bi-inhā al-maʿārik', *Mareb Press*, 14 May 2007, http://marebpress.net/news_details.php?lng=arabic&sid=5905, last accessed 22 July 2016.
163. 'Al-shaykh Fayṣal bin ʿArīj li-l-jumhūr: al-iṣlāḥ yuʾajjij al-ḥarb wa yatamannā hilāk al-ṭarfayn', *Al-Jumhor*, 12 December 2009, http://www.aljumhor.net/portal/print.php?id=1484, last accessed 22 July 2016.
164. 'Al-Miṣrī: la ʿawdah li-marḥalat taqbīl al-aqdām', *Al-Methaq*, 18 May 2007, http://www.almethaq.net/news/news-3138.htm, last accessed 22 July 2016.
165. What was said during this meeting has been reconstructed on the basis of several interviews with persons involved.

166. 'Muwājahāt musallaḥah bayn quwwāt al-shurṭah wa l-amn al-markazī dākhil Ṣa'dah', *Al-Majalis*, 25 May 2007, http://al-majalis.com/forums/viewtopic.php?f=18&t=6152&start=525, last accessed 22 July 2016.
167. 'Al-jaysh yuwajjih ḍarabāt li-kull man tasawwal lahu nafsihi li-musā'adat al-Ḥūthiyyīn', *Al-Majalis*, 5 June 2007, http://www.almajalis.org/forums/viewtopic.php?f=18&t=6152&start=435, last accessed 22 July 2016.
168. Brandt 2012: 63.
169. Hamidi 2009: 173.
170. 'Risālat tahdīd wajjahahā 'Abd al-Malik al-Ḥūthī ilā mashāyikh Ṣa'dah', *Akhbaralyom*, 1 June 2007, http://akhbaralyom.net/news_details.php?sid=21972, last accessed April 2012.
171. 'Saada: Calls for dialogue abound, but fighting continues', Wikileaks, 29 May 2007, https://wikileaks.org/plusd/cables/07SANAA1022_a.html, last accessed 22 July 2016.
172. 'Akthar min thalāthīn alf nāziḥ min jaḥīm Ṣa'dah', *Mareb Press*, 29 April 2007, http://marebpress.net/news_details.php?lng=arabic&sid=5673, last accessed 2 July 2016.
173. Interview, July 2014.
174. 'Saada: War is over, but can RoYG now win the peace?', Wikileaks, 18 June 2007, https://wikileaks.org/plusd/cables/07SANAA1133_a.html, last accessed 22 July 2016.
175. 'Fī ẓill anbā' 'an tawjīhāt amrīkiyyah li-ṭayy milaff Ṣa'dah', *Mareb Press*, 8 May 2007, http://marebpress.net/news_details.php?lng=arabic&sid=5820, last accessed 22 July 2016.
176. 'Saada: Calls for dialogue abound, but fighting continues', Wikileaks, 29 May 2007, https://wikileaks.org/plusd/cables/07SANAA1022_a.html, last accessed 22 July 2016.
177. Peterson 2006; Kamrava 2011; Fattah 2014.
178. The provisions of the First Doha Agreement, according to Salmoni et al. 2010: 315–16:
    1. Cessation of military operations; and adherence, of the Ḥūthī and those with him ['Abdulmalik], to the republican order [system], the constitution and the laws in force in the country.
    2. Ending of the rebellion; implementation of the general amnesty decision; and the release of prisoners, except for those charged in cases turned over to the general prosecutor or under consideration by the courts; and search for [discovery of] the missing people and care for injured/wounded people; and release of corpses by whomever possesses them.
    3. Life [should] return to normal in the regions [of conflict], and everyone [should] return to his area, and live as safe citizens, as all the other citizens in the regions of the republic.

4. Extension of the state's general order in the region, as in all other regions of the republic.
5. The relinquishment of medium weapons, along with their ammunition, to the state.
6. Respect for freedom of opinion, to include the right to establish a political party in accordance with the constitution and the laws in force in the country.
7. The arrival of ʿAbdulmalik al-Ḥūthī, Yaḥyā al-Ḥūthī, ʿAbdulkarīm al-Ḥūthī, and ʿAbdullah al-Razzāmī to Qatar, without undertaking any political or media activity hostile to Yemen and without leaving Qatar except after the agreement of the Yemeni government.
8. Cessation of all matter of media campaigns and acts of provocative incitement.
9. The Yemeni government will undertake the reconstruction of what the war has destroyed and the treatment of its effects; the praiseworthy state of Qatar will undertake to contribute to a fund for the rebuilding of the affected areas and for the compensation of those affected [by the fighting], and this fund will be open to the contributions of Arab and friendly states.

179. International Crisis Group 2009: 22.
180. 'Maṣdar masʾūl yuʾakkid taʿlīq al-ʿamaliyyāt al-ʿaskariyyah bi-Ṣaʿdah', *26 September*, 16 June 2007, http://26sep.net/news_details.php?sid=28963, last accessed 22 July 2016.
181. Interview, October 2015.
182. On Aḥmad Dahbāsh Miṭrī, see Brandt 2012.
183. "Abd al-Malik al-Ḥūthī jarfuḍ taslīm al-asliḥah al-thaqīlah', *Mareb Press*, 2 July 2007, http://marebpress.net/news_details.php?lng=arabic&sid=6581, last accessed 22 July 2016.
184. 'Qādat al-Ḥūthiyyūn yughādirūna ilā Qatar', *Mareb Press*, 16 June 2007, http://marebpress.net/news_details.php?lng=arabic&sid=6356, last accessed 22 July 2016.
185. 'Bayān lajnat Ṣaʿdah yuthīr al-tawattur', *Al-Eshteraky*, 6 July 2007, http://aleshteraky.com/archive/news_details.php?lng=arabic&sid=2439, last accessed 22 July 2016.
186. 'Akkada khallāfah maʿ al-sulṭah miʾat fī l-miʾah', *Mareb Press*, 28 July 2007, http://marebpress.net/news_details.php?lng=arabic&sid=6991, last accessed 22 July 2016.
187. "Abd al-Malik al-Ḥūthī: ... lajnat al-ittifāq tatajāhal khatwātnā', *Al-Eshteraky*, http://aleshteraky.com/archive/news_details.php?lng=arabic&sid=2461, 9 July 2007, last accessed 22 July 2016.
188. "Abd al-Malik al-Ḥūthī: ... ṭābūr thālith aṭlaqa al-nār ʿalā lajnat al-ittifāq', *Al-Eshteraky*, http://aleshteraky.com/archive/news_details.php?lng=arabic&sid=2498, 15 July 2007, last accessed 22 July 2016.

189. 'Saada: Ceasefire fragile, but holding', Wikileaks, https://wikileaks.org/plusd/cables/07SANAA1414_a.html, 23 July 2007, last accessed 22 July 2016.
190. 'Al-Ḥūthiyyūn yu'akkidūn istimrār qaṣf al-jaysh al-yamanī li-manāṭiq sakaniyyah', *Mareb Press*, http://marebpress.net/news_details.php?lng=arabic&sid=8228, 8 November 2007, last accessed 22 July 2016.
191. 'Qā'id al-ḥaras al-khāṣṣ maʿ wafd murāfiq fī Mūskū', *Mareb Press*, 11 March 2007, http://marebpress.net/news_details.php?lng=arabic&sid=5013, last accessed 22 July 2016.
192. Interview with an observer close to the Mujallī family, November 2012.
193. 'Qabā'il muḥāfaẓat Ṣaʿdah tuṭālib bi-surʿah muḥākamat al-junāt...', *Mareb Press*, 18 December 2007, http://marebpress.net/news_details.php?sid=8764&lng=arabic, last accessed 22 July 2016.
194. 'Nā'ib barlamānī yuhaddid bi-taṣfiyat kibār mas'iūlī al-dawlah wa ḍarab ʿumq al-niẓām', *Nabanews*, 19 December 2007, http://www.nabanews.net/2009/12066.html, last accessed 22 July 2016.
195. Ibid. On 'rifles of good faith', see Dresch 1989: 87–8; Abū Ghānim 1991: 269; Heinze 2014a: 85–7.
196. 'Al-dawlah takhsur bi-kartihā al-akhīr fī Ṣaʿdah', *Newyemen*, 1 January 2008, http://www.newyemen.net/dgNews/news-736.htm, last accessed 22 July 2016.
197. Interview with an observer close to the Mujallī family, November 2012.
198. Al-Zwaini 2006: 13.
199. 'Al-Ḥūthiyyūn aṣbaḥū akthar quwwah', *Mareb Press*, 26 January 2008, http://marebpress.net/news_details.php?lng=arabic&sid=9341, last accessed 22 July 2016.
200. 'Saada Update: It's Not Quiet On Yemen's Northwestern Frontier', Wikileaks, 13 January 2008, http://wikileaks.org/cable/2008/01/08SANAA67.html, last accessed 22 July 2016.
201. Jabal al-Tha'r marks the eastern terminus of the 1934 Ṭā'if Line, see al-Enazy 2005.
202. 'Qabā'il Wā'ilah lā taʿtarif bi-l-khaṭṭ al-ḥudūdī al-jadīd', *Mareb Press*, 21 June 2006, http://marebpress.net/news_details.php?sid=2054&lng=arabic, last accessed 22 July 2016.
203. 'Al-Huthiyyun yuṭālibun al-Saʿūdiyyah an yaʿlimū aghrāḍahum', *Mareb Press*, 9 January 2007, https://marebpress.net/news_details.php?lng=arabic&sid=4130, last accessed 22 July 2016.
204. 'Parliament in Crisis over Abu Ras Resignation Allegations', *Yemen Observer*, 24 September 2005, http://www.yobserver.com/reports/1008216.html, last accessed March 2012.
205. 'al-Nāziḥīn min qabā'il Dahm yushīdū awwal mukhayamah ʿalā al-ḥudūd al-yamaniyyah al-saʿūdiyyah', *Mareb Press*, 3 October 2007, http://www.marebpress.net/news_details.php?sid=7836, last accessed 22 July 2016.

206. Dahlgren 2008; Dahlgren 2010.
207. 'Efforts underway to revive Qatari mediation', Wikileaks, 18 November 2007, https://wikileaks.org/plusd/cables/07SANAA2124_a.html, last accessed 23 July 2016.
208. Provision 7 of the First Doha Agreement corresponds to Provision 12 of the Second Doha Agreement. For the exact wording of the Second Doha Agreement, see 'Naṣṣ wathīqat al-Dawḥah', *Mareb Press*, 21 March 2008, http://marebpress.net/news_details.php?lng=arabic&sid=10317, last accessed 23 July 2016.
209. Ibid.
210. 'Al-sulṭah wa l-Ḥūthiyyūn yatabādalān ittihāmāt', *al-Ayyam*, 19 April 2008, http://www.al-ayyam.info/default.aspx?NewsID=307918ac-facd-4129–9d55–927a1ac7b2b1, last accessed December 2011.
211. 'Maṣraʿ sabʿah min anṣār al-Ḥūthī wa suqūṭ mirwaḥiyyah bi-Ḥaydān', *Mareb Press*, 3 February 2008, http://marebpress.net/news_details.php?lng=arabic&sid=9463, last accessed 23 July 2016.
212. The Bukhtān clan subscribed to different political loyalties; see the present chapter's section on 'The Fourth War: The Jews of Āl Sālim'.
213. 'Taʿqīdāt jadīdah fī qaḍiyyah Ṣaʿdah', *Mareb Press*, 4 March 2008, http://marebpress.net/news_details.php?lng=arabic&sid=10047, last accessed 23 July 2016.
214. Barakat 2014: 15.
215. See Chapter 2's section on 'Tribal Allegiances during the Civil War'.
216. See Chapter 5's section on 'The First War: War Course'.
217. 'Al-sulṭah wa l-Ḥūthiyyūn yatabādalān ittihāmāt', *al-Ayyam*, 19 April 2008, http://www.al-ayyam.info/default.aspx?NewsID=307918ac-facd-4129–9d55–927a1ac7b2b1, last accessed December 2011.
218. Ibid.
219. See Chapter 4's section 'From Zaydi Revivalism to Political Competition'.
220. According to other sources this incident was an 'accident'. Nonetheless, the blood feud evolved.
221. Lichtenthäler 2003: 63–4.
222. Interview, May 2014.
223. 'Al-sulṭah wa l-Ḥūthiyyūn yatabādalān ittihāmāt', *al-Ayyam*, 19 April 2008, http://www.al-ayyam.info/default.aspx?NewsID=307918ac-facd-4129–9d55–927a1ac7b2b1, last accessed December 2011.
224. 'Al-Qatariyyūn yastānifūna masāʿī "al-furṣah al-akhīrah"', *Mareb Press*, 20 April 2008, http://marebpress.net/news_details.php?lng=arabic&sid=10799, last accessed 23 July 2016.
225. Worth 2008. On Imam Aḥmad's quote, see vom Bruck 2005: 56.
226. "Abd al-Malik al-Ḥūthī yuhaddid al-sulṭah', *Al-Eshteraky*, 5 May 2008, http://aleshteraky.com/archive/news_details.php?lng=arabic&sid=3962, last accessed 23 July 2016.

227. Peterson 2008a: 11; Dorlian 2011: 188.
228. "'Abd al-Malik al-Ḥūthī yuhaddid al-sulṭah', *Al-Eshteraky*, 5 May 2008, http://aleshteraky.com/archive/news_details.php?lng=arabic&sid=3962, last accessed 23 July 2016.
229. 'Quwwat al-ḥaras al-jumhūrī tadkhul khaṭṭ al-mawājahah fī Ṣa'dah', *Mareb Press*, 7 May 2008, http://marebpress.net/news_details.php?lng=arabic&sid=11125, last accessed 23 July 2016.
230. 'Suqūt 18 qatīlān fī muwājahāt sharisah', *Al-Riyadh*, 5 May 2008, http://www.alriyadh.com/2008/05/05/article340160.html, last accessed 23 July 2016.
231. 'Mudīr amn muḥāfaẓat Ṣan'ā' lā yazāl muḥāṣar fī Banī Ḥushaysh', *Mareb Press*, 14 May 2008, http://marebpress.net/news_details.php?lng=arabic&sid=11261, last accessed 23 July 2016.
232. 'Tamarrud khatīr bi-ḍawāḥī Ṣan'ā'', *Mareb Press*, 15 May 2008, http://marebpress.net/news_details.php?lng=arabic&sid=11284, last accessed 23 July 2016.
233. For a detailed account of the tribal society of Banī Ḥushaysh after the 1960s civil war, see Dostal 1974. Sana'a city is a separate governorate.
234. 'Al-quwwāt al-ḥukūmiyyah tuḥāṣir manāṭiq fī Banī Ḥushaysh', *Mareb Press*, 26 May 2008, http://marebpress.net/news_details.php?lng=arabic&sid=11491, last accessed 23 July 2016.
235. Interview, November 2012.
236. The widespread rumours that the fighting in Banī Ḥushaysh was a power struggle between various army units or even an 'aborted coup' led by 'Alī Muḥsin against President Salih could not be confirmed.
237. 'Tajaddud al-muwājahāt bayn al-Ḥūthiyyūn wa l-quwwāt al-ḥukūmiyyah 'alā mashārif Ṣan'ā', *Mareb Press*, 1 June 2008, http://marebpress.net/news_details.php?lng=arabic&sid=11591, last accessed 23 July 2016.
238. Ibid.
239. The Ashrāf tribe claims descent from the Prophet Muhammad. Despite maintaining a degree of independence from the tribal environment within which they live, the Āl Ashrāf nonetheless maintain many of the structural characteristics of a conventional tribe; see vom Bruck 2005: 141–2.
240. 'Jawf, Forgotten Governorate', Saba News, 20 August 2009, http://www.sabanews.net/en/news191906.htm, last accessed 22 July 2016.
241. CTC 2011: 77–9.
242. See Brandt 2016.
243. Brandt 2016. Al-Dawsari cites a woman from al-Jawf saying that the revenge killings 'affect the entire community: houses are destroyed, children are turned orphans, young women turned widows, and the blood of the killed is more than the water [in] Al-Jawf'; see al-Dawsari et al. 2012: 13.
244. Dresch 2006 passim.
245. Interview with a senior Baraṭ shaykh, September 2013.

246. Interview, April 2014.
247. Serjeant 1977: 228–9; Dresch 1989: 366–72; Caton 1990: 11.
248. See Chapter 3's section on 'Boundary Fortifications'.
249. CTC 2011: 82. Qā'id (Abū ʿAlī) al-Ḥārithī was suspected of having been involved in the October 2000 USS Cole bombing. He was killed by a US Predator drone on 3 November 2002.
250. CTC 2011: 83.
251. Before that, Ṣādiq Abū Rās held the posts of minister of state, minister of agriculture, minister of civil service, minister of local administration, and governor of Taʿiz. He was an influential member of the Salih regime's inner circle and was among those injured in the blast within the presidential compound's mosque in June 2011, as a result of which he lost a foot. Sources indicated that this career was opened to him to prevent him from 're-opening the files on his father's death'.
252. See the present chapter's section 'Fourth Interim: The Government Loses Its Last Cards'.
253. ʿAbdulwāḥid Abū Rās was a distant cousin of Fayṣal and Ṣādiq, the sons of Amīn Abū Rās (d. 1978), who belong to the main line. In 2003, ʿAbdulwāḥid competed with Fayṣal for the parliamentary seat of Baraṭ al-ʿInān and al-Marāshī. When Fayṣal won, ʿAbdulwāḥid joined the Houthi movement. In 2004, he was arrested and tortured in the Political Security Prison.
254. Interview, November 2013.
255. According to sources from the Baraṭ region, in the 1990s Badr al-Dīn al-Ḥūthī spent some time among the Dhū Muḥammad in al-Zāhir district.
256. See Chapter 4's section on 'The al-Ḥūthī Family'.
257. Interview, October 2015.
258. Interview, October 2015.
259. 'Nāziḥū Ḥarf Sufyān yattajihūna ilā muḥāfaẓat al-Jawf', *Mareb Press*, 1 June 2008, http://marebpress.net/news_details.php?lng=arabic&sid=11598, last accessed 23 July 2016.
260. Interview with a Houthi veteran from al-Jawf, October 2015.
261. 'Qabā'il fī l-Jawf tashtabik maʿ al-Ḥūthiyyīn', *Mareb Press*, 25 June 2008, http://marebpress.net/news_details.php?lng=arabic&sid=11957, last accessed 23 July 2016.
262. Interview, October 2015.
263. Parts of this chapter are based on Brandt 2013.
264. Dresch 1989: 254, 258.
265. On the Sufyān's tribal structure, see Chapter 1's section on 'Estates of Society: The Tribes of Saʿdah, Sufyān and al-Jawf'.
266. The Ḥubaysh lineage is of very long standing and is famous for having supported the imams; see Dresch 1989: 202, 207, 211.
267. Kahlān Abū Shawārib was elected on 17 May 2008 as governor of ʿAmrān. On these elections, see the following section.

268. 'Al-Ḥūthiyyūn yufridūna ḥiṣārān ʿalā muḥāfiẓ ʿAmrān dākhil muʿaskar al-Jabal al-Aswad bi-Ḥarf Sufyān', *al-Wahdawi*, 30 June 2008, http://www.alwahdawi.net/news_details.php?sid=4279, last accessed 23 July 2016.
269. 'Ḥarf Sufyān: kayfa ukhturiqat maqarrāt al-aḥzāb', *Mareb Press*, 27 June 2008, http://marebpress.net/articles.php?id=3882&lng=arabic, last accessed 23 July 2016.
270. Interview, August 2012.
271. Muḥsin Maʿqil himself, who was also secretary-general of Sufyān's Local Council, remained unwavering in his loyalty to the government and disappeared without a trace. His fate remains uncertain.
272. Interview, November 2012.
273. Interview, November 2012.
274. See the present chapter's section 'Fourth Interim: A Memorable Funeral'.
275. *Marāghah* is the title of a judicial office; the *marāghah* is considered the specialist par excellence in customary law. Among the tribes of Hamdān, the *marāghah* is the most senior shaykh in the process of tribal appeal and his verdict is final. The title *naqīb* is used as a hereditary title for exceptionally influential shaykhly families, most of them of Bakīlī stock. For further details, see Brandt 2014c: 104–5.
276. See the present chapter's section 'War mongers: The Gaddafi Issue'.
277. Interview with a Sufyān tribesman, June 2015.
278. Interview, November 2012. The al-Qaʿūd family, too, was politically divided: some parts were with the Houthis, some were friends of Ṣaghīr.
279. Interview, June 2015.
280. 'Al-shaykh Ṣaghīr bin ʿAzīz yakhshif al-tafāṣil al-kāmilah li-ḥarb Ḥarf Sufyān', *Baraqish Net*, 12 August 2010, http://www.barakish.net/news02.aspx?cat=0&sub=0&id=10286, last accessed 23 July 2016. It should be noted that despite his high army rank Ṣaghīr did not become involved in the Houthi conflict as a regular army officer, but rather as the leader of a local militia.
281. 'Ikhtiṭāf al-ṭifl Amīn ʿAbd al-Qādir Badr al-Dīn al-Ḥūthī (13 sanah) fī Ṣanʿā'', *Al-Eshteraky*, 13 April 2007, http://aleshteraky.com/archive/news_details.php?lng=arabic&sid=2044, last accessed 22 July 2016.
282. 'Jughrāfiyyah al-ḥarb al-khāmisah', *Mareb Press*, 5 June 2008, http://marebpress.net/nprint.php?sid=11653, last accessed 23 July 2016.
283. Dresch 1989: 258–61.
284. See the present chapter's sections 'Fifth Interim: Sufyān' and 'The Sixth War: Ceasefire Sequencing'.
285. Romeo and El Mensi 2008: 35.
286. Day 2012: 236.
287. Day 2012: 237.
288. On Fāris' mediation in Marrān, see the following section 'Mediation and Unilateral Ceasefire'.

289. See the present chapter's section 'Fourth Interim: The Government Loses its Last Cards'.
290. 'Fawz murashshaḥ mu'tamarī Ḥasan Manāʿ fī Ṣaʿdah', *al-Methaq*, 17 May 2008, http://www.almethaq.net/news/news-6933.htm, last accessed 23 July 2016.
291. Interview, November 2015.
292. See the present chapter's section on 'The Sixth War: The Manāʿ Case'.
293. See also 'Suqūt 18 qatīlān fī muwājahāt sharisah', *Al-Riyadh*, 5 May 2008, http://www.alriyadh.com/2008/05/05/article340160.html, last accessed 23 July 2016.
294. Peterson 2008a: 11–14. See also 'Ra'īs al-jumhūriyyah yukallif Ḥusayn al-Aḥmar wa ʿadad min qādat al-taḍāmun bi-l-tawassuṭ', *Mareb Press*, 7 May 2008, http://marebpress.net/news_details.php?lng=arabic&sid=11125, last accessed 23 July 2016. On the National Solidarity Council, see Phillips 2011b: 41.
295. 'Yemen's sheikhs disown the so-called Solidarity Council', *Al-Motamar*, 13 August 2007, http://www.almotamar.net/en/3200.htm, last accessed 22 July 2016.
296. The following reconstruction of the events in Marrān is partly based on 'Al-ʿamīd ʿAbd al-ʿAzīz al-Shahārī ṣakhrah ṣumūd fī Jibāl Ḥaydān', *Mareb Press*, 1 July 2008, http://marebpress.net/news_details.php?lng=arabic&sid=12029, last accessed 23 July 2016.
297. 'Al-ʿamīd ʿAbd al-ʿAzīz al-Shahārī: al-hazā'im al-qāsiyah li-l-irhābiyyīn jaʿlathum yakhtaliqūna al-akādhīb', *26 September Net*, 26 June 2008, http://www.26sep.net/news_details.php?sid=43144, last accessed 23 July 2016.
298. 'Taklīf Manāʿ badlan ʿan al-Aḥmar baʿd iʿtirāḍ qablī', *Mareb Press*, 15 June 2008, http://marebpress.net/news_details.php?lng=arabic&sid=11794, last accessed 23 July 2016.
299. Muḥammad ʿAbdullah Muṣliḥ was killed in September 2015 during the Houthi incursions in Jīzān.
300. Interview, October 2015.
301. Markaz 2008: 236–7.
302. Hamidi 2009: 182.
303. Human Rights Watch 2008b.
304. 'Ḥusayn al-Aḥmar yusallim maṭālib 15 shaykh li-l-ra'īs', *Newsyemen*, 10 July 2008, http://www.newsyemen.net/view_news.asp?sub_no=1_2008_07_10_20863, last accessed March 2012.
305. Clarke 2010: 175.
306. William Shakespeare, *Macbeth*: Act 3, Scene 2.
307. Human Rights Watch 2008b.
308. International Crisis Group 2009: 22–4.
309. Salmoni et al. 2010: 248.
310. International Crisis Group 2009: 24.
311. International Crisis Group 2009: 23.
312. International Crisis Group 2009: 22–4.

313. Human Rights Watch 2008b.
314. 'Iqṣā' Hilāl min muhimmat al-salām bi-Ṣa'dah', *Mareb Press*, 4 September 2008, http://marebpress.net/news_details.php?lng=arabic&sid=12932, last accessed 23 July 2016.
315. International Crisis Group 2009: 22–4.
316. 'Al-Ḥūthiyyūn yarfuḍūna al-Marrānī ra'īsan li-lajnat al-wisāṭah', *Mareb Press*, 24 November 2008, http://marebpress.net/news_details.php?lng=arabic&sid=13977, last accessed 23 July 2016.
317. 'Ayna taqif Ṣa'dah al-ān?', *Mareb Press*, 11 September 2008, http://marebpress.net/news_details.php?lng=arabic&sid=13023, last accessed 23 July 2016,
318. Interviews, Summer 2015.
319. The description of events in Āl al-Ḥamāṭī is partly based on 'Fī Ṣa'dah... al-Ḥamāṭī wa l-Ḥūthī muwājahāt ghayr mutakāfi'ah', *Yemeress*, 29 December 2008, http://www.yemeress.com/akhbaralyom/6429, last accessed 23 July 2016.
320. 'Al-Ḥūthiyyūn: musta'idūn li-l-difā' 'an anfusinā fī ayy waqt', *Mareb Press*, 3 April 2009, http://marebpress.net/news_details.php?lng=arabic&sid=15915, last accessed 23 July 2016.
321. Gingrich 2011: 41.
322. Gingrich 1994a: 26; Gingrich 2011; Brandt 2012.
323. See the present chapter's section 'Fourth Interim: The Government Loses its Last Cards'.
324. Interviews, September 2013.
325. 'Al-jaysh yuwajjih ḍarabāt li-kull man tasawwal lahu nafsihi li-musā'adat al-Ḥūthiyyīn', *Al-Majalis*, 5 June 2007, http://www.almajalis.org/forums/viewtopic.php?f=18&t=6152&start=435, last accessed 22 July 2016.
326. 'Al-jaysh wa 'anāṣir al-Ḥūthī yujrīān taḥarrukāt', *al-Ayyam*, 5 April 2009, http://www.al-ayyam.info/default.aspx?NewsID=da7c30a4-b7a3-47c8-b96d-fb40e-929a3bf, last accessed January 2012.
327. 'Al-Ḥūthiyyūn: musta'idūn li-l-difā' 'an anfusinā fī ayy waqt', *Mareb Press*, 3 April 2009, http://marebpress.net/news_details.php?lng=arabic&sid=15915, last accessed 23 July 2016.
328. 'Al-Ḥūthiyyūn yusayṭirūna 'alā mujamm' mūdīriyyat Shidā'', *Mareb Press*, 4 August 2009, http://marebpress.net/news_details.php?sid=17958&lng=arabic, last accessed 23 July 2016.
329. See Chapter 3's section on 'Border Guards'.
330. 'Mawājahāt 'anīfah fī Bāqim', *Al-Eshteraky*, 5 August 2009, http://www.aleshteraki.net/news_details.php?lng=arabic&sid=6533, last accessed 21 September 2012.
331. 'Ṣa'dah: ḥarūqāt jadīdah', *al-Badell*, 24 April 2009, http://albadell.net/details.asp?id=2931&catid=1#top, last accessed January 2012.
332. Parts of this chapter are based on Brandt 2013.

333. ʻWazīr al-difāʻ wa ʻAlī Muḥsin yabḥathān fī ʻAmrān tadāʻiyāt maqtal anāṣir min al-ḥaras al-jumhūrīʼ, *Mareb Press*, 18 October 2008, http://marebpress.net/news_details.php?lng=arabic&sid=13476, last accessed 23 July 2016.
334. ʻMaqtal 5 ʻaskariyyīn wa iḥrāq 4 nāqilāt junūd wa taqmayn fī Sufyānʼ, *Mareb Press*, 13 October 2008, http://marebpress.net/news_details.php?lng=arabic&sid=13402, last accessed 23 July 2016.
335. ʻWazīr al-difāʻ wa ʻAlī Muḥsin yabḥathān fī ʻAmrān tadāʻiyāt maqtal anāṣir min al-ḥaras al-jumhūrīʼ, *Mareb Press*, 18 October 2008, http://marebpress.net/news_details.php?lng=arabic&sid=13476, last accessed 23 July 2016.
336. Dresch and Haykel 1995: 416.
337. On the tribal concept of ʻhonourʼ, see Chapter 1's section on ʻEstates of Society: Yemen's Tribal Systemʼ.
338. ʻBaʻd akthar min 40 qatīl fī ḥarb al-ʻUṣaymāt wa Sufyān bawādir ittisāʻ ruqʻat al-ḥarb li-tashmil Bakīl wa Ḥāshidʼ, *Mareb Press*, 30 December 2008, http://marebpress.net/news_details.php?lng=arabic&sid=14441, last accessed 23 July 2016.
339. "Adad al-qatlā tjāwaz al-80 wa miʼāt al-jarḥā baynahum nisāʼ wa aṭfālʼ, *Sawtshouraonline*, 3 March 2009, http://sawtshouraonline.com/index.php?option=com_k2&view=item&id=6663, last accessed February 2013.
340. Ibid.
341. ʻBaʻd akthar min 40 qatīl fī ḥarb al-ʻUṣaymāt wa Sufyān bawādir ittisāʻ ruqʻat al-ḥarb li-tashmil Bakīl wa Ḥāshidʼ, *Mareb Press*, 30 December 2008, http://marebpress.net/news_details.php?lng=arabic&sid=14441, last accessed 23 July 2016. Ḥaydar here refers to the inauguration of President Salih, who belongs to the Ḥāshid tribe.
342. "Adad al-qatlā tajāwaz al-80 wa miʼāt al-jarḥā baynahum nisāʼ wa aṭfālʼ, *Sawtshouraonline*, 3 March 2009, http://sawtshouraonline.com/index.php?option=com_k2&view=item&id=6663, last accessed February 2013.
343. Weir 2008: 134.
344. This statement was indeed sent to the press and published by some newspapers; see ʻBayān ṣādir min qibal mashāyikh ahl al-Jawf yadīnūna fīhi aʻmāl al-Sharīfʼ, *Soutalgnoub*, http://soutalgnoub.com/home/index.php?view=article&catid=62:yemen-brother&id=4769&format=pdf, 29 July 2009, last accessed 23 July 2016
345. ʻAl-Raʼīs yaltaqī bi-l-shaykh Amīn al-ʻUkaymīʼ, *Mareb Press*, 31 January 2009, http://marebpress.net/news_details.php?lng=arabic&sid=14891, last accessed 23 July 2016.
346. Ibid. In this interview, al-ʻUkaymī blames the Ministry of Education for the spread of the Houthi movement in al-Jawf, as it had not provided a sufficient number of ʻScientific Institutesʼ (Iṣlāḥ educational institutions) in the governorate.
347. ʻAl-raʼīs yuṭālib mashāyikh Maʼrib taslīm al-maṭlūbīn wa ʻadam mujāmilatihimʼ,

Mareb Press, 3 February 2009, http://marebpress.net/news_details.php?lng=arabic&sid=14948, last accessed 23 July 2016.

348. Zayd al-al-Ḍumayn was a brother of the murdered ʿAbdulwahhāb al-Ḍumayn. While ʿAbdulwahhāb had been active for the government, Zayd fought for the Houthis—another example of different loyalties within the same family.
349. "ʿAbd al-Malik al-Ḥūthī yattahim mīlishiyāt al-sulṭah bi-tanfīdh al-kamīn', *Mareb Press*, 12 February 2009, http://marebpress.net/news_details.php?lng=arabic&sid=15078, last accessed 23 July 2016.
350. 'Khālid al-Sharīf yarfuḍ ittihāmāt al-Ḥūthī', *Mareb Press*, 14 February 2009, http://marebpress.net/news_details.php?lng=arabic&sid=15104, last accessed 23 July 2016.
351. "ʿAbd al-Malik al-Ḥūthī yattahim mīlishiyāt al-sulṭah bi-tanfīdh al-kamīn', *Mareb Press*, 12 February 2009, http://marebpress.net/news_details.php?lng=arabic&sid=15078, last accessed 23 July 2016.
352. Interview, October 2015.
353. See the present chapter's section on 'The Fourth War: The Popular Army'.
354. 'Bi-sabab al-Ḥūthī... al-raʾīs yaltaqī mashāyikh Dahm', *Mareb Press*, 17 February 2009, http://marebpress.net/news_details.php?lng=arabic&sid=15149, last accessed 23 July 2016.
355. 'Al-Ḥūthiyyūn yataʿrradūna li-ḍarb fī aḥad faʿāliyāt al-iṣlāḥ fī l-Jawf', *Mareb Press*, 13 May 2009, http://marebpress.net/news_details.php?lng=arabic&sid=16550, last accessed 23 July 2016.
356. 'Majlis taḥālif qabāʾil Maʾrib wa l-Jawf wa wusṭāʾ min Sufyān yaltaqūna li-baḥth ʿan tahdiʾah', *Mareb Press*, 9 August 2009, http://marebpress.net/news_details.php?lng=arabic&sid=18047, last accessed 23 July 2016.
357. 'Al-Qabīlah tuwājih al-Ḥūthiyyīn wa l-dawlah tatafarraj', *Mareb Press*, 13 February 2009, http://marebpress.net/news_details.php?lng=arabic&sid=15092, last accessed 23 July 2016.
358. Description given by German Deputy Ambassador Michael Reuss to the US Embassy, see 'Theories proliferate regarding Saada kidnapping/murder', Wikileaks, 24 June 2009, https://wikileaks.org/plusd/cables/09SANAA1153_a.html, last accessed 22 July 2016.
359. 'Al-shaykh Mujallī: al-Ḥūthiyyūn yataḥaffaẓūna ʿalā al-rahāʾin', *al-Masdar*, 23 June 2009, http://almasdaronline.com/article/977, last accessed 23 July 2016.
360. 'Entführung im Jemen: Innenminister verspricht schonungslose Jagd auf Geiselnehmer', *Der Spiegel*, 20 June 2009, http://www.spiegel.de/politik/ausland/entfuehrung-im-jemen-innenminister-verspricht-schonungslose-jagd-auf-geiselnehmer-a-631573.html, last accessed 22 July 2016.
361. Interviews, December 2015.
362. 'Anṣār al-Ḥūthī yataẓāharūna fī Ṣaʿdah iḥtijājān ʿalā khaṭf wa qatl al-aṭibbāʾ', *Mareb Press*, 17 June 2009, http://marebpress.net/news_details.php?lng=arabic&sid=17115, last accessed 23 July 2016.

363. 'Theories proliferate regarding Saada kidnapping/murder', Wikileaks, 24 June 2009, https://wikileaks.org/plusd/cables/09SANAA1153_a.html, last accessed 22 July 2016.
364. Ibid.
365. 'Entführung im Jemen: Muslim stritt mit Deutschem über Missionierung', *Der Spiegel*, 20 June 2009, http://www.spiegel.de/politik/ausland/entfuehrung-im-jemen-muslim-stritt-mit-deutschem-ueber-missionierung-a-631527.html, last accessed 22 July 2016.
366. 'Theories proliferate regarding Saada kidnapping/murder', Wikileaks, 24 June 2009, https://wikileaks.org/plusd/cables/09SANAA1153_a.html, last accessed 22 July 2016.
367. 'Entführung im Jemen: Deutsche Geiseln setzten Hilferuf per Handy ab', *Der Spiegel*, 18 June 2009, http://www.spiegel.de/politik/ausland/entfuehrung-im-jemen-deutsche-geiseln-setzten-hilferuf-per-handy-ab-a-631245.html, last accessed 22 July 2016.
368. Brandt forthcoming (a).
369. 'Hudnah jadīdah bayn al-qāʿidah wa l-niẓām', *al-Masdar*, 24 July 2009, http://almasdaronline.com/article/1400, last accessed 23 July 2016.
370. 'In Gottes Namen', *Der Spiegel*, 22 June 2009, http://www.spiegel.de/spiegel/print/d-65794346.html, last accessed 22 July 2016.
371. Boucek 2010: 8.
372. 'Geiseldrama: Die seltsamste Entführung, die es je im Jemen gab', *Der Spiegel*, 21 June 2009, http://www.spiegel.de/politik/ausland/geiseldrama-die-seltsamste-entfuehrung-die-es-je-im-jemen-gab-a-631646.html, last accessed 22 July 2016.
373. 'Jemen: Geiselnehmer verlangen Freilassung von Terroristen', *Der Spiegel*, 16 January 2010, http://www.spiegel.de/politik/ausland/jemen-geiselnehmer-verlangen-freilassung-von-terroristen-a-672301.html, last accessed 22 July 2016.
374. See the present chapter's section on 'The Sixth War: The Struggle for Peace'.
375. Interview, November 2012.
376. 'Arbaʿah min nuwwāb Ṣaʿdah ʿan al-muʾtamar al-ḥākim yuqaddimūn istiqālātahum', *Mareb Press*, 12 July 2009, http://www.marebpress.net/news_details.php?lng=arabic&sid=17491, last accessed 23 July 2016.
377. 'Ḥamīd al-Aḥmar ʿabr qanāt al-jazīrah yuwajjih al-naṣāʾiḥ li-ʿAlī Sālim al-Bayḍ', *Mareb Press*, 5 August 2009, l http://marebpress.net/news_details.php?lng=arabic&sid=17985, last accessed 23 July 2016.
378. 'Al-Ḥūthī yarudd ʿalā Ḥamīd al-Aḥmar', *Mareb Press*, http://marebpress.net/news_details.php?lng=arabic&sid=17987, 6 August 2009, last accessed 23 July 2016.
379. 'Munaẓẓamāt: akthar min miʾat alf nāziḥ fī Ṣaʿdah', *Mareb Press*, http://marebpress.net/news_details.php?lng=arabic&sid=17896, 1 August 2009, last accessed 23 July 2016.

380. 'Al-Ḥūthī: katībah yamaniyyah tadkhul al-arāḍī al-sa'ūdiyyah li-l-iltifāf 'alā minṭaqat al-Ḥaṣāmah', *Mareb Press*, 3 August 2009, http://marebpress.net/news_details.php?lng=arabic&sid=17934, last accessed 23 July 2016.
381. Interview with a Houthi field commander in al-Jawf, October 2015.
382. See, for example, Phillips 2011b: 36.
383. 'Saudi Arabia: Renewed assurances on satellite imagery', Wikileaks, 7 February 2010, https://wikileaks.org/plusd/cables/10RIYADH159_a.html, last accessed 22 July 2016; see also Day 2012: 218.
384. 'Al-Ḥūthī yu'akkid al-sayṭarah 'alā mawqi' qurb mu'askar al-kamb', *Mareb Press*, 11 September 2009, http://marebpress.net/news_details.php?lng=arabic&sid=18723, last accessed 23 July 2016.
385. 'Fāris Manā' wa mashāyikh Saḥār ya'tazimūna 'aqr 20 'ijlān amām ri'āsat al-jumhūriyyah', *Mareb Press*, 12 October 2009, http://marebpress.net/news_details.php?lng=arabic&sid=19316, last accessed 23 July 2016.
386. 'Nuzūḥ ahālī minṭaqat Bāqim', *Mareb Press*, 13 September 2009, http://marebpress.net/news_details.php?lng=arabic&sid=18786, last accessed 23 July 2016.
387. 'Iṣābat al-shaykh Ḥusayn Ḥaydar ... wa l-sa'ūdiyyah tughliq sharīṭahā al-ḥudūdī ma' al-yaman', *Mareb Press*, 14 September 2009, http://marebpress.net/news_details.php?lng=arabic&sid=18791, last accessed 23 July 2016.
388. 'Al-jaysh yaqṣaf bi-l-dabbābāt ma'āqil al-Ḥūthiyyīn bi-Ṣa'dah al-qadīmah', *Mareb Press*, 6 September 2009, http://marebpress.net/news_details.php?lng=arabic&sid=18617, last accessed 23 July 2016.
389. ''Amaliyyāt 'askariyyah li-l-ḥaras al-jumhūrī fī Ṣa'dah', *Mareb Press*, 8 December 2009, http://marebpress.net/news_details.php?lng=arabic&sid=20546, last accessed 23 July 2016.
390. Interview with a shaykh from the Dammāj region, November 2015.
391. Bonnefoy and Kuschnitzki 2015: 44.
392. This chapter is partly based on Brandt 2013.
393. See the present chapter's section on 'The Fourth War: The Popular Army'.
394. 'Al-shaykh Sufyān Mujāhid Ḥaydar: idhā lam takuf al-dawlah fī ishtirākiha ma' Ḥāshid fī muqātilatinā fa-innā sa-naqif ma' al-Ḥūthiyyīn', *Mareb Press*, 29 August 2009, http://marebpress.net/news_details.php?lng=arabic&sid=18456, last accessed 23 July 2016.
395. Ibid.
396. Salmoni et al. 2010: 162.
397. 'Hamid al-Ahmar tries his hand at coordinating Houthi, Southern Movement efforts', Wikileaks, 12 October 2009, https://wikileaks.org/plusd/cables/09SANAA1882_a.html, last accessed 22 July 2016.
398. 'Yushārik fīhā al-'amāliqah wa l-ḥaras al-jumhūrī wa l-liwā' 119', *Mareb Press*, 8 September 2009, http://marebpress.net/news_details.php?lng=arabic&sid=18665, last accessed 23 July 2016.

399. 'Akthar min 100 juththah li-'anāṣir ḥūthiyyah muta'affinah 'alā jawānib al-turuqāt', *Mareb Press*, 23 August 2009, http://marebpress.net/news_details.php?lng=arabic&sid=18313, last accessed 23 July 2016.
400. 'Saada War: Despite claims of ceasefire, civilians suffer, no end to the fighting in sight', Wikileaks, 26 August 2009, https://wikileaks.org/plusd/cables/09SANAA1599_a.html, last accessed 22 July 2016.
401. See the present chapter's section on 'The Sixth War: Ceasefire Sequencing and Third Doha Agreement'.
402. 'Kashaf 'an ḥaqīqat al-mawāqif al-qabaliyyah min ḥarb Ṣa'dah', *Mareb Press*, 20 August 2009, http://marebpress.net/news_details.php?lng=arabic&sid=18264, last accessed 23 July 2016.
403. The Bakīl Council for Peace and Reform was established in October 1986. Its membership comprises more than seventy Bakīl shaykhs.
404. In 2010, when the fighting in al-Jawf took on an openly sectarian character, Amīn al-'Ukaymī also personally participated in the battles. He took a particularly proactive role from the start of Operation Decisive Storm in 2015, when he fought on the side for the Saudi-led coalition forces.
405. On Khālid al-Sharīf's role in al-Jawf, see the present chapter's section 'Fifth Interim: Al-Jawf'.
406. 'Wisāṭah qabaliyyah li-inhā' muwājahāt al-Shawlān wa Banī Hamdān', *Mareb Press*, 4 January 2010, http://marebpress.net/news_details.php?lng=arabic&sid=21209, last accessed 23 July 2016.
407. Interview, July 2015.
408. This section is also called the al-Ṣaqrān.
409. 'Al-Jawf: al-Ḥūthiyyūn yaqṣafūna al-qabā'il bi-dabbābah', *Mareb Press*, 8 January 2010, http://marebpress.net/news_details.php?lng=arabic&sid=21320, last accessed 23 July 2016.
410. CTC 2011: 81 n. 231.
411. 'Khālid al-Sharīf wa qabā'il Dhū Ḥusayn taqūm bi-ṭard niqāṭ taqaṭṭu' al-Ḥūthiyyīn fī l-Jawf', *Mareb Press*, 2 January 2010, http://marebpress.net/news_details.php?lng=arabic&sid=21164, last accessed 23 July 2016.
412. Interview with a member of the Houthi leadership in Sa'dah, November 2015.
413. Al-Dawsari 2014.
414. CTC 2011: 60.
415. This chapter is partly based on Brandt 2012.
416. On the system of delegation of war leadership prevalent in Munabbih, see Gingrich 1994a: 26 and 2011; Brandt 2012 and the present chapter's section 'Fifth Interim: The Western Mountains'.
417. See the present chapter's section on 'The Fourth War: The First Doha Agreement'.
418. Interview, November 2012.
419. 'Al-shaykh Ḥusayn 'Alī al-Munabbihī li-l-Jumhūr: Al-Ḥūthī adāt īrāniyyah... wa

Munabbih wa Qaṭābir maqbarat li-l-tamarrud', *Yemeress*, 27 December 2009, http://www.yemeress.com/aljumhor/1602, last accessed 23 July 2016.

420. On *qabyalah*, see the section in Chapter 1 of this volume on 'Estates of Society: Yemen's Tribal System'.
421. Jamous 1991.
422. 'Al-Ḥūthī yaqūl annahum sayṭarū ʿalā al-liwā' 105 fī asfal Marrān', *Mareb Press*, 31 August 2009, http://marebpress.net/news_details.php?lng=arabic&sid=18485, last accessed 31 July 2016.
423. 'Al-istikhbārāt al-ʿaskariyyah tulqī al-qabḍ ʿalā arkān ḥarb liwā' 105', *Mareb Press*, 1 September 2009, http://marebpress.net/news_details.php?lng=arabic&sid=18511, last accessed 23 July 2016.
424. See Chapter 3's section 'A Contested Boundary'.
425. Badeeb 1986: 51–2.
426. 'Al-Ḥūthī yattahim al-ṭayarān al-saʿūdī bi-l-ighārah ʿalā mudīriyyat al-Malāḥīṭ', *Mareb Press*, 27 August 2009, http://marebpress.net/news_details.php?lng=arabic&sid=18401, last accessed 23 July 2016.
427. 'Maṣdar rasmī yanfī wujūd ghurfat ʿamaliyyāt mushtarakah bayn al-Yaman wa l-Saʿūdiyyah', *Mareb Press*, 23 August 2009, http://marebpress.net/news_details.php?lng=arabic&sid=18314, last accessed 23 July 2016.
428. 'Al-Ḥūthī yattahim al-Saʿūdiyyah bi-daʿm al-jaysh al-yamanī', *Mareb Press*, 2 November 2009, http://marebpress.net/news_details.php?lng=arabic&sid=19804, last accessed 23 July 2016.
429. 'Sa'ada, month five: Is Saleh serious about ending the war?', Wikileaks, 16 December 2009, https://wikileaks.org/cable/2009/12/09SANAA2227.html, last accessed 22 July 2016.
430. 'Saudis 'in a panic mode' as Shi'ite rebels move North from Yemen', *World Tribune*, 4 December 2009, http://www.worldtribune.com/worldtribune/WTARC/2009/me_jordan0940_12_04.asp, last accessed 22 July 2016.
431. Ibid.
432. For a detailed list of troop movements in Saudi Arabia, see 'Saudis will do what it takes to secure border, 8 November 2009', Wikileaks, 8 November 2009, https://wikileaks.org/plusd/cables/09RIYADH1490_a.html, last accessed 22 July 2016.
433. 'Ikhlā' 400 qariyah', *Mareb Press*, 18 November 2009, http://marebpress.net/news_details.php?lng=arabic&sid=20198, last accessed 23 July 2013.
434. 'Al-Ḥūthiyyūn yuhājimūn al-Saʿūdiyya', *Mareb Press*, 4 November 2009, http://marebpress.net/news_details.php?lng=arabic&sid=19845, last accessed 23 July 2016.
435. 'Saudis "in a panic mode" as Shi'ite rebels move North from Yemen', *World Tribune*, 4 December 2009, http://www.worldtribune.com/worldtribune/WTARC/2009/me_jordan0940_12_04.asp, last accessed 22 July 2016.

436. 'Saudi airstrikes at Yemen border', Wikileaks, 9 November 2009, https://wikileaks.org/plusd/cables/09SANAA2040_a.html, last accessed 22 July 2016.
437. 'Al-intikhābāt al-takmīliyyah: al-tawrīth wa l-qurābah wa l-fanādiq ta'shīrāt al-mu'tamar', *Mareb Press*, 9 December 2009, http://marebpress.net/news_details.php?lng=arabic&sid=20580, last accessed 23 July 2016.
438. Interview, December 2015.
439. For details see, for example, 'Al-intikhābāt al-takmīliyyah: al-tawrīth wa l-qurābah wa l-fanādiq ta'shīrāt al-mu'tamar', *Mareb Press*, 9 December 2009, http://marebpress.net/news_details.php?lng=arabic&sid=20580, last accessed 23 July 2016.
440. 'Ṣa'dah: ijrā' al-intikhābāt dākhil funduq fī l-madīnah wa bi-ghiyāb al-muṣawwitīn', *al-Masdar*, 10 December 2009, http://almasdaronline.com/article/print/3456, last accessed 23 July 2016.
441. Ibid.
442. On the blood feud between the Mujallī and Dughsān clans, see the present chapter's section 'Fourth Interim: A Memorable Funeral'.
443. 'Ṣa'dah: ijrā' al-intikhābāt dākhil funduq fī l-madīnah wa bi-ghiyāb al-muṣawwitīn', *al-Masdar*, 10 December 2009, http://www.almasdaronline.net/print.php?news_id=3456, last accessed 23 July 2016.
444. Ibid.
445. See Chapter 2's section 'Shadow Economy'.
446. For details see: 'Saudi Ambassador provides information on Yemeni arms dealer Faris Mana', Wikileaks, 8 December 2008, https://wikileaks.org/plusd/cables/08SANAA1973_a.html, last accessed 22 July 2016.
447. See the present chapter's section on 'War mongers: The Gaddafi Issue'.
448. See the present chapter's section on 'The Fifth War: Mediation and Unilateral Ceasefire'.
449. 'ROYG issues blacklist of Sa'ada arms traffickers', Wikileaks, 12 October 2009, https://wikileaks.org/plusd/cables/09SANAA1870_a.html, last accessed 22 July 2016.
450. Ibid.
451. 'Qā'imah sawdā' bi-tijār al-silāḥ 'alā ra'sihim Fāris Manā'', Nashwan News, 5 October 2009, http://m.nashwannews.com/news.php?action=view&id=2451, last accessed 23 July 2016.
452. See Chapter 2's section 'Shadow Economy'.
453. 'ROYG issues blacklist of Sa'ada arms traffickers', Wikileaks, 12 October 2009, https://wikileaks.org/plusd/cables/09SANAA1870_a.html, last accessed 22 July 2016.
454. United Nations Security Council Report S/2015/401: 31.
455. 'ROYG reports seizure of Iranian-crewed ship with Houthi-bound weapons', Wikileaks, 27 October 2009, https://wikileaks.org/plusd/cables/09SANAA1965_a.html, last accessed 22 July 2016.

456. 'Sa'ada War: Despite claims of ceasefire, civilians suffer, no end to the fighting in sight', Wikileaks, 26 August 2009, https://wikileaks.org/plusd/cables/09SANAA1599_a.html, last accessed 22 July 2016.
457. Interviews, November 2015.
458. 'Al-shaykh Fāyiz al-ʿAwjarī: tujjār al-ḥurūb wa l-silāḥ yaʿmalūna ʿalā iṭālat amad al-ḥarb', *al-Mithaq*, 9 November 2009, http://www.almethaq.net/news/news-12516.htm, last accessed 23 July 2016.
459. 'Al-qaṣf yastahdif makhzan asliḥah bi-manzil Manāʿ', YE1, 30 December 2009, http://www.ye1.org/forum/threads/469400/page-2, last accessed 23 July 2016.
460. 'Muḥāfiẓ Ṣaʿdah: mubādarat al-Ḥūthiyyīn kadhib wa khidāʿ', *Al-Sharq al-Awsat*, 3 February 2010, http://www.aawsat.com/details.asp?section=4&article=555631&issueno=11390, last accessed 23 July 2016.
461. 'Iqālat muḥāfiẓ Ṣaʿdah wa Hājir khalafān lahu', *Mareb Press*, 6 February 2010, http://marebpress.net/news_details.php?lng=arabic&sid=22191, last accessed 23 July 2016.
462. See the present chapter's section on 'The Fifth War: Gubernatorial Elections'.
463. 'Baʿd iʿtiṣām ṭālaba bi-ifrāj ʿan Manāʿ', *Mareb Press*, 20 February 2010, http://marebpress.net/news_details.php?lng=arabic&sid=22553, last accessed 23 July 2016.
464. This was a rather dubious assembly, since almost all shaykhs mentioned were known for either arms trading or links to radical Sunnism.
465. 'Baʿd iʿtiṣām ṭālaba bi-ifrāj ʿan Manāʿ', *Mareb Press*, http://marebpress.net/news_details.php?lng=arabic&sid=22553, 20 February 2010, last accessed 23 July 2016.
466. 'Al-nā'ib Fāyiz al-ʿAwjarī: Fāris Manāʿ 'Ḥūthī' sallama al-mutamarridīn makhzan aṣliḥah', *al-Jumhor*, http://www.aljumhor.net/portal/news-1864.htm, 30 January 2010, last accessed 23 July 2016.
467. 'Ḥasan Manāʿ yattahim qiyādāt amniyyah bi-daʿm al-Ḥūthiyyīn bi-l-silāḥ', *Mareb Press*, http://marebpress.net/news_details.php?lng=arabic&sid=22573, 21 February 2010, last accessed 23 July 2016.
468. UN Security Council, 'Security Council Committee on Somalia and Eritrea Issues List of Individuals Identified Pursuant to Paragraph 8 of Resolution 1844 (2008)', press release, 12 April 2010, http://www.un.org/News/Press/docs/2010/sc9904.doc.htm, last accessed 22 July 2016.
469. Ibid.
470. See the present chapter's section on 'The Sixth War: Seizure of Saʿdah City'.
471. 'Ma'rib Press tanshur shurūṭ al-lajnah al-amniyyah al-ʿuliyā', *Mareb Press*, http://marebpress.net/news_details.php?lng=arabic&sid=18123, 13 August 2009, last accessed 23 July 2016.
472. Interview with a member of the Houthi leadership in Saʿdah, June 2015.
473. 'Al-Ḥūthī yarfaḍ al-shurūṭ al-sittah', *Mareb Press*, http://marebpress.net/news_details.php?lng=arabic&sid=18129, 13 August 2009, last accessed 23 July 2016.

474. 'Al-ra'īs yuʿadd bi-saḥq ḥarakat al-tamarrud al-ḥūthiyyah', *Mareb Press*, http://marebpress.net/news_details.php?lng=arabic&sid=18248, 19 August 2009, last accessed 23 July 2016.
475. 'Al-ḥukūmah tuqarrir taʿlīq al-ʿamaliyyāt al-ʿaskariyyah bi-Ṣaʿdah', *Mareb Press*, http://marebpress.net/news_details.php?lng=arabic&sid=18578, 4 September 2009, last accessed 24 July 2016.
476. See Terrorism Monitor 7/28: 1, 2009, http://www.jamestown.org/uploads/media/TM_007_90.pdf, last accessed 22 July 2016.
477. A Houthi leader joked about it: 'Muqtadā's mediation initiative was not very serious. He knew from the outset that his interference in Saʿdah had the potential to provoke the Third World War'; Interview, June 2015.
478. Interview, March 2009.
479. 'Abnā' muḥāfaẓat Ṣaʿdah yarfiḍūna ay wisāṭah', *26 September Net*, http://www.26sep.net/news_details.php?lng=arabic&sid=57080, 26 October 2009, last accessed 24 July 2016.
480. 'Al-wisāṭāt tastafizz al-qabā'il', YE1, http://www.ye1.org/forum/threads/424969/, 14 September 2009, last accessed 24 July 2016.
481. 'Ma'rib Press yanshur naṣṣ risālat al-Ḥūthī', *Mareb Press*, http://marebpress.net/news_details.php?lng=arabic&sid=18857, 17 September 2009, last accessed 24 July 2016.
482. 'Naṣr Allah yadʿū Ṣāliḥ li-waqf al-qitāl bi-Ṣaʿdah', *Mareb Press*, http://marebpress.net/news_details.php?lng=arabic&sid=18880, 18 December 2009, last accessed 24 July 2016.
483. 'Raddān ʿalā Irān...', *Mareb Press*, http://marebpress.net/news_details.php?lng=arabic&sid=20006, 10 November 2009, last accessed 24 July 2016.
484. 'Al-khārijiyyah al-yamaniyyah tarfuḍ al-wiṣāyah al-īrāniyyah', *Mareb Press*, http://marebpress.net/news_details.php?lng=arabic&sid=20016, 11 November 2009, last accessed 24 July 2016.
485. 'Sa'ada ceasefire discussions underway', Wikileaks, https://wikileaks.org/plusd/cables/09SANAA2117_a.html, 23 November 2009, last accessed 22 July 2016.
486. Ibid.
487. 'Al-Ḥūthiyyūn yaqbilūna bi-shurūṭ al-tahdi'ah', *Mareb Press*, http://marebpress.net/news_details.php?lng=arabic&sid=20546, 8 December 2009, last accessed 24 July 2016.
488. 'Yemen security high on the GCC agenda summit', *Gulf News*, http://gulfnews.com/news/gulf/yemen/yemen-security-high-on-the-gcc-agenda-summit-1.528709, 17 November 2009, last accessed 22 July 2016.
489. 'Sa'ada, month five: Is Saleh serious about ending the war?', Wikileaks, https://wikileaks.org/plusd/cables/09SANAA2227_a.html, 16 December 2009, last accessed 22 July 2016.
490. Ibid.
491. 'Yemen's counter terrorism unit stretched thin by war against Houthis', Wikileaks,

https://wikileaks.org/cable/2009/12/09SANAA2230.html, 17 December 2009, last accessed 22 July 2016.

492. 'Al-ra'īs yad'ū al-Ḥūthiyyīn wa l-Qā'idah ilā ilqā' al-silāḥ', *Mareb Press*, http://marebpress.net/news_details.php?lng=arabic&sid=21141, 1 January 2010, last accessed 24 July 2016.
493. 'Al-tamarrud yu'lin isti'adādahu waqf al-qitāl… wa abnā' Ṣa'dah yarfuḍūna', *al-Jumhor*, http://www.aljumhor.net/portal/news-1713.htm, 11 January 2010, last accessed 24 July 2016.
494. "Abd al-Malik al-Ḥūthī yu'lin waqf al-ḥarb ma' al-Sa'ūdiyyah', *Mareb Press*, http://marebpress.net/news_details.php?lng=arabic&sid=21807, 25 January 2010, last accessed 24 July 2016.
495. Brehony 2015: 240.
496. 'Mu'tamar London qaddama al-jānib al-'askarī 'alā ahamm mashākil al-Yaman', *Mareb Press*, http://marebpress.net/news_details.php?lng=arabic&sid=22180, 6 February 2010, last accessed 24 July 2016.
497. 'Rebels announce ceasefire with Saudi… Is a Yemen peace deal next?', Wikileaks, https://wikileaks.org/cable/2010/01/10SANAA168.html, 26 January 2010, last accessed 22 July 2016.
498. Human Rights Watch 2010.
499. Interviews with sources from the Sa'dah region, November 2015.
500. 'Ṣa'dah: najāt wakīl wizārat al-dākhiliyyah min muḥāwalat ightiyāl', *Mareb Press*, http://marebpress.net/news_details.php?lng=arabic&sid=22345, 12 February 2010, last accessed 24 July 2016.
501. 'Najāt mudīr mudīriyyat al-Maṭammah min muḥāwalat ightiyāl', *Mareb Press*, http://marebpress.net/news_details.php?lng=arabic&sid=22364, 13 February 2010, last accessed 24 July 2016. On the conflict between the Houthis and the Āl Ṣaqrah, see the present chapter's section on 'The Sixth War: Al-Jawf'.
502. Interview with a Rāziḥ shaykh, November 2015.
503. Interview with a Sufyān shaykh, November 2015.
504. Interview, November 2015.
505. 'Nuwwāb Ṣa'dah ya'taṣimūna iḥtijājan 'alā muḥāṣarat al-Ḥūthiyyīn li-manzil Bin 'Azīz', Nashwan News, http://m.nashwannews.com/news.php?action=view&id=6428, 20 July 2010, last accessed 24 July 2016.
506. 'At least 49 killed in north Yemen clashes: rebels, 21 July 2010', ReliefWeb, http://reliefweb.int/report/yemen/least-49-killed-north-yemen-clashes-rebels, 21 July 2010, last accessed 22 July 2016.
507. 'Yemen truce under threat as fighting flares again', *The National*, http://www.thenational.ae/news/world/yemen-truce-under-threat-as-fighting-flares-again, 22 July 2010, last accessed 22 July 2016.
508. 'Yemen officials, rebels reach peace deal in Qatar', Reuters, http://mobile.reuters.com/article/idUSTRE67Q39T20100827, 27 August 2010, last accessed 22 July 2016.

509. Terrill 2011: 20–1.
510. Kamrava 2011: 550–2.
511. 'Naql Bin 'Azīz ilā Ṣan'ā'', *Mareb Press*, http://marebpress.net/news_details.php?sid=26509&lng=arabic, 27 July 2010, last accessed 24 July 2016.
512. 'Ṣa'dah: maqtal al-shaykh al-'Awjarī 'alā yadd al-Ḥūthiyyīn fī l-Ṣafrā'', *Mareb Press*, http://marebpress.net/news_details.php?sid=27201, 28 August 2010, last accessed 24 July 2016.
513. Interview, March 2015.
514. Gingrich 1989a: 127–8; Gingrich 1994a: 21.
515. 'Al-shaykh Muqīt: ta'sīs ḥilf qablī jā' 'alā raghbat min mashāyikh wa abnā' al-qabā'il', *Aden News*, http://aden-news.net/news_details.php?sid=1629, 9 March 2010, last accessed November 2012.
516. Interview with a shaykh directly involved in the Tribal Alliance, January 2016.
517. Interview with a member of the Houthi leadership in Sa'dah, December 2015.
518. Interview, December 2015.
519. 'Qabā'il Ṣa'dah tu'lin tashkīl ḥilf qablī li-muwājahāt al-Ḥūthiyyīn', *NewsYemen*, http://www.newsyemen.net/view_news.asp?sub_no=1_2010_06_16_44812, 16 June 2010, last accessed December 2010.
520. 'Al-nā'ib Bin 'Arīj: al-Ḥūthī yata'āmal ma' abnā' Ṣa'dah min wāq' al-muntaṣir', *al-Jumhor*, http://www.aljumhor.net/portal/news-2825.htm, 20 June 2010, last accessed 24 July 2016.
521. 'Al-mutamarridūn yashunnūn hujūmān 'alā aṣḥāb al-shaykh Dahbāsh fī Munabbih', *Akhbaralyom*, http://www.akhbaralyom.net/news_details.php?lng=arabic&sid=32029, 9 November 2010, last accessed 24 July 2016.
522. 'Maqtal 30 Ḥūthiyān wa 20 min ittibā' Qamshah', *Saadahnews*, www.saadahnews.net/?Article=579, 12 December 2010, last accessed January 2012.
523. 'Najāt qā'id al-taḥāluf al-qabalī bi-Ṣa'dah min muḥāwalat ightiyāl', *Saadahnews*, http://www.saadahnews.net/?Article=618, 17 June 2011, last accessed January 2012.
524. Interview, January 2015.
525. On the Arab Spring movement in Yemen, see Chapter 7.
526. International Crisis Group 2013: 12.
527. Yadav 2014a.
528. "Asharāt al-qatlā wa l-jarḥā fī muwājahāt bayn Ḥūthiyyīn wa musallaḥīn qabaliyyīn', *Yemenress*, http://www.yemeress.com/alwatan/65697, 4 March 2011, last accessed 24 July 2016.
529. Carvajal 2011.
530. Interviews, January 2016.
531. 'Ṣa'dah tanṣib Fāris Manā' muḥāfiẓ jadīd', *Alnashernews*, http://www.alnashernews.com/news/news.php?action=view&id=5104, 18 May 2011, last accessed February 2012.

532. Interview with a member of Saʿdah's Local Council, February 2016.
533. In summer 2005, ʿAbdullah al-Ḥākim had been arrested on suspicion of being member of the so-called 'Sanaʿa terrorist cell'; in January 2006 he escaped from the prison. See Chapter 5's section on 'The Third War: War Course'. On 7 November 2014, the Security Council 2140 Sanctions Committee designated him (together with Ali Abdullah Salih and ʿAbdulkhāliq al-Ḥūthī) as subject to an assets freeze and travel ban.
534. During the December 2008 battles with Āl al-Ḥamāṭī in Majz (see the present chapter's section 'Fifth Interim: The Western Mountains'), he allegedly thwarted all mediation initiatives by saying: 'If you are men, we meet on the battlefield'. He was known for his threats towards critical journalists. During the 2011 Dammāj battles, he shocked an entire delegation of journalists and human rights activists from the capital with the threat of cutting off tongues and burning critical journalists; see 'Al-qāʾid al-ʿaskarī li-l-Ḥūthiyyīn yuhaddid bi-iḥrāq al-wafd al-ṣaḥafī', *Mareb Press*, http://marebpress.net/news_details.php?sid=38180, 27 November 2011, last accessed 24 July 2016. His relation with the press, in particular with *Mareb Press*, has been seriously disturbed ever since.

7. FAUSTIAN BARGAINS: 2011–14

1. Interview, March 2012.
2. Bonnefoy and Kuschnitzki 2015.
3. International Crisis Group 2014: 3–4; Brandt forthcoming (a).
4. Brandt 2013; International Crisis Group 2014: 7–8.
5. International Crisis Group 2014: 8–9.
6. Heinze 2014b.
7. Carapico and Yadav 2014; Wilson 2014.
8. 'Houthis look to establish Shiite state along Saudi border', *Yemen Times*, http://yementimes.com/defaultdet.aspx?SUB_ID=34879, 29 November 2011, last accessed April 2013.
9. 'Al-asbāb al-ḥaqīqiyyah li-rafḍ al-Ḥūthiyyīn li-haykalat al-jaysh', *Mareb Press*, http://marebpress.net/articles.php?id=18561&lng=arabic, 25 December 2012, last accessed 24 July 2016. On the 2012 security sector reform, see also Albrecht 2013; International Crisis Group 2013.
10. 'Yemen leak: Collusion between Houthis and ex-president Saleh', *Middle East Eye*, http://www.middleeasteye.net/news/yemen-leak-collusion-between-houthis-and-ex-president-saleh-1125273454#sthash.FUuXSyTO.dpuf, 22 January 2015, last accessed 22 July 2016.
11. Gaston 2014; Schmitz 2014.
12. Al-Bukhaytī 2014.
13. Brandt forthcoming (b).
14. Brandt forthcoming (b).
15. Thiel 2015.

CONCLUSION

1. Geertz 1972: 460.
2. Eickelman 2002; Eickelman and Piscatori 2004.
3. Mundy 1995: 5.
4. Jamous 1991.
5. Gingrich 2014b: 119.

BIBLIOGRAPHY

Abū Ghānim, Faḍl. 1991. *Al-bunyah al-qabaliyyah fī l-Yaman bayna al-istimrār wa l-taghayyur*, Sanaʿa: Dār al-Ḥikmah al-Yamāniyyah.

Adra, Najwa. 1982. *Qabyala: The Tribal Concept in the Central Highlands of the Yemen Arab Republic*, Ph.D. thesis, Temple University.

Ahroni, Reuben. 2001. *Jewish Emigration from the Yemen, 1951–98: Carpet Without Magic*, London: Routledge.

al-ʿAbbāsī al-ʿAlawī, ʿAlī b. Muḥammad b. ʿUbayd Allah. 1981. *Sīrat al-Hādī ilā al-Ḥaqq Yaḥyā b. al-Ḥusayn b. al-Qāsim*, Beirut: Dār al-fikr li-l-ṭibāʿah wa l-nashr wa l-tawzīʿ.

Al-Aḥmadī, ʿĀdil. 2006. *Al-zahr wa l-ḥajar: al-tamarrud al-shīʿī fī l-yaman*, Sanaʿa: Markaz Nashwān al-Ḥimyarī li-l-dirāsāt wa l-nashr.

Al-Aḥmar, ʿAbdullah. 2007. *Mudhakkirāt al-shaykh ʿAbdullah b. Ḥusayn al-Aḥmar: qaḍāyā wa mawāqif*, 10 volumes, Sanaʿa: al-Āfāq li-l-ṭibāʿah wa l-nashr.

al-Akwaʿ, Ismāʿīl. 1987. 'Nashwān Ibn Saʿīd al-Ḥimyarī and the Spiritual, Religious and Political Conflicts of his Era' in Werner Daum (ed.), *Yemen: 3000 Years of Art and Civilization in Arabia Felix*, Frankfurt am Main: Umschau-Verlag, pp. 2012–231.

——— 1996. *Les hijra et les forteresses du savoir au Yémen*, Sanaʿa: Centre Français d'Études Yéménites.

Albergoni, Gianni and Bédoucha, Geneviève. 1991. 'Hiérarchie, médiation et tribalisme en Arabie du Sud: la hijra yéménite', *L'Homme* 118: 31/2, pp. 7–36.

Albrecht, Holger. 2013. 'The Security Sector in Yemen: No State, No Problem?', *Peacebrief* 142, 21 March 2013, United States Institute for Peace, http://www.usip.org/sites/default/files/PB142-Security-Sector-in-Yemen.pdf, last accessed 10 February 2017.

al-Bukhaytī, ʿAlī. 2014. 'Ma bayn mamlaka al-sayyid wa jumhūriyyah al-shaykh', *Barakish Net*, 8 January 2014, http://www.barakish.net/news02.aspx?cat=12&sub=14&id=61418, last accessed 10 February 2017.

Al-Dawlah, Ḥasan. 2009. 'Ṣaʿdah wa ḥarb al-thamānī sanawāt 1962–1969', *Al-Gomhoriah*, 14571, 26 September 2009, http://www.algomhoriah.net/newsweekprint.php?sid=93533, last accessed 10 February 2017.

Al-Dawsari, Nadwa. 2014. 'Sectarian War Going Unnoticed in East Yemen', *MENA Source*, Atlantic Council, http://www.atlanticcouncil.org/blogs/menasource/sectarian-war-going-unnoticed-in-east-yemen, last accessed 10 February 2017.

Al-Dawsari, Nadwa, Kolarova, Daniela and Pedersen, Jennifer. 2012. 'Yemen Community-Based Conflict Mitigation Program', *PDCI*, http://www.pdci-network.org/wp-content/uploads/2013/10/baseline-assessment-without-annexes.pdf.

Al-Dirwānī, Ṣabrī Muḥammad. 2013. *Ṣaʿdah al-ḥarb al-ūlā: al-asbāb wa l-tadāʿiāt*, Sanaʿa: Author's edition.

Al-Enazy, Askar Halwan. 2005. *The Long Road from Taif to Jeddah. Resolution of a Saudi-Yemeni Boundary Dispute*, Abu Dhabi: ECSSR.

al-Ḥajrī, Muḥammad. 1984. *Majmuʿ buldān al-yaman wa qabāʾil-hā*, (ed.) Ismāʿīl b. ʿAlī al-Akwaʿ, Sanaʿa: Wizārāt al-iʿlām wa l-thaqāfah.

Al-Hilaly, Khaled. 2009. 'Saudi Arabia to build a border security system', *Yemen Times*, 6 July 2009.

Al-Ḥūthī, Ḥusayn. 2002a. 'Al-ṣarkhah fī wajh al-mustakbirīn', transcript of public lecture given in Saʿdah.

—— 2002b. 'Sūrat al-māʾidah (1)', transcript of public lecture given in Saʿdah.

—— 2002c. 'Khatr dukhūl Amrīkā al-Yaman', transcript of public lecture given in Saʿdah.

—— 2002d. 'Latahdhanna ḥadhwa Banī Isrāʾīl', transcript of public lecture given in Saʿdah.

Al-Mujāhid, ʿAbdulraḥman. 2007a. *Al-tashīʿ fī Ṣaʿdah: Dirāsah mīdāniyyah (al-juzʾ al-awwal)*, vol. 1, Sanaʿa: Al-afāq li-l-ṭabāʿah wa l-nashr.

—— 2007b. *Al-tashīʿ fī Ṣaʿdah: Afkār al-shabāb al-muʾmin fī l-mīzān (al-juzʾ al-thānī)*, vol. 2, Sanaʿa: Al-afāq li-l-ṭabāʿah wa l-nashr.

al-Rammah, Khalid A. and Awass, Aish A. 2009. 'Yemeni-Saudi Experience of Joint Border Management: A Paper to be Presented to Mass Destruction Weapons and Border Security Group', Sanaʿa: Sheba Center for Strategic Studies.

al-Rasheed, Madawi. 2007. *Contesting the Saudi state: Islamic voices from a new generation*, Cambridge: Cambridge University Press.

al-Rasheed, Madawi and Vitalis, Robert. 2004. 'Introduction', in Madawi al-Rasheed and Robert Vitalis (eds), *Counter-Narratives: History, Contemporary Society, and Politics in Saudi Arabia and Yemen*, New York: Palgrave Macmillan, pp. 1–10.

Al-Ṣanʿānī, ʿAbdullah Muḥammad. 2005. *Al-ḥarb fī Ṣaʿdah: min awwal ṣayḥah... ilā ākhir ṭalqah*, Cairo: Dār al-Amal.

al-Saqqaf, Abou Bakr. 1999. 'The Yemeni Unity: Crisis in Integration', in Remy Leveau, Franck Mermier, and Udo Steinbach (eds), *Le Yémen Contemporain*, Paris: Éditions Karthala, pp. 141–59.

al-Sufyānī, Khālid. 2004. *Taʾrīkh Ṣaʿdah*, 2 Vols., Sanaʿa: Markaz ʿAbbādī li-l-Dirāsat wa l-Nashr.

al-Wādiʿī, Muqbil. 1999. *Tarjamat Abī ʿAbd al-Raḥman Muqbil b. Hādī al-Wādiʿī*, Sanaʿa: Maktabat Ṣanʿāʾ al-Athariyyah.

Al-Wardī, ʿAlī. 1962. *Mantiq Ibn Khaldūn*, al-Qāhira: Jāmiʿat al-Duwal al-ʿArabiyyah.

Al-Zwaini, Layla. 2006. 'State and Non-State Justice in Yemen', paper presented at the Conference on the Relationship between State and Non-State Justice Systems in Afghanistan, 10–14 December 2006, United States Institute for Peace.

——— 2012. 'The rule of law in Yemen: Prospects and challenges', The Hague: Rule of Law Quick Scan Series Yemen.

ʿĀmir, Jamāl. 2005. 'Badr al-Dīn al-Ḥūthī li-l-Wasaṭ: Al-raʾīs khāfa ʿan yākhudh Ḥusayn minhu al-wilāyah', *al-Wasaṭ*, 19 March 2005.

Arendonk, Cornelis van. 1919. *De Opkomst van het Zaidietische Imamaat in Yemen*, Leiden: Brill.

——— 1960. *Les Débuts de l'Imamat Zaidite au Yémen*, Leiden: Brill.

Augustin, Amira. 2015. 'Spaces in the Making: Peripheralization and Spatial Injustice in Southern Yemen', *Middle East—Topics and Arguments* 5, pp. 47–55.

Badeeb, Saeed. 1986. *The Saudi-Egyptian Conflict over North Yemen, 1962–1970*, Boulder: Westview Press.

Baldry, John. 1977. 'Anglo-Italian rivalry in Yemen and ʿAsir, 1900–1934', *Die Welt des Islams* XVII: 1–4, pp. 156–93.

Bang, Anne. 1996. *The Idrisi State of Asir 1906–1934: Politics, Religion and Personal Prestige as State-building factors in Early Twentieth Century Arabia*, Bergen: Studies on the Middle East and Africa.

Barakat, Sultan. 2014. 'Qatari Mediation: Between Ambition and Achievement', *Brookings Doha Center Analysing Paper 12*, Doha: Brookings Institution.

Baud, Michiel and van Schendel, Willem. 1997. 'Toward a Comparative History of Borderlands', *Journal of World History* 8: 2, pp. 211–42.

Bauman, Zygmunt. 2000. *Liquid Modernity*, Hoboken: Blackwell.

Bédoucha, Geneviève. 1987. 'Une Tribu sédentaire: La tribu des hautes plateaux yéménites', *L'Homme* 102: 27, pp. 139–50.

Behnstedt, Peter. 1987a. 'Anmerkungen zu den Dialekten der Gegend von Ṣaʿdah (Nord-Jemen)', *Zeitschrift für arabische Linguistik* 16, pp. 93–107.

——— 1987b. *Die Dialekte in der Gegend von Ṣaʿdah (Nord-Jemen)*, Wiesbaden: Harrassowitz.

Blumi, Isa. 2003. 'Thwarting the Ottoman Empire: Smuggling through the Empire's New Frontiers in Ottoman Yemen and Albania, 1878–1910', *International Journal of Turkish Studies*, 9: 1–2, pp. 255–74.

——— 2009a. 'Unique Authoritarianism: Shifting Fortunes and the Malleability of the Salih Regime in Yemen, 1990–present', *EUI Working Paper RSCAS* 2009/10, Florence: European University Institute.

—— 2009b. 'The Frontier as a Measure of Modern Power: Local Limits to Empire in Yemen, 1872–1914' in A. C. S. Peacock (ed.), *The Frontiers of the Ottoman World*, Oxford: Oxford University Press, pp. 289–304.

—— 2010. 'Illicit trade and the emergence of Albania and Yemen' in I. William Zartman (ed.), *Understanding Life in the Borderlands: Boundaries in Depth and in Motion*, Athens: University of Georgia Press.

—— 2011. *Chaos in Yemen: Societal Collapse and the New Authoritarianism*; London: Routledge.

Boellstorff, Tom. 2012. 'Rethinking Digital Anthropology' in H. A. Horst and D. Miller (eds.), *Digital Anthropology*, New York: Berg Publishers, pp. 39–60.

Bolt, Maxim. 2012. 'Waged entrepreneurs, policed informality: work, the regulation of space and the economy of the Zimbabwean-South African border', *Africa: The Journal of the International African Institute* 82:1, pp. 111–30.

Bonnefoy, Laurent. 2008. 'Salafism in Yemen: A 'Saudisation'?' in Madawi al-Rasheed (ed.), *Kingdom Without Borders: Saudi Expansion in the World*, London: Hurst, pp. 245–62.

—— 2009a. 'How Transnational is Salafism in Yemen?' in Roel Meijer (ed.), *Global Salafism. Islam's New Religious Movement*, London: Hurst, pp. 321–41.

—— 2009b. 'Varieties of Islamism in Yemen: The Logic of Integration Under Pressure', *Middle East Review of International Affairs* 13:1.

—— 2009c. 'Deconstructing Salafism in Yemen', *CTC Sentinel* 2:2.

—— 2011. *Salafism in Yemen: Transnationalism and Religious Identity*, London: Hurst.

Bonnefoy, Laurent and Ibn Cheikh, Fayçal. 2001. 'Le Rassemblement yéménite pour la réforme (al-Islâh) face à la crise du 11 septembre 2001 et la guerre en Afghanistan', *Chroniques yéménites* 9, http://cy.revues.org/73, last accessed 10 February 2017.

Bonnefoy, Laurent and Kuschnitzki, Judit. 2015. 'Salafis and the "Arab Spring" in Yemen: Progressive Politicization and Resilient Quietism', *Arabian Humanities* 4, https://cy.revues.org/2811, last accessed 17 February 2017.

Bonnefoy, Laurent and Poirier, Marine. 2010. 'The Yemeni Congregation for Reform (al-Islâh): The Difficult Process of Building a Project for Change', in K. Karam and M. Catusse (eds), *Returning to Political Parties? Political Party Development in the Arab World*, Beirut: Lebanese Center for Policy Studies.

Bonte, Paul and Conte, Édouard. 1991. 'La tribu arabe: approches anthropologiques et orientalistes', in Paul Bonte, Édouard Conte, Constant Hamès and A. W. Ould Cheikh (eds), *Al-Ansāb: La quête des origines. Anthropologie historique de la société tribale arabe*, Paris: Éditions de la Maison des Sciences de l'Homme, pp. 13–48.

Boucek, Christopher. 2010. 'War in Saada: From Local Insurrection to National Challenge', *Carnegie Paper* 110, Washington DC: Carnegie Endowment for International Peace.

Brandt, Marieke. 2006. 'Ḥamūd al-Hitār und die Praxis des kommunikativen Handelns', *Jemen-Report* 37:2, pp. 4–8.

——— 2012. 'Friedens-Šayḫ und Kriegs-Šayḫ: Der Übergang von Kriegsführerschaft bei den Banū Munebbih im Ḥūṯī-Konflikt in Nordwest-Jemen', *Anthropos* 107, pp. 49–69.

——— 2013. 'Sufyān's "hybrid" war: Tribal politics during the Ḥūthī conflict', *Journal of Arabian Studies* 3:1, pp. 120–38.

——— 2014a. 'The Irregulars of the Ṣa'dah War: "Colonel Shaykhs" and "Tribal Militias" in Yemen's Ḥūthī Conflict (2004–2010)' in Helen Lackner (ed.), *Why Yemen Matters: A Society in Transition*, London: Saqi, pp. 105–22.

——— 2014b. 'The Contemporary Structures and Historical Formation of the Khawlān and Jumā'ah Tribes in Ṣa'dah, Northwest Yemen', *Anthropology of the Middle East* 9:1, pp. 59–82.

——— 2014c. 'Inhabiting Tribal Structures: Leadership Hierarchies in Tribal Upper Yemen (Hamdān & Khawlān b. 'Āmir)' in Andre Gingrich and Siegfried Haas (eds), *Southwest Arabia across History: Essays to the Memory of Walter Dostal*, Vienna: Verlag der Österreichischen Akademie der Wissenschaften, pp. 91–116.

——— 2016. 'Heroic history, disruptive genealogy: Al-Ḥasan al-Hamdānī and the historical formation of the Shākir tribe (Wā'ilah and Dahm) in al-Jawf, Yemen', *Medieval Worlds* 3, pp. 116–45.

——— forthcoming (a): 'The Global and the Local: Al-Qaeda and Yemen's Tribes', in Virginie Collombier and Olivier Roy (eds), *Tribes and Global Jihadism*, London: Hurst.

——— forthcoming (b): 'The Huthi Enigma: Ansar Allah and the "Second Republic"', in Marie-Christine Heinze (ed.), *Yemen and the Path to War: Power, Politics and Society in the Twenty-First Century*, London: IB Tauris.

Braudel, Fernand. 1958. 'Histoire et sciences sociales. La longue durée', *Annales* 18:4, pp. 725–53.

Brehony, Noel. 2015. 'Yemen and the Huthis: Genesis of the 2015 Crisis', *Asian Affairs*, XLVI:II, pp. 232–50.

Burgat, François. 2006. 'Le Yémen après le 11 septembre 2001: entre construction de l'État et rétrécissement du champ politique', *Critique Internationale* 32, pp. 9–21.

Burgat, François and Sbitli, Muhammad. 2002. 'Les Salafis au Yémen ou… La modernisation malgré tout', *Chroniques Yéménites* 10, pp. 123–152, http://cy.revues.org/137#tocto1n1, last accessed 10 February 2017.

Burke, Edward. 2012. 'One blood and one destiny? Yemen's relations with the Gulf Cooperation Council', *Kuwait Programme on Development, Governance and Globalisation in the Gulf States* 23, London: LSE, http://www.cer.org.uk/sites/default/files/Yemen-and-the-GCC_burke_june12.pdf, last accessed 10 February 2017.

Burrowes, Robert D. 1987. *The Yemen Arab Republic: The Politics of Development 1962–1986*, Colorado: Westview Press.

Burrowes, Robert and Kasper, Catherine. 2007. 'The Salih Regime and the Need for a Credible Opposition', *Middle East Journal* 61:2, pp. 263–80.

Campbell, Howard. 2009. *Drug War Zone: Frontline Dispatches from the Streets of El Paso and Juárez*, Austin: University of Texas Press.

Carapico, Sheila. 1993a. 'Campaign Politics and Coalition-Building: The 1993 Parliamentary Elections', *Yemen Update* 33, pp. 37–39.

—— 1993b. 'Elections and Mass Politics in Yemen', *Middle East Report* 185, pp. 2–6.

—— 1998. *Civil Society in Yemen: The Political Economy of Activism in Modern Arabia*, Cambridge University Press.

Carapico, Sheila and Yadav, Stacey Philbrick. 2014. 'The Breakdown of the GCC Initiative', MERIP 273, http://www.merip.org/mer/mer273/breakdown-gcc-initiative, last accessed 10 February 2017.

Carvajal, Fernando. 2011. 'Houthi Expansion and Marginalization', *The Yemen Peace Project*, 27 November 2011, http://www.yemenpeaceproject.org/blogpost/analysis-commentary/houthi-expansion-and-marginalization/, last accessed 10 February 2017.

Caton, Steven. 1987. 'Power, persuasion, and language: A Critique of the segmentary model in the Middle East', *IJMES* 19, pp. 77–102.

—— 1990. *Peaks of Yemen I Summon: Poetry as Cultural Practice in a North Yemeni Tribe*, Berkeley: University of California Press.

Ceccato, Vania and Haining, Robert. 2004. 'Crime in Border Regions: The Scandinavian Case of Öresund', *Annals of the Association of American Geographers* 94:4, pp. 807–26.

Chapin Metz, Helen (ed.). 1987. *Libya: A Country Study*, Washington DC: GPO for the Library of Congress, http://countrystudies.us/libya/, last accessed 10 February 2017.

Clarke, Victoria. 2010. *Yemen: Dancing on the Heads of Snakes*, New Haven: Yale University Press.

Cook, Michael. 2000. *Commanding Right and Forbidding Wrong in Islamic Thought*, Cambridge: Cambridge University Press.

CTC (Combating Terrorism Center at West Point). 2011. 'A False Foundation? AQAP, tribes, and ungoverned spaces in Yemen', Gabriel Koehler-Derrick (ed.), West Point: Combating Terrorism Center, https://www.ctc.usma.edu/posts/a-false-foundation-aqap-tribes-and-ungoverned-spaces-in-yemen, last accessed 10 February 2017.

Dahlgren, Susanne. 2008. 'The Southern Movement in Yemen', *ISIM Review* 22, pp. 50–51.

—— 2010. 'The Snake with a Thousand Heads: The Southern Cause in Yemen', *MERIP* 256, http://www.merip.org/mer/mer256/snake-thousand-heads, last accessed 10 February 2017.

Day, Stephen. 2012. *Regionalism and Rebellion in Yemen: A Troubled National Union*, Cambridge: Cambridge University Press.

de Gaury, Gerald. 1967. *Faisal, King of Saudi Arabia*, New York/Washington: Praeger.

de Regt, Marina. 2015. 'Noura and Me: Friendship as Method in Times of Crisis', *Urban Anthropology and Studies of Cultural Systems and World Economic Development* 44, 1/2, pp. 43–70.

Detalle, Renaud. 1993a. 'The Yemeni Elections Up Close', *Middle East Report* 185, pp. 8–12.

——— 1993b. 'Yemen: les élections législatives du 27 avril 1993', *Maghreb-Machrek* 141, pp. 3–26.

——— 1997. 'Les islamistes yéménites et l'état: Vers l'émancipation?' in Basma Kodmani-Darwish and May Chartouni-Dubarry (eds), *Les États arabes face à la contestation islamiste*, Paris: Armand Colin, pp. 278–9.

——— 2000. 'The Yemeni-Saudi Conflict: Bilateral Transactions and Interactions' in Renaud Detalle (ed.), *Tensions in Arabia: The Saudi-Yemeni Fault Line*, Baden-Baden: Nomos, pp. 52–79.

DeWalt, K. M., DeWalt, B. R. and Wayland, C. B. 1998. 'Participant observation' in H. R. Bernard (ed.), *Handbook of Methods in Cultural Anthropology*, Walnut Creek, CA: AltaMira, pp. 259–99.

Dorlian, Samy. 2011. 'The Ṣaʿda War in Yemen: Between Politics and Sectarianism', *The Muslim World* 101, pp. 182–201.

——— 2013. *La mouvance zaydite dans le Yémen contemporain: une modernisation avortée*, Paris: Harmattan.

Dostal, Walter. 1974. 'Sozio-ökonomische Aspekte der Stammesdemokratie in Nordost-Yemen', *Sociologus* 24/I, pp. 1–15.

——— 1983. *Ethnographic Atlas of ʿAsīr: Preliminary Report*, Vienna: Österreichische Akademie der Wissenschaften.

——— 2006. 'Vorbemerkung' in Walter Dostal (ed.), *Tribale Gesellschaften der südwestlichen Regionen des Königreiches Saudi Arabien*, Vienna: Verlag der Österreichischen Akademie der Wissenschaften.

——— 2008. *Von Mohammed bis al-Qaida: Einblicke in die Welt des Islam*, Wien: Passagen.

Dresch, Paul. 1981. 'The several peaces of Yemeni Tribes', *Journal of the Anthropological Society of Oxford* 12:2, pp. 73–86.

——— 1984a. 'The position of Shaykhs among the northern tribes of Yemen', *Man* 19/1, pp. 31–49.

——— 1984b. 'Tribal relations and political history in Upper Yemen' in B. R. Pridham (ed.), *Contemporary Yemen: Politics and Historical Background*, London: Croon Helm, pp. 154–74.

——— 1986. 'The significance of the course events take in segmentary systems', *American Ethnologist* 13:2, pp. 309–24.

——— 1989. *Tribes, Government, and History in Yemen*, Oxford: Clarendon Press.

——— 1990. 'Imams and Tribes: The Writing and Acting of History in Upper Yemen', in Philip S. Khoury and Joseph Kostiner (eds.), *Tribes and State Formation in the Middle East*, Berkeley: University of California Press, pp. 252–87.

——— 1995. 'A Fragment of the Yemeni Past: ʿAlī Nāṣir al-Qardaʿī and the Shabwah Incident, *Journal of Arabic Literature* 26:3, pp. 232–54.

——— 2000. *A History of Modern Yemen*, Cambridge: Cambridge University Press.

——— 2006. *The Rules of Baraṭ: Tribal Documents from Yemen*, Sanaʿa: CEFAS/DAI.

Dresch, Paul and Haykel, Bernard. 1995. 'Stereotypes and Political Styles: Islamists and Tribesfolk in Yemen', *IJMES* 27, pp. 405–31.

du Bouchet, Ludmila. 2007. 'The State, Political Islam and Violence: The Reconfiguration of Yemeni Politics since 9/11' in A. Blom, L. Bucaille and L. Martinez (eds), *The Enigma of Islamist Violence*, London: Hurst, pp. 137–64.

Dupret, B. 2000a. 'Systèmes coutumiers, centralisme juridique de l'Etat et usage du droit', *Chroniques Yéménites* 8, Sana'a: CEFAS, pp. 67–8.

——— 2000b. 'Les procédures de la justice tribale. Extrait de Rashād al-ʿAlīmī, « La justice tribale dans la société yéménite », traduit de l'arabe', *Chroniques Yéménites* 8, Sana'a: CEFAS, pp. 69–80.

Durac, Vincent. 2011. 'The joint meeting parties and the politics of opposition in Yemen', *British Journal of Middle Eastern Studies* 38:3, pp. 343–65.

Eickelman, Dale F. 2002. *The Middle East and Central Asia: An Anthropological Approach*, 4th edn, New Jersey: Prentice Hall.

Eickelman, Dale F. and Piscatori, James. 2004. *Muslim Politics*, Princeton: Princeton University Press, 2004.

Emerson, R. M; Fretz, R. I. and Shaw, L. L. 2001. 'Participant Observation and Fieldnotes', in P. Atkinson et al. (eds), *Handbook of Ethnography*, Thousand Oaks: Sage, pp. 356–7.

European Union Election Observation Mission (EOM) Yemen. 2006. 'Election Observation Mission Yemen 2006 Final Report', http://www.eods.eu/library/FR%20YEMEN%202006_en.pdf, last accessed 10 February 2017.

Evans-Pritchard, Edward. 1940. *The Nuer: A Description of the Modes of Livelihood and Political Institutions of a Nilotic People*, Oxford: Clarendon Press.

Fattah, Khaled. 2010. 'A Political History of Civil-Military Relations in Yemen', *Alternative Politics*, Special Issue 1, pp. 25–47.

——— 2014. 'The Repercussions of the GCC Tension in Yemen', Carnegie Endowment for International Peace, http://carnegieendowment.org/sada/?fa=55276, last accessed 10 February 2017.

Feldner, Yotam. 2004. 'The Saudi Separation Fence', *MEMRI* 162, http://www.israpost.com/Community/articles/show.php?articleID=2410, last accessed 10 February 2017.

Fischer-Tahir, Andrea and Naumann, Matthias. 2013. *Peripheralization: The Making of Spatial Dependencies and Social Injustice*, Berlin: Springer.

Flick, Uwe. 2008. *Triangulation: Eine Einführung*, Wiesbaden: VS Verlag.

Forrer, Ludwig. 1942. *Südarabien nach al-Hamdānī's 'Beschreibung der Arabischen Halbinsel'*, Leipzig: Deutsche Morgenländische Gesellschaft.

Fustier, Nathalie. 2000. 'The Saudi Perspective and US Interests', in Renaud Detalle (ed.), *Tensions in Arabia. The Saudi-Yemeni Fault Line*, Baden-Baden: Nomos, pp. 99–114.

Gale, Ivan. 2009. 'EADS wins Saudi border security contract', *The National*, 2 July 2009, http://www.thenational.ae/news/uae-news/technology/eads-wins-saudi-border-security-contract, last accessed 10 February 2017.

Gaston, Erica. 2014. 'Process Lessons Learned in Yemen's National Dialogue', Washington DC: United States Institute of Peace, *Special Report 342*.

Gatter, Peer. 2012. *Politics of Qat: The Role of a Drug in Ruling Yemen*, Wiesbaden: Reichert.

Gause, F. Gregory. 1990. *Saudi-Yemeni Relations: Domestic Structures and Foreign Influence*, New York: Columbia University Press.

——— 2011. 'Saudi Arabia's Regional Security Strategy', in Mehran Kamrava (ed.), *International Politics of the Persian Gulf*, Syracuse NY: Syracuse University Press.

Geertz, Clifford. 1972. 'Comments', in Richard Antoun and Ilya Harik (eds), *Rural Politics and Social Change in the Middle East*, Bloomington and London: University of Indiana Press.

Gellner, Ernest, 1969, *Saints of the Atlas*, London: Weidenfeld and Nicolson.

——— 1981. *Muslim Society*, Cambridge: Cambridge University Press.

Gerholm, Thomas. 1977. *Market, Mosque and Mafraj: Social Inequality in a Yemeni Town*, Stockholm: Stockholm University Press.

Ghanem, Isam. 1990. 'The Legal History of 'Asir (Al-Mikhlaf Al-Sulaymani)', *Arab Law Quarterly* 5:3, pp. 211–14.

Gingrich, Andre. 1987. 'Die Banu Munebbih des nördlichen Khawlān: Einige vorläufige Ergebnisse ethnologischer Forschung in der AR Jemen', *Sociologus* 1:37, pp. 89–93.

——— 1989a. *Der Agrarkalender der Munebbih: Eine ethnologische Studie zu sozialem Kontext und regionalem Vergleich eines tribalen Sternenkalenders in Südwestarabien*, Habilitation thesis, Vienna University.

——— 1989b. 'The guest meal among the Munebbih: Some considerations on tradition and change in aysh wa milh in north-western Yemen', *Peuples Méditerranéens* 46, pp. 129–49.

——— 1989c. 'Kalender, Regenzeit und Stieropfer in Nordwest-Jemen' in Bernhard Scholz (ed.), *Der orientalische Mensch und seine Beziehungen zur Umwelt: Beiträge zum 2. Grazer Morgenländischen Symposium (2.-5. März 1989)*, Graz: Grazer Morgenländische Studien 2, pp. 353–70.

——— 1989d. 'How the chiefs' daughters marry: Tribes, marriage patterns and hierarchies in Northwest-Yemen' in Andre Gingrich, Sylvia Haas and Gabriele Paleczek (eds), *Kinship, Social Change and Evolution: Proceedings of a Symposium Held in Honour of W. Dostal*, Horn: Berger, pp. 75–85.

—— 1989e. 'Les Munebbih du Yémen perçus par leur voisins: Description d'une société par le corps et sa parure', *Techniques et culture* 13, pp. 127–39.

—— 1993. 'Tribes and rulers in northern Yemen', in Andre Gingrich, Sylvia Haas, Gabriele Paleczek and Thomas Fillitz (eds), *Studies in Oriental Culture and History: Festschrift für Walter Dostal*, Frankfurt am Main etc: Lang, pp. 253–80.

—— 1994a. *Südwestarabische Sternenkalender: Eine ethnologische Studie zu Struktur, Kontext und regionalem Vergleich des tribalen Agrarkalenders der Munebbih im Jemen*, Vienna: WUV-Univ.-Verlag.

—— 1994b. 'Nationalismus und Staatenbildung in der arabischen Welt am Beispiel des Jemen', in E. Bruckmüller, S. Linhart and C. Mährdel (eds), *Nationalismus: Wege der Staatenbildung in der außereuropäischen Welt*, Vienna: Verlag für Gesellschaftskritik, pp. 101–18.

—— 1996. 'Spirits of the Border: Some Remarks on the Connotation of Jinn in North-Western Yemen', *Quaderni Studi Arabi* 13, pp. 199–212.

—— 2001. 'Ehre, Raum und Körper: Zur sozialen Konstruktion der Geschlechter im Nordjemen', in U. Davis-Sulikowski, H. Diemberger, A. Gingrich and J. Helbling (eds), *Körper, Religion und Macht: Sozialanthropologie der Geschlechterbeziehungen*, Frankfurt/Main: Campus, pp. 221–93.

—— 2002. 'Regen Gottes, Land der Ehre: Konzeptualisierungen von Natur bei den Munebbih des Nordwestjemen', in Andre Gingrich and Elke Mader (eds), *Metamorphosen der Natur: Sozialanthropologische Untersuchungen zum Verhältnis von Weltbild und natürlicher Umwelt*, Wien/Köln/Weimar: Böhlau, pp. 143–59.

—— 2011. 'Warriors of Honor, Warriors of Faith: Two historical male role models from south-western Arabia' in Maria Six-Hohenbalken and Nerina Weiss (eds), *Violence Expressed: An Anthropological Approach*, London: Ashgate, pp. 37–54.

—— 2014a. 'Connecting and Disconnecting: Intentionality, Anonymity, and Transnational Networks in Upper Yemen', in Thomas Hylland Eriksen, Christina Garsten and Shalini Randeria (eds), *Anthropology Now and Next: Essays in Honor of Ulf Hannerz*, pp. 48–69.

—— 2014b. 'Galactic Polities: Anthropological Insights for Understanding States in Yemen's pre-Ottoman Past', in Andre Gingrich and Siegfried Haas (eds), *Southwest Arabia across History: Essays to the Memory of Walter Dostal*, Vienna: Verlag der Österreichischen Akademie der Wissenschaften, pp. 117–24.

—— 2015. 'Tribe', in James D. Wright (ed.), International Encyclopedia of the Social & Behavioral Sciences, 2nd edition, Vol. 24, Oxford: Elsevier, pp. 645–7.

—— forthcoming. 'The Use and Abuse of Civilization: An Assessment from Historical Anthropology for South Arabia's History', in Johan P. Arnason and Christopher Hann (eds), *Anthropology and Civilizational Analysis: Eurasian Explorations*, Chicago: University of Chicago Press.

Gingrich, Andre and Heiss, Johann. 1986. *Beiträge zur Ethnographie der Provinz Ṣaʿda, Nordjemen*, Vienna: Verlag der Österreichischen Akademie der Wissenschaften.

Glaser, Eduard. 1913. *Eduard Glasers Reise nach Marib*, ed. D. H. Müller, Vienna: Hölder.

Glosemeyer, Iris. 1993. 'The first Yemeni parliamentary elections in 1993', *Orient* 34, pp. 439–51.

——— 1995. *Liberalisierung und Demokratisierung in der Republik Jemen, 1990–1994: Einführung und Dokumente*, Hamburg: Deutsches Orient-Institut.

——— 2001. *Politische Akteure in der Republik Jemen: Wahlen, Parteien und Parlamente*, Hamburg: Deutsches Orient-Institut.

Glosemeyer, Iris and Reneau, Don. 2004. 'Local Conflict, Global Spin: An Uprising in the Yemeni Highlands', *Middle East Report* 232, pp. 44–6.

Gochenour, David Thomas. 1984. *The Penetration of Zaydī Islam into Early Medieval Yemen*, Ph.D. thesis, Harvard University.

Government of Yemen. 2006. 'Statistical Semi-Final Report of the Presidential Elections on Local Constituencies' Level' [iḥṣā'iyyah shibh nihā'iyyah li-natā'ij al-intikhābāt al-ri'āsiyyah 'āmm 2006 'alā mustawā al-dawā'ir al-maḥalliyyah], Sana'a.

Halliday, Fred. 1977. 'Labor Migration in the Middle East', *MERIP Reports* 10:56.

Hamidi, Ayman. 2009. 'Inscriptions of Violence in Northern Yemen: Haunting Histories, Unstable Moral Spaces', *Middle Eastern Studies* 45:2, pp. 165–87.

Hart-Davis, Duff. 2012. *The War That Never Was: The True Story of the Men who Fought Britain's Most Secret Battle*, London: Arrow.

Haykel, Bernard. 1995. 'A Zaydi Revival?', *Yemen Update* 36, pp. 20–1.

——— 1999. 'Rebellion, Migration or Consultative Democracy? The Zaydis and their detractors in Yemen', in Remy Leveau, Franck Mermier, and Udo Steinbach (eds), *Le Yémen Contemporain*, Paris: Éditions Karthala, pp. 193–201.

——— 2002. 'The Salafis in Yemen at a Crossroads: An Obituary of Shaykh Muqbil al-Wādi'ī of Dammāj (d. 1422/2001)', *Jemen Report* 1, pp. 28–31.

——— 2003. *Revival and Reform in Islam: The Legacy of Muḥammad al-Shawkānī*, Cambridge: Cambridge University Press.

Hegghammer, Thomas and Lacroix, Stéphane. 2007. 'Rejectionist Islamism in Saudi Arabia: The Story of Juhayman al-'Utaybi revisited', *IJMES* 39, pp. 103–22.

Heinze, Marie-Christine. 2010. 'Die Grenzproblematik zwischen dem Jemen und Saudi-Arabien', in Conrad Schetter, Stephan Conermann and Bernd Kuzmits (eds), *Die Grenzen Asiens zwischen Globalisierung und staatlicher Fragmentierung*, Berlin: EB-Verlag, pp. 137–78.

——— 2014a. 'On "Gun Culture" and "Civil Statehood" in Yemen', *Journal of Arabian Studies* 4:1, pp. 70–95.

——— 2014b. 'The triumphant advance of the Houthi rebels', *Qantara*, 24 September 2014, http://en.qantara.de/content/political-upheaval-in-yemen-the-triumphant-advance-of-the-houthi-rebels, last accessed 10 February 2017.

——— 2015. *Yemen through the janbiya. The social lives of daggers in 'South Arabia'*, Ph.D. thesis, Bielefeld University.

Heiss, Johann. 1989. 'War and Mediation for Peace in a Tribal Society (Yemen, 9th Century)', in Andre Gingrich, Sylvia Haas and Gabriele Paleczek (eds), *Kinship, Social Change and Evolution: Proceedings of a Symposium Held in Honour of W. Dostal*, Horn: Berger, pp. 63–74.

——— 1998. *Tribale Selbstorganisation und Konfliktregelung: Der Norden des Jemen zur Zeit des ersten Imams (10. Jahrhundert)*, Ph.D. thesis, University of Vienna.

——— 2014. 'Sa'da revisited', in Andre Gingrich and Siegfried Haas (eds), *Southwest Arabia across History: Essays to the Memory of Walter Dostal*, Vienna: Verlag der Österreichischen Akademie der Wissenschaften, pp. 79–89.

Herzfeld, Michael. 1987. *Anthropology through the looking-glass: Critical ethnography on the margins of Europe*, Cambridge: Cambridge University Press.

Herzog, Lawrence A. 1990. *Where North Meets South: Cities, Space, and Politics on the United States-Mexico Border*, Austin: Center for Mexican American Studies.

Hovden, Eirik. 2018. *Constructions of Validity in Zaydi Waqf Law: Administration, Codification and Legal Knowledge*, Leiden: Brill.

Human Rights Watch. 2008a. 'The Ismailis of Najran: Second-Class Saudi Citizens', www.hrw.org/en/reports/2008/09/22/ismailis-najran, last accessed 14 May 2013.

——— 2008b. 'Disappearances and Arbitrary Arrests in the Armed Conflict with Huthi Rebels in Yemen', https://www.hrw.org/report/2008/10/24/disappearances-and-arbitrary-arrests-armed-conflict-huthi-rebels-yemen, last accessed 10 February 2017.

——— 2010. 'All Quiet on the Northern Front? Uninvestigated Laws of War Violations in Yemen's War with Huthi Rebels', https://www.hrw.org/report/2010/04/07/all-quiet-northern-front/uninvestigated-laws-war-violations-yemens-war-huthi, last accessed 10 February 2017.

Ingrams, Doreen and Ingrams, Leila (eds). 1993. *Records of Yemen: 1798–1960*, Vol. 9: 1933–1945, London: Archive Editions.

International Crisis Group. 2009. 'Defusing the Saada Time Bomb', *Middle East Report* 86.

——— 2013. 'Yemen's Military-Security Reform: Seeds of New Conflict?', *Middle East Report* 139.

——— 2014. 'The Huthis: From Saada to Sanaa', *Middle East Report* 154.

Jamous, Raymond. 1991. 'From the Death of Men to the Peace of God: Violence and Peace-Making in the Rif', in J. G. Peristiany and J. Pitt-Rivers (eds), *Honor and Grace in Anthropology*, Cambridge: Cambridge University Press, pp. 167–92.

Jarvis, M. 2010. *In the Eye of All Trade: Bermuda, Bermudians and the Maritime Atlantic World*, Chapel Hill: University of North Carolina Press.

Jellissen, Susan M. and Gottheil, Fred M. 2013. 'On the utility of security fences along international borders', *Defense & Security Analysis* 29:4, pp. 266–79.

Jenkins, Timothy. 1994. 'Fieldwork and the Perception of Everyday Life', *Man* 29:2, pp. 433–55.

Johnsen, Gregory. 2013. *The Last Refuge: Yemen, Al-Qaeda, and the Battle for Arabia*, London: Oneworld.

Jones, Stephen B. 1945. *Boundary Making: A Handbook for Statesmen, Treaty Editors and Boundary Commissioners*, Washington, DC: Carnegie Endowment for International Peace.

Kamrava, Mehran. 2011. 'Mediation and Qatari Foreign Policy', *The Middle East Journal* 65:4, pp. 539–56.

King, James. 2012. *Zaydis in a post-Zaydi Yemen: contemporary 'ulama reactions to Zaydism's marginalization in the Republic of Yemen*, M.A. thesis, Columbia University.

Knupp, Marcus. 2000. *Wochenmärkte im Jemen: Ein traditionelles Versorgungssystem als Indikator gesellschaftlichen Wandels*, Köln: Geographisches Institut der Universität zu Köln.

Kohlberg, Etan. 1976. 'Some Zaydī Views on the Companions of the Prophet', *Bulletin of the School of Oriental and African Studies* 39:1, pp. 91–8.

Kopp, Horst. 1981. *Agrargeographie der Arabischen Halbinsel*, Erlangen: Selbstverlag der Fränkischen Geographischen Gesellschaft.

——— 2000. 'Water and Mineral Resources in Yemen and Saudi Arabia', in Renaud Detalle (ed.). *Tensions in Arabia: The Saudi-Yemeni Fault Line*; Baden-Baden: Nomos, pp. 80–95.

——— (ed.) 2005. *Länderkunde Jemen*, Wiesbaden: Reichert.

Kopp, Horst and Schweizer, Günther (eds). 1984. *Entwicklungsprozesse in der Arabischen Republik Jemen*, Wiesbaden: Reichert.

Koszinowski, Thomas. 1993. 'Abdallah Ibn Hussain al-Ahmar (Kurzbiographie)', *Orient* 34:3, pp. 335–41.

——— 1999. 'Yemeni Foreign Policy since Unification and the Part Played by Saudi Arabia', in Remy Leveau, Franck Mermier, and Udo Steinbach (eds), *Le Yémen Contemporain*, Paris: Éditions Karthala, pp. 61–78.

Kuczynski, Liliane. 1985. 'Les juifs du Yémen: approche ethnologique', in Joseph Chelhod (ed.), *L'Arabie du Sud, Historie et Civilisation. Tome III: Culture et institutions du Yémen*, Paris: Editions G.-P. Maisonneuve et Larose, pp. 277–302.

Lichtenthäler, Gerhard. 2003. *Political Ecology and the Role of Water: Environment, Society and Economy in Northern Yemen*, Aldershot: Ashgate.

Longley Alley, April. 2007. 'The High Watermark of Islamist Politics? The Case of Yemen', *The Middle East Journal* 61:2, pp. 240–60.

Lux, Abdullah. 2009. 'Yemen's last Zaydī Imām: The shabāb al-mu'min, the Malāzim, and 'ḥizb allāh' in the thought of Ḥusayn Badr al-Dīn al-Ḥūthī', *Contemporary Arab Affairs* 2:3, pp. 369–434.

Madelung, Wilferd. 1965. *Der Imam al-Qāsim ibn Ibrāhīm und die Glaubenslehre der Zaiditen*, Berlin: de Gruyter.

——— 1991. 'The origins of the Yemenite hijra', in Alan Jones (ed.), *Arabicus Felix*,

Luminousis Britannicus: Essays in Honour of A. F. L. Beeston on his Eightieth Birthday, Reading: Ithaca, pp. 25–44.

Markaz al-jazīrah al-ʿarabiyyah li-l-dirāsah wa l-buḥūth. 2008. *Al-Ḥūthiyyah fī l-Yaman*, Sanaʿa.

Martin, Denis-Constant. 2002. *A la Recherche des OPNI*, Paris: Karthala.

Martínez, Oscar. 1994. *Border People: Life and Society in the U.S.-Mexico Borderlands*, Tucson: University of Arizona Press, pp. 5–10.

McGregor, Andrew. 2004. 'Shi'ite Insurgency in Yemen: Iranian Intervention or Mountain Revolt?', *Terrorism Monitor* 2:16.

Meir-Glitzenstein, Esther. 2011. 'Operation Magic Carpet: Constructing the Myth of the Magical Immigration of Yemenite Jews to Israel', *Israel Studies* 16:3, pp. 149–73.

—— 2012. *The Exodus of the Yemenite Jews: Failed Operation and Formative Myth*, Tel Aviv: Resling.

Meissner, Jeffrey. 1987. *Tribes at the Core: Legitimacy, Structure and Power in Zaydī Yemen*, Ph.D. thesis, Columbia University.

Mermier, Franck. 1985. 'Patronyme et hiérarchie sociale à Sanaa (République Arabe du Yémen)', in *Peuples Méditerranéens* 33, pp. 33–41.

—— 1991. 'Récit d'origine et rituel d'allégeance: Le jour de *ghadīr khumm* et la cérémonie de nushūr au Yémen", *Peuples Méditerranéens* 56–57, pp. 177–80.

—— 1993. 'La commune de Sanaa: Pouvoir citadin et légitimité religieuse au XIX siècle', in Andre Gingrich, Sylvia Haas and Gabriele Paleczek (eds), *Studies in Oriental Culture and History: Festschrift for Walter Dostal*, Frankfurt: Lang, pp. 242–52.

—— 1997. 'L'Islam politique au Yémen ou la « Tradition » contre les traditions?', *Monde Arabe Maghreb-Machrek* 155, pp. 6–19.

Messick, Brinkley. 1993. *The Calligraphic State. Textual Domination and History in a Muslim Society*, Berkeley: University of California Press.

Moberg, Axel. 1924. *The Book of the Himyarites: Fragments of a Hitherto Unknown Syriac Work*, London et al.: Lund.

Mundy, Martha. 1995. *Domestic government: kinship, community and polity in North Yemen*, London: I.B. Tauris.

Niewöhner-Eberhard, Elke. 1976. 'Täglicher Suq und Wochenmarkt in Sa'da, Jemen', *Erdkunde*, pp. 24–7.

—— 1985. *Ṣaʿda: Bauten und Bewohner in einer traditionellen islamischen Stadt*, Wiesbaden: Reichert.

—— 1988. Veränderungen im Maktangebot: Der Sūq von Ṣaʿda n den Jahren 1973 und 1983, *Baessler-Archiv* 35, pp. 357–81.

O'Ballance, Edgar. 1971. *The War in the Yemen*, Hamden: Archon Books.

Padnos, Theo. 2011. *Undercover Muslim: A Journey Into Yemen*, London: Bodley Head.

Parfitt, Tudor. 1996. *The Road to Redemption: The Jews of the Yemen 1900–1950*, Leiden: Brill.

Pawelke, Günther. 1959. *Jemen: Das verbotene Land*, Düsseldorf: Econ.

Peterson, John E. 1982. *Yemen: The Search for a Modern State*, Baltimore/London: The Johns Hopkins University Press.

——— 2006. 'Qatar and the World: Branding for a Micro-State, *Middle East Journal* 60:4, pp. 733–48.

——— 2008a. 'The al-Huthi Conflict in Yemen', *Arabian Peninsula Background Note* APBN-006, www.JEPeterson.net.

——— 2008b. 'Tribes and Politics in Yemen', *Arabian Peninsula Background Note* APBN-007, www.JEPeterson.net.

Philby, H. St. J. B., 1952. *Arabian Highlands*, Ithaca: Cornell University Press.

Phillips, Sarah. 2005. 'Cracks in the Yemeni System', *Middle East Research and Information Project*, http://www.merip.org/mero/mero072805, last accessed 10 February 2017.

——— 2008. *Yemen's Democracy Experiment in Regional Perspective: Patronage and Pluralized Authoritarianism*, New York: Palgrave Macmillan.

——— 2010. 'What Comes Next in Yemen? Al-Qaeda, the Tribes, and State-Building', *Carnegie Paper* 107, http://carnegieendowment.org/files/yemen_tribes.pdf, last accessed 10 February 2017.

——— 2011a. *Yemen and the Politics of Permanent Crisis*, London: Routledge.

——— 2011b. 'Developmental Dysfunction and Yemen: Division in a Crisis State', Research Paper 14, Birmingham: Development Leadership Program.

Platt, Tristan. 2012. 'Between Routine and Rupture: the Archive as Field Event', in R. Fardon et al. (eds), *Sage Handbook of Social Anthropology*, Thousand Oaks: Sage, pp. 65–78.

Poirier, Marine. 2008. 'Yémen nouveau, futur meilleur? Retour sur l'élection présidentielle de 2006', *Chroniques yéménites* 15, pp. 129–59.

Puin, Gerd-Rüdiger. 1984. 'The Yemeni hijrah concept of tribal protection', in T. Khalidi (ed.), *Land Tenure and Social Transformation in the Middle East*, Beirut: AUB, pp. 483–94.

Rathjens, Carl. 1951. 'Taghut gegen scheri'ah', *Jahrbuch des Linden-Museums*, Stuttgart: Linden-Museum.

Reissner, Johannes. 1981. 'Die Idrīsīden in ʿAsīr. Ein historischer Überblick', *Die Welt des Islams* 21, 1:4, pp. 164–92.

Robben, Antonius (ed.). 2009. *Iraq at a Distance: What Anthropologists Can Teach Us About the War*, Philadelphia: University of Pennsylvania Press.

——— 2011. 'Neue Kriege', in Fernand Kreff, Eva-Maria Knoll and Andre Gingrich (eds), *Lexikon der Globalisierung*, Bielefeld: Transcript, pp. 296–99.

Romeo, Leonardo G.; El Mensi, Mohamed. 2008. 'The Difficult Road to Local Autonomy in Yemen', *International Studies Program Working Paper 08–34*, http://icepp.gsu.edu/files/2015/03/ispwp0834.pdf, last accessed 10 February 2017.

Rondot, Philippe. 1978. 'La mort du chef d'état du Yémen du Nord', *Maghreb-Machrek* 79, pp. 10–14.

Rupert, Linda M. 2012. *Creolization and Contraband: Curaçao in the Early Modern Atlantic World*, Athens, GA: University of Georgia Press.

Sanjek, Roger and Tratner, Susan (eds). 2015. *eFieldnotes: The Makings of Anthropology in the Digital World*, Philadelphia: University of Pennsylvania Press.

Salisbury, Peter. 2015. 'Yemen and the Saudi-Iranian Cold War', London: Chatham House Middle East and North Africa Programme, https://www.chathamhouse.org/sites/files/chathamhouse/field/field_document/20150218YemenIranSaudi.pdf, last accessed 10 February 2017.

Salmoni, Barak, Loidolt, Bryce and Wells, Madeleine. 2010. *Regime and periphery in Northern Yemen: The Huthi phenomenon*, Santa Monica: RAND.

Sarī al-Dīn, 'Āyyidah. 2010. *Al-Ḥūthiyyūn fī l-Yaman bayn al-siyāsah wa l-wāq'*, Beirut: Bīssān li-l-nashr wa l-tawzī' wa l-i'alām.

Schmitt, Eric and Worth, Robert. 2012. 'With Arms for Yemen Rebels, Iran Seeks Wider Mideast Role', *The New York Times*, 15 March 2012.

Schmitz, Charles. 2014. 'Yemen's National Dialogue', *MEI Policy Paper 1*, Washington DC: Middle East Institute.

Schofield, Richard. 1992. *Arabian boundary disputes: Vol. 20: Saudi Arabia—Yemen: 1913—1992*, Slough: Archive Editions.

—— 1999. 'Negotiating the Saudi-Yemeni International Boundary', talk to the British-Yemeni Society (abridged version), 31 March 1999, http://www.al-bab.com/bys/articles/schofield00.htm, last accessed 10 February 2017.

—— 2000. 'The International Boundary between Yemen and Saudi Arabia', in Renaud Detalle (ed.), *Tensions in Arabia. The Saudi-Yemeni Fault Line*, Baden-Baden: Nomos, pp. 15–48.

Schwedler, Jillian. 1998. 'Democratic Institutions and the Practice of Power in Yemen: The Changing Role of the Islâh Party', in *Yemen: The Challenge of Social, Economic and Democratic Development*, Conference Proceedings, Exeter: Centre for Arabic Studies, University of Exeter, pp. 1–25.

—— 2008. *Faith in Moderation: Islamist Parties in Jordan and Yemen*, Cambridge: Cambridge University Press.

Schweizer, Günther. 1984. 'Social and economic change in the rural distribution system: Weekly markets in the Yemen Arab Republic', in B. R. Pridham (ed.), *Contemporary Yemen: Politics and Historical Background*, London and Sydney: Croom Helm, pp. 107–21.

Seitz, Adam. 2014. 'Ties that bind and divide: The "Arab Spring" and Yemeni civil-military relations', in Helen Lackner (ed.), *Why Yemen Matters: A Society in Transition*, London: Saqi, pp. 50–67.

—— 2016. 'Patronage Politics in Transition: Political and Economic Interests of the Yemeni Armed Forces', in E. Grawert and Z. Abdul-Magd (eds), *Businessmen in*

Arms: How the Military and Other Armed Groups Profit in the MENA Region, Lanham: Rowman & Littlefield, pp. 157–73.

Selznick, Philip. 1949. *TVA and the Grass Roots: A Study in the Sociology of Formal Organization*, Berkeley and Los Angeles: University of California Press.

Serjeant, R.B. 1962. 'Ḥaram and ḥawṭah, the sacred enclave in Arabia', in A. al-Badawi (ed.), *Melanges Taha Husain*, Cairo: Dār al-Maʿārif, pp. 41–58.

——— 1969. 'The Zaydīs', in A. J. Arberry (ed.), *Religion in the Middle East*, Cambridge: Cambridge University Press, pp. 285–301.

——— 1977. 'South Arabia', in C. van Nieuwenhuijze (ed.), *Commoners, Climbers and Notables*, Leiden: Brill, pp. 226–47.

——— 1982. 'The interplay between tribal affinities and religious (Zaydī) authority in the Yemen', *al-Abḥāth* 30, Beirut: American University of Beirut, pp. 11–50.

——— 1983. 'The Post Medieval and Modern History of Ṣanʿāʾ and the Yemen, ca. 853–1382/1515–1962', in R.B. Serjeant and Ronald Lewcock (eds), *Sanaʿa: An Arabian Islamic City*, London: World of Islam Festival Trust, pp. 68–107.

Sharaf al-Dīn, ʿAlī ʿAbd al-Karīm al-Faḍīl. 1995. *Al-Aghṣān li-mushajjarāt insāb ʿAdnān wa Qaḥṭān*, al-Riyāḍ.

Shuja al-Deen, Maysaa. 2009. 'Media absent from Yemen's forgotten war', *Arab Media and Society*, Spring 2009, http://www.arabmediasociety.com/articles/downloads/20090506152723_AMS8_Maysaa_Shuja_al-Deen.pdf, last accessed 10 February 2017.

Shuwayṭ, Qaid. 2006. 'Qātaltu wa ḥūṣartu wa hudimat manāzilī li-thalāthi marrāt', *14th October*, 3 October 2006.

Smith, Rupert. 2005. *The Utility of Force: The Art of War in the Modern World*, London: Allen Lane.

Steffen, H. 1978. *Yemen Arab Republic: Final Report on the Airphoto Interpretation Project of the Swiss Technical Co-Operation Service*, Zurich: Bern.

Stenslie, Stig. 2013. 'Not too strong, not too weak: Saudi Arabia's policy towards Yemen', *NOREF Policy Brief*, Oslo: Norwegian Peacebuilding Resource Centre.

Stevenson, Thomas. 1985. *Social Change in a Yemeni Highlands Town*; Salt Lake City: University of Utah Press.

——— 1993. 'Yemeni Workers Come Home: Reabsorbing One Million Migrants', *Middle East Report* 181, pp. 15–20.

Stookey, Robert W. 1974. 'Social structure and politics in the Yemen Arab Republic, Parts I and II, *Middle East Journal* 28:3, pp. 248–60, 409–18.

——— 1978. *Yemen: The Politics of the Yemen Arab Republic*, Boulder: Westview Press.

Swagman, Charles. 1988. *Development and Change in Highland Yemen*, Salt Lake City: University of Utah Press.

Swanson, Jon and Hebert, Mary. 1982. *Rural Society and Participatory Development: Case Studies of Two Villages in the Yemen Arab Republic*; Ithaca: Cornell University & USAID/Y Project.

Tapper, Richard. 1991. 'Anthropologists, Historians, and Tribespeople on Tribe and State Formation in the Middle East', in Phillip. S. Khoury and Joseph Kostiner (eds), *Tribes and State Formation in the Middle East*, London: I.B. Tauris, pp. 48–73.

Terrill, W. Andrew. 2011. *The Conflicts in Yemen and U.S. National Security*, SSI Monograph, Carlisle Barracks, Pennsylvania: Strategic Studies Institute, http://www.strategicstudiesinstitute.army.mil/pdffiles/PUB1040.pdf, last accessed 10 February 2017.

——— 2014. 'Iranian Involvement in Yemen', *Orbis* 58:3, pp. 429–40.

Thiel, Tobias. 2015. 'Yemen's Imposed Federal Boundaries', 20 July 2015, Washington DC: Middle East Research and Information Project, http://www.merip.org/yemens-imposed-federal-boundaries, last accessed 10 February 2017.

Toren, Christina and de Pina-Cabral, João (eds). 2011. *The Challenge of Epistemology: Anthropological Perspectives*, New York/Oxford: Berghahn.

Tuchscherer, Michel. 1992. *Imams, Notables et Bédouins du Yémen au XVIIIe siècle*, Cairo: IFAO.

Tutwiler, Richard. 1984. 'Taʿāwun Maḥwīt: A case study of a Local Development Association in Highland Yemen', in L. Cantori and I. Harik (eds), *Local Politics and Development in the Middle East*, Boulder: Westview.

Tutwiler, Richard and Carapico, Sheila. 1981. *Yemeni Agriculture and Economic Change*, Sanaʿa: American Institute for Yemeni Studies.

United Nations Security Council Report S/2015/401, New York, http://www.securitycouncilreport.org/atf/cf/%7B65BFCF9B-6D27-4E9C-8CD3-CF6E4FF96FF9%7D/s_2015_401.pdf, last accessed 10 February 2017.

USAID. 2006. 'Yemen Corruption Assessment', https://yemen.usembassy.gov/root/pdfs/reports/yemen-corruption-assessment.pdf, last accessed 10 February 2017.

Vaglieri. L. Veccia. 1983. 'Ghadīr Khumm', in *EI II*.

Van Hear, Nicholas. 1994. 'The Socio-Economic Impacts of the Involuntary Mass Return to Yemen in 1990', *Journal of Refugee Studies* 7:1, pp. 18–38.

Volkan, Vamik. 2004. 'Chosen Trauma: The Political Ideology of Entitlement and Violence', paper presented at the Berlin Meeting, Germany, 10 June 2004, http://vamikvolkan.com/Chosen-Trauma,-the-Political-Ideology-of-Entitlement-and-Violence.php, last accessed 10 February 2017.

vom Bruck, Gabriele. 1998. 'Disputing descent-based authority in the idiom of religion: the case of the Republic of Yemen', *Die Welt des Islam* 38:2, pp. 149–91.

——— 1999. 'Being a Zaydī in the absence of an Imām: Doctrinal revisions, religious instruction, and the (re-) invention of ritual', in Remy Leveau, Franck Mermier, and Udo Steinbach (eds), *Le Yémen Contemporain*, Paris: Éditions Karthala, pp. 169–92.

——— 2005. *Islam, Memory, and Morality in Yemen: Ruling Families in Transition*, New York: Palgrave Macmillan.

——— 2010. 'Regimes of Piety Revisited: Zaydī Political Moralities in Republican Yemen', *Die Welt des Islams* 50:2, pp. 185–223.

Wachowski, Markus. 2012. *Rationale Schiiten: Ismailitische Weltsichten nach einer postkolonialen Lektüre von Max Webers Rationalismusbegriff*, Berlin/New York: De Gruyter.

Wedeen, Lisa. 2008. *Peripheral Visions: Publics, Power and Performance in Yemen*, Chicago: University of Chicago Press.

Weir, Shelagh. 1985. *Qat in Yemen: Consumption and Social Change*, London: British Museum Publications.

——— 1986. 'Tribe, hijrah and madinah in North-West Yemen', in K. Brown, M. Jole, S. Zubaida (eds), *Middle Eastern Cities in Comparative Perspective*, London/New York: Ithaca, pp. 225–39.

——— 1997. 'A clash of fundamentalisms: Wahhabism in Yemen', *MERIP* 204, 27:3.

——— 2007. *A Tribal Order: Politics and Law in the Mountains of Yemen*, Austin: University of Texas Press.

——— 2011. 'The end of Bayt Zayd', *The Middle East in London*, October–November 2011, pp. 7–9.

Wells Goldburt, Madeleine. 2013. 'Huthis as "Foreign": Threat Perception and Yemeni Regime Decision-Making about Sa'dah, 2004–2010', paper presented at the conference *Yemen: Challenges for the Future*, BYS/SOAS, London, 11–12 January 2013.

Wenner, Manfred W. 1967. *Modern Yemen 1918–1966*, Baltimore: Johns Hopkins University Press.

Whitaker, Brian. 1995. 'Crisis over the border', *Middle East International*, 29 January 1995, https://al-bab.com/albab-orig/albab/yemen/artic/mei10.htm, last accessed 10 February 2017.

——— 1997. 'Border Deal Nearer', *Middle East International*, 26 September 1997, http://al-bab.com/albab-orig/albab/yemen/artic/mei27.htm, last accessed 10 February 2017.

——— 1998a. 'Border Dispute Flares', *Middle East International*, 5 June 1998, http://al-bab.com/articles-section/border-dispute-flares, last accessed 10 February 2017.

——— 1998b. 'Border Row with the Saudis', *Middle East International*, 31 July 1998, http://al-bab.com/articles-section/border-row-saudis, last accessed 10 February 2017.

Wiegand, Bruce. 1993. 'Petty smuggling as "social justice": Research findings from the Belize-Mexico Border', Social *and Economic Studies* 42:1, pp. 171–93.

Wilson, Robert. 2014. 'Yemen's National Dialogue Conference, a triumph for optimism?', *British-Yemeni Society Journal* 22, pp. 8–14.

Worth, Robert F. 2008. 'An Interview with President Ali Abdullah Saleh', 22 June 2008, *The New York Times*, http://www.nytimes.com/2008/06/28/world/middleeast/28saleh-interview.html?pagewanted=all&_r=0, last accessed 10 February 2017.

—— 2010. 'Saudi Border With Yemen Is Still Inviting for Al Qaeda', *The New York Times*, 26 October 2010, http://www.nytimes.com/2010/10/27/world/middleeast/27saudi.html?pagewanted=all&_r=2&, last accessed 10 February 2017.

Yadav, Stacey Philbrick. 2013. *Islamists and the state: legitimacy and institutions in Yemen and Lebanon*, London: I.B. Tauris.

—— 2014a. 'The limits of the "sectarian" framing in Yemen', *The Washington Post*, 25 September 2014, https://www.washingtonpost.com/blogs/monkey-cage/wp/2014/09/25/the-limits-of-the-sectarian-framing-in-yemen/, last accessed 10 February 2017.

—— 2014b. 'Mapping the Terrain of Reform in Yemen: Islah over Two Decades', in Quinn Mecham, Julie Chernov-Hwang (eds), *Islamist parties and political normalization in the Muslim world*, Philadelphia: University of Pennsylvania Press.

Yamani, Mai. 2008. 'The Two Faces of Saudi Arabia', *Survival: Global Politics and Strategy* 50:1, pp. 143–156.

INDEX

al-Miṣrī, Muṭahhar, 229, 235, 239, 243, 245, 250, 251, 272, 290, 295
Miṭrī, Aḥmad, 85, 93, 126, 128, 227, 240, 281, 305, 307, 331
Miṭrī, Dahbāsh, 47, 56, 85
Miṭrī, Yūsif, 93, 307, 320, 330, 331
'mosque grabbing', 112
Mottaki, Manouchehr, 207, 321
Mu'ayyad, ʿAbdullah Ḥusayn, 189, 191
Mu'ayyad, Ḥamūd ʿAbbās, 113, 119, 139, 165, 228
al-Mu'ayyadī, Majd al-Dīn, 53, 106, 113–15, 117–18, 123–4, 131–2, 145
Muhammad, Prophet of Islam, 21, 101
Muḥammad al-Badr, Zaydi Imam, 42, 43, 44, 45, 48
Muḥammad Ḥusayn, Prince of Yemen, 47
muḥtasib, 115
al-Mujāhid, ʿAbdulraḥman, 149
Mujallī family, 41–2, 50, 51, 55, 174–5, 251, 272
  Dughsān, feud with, 251, 313
  Fāris Manāʿ, relations with, 314, 317
  investment, 65, 174
  Saʿdah wars, 174–5, 251
Mujallī, Fāyid, 41, 46, 55, 63, 108, 110, 174
Mujallī, Ḥamūd, 42, 43, 46
Mujallī, Ḥusayn, 41–2, 51, 55, 63, 65, 108, 110, 122, 174
Mujallī, Ṭaha, 243
Mujallī, ʿUmar, 65, 271, 272, 313
Mujallī, ʿUthmān, 51, 65, 108, 110, 174
  and Ahl Dammāj, 110–11
  elections, 127, 128, 129, 272
  and Jews, expulsion of (2007), 219
  and mediation (2007), 243
  resignation from GPC (2009), 293
  Saʿdah war, first (2004), 110, 164
  Saʿdah war, fourth (2007), 236
  Saʿdah war, sixth (2009–2010), 320, 324, 327–8
  Yāsir, assassination attempt on (2007), 243–5
Mujallī, Yāsir, 127, 236, 243–5
Munabbih, ix, 12, 20, 24, 25, 26, 27, 28–9, 343
  Border Guard, 85–6, 91, 93
  civil war (1962–70), 46, 47, 50, 55, 56, 84
  Doha Agreement (2007), 240
  elections, 126, 128, 129, 196, 312
  development, 65–6
  and hostage system, 41
  Houthi movement, resistance to, 145, 280
  and patronage, 60
  presidential and municipal elections (2006), 196–7
  Saʿdah war, third (2005–2006), 184, 191
  Saʿdah war, fourth (2007), 214, 226, 227, 236, 281
  Saʿdah war, fifth (2008), 254
  Saʿdah war, sixth (2009–2010), 200, 282, 305–7, 309, 335, 351
  and *sādah*, 29, 47, 60, 95, 149
  and Saudi border, 79, 80, 91, 93–5
  Tribal Alliance of the Sons of Saʿdah, 330, 331
Munabbih (Rāziḥ), 28
al-Munabbihī family, 55
  ʿAlī Ḥusayn, 55, 66, 86, 93, 128–9, 164, 227, 281–2, 305–7, 312
  Ḥusayn ʿAlī, 313, 317, 320, 330
Muqīt family, 54, 91–2, 95, 236–7, 326
  ʿAbdullah, 332
  Bandar, 92, 281–2, 297
  Ḥasan, 91–2, 120, 126, 128, 224, 232, 236, 281, 297, 320, 330